Introduction to Financial Accounting

Second Canadian Edition

Introduction to Financial Accounting

Second Canadian Edition

Charles T. Horngren
Stanford University

Gary L. Sundem
University of Washington—Seattle

John A. Elliott
Cornell University

Howard D. Teall
Wilfrid Laurier University

 Prentice Hall Canada Inc. Scarborough, Ontario

Canadian Cataloguing in Publication Data

Main entry under title:

Introduction to financial accounting

2nd Canadian ed.
Includes index.
ISBN 0-13-862954-4

1. Accounting. I. Horngren, Charles T., 1926–

HF5635.I577 1998   657   C97-931199-8

© 1998, 1995 Prentice-Hall Canada Inc., Scarborough, Ontario
A Division of Simon & Schuster/A Viacom Company

Prentice-Hall, Inc., Upper Saddle River, New Jersey
Prentice-Hall International (UK) Limited, London
Prentice-Hall of Australia, Pty. Limited, Sydney
Prentice-Hall Hispanoamericana, S.A., Mexico City
Prentice-Hall of India Private Limited, New Delhi
Prentice-Hall of Japan, Inc., Tokyo
Simon & Schuster Southeast Asia Private Limited, Singapore
Editora Prentice-Hall do Brasil, Ltda., Rio de Janeiro

ISBN 0-13-862954-4

Publisher: Patrick Ferrier
Senior Marketing Manager: Ann Byford
Senior Developmental Editor: Lesley Mann
Copy Editor: Shirley Corriveau
Production Editor: Mary Ann McCutcheon
Production Coordinator: Deborah Starks
Cover Design: Gary Beelik
Cover Image: Ann Cutting/Photonica
Page Layout: Joan Wilson

Original English Language edition published by Prentice-Hall, Inc.,
Englewood Cliffs, New Jersey
Copyright © 1996.

   2 3 4 5   CC   02 01 00 99 98

Printed and bound in U.S.A.

Every reasonable effort has been made to obtain permissions for all articles and data used in this edition. If errors or omissions have occurred, they will be corrected in future editions provided written notification has been received by the publisher.

The Hudson's Bay Company's 1996 Annual Report (including all trade-marks, text, photographs, images and drawings therein) utilized in this textbook is used by Prentice Hall Canada Inc. under license by Hudson's Bay Company. The licensed use of Hudson's Bay Company's 1996 Annual Report in this textbook should not be construed in any way as the agreement or consent, tacit or otherwise, of the company or its shareholders with the methodologies, approach and subject matter of this textbook.

Visit the Prentice Hall Canada Web site! Send us your comments, browse our catalogues, and more. **www.phcanada.com** Or reach us through e-mail at **phcinfo_pubcanada@prenhall.com**

To my parents
George and Wilma

■ **Charles T. Horngren** is the Edmund W. Littlefield Professor of Accounting at Stanford University. A graduate of Marquette University, he received his MBA from Harvard University and his Ph.D. from the University of Chicago. He is also the recipient of honorary doctorates from Marquette University and De Paul University.

A Certified Public Accountant, Horngren has served on the Accounting Principles Board, the Financial Accounting Standards Board Advisory Council, the Council of the American Institute of Certified Public Accountants, and as a trustee of the Financial Accounting Foundation.

A member of the American Accounting Association, Horngren has been its President and its Director of Research. He received the Outstanding Accounting Educator Award in 1973. The California Certified Public Accountants Foundation gave Horngren its Faculty Excellence Award in 1975 and its Distinguished Professor Award in 1983. In 1985 the American Institute of Certified Public Accountants presented its first Outstanding Educator Award to Horngren. In 1990 he was elected to the Accounting Hall of Fame.

Professor Horngren is also a member of the National Association of Accountants. He was a member of the Board of Regents, Institute of Certified Management Accountants, which administers the CMA examinations.

Horngren is the co-author of six other books published by Prentice Hall including: *Cost Accounting: A Managerial Emphasis*, Eighth Edition (with George Foster and Srikant M. Datar); *Introduction to Management Accounting*, Tenth Edition (with Gary L. Sundem and William O. Stratton); *Accounting*, Third Edition (with Walter T. Harrison Jr. and Michael A Robinson), and *Financial Accounting,* Second Edition (also with Harrison). In addition he is the Consulting Editor for the Prentice Hall Series in Accounting.

■ **Gary L. Sundem** is Professor of Accounting at the University of Washington, Seattle. He received his B.A. degree from Carleton College and his MBA and Ph.D. degrees from Stanford University.

Professor Sundem was the 1992–93 President of the American Accounting Association, served as Executive Director of the Accounting Education Change Commission, 1989–91, and as Editor of *The Accounting Review*, 1982–86.

A member of the National Association of Accountants, Sundem is past-president of the Seattle chapter. He has served on NAA's national Board of Directors, Committee on Academic Relations, and the Research Committee.

Professor Sundem has numerous publications in accounting and finance journals, including *Issues in Accounting Education, The Accounting Review, Journal of Accounting Research*, and *The Journal of Finance*. He received an award for the most notable contribution to accounting literature in 1978. He was selected as the Outstanding Accounting Educator by the Washington Society of CPAs in 1987. He has made more than 100 presentations at universities in the United States and abroad.

■ **John A. Elliott** is an Associate Professor of Accounting at the Johnson Graduate School of Management at Cornell University. He received his B.S. and MBA degrees from the University of Maryland and his Ph.D. degree from Cornell University. He is currently Director of the Ph.D. program at the Johnson School and has acted as associate dean for academic affairs.

A certified public accountant, Elliott worked for Arthur Anderson & Co. and for Westinghouse before returning for his advanced degrees. He currently teaches financial accounting and international accounting at the Johnson School. Prior teaching has included auditing and taxation as well as intermediate accounting and financial statement analysis. Over 25 years as an educator, Professor Elliott has taught at the University of Maryland, St. Lawrence University, Central Washington State College, and the University of Chicago. In addition to executive teaching for Cornell, he has conducted various corporate training programs in the United States and internationally.

As a member of the American Accounting Association, he was the founding president of the Financial Accounting and Reporting Section. As a member of the Financial Accounting Standards Committee he has frequently responded to FASB exposure drafts and worked to integrate academic study with practice. His research has been published in accounting and economics journals and deals primarily with the use of accounting information to assess the financial condition of an enterprise.

Professor Elliott served on the Hangar Theatre Board of Trustees for nine years, and was president for four of those years. He currently serves as Treasurer of the Board of the Cayuga Medical Center at Ithaca.

■ **Howard D. Teall** is an Associate Professor in the School of Business and Economics at Wilfrid Laurier University. He is currently serving as Associate Dean of Business: Academic Programs and as President of the Canadian Academic Accounitng Association. He received HBA, MBA, and Ph.D. degrees from the School of Business Administration at the University of Western Ontario, and a CA designation while employed with Price Waterhouse.

Previous university positions have been held at the Helsinki School of Economics and Business Administration, INSEAD (The European Institute of Business Administration), The International University of Japan and The University of Western Ontario.

Professor Teall has published articles in both financial and managerial fields including research into the impacts of financial disclosures in the oil and gas industry and management control issues. He has co-authored with Charles Horngren, Gary Sundem and William Stratton, *Management Accounting*, Second Canadian Edition and with Charles Horngren, George Foster, and Srikant Datar, *Cost Accounting: A Managerial Emphasis*, Canadian Edition, also published by Prentice Hall Canada.

Professor Teall has provided management training programs and consulting for IBM Canada Ltd., Ontario Hydro, B.F. Goodrich Canada Limited, Petro-Canada, General Motors of Canada Limited, General Motors Corporation, the Federal Business Development Bank, the Canadian Department of Industry, Science and Technology Canada, The Liquor Control Board of Ontario, The Banff Centre for Management, Polysar Rubber Corporation, Royal Bank of Trinidad and Tobago and professional qualification programs for Coopers and Lybrand, Deloitte & Touche, the Chartered Accountants Students' Association of Ontario, the Institute of Chartered Accountants of Ontario, the Atlantic Provinces Association of Chartered Accountants; and the Society of management Accountants of Ontario.

Brief Contents

inventory Goods held by a company for the purpose of sale to customers.

amount. **Inventory** refers to goods held by the company for the purpose of sale to customers. The form of the assets changed, but the total amount of assets is unchanged. Moreover, the right-side items are completely unchanged.

After any transaction has been completed, Biwheels can prepare a balance sheet.

Biwheels Company
Balance Sheet
January 2, 19X2

Assets		Liabilities and Owner's Equity	
Cash	$350,000	Liabilities (note payable)	$100,000
Merchandise inventory	150,000	Smith, capital	400,000
Total assets	$500,000	Total liabilities and owner's equity	$500,000

Transaction Analysis

account A summary record of the changes in a particular asset, liability, or owners' equity.

Accountants record transactions in an organization's *accounts*. An **account** is a summary record of the changes in a particular asset, liability, or owners' equity, and the *account balance* is the net total of all entries to the account to date. The analysis of transactions is the nucleus of accounting. For each transaction, the accountant determines (1) which specific accounts are affected, (2) whether the account balances are increased or decreased, and (3) the amount of the change in each account balance.

Exhibit 1-1 shows how a series of transactions may be analyzed using the balance sheet equation. The transactions are numbered for easy reference. Please examine how the first three transactions that were discussed earlier are analyzed in Exhibit 1-1.

Consider how each of the following additional transactions is analyzed:

4. Jan. 3. Biwheels buys bicycles for $10,000 from a manufacturer. The manufacturer requires $4,000 by January 10 and the balance in thirty days.

5. Jan. 4. Biwheels acquires assorted store equipment for a total of $15,000. A cash down payment of $4,000 is made. The remaining balance must be paid in sixty days.

6. Jan. 5. Biwheels sells a store showcase to a business neighbour after Smith decides he dislikes it. Its selling price, $1,000, happens to be exactly equal to its cost. The neighbour agrees to pay within thirty days.

7. Jan. 6. Biwheels returns some inventory (which had been acquired on January 3 for $800) to the manufacturer for full credit (an $800 reduction of the amount that Biwheels owes the manufacturer).

8. Jan. 10. Biwheels pays $4,000 to the manufacturer described in transaction 4.

9. Jan. 12. Biwheels collects $700 of the $1,000 owed by the business neighbour for transaction 6.

10. Jan. 12. Smith remodels his home for $35,000, paying by cheque from his personal bank account.

To check your comprehension, use the format in Exhibit 1-1 to analyze each transaction. Try to do your own analysis of each transaction before looking at the entries shown for it in the exhibit. For example, you could cover the numerical entries with a sheet of paper or a ruler and then proceed through each transaction, one by one.

Exhibit 1-1

Biwheels Company
Analysis of Transactions for December 31, 19X1–
January 12, 19X2

Description of Transactions	Cash	+ Accounts Receivable +	Merchandise Inventory	+ Store Equipment =	Note Payable	+ Accounts Payable +	Smith, Capital
Assets				**=**	**Liabilities + Owner's Equity**		
(1) Initial investment	+400,000			=			+400,000
(2) Loan from bank	+100,000			=	+100,000		
(3) Acquire inventory for cash	−150,000		+150,000	=			
(4) Acquire inventory on credit			+10,000	=		+10,000	
(5) Acquire store equipment for cash plus credit	−4,000			+15,000 =		+11,000	
(6) Sale of equipment		+1,000		−1,000 =			
(7) Return of inventory acquired on January 3			−800	=		−800	
(8) Payments to creditors	−4,000			=		−4,000	
(9) Collections from debtors	+700	−700					
Balance, January 12, 19X2	342,700	+300	+159,200	+14,000 =	100,000 +	16,200 +	400,000
		516,200			516,200		

Transaction 4, Purchase on Credit. The vast bulk of purchases among manufacturers, wholesalers, and retailers throughout the world is conducted on a *credit* basis rather than on a *cash* basis. An authorized signature of the buyer is usually sufficient to assure payment; no formal promissory note is necessary. This practice is known as buying on **open account**; the debt is shown on the buyer's balance sheet as an **account payable**. Thus an account payable is a liability that results from a purchase of goods or services on open account. As Exhibit 1-1 shows for this merchandise purchase on account, the merchandise inventory (an asset account) of Biwheels is increased and an account payable (a liability account) is also increased in the amount of $10,000 to keep the equation in balance.

open account Buying or selling on credit, usually by just an "authorized signature" of the buyer.

account payable A liability that results from a purchase of goods or services on open account.

	Cash	Merchandise Inventory	Note Payable	Accounts Payable	Smith, Capital
	Assets		**= Liabilities**	**+ Owner's Equity**	
Bal.	350,000	150,000	= 100,000		400,000
(4)		+10,000	=	+10,000	
Bal.	350,000	160,000	= 100,000	10,000	400,000
		510,000		510,000	

compound entry A transaction that affects more than two accounts.

Transaction 5, Purchase for Cash Plus Credit. This transaction illustrates a **compound entry** because it affects more than two balance sheet accounts (two asset accounts and one liability account in this case). Store equipment is increased by the full amount of its cost regardless of whether payment is made in full now, in full later, or partially now and partially later. Therefore Biwheels' Store Equipment (an asset account) is increased by $15,000, Cash (an asset account) is decreased by $4,000, and Accounts Payable (a liability account) is increased by the difference, $11,000.

		Assets		=	Liabilities	+	Owner's Equity
	Cash	Merchandise Inventory	Store Equipment		Note Payable	Accounts Payable	Smith, Capital
Bal.	350,000	160,000		=	100,000	10,000	400,000
(5)	− 4,000		+ 15,000	=		+ 11,000	
Bal.	346,000	160,000	15,000	=	100,000	21,000	400,000
		521,000				521,000	

Transaction 6, Sale on Credit.   This transaction is similar to a purchase on credit except that Biwheels is now the seller. Accounts Receivable (an asset account) of $1,000 is created, and Store Equipment (an asset account) is decreased by $1,000. We are purposely avoiding transactions that result in profits or losses until the next chapter. Instead we are concentrating on elementary changes in the balance sheet equation. In this case, the transaction affects assets only; liabilities and owner's equity are unchanged.

			Assets		=	Liabilities	+	Owner's Equity
	Cash	Accounts Receivable	Merchandise Inventory	Store Equipment		Note Payable	Accounts Payable	Smith, Capital
Bal.	346,000		160,000	15,000	=	100,000	21,000	400,000
(6)		+1,000		− 1,000	=			
Bal.	346,000	1,000	160,000	14,000	=	100,000	21,000	400,000
		521,000					521,000	

Transaction 7, Return of Inventory to Supplier.   When a company returns merchandise to its suppliers for credit, its merchandise inventory account is reduced and its liabilities are reduced. In this instance, the amount of the decrease on each side of the equation is $800.

			Assets		−	Liabilities	+	Owner's Equity
	Cash	Accounts Receivable	Merchandise Inventory	Store Equipment		Note Payable	Accounts Payable	Smith, Capital
Bal.	346,000	1,000	160,000	14,000	=	100,000	21,000	400,000
(7)			− 800		=		− 800	
Bal.	346,000	1,000	159,200	14,000	=	100,000	20,200	400,000
		520,200					520,200	

creditor One to whom money is owed.

Transaction 8, Payments to Creditors. A **creditor** is one to whom money is owed. The manufacturer is an example of a creditor. These payments decrease both assets (Cash) and liabilities (Accounts Payable) by $4,000.

		Assets			=	Liabilities		+	Owner's Equity
	Cash	Accounts Receivable	Merchandise Inventory	Store Equipment		Note Payable	Accounts Payable		Smith, Capital
Bal.	346,000	1,000	159,200	14,000	=	100,000	20,200		400,000
(8)	– 4,000				=		– 4,000		
Bal.	342,000	1,000	159,200	14,000	=	100,000	16,200		400,000
		516,200					516,200		

debtor One who owes money.

Transaction 9, Collections from Debtors. A **debtor** is one who owes money. Here the business neighbour is the debtor, and Biwheels is the creditor. These collections increase one of Biwheels' assets (Cash) and decrease another asset (Accounts Receivable) by $700.

		Assets			=	Liabilities		+	Owner's Equity
	Cash	Accounts Receivable	Merchandise Inventory	Store Equipment		Note Payable	Accounts Payable		Smith, Capital
Bal.	342,000	1,000	159,200	14,000	=	100,000	16,200		400,000
(9)	+ 700	– 700			=				
Bal.	342,700	300	159,200	14,000	=	100,000	16,200		400,000
		516,200					516,200		

Note that transactions 4 through 9 illustrate the entity concept in that they all relate to Smith's *business* entity, the Biwheels Company. When Smith remodels his home for $35,000, paying by cheque from his personal bank account, the transaction is a nonbusiness transaction of Smith's *personal* entity. It is not recorded by the business. Our focus is solely on the business entity.

Preparing the Balance Sheet

A cumulative total may be drawn at *any* date for each *account* in Exhibit 1-1. The following balance sheet uses the totals at the bottom of Exhibit 1-1. Observe once again that a balance sheet represents the financial impact of an accumulation of transactions at a specific point in time, here January 12, 19X2.

Biwheels Company
Balance Sheet
January 12, 19X2

Assets		Liabilities and Owners' Equity	
Cash	$342,700	Note payable	$100,000
Accounts receivable	300	Accounts payable	16,200
Merchandise		Total liabilities	$116,200
inventory	159,200		
Store equipment	14,000	Smith, capital	400,000
Total	$516,200	Total	$516,200

As noted earlier, Biwheels could prepare a new balance sheet after each transaction. Obviously, such a practice would be awkward and unnecessary. Therefore balance sheets are usually produced once a month.

Examples of Actual Corporate Balance Sheets

To become more familiar with the balance sheet and its equation, consider the following condensed excerpts from two actual recent financial reports. Some terms vary among organizations, but the essential balance sheet equation does not.

Maritime Telegraph and Telephone Company Limited (in thousands) December 31, 1995

Assets		Liabilities and Owners' Equity	
Cash	$ 5,949	Notes payable	$ 696,085
Accounts receivable	124,800	Accounts payable	41,437
Telecommunications property	1,284,948	Other liabilities	254,016
		Total liabilities	$ 991,538
Other assets	107,418	Owners' equity	531,577
		Total liabilities and	
Total assets	$1,523,115	owners' equity	$1,523,115

The Maritime Telephone and Telegraph 1995 balance sheet illustrates the prominence of telecommunications property and equipment as a major component of a telephone company's assets. Moreover, the total liabilities exceed the owners' equity, which is commonplace for utilities, but not for most large industrial and service organizations. The other liabilities consist largely of long-term debt that usually arises in conjunction with the acquisition of long-term assets.

Canadian Tire (in thousands) December 31, 1994

Assets		Liabilities and Owners' Equity	
Cash	$ 156,038	Notes payable	$ 699,841
Accounts receivable	1,050,205	Accounts payable	443,797
Inventories	417,688	Other liabilities	373,119
Property, plant, and		Total liabilities	$1,516,757
equipment	972,007	Owners' equity	1,152,106
Other assets	72,925	Total liabilities and	
Total assets	$2,668,863	owners' equity	$2,668,863

Canadian Tire has a significant amount of inventories. The accounts receivable exists because the retail stores are franchised and thus the stores purchase from Canadian Tire on credit. Canadian Tire's total liabilities of $1,516,757 exceed the owners' equity of $1,152,106.

Appendix A at the end of this book contains a complete set of the actual 1996–97 financial statements of the Hudson's Bay Company. As you proceed from chapter to chapter, you should examine the pertinent parts of the Hudson's Bay Company financial statements. In this way, you will become increasingly comfortable with actual financial reports. For example, the general format and major items in the Hudson's Bay Company balance sheet should be familiar by now. Details will gradually become understandable as each chapter explains the nature of the various major financial statements.

Canadian Tire
www.canadiantire.com

Hudson's Bay Company
www.hbc.com/hom.asp

■ TYPES OF OWNERSHIP

Business entities can take one of three forms. Owners must decide whether to organize as sole proprietorships, partnerships, or corporations.

Sole Proprietorships

sole proprietorship
A separate organization with a single owner.

A **sole proprietorship** is a separate organization with a single owner. Most often the owner is also the manager. Therefore sole proprietorships tend to be small retail establishments and individual professional businesses such as those of dentists, physicians, and lawyers. From an *accounting* viewpoint, each sole proprietorship is an individual entity that is separate and distinct from the proprietor.

Partnerships

partnership A special form of organization that joins two or more individuals together as co-owners.

A **partnership** is a special form of organization that joins two or more individuals together as co-owners. Many retail establishments, as well as dentists, physicians, lawyers, and accountants, conduct their activities as partnerships. Indeed, partnerships can sometimes be gigantic. For instance, the largest independent accounting firms have hundreds of partners. Again, from an *accounting* viewpoint, each partnership is an individual entity that is separate from the personal activities of each partner.

Corporations

corporation An organization that is an "artificial being" created by individual provincial or federal laws.

Corporations are organizations created under provincial or federal law in Canada. Individuals form a corporation by applying to the government for approval of the company's *articles of incorporation*, which include information on shares of ownership. Most large corporations are **publicly owned** in that shares in the ownership are sold to the public. The owners of the corporation are then identified as *shareholders* (or *stockholders*). Large publicly owned corporations can have thousands of shareholders. Some corporations are **privately owned** by families, small groups of shareholders, or a single individual, and shares of ownership are not publicly sold.

publicly owned
A corporation in which shares in the ownership are sold to the public.

In Canada, there are both federal and provincial laws governing the creation of corporations. Federally, the Canada Business Corporations Act regulates the rights and responsibilities of federally incorporated companies while provincially an act, normally called the Business Corporations Act or the Corporations Act performs the same function for companies incorporated by a province.

privately owned
A corporation owned by a family, a small group of shareholders, or a single individual, in which shares of ownership are not publicly sold.

In addition, certain corporations are owned by the government and are called Crown corporations. For example, Ontario Hydro is a Crown corporation owned by the Ontario provincial government which has been incorporated to meet the objectives of providing hydro across the province. Today, many governments are evaluating the sale of their shares in the Crown corporations. This process in which a Crown corporation becomes a publicly owned corporation is called privatization. Air Canada and Petro-Canada are two publicly owned companies that were previously Crown corporations owned by the federal government.

Internationally, distinct legal organizations are very common. In the United Kingdom they are frequently indicated by the word *limited* (Ltd) in the name. In

Ontario Hydro
www.hydro.on.ca

many countries whose laws trace back to Spain, the initials *S.A.* refer to a "society anonymous" in which multiple owners stand behind the company. A necessary condition for modern market economies is a mechanism that permits investment capital to be accumulated in support of larger economic efforts. A corporate type of form has proven effective worldwide.

Once a corporation has been established, it is a *legal* entity apart from its owners. The management and business activities are conducted completely apart from the activities of the owners. The corporation is also, of course, an *accounting* entity.

Advantages and Disadvantages

The corporate form of organization has many advantages. Perhaps most notable is the **limited liability** of owners, which means that corporate creditors (such as banks or suppliers) ordinarily have claims against the corporate assets only. Therefore, if a corporation drifts into financial trouble, its creditors cannot look for repayment beyond the corporate entity; that is, generally the owners' personal assets are not subject to the creditors' grasp. In contrast, the owners of proprietorships and partnerships typically have *unlimited liability*, which means that business creditors can look to the owners' personal assets for repayment. For example, if Biwheels were a partnership, *each* partner would bear a personal liability for full payment of the $100,000 bank loan.

Another advantage of the corporation is easy transfer of ownership. In selling shares in its ownership, the corporation usually issues **capital stock certificates** (often called simply **stock certificates**) as formal evidence of ownership. These shares may be sold and resold among present and potential owners. Stock exchanges make trading of shares easy. Millions of shares are bought and sold on an average day on the Toronto Stock Exchange (TSE) alone. Shares of many large firms are also traded on international exchanges such as those in New York, Tokyo and London.

In contrast to proprietorships and partnerships, corporations have the advantage of ease in raising ownership capital from hundreds or thousands of potential shareholders. Indeed, AT&T has nearly 2.5 million shareholders, owning a total of over 1 billion shares of stock.

The corporation also has the advantage of continuity of existence. Life is indefinite in the sense that it continues even if its ownership changes. In contrast, proprietorships and partnerships officially terminate upon the death or complete withdrawal of an owner.

The effects of the form of ownership on income taxes may vary significantly. For example, a corporation is taxed as a separate entity (as a corporation). But no income taxes are levied on a proprietorship (as a proprietorship) or on a partnership (as a partnership). Instead the income earned by proprietorships and partnerships is attributed to the owners as personal taxpayers. In short, the income tax laws regard corporations as being taxable entities, but proprietorships or partnerships as not being taxable entities. Whether the corporation provides tax advantages depends heavily on the personal tax situations of the owners.

Regardless of the economic and legal advantages or disadvantages of each type of organization, some small-business owners incorporate simply for prestige. That is, they feel more important if they can refer to "my corporation" and if they can refer to themselves as "chairman (chairperson) of the board" or "president" instead of "business owner" or "partner."

limited liability
A feature of the corporate form of organization whereby corporate creditors ordinarily have claims against the corporate assets only. The owners' personal assets are not subject to the creditors' grasp.

capital stock certificate (stock certificate) Formal evidence of ownership of shares in a corporation.

Toronto Stock Exchange
www.telenium.ca/TSE/

Objective 5

Understand the advantages and disadvantages of the three types of business organizations and how to account for each.

In terms of numbers of entities, there are fewer corporations in Canada than there are proprietorships or partnerships. However, the corporation has far more economic significance. Corporations conduct a sheer money volume of business that dwarfs the volume of other forms of organization. Moreover, almost every reader of this book interacts with, owes money to, or invests in corporations. For these reasons, this book emphasizes the corporate entity.

capital A term used to identify owners' equities for proprietorships and partnerships.

Accounting for Owners' Equity

The basic accounting concepts that underlie the owners' equity are unchanged regardless of whether the organization is a proprietorship, a partnership, or a corporation. However, owners' equities for proprietorships and partnerships are often identified by the word **capital**. In contrast, owners' equity for a corporation is usually called **shareholders' equity** or **stockholders' equity**. Examine the possibilities for the Biwheels Company that are shown in the accompanying table.

shareholders' equity (stockholders' equity) Owners' equity of a corporation. The excess of assets over liabilities of a corporation.

Owners' Equity for Different Organizations

Owner's Equity for a Proprietorship (Assume George Smith is the sole owner)	
George Smith, capital	$400,000

Owners' Equity for a Partnership (Assume Smith has two partners)	
George Smith, capital	$320,000
Alex Handl, capital	40,000
Susan Eastman, capital	40,000
Total partners' capital	$400,000

Owners' Equity for a Corporation	
Shareholders' equity:	
Capital stock, 10,000 shares issued	$400,000

paid-in capital The total capital investment in a corporation by its owners at the inception of business and subsequently.

The accounts for the proprietorship and the partnership show owners' equity as straightforward records of the *capital* invested by the owners. For a corporation, the total capital investment in a corporation by its owners at the inception of business and subsequently is called **paid-in capital**. It is recorded in two parts: capital stock at par value and paid-in capital in excess of par value.

par value (stated value) The nominal dollar amount printed on stock certificates.

The Meaning of Par Value

Originally, par value was conceived as a measure of protection for creditors because it established the minimum legal liability of a shareholder. In this way, the creditors would be assured that the corporation would have at least a minimum amount of ownership capital ($10 for each share issued). Indeed, the shareholder had a commitment to invest at least $10 per share in the corporation.

paid-in capital in excess of par value When issuing stock, the difference between the total amount received and the par value.

The amount of $10 is determined by the board of directors and is usually called **par value** or **stated value**. Typically, the stock is sold at a price that is higher than its par value. The difference between the total amount received for the stock and the par value is called **paid-in capital in excess of par value**.

To alter our example to the corporate form, assume 10,000 shares of Biwheels stock have been sold for $40 per share. The par value is $10 per share, and therefore the paid-in capital in excess of par value is $30 per share. Thus, the total ownership claim of $400,000 arising from the investment is split between two equity claims, one for $100,000 "capital stock, at par" and one for $300,000 "paid-in capital in excess of par" or "additional paid-in capital."

The following formulas show these components of the total paid-in capital account:

$$\text{Total paid-in capital} = \text{Capital stock at par} + \text{Paid-in capital in excess of par}$$

$$\$400,000 = \$100,000 + \$300,000$$

$$\text{Capital stock at par} = \text{Number of shares issued} \times \text{Par value per share}$$

$$\$100,000 = 10,000 \times \$10$$

$$\text{Paid-in capital in excess of par} = \text{Total paid-in capital} - \text{Common stock at par}$$

$$\$300,000 - \$400,000 \quad \$100,000$$

$$\text{Total paid-in capital} = \text{Number of shares issued} \times \text{Average issue price per share}$$

$$\$400,000 = 10,000 \times \$40$$

common stock Stock representing the class of owners having a "residual" ownership of a corporation.

The par (or stated) values are usually set far below the full market price of the shares upon issuance, as illustrated by the following excerpts from recent actual corporate balance sheets. The excerpts use the term *common stock* to describe capital stock. Sometimes more than one type of capital stock is issued by a corporation (as explained in Chapter 11). But there is always **common stock**, which represents the "residual" ownership.

Sun Microsystems, Inc.

Common stock, $0.00067 par value, 300,000,000 shares authorized; issued 106,394,200 shares	$	72,000
Additional paid-in capital		1,066,571,000

The extremely small amount of par value in comparison with the additional paid-in capital is common and illustrates the insignificance of "par value" in today's business world. Also note the use of a frequently encountered term, "additional paid-in capital," as a short synonym for "paid-in capital in excess of par value of common stock." Finally, note that the number of "shares authorized" is the maximum number of shares that the company can issue as designated by the company's articles of incorporation.

Microsoft

Common stock and paid-in-capital— shares authorized 2,000,000,000 issued and outstanding 581,000,000	$1,086,000,000

Microsoft does not split the paid-in capital into two lines and does not even mention the par value, which is $.00001 per share. Inasmuch as par value is usually small and has little significance, this approach is praiseworthy.

In summary, both of these actual corporate presentations can be described accurately with a simple term, *total paid-in capital*, which will be distinguished from other ownership equity arising from profitable operations in later chapters.

■ CREDIBILITY AND THE ROLE OF AUDITING

The credibility of financial statements is the ultimate responsibility of the managers who are entrusted with the resources under their command. In proprietorships, the owner is usually the top manager. In partnerships, top management may be shared by the owners. In corporations, the ultimate responsibility for management is delegated by shareholders to the *board of directors*, as indicated in the following diagram:

An advantage of the corporate form of organization is separation of ownership and management. Shareholders invest resources but do not need to devote time to managing, and managers can be selected for their managerial skills, not their ability to invest large sums in the firm. The board of directors is the link between shareholders and the actual managers. It is the board's duty to ensure that managers act in the interests of shareholders.

The board of directors is elected by the shareholders, but the slate of candidates is often selected by management. Sometimes, the chairman of the board is also the top manager and the major shareholder. For example, for over thirty years Henry Ford II was the major shareholder, the chairman of the board, and the chief executive officer (CEO) of the Ford Motor Company. Other top managers such as the president, financial vice president, and marketing vice president are routinely elected to the board of directors of the company they manage. Therefore, the interests of both shareholders and managers are usually represented on the board of directors.

Membership on a board of directors is often extended to CEOs and presidents of other corporations, to university presidents and professors, and to lawyers. For example, the eight-member board of Electrohome includes two Electrohome executives, five present or former CEOs or directors of other companies, and one former professor and university president. In many cases, these members of the board are also shareholders of the corporation.

In fulfilling its management responsibilities, the board of directors relies on financial statements to assess the corporation's performance. Because financial statements are prepared by managers (or by accountants employed

Canadian Institute of Chartered Accountants (CICA) A professional accounting organization of Chartered Accountants (CA).

Certified General Accountants Association of Canada (CGAAC) A professional accounting organization of Certified General Accountants (CGA).

Society of Management Accountants of Canada (SMAC) A professional accounting organization of Certified Management Accountants (CMA).

audit An examination of transactions and financial statements made in accordance with generally accepted auditing standards.

auditor's opinion (independent opinion) A report describing the auditor's examination of transactions and financial statements. It is included with the financial statements in an annual report issued by the corporation.

by the managers), there is a chance that the statements will portray an overly rosy picture of the firm—thereby enhancing the image of management. Long ago shareholders, as well as external parties such as banks who lend money to the firm, wanted some third-party assurance about the credibility of the financial statements. The profession of public accounting arose to serve this purpose—to provide a means for examining financial statements and the transactions underlying them and to provide an opinion on the statements' credibility.

Professional Accountants

Public accountants' opinions on financial statements will add credibility only if such accountants have a reputation for expertise and integrity and provide assurance that their examination of the financial statements was thorough. To assure expertise and integrity, professional accountants are certified.

In Canada, there are three professional accounting designations that have national coordinating organizations but have provincial bodies that regulate the education and membership requirements. The Chartered Accountant (CA) designation, certified by the **Canadian Institute of Chartered Accountants (CICA)** and its provincial institutes, and the **Certified General Accountant (CGA)**, certified by the **Certified General Accountants Association of Canada (CGAAC)** and its provincial associations, are primarily focused on external financial reporting. **The Certified Management Accountant (CMA)** designation as offered by the **Society of Management Accountants of Canada (SMAC)** and its provincial societies is primarily focused on internal management accounting.

The Auditor's Opinion

To assess management's financial disclosure, public accountants conduct an **audit**, which is an examination of transactions and financial statements made in accordance with generally accepted auditing standards developed primarily by the CICA. This audit includes miscellaneous tests of the accounting records, internal control systems, and other auditing procedures as deemed necessary. The examination is described in the **auditor's opinion** (also called an **independent opinion**) that is included with the financial statements in an annual report issued by the corporation. Standard phrasing is used for auditors' opinions, as illustrated by the following opinion rendered by a large CA firm, Arthur Andersen & Co., for Consumers Packaging Inc.

Auditors' Report
To the Shareholders of Consumers Packaging Inc.:

We have audited the balance sheet of Consumers Packaging Inc. as at December 31, 1995 and the statements of earnings, deficit and cash flow for the year then ended. These financial statements are the responsibility of the Company's management. Our responsibility is to express an opinion on these financial statements based on our audit.

We conducted our audit in accordance with generally accepted auditing standards. Those standards require that we plan and perform an audit to obtain reasonable assurance whether the financial statements are free of material misstatement. An audit includes examining, on a test basis, evidence supporting the amounts and disclosures in the financial statements. An audit also includes assessing the accounting principles used and significant estimates made by management, as well as evaluating the overall financial statement presentation.

In our opinion, these financial statements present fairly, in all material respects, the financial position of the Company as at December 31, 1995 and the results of its operations and its cash flow for the year then ended in accordance with generally accepted accounting principles.

Toronto, Ontario   Arthur Andersen & Co.
February 6, 1996   Chartered Accountants

This book will explore the meaning of such phrases as "present fairly" and "generally accepted accounting principles." For now, reflect on the fact that auditors do not prepare a company's financial statements. Rather, the auditor's opinion is the public accountant's stamp of approval on *management's* financial statements.

■ THE ACCOUNTING PROFESSION

public accounting
The field of accounting to which services are offered to the general public on a fee basis.

private accounting
Accountants who work for businesses, government agencies, and other nonprofit

The accounting profession can be classified in many ways. A major classification is **public accounting** and **private accounting**. "Public" accountants are those whose services are offered to the general public on a fee basis. Such services include auditing, income taxes, and management consulting. "Private" accountants are all the rest. They consist not only of those individuals who work for businesses but also of those who work for government agencies, including Revenue Canada, and other nonprofit organizations.

Public Accounting Firms

Public accounting firms vary in size and in the type of accounting services performed. There are small proprietorships, where auditing may represent as little as 10% or less of annual billings. *Billings* are the total amounts charged to clients for services rendered to them. The bulk of the work of these firms is income taxes and "write-up" work (the actual bookkeeping services for clients who are not equipped to do their own accounting).

There are also a handful of gigantic firms that have over two thousand partners with offices located throughout the world. Such enormous firms are necessary because their clients are also enormous. For instance, a large firm has reported that its annual audit of one client takes the equivalent of seventy-two accountants working a full year. Another client has three hundred separate corporate entities in forty countries that must ultimately be consolidated into one set of overall financial statements.

The six largest public international accounting firms are known collectively as the "Big-Six":

Objective 7

Describe public and private accounting and the role of ethics in the accounting profession.

- Arthur Andersen & Co.
- Coopers & Lybrand
- Deloitte & Touche
- Ernst & Young
- KPMG Peat Marwick
- Price Waterhouse

In Canada, two additional firms are among the largest firms: Doane Raymond Grant Thornton and BDO Dunwoody. Many of the companies listed on the TSE are clients of these eight firms. These accounting firms have annual billings in excess of a billion dollars each. A majority of the billings is attributable to auditing services. The top partners in big accounting firms are compensated on about the same scale as their corporate counterparts. Huge accounting firms tend to receive more publicity than other firms. However, please remember that there are thousands of other able accounting firms, varying in size from sole practitioners to giant international partnerships.

Canada's Big Eight CA Firms: 1996 Revenues Rise

Canada's Big Eight accounting firms had a good year in fiscal 1996, increasing their revenue by an average of 7.6 percent, according to industry newspaper *The Bottom Line*.

There were no changes in ranking among the top eight, with KPMG remaining the country's largest firm with revenue of $524.7-million, up 6.5 percent from the previous year.

The biggest gains were made by: No. 2-ranked Deloitte & Touche, with revenue of $499-million, up 13.1 percent; Coopers & Lybrand, the fourth-ranked firm, up 11.6 percent to $336.4-million; and Price Waterhouse, up 10 percent to nearly $276-million for sixth place.

Standard audit work remains flat at many firms, the newspaper reports. This is partly because of corporate mergers and partly the effect of 1994 changes to the Canada Business Corporations Act which mean that large, privately held Canadian subsidiaries no longer have to be audited.

Growth areas included consulting and special services such as forensic accounting, insolvency and alternative dispute resolution.

Most of the big firms were stable in staffing levels last year, although Ernst & Young lost 48 partners, partly because of a divestment of services it considered non-core. Deloitte & Touche lost 15 partners but gained 171 professional staff, the largest staff increase of any firm.

The top 10 in order are: KPMG, Deloitte & Touche, Ernst & Young ($415-million); Coopers & Lybrand, Andersen Worldwide ($300-million); Price Waterhouse, Doane Raymond Grant Thornton ($202.9-million); BDO Dunwoody ($132.3-million); Richter Usher & Vineberg ($62-million); and Collins Barrow ($31.1 million).

Doane Raymond is an association of firms rather than a fully integrated partnership.

Source: "Accounting revenue rises 7.6%", The Globe and Mail (April 14, 1997). Reprinted with permission from The Globe and Mail.

Coopers & Lybrand
www.ca.coopers.com

Deloitte & Touche
www.deloitte.ca

Ernst & Young
www.eycan.com

Other Opportunities for Accountants

In the accompanying diagram, the long arrows indicate how accountants often move from public accounting firms to positions in business or government. Obviously, these movements can occur at any level or in any direction.

Accounting cuts across all management functions, including purchasing, manufacturing, wholesaling, retailing, and a variety of marketing and transportation activities. It provides an excellent opportunity for gaining broad knowledge. Senior accountants or controllers in a corporation are

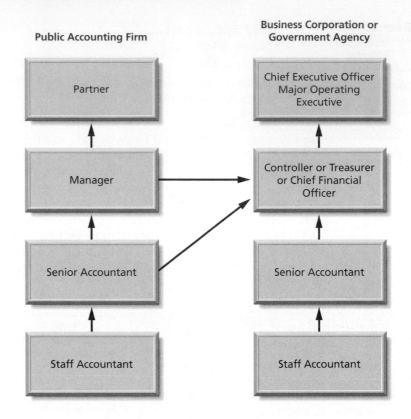

sometimes picked as production or marketing executives. Why? Because they may have impressed other executives as having acquired general management skills.

Accounting was recently ranked as the most important business school course for future managers. *Business Week* recently reported that "more CEOs [chief executive officers] started out in finance or accounting than in any other area."

Professional Ethics

Professional accountants must abide by codes of professional conduct. Surveys of public attitudes toward professional accountants have consistently ranked the accounting profession as having high ethical standards. The codes of professional conduct are especially concerned with integrity and independence. For example, independent auditors are forbidden to own shares of their client corporations. Moreover, the auditors must satisfy themselves that their clients' financial statements are prepared in accordance with GAAP.

Summary Problems for Your Review

Problem One

Review Exhibit 1-1 (p. 12). Analyze the following additional transactions of Biwheels Company. Begin with the balances shown for January 12, 19X2, in Exhibit 1-1. Prepare an ending balance sheet for Biwheels Company (say, on January 16 after these additional transactions).

i. Biwheels pays $10,000 on the bank loan (ignore interest).
ii. Smith buys furniture for his home for $5,000, using his family charge account at Eaton's.
iii. Biwheels buys merchandise inventory for $50,000. Half the amount is paid in cash, and half is owed on open account.
iv. Biwheels collects $200 more from its business debtor.

Exhibit 1-2

Biwheels Company
Analysis of Additional January Transactions

Description of Transaction		Assets			=	Liabilities + Owner's Equity		
	Cash	+ Accounts Receivable +	Merchandise Inventory +	Store Equipment =	Note Payable +	Accounts Payable +	Smith, Capital
Balance, January 12, 19X2	342,700 +	300 +	159,200 +	14,000 =	100,000 +	16,200 +	400,000
(i) Payment on bank loan	– 10,000				=– 10,000		
(ii) Personal; no effect							
(iii) Acquire inventory, half for cash	– 25,000		+ 50,000	=		+ 25,000	
Collection of receivable	+ 200	– 200					
Balance, January 16	307,900 +	100 +	209,200 +	14,000 =	90,000 +	41,200 +	400,000
			531,200		=	531,200	

Exhibit 1-3

Biwheels Company
Balance Sheet
January 16, 19X2

Assets		Liabilities and Owner's Equity	
		Liabilities:	
Cash	$307,900	Note payable	$ 90,000
Accounts receivable	100	Accounts payable	41,200
Merchandise inventory	209,200	Total liabilities	$131,200
Store equipment	14,000	Smith, capital	400,000
Total	$531,200	Total	$531,200

Solution to Problem One

See Exhibits 1-2 and 1-3. Note that transaction (ii) is ignored because it is wholly personal. However, visualize how Smith's personal balance sheet would be affected. His assets, Home Furniture, would rise by $5,000 and his liabilities, Accounts Payable, would also rise by $5,000.

Problem Two

"If I purchase 100 shares of the outstanding stock of Air Canada (or Biwheels Company), I invest my money directly in that corporation. Air Canada must record that event." Do you agree? Explain.

Solution to Problem Two

Money is invested directly in a corporation when the entity originally issues the stock. For example, 100,000 shares of stock may be issued at $80 per share, bringing in $8 million to the corporation. This is a transaction between the corporation and the shareholders. It affects the corporate financial position:

Cash <u>$8,000,000</u>   Shareholders' equity <u>$8,000,000</u>

Subsequently, 100 shares of that stock may be sold by an original shareholder (Wayne Gretzky) to another individual (Meg Ryan) for $130 per share. This is a private transaction; no cash is received by the corporation. Of course, the corporation records the fact that 100 shares originally owned by Gretzky are now owned by Ryan, but the corporate financial position is unchanged. Accounting focuses on the business entity; subsequently, private dealings of the owners have no effect on the financial position of the entity, although the corporation records the owners' identities.

Problem Three

"One individual can be an owner, an employee, and a creditor of a corporation." Do you agree? Explain.

Solution to Problem Three

Yes. The corporation enters contracts, hires employees, buys buildings, and conducts other business. The chairman of the board, the president, the other officers, and all the workers are employees of the corporation. Thus Robert Astley could own some of the capital stock of the Mutual Life Assurance Company of Canada and also be an employee (CEO). Since money owed to employees for salaries is a liability, he could be an owner, an employee, and a creditor. Similarly, an employee of a telephone company who is a shareholder of the company could also be receiving telephone services from the same company. He is an owner, employee, *customer*, and debtor of the company.

Highlights to Remember

Financial statements provide information for decision making to managers, creditors, and owners of all types of organizations. The balance sheet (or statement of financial position) provides a "snapshot" of the financial position of an organization at any instant. That is, it answers the basic question, Where are we? The balance sheet equation is Assets = Liabilities + Owners' Equity. This equation must always be in balance.

Using the entity concept, the accountant relates transactions to a sharply defined area of accountability. Entities may take different forms, including proprietorships, partnerships, or corporations. There are also entities within entities. For example, the University of Quebec contains various schools and departments within schools. The department is an accounting entity nested within the school, which is a larger entity nested within the university.

Transaction analysis is the heart of accounting. Transactions are events that require recording in an organization's accounts. For each transaction, an accountant must determine what accounts are affected and by how much. The transactions of a personal entity should not be mingled with those of a business entity.

Corporations are especially important entities because so much business is conducted by corporations. The ownership equity of a corporation is usually called shareholders' equity.

Separation of ownership from management in corporations creates a demand for auditing, a third-party examination of financial statements. The public accounting profession gives credibility to audits by specifying qualifications for certified public accountants, including ethical standards, and by developing generally accepted auditing standards to ensure thoroughness of audits. Because accountants work with managers in all management functions, accounting positions are fertile training grounds for future top managers.

Assignment Material

The assignment material for each chapter is divided into Questions, Exercises, Problems, Critical Thinking Problems (in most chapters), and Company Cases. The assignment material contains problems based on fictitious companies and problems based on real-life situations. We hope our use of actual companies and news events enhances your interest in accounting.

Problems based on real companies are identified with a logo in the margin while Company Cases are all based on real companies. These problems and cases underscore a major objective of this book: to increase the reader's ability to read, understand, and use published financial reports and news articles. In later chapters, these problems and cases provide the principal means of reviewing not only the immediate chapter but also the previous chapters. In particular, note the Hudson's Bay Company and Annual Report Disclosure cases at the end of each chapter's assignment material.

Spreadsheet Templates for problems flagged with a disk icon are available as a supplement to this text.

QUESTIONS

1-1. Give three examples of decisions that are likely to be influenced by financial statements.

1-2. Give three examples of users of financial statements.

1-3. Briefly distinguish between *financial accounting* and *management accounting*.

1-4. Give four examples of accounting entities.

1-5. Give two synonyms for *balance sheet*.

1-6. Explain the difference between a *note payable* and an *account payable*.

1-7. Give two synonyms for *owners' equity*.

1-8. Explain the meaning of *limited liability*.

1-9. Why does this book emphasize the corporation rather than the proprietorship or the partnership?

1-10. "The idea of par value is insignificant." Explain.

1-11. Name three professional accounting designations and their national body.

EXERCISES

1-12 Describing Underlying Transactions

LTC Company, which was recently formed, is engaging in some preliminary transactions before beginning full-scale operations for retailing laptop computers. The balances of each item in the company's accounting equation are given below for May 10 and for each of the next nine business days.

Required State briefly what you think took place on each of these nine days, assuming that only one transaction occurred each day.

	Cash	Accounts Receivable	Computer Inventory	Store Fixtures	Accounts Payable	Owners' Equity
May 10	$ 6,000	$4,000	$18,000	$ 3,000	$ 4,000	$27,000
11	11,000	4,000	18,000	3,000	4,000	32,000
12	11,000	4,000	18,000	7,000	4,000	36,000
15	8,000	4,000	21,000	7,000	4,000	36,000
16	8,000	4,000	26,000	7,000	9,000	36,000
17	11,000	1,000	26,000	7,000	9,000	36,000
18	6,000	1,000	26,000	14,000	11,000	36,000
19	3,000	1,000	26,000	14,000	8,000	36,000
22	3,000	1,000	25,600	14,000	7,600	36,000
23	1,000	1,000	25,600	14,000	7,600	34,000

1-13 Describing Underlying Transactions

The balances of each item in Lansdown Company's accounting equation are given below for August 31 and for each of the next nine business days.

Required State briefly what you think took place on each of these nine days, assuming that only one transaction occurred each day.

	Cash	Accounts Receivable	Computer Inventory	Store Fixtures	Accounts Payable	Owners' Equity
Aug. 31	$2,000	$8,000	$ 9,000	$ 7,500	$ 5,500	$21,000
Sept. 1	4,000	6,000	9,000	7,500	5,500	21,000
2	4,000	6,000	9,000	10,000	8,000	21,000
3	1,000	6,000	9,000	10,000	8,000	18,000
4	2,000	9,000	5,000	10,000	8,000	18,000
5	2,000	9,000	10,000	10,000	8,000	23,000
8	1,500	9,000	10,000	10,000	7,500	23,000
9	1,000	9,000	10,000	13,000	10,000	23,000
10	1,000	9,000	10,000	12,700	9,700	23,000
11	4,000	6,000	10,000	12,700	9,700	23,000

1-14 Prepare Balance Sheet

Sunshine Corporation's balance sheet at March 30, 19X1, contained only the following items (arranged here in random order):

Cash	$10,000	Accounts payable	$ 7,000
Notes payable	10,000	Furniture and fixtures	3,000
Merchandise inventory	40,000	Long-term debt payable	12,000
Paid-in capital	81,000	Building	20,000
Land	6,000	Notes receivable	2,000
Accounts receivable	14,000	Machinery and equipment	15,000

On March 31, 19X1, these transactions and events took place:

1. Purchased merchandise on account, $2,500.
2. Sold at cost for $1,000 cash some furniture that was not needed.
3. Issued additional capital stock for machinery and equipment valued at $12,000.
4. Purchased land for $25,000, of which $5,000 was paid in cash, the remaining being represented by a five-year note (long-term debt).
5. The building was valued by professional appraisers at $50,000.

Required   Prepare in good form a balance sheet for March 31, 19X1, showing supporting computations for all new amounts.

1-15   Prepare Balance Sheet

Geary Corporation's balance sheet at November 29, 19X1 contained only the following items (arranged here in random order):

Paid-in capital	$195,000	Machinery and equipment	$ 20,000
Notes payable	20,000	Furniture and fixtures	8,000
Cash	21,000	Notes receivable	8,000
Accounts receivable	10,000	Accounts payable	15,000
Merchandise inventory	29,000	Building	230,000
Land	46,000	Long-term debt payable	142,000

On the following day, November 30, these transactions and events occurred:

1. Purchased machinery and equipment for $14,000, paying $3,000 in cash and signing a ninety-day note for the balance.
2. Paid $5,000 on accounts payable.
3. Sold on account some land that was not needed for $6,000, which was the Geary Corporation's acquisition cost of the land.
4. The remaining land was valued at $240,000 by professional appraisers.
5. Issued capital stock as payment for $23,000 of the long-term debt, that is, debt due beyond one year.

Required   Prepare in good form a balance sheet for November 30, 19X1, showing supporting computations for all new amounts.

PROBLEMS

1-16   Prepare Balance Sheet

Alexis Brentano is a realtor. She buys and sells properties on her own account, and she also earns commissions as a real estate agent for buyers and sellers. Her business was organized on November 24, 19X1, as a sole proprietorship. Brentano also owns her own personal residence. Consider the following on November 30, 19X1:

1. Brentano owes $90,000 on a mortgage on some undeveloped land which was acquired by her business for a total price of $175,000.
2. Brentano had spent $15,000 cash for a Century 21 real estate franchise. Century 21 is a national affiliation of independent real estate brokers. This franchise is an asset.
3. Brentano owes $100,000 on a personal mortgage on her residence which was acquired on November 20, 19X1 for a total price of $180,000.
4. Brentano owes $2,800 on a personal charge account with Nordstrom's Department Store.
5. On November 28, Brentano hired David Goldstein as her first employee. He was to begin work on December 1. Brentano was pleased because Goldstein was one of the best real estate salesmen in the area. On November 29, Goldstein was killed in an automobile accident.

6. Business furniture of $17,000 was acquired on November 25 for $6,000 on open account plus $11,000 of business cash. On November 26, Brentano sold a $1,000 business chair for $1,000 to her next-door business neighbour on open account.

7. Brentano's balance at November 30 in her business chequing account after all transactions was $9,500.

Required   Prepare a balance sheet as of November 30, 19X1, for Alexis Brentano, realtor.

1-17   Analysis of Transactions

Use the format of Exhibit 1-1 (p. 12) to analyze the following transactions for April of Kijewski Cleaners. Then prepare a balance sheet as of April 30, 19X1. Kijewski was founded on April 1.

1. Issued 1,000 shares of $1 par common stock for cash, $60,000.
2. Issued 1,000 shares of $1 par common stock for equipment, $60,000.
3. Borrowed cash, signing a note payable for $30,000.
4. Purchased equipment for cash, $20,000.
5. Purchased office furniture on account, $10,000.
6. Disbursed cash on account (to reduce the account payable), $4,000.
7. Sold equipment on account at cost, $8,000.
8. Discovered that the most prominent competitor in the area was bankrupt and was closing its doors on April 30.
9. Collected cash on account, $3,000. See transaction 7.

1-18   Analysis of Transactions

Consider the following January transactions:

1. ABC Corporation is formed on January 1, 19X1, by three persons, Aldor, Binge, and Chin. ABC will be a wholesale distributor of electronic games. Each of the three investors is issued 20,000 shares of common stock ($2 par value) for $10 cash per share. Use two shareholders' equity accounts: Capital Stock (at par) and Additional Paid-in Capital.
2. Merchandise inventory of $200,000 is acquired for cash.
3. Merchandise inventory of $85,000 is acquired on open account.
4. Unsatisfactory merchandise that cost $11,000 in transaction 3 is returned for full credit.
5. Equipment of $40,000 is acquired for a cash down payment of $10,000 plus a three-month promissory note of $30,000.
6. As a favour, ABC sells equipment of $4,000 to a business neighbour on open account. The equipment had cost $4,000.
7. ABC pays $20,000 on the account described in transaction 3.
8. ABC collects $2,000 from the business neighbour. See transaction 6.
9. ABC buys merchandise inventory of $100,000. One-half of the amount is paid in cash, and one-half is owed on open account.
10. Chin sells half of his common stock to Loring for $13 per share.

Required   1. Using a format similar to Exhibit 1-1 (p. 12), prepare an analysis showing the effects of January transactions on the financial position of ABC Corporation.

2. Prepare a balance sheet as of January 31, 19X1.

1-19   Analysis of Transactions

You began a business as a wholesaler of gloves, scarves, and caps. The following events have occurred:

1. On March 1, 19X1, you invested $150,000 cash in your new sole proprietorship, which you call Yukon Products.
2. Acquired $20,000 inventory for cash.
3. Acquired $8,000 inventory on open account.
4. Acquired equipment for $15,000 in exchange for a $5,000 cash down payment and a $10,000 promissory note.
5. A large retail store, which you had hoped would be a big customer, discontinued operations.
6. You take gloves home for your family. The gloves were carried in Yukon's inventory at $600. (Regard this as a borrowing by you from Yukon Products.)
7. Gloves that cost $300 in transaction 2 were of the wrong style. You returned them and obtained a full cash refund.
8. Gloves that cost $800 in transaction 3 were of the wrong colour. You returned them and obtained gloves of the correct colour in exchange.
9. Caps that cost $500 in transaction 3 had an unacceptable quality. You returned them and obtained full credit on your account.
10. Paid $5,000 on promissory note.
11. You use your personal cash savings of $5,000 to acquire some equipment for Yukon. You consider this as an additional investment in your business.
12. Paid $3,000 on open account.
13. Two scarf manufacturers who are suppliers for Yukon announced a 7% rise in prices, effective in sixty days.
14. You use your personal cash savings of $1,000 to acquire a new TV set for your family.
15. You exchange equipment that cost $4,000 in transaction 4 with another wholesaler. However, the equipment received, which is almost new, is smaller and is worth only $1,500. Therefore the other wholesaler also agrees to pay you $500 in cash now and an additional $2,000 in cash in sixty days. (No gain or loss is recognized on this transaction.)

Required

1. Using Exhibit 1-1 (p. 12) as a guide, prepare an analysis of Yukon's transactions for March. Confine your analysis to the effects on the financial position of Yukon Products.
2. Prepare a balance sheet for Yukon Products as of March 31, 19X1.

1-20 Personal and Professional Entities

Kate Green, a recent graduate of a law school, was penniless on December 25, 19X1.

1. On December 26, Green inherited an enormous sum of money.
2. On December 27, she placed $80,000 in a business chequing account for her unincorporated law practice.
3. On December 28, she purchased a home for a down payment of $100,000 plus a home mortgage payable of $250,000.
4. On December 28, Green agreed to rent a law office. She provided a $1,000 cash damage deposit (from her business cash), which will be fully refundable when she vacates the premises. This deposit is a business asset. Rental payments are to be made in advance on the first business day of each month. (The first payment of $700 is not to be made until January 2, 19X2.)
5. On December 28, Green purchased a computer for her law practice for $5,000 cash plus a $5,000 promissory note due in ninety days.
6. On December 28, she also purchased legal supplies for $1,000 on open account.

7. On December 28, Green purchased office furniture for her practice for $4,000 cash.

8. On December 29, Green hired a legal assistant receptionist for $380 per week. He was to report to work on January 2.

9. On December 30, Green's law practice lent $2,000 of cash in return for a one-year note from G. Keefe, a local candy store owner. Keefe had indicated that she would spread the news about the new lawyer.

Required

1. Use the format demonstrated in Exhibit 1-1 (p. 12) to analyze the transactions of Kate Green, lawyer. To avoid crowding, put your numbers in thousands of dollars. Do not restrict yourself to the account titles in Exhibit 1-1.

2. Prepare a balance sheet as of December 31, 19X1.

1-21   Bank Balance Sheet

Consider the following balance sheet accounts of Bank of North America (in millions):

Assets		Liabilities and Shareholders' Equity	
Cash	$ 13,470	Deposits	$ 141,618
Government and		Other liabilities	28,171
other securities	32,162	Total liabilities	$ 169,789
Loans receivable	122,871	Shareholders' equity	17,144
Premises and equipment	3,631		
Other assets	14,799	Total liabilities and	
Total assets	$186,933	shareholders' equity	$186,933

This balance sheet illustrates how banks gather and use money. Nearly 75% of the total assets are in the form of investments in loans, and over 80% of the total liabilities and shareholders' equity are in the form of deposits, the major liability. That is, these financial institutions are in the business of raising funds from depositors and, in turn, lending those funds to businesses, homeowners, and others. The shareholders' equity is usually tiny in comparison with the deposits (only about 6% in this case).

Required

1. What Bank of North America accounts would be affected if you deposited $1,000?
2. Why are deposits listed as liabilities?
3. What accounts would be affected if the bank loaned Joan Kessler $50,000 for home renovations?
4. What accounts would be affected if Isabel Garcia withdrew $4,000 from her savings account?

1-22   Accounting and Ethics

A survey of high school, college, and university students showed that accountants are given high marks for their ethics. Professional associations for both internal accountants and external auditors place much emphasis on their standards of ethical conduct. Discuss why maintaining a reputation for ethical conduct is important for (1) accountants within an organization, and (2) external auditors. What can accountants do to foster a reputation for high ethical standards and conduct?

COMPANY CASES

1-23   Analysis of Transactions

Walgreen Company is a well-known drugstore chain. A condensed balance sheet for August 31, 1993 follows (in thousands):

Assets		Liabilities and Shareholders' Equity	
Cash	$ 91,597	Notes payable	$ 99,590
Accounts receivable	139,313	Accounts payable	427,185
Inventories	1,094,053	Other liabilities	629,665
Property and		Shareholders' equity	1,378,751
other assets	1,210,228		
Total	$2,535,191	Total	$2,535,191

Required Use a format similar to Exhibit 1-1 (p. 12) to analyze the following transactions for the first two days of September. (Dollar amounts are in thousands.) Then prepare a balance sheet as of September 2.

1. Issued 1,000 shares of common stock to employees for cash, $22.
2. Issued 1,500 shares of common stock for the acquisition of special equipment from a supplier, $33.
3. Borrowed cash, signing a note payable for $120.
4. Purchased equipment for cash, $125.
5. Purchased inventories on account, $90.
6. Disbursed cash on account (to reduce the accounts payable), $354.
7. Sold display equipment to retailer on account at cost, $14.
8. Collected cash on account, $84.

1-24 Analysis of Transactions
Nike, Inc. had the following condensed balance sheet on May 31, 1994 (in thousands):

Assets		Liabilities and Owners' Equity	
Cash	$ 518,816	Notes payable	$ 127,378
Accounts receivable	703,682	Accounts payable	210,578
Inventories	470,023	Other liabilities	294,910
Equipment and		Total liabilities	$ 632,866
other assets	681,294	Owners' equity	1,740,949
		Total liabilities and	
Total assets	$2,373,815	owners' equity	$2,373,815

Consider the following transactions that occurred during the first three days of June (in thousands of dollars):

1. Inventories were acquired for cash, $150.
2. Inventories were acquired on open account, $200.
3. Unsatisfactory shoes acquired on open account in March were returned for full credit, $40.
4. Equipment of $120 was acquired for a cash down payment of $30 plus a six-month promissory note of $90.
5. To encourage wider displays, special store equipment was sold on account to Montreal area stores for $400. The equipment had cost $400 in the preceding month.

6. Michael J. Fox produced, directed, and starred in a movie. As a favour to a Nike executive, he agreed to display Nike shoes in a basketball scene. No fee was paid by Nike.
7. Cash was disbursed on account (to reduce accounts payable), $170.
8. Collected cash on account, $180.
9. Borrowed cash from a bank, $500.
10. Sold additional common stock for cash to new investors, $900.
11. The president of the company sold 5,000 shares of his personal holdings of Nike stock through his stockbroker.

Required

1. Using a format similar to Exhibit 1-1(p. 12), prepare an analysis showing the effects of the June transactions on the financial position of Nike.
2. Prepare a balance sheet as of June 3.

1-25   Presenting Paid-in Capital

Consider excerpts from two balance sheets (amounts in thousands):

Common stock, $0.20 par value; authorized	
400 million shares; shares outstanding 305,603,000	$ 61,000
Additional paid-in capital	5,212,000

Common stock par value—$1.25 —outstanding 581,388,475	
shares (includes capital in excess of par value)	$6,980,000

1. How would the presentation of the first company's shareholders' equity accounts be affected if one million more shares were issued for $50 cash per share?
2. How would the presentation of the second company's shareholders' equity accounts be affected if one million more shares were issued for $50 cash per share? Be specific.

1-26   Presenting Paid-in Capital

Honeywell, Inc., maker of thermostats and a variety of complex control systems, presented the following in its balance sheet of January 1, 1994:

Common stock—$1.50 par value, 188,328,570 shares issued	?
Additional paid-in capital	$431,500,000

What amount should be shown on the common stock line? What was the average price per share paid by the original investors for the Honeywell common stock? How do your answers compare with the $31 market price of the stock on January 2, 1995? Comment briefly.

1-27   Presenting Paid-in Capital

Mitsubishi Kasei Corporation is Japan's premier integrated chemical company. The following items were presented in its balance sheet of March 31, 1991:

Common stock— ¥50 par value, 1,408 million shares issued	
and outstanding	?
Additional paid-in capital (in millions of yen)	¥105,982

Note: ¥ is the symbol for Japanese yen.

1. What amount should be shown on the common stock line?
2. What was the average price per share paid by the original investors for the Mitsubishi Kasei common stock?
3. How do your answers compare with the ¥580 market price of the stock? Comment briefly.

1-28 Prepare Balance Sheet

Microsoft is the world's leading software company. Microsoft's 1994 annual report included the following balance sheet items (in millions of dollars):

Property, plant, and equipment	867
Accounts payable	239
Inventories	127
Capital stock	1,086
Cash	?
Total shareholders' equity	?
Long-term debt	0
Total assets	3,805
Accounts receivable	338
Other assets	310
Additional shareholders' equity	?
Other liabilities	324

Required   Prepare a condensed balance sheet, including amounts for

1. Cash.
2. Additional and total shareholders' equity.
3. Total liabilities.

1-29 Prepare Balance Sheet

Procter & Gamble Company has many popular products, including Tide, Jif, and Crest. Its balance sheet of June 30, 1994, contained the following items (in millions):

Long-term debt payable	$ 4,980
Cash	(1)
Total shareholders' equity	(2)
Total liabilities	(3)
Accounts receivable	3,115
Common stock	684
Inventories	2,877
Accounts payable	3,264
Property, plant, and equipment	10,024
Additional shareholders' equity	8,148
Other assets	7,146
Other liabilities	8,459
Total assets	25,535

Required   Prepare a condensed balance sheet, including amounts for

1. Cash. What do you think of its relative size?
2. Total shareholders' equity.
3. Total liabilities.

1-30 Hudson's Bay Company Annual Report

This and similar problems in succeeding chapters focus on the financial statements of an actual company. The Hudson's Bay Company is the largest retailer in Canada.

As each homework problem is solved, readers gradually strengthen their understanding of actual financial statements in their entirety.

Refer to the Hudson's Bay Company balance sheet in Appendix A at the end of the book and answer the following questions:

1. How much cash did the Hudson's Bay Company have on January 31, 1997? (Include cash equivalent as part of cash.) 24,841,000
2. What were the total assets on January 31, 1997? 3,816,269
3. Write the company's accounting equation as of January 31, 1997, by filling in the dollar amount:

   Assets = Liabilities + Shareholders' equity. Consider deferred income taxes and contingencies to be liabilities.

1-31   Annual Report Disclosure

Each chapter will have one problem that requires use of a company's annual report. Select a company of your choice (or as directed by your professor), obtain a copy of a recent annual report, and answer the questions noted as "Annual Report Disclosure" at the end of each chapter.

Select the financial statements of any company and focus on the balance sheet.

Required

1. Identify the amount of cash (including cash equivalents, if any) shown on the most recent balance sheet.
2. What were the total assets shown on the most recent balance sheet? The total liabilities plus shareholders' equity? How do these two amounts compare?
3. Compute total liabilities and total shareholders' equity. (Assume that all items on the right side of the balance sheet that are not explicitly listed as shareholders' equity are liabilities.) Compare the size of the liabilities to shareholders' equity and comment on the comparison. Write the company's accounting equation as of the year-end by filling in the dollar amounts.

2

Income Measurement: The Accrual Basis

Learning Objectives

After studying this chapter, you should be able to

1 Explain how revenues and expenses combine to measure income for an accounting time period.

2 Compare the accrual basis and cash basis accounting methods and use the concepts of recognition, matching, and cost recovery to record revenues and expenses.

3 Prepare an income statement and show how it is related to a balance sheet.

4 Prepare a statement of changes in financial position and show how it differs from an income statement.

5 Account for cash dividends and prepare a statement of retained earnings.

6 Identify the major organizations that influence generally accepted accounting principles.

7 Compute and explain earnings per share, price-earnings ratio, dividend-yield ratio, and dividend-payout ratio.

The measurement of income is one of the most important and controversial topics in accounting. This chapter presents the rudiments of measuring income, including a discussion of revenues and expenses. It also defines three basic financial statements prepared by accountants: *the income statement, statement of changes in financial position,* and *statement of retained earnings.* We enlarge our understanding of generally accepted accounting principles (GAAP) and how they are determined. Finally, four financial ratios that decision makers use to analyze the performance and prospects of a business entity are introduced.

Income is a measure of accomplishment—a means of evaluating an entity's performance over a period of time. Although income could be measured many ways, accountants have agreed to use the accrual basis in reporting an entity's net income, so that is the major focus of this chapter. An alternative, the cash basis, has supporters, and accountants prepare another statement, the statement of changes in financial position, to provide information about how the company obtains and uses cash.

Many different groups of people have an interest in a company's net income. Investors eagerly await reports about a company's annual income. Stock prices generally reflect investors' expectations about income, but often actual reported income differs from what was expected. When this happens, stock prices can have large swings. Government regulators and tax authorities are interested in a company's net income. Company management may be rewarded with bonuses based on reported income. A company's net income is of interest to a wide range of persons.

■ INTRODUCTION TO INCOME MEASUREMENT

Objective 1

Explain how revenues and expenses combine to measure income for an accounting time period.

Almost all of us have a reason for learning about how accountants measure income. For example, we want to know how we are doing as individuals, as corporations, as hospitals, or as universities. Even nonprofit institutions use a concept of income as a way of determining how much they can afford to spend to accomplish their objectives. Investors use a concept of income to measure their successes and failures and to compare the performance of their existing and potential holdings. Indeed, *income* is the primary way of evaluating the economic performance of people, corporations, other entities, and economies as a whole.

The accountant's measurements of income are the major means of evaluating a business entity's performance. But measuring income is not straightforward. Most people agree that income should be a measure of the increase in the "wealth" of an entity over a period of time. However, disputes arise over how to define wealth and how to measure the increase in wealth for a specific entity for a specific time period. These disputes will never be fully resolved. Nevertheless, accountants have decided that a common set of rules for measuring income should be applied by all companies so that decision makers such as investors can more easily compare the performance of one company with that of another. These rules provide the basis for the following discussion of income measurement. We begin by discussing the time period over which income is measured and then proceed to measures of accomplishments (revenues) and efforts (expenses).

Operating Cycle

operating cycle
The time span during which cash is used to acquire goods and services, which in turn are sold to customers, who in turn pay for their purchases with cash.

Most corporations and business entities follow a similar, somewhat rhythmical, pattern of economic activity during which income is measured. An **operating cycle** (also called a *cash cycle* or *earnings cycle*) is the time span during which cash is used to acquire goods and services, which in turn are sold to customers, who in turn pay for their purchases with cash. Consider the following example. A retail business usually engages in some version of the operating cycle in order to earn profits:

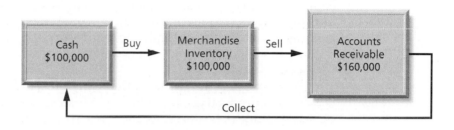

The box for Accounts Receivable (amounts owed to the entity by customers) is larger than the other two boxes because the objective is to sell goods at a price higher than the acquisition cost. Retailers and nearly all other businesses buy goods and services and perform acts (such as placing them in a convenient location or changing their form) that merit selling prices that yield an expected profit. The total amount of profit earned during a particular period depends on the excess of selling prices over costs of the goods and additional expenses and on the speed of the operating cycle.

The Accounting Time Period

The only way to be certain of how successfully a business has performed is to close its doors, sell all its assets, pay all liabilities, and return any leftover cash to the owner. Indeed in the 1400s, Venetian merchant traders did exactly that. For each voyage, cash was invested, goods were acquired and exported to foreign markets, and sold for cash. The proceeds were distributed to the original investors. Today, however, owners, managers, and others want periodic reports on how well an entity has performed before the entity is terminated. The accountant's measurements of income are a major means of evaluating progress during the accounting time period.

fiscal year The year established for accounting purposes.

The calendar year is the most popular time period for measuring income or profits. However, many companies use a **fiscal year**, which is the year established for accounting purposes, that ends on some date other than December 31. The fiscal year-end date is often the low point in annual business activity. For example, Bombardier Inc. has a fiscal year-end of January 31 and Andrés Wines a year-end of March 31.

Users of financial statements also want to know how well the business is doing each month, each quarter, and each half-year. Therefore, companies

interim periods The time spans established for accounting purposes that are less than a year.

prepare financial statements for **interim periods**, which are the time spans established for accounting purposes that are less than a year.

Revenues and Expenses

revenues Gross increases in owners' equity arising from increases in assets received in exchange for the delivery of goods or services to customers.

expenses Decreases in owners' equity that arise because goods or services are delivered to customers.

income (profit, earnings) The excess of revenues over expenses.

retained earnings Additional owners' equity generated by income or profits.

Revenues and expenses are the key components in measuring income. These terms apply to the inflows and outflows of assets that occur during a business entity's operating cycle. More specifically, **revenues** are gross increases in owners' equity arising from increases in assets received in exchange for the delivery of goods or services to customers. **Expenses** are decreases in owners' equity that arise because goods or services are delivered to customers. Together these items define the fundamental meaning of **income** (or **profit** or **earnings**), which can simply be defined as the excess of revenues over expenses. The additional owners' equity generated by income or profits is **retained earnings**.

Consider again the Biwheels Company presented in Chapter 1. Exhibit 2-1 is a direct reproduction of Exhibit 1-1, which summarized the nine transactions of George Smith's business. Assume now that Smith has incorporated his business so that the company is a corporation instead of a sole proprietorship. That is, the owner's equity account is no longer George Smith, Capital. In Exhibit 2-1, it is shareholders' equity.

Now consider some additional transactions. Suppose Biwheels' sales for the entire month of January amount to $160,000 on open account. The cost to Biwheels of the inventory sold is $100,000. Note that the January sales and other transactions illustrated here are recorded as *summarized* transactions. The company's sales do not all take place at once, nor do purchases of inventory, collections from customers, or disbursements to suppliers.

The accounting for the summarized sales transaction has two phases, a *revenue phase* (10a) and an *expense phase* (10b):

	Assets		=	Liabilities	+	Shareholders' Equity
	Accounts Receivable	*Merchandise Inventory*				*Retained Earnings*
(10a) Sales on open account	+160,000		=			+160,000 (sales revenues)
(10b) Cost of merchandise inventory sold		−100,000	=			−100,000 (cost of goods sold expenses)

This transaction records the $160,000 sale on open account of inventory that had cost $100,000. Two things happen simultaneously in the balance sheet equation: an inflow of assets in the form of accounts receivable (10a) in *exchange* for an outflow of assets in the form of merchandise inventory (10b). Liabilities are completely unaffected, so shareholders' equity rises by $160,000 (sales revenues) − $100,000 (cost of goods sold expense), or $60,000.

Exhibit 2-1

Biwheels Company

Analysis of Transactions for December 31, 19X1–
January 12, 19X2 (in dollars)

Description of Transactions	Cash	+ Accounts Receivable	+ Merchandise Inventory	+ Store Equipment	=	Note Payable	+ Accounts Payable	+ Shareholders' Equity
(1) Initial investment	+400,000				=			+400,000
(2) Loan from bank	+100,000				=	+100,000		
(3) Acquire inventory for cash	–150,000		+150,000		=			
(4) Acquire inventory on credit			+ 10,000		=		+10,000	
(5) Acquire store equipment for cash plus credit	– 4,000			+15,000	=		+11,000	
(6) Sales of equipment		+1,000		– 1,000	=			
(7) Return of inventory acquired on January 3			– 800		=		– 800	
(8) Payments to creditors	– 4,000				=		– 4,000	
(9) Collections from debtors	+ 700	– 700			=			
Balance, January 12, 19X2	342,700	+ 300	+ 159,200	+ 14,000	=	100,000	+ 16,200	+ 400,000
			516,200				516,200	

As entries 10a and 10b show, revenue from sales is recorded as an increase in assets, namely, Accounts Receivable, and an increase in Retained Earnings, a shareholders' equity account. In contrast, the expense of the goods sold is recorded as a decrease in assets, namely, the Merchandise Inventory account, and a decrease in Retained Earnings. So expenses are negative entries to shareholders' equity accounts. These relationships can be illustrated as follows:

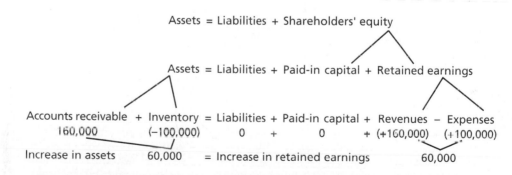

Revenue is recorded when a sale on open account is made and an asset, accounts receivable, is recorded; recording is not delayed until cash is received. Likewise, expenses are recorded when goods or services are delivered or assets are used for operations, not when items are purchased or when payments are made. Therefore, accountants measure income by the increases and decreases in assets, not solely by cash receipts and cash disbursements.

accrual basis Accounting method that recognizes the impact of transactions on the financial statements in the time periods when revenues and expenses occur.

cash basis Accounting method that recognizes the impact of transactions on the financial statements only when cash is received or disbursed.

Objective 2

Compare the accrual basis and cash basis accounting methods and use the concepts of recognition, matching, and cost recovery to record revenues and expenses.

■ METHODS FOR MEASURING INCOME

Accrual Basis and Cash Basis

Income measurement is anchored to the **accrual basis** of accounting, as distinguished from the cash basis. The accrual basis recognizes the impact of transactions on the financial statements in the time periods when revenues and expenses occur. That is, revenue is recorded as it is earned, and expenses are recorded as they are incurred—not necessarily when cash changes hands.

In contrast, the **cash basis** recognizes the impact of transactions on the financial statements only when cash is received or disbursed.

For many years accountants debated the merits of accrual basis versus cash-basis accounting. Supporters of the accrual basis maintained that the cash basis provides an incomplete measure of performance—it ignores activities that increase or decrease assets other than cash. Supporters of the cash basis pointed out that companies with good records of income went bankrupt because they did not generate enough cash to meet their obligations. Both camps were right. Income under the accrual basis is the better measure for relating overall operating accomplishments to efforts. Why? Because it includes a more complete summary of the entity's value-producing activities. The cash basis focuses on the narrow but important issue of an entity's ability to generate cash from its current operations. The cash flow from operations is an important part of the statement of changes in financial position to be introduced later in this chapter.

Accrual versus Cash Accounting for Governments

Most governments in the world use cash-basis, not accrual-basis, accounting. Many accountants and economists claim that the cash-basis system does not give a true picture of the financial health of a national economy.

Using cash-basis accounting, the economic performance of a country is measured by the difference between its cash receipts and cash disbursements. During the mid-1980s many countries had large annual deficits, meaning that disbursements greatly exceeded receipts. The difference had to be made up by heavy borrowing.

By the 1990s many European countries, such as Britain and Germany, had reduced their annual deficits so that their economic picture looked rosier, at least according to their cash-basis accounting records. But much of the deficit reduction came from delaying expenditures on assets such as roads, bridges, and education. At the same time, they were using up assets that had been purchased in the past. Their cash-basis accounting system did not measure this depletion in the countries' asset bases. If companies ignored depletion of their assets, they would soon be out of business. Governments must also face this reality sooner or later.

Accrual accounting separates outlays for assets, which have value that carries over into future years, from outlays for resources that are consumed immediately. If these governments had used accrual accounting, they would have learned the extent of the negative impact of using up more assets than are being replaced. National wealth was decreasing even though cash disbursements did not greatly exceed cash receipts.

One government—New Zealand's—has recently changed to an accrual-accounting system. The government leaders believe the accrual balance sheet and income statement will provide a better measure of the financial performance and position of the country than did the cash-basis system. ■

Sources: "Budget by Balance Sheet," The Economist (January 25, 1992), p. 18; R. Khalaf, "Lies, Damned Lies, and the Budget Deficit," Forbes (December 9, 1991), p. 71.

Recognition of Revenues

recognition A test for determining whether revenues should be recorded in the financial statements of a given period. To be recognized, revenues must be earned and realized.

A major convention accountants use to measure income on an accrual basis is **recognition** of revenues, which is a test for determining whether revenues should be recorded in the financial statements of a given period. To be recognized, revenues must ordinarily meet *two* criteria:

1. Be *earned*. For revenues to be earned, the goods or services must be fully rendered. The usual evidence is delivery to customers.
2. Be *realized*. Revenues are realized when cash or claims to cash are received in exchange for goods or services. The usual evidence is a market transaction whereby the buyer pays or promises to pay cash and the seller delivers merchandise or services. If cash is not received directly, the eventual collectibility of cash must be reasonably assured.

Revenue recognition for most retail companies such as Loblaw, Oshawa Group, and Mark's Work Wearhouse is straightforward. Revenue is both earned and realized at the point of sale. For other companies, revenue may be earned and realized at different times. When this occurs, revenue recognition is delayed until the second event. Consider the following examples:

- *The Financial Post* receives prepaid subscriptions. The revenue is realized when the subscription is received, but it is not earned until delivery of each issue.
- A real estate company "sells" land in the Yukon on an installment basis but without credit investigations. Often when collectibility is questionable, revenue recognition may be delayed until cash is received.

Matching and Cost Recovery

product costs Costs that are linked with revenues and are charged as expenses when the related revenue is recognized.

matching The recording of expenses in the same time period as the related revenues are recognized.

period costs Items identified directly as expenses of the time period in which they are incurred.

cost recovery The concept by which some purchases of goods or services are recorded as assets because their costs are expected to be recovered in the form of cash inflows (or reduced cash outflows) in future periods.

Expenses are recognized and recorded in the financial statements of the period in which their economic benefits are consumed or used up. Expenses of any period are of two types: (1) those linked with the revenues earned that period, and (2) those linked with the time period itself.

Some costs, such as cost of goods sold or sales commissions, are naturally linked with revenues. If there are no revenues, there is no cost of goods sold or sales commissions. Such costs are called **product costs** and are charged as expenses when revenue from the goods is recognized. The concept of *matching*, a favourite buzzword of accountants, describes the recognition of these product costs. **Matching** is the recording of expenses in the same time period as the related revenues are recognized.

Other expenses, such as rent expense and many administrative expenses, occur regardless of the level of sales in a particular period. Their benefits are consumed by the passage of time rather than the level of sales. Such items are identified directly as expenses of the time period and are called **period costs**.

The heart of recognizing expense in the accounts is the *cost recovery* concept. Under **cost recovery**, some purchases of goods or services are recorded as assets because the costs are expected to be recovered in the form of cash inflows (or reduced cash outflows) in future periods. For example, the purchase price of goods or services that are acquired in the current period but will not be fully used until a future period should be initially recorded as an asset. When the good or service is used, the accountant reduces the asset account and records an expense. Rent paid in advance is such an asset. Suppose a firm pays an annual rental of $12,000 on January 1. An asset account, *prepaid rent*, is increased by $12,000 because the rental services have not yet been used. Each month the prepaid rent account is reduced by $1,000, and rent expense is increased by $1,000, recognizing the using up of the prepaid rent asset.

Notice that prepaid rent is an *intangible* asset. Assets are defined as economic resources. They are not confined to tangible items that you can see or touch, such as cash or inventory. Assets also include the intangible legal rights to future services, such as the use of facilities.

Applying Matching and Cost Recovery

To focus on the matching and cost recovery concepts, assume that the Biwheels Company has only two expenses other than the cost of goods sold: rent expense and amortization[1] expense. Transaction 11 (see Exhibit 2-2, which merely continues Exhibit 2-1) is the payment of store rent of $6,000 covering January, February, and March of 19X2. Rent is $2,000 per month, payable quarterly in advance. (Assume that this initial payment was made on January 16, although rent is commonly paid at the start of the rental period.)

The rent disbursement acquires the right to use store facilities for the next three months. The $6,000 measures the *future* benefit from these services, so the amount is recorded in an asset account, Prepaid Rent:

	Assets		= Liabilities +	Shareholders' Equity
	Cash	Prepaid Rent		Retained Earnings
(11) Pay rent in advance	−6,000	+6,000 =		
(12) Recognize rent expense		−2,000 =		−2,000 (increase rent expense)

Transaction 11, made at the time of disbursement, shows no effect on shareholders' equity in the balance sheet equation. One asset, cash, is simply exchanged for another, prepaid rent.

Transaction 12 is recorded at the end of January. It recognizes that one-third of the rental services has expired, so the asset is reduced, and shareholders' equity is also reduced by $2,000 as rent expense for January. This recognition of rent *expense* means that $2,000 of the asset, Prepaid Rent, has been "used up" in the conduct of operations during January.

Prepaid rent of $4,000 is carried forward as an asset as of January 31 because the accountant was virtually certain of cost recovery. Why? Because without the prepayment, cash outflows of $2,000 each would have to be made for February and March. So the cost of the prepayment will be recovered in the sense that future cash outflows will be reduced by $4,000. Furthermore, future revenues (sales) are expected to be high enough to ensure the recovery of the $4,000.

---

[1]The term amortization is used in this book to be consistent with the *CICA Handbook*, s. 3060. It is synonymous with depreciation and depletion.

Exhibit 2-2

Biwheels Company Analysis of Transactions for January 19X2 (in dollars)

Description of Transactions	Assets						=	Liabilities		+	Shareholders' Equity	
	Cash	+ Accounts Receivable	+ Merchandise Inventory	+ Prepaid Rent	+ Store Equipment		=	Note Payable	+ Accounts Payable	+	Paid-in Capital	+ Retained Earnings
(1)–(9) See Exhibit 2-1 Balance, January 12, 19X2	342,700	+ 300	+ 159,200		+ 14,000		=	100,000	+ 16,200	+	400,000	
(10a) Sales on open account (inflow of assets)		+160,000					=					+ 160,000 (sales revenue)
(10b) Cost of merchandise inventory sold (outflow of assets)			−100,000				=					− 100,000 (increase cost of goods sold expense)
(11) Pay rent in advance	− 6,000			+6,000			=					
(12) Recognize expiration of rental services				−2,000			=					− 2,000 (increase rent expense)
(13) Recognized expiration of equipment services (amortization)					− 100		=					− 100 (increase amortization expense)
Balance, January 31, 19X2	336,700	+ 160,300	+ 59,200	+ 4,000	+ 13,900		=	100,000	+ 16,200	+	400,000	+ 57,900
	574,100						=				574,100	

amortization The systematic allocation of the acquisition cost of long-lived or fixed assets to the expense accounts of particular periods that benefit from the use of the assets.

The same matching and cost recovery concepts that underlie the accounting for prepaid rent apply to **amortization**, which is the systematic allocation of the acquisition cost of *long-lived* or *fixed assets* to the expense accounts of particular periods that benefit from the use of the assets. These assets are tangible physical assets such as buildings, equipment, furniture, and fixtures owned by the entity. Land is not subject to amortization.

In both prepaid rent and amortization, the business purchases an asset that gradually wears out or is used up. As the asset is being used, more and more of its original cost is transferred from an asset account to an expense account. The sole difference between amortization and prepaid rent is the length of time taken before the asset loses its usefulness. Buildings, equipment, and furniture remain useful for many years; prepaid rent and other prepaid expenses usually expire within a year.

Transaction 13 in Exhibit 2-2 records the amortization expense for the Biwheels equipment. A portion of the original cost of $14,000 becomes amortization expense in each month of the equipment's useful life, say, 140 months. Under the matching concept, the amortization expense for January is $14,000 / 140 months, or $100 per month:

	Assets	=	Liabilities +	Shareholders' Equity
	Store Equipment			*Retained Earnings*
(13) Recognize amortization expense	−100	=		−100 (increase amortization expense)

In this transaction, the asset account, Store Equipment, is decreased as is the shareholders' equity account, Retained Earnings. The general concept of expense should be clear by now. The purchase and use of goods and services (for example, inventories, rent, equipment) ordinarily consist of two basic steps: (1) the *acquisition* of the assets (transactions 3, 4, and 5 in Exhibit 2-1 and transaction 11 in Exhibit 2-2), and (2) the *expiration* of the assets as *expenses* (transactions 10b, 12, and 13 in Exhibit 2-2). As these examples show, when prepaid expenses and fixed assets are used up, the total assets and owners' equity are decreased. When sales to customers bring new assets to the business, its total assets and owners' equity are increased. Expense accounts are basically deductions from shareholders' equity. Similarly, revenue accounts are basically additions to shareholders' equity.

Recognition of Expired Assets

Assets such as inventory, prepaid rent, and equipment may be thought of as stored costs that are carried forward to future periods rather than immediately charged against revenue:

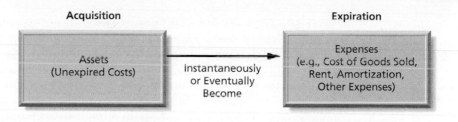

Thus, assets are unexpired costs held back from the expense stream and carried in the balance sheet to await expiration in future periods. Assets have future potential to produce revenue.

The analysis of the inventory, rent, and amortization transactions in Exhibit 2-2 distinguishes between acquisition and expiration. The unexpired costs of inventory, prepaid rent, and equipment are assets until they are used up and become expenses.

Services such as advertising are often acquired and used almost instantaneously. Conceptually, these costs should, at least momentarily, be viewed as assets upon acquisition before being written off as expenses. For example, suppose newspaper advertising was acquired for $1,000 cash. To abide by the acquisition-expiration sequence, the transaction could be analyzed in two phases; see alternative 1 below.

	Assets			= Liabilities +		Shareholders' Equity	
Transaction	Cash +	Other Assets +	Prepaid Advertising =			Paid-in Capital +	Retained Earnings
ALTERNATIVE 1: TWO PHASES							
Phase (a) Prepay for advertising	−1,000		+1,000	=			
Phase (b) Use up advertising			1,000	−			−1,000 (advertising expense)
ALTERNATIVE 2: ONE PHASE							
Phases (a) and (b) together	−1,000			=			−1,000 (advertising expense)

In practice, however, many services are acquired and used up so quickly that accountants do not bother recording the asset, Prepaid Advertising. Instead the shortcut in alternative 2 is usually recorded. When financial statements are prepared, this presents the correct result, but the two-step alternative 1 underscores what the entity actually does. The entity acquires goods and services, not expenses per se. These goods and services become expenses as they are used to generate revenue.

Some of the most difficult issues in accounting centre on *when* an unexpired cost expires and becomes an expense. For example, some accountants believe that research and development costs should be accounted for as unexpired costs, shown on balance sheets among the assets, and written off to expense in some systematic manner over a period of years. After all, companies engage in research and product development activities because they expect them to create future benefits. In Canada, companies are allowed to record development on the balance sheet if certain conditions are met, while research costs must be expensed as incurred. Regulators in the United States and most other countries have ruled that such costs have vague future benefits that are difficult to measure reliably and thus have required writing them off as expenses immediately. In such cases, research costs are not found on balance sheets. In contrast, Italy and Spain allow research and development costs to be recognized initially as an asset and to be shown on the balance sheet.

Analyzing the Balance Sheet Equation

Recall from page 43:

1) Assets (A) = Liabilities (L) + Shareholders' equity (SE)

2) Assets   = Liabilities + Paid-in capital + Retained earnings

3) Assets   = Liabilities + Paid-in capital + Revenue − Expenses

Revenue and expense accounts are nothing more than subdivisions of shareholders' equity—temporary shareholders' equity accounts, as it were. Their purpose is to summarize the volume of sales and the various expenses so that income can be measured.

The analysis of each transaction in Exhibits 2-1 and 2-2 illustrates the dual nature of the balance sheet equation, which is always kept in balance. If the items affected are confined to one side of the equation, the total amount added is equal to the total amount subtracted on that side. If the items affected are on both sides, then equal amounts are simultaneously added or simultaneously subtracted on each side.

The striking feature of the balance sheet equation is its universal applicability. No transaction has ever been conceived, no matter how simple or complex, that cannot be analyzed via the equation. Business leaders and accountants employ the balance sheet equation constantly to be sure they understand the effects of business transactions they are planning.

income statement
A report of all revenues and expenses pertaining to a specific time period.

net income The remainder after all expenses have been deducted from revenues.

■ THE INCOME STATEMENT

Chapter 1 showed that a balance sheet is a summary of the net result of all of the transactions recorded in an entity's accounts. Another basic financial statement, the *income statement*, focuses on the revenue and expense transactions recorded in the retained earnings account. An **income statement** is a report of all revenues and expenses pertaining to a specific time period. **Net income** is the famous "bottom line" on an income statement—the remainder after *all* expenses (including income taxes, which are illustrated later) have been deducted from revenue.

Exhibit 2-3

Biwheels Company
Income Statement
for the Month Ended
January 31, 19X2

Sales (revenues)		$ 160,000
Deduct expenses:		
Cost of goods sold	$100,000	
Rent	2,000	
Amortization	100	
Total expenses		102,100
Net income		$ 57,900

Look back at Exhibit 2-2 and notice that four transactions affect the Biwheels Company's retained income account: sales revenue, cost of goods sold expense, rent expense, and amortization expense. Exhibit 2-3 shows how an income statement displays these transactions. The net income is $57,900.

Notice that the income statement measures performance for a *span of time*, whether it be a month, a quarter, or longer. Therefore the income statement must always indicate the exact period covered. In Exhibit 2-3, the Biwheels income statement clearly shows it is for the *month* ended January 31, 19X2. Recall that the balance sheet shows the financial position at an *instant of time*, and therefore the balance sheet must always indicate the exact date, not a period of time.

Public companies in Canada generally publish income statements quarterly. In some other countries, only semi-annual or annual statements are published. Nevertheless, most companies prepare such statements monthly or weekly for internal management purposes. Some top managers even insist on a daily income statement to keep up to date on the performance of their operations.

Decision makers use the income statement to assess the performance of an entity or its management over a span of time. The income statement shows how the entity's operations for the period have increased net assets through revenues and decreased net assets by consuming resources (expenses). *Net income* measures the amount by which the increase in assets exceeds the decrease. (A *net loss* means that the value of the assets used exceeded the revenues.) In essence, net income is one measure of the wealth created by an entity during the accounting period. By tracking net income from period to period, comparing changes in net income to economy-wide and industry averages, and examining changes in the revenue and expense components of net income, investors and other decision makers can evaluate the success of the period's operations.

For example, the management of Dominion Textile Inc. explained its decrease in net income in 1996 as follows:

> 1996 was a disappointing year with mixed results. The year was characterized by difficult conditions including a temporary oversupply situation in the North American denim sector; excess inventories at some European garment manufacturers and poor market conditions in certain countries in Europe; an aggressive pricing environment in basic workwear and cable wrap; and historically high cotton prices. On the positive side, demand remained strong for denim and hygiene nonwovens. Our core business units continued to develop new products and enhance partnerships with key customers.
>
> The corporation recorded a net loss of $48.5 million, or $1.28 per share, versus a profit of $33.8 million, or $0.70 per share, in 1995. Net earnings from continuing operations were $5.5 million, or $0.02 per share, versus $24.1 million, or $0.46 per share, in 1995.[2]

Dominion Textile is a Canadian company whose income statement reflects Canadian GAAP. However, income statements throughout the world have the same basic format, although international differences in terminology do arise. For example, the British use the term *turnover* instead of *revenues*. Thus, the first line of British Petroleum's income statement reads (where £ is the British monetary unit, the pound):

Turnover £ 34,950,000,000

Objective 3

Prepare an income statement and show how it is related to a balance sheet.

Dominion Textiles Inc.
www.domtex.com/

---

[2]Dominion Textile Inc. 1996 *Annual Report.*

Relationship Between Income Statement and Balance Sheet

The income statement is the major link between two balance sheets:

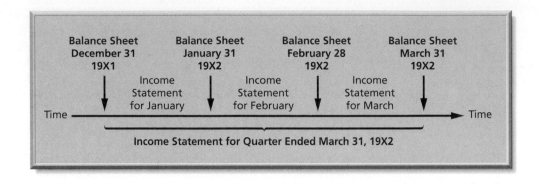

Remember that the balance sheet provides a snapshot of an entity's financial position at an *instant* of time; in contrast, the income statement provides a moving picture of events over a *span* of time.

For example, the Biwheels Company balance sheet for December 31, 19X1 was given in Chapter 1, page 12. At that date, the balance sheet showed assets of $500,000 and, to balance the equation, liabilities of $100,000 plus shareholders' equity of $400,000. There was no retained earnings. The January transactions analyzed in Exhibit 2-2 showed revenues of $160,000 and expenses of $102,100 recorded in the retained earnings account. The income statement in Exhibit 2-3 displays these revenues and expenses for the time span, the month of January. The next balance sheet, on January 31, 19X2, will include these changes in retained earnings (sales revenue of $160,000 and expenses of $102,100). The shareholders' equity account, Retained Earnings, will be $160,000 – $102,100 = $57,900 greater on January 31, 19X2 than it was on December 31, 19X1.

■ STATEMENT OF CHANGES IN FINANCIAL POSITION

Income versus Cash Flows

Recall what triggers the recognition of revenues when measuring income: the receipt of any asset, such as an account receivable, not just the receipt of cash. Revenues should eventually entail a cash receipt, but the important factor in assessing an entity's performance is the generation of a new asset, not the conversion of the asset into cash. Likewise, expenses are recorded when an entity gives up or uses up an asset, not when it acquires or pays for the asset. For example, when Eaton's purchases and pays for inventory, it is exchanging one asset, cash, for another, inventory. Value is neither created

Objective 4

Prepare a statement of changes in financial position and show how it differs from an income statement.

statement of changes in financial position (cash flow statement)
A required statement that reports the cash receipts and cash payments of an entity during a particular period.

nor lost. But when a product is delivered to a customer, an asset is given up (in exchange for a promise to pay for it), and the expense should be matched with revenues to calculate the income that we use for evaluating performance.

You can think of income as a measure of the entity's performance in generating net assets (that is, assets less liabilities). Increases in retained earnings are accompanied by increases in assets or decreases in liabilities. However, income does not measure the entity's performance in generating cash.

Because a business enterprise is usually formed to return cash to the owners, and because creditors must be paid in cash, many decision makers want a financial statement focused on cash in addition to the income statement that focuses on changes in net assets. The *statement of changes in financial position* is prepared to fill this need. The **statement of changes in financial position** reports the cash receipts and cash payments of an entity during a particular period. Like the income statement, it summarizes activities over a *span of time*, so it must be labelled with the exact period covered. Furthermore, like the income statement, which shows changes in retained income, the statement of changes in financial position details the changes in one balance sheet account, the cash account.

Introduction to Statement of Changes in Financial Position

The fundamental approach to the statement of changes in financial position is simple: (1) list the activities that increased cash (that is, cash inflows) and those that decreased cash (cash outflows), and (2) place each cash inflow and outflow into one of three categories according to the type of activity that caused it: operating activities, investing activities, and financing activities.

Operating activities include the sale and the purchase or production of goods and services, including collections from customers, payments to suppliers or employees, and payments for items such as rent, taxes, and interest. *Investing activities* include acquiring and selling long-term assets and securities held for long-term investment purposes. *Financing activities* include obtaining resources from owners and creditors and repaying amounts borrowed.

Consider our Biwheels example from its inception in December 19X1 through the end of January 19X2. Part I of Exhibit 2-4 lists the transactions that affect cash, and Part II shows the statement of changes in financial position. Notice that at the bottom of the statement the changes in cash during the month are added to the beginning balance to give the January 31, 19X2 balance in the cash account.

Exhibit 2-4

Biwheels Company
Statement of
Changes in Financial
Position for the One
Month Ended
January 31, 19X2

PART I: TRANSACTIONS AFFECTING CASH		
Transaction	*Amount*	*Type of Activity*
(1) Initial investment	$400,000	Financing
(2) Loan from bank	100,000	Financing
(3) Acquire inventory for cash	(150,000)	Operating
(5) Acquire store equipment for cash	(4,000)	Investing
(8) Payments to trade creditors	(4,000)	Operating
(9) Sale of store equipment	700	Investing
(11) Pay rent in cash	(6,000)	Operating

PART II: STATEMENT OF CHANGES IN FINANCIAL POSITION	
CASH FLOWS FROM OPERATING ACTIVITIES	
Cash payments to suppliers	$ (154,000)
Cash payments for rent	(6,000)
Net cash used for operating activities	$(160,000)
CASH FLOWS FROM INVESTING ACTIVITIES	
Cash payments for purchases of equipment	$ (4,000)
Cash receipts from sales of equipment	700
Net cash used for investing activities	$ (3,300)
CASH FLOWS FROM FINANCING ACTIVITIES	
Proceeds from initial investment	$ 400,000
Proceeds from bank loan	100,000
Net cash provided by financing activities	$ 500,000
Net increase in cash	$ 336,700
Cash balance, December 1, 19X1	0
Cash balance, January 31, 19X2	$ 336,700

The statement of changes in financial position gives a direct picture of where cash came from and where it went. The dominant reason that cash increased by $336,700 is that $500,000 of new financing was obtained. A total of $160,000 was paid to support operating activities. It is not unusual to have large cash outflows for operating activities in the early periods of a business's life or when an entity is growing quickly. Cash payments for inventories and prepayments for operating expenses often exceed receipts. In the Biwheels example, all sales were on open account and no cash was received before the end of January, so all operating cash flows were outflows. Despite income of $57,900 for January, Biwheels has not yet started to generate any cash from operating activities.

Summary Problem for Your Review

If you have never studied accounting before, or if you studied it long ago, do not proceed further until you have solved the following problem. There are no shortcuts. Pushing a pencil is an absolute necessity for becoming comfortable with accounting concepts. The cost-benefit test will easily be met: your gain in knowledge will exceed your investment of time. Please do the work on your own. In particular, do not ask for help from professional accountants or advanced accounting students. They might introduce new terms beyond those already covered that will only confuse, not clarify, at this stage. Instead, scrutinize Exhibits 2-1 through 2-4. Note how each transaction affects the balance sheet equation and how the financial statements are prepared. Then solve the problem that follows.

Problem One

Biwheels' transactions for January were analyzed in Exhibits 2-1 and 2-2, pages 41 and 45. The balance sheet, January 31, 19X2, is

Biwheels Company
Balance Sheet
January 31, 19X2

Assets		Liabilities and Shareholders' Equity		
Cash	$ 336,700	Liabilities:		
Accounts receivable	160,300	Note payable		$ 100,000
Merchandise		Accounts payable		16,200
inventory	59,200	Total liabilities		$ 116,200
Prepaid rent	4,000	Shareholders' equity:		
Store equipment	13,900	Paid-in capital	$400,000	
		Retained earnings	57,900	
		Total shareholders' equity		457,900
		Total liabilities and		
Total assets	$574,100	shareholders' equity		$574,100

The following series of transactions occurred during February:

(14) Collection of accounts receivable, $130,000.

(15) Payments of accounts payable, $15,000.

(16) Acquisitions of inventory on open account, $80,000, and for cash, $10,000.

(17) Merchandise carried in inventory at a cost of $110,000 was sold for $176,000, of which $125,000 was on open account and $51,000 was for cash.

(18) Recognition of rent expense for February.

(19) Recognition of amortization expense for February.

(20) Borrowing of $10,000 from the bank was used to buy $10,000 of store equipment on February 28.

Required

1. Prepare an analysis of transactions, employing the equation approach demonstrated in Exhibit 2-2.
2. Prepare a balance sheet as of February 28, 19X2, and an income statement and statement of changes in financial position for the month of February.

Solution to Problem One

1. *Analysis of transactions.* The answer is in Exhibit 2-5. All transactions are straightforward extensions or repetitions of the January transactions.
2. *Preparation of financial statements.* Exhibit 2-6 contains the balance sheet, income statement, and statement of changes in financial position, which have been described earlier. Notice that the balance sheet lists the ending balances in all the accounts in Exhibit 2-5. The income statement summarizes the revenue and expense entries in retained income, and the statement of changes in financial position summarizes the entries to the cash account.

Exhibit 2-5   Biwheels Company   Analysis of Transactions for February 19X2 (in dollars)

Description of Transactions	Assets					=	Liabilities		+	Owners' Equity	
							Liabilities			Shareholders' Equity	
	Cash	Accounts Receivable	Merchandise Inventory	Prepaid Rent	Store Equipment	=	Notes Payable	Accounts Payable	+	Paid-in Capital	Retained Earnings
Balance, January 31, 19X2	336,700	+ 160,300	+ 59,200	+ 4,000	+ 13,900	=	100,000	+ 16,200	+	400,000	+ 57,900
(14) Collection of accounts receivable	+130,000	−130,000									
(15) Payments of accounts payable	− 15,000					=		−15,000			
(16) Acquisitions of inventory on open account and for cash	− 10,000		+ 90,000			=		+80,000			
(17a) Sales on open account and for cash	+ 51,000	+125,000				=					+ 176,000 (increase sales revenue)
(17b) Cost of inventory sold			−110,000			=					− 110,000 (increase cost of goods sold expense)
(18) Recognize expiration of rental services				−2,000		=					− 2,000 (increase rent expense)
(19) Recognize expiration of equipment services (amortization)					− 100	=					− 100 (increase amortization expense)
(20a) Borrow from bank	+ 10,000					=	+10,000				
(20b) Purchase store equipment	− 10,000				+10,000	=					
Balance, February 28, 19X2	492,700	+ 155,300	+ 39,200	+ 2,000	+ 23,800	=	110,000	+ 81,200	+	400,000	+ 121,800
	713,000						713,000				

Exhibit 2-6	Assets		Liabilities and Shareholders' Equity		
Biwheels Company	Cash	$492,700	Liabilities:		
Balance Sheet	Accounts receivable	155,300	Notes payable	$110,000	
February 28, 19X2	Merchandise		Accounts payable	81,200	$191,200
	inventory	39,200			
	Prepaid rent	2,000	Shareholders' equity:		
	Store equipment	23,800	Paid-in capital	$400,000	
			Retained earnings	121,800	521,800
	Total	$ 713,000	Total		$713,000

Biwheels Company	Sales		$176,000
Income Statement	Deduct expenses:		
for the Month Ended	Cost of goods sold	$110,000	
February 28, 19X2	Rent	2,000	
	Amortization	100	112,100
	Net income		$ 63,900

Biwheels Company	CASH FLOWS FROM OPERATING ACTIVITIES	
Statement of	Cash collections from customers	$181,000
Changes in Financial	Cash payments to suppliers	(25,000)
Position for the	Net cash provided by operating activities	$156,000
Month Ended	CASH FLOWS FROM INVESTING ACTIVITIES	
February 28, 19X2	Purchase of store equipment	$ (10,000)
	Net cash used for investing activities	$ (10,000)
	CASH FLOWS FROM FINANCING ACTIVITIES	
	Loan from bank	$ 10,000
	Net cash provided by financing activities	$ 10,000
	Net increase in cash	$156,000
	Cash balance, February 1, 19X2	336,700
	Cash balance, February 28, 19X2	$492,700

■ ACCOUNTING FOR DIVIDENDS AND RETAINED EARNINGS

A corporation's revenues and expenses for a particular time period are recorded in the shareholders' equity account, Retained Earnings. Because net income is the excess of revenues over expenses, retained earnings increase by the amount of net income reported during the period. (If expenses exceed revenues, retained earnings decrease by the amount of the period's net loss.)

Cash Dividends

cash dividends
Distributions of cash to shareholders that reduce retained earnings.

In addition to revenues and expenses, cash dividends are recorded in the Retained Earnings account. **Cash dividends** are distributions of cash to shareholders that reduce retained earnings. Corporations pay out cash dividends to shareholders to provide a return on the shareholders' investment in the corporation. The ability to pay dividends is fundamentally a result of profitable operations. Retained earnings increase as profits accumulate, and they decrease as dividends are paid out.

Although cash dividends decrease retained earnings, they are not expenses like rent and amortization. They should not be deducted from revenues because dividends are not directly linked to the generation of revenue or the costs of operating activities. For example, assume that on February 28, cash dividends of $50,000 are declared by the Biwheels board of directors and are disbursed to shareholders. This transaction (21) is analyzed as follows:

	Assets	= Liabilities	+	Shareholders' Equity
	Cash			*Retained Earnings*
(21) Declaration and payment of cash dividends	−50,000	=		−50,000 (dividends)

Transaction 21 shows the decrease in Retained Earnings and the decrease in Cash.

Cash dividends distribute some of the company's assets (cash) to shareholders, thus reducing their residual interest in Biwheels. Sufficient cash must be available for dividends to be paid. Because of the need for cash, many companies try to avoid paying dividends that exceed the amount of cash provided by operating activities.

As a successful company grows, the Retained Earnings account can soar enormously if dividends are not paid. It can easily be the largest shareholders' equity account. Its balance is the cumulative, lifetime earnings of the company less its cumulative, lifetime losses and dividends. For example, at October 31, 1996, Bank of Montreal's retained earnings are $3,740 million compared with common share capital of $2,989 million.

The amount of cash dividends declared by the board of directors of a company depends on many factors. For example, the amount of a dividend often is some fraction of net income, but dividends are not necessarily tied to current net income. Although profitable operations and the existence of a balance in Retained Earnings are generally essential, dividend policy is also influenced by the company's cash position and future needs for cash to pay debts or to purchase additional assets. Dividends are also influenced by whether the company is committed to a stable dividend policy or to a policy that normally ties dividends to fluctuations in net income. Under a stable policy, dividends may be paid consistently even if a company encounters a few years of little or no net income. Many companies maintain a stable dividend from year to year because it gives shareholders the ability to plan on a steady cash return from their investment. (More is said about dividends in Chapter 11.)

Dividends or withdrawals are often spoken of as "distributions of profits" or "distributions of retained earnings." Dividends are often erroneously described as being "paid out of retained earnings." In reality, cash dividends are distribu-

Bank of Montreal
www.bmo.com/

tions of assets that reduce a portion of the ownership claim. The distribution is made possible by both profitable operations and the existence of cash.

Dividend Transactions

Transaction 21 combined the declaration and payment of a dividend into a single transaction as if everything had occurred on the same day. However, corporations usually approach dividend matters in steps. The board of directors declares a dividend on one date (declaration date) payable to those shareholders on record as owning the stock on a second date (record date) and actually pays the dividend on a third date (payment date).

Such dividend actions entail two accounting transactions. First, the *declaration* affects the corporation's financial position because the shareholders also become creditors for the amount of the legally declared dividend. Second, the resulting liability is reduced only when the cash is disbursed. Consequently, transaction 21 must be divided into two phases:

	Assets	=	Liabilities	+	Shareholders' Equity
	Cash	−	Dividends Payable	+	Retained Earnings
(21a) Date of declaration		=	+50,000		−50,000 (dividends)
(21b) Date of payment	−50,000	=	−50,000		
The net effect is eventually the same as in 21 above	−50,000	=	0		−50,000

Although the ultimate effect is the same as that shown originally in transaction 21, a balance sheet prepared *between* the date of declaration and the date of payment must show dividends payable as a *liability*. Note too that although a corporation may be expected to pay dividends, no legal liability occurs until a board of directors formally declares a dividend.

Retained Income and Cash

The existence of retained income enables a board of directors to *declare* a dividend. The existence of cash enables the corporation to *pay* the dividend. Cash and Retained Earnings are two entirely separate accounts sharing no necessary relationship. Consider the following illustration:

Step 1. Assume an opening balance sheet of

Cash	$ 100	Paid-in capital	$100

Step 2. Purchase inventory for $50 cash. The balance sheet now reads

Cash	$ 50	Paid-in capital	$100
Inventory	50		
Total assets	$ 100		

Step 3. Now sell the inventory for $80 cash, which produces a retained income of $80 – $50 = $30:

Cash	$ 130	Paid-in capital	$100
		Retained earnings	30
		Total owners' equity	$ 130

At this stage, the retained earnings might be reflected by a $30 increase in cash. But the $30 in retained earnings connotes only a *general* claim against *total assets*. This can be clarified by the transaction that follows.

Step 4. Purchase inventory and equipment, in the amounts of $60 and $50, respectively. Now,

Cash	$ 20	Paid-in capital	$100
Inventory	60	Retained earnings	30
Equipment	50		
Total assets	$ 130	Total owners' equity	$ 130

Where is the $30 in retained earnings reflected? Is it reflected in Cash, in Inventory, or in Equipment? The answer is indeterminate. Since there is only $20 in Cash, and Retained Earnings are $30, the claim is not exclusively on Cash. Part of the results of profitable sales have been reinvested in inventory and equipment. This example helps to explain the nature of the Retained Earnings account. It is a *residual claim*, not a pot of gold. Retained earnings are increased by profitable operations, but the cash inflow from sales may be used to buy more inventory or equipment (Step 4). Retained earnings (and also paid-in capital) are a *general* claim against, or *undivided* interest in, *total* assets, *not* a specific claim against cash or against any other particular asset. Do not confuse the assets themselves with the claims against the assets.

Statement of Retained Earnings

statement of retained earnings A statement that lists the beginning balance in retained earnings, followed by a description of any changes that occurred during the period, and the ending balance.

Exhibit 2-7 shows another financial statement prepared by accountants. The **statement of retained earnings** lists the beginning balance (in this case, January 31) in Retained Earnings, followed by a description of any major changes (in this case, net income and dividends) that occurred during the period, and the ending balance (February 28) for the Biwheels Company.

Exhibit 2-7		
Biwheels Company	Retained earnings, January 31, 19X2	$ 57,900
Statement of	Net income for February	63,900
Retained Earnings	Total	$121,800
for the Month Ended	Dividends declared	50,000
February 28, 19X2	Retained earnings, February 28, 19X2	$ 71,800

statement of earnings and retained earnings A statement that includes a statement of retained income at the bottom of an income statement.

Frequently, the statement of retained earnings is added to the bottom of the income statement. If that is done, the combined statements are called a **statement of income and retained earnings**. For example, the income statement in Exhibit 2-6 combined with Exhibit 2-7 and retitled appears as shown in Exhibit 2-8.

Note how Exhibit 2-8 is anchored to the balance sheet equation:

$$\text{Assets} = \text{Liabilities} + \text{Paid-in capital} + \text{Retained earnings}$$

$$\text{Ending balance} = \left[\text{Beginning balance} + \text{Revenues} - \text{Expenses} - \text{Dividends} \right]$$

$$\text{Bal. Feb. 28 after dividends} = \left[57,900 + 176,000 - 112,100 - \$50,000 \right] = 71,800$$

Exhibit 2-8		
Biwheels Company	Sales		$176,000
Statement of Income	Deduct expenses:		
and Retained	Cost of goods sold	$110,000	
Earnings for the	Rent	2,000	
Month Ended	Amortization	100	112,100
February 28, 19X2	Net income		$ 63,900 *
	Retained earnings, January 31, 19X2		57,900
	Total		$121,800
	Dividends declared		50,000
	Retained earnings, February 28, 19X2		$ 71,800

* Note how the income statement ends here. The $63,900 simultaneously becomes the initial item on the statement of retained earnings portion of this combined statement.

Customs of Presentation

Exhibits 2-7 and 2-8 illustrate some customs that accountants follow when they prepare financial statements. To save space accountants often place a subtotal on the right side of the final number in a column, as is illustrated by the $112,100 in Exhibit 2-8. Under this arrangement, the expenses caption is used only once.

Dollar signs are customarily used at the beginning of each column of dollar amounts and for net income. Some statements also use dollar signs with the subtotals, the $63,900 and the $121,800 in Exhibit 2-8. Double-underscores (double rulings) are typically used to denote final numbers.

Summary Problem for Your Review

Problem Two

(The first problem appeared earlier in the chapter.)

The following interpretations and remarks are frequently encountered with regard to financial statements. Do you agree or disagree? Explain fully.

1. "Sales show the cash coming in from customers, and the various expenses show the cash going out for goods and services. The difference is net income."
2. Consider the following January 27, 1996, accounts of The Oshawa Group Limited, a leading Canadian retail food franchiser:

	(000's)
Common shares	$ 252,200
Retained earnings	544,600
Total shareholders' equity	$ 796,800

A shareholder commented, "Why can't that big company pay higher wages and dividends too? It can use its hundreds of millions of dollars of retained earnings to do so."

3. "The total Oshawa Group's shareholders' equity measures the amount that the shareholders would get today if the corporation were liquidated."

Solution to Problem Two

1. Cash receipts and disbursements are not the fundamental basis for the accounting recognition of revenues and expenses. Credit, not cash, lubricates the economy. Therefore, if services or goods have been delivered to a customer, a legal claim to future cash in the form of a receivable is deemed sufficient justification for recognizing revenue. Similarly, if services or goods have been used up, a legal obligation in the form of a payable is justification for recognizing expense.

   This approach to the measurement of net income is known as the accrual method. Revenue is recognized as it is (a) earned by goods or services rendered and (b) realized. Expenses are recorded when goods or services are used up in the obtaining of revenue (or when such goods or services cannot justifiably be carried forward as an asset because they have no potential future benefit). The expenses and losses are deducted from the revenue, and the result of this matching process is net income, the net increase in shareholders' equity from the conduct of operations. Cash flow from operations can be larger or smaller than net earnings.

2. As the chapter indicated, retained earnings are not cash. They are a shareholders' equity account that represents the accumulated increase in ownership claims due to profitable operations. This claim or interest may be partially liquidated by the pay-

ment of cash dividends, but a growing company will reinvest cash in receivables, inventories, plant, equipment, and other assets so necessary for expansion. As a result, the ownership claims measured by retained earnings may become "permanent" in the sense that, as a practical matter, they will never be liquidated as long as the company remains a going concern.

The fallacy of linking retained earnings and cash is illustrated by the fact that Oshawa's cash was less than $45 million on the balance sheet date when its retained earnings exceeded $544 million.

3. Shareholders' equity is a difference, the excess of assets over liabilities. If the assets were carried in the accounting records at their liquidating value today and the liabilities were carried at the exact amounts needed for their extinguishment, the remark would be true. But such valuations would be coincidental because assets are customarily carried at *historical cost* expressed in an unchanging monetary unit. Intervening changes in markets and general price levels in inflationary times may mean that the assets are woefully understated. Investors may make a critical error if they think that balance sheets indicate current values.

Furthermore, the "market values" for publicly owned shares are usually determined by daily trading conducted in the financial marketplaces such as the Toronto Stock Exchange. These values are affected by numerous factors, including the *expectations* of (a) price appreciation and (b) cash flows in the form of dividends. The focus is on the future; the present and the past are examined as clues to what may be forthcoming. Therefore the present shareholders' equity is usually of only incidental concern.

■ THE LANGUAGE OF ACCOUNTING IN THE REAL WORLD

Unfortunately for the new student of accounting, organizations use different terms to describe the same concept or account, creating a multitude of synonyms. These terms are not introduced here to confuse you. Our objective is to acquaint you with the real world of accounting vocabulary so that you will not be surprised when a company's financial statement uses different terms than you learned initially.

retained income (reinvested earnings) A synonym for retained earnings.

As Exhibit 2-9 shows, the terms *income, earnings,* and *profits* are often used interchangeably. Indeed, many companies will use net *income* on their income statements but will refer to retained income as retained *earnings*. In short, retained income is usually called **retained earnings** or **reinvested earnings**.

statement of income (statement of operations, results of operations, statement of earnings, operating statement, statement of revenues and expenses, P&L statement) A synonym for income statement.

The term *earnings* is becoming increasingly popular because it has a preferable image. *Earnings* apparently implies compensation for honest toil, whereas *income* or *profit* evidently inspires cartoonists to portray managers as greedy, evil-looking individuals.

The income statement is frequently called the **statement of income, statement of operations, results of operations,** or **statement of earnings.** Other terms sometimes encountered are the **operating statement** and **statement of revenues and expenses**. For many years, the most popular name for this statement was statement of profit and loss, often termed the **P&L statement**. Such a label is justifiably fading into oblivion. After all, the ultimate result is either a profit *or* a loss.

sales (sales revenues) Part of revenues.

The terms **sales** and **sales revenues** are included in revenues.

cost of goods sold (cost of sales) The original acquisition cost of the inventory that was sold to customers during the reporting period.

The term **cost of sales** is a synonym for **cost of goods sold**. For example, Bethlehem Steel Corporation uses *cost of sales*, not *cost of goods sold*. Both terms mean the entity's original acquisition cost of the inventory that was sold to customers during the reporting period.

Fortunately, some accounting terms have no synonyms. Examples are *expenses* and *dividends*.

Exhibit 2-9

Some Synonyms in Accounting

Term Initially Used in This Book	Examples of Synonyms	Example of Companies
1. Net income		Anheuser-Busch, Mitel Corporation, Colgate-Palmolive
	Net earnings	Moore Corporation, Norcen Energy, National Sea Products
	Profit	Caterpillar
2. Retained earnings	Retained income	Norcen Energy, Andrés Wine, Moore Corporation
		General Motors
	Reinvested earnings	Scott Paper, Coca-Cola
	Earnings retained for use in the business	Ford Motor
	Profit employed in the business	Caterpillar

■ MORE ON NONPROFIT ORGANIZATIONS

The examples in this chapter have focused on profit-seeking organizations, but balance sheets and income statements are also used by nonprofit organizations. For example, hospitals and universities have income statements, although they are called statements of *revenue* and *expense*. The "bottom line" is frequently called "excess of revenue over expense" or "net financial result" rather than "net income."

The basic concepts of assets, liabilities, revenue, expense, and operating statements are applicable to all organizations, whether they be utilities, symphony orchestras, private, public, Canadian, American, or Asian. However, some nonprofit organizations have been slow to adopt some ideas that are widely used in progressive companies. For example, many government organizations use only the cash basis of accounting, not the accrual basis. This practice hampers the evaluation of the performance of such organizations. A recent annual report of the New York Metropolitan Museum of Art stated: "As the Museum's financial operations have begun to resemble in complexity those of a corporation, it has become necessary to make certain changes in our accounting.... Operating results are reported on an accrual rather than the previously followed cash basis. Thus, revenue and expenses are recorded in the proper time period."

New York Metropolitan Museum of Art
www.metmuseum.org/

An article in *Forbes* commented:

> Shoddy, misleading accounting has not been the cause of our cities' problems but it has prevented us from finding solutions. Or even looking for solutions until it's too late. Chicago's schools, for example, suddenly found themselves unable to pay their teachers. Had the books been kept like any decent corporation's, that could never have happened. The most basic difference is in the common use of cash accounting rather than the accrual method that nearly all businesses use.

■ MORE ON GENERALLY ACCEPTED ACCOUNTING PRINCIPLES (GAAP)

This section continues our study of accounting principles. So far in this chapter, the accrual basis and the concepts of recognition, matching, and cost recovery have been discussed.

Stable Monetary Unit

Objective 6

Identify the major organizations that influence generally accepted accounting principles.

The monetary unit (called the dollar in Canada, the United States, Australia, New Zealand, and elsewhere) is the principal means for measuring assets and equities. It is the common denominator for quantifying the effects of a wide variety of transactions. Accountants record, classify, summarize, and report in terms of the monetary unit.

Such measurement assumes that the monetary unit, the dollar, is an unchanging yardstick. Yet we all know that a 1995 dollar did not have the same purchasing power that a 1985 or a 1975 dollar had. Furthermore, the change in the purchasing power of the monetary unit varies among countries. During the 1980s, the Canadian dollar lost 5.0% of its purchasing power per year, while the U.S. dollar lost 5.0%, the Japanese yen lost only 2.2%, and the Italian lira lost 10.1%. Therefore, accounting statements that include assets measured in different years must be interpreted and compared with full consciousness of the limitations of the basic measurement unit.

Accounting Standard-Setting Bodies

Accounting Standards Board (ASB) A committee of the CICA empowered to establish Canadian generally accepted accounting standards.

Financial Accounting Standards Board (FASB) A private-sector body that determines generally accepted accounting standards in the United States.

Accounting Principles Board (APB) The predecessor to the Financial Accounting Standards Board.

The existence of generally accepted accounting principles (GAAP) implies that someone must decide which principles are generally accepted and which are not. This decision falls to regulatory agencies, professional associations or government bodies.

In Canada, the **Accounting Standards Board (ASB)** of the Canadian Institute of Chartered Accountants (CICA) provides significant guidance in the determination of GAAP through the pronouncements of the *CICA Handbook*.

In the United States, generally accepted accounting principles have been determined primarily by two private-sector bodies, the **Financial Accounting Standards Board (FASB)** and its predecessor, the **Accounting Principles Board (APB)**.

The FASB is an independent creature of the private sector and is financially supported by various professional accounting associations (such as the leading

AICPA American Institute of Certified Public Accountants, the leading organization of the auditors of corporate financial

FASB Statements The FASB's rulings on generally accepted accounting principles.

International Accounting Standards Committee (IASC) An organization representing over one hundred accountancy boards from over seventy-five countries that is developing a common set of accounting standards to be used throughout the world.

organization of auditors, the American Institute of Certified Public Accountants, also known as the **AICPA**). The FASB's rulings on GAAP are called **FASB Statements**.

Recent years have seen a growing interest in developing a common set of accounting principles throughout the world. Often called *harmonization of accounting standards*, the movement seeks to eliminate differences in accounting principles that are not caused by cultural or environmental differences between countries. Leading the way is the **International Accounting Standards Committee (IASC)**, which represents more than one hundred accountancy bodies from over seventy-five countries. Like the CICA, the IASC is a private-sector body that issues standards—so far over thirty of them. Although compliance with IASC standards is voluntary, a growing number of countries and multinational companies are adopting the methods advocated by the IASC.

Also affecting international accounting standards is the European (Economic) Community (EC). Via a series of *Directives*, which have the force of law, the EC is reducing the variations in financial statements of companies in its twelve member nations.

■ FOUR POPULAR FINANCIAL RATIOS

To underscore how financial statements are used, this book will gradually introduce you to various financial ratios. Because stock market prices are quoted on a per-share basis, many ratios are expressed per share (and after income taxes).

A financial ratio is computed by dividing one number by another. For a set of complex financial statements, literally hundreds of ratios can be computed if desired. Every analyst has a set of favourite ratios, but one is so popular that it dwarfs all others: earnings per share of common stock (EPS).

A primary focus of financial reporting is on earnings. The income statement and its accompanying earnings per share are paramount to many users of financial reports, so accounting authorities have specified how various items therein must be displayed.

The accounting standard setting bodies have promulgated the requirement that EPS data appear on the face of the income statement of publicly held corporations. This is the only instance where a financial ratio is required as a part of the body of financial statements.

Objective 7

Compute and explain earnings per share, price-earnings ratio, dividend-yield ratio, and dividend-payout ratio.

Earnings per Share (EPS)

When the owners' equity is relatively simple, the computation of EPS is straightforward. For example, consider Mark's Work Wearhouse, the well-known clothing retailer. The bottom of two of its income statements showed:

	1996	1995
Net income	$3,117,000	$ 6,315,000
Net income per share of common stock	$ 0.13	$ 0.27

The earnings per share (called *net income per share* by Mark's Work Wearhouse) was calculated as follows:

$$EPS = \frac{\text{Net income}}{\text{Weighted average number of shares outstanding}}$$

$$1996\,EPS = \frac{\$3,117,000}{24,514,605} = \$0.13 \quad 1995\,EPS = \frac{\$6,315,000}{23,186,745} = \$0.27$$

The Mark's Work Wearhouse computation is relatively simple because the company has only one type of capital stock, little fluctuation of shares outstanding throughout the year, and no unusual items affecting the computation of net income. EPS calculations can become more difficult when such complications arise. See Chapter 13 for further discussion.

Price-Earnings (P-E) Ratio

Another popular ratio is the price-earnings (P-E) ratio:

$$\text{P-E Ratio} = \frac{\text{Market price per share of common stock}}{\text{Earnings per share of common stock}}$$

The numerator is typically today's market price; the denominator, the EPS for the most recent twelve months. Thus the P-E ratio varies throughout a given year, depending on the fluctuations in the stock price. For example, Mark's Work Wearhouse P-E ratio would be:

1995 P-E	$\dfrac{\$1.70}{\$0.27}$ =	6.30
1996 P-E	$\dfrac{\$1.25}{\$0.13}$ =	9.62

Finance newspapers publishes P-E ratios daily on their stock pages. P-E ratios are rarely carried out to any decimal places when published in the business press. The P-E ratio is sometimes called the *earnings multiple*. It measures how much the investing public is willing to pay for the company's prospects for earnings. Note especially that the P-E ratio is a consensus of the marketplace. This earnings multiplier may differ considerably for two companies within the same industry. It may also change for the same company through the years. Glamour stocks often have astronomical ratios. In general, a high P-E ratio indicates that investors predict that the company's net income will grow at a fast rate. Consider Microsoft's 1995 ratio of 30 compared to the 8 for the Bank of Montreal.

Dividend-Yield Ratio

Individual investors are usually interested in the profitability of their personal investments in common stock. That profitability takes two forms: cash dividends and market-price appreciation of the stock. Two popular ratios are the *dividend-yield ratio* (the current dividend per share divided by the current market price of the stock) and the price-earnings ratio (just discussed). The *dividend-yield ratio* (or *dividend-yield percentage*), also simply called *dividend yield*, is computed as follows:

$$\text{Dividend yield} = \frac{\text{Common dividends per share}}{\text{Market price per share}}$$

The following dividend yields for the Bank of Montreal are computed as follows:

	Using Highest Market Price During Fourth Quarter	Using Lowest Market Price During Fourth Quarter
1995 Dividend yield =	$\dfrac{\$.33}{\$31} = 1.1\%$	$\dfrac{\$.33}{\$27.875} = 1.2\%$
1996 Dividend yield =	$\dfrac{\$.40}{\$41.65} = 1.0\%$	$\dfrac{\$.40}{\$32.75} = 1.2\%$

When published in the business press, dividend yields are ordinarily carried to one decimal place. Dividend ratios may be of particular importance to those investors in common stock who seek regular cash returns on their investments. For example, an investor who favoured high current returns would not buy stock in growth companies. Growth companies have conservative dividend policies because they are using most of their profit-generated resources to help finance expansion of their operations.

Market prices at which stocks are traded in organized marketplaces, such as the Toronto Stock Exchange, are quoted in the daily newspapers. The dividend yields are also published, as measured by annual disbursements based on the last quarterly dividends.

Consider the following stock quotations published by *The Globe and Mail* for the Bank of Montreal regarding trading on a particular day in 1997:

52 Weeks										
High	Low	Stock	Div.	High	Low	Close	Net Chg.	Vol. 100s	Yld. %	P-E Ratio
55.80	31¼	Bank Mtl	1.60	49.30	48.10	48.95	−0.25	7607	3.3	11.3

Starting from left to right, the highest price at which the Bank of Montreal common stock was traded in the preceding fifty-two weeks was $55.80 per share; the lowest price, $31.25. The current dividend rate for twelve months is $1.60 per share, producing a yield of 3.3% based on the day's closing price of the stock. The P-E ratio is 11.3, also based on the closing price. Total sales for the day were 760,700 shares. The highest price at which the stock was traded was $49.30 per share; the lowest $48.10. The closing price was that of the last trade for the day, $48.95, which was $.25 lower than the preceding day's last trade.

Keep in mind that transactions in publicly traded shares are between *individual investors* in the stock, not between the *corporation* and the individuals. Thus a "typical trade" results in the selling of, say, 100 shares of the Bank of Montreal stock held by Ms. Johnson in Vancouver to Ms. Davis in Halifax for $4,895 cash. These parties would ordinarily transact the trade through their respective stockbrokers, who represent individual shareholders. The Bank of Montreal would not be directly affected by the trade except that its records of shareholders would be changed to show the 100 shares were now held by Davis, not Johnson.

Dividend-Payout Ratio

Although not routinely published, the dividend-payout ratio also receives much attention from analysts. Consider McDonald's, the well-known fast-food chain. The formula for its payout computation is given below, followed by McDonald's ratio, using figures from a recent annual report:

McDonald's Corp.
www.mcdonalds.com

$$\text{Dividend-payout ratio} = \frac{\text{Common dividends per share}}{\text{Earnings per share}}$$

$$\text{Dividend-payout ratio} = \frac{\$.42}{\$2.91} = 14\%$$

McDonald's fits into the category of a low-payout company. As long as McDonald's continues its worldwide expansion, a minimal payout can be anticipated. Some fast-growing companies such as Microsoft pay no dividends. In contrast, companies without exceptional growth tend to pay a higher percentage of their earnings as dividends. Public utilities will ordinarily have a payout ratio of 60% to 70%.

Highlights to Remember

This chapter focused on how accountants measure income, the excess of revenues over expenses for a particular time period, on an accrual basis. In accrual accounting, revenue is seldom accompanied by an immediate cash receipt; therefore, *revenue* should not be confused with the term *cash receipt*. Similarly, an expense is seldom accompanied by an immediate cash disbursement; *expense* should not be confused with the term *cash disbursement*.

The concept of recognition means that revenues are assigned to the period in which they are earned and realized. Under the concepts of matching and cost recovery, expenses are assigned to a period in which the pertinent goods and services are either used or appear to have no future benefit. Revenues and expenses are components of shareholders' equity. Revenues increase shareholders' equity; expenses decrease shareholders' equity.

An income statement shows an entity's revenues and expenses for a particular span of time. The net income links to the balance sheet because it is an addition to retained income.

Income based on accrual accounting focuses on an entity's performance in generating net assets. In contrast, the statement of changes in financial position focuses on an entity's ability to generate and use cash. A focus on cash is too narrow to provide a measure of overall performance, but it provides valuable information on the important function of cash generation and use.

Cash dividends are not expenses. They are distributions of cash to shareholders that reduce retained income. Corporations are not obligated to pay dividends, but once dividends are declared by the board of directors they become a legal liability until paid in cash.

International Accounting Standards Committee
www.iasc.org.uk/

Generally accepted accounting principles (GAAP) are based on many concepts. Among those covered in this chapter are the accounting time period, recognition, matching, cost recovery, and stable monetary unit. GAAP in Canada is generally determined by the Canadian Institute of Chartered Accountants. Growing interest in a common international GAAP has moved the International Accounting Standards Committee (IASC) to the forefront of standard setting.

Assignment Material

QUESTIONS

2-1. "Expenses are negative shareholders' equity accounts." Explain.

2-2. What are the two tests of recognition of revenue?

2-3. Give two examples in which revenue is not recognized at the point of sale, one in which recognition is delayed because the revenue is not yet earned, and one because it is not yet realized.

2-4. "Expenses are assets that have been used up." Explain.

2-5. "The manager acquires goods and services, not expenses per se." Explain.

2-6. "Cash dividends are not expenses." Explain.

2-7. Identify the three categories of cash flows found on the statement of changes in financial position and list two activities that might appear in each of the categories.

2-8. What are the major defects of the cash basis?

2-9. "Retained earnings are not a pot of gold." Explain.

2-10. What is the meaning of a *general claim*?

2-11. Give two synonyms for *income statement*.

2-12. Give two synonyms for *net income*.

2-13. Give two synonyms for *retained earnings*.

2-14. "The term *earnings* is becoming increasingly popular because it has a preferable image." Explain.

2-15. "Changes in the purchasing power of the dollar hurt the credibility of financial statements." Do you agree? Explain.

2-16. Distinguish between GAAP, FASB, SEC, and APB.

2-17. Countries have different ways of choosing Accounting Standards. Outline at least one alternative to the Canadian approach.

2-18. What function does the International Accounting Standards Committee (IASC) have in setting GAAP?

EXERCISES

2-19 Synonyms and Antonyms

Consider the following terms: (1) unexpired costs, (2) reinvested earnings, (3) expenses, (4) net earnings, (5) prepaid expenses, (6) undistributed earnings, (7) statement of earnings, (8) used-up costs, (9) net profits, (10) net income, (11) revenues, (12) retained income, (13) sales, (14) statement of financial condition, (15) statement of income, (16) statement of financial position, (17) retained earnings, (18) statement of operations, and (19) cost of goods sold.

Required

Group the items into two major categories, the income statement and the balance sheet. Answer by indicating the numbered items that belong in each group. Specify items that are assets and items that are expenses.

2-20 Special Meanings of Terms

A news story described the disappointing sales of a new model car, the Nova. An auto dealer said: "Even if the Nova is a little slow to move out of dealerships, it is more of a plus than a minus.... We're now selling 14 more cars per month than before. That's revenue. That's the bottom line."

Required

Is the dealer confused about accounting terms? Explain.

2-21 Nature of Retained Earnings

This is an exercise on the relationships between assets, liabilities, and ownership equities. The numbers are small, but the underlying concepts are large.

1. Assume an opening balance sheet of:

Cash	$1,500	Paid-in capital	$1,500

2. Purchase inventory for $600 cash. Prepare a balance sheet. A heading is unnecessary in this and subsequent requirements.
3. Sell the entire inventory for $850 cash. Prepare a balance sheet. Where is the retained earnings in terms of relationships within the balance sheet? That is, what is the meaning of the retained earnings? Explain in your own words.
4. Buy inventory for $400 cash and equipment for $700 cash. Prepare a balance sheet. Where are the retained earnings in terms of relationships within the balance sheet? That is, what is the meaning of the retained earnings? Explain in your own words.
5. Buy inventory for $500 on open account. Prepare a balance sheet. Where are the retained earnings and account payable in terms of the relationships within the balance sheet? That is, what is the meaning of the account payable and the retained earnings? Explain in your own words.

2-22   Asset Acquisition and Expiration
The Lougee Company had the following transactions:

a. Paid $18,000 cash for rent for the next six months.
b. Paid $2,000 for stationery and wrapping supplies.
c. Paid $3,000 cash for an advertisement in the *Calgary Herald*.
d. Paid $9,000 cash for a training program for employees.

Required   Show the effects on the balance sheet equation in two phases: at acquisition and upon expiration at the end of the month of acquisition. Show all amounts in thousands.

2-23   Find Unknowns
The following data pertain to the Mosimar Corporation. Total assets at January 1, 19X1 were $100,000; at December 31, 19X1 $124,000. During 19X1, sales were $304,000, cash dividends were $4,000, and operating expenses (exclusive of cost of goods sold) were $150,000. Total liabilities at December 31, 19X1, were $55,000; at January 1, 19X1, $40,000. There was no additional capital paid in during 19X1.

Required   1. Shareholders' equity, January 1, 19X1
2. Net income for 19X1
3. Cost of goods sold for 19X1

2-24   Income Statement
A statement of an automobile dealer for the year ending December 31, 19X3 follows:

Revenues:		
Sales	$1,000,000	
Increase in market value of land and building	200,000	$1,200,000
Deduct expenses:		
Advertising	$ 100,000	
Sales commissions	50,000	
Utilities	20,000	
Wages	150,000	
Dividends	100,000	
Cost of cars purchased	700,000	1,120,000
Net profit		$ 80,000

Required List and describe any shortcomings of this statement.

2-25 Balance Sheet Equation

(Alternates are 2-37 and 2-44.) For each of the following independent cases, compute the amounts (in thousands) for the items indicated by letters, and show your supporting computations:

	Case 1	Case 2	Case 3
Revenues	$140	$ K	$290
Expenses	120	200	250
Dividends declared	–0–	5	Q
Additional investment by shareholders	–0–	40	35
Net income	E	20	P
Retained earnings:			
Beginning of year	30	60	100
End of year	D	J	110
Paid-in capital:			
Beginning of year	15	10	N
End of year	C	H	85
Total assets:			
Beginning of year	85	F	L
End of year	100	280	M
Total liabilities:			
Beginning of year	40 A	90	105
End of year	B	G	95

2-26 Nonprofit Operating Statement

Examine the accompanying Income Statement for the fiscal year 19X1–X2 of the Oxbridge University Faculty Club. Identify the Oxbridge classifications and terms that would not be used by a profit-seeking hotel and restaurant. Suggest terms that the profit-seeking entity would use instead. (£ is the British pound.)

Food Service:

Sales		£545,128	
Expenses:			
Food	£287,088		
Labour	272,849		
Operating costs	30,535	590,472	
Deficit			£(45,344)

Bar:

Sales		£ 90,549	
Expenses:			
Cost of liquor	£ 29,302		
Labour	5,591		
Operating costs	6,125	41,018	
Surplus			49,531

continued

Hotel:

Sales	£ 33,771	
Expenses	23,803	
Surplus		9,968
Surplus from operations		£ 14,155
General income (members' dues, room fees, etc.)		95,546
General administration and operating expenses		(134,347)
Deficit before university subsidy		£ (24,646)
University subsidy		30,000
Net surplus after university subsidy		£ 5,354

PROBLEMS →

2-27 Fundamental Revenue and Expense

Inkwell Corporation was formed on June 1, 19X2, when some shareholders invested $100,000 in cash in the company. During the first week of June, $85,000 cash was spent for merchandise inventory (sportswear). During the remainder of the month, total sales reached $110,000, of which $70,000 was on open account. The cost of the inventory sold was $60,000. For simplicity, assume that no other transactions occurred except that on June 28 Inkwell Corporation acquired $25,000 additional inventory on open account.

Required

1. Using the balance sheet equation approach demonstrated in Exhibit 2-2 (p. 45), analyze all transactions for June. Show all amounts in thousands.
2. Prepare a balance sheet, June 30, 19X2.
3. Prepare two statements for June, side by side. The first should use the accrual basis of accounting to compute net income, and the second the cash basis to compute net cash provided by (or used by) operating activities. Which basis provides a more informative measure of economic performance? Why?

2-28 Accounting for Prepayments

(Alternates are 2-30, 2-33, 2-40, and 2-42.) The Lopez Company, a wholesale distributor of home appliances, began business on July 1, 19X2. The following summarized transactions occurred during July:

1. Lopez's shareholders contributed $220,000 in cash in exchange for their common stock.
2. On July 2, Lopez signed a one-year lease on a warehouse, paying $60,000 cash in advance for occupancy of twelve months.
3. On July 2, Lopez acquired warehouse equipment for $100,000. A cash down payment of $40,000 was made and a note payable was signed for the balance.
4. On July 2, Lopez paid $24,000 cash for a two-year insurance policy covering fire, casualty, and related risks.
5. Lopez acquired assorted merchandise for $35,000 cash.
6. Lopez acquired assorted merchandise for $190,000 on open account.
7. Total sales were $200,000, of which $30,000 were for cash.
8. Cost of inventory sold was $160,000.
9. Rent expense was recognized for the month of July.
10. Amortization expense of $2,000 was recognized for the month.
11. Insurance expense was recognized for the month.
12. Collected $35,000 from credit customers.
13. Disbursed $80,000 to trade creditors.

For simplicity, ignore all other possible expenses.

1. Using the balance sheet equation format demonstrated in Exhibit 2-2 (p. 45), prepare an analysis of each transaction. Show all amounts in thousands. What do transactions 8 to 11 illustrate about the theory of assets and expenses? (Use a Prepaid Insurance account, which is not illustrated in Exhibit 2-2.)
2. Prepare an income statement for July on the accrual basis.
3. Prepare a balance sheet, July 31, 19X2.

2-29 Net Income and Cash Flows from Operating Activities

(Alternates are 2-31, 2-41, and 2-43.) Refer to the preceding problem. Suppose Lopez measured performance on the cash basis instead of the accrual basis. Compute the net cash provided by (or used for) operating activities. Which measure, net income or net cash provided by (or used for) operating activities, provides a better measure of overall performance? Why?

2-30 Analysis of Transactions, Preparation of Statements

(Alternates are 2-28, 2-33, 2-40, and 2-42.) The Philips Company was incorporated on April 1, 19X2. Philips had ten holders of common stock. Rita Philips, who was the president and chief executive officer, held 51% of the shares. The company rented space in chain discount stores and specialized in selling ladies' shoes. Philips' first location was in a store that was part of Century Market Centres Limited.

The following events occurred during April:

1. The company was incorporated. Common shareholders invested $140,000 cash.
2. Purchased merchandise inventory for cash, $45,000.
3. Purchased merchandise inventory on open account, $35,000.
4. Merchandise carried in inventory at a cost of $37,000 was sold for cash for $25,000 and on open account for $65,000, a grand total of $90,000. Philips (not Century) carries and collects these accounts receivable.
5. Collection of the above accounts receivable, $15,000.
6. Payments of accounts payable $28,000. See transaction 3.
7. Special display equipment and fixtures were acquired on April 1 for $36,000. Their expected useful life was thirty-six months. This equipment was removable. Philips paid $12,000 as a down payment and signed a promissory note for $24,000. Also see transaction 11.
8. On April 1, Philips signed a rental agreement with Century. The agreement called for a flat $2,000 per month, payable quarterly in advance. Therefore Philips paid $6,000 cash on April 1.
9. The rental agreement also called for a payment of 10% of all sales. This payment was in addition to the flat $2,000 per month. In this way, Century would share in any success of the venture and be compensated for general services such as cleaning and utilities. This payment was to be made in cash on the last day of each month as soon as the sales for the month had been tabulated. Therefore Philips made the payment on April 30.
10. Employee wages and sales commissions were all paid for in cash. The amount was $35,000.
11. Amortization expense of $1,000 was recognized ($36,000 / 36 months). See transaction 7.
12. The expiration of an appropriate amount of prepaid rental services was recognized. See transaction 8.

1. Prepare an analysis of Philips Company's transactions, employing the equation approach demonstrated in Exhibit 2-2 (p. 45). Show all amounts in thousands.
2. Prepare a balance sheet as of April 30, 19X2, and an income statement for the month of April. Ignore income taxes.

3. Given these sparse facts, analyze Philips' performance for April and its financial position as of April 30, 19X2.

2-31 Net Income and Cash Flows from Operating Activities

(Alternates are 2-29, 2-41, and 2-43.) Refer to the preceding problem. Suppose Philips measured performance on the cash basis instead of the accrual basis. Compute the net cash provided by (or used for) operating activities. Which measure, net income or net cash provided by (or used for) operating activities, provides a better measure of overall performance? Why?

2-32 Prepare Financial Statements

The Lazolli Corporation does not use the services of a professional accountant. However, at the end of its second year of operations, 19X2, the company's financial statements were prepared by its office manager. Listed below in random order are the items appearing in these statements:

Accounts receivable	$ 27,700	Office supplies inventory	$2,000
Paid-in capital	100,000	Notes payable	7,000
Trucks	33,700	Merchandise inventory	61,000
Cost of goods sold	156,000	Accounts payable	14,000
Salary expense	86,000	Notes receivable	2,500
Unexpired insurance	1,800	Utilities expenses	5,000
Rent expense	19,500	Net income	4,200
Sales	280,000	Retained earnings	
Advertising expense	9,300	January 1, 19X2	18,000
Cash	14,500	December 31, 19X2	22,200

You are satisfied that the statements in which these items appear are correct except for several matters that the office manager overlooked. The following information should have been entered on the books and reflected in the financial statements:

a. The amount shown for rent expense includes $1,500 that is actually prepaid for the first month in 19X3.

b. Of the amount shown for unexpired insurance, only $800 is prepaid for periods after 19X2.

c. Amortization of trucks for 19X2 is $5,000.

d. About $1,200 of the office supplies in the inventory shown above was actually issued and used during 19X2 operations.

e. Cash dividends of $3,000 were declared in December 19X2 by the board of directors. These dividends are to be distributed in February 19X3.

Required Prepare in good form the following corrected financial statements, ignoring income taxes:

1. Income statement for 19X2
2. Statement of retained earnings for 19X2
3. Balance sheet at December 31, 19X2

It is not necessary to prepare a columnar analysis to show the transaction effects on each of the elements of the accounting equation.

2-33 Transaction Analysis and Financial Statements, Including Dividends

(Alternates are 2-28, 2-30, 2-40, and 2-42.) Consider the following balance sheet at December 31, 19X1 of a wholesaler of party supplies:

Assets		Liabilities and Shareholders' Equity		
		Liabilities:		
Cash	$ 200,000	Accounts payable		$ 700,000
Accounts receivable	$ 400,000	Shareholders' equity:		
Merchandise inventory	860,000	Paid-in capital	$300,000	
Prepaid rent	40,000	Retained earnings	600,000	
Equipment	100,000	Total shareholders'		
		equity		900,000
Total	$1,600,000	Total		$1,600,000

The following is a summary of transactions that occurred during 19X2:

a. Acquisitions of inventory on open account, $1 million.

b. Sales on open account, $1.4 million; and for cash, $200,000. Therefore, total sales were $1.6 million.

c. Merchandise carried in inventory at a cost of $1.2 million was sold as described in b.

d. The warehouse twelve-month lease expired on September 1, 19X2. However, the lease was immediately renewed at a rate of $84,000 for the next twelve-month period. The entire rent was paid in cash in advance.

e. Amortization expense for 19X2 for the warehouse equipment was $20,000.

f. Collections on accounts receivable, $1.25 million.

g. Wages for 19X2 were paid in full in cash, $200,000.

h. Miscellaneous expenses for 19X2 were paid in full in cash, $70,000.

i. Payments on accounts payable, $900,000.

j. Cash dividends for 19X2 were paid in full in December, $100,000.

Required

1. Prepare an analysis of transactions, employing the equation approach demonstrated in Exhibit 2-2 (p. 45). Show the amounts in thousands of dollars.

2. Prepare a balance sheet, statement of income, and statement of retained earnings. Also prepare a combined statement of income and retained earnings.

3. Reconsider transaction j. Suppose the dividends were declared on December 15, payable on January 31, 19X3, to shareholders of record on January 20. Indicate which accounts and financial statements in requirement 2 would be changed and by how much. Be complete and specific.

2-34   Statement of Changes in Financial Position

Kang Company imports Asian goods and sells them in eight import stores on the West Coast. On August 1, 19X4, Kang's cash balance was $164,000. Summarized transactions during August were:

1. Sales on open account, $580,000.

2. Collections of accounts receivable, $450,000.

3. Purchases of inventory on open account, $305,000.

4. Payment of accounts payable, $280,000.

5. Cost of goods sold, $325,000.

6. Salaries and wages expense, $105,000, of which $90,000 was paid in cash and $15,000 remained payable on August 31.

7. Rent expense for August, $35,000, paid in advance in July.

8. Amortization expense, $46,000.

9. Other operating expenses, $60,000, all paid in cash.

10. Borrowed from bank on August 31, $50,000, with repayment (including interest) due on December 31.

11. Purchased fixtures and equipment for San Diego store on August 31, $120,000; half paid in cash and half due in October.

Required

1. Prepare a statement of changes in financial position, including the cash balance on August 31.

2. Prepare an income statement.

3. Explain why net income differs from net cash provided by (or used for) operating activities.

2-35   Two Sides of a Transaction

For each of the following transactions, show the effects on the entities involved. As was illustrated in the chapter, use the A = L + OE equation to demonstrate the effects. Also name each amount affected, show the dollar amount, and indicate whether the effects are increases or decreases. The following transaction is completed as an illustration.

Illustration

The Provincial General Hospital collects $1,000 from the Blue Cross Health Care Plan.

		A		=	L	+ OE
Entity	Cash	Receivables	Trucks		Payables	
Hospital	+1,000	−1,000		=		
Blue Cross	−1,000			=	−1,000	

1. Borrowing of $100,000 on a home mortgage from Federal Savings by Evan Porteus.

2. Payment of $10,000 principal on the above mortgage. Ignore interest.

3. Purchase of a two-year subscription to *Maclean's* magazine for $80 cash by Carla Bonini.

4. Purchase of trucks by Canada Post for $10 million cash. The trucks were carried in the Treasury Board's accounts at $10 million.

5. Purchase of government bonds for $100,000 cash by Lockheed Corporation.

6. Cash deposits of $10 on the returnable bottles sold by Loblaw Stores to a retail customer, Philomena Simon.

7. Collections on open account of $100 by Sears store from a retail customer, Kenneth Arrow.

8. Purchase of traveller's checks of $1,000 from CIBC by Michael Harrison.

9. Cash deposit of $500 in a chequing account in Bank of Montreal by David Kreps.

10. Purchase of an Air Canada "super-saver" airline ticket for $500 cash by Robert Wilson on June 15. The trip will be taken on September 10.

CRITICAL THINKING PROBLEM

2-36   Financial Ratios

Following is a list of selected financial data:

	Per-share Data			Ratios and Percentages		
Company	Price	Earnings	Dividends	Price-Earnings	Dividend Yield	Dividend-Payout
A	$17	$1.76	$ —	$ —	—%	17%
B	37	—	2.12	—	—	42
C	—	5.30	1.80	6.4	—	—
D	34	—	2.32	12.0	6.8	—
E	60	5.18	—	—	5.3	—
F	30	3.14	1.40	—	—	—
G	—	—	4.00	—	6.8	30

The missing figures for this schedule can be computed from the data given.

Required

1. Compute the missing figures and identify the company with
   a. The highest dividend yield
   b. The highest dividend-payout percentage
   c. The lowest market price relative to earnings
2. Based on these data, which company would you choose as
   a. The most attractive investment? Why?
   b. The least attractive investment? Why?

COMPANY CASES

2-37   Balance Sheet Equation

(Alternates are 2-25 and 2-44.) Reebok International's actual terminology and actual data (in millions of dollars) follow for a recent fiscal year:

Cost and expenses	B
Net income	$ 177
Dividends	34
Additional investments by shareholders	4
Assets, beginning of period	1,166
Assets, end of period	E
Liabilities, beginning of period	A
Liabilities, end of period	1,403
Paid-in capital, beginning of period	276
Paid-in capital, end of period	D
Retained earnings, beginning of period	565
Retained earnings, end of period	C
Revenues	2,159

Required

Find the unknowns (in millions), showing computations to support your answers.

2-38   Earnings and Dividend Ratios

Procter & Gamble's brand names include Tide, Crest, Jif, and Prell. The company's 1994 annual report showed earnings of $2,211 million. Cash dividends per share were $1.24. Procter & Gamble had 683,100,000 average number of common shares outstanding. No other type of stock was outstanding. The market price of the stock at the end of the year was $62 per share.

Required   Compute (1) earnings per share, (2) price-earnings ratio, (3) dividend yield, and (4) dividend-payout ratio.

2-39   Earnings and Dividend Ratios

Chevron Corporation is one of the largest oil companies in the world. The company's revenue in 1994 was $37 billion. Net income was $1,285,000,000. EPS was $3.89. The company's common stock is the only type of shares outstanding.

Required   1. Compute the average number of common shares outstanding during the year.
2. The dividend-payout ratio was 90%. What was the amount of dividends per share?
3. The average market price of the stock for the year was $44 per share. Compute (a) dividend yield and (b) price-earnings ratio.

2-40   Analysis of Transactions, Preparation of Statements

(Alternates are 2-28, 2-30, 2-33, and 2-42.) Loblaw Companies Limited's actual condensed balance sheet data for December 30, 1995, follows (in millions):

Cash	$ 692.1	Accounts payable	$ 936.7
Accounts receivable	164.4	Other liabilities	1,101.5
Inventories	609.5	Paid-in capital	258.2
Other assets	240.4	Retained earnings	901.7
Property, plant, and equipment	1,490.7		
Total	$3,197.1	Total	$3,197.1

The following summarizes some transactions during January (in millions):

1. Groceries carried in inventory at a cost of $3 were sold for cash of $2 and on open account of $8, a grand total of $10.
2. Acquired inventory on account, $5.
3. Collected receivables, $3.
4. On May 2, used $12 cash to prepay some rent and insurance for 12 months.
5. Payments on accounts payable (for inventories), $2.
6. Paid selling and administrative expenses in cash, $1.
7. Prepaid expenses of $1 for rent and insurance expired in May.
8. Amortization expense of $1 was recognized for May.

Required   1. Prepare an analysis of Loblaw's transactions, employing the equation approach demonstrated in Exhibit 2-2 (p. 45). Show all amounts in millions. (For simplicity, only a few transactions are illustrated here.)

2. Prepare a statement of earnings for the month ended January 31 and a balance sheet, January 31. Ignore income taxes.

2-41   Net Income and Cash Flows from Operating Activities

(Alternates are 2-29, 2-31, and 2-43.) Refer to the preceding problem. Suppose Loblaw's measured performance on the cash basis instead of the accrual basis. Compute the net cash provided by (or used for) operating activities. Which measure, net income or net cash provided by (or used for) operating activities, provides a better measure of overall performance? Why?

2-42   Analysis of Transactions, Preparation of Statements

(Alternates are 2-28, 2-30, 2-33, and 2-40.) Wm. Wrigley Jr. Company manufactures and sells chewing gum. The company's actual condensed balance sheet data for a recent December 31 follow (in millions):

Cash	$ 86	Accounts payable	$ 63
Receivables	118	Dividends payable	12
Inventories	177	Other liabilities	158
Other current assets	121	Paid-in capital	17
Property, plant, and equipment	240	Retained earnings	565
Other assets	73		
Total	$815	Total	$815

The following summarizes some major transactions during January (in millions):

1. Gum carried in inventory at a cost of $40 was sold for cash of $20 and on open account of $52, a grand total of $72.
2. Collection of receivables, $50.
3. Amortization expense of $2 was recognized.
4. Selling and administrative expenses of $24 were paid in cash.
5. Prepaid expenses of $5 expired in January. These included fire insurance premiums paid in the previous year that applied to future months. The expiration increases selling and administrative expense and reduces other current assets.
6. The December 31 liability for dividends was paid in cash on January 25.
7. On January 30, the company declared a $2 dividend, which will be paid on February 25.

Required

1. Prepare an analysis of Wrigley's transactions, employing the equation approach demonstrated in Exhibit 2-2 (p. 45). Show all amounts in millions. (For simplicity, only a few major transactions are illustrated here.)
2. Prepare a statement of earnings and also a statement of retained earnings for the month ended January 31. Also prepare a balance sheet, January 31. Ignore income taxes.

2-43 Net Income and Cash Flows from Operating Activities
(Alternates are 2-29, 2-31, and 2-41.) Refer to the preceding problem. Suppose Wrigley measured performance on the cash basis instead of the accrual basis. Compute the net cash provided by (or used for) operating activities. Which measure, net income or net cash provided by (or used for) operating activities, provides a better measure of overall performance? Why?

2-44   Balance Sheet Equation
(Alternates are 2-25 and 2-37.) Nordstrom, Inc., the fashion retailer, had the following actual data for its 1994 fiscal year (in millions):

Assets, beginning of period	$2,053
Assets, end of period	2,177
Liabilities, beginning of period	A
Liabilities, end of period	E
Paid-in capital, beginning of period	155
Paid-in capital, end of period	D
Retained earnings, beginning of period	897
Retained earnings, end of period	C
Sales and other revenues	3,590
Cost of sales, and all other expenses	3,450
Net earnings	B
Dividends	28
Additional investment by shareholders	2

Required   Find the unknowns (in thousands), showing computations to support your answers.

2-45   Net Income and Retained Income

McDonald's Corporation is a well-known fast-food restaurant company. The following data are from a recent annual report (in millions):

Retained earnings,		Dividends paid	$ 197.2
beginning of year	$6,727.3	General, administrative,	
Revenues	7,408.1	and selling expenses	941.1
Interest and other		Franchise expenses	318.4
non-operating expenses	308.3	Retained earnings,	
Provisions for income taxes	593.2	end of year	7,612.6
Food and packaging	1,735.1	Occupancy and other	
Wages and salaries	1,291.2	operating expenses	1,138.3

Required
1. Prepare the following for the year:
   a. Income statement. The final three lines of the income statement were labelled as income before provision for income taxes, provision for income taxes, and net income.
   b. Statement of retained earnings.
2. Comment briefly on the relative size of the cash dividend.

2-46   Earnings Statement, Retained Earnings

The Procter & Gamble Company has many well-known products. Examples are Tide, Crest, Jif, and Prell. The following amounts were in the financial statements contained in its 1994 annual report (in millions):

Net sales and other income	$30,296	Retained earnings at	
Cash	2,373	beginning of year	6,248
Interest expense and other	234	Cost of products sold	17,355
Income taxes	1,135	Dividends to shareholders	847
Accounts payable—Trade	2,604	Marketing, administrative,	
Cash provided by operations	3,649	and other expenses	9,361

Required   Choose the relevant data and prepare (1) the income statement for the year and (2) the statement of retained income for the year. The final three lines of the income statement were labelled as earnings before income taxes, income taxes, and net earnings.

2-47   Classic Case of the President's Wealth

This is a classic case in accounting. From the *Chicago Tribune*, August 20, 1964:

- Accountants acting on President Johnson's orders today reported his family wealth totalled $3,484,098.

- The statement of capital, arrived at through conservative procedures of evaluation, contrasted with a recent estimate published by *Life* magazine, which put the total at 14 million dollars.

- The family fortune, which is held in trust while the Johnsons are in the White House, was set forth in terms of book values. The figures represent original cost rather than current market values on what the holdings would be worth if sold now.

- Announced by the White House press office, but turned over to reporters by a national accounting firm at their Washington branch office, the financial statement apparently was intended to still a flow of quasi-official and unofficial estimates of the Johnson fortune....

Assets:		
Cash		$ 132,547
Bonds		398,540
Interest in Texas Broadcasting Corp		2,543,838
Ranch properties and other real estate		525,791
Other assets, including insurance policies		82,054
Total assets		$3,682,770
Liabilities:		
Note payable on real estate holding, 5 percent due 1971	$150,000	
Accounts payable, accrued interest, and income taxes	48,672	
Total liabilities		$198,672
Capital		**$3,484,098**

- The report apportions the capital among the family, with $37,081 credited to the President; $2,126,298 to his wife Claudia T., who uses the name Lady Bird; $490,141 to their daughter Lynda Bird; and $489,578 to their daughter Luci Baines.

- The statement said the family holdings—under the names of the President, his wife, and his two daughters, Lynda Bird and Luci Baines—had increased from $737,730 on January 1, 1954, a year after Johnson became Democratic leader of the Senate, to $3,484,098 on July 31 this year, a gain of $2,746,368....

- A covering letter addressed to Johnson said the statement was made "in conformity with generally accepted accounting principles applied on a consistent basis."

- By far the largest part of the fortune was listed as the Johnsons' interest in the Texas Broadcasting Corporation, carried on the books as worth $2,543,838.

- The accountants stated that this valuation was arrived at on the basis of the cost of the stock when the Johnsons bought control of the debt-ridden radio station between 1943 and 1947, plus accumulated earnings ploughed back as equity, less 25% capital gains tax.[1]

Editorial, Chicago Tribune, August 22, 1964:

- An accounting firm acting on Mr. Johnson's instructions and employing what it termed "generally accepted auditing standards" has released a statement putting the current worth of the Lyndon Johnson family at a little less than 3½ million dollars....

---

[1] You need not be concerned about the details of this method of accounting until you study in more advanced courses. In brief, when an investor holds a large enough stake in a corporation, such investment is accounted for at its acquisition cost plus the investor's pro rata share of the investee's net income (or net loss) minus the investor's share of dividends. For example, suppose the Texas Broadcasting Corporation earned $500,000 in a given year and that Johnson owned 20% of the corporation. In this situation, the Johnson financial statements would show an increase in Interest in Texas Broadcasting Corp. of $100,000 less the $25,000 income tax that would become payable upon disposition of the investment. (Today's accountants would prefer to increase the Investment account by the full $100,000 and the liabilities by $25,000. See the Carter financial statements.)

Exhibit 2-10

Perry, Chambliss,
Sheppard and
Thompson
Certified Public
Accountants
Americus, Georgia
James Earl Carter, Jr.
and Rosalynn Carter
Statement of Assets
and Liabilities
December 31, 1977
(unaudited)

Assets	Cost Basis	Estimated Current Value
Cash	$204,979.04	$ 204,979.04
Cash Value of Life Insurance	45,506.88	45,506.88
U.S. Savings Bonds, Series E	1,425.00	1,550.94
Loan receivable	50,000.00	50,000.00
Overpayment of 1977 Income Taxes	51,121.27	51,121.27
Personal Assets Trust—Note 3	151,097.87	557,717.11
Residence, Plains, Georgia	45,000.00	54,090.00
Lot in Plains, Georgia	1,100.00	3,155.00
Automobile	4,550.75	2,737.50
Total assets	$554,780.81	$ 970,857.74

Liabilities and Capital		
Miscellaneous accounts payable, estimated	$ 1,500.00	$ 1,500.00
Provision for possible income taxes on unrealized asset appreciation—Note 4	–0–	174,000.00
Total liabilities	$ 1,500.00	$ 175,500.00
Excess of assets over liabilities (Capital)	$553,280.81	$ 795,357.75

NOTE 1: Estimated market values of real estate are 100% of the fair market values as determined by county tax assessors except as to certain assets held in the personal assets trust, which are stated at book value.
NOTE 2: This statement excludes campaign fund assets and liabilities.
NOTE 3: The interest in Carter's Warehouse partnership, the capital stock of Carter's Farms, Inc., the remainder interest in certain real estate and securities and a commercial lot in Plains, Georgia, were transferred to a personal assets trust in January, 1977. The primary purpose of the trust is to isolate the President from those of his assets which are most likely to be affected by actions of the federal government. The President was responsible as a general partner for obligations of the partnership before his partnership interest was transferred to the trust. The transfer to the trust did not affect such responsibility.
NOTE 4: If the market values of the assets were realized, income taxes would be payable at an uncertain rate. A provision for such income taxes has been made at rates in effect for 1977.
NOTE 5: The amounts in the accompanying statements are based principally upon the accrual basis method of accounting.

- Dean Burch, chairman of the Republican National Committee, has remarked that the method used to list the Johnson assets was comparable to placing the value of Manhattan Island at $24, the price at which it was purchased from the Indians. The Johnson accounting firm conceded that its report was "not intended to indicate the values that might be realized if the investment were sold."
- In fact, it would be interesting to observe the response of the Johnson family if a syndicate of investors were to offer to take Texas Broadcasting off the family's hands at double the publicly reported worth of the operation....

Required

1. Evaluate the criticisms, making special reference to fundamental accounting concepts or "principles."
2. The financial statements of President and Mrs. Carter are shown in Exhibit 2-10. Do you prefer the approach taken by the Carter statements as compared with the Johnson statements? Explain.
3. The Carter statements in Exhibit 2-10 indicate that the Carter residence cost $45,000. Its estimated current value is shown as $54,090. Which number do you

believe is more accurate? More relevant? Which number, $45,000 or $54,090, would be used by a business in its statement of assets?

4. Have the Carters earned income of $54,090 – $45,000 on their residence?
5. Suppose you were asked tomorrow to prepare your family's (or your individual) statement of assets and liabilities. Could you do it? How would you measure your wealth?

2-48   Revenue Recognition and Ethics
Kendall Square Research Corporation (KSR), located in Waltham, Massachusetts, produced high-speed computers and competed against companies such as Cray Research and Sun Microsystems.

In August 1993 the common stock of KSR reached an all-time high of $25.75 a share; by mid-December it had plummeted to $5.25. Its financial policies were called into question in an article in *Financial Shenanigan Busters*, Winter 1994, p. 3. The main charge was that the company was recording revenues before it was appropriate.

KSR sold expensive computers to universities and other research institutions. Often the customers took delivery before they knew how they might pay for the computers. Sometimes they anticipated receiving grants that would pay for the computers, but other times they had no prospective funding. KSR also recorded revenue when computers were shipped to distributors who did not yet have customers to buy them and when computers were sold contingent on future upgrades.

Required   Comment on the ethical implications of KSR's revenue recognition practices.

2-49   Hudson's Bay Company Annual Report

Refer to the financial statements of the actual company, the Hudson's Bay Company, in Appendix A at the end of the text and answer the following questions:

Required
1. What was the amount of total revenues for the 1997 fiscal year? The net income?
2. What was the total amount of cash dividends for the 1997 fiscal year?
3. What was the title of the financial statement that contained the dividend amount? Did it differ from the title you expected? Explain.

2-50   Annual Report Disclosure
Select the financial statements of any company of your choice.

Required
1. What was the amount of sales or total revenues for the most recent year? The net income?
2. What was the total amount of cash dividends for the most recent year?
3. What was the amount of cash provided by (or used for) operating activities in the most recent year? Compare the amount to the net income.
4. What was the ending balance in retained income in the most recent year? What were the two most significant items during the year that affected the retained income balance?

3

The Recording Process: Journals and Ledgers

Learning Objectives

After studying this chapter, you should be able to

1. Explain the double-entry accounting system, the role of ledger accounts, and the meaning of debits and credits.

2. Describe the sequence of steps in recording transactions and explain how transactions are journalized and posted.

3. Analyze transactions for journalizing and posting and explain the relationship of revenues and expenses to shareholders' equity.

4. Prepare journal entries and post them to the ledger.

5. Prepare a trial balance and understand its role relative to the income statement and balance sheet.

6. Correct erroneous entries and describe how errors affect accounts.

7. Use T-accounts to aid the discovery of unknown amounts.

8. Understand the significance of computers in data processing.

9. Explain the meaning of the concepts going concern, materiality, and cost-benefit.

To intelligently use the reports prepared by accountants, decision makers must understand the methods used to record and analyze accounting data. This chapter focuses on the double-entry accounting system that is universally used to record and process information about an entity's transactions. We concentrate primarily on specific procedures and techniques instead of new accounting concepts.

The chapter begins by describing the building blocks of a double-entry system—ledgers and journals. It then defines terms that accountants use daily, such as *debit* and *credit*, but that often seem strange to nonaccountants. Next, the chapter traces the process of recording transactions, from the original entry into the accounts to the completed financial statements. It includes treatment of errors in the records and methods for creating entries from incomplete files and data sources. Finally, the gradual introduction of basic concepts continues with coverage of the going concern convention, materiality, and the cost-benefit criterion.

Methods of processing accounting data have changed dramatically in the last decade or two, as computerized systems have replaced manual ones. However, the steps in recording, storing, and processing accounting data have not changed. Moving from pencil-and-paper accounting records to computerized ones is like starting to drive a car with an automatic transmission after driving one with a manual transmission. Less time must be spent on routine tasks, but a basic understanding of the system is still required. Whether data are entered into the system by pencil, keyboard, or optical scanner, the same basic data are required. Whether reports are automatically produced by a computer or painstakingly assembled by hand, understanding and interpreting the reports requires basic knowledge about how the underlying data were processed. Therefore, this chapter is important to anyone who *uses* accounting reports, as well as to someone who plans to *produce* such reports.

■ THE DOUBLE-ENTRY ACCOUNTING SYSTEM

double-entry system
The method usually followed for recording transactions, whereby at least two accounts are always affected by each transaction.

In a large business such as an Eaton's or The Bay store, hundreds or thousands of transactions occur hourly. Accounting procedures must be used to keep track of these transactions in a systematic manner. The method usually followed for recording all of a business entity's transactions is the **double-entry system**, whereby at least two accounts are always affected by each transaction. Each transaction must be analyzed to determine which accounts are involved, whether the accounts are increased or decreased, and the amount of the change in each account balance.

Recall the first three transactions of the Biwheels Company introduced in Chapter 1:

Objective 1

Explain the double-entry accounting system, the role of ledger accounts, and the meaning of debits and credits.

	A		=	L	+	SE
	Cash	Merchandise Inventory		Note Payable		Paid-in Capital
(1) Initial investment by owner	+400,000		=			+400,000
(2) Loan from bank	+100,000		=	+100,000		
(3) Acquire inventory for cash	−150,000	+150,000	=			

This balance sheet equation illustrates the basic concepts of the double-entry system by showing two entries for each transaction. It also emphasizes that the equation Assets = Liabilities + Shareholders' Equity must always remain in balance.

The balance sheet equation approach is unwieldy as a means for recording each and every transaction that occurs. In practice, *ledgers* are used to record the individual transactions in the proper accounts.

Ledger Accounts

ledger A group of related accounts kept current in a systematic manner.

general ledger The collection of accounts that accumulates the amounts reported in the major financial statements.

T-account Simplified version of ledger accounts that takes the form of the capital letter T.

A **ledger** contains a group of related accounts kept current in a systematic manner. The ledger may be in the form of a bound record book, a loose-leaf set of pages, or some kind of electronic storage element such as magnetic tape or disk. You can think of a ledger as a book with one page for each account. When you hear reference to "keeping the books" or "auditing the books," the word *books* refers to the ledgers. A firm's **general ledger** is the collection of accounts that accumulates the amounts reported in the firm's major financial statements.

The ledger accounts used here are simplified versions of those used in practice. They are called **T-accounts** because they take the form of the capital letter T. The vertical line in the T divides the account into left and right sides for recording increases and decreases in the account. The account title is on the horizontal line. For example, consider the format of the Cash account:

Cash	
Left side	Right side
Increases in cash	Decreases in cash

The T-accounts for the first three Biwheels Company transactions are as follows:

Assets	=	Liabilities + Shareholders' Equity

Cash				Note Payable	
Increases		Decreases		Decreases	Increases
(1)	400,000	(3)	150,000		(2)	100,000
(2)	100,000				

Merchandise Inventory				Paid-in Capital	
Increases		Decreases		Decreases	Increases
(3)	150,000				(1)	400,000

These entries are in accordance with the rules of the double-entry system. Two accounts are affected by each transaction.

In practice, accounts are created as needed. The process of writing a new T-account in preparation for recording a transaction is called *opening the account*. For transaction 1, we opened Cash and Paid-in Capital. For transaction 2, we opened Note Payable, and for transaction 3 we opened Merchandise Inventory.

Each T-account summarizes the changes in a particular asset, liability, or shareholders' equity. Each transaction is keyed in some way, such as by the numbering used in this illustration or by the date or by both. This keying helps

balance The difference between the total left-side and right-side amounts in an account at any particular time.

the rechecking (auditing) process by aiding the tracing of entries in the ledger account to the original transactions. A **balance** is the difference between the total left-side and right-side amounts in an account at any particular time.

Asset accounts have *left-side balances*. They are increased by entries on the left side and decreased by entries on the right side. Liabilities and owners' equity accounts have *right-side balances*. They are increased by entries on the right side and decreased by entries on the left side.

Consider the analysis and entries for each Biwheels transaction. Notice that each transaction has a left-side entry and a right-side entry of the same amount.

1. Transaction: Initial investment by owners, $400,000 cash.
    Analysis: The asset **Cash** is increased.
                The shareholders' equity **Paid-in Capital** is increased.
    Entry:

Cash		Paid-in Capital	
(1) 400,000			(1) 400,000

2. Transaction: Loan from bank, $100,000.
    Analysis: The asset **Cash** is increased.
                The liability **Note Payable** is increased.
    Entry:

Cash		Note Payable	
(1) 400,000			(2) 100,000
(2) 100,000			

3. Transaction: Acquired inventory for cash, $150,000.
    Analysis: The asset Cash is decreased.
                The asset Merchandise Inventory is increased.
    Entry:

Cash		
(1) 400,000	(3)	150,000
(2) 100,000		

Merchandise Inventory	
(3) 150,000	

Accounts such as these exist to keep an up-to-date record of the changes in specific assets and equities. Financial statements can be prepared at any instant if the account balances are up-to-date. The information accumulated in the accounts provides the necessary summary balances for the financial statements. For example, the balance sheet after the first three transactions contains the following account balances:

Assets		Liabilities + Shareholders' Equity	
Cash	$350,000	Liabilities:	
Merchandise		Note payable	$100,000
inventory	150,000	Shareholders' equity:	
		Paid-in capital	400,000
Total	$500,000	Total	$500,000

■ THE DEBIT-CREDIT LANGUAGE

debit An entry or balance on the left side of an account.

credit An entry or balance on the right side of an account.

charge A word often used instead of debit.

You have just seen that the double-entry system features entries on left sides and right sides of various accounts. Accountants use the term **debit** to denote the left-side entries and the term **credit** to denote right-side entries. For instance, suppose a professional accountant was asked how to analyze and record transaction 1. She would say, "That's easy. Debit Cash and credit Paid-in Capital." By so doing, she enters $400,000 on the *left* side of Cash and $400,000 on the *right* side of Paid-in Capital.

In short, *debit* means *left* and *credit* means *right*. The word **charge** is often used instead of *debit*, but no single word is used as a synonym for credit. Abbreviations may be used—*dr.* for debit and *cr.* for credit.

The words *debit* and *credit* have a Latin origin. They were used when double-entry bookkeeping was introduced in 1494 by Pacioli, an Italian monk. (Indeed, it has been said, probably by an accountant, that the most important event of the 1490s was the creation of double-entry bookkeeping, not Columbus's ocean crossing.) Even though *left* and *right* are more descriptive words, *debit* and *credit* are too deeply entrenched to avoid.

Debit and *credit* are used as verbs, adjectives, and nouns. "Debit $1,000 to cash, and credit $1,000 to accounts receivable" are examples of uses as verbs, meaning that $1,000 should be placed on the left side of the Cash account and on the right side of the Accounts Receivable account. Similarly, in phrases such as "a debit is made to cash" or "cash has a debit balance of $12,000," the word *debit* is a noun or an adjective that describes the status of a particular account. Thus *debit* and *credit* are short words packed with meaning.

In our everyday conversation, we sometimes use the words *debit* and *credit* in a general sense that may completely diverge from their technical accounting uses. For instance, we may give praise by saying, "She deserves plenty of credit for her good deed," or we may give criticism by saying, "That misplay is a debit on his ledger." When you study accounting, forget these general uses and misuses of the words. Merely think right or left—that is, right side or left side.

■ RECORDING TRANSACTIONS: JOURNALS AND LEDGERS

Although Biwheels transactions 1, 2, and 3 were entered directly in the ledger in the previous section, in actual practice the recording process does not start with the ledger. The sequence of steps in recording transactions is as follows:

Transactions → Documentation → Journal → Ledger → Trial Balance → Financial Statements

source documents The supporting original records of any transaction; they are memoranda of what happened.

The recording steps begin when the transaction is substantiated by **source documents**. These are supporting original records of any transaction. Examples of source documents include sales slips or invoices, cheque stubs, purchase orders, receiving reports, cash receipt slips, and minutes of the board of directors. Source documents are kept on file so they can be used to verify the accuracy of recorded transactions if necessary.

Exhibit 3-1   Journal Entries—Recorded in General Journal and Posted to General Ledger Accounts

General Journal

Date	Entry No.	Accounts and Explanation	Post Ref.	Debit	Credit
19X1					
12/31	1	Cash	100	400,000	
		Paid-in capital	300		400,000
		Capital stock issued to Smith			
12/31	2	Cash	100	100,000	
		Note payable	202		100,000
		Borrowed at 9% interest on a			
		one year note.			
19X2					
1/2	3	Merchandise inventory	130	150,000	
		Cash	100		150,000
		Acquired inventory for cash.			

General Ledger

CASH   Account No. **100**

Date	Explanation	Journ. Ref.	Debit	Date	Explanation	Journ. Ref.	Credit
19X1				19X2			
12/31	(often blank because			1/2		3	150,000
	the explanation is						
	already in the journal)	1	400,000				
12/31		2	100,000				

MERCHANDISE INVENTORY   Account No. 130

Date	Explanation	Journ. Ref.	Debit	Date	Explanation	Journ. Ref.	Credit
19X2							
1/2		3	150,000				

NOTE PAYABLE   Account No. 202

Date	Explanation	Journ. Ref.	Debit	Date	Explanation	Journ. Ref.	Credit
				19X1			
				12/31		2	100,000

PAID-IN CAPITAL   Account No. 300

Date	Explanation	Journ. Ref.	Debit	Date	Explanation	Journ. Ref.	Credit
				19X1			
				12/31		1	400,000

book of original entry A formal chronological record of how the entity's transactions affect the balances in pertinent accounts.

general journal The most common example of a book of original entry; a complete chronological record of transactions.

In the second step, an analysis of the transaction is placed in a **book of original entry**, which is a formal chronological record of how each transaction affects the balances in particular accounts. The most common example of a book of original entry is the **general journal**. An entire transaction is recorded in one place in the journal, in contrast to the ledger, where only part of a transaction is recorded in a particular ledger account. The general journal is thus a complete, chronological record that can be likened to a diary of all of the events in an entity's life.

The timing of the steps will differ. Transactions occur constantly and documentation is prepared continuously. Depending on the size and nature of the organization, the accounting operation may be very large and transaction analysis may also occur continuously or the operation may be small and the analysis of transactions and recording in the journal may be less frequent. As discussed previously, the ledger is the collection of information about specific accounts. Information in the ledger is updated periodically by recording each piece of each transaction in the ledger account where it belongs. This process might occur weekly or even less frequently in very small organizations.

The fourth step, preparation of the trial balance, serves two purposes. It verifies clerical accuracy and assists in preparing financial statements. Thus it occurs as needed, perhaps each month or each quarter as the firm prepares its financial statements. The final step, the preparation of financial statements, occurs at least once a quarter for publicly traded companies in Canada. These statements, which include the balance sheet, the income statement, the statement of changes in financial position, and the statement of changes in retained earnings were described in Chapter 2.

Some companies prepare financial statements more frequently for management's benefit. Recently many companies were watching results at Springfield ReManufacturing Corp in the Ozark mountains of southern Missouri. Springfield is a leader in "open-book management." The phrase "open books" refers to the company's accounting results. Management and all employees meet monthly to examine the results in detail. Extensive training is provided to employees on how the accounting process works and what the numbers mean. This new management process increased efficiency and profitability at Springfield. In summary, the timing of the steps in the accounting cycle must conform to the needs of the users of the data.

journalizing The process of entering transactions into the journal.

journal entry An analysis of the effects of a transaction on the accounts, usually accompanied by an explanation.

Journalizing Transactions

The process of entering transactions into the journal is called **journalizing**. A **journal entry** is an analysis of the effects of a transaction on the accounts, usually accompanied by an explanation. The accounts to be debited and credited are identified. For example, the top of Exhibit 3-1 shows how the opening three transactions for Biwheels are journalized.

The conventional form of the general journal includes the following:

1. The date and identification number of the entry make up the first two columns.

2. The accounts affected are shown in the next column, Accounts and Explanation. The title of the account or accounts to be *debited* is placed flush left. The title of the account or accounts to be *credited* is indented in a consistent way. The journal entry is followed by the narrative explanation, which can be brief or extensive. The length of the explanation depends on the complexity of the transaction and whether management wants the journal itself to contain all relevant information. Most often, explanations are brief and details are available in the file of supporting documents.

3. The Post Ref. (posting reference) column in Exhibit 3-1 contains the number that is assigned to each account and is used for cross-referencing to the ledger accounts.

4. The money columns are for recording the amounts in the debit (left) or credit (right) columns for each account. No dollar signs are used.

Objective 2

Describe the sequence of steps in recording transactions and explain how transactions are journalized and posted.

Chart of Accounts

chart of accounts
A numbered or coded list of all account titles.

Organizations have a **chart of accounts**, which is normally a numbered or coded list of all account titles. These numbers are used as references in the Post Ref. column of the journal, as Exhibit 3-1 demonstrates. The following is the chart of accounts for Biwheels:

Account Number	Account Title	Account Number	Account Title
100	Cash	202	Note payable
120	Accounts receivable	203	Accounts payable
		300	Paid-in capital
130	Merchandise inventory	400	Retained earnings
140	Prepaid rent	500	Sales revenues
170	Store equipment	600	Cost of goods sold
170A	Accumulated amortization, store equipment (explained later)	601	Rent expense
		602	Amortization expense

Although an outsider may not know what the code means, accounting employees become so familiar with the code that they think, talk, and write in terms of account numbers instead of account names. Thus an outside auditor may find entry 3, the acquisition of Merchandise Inventory (Account 130) for Cash (Account 100), journalized as follows:

MONEY COLUMNS

19X2		dr.	cr.
Jan. 2	130	150,000	
	100		150,000

This journal entry is the employee's shorthand. Its brevity and lack of explanation would hamper any outsider's understanding of the transaction, but the entry's meaning would be clear to anyone within the organization.

Posting Transactions to the Ledger

posting The transferring of amounts from the journal to the appropriate accounts in the ledger.

Posting is the transferring of amounts from the journal to the appropriate accounts in the ledger. It is a mechanical process that is ideally suited to computers. The accountant places the journal entry in the general journal, and the computer is programmed to transfer the relevant information to the ledger. To demonstrate, consider transaction 3 for Biwheels. Exhibit 3-1 shows with bold arrows how the credit to cash is posted.

The sample of the general ledger in Exhibit 3-1 is in the form of elaborate T-accounts; that is, debits are on the left side and credits on the right side. Note how cross-referencing occurs between the journal and the ledger. The date is recorded in the journal and the ledger, and the journal entry number is placed in the reference column of the ledger. The process of numbering or otherwise specifically identifying each journal entry and each posting is known as the **keying of entries**, or **cross-referencing**. It allows users to find the other parts of the transactions no matter where they start. It also helps auditors to find and correct errors and reduces the frequency of initial errors.

keying of entries (cross-referencing) The process of numbering or otherwise specifically identifying each journal entry and each posting.

Professional accountants and financial managers frequently think about complicated transactions in terms of how they would be analyzed in a journal or in T-accounts. These bookkeeping devices become models of the organization. Accountants or managers often ask, "How would you journalize that transaction?" or "How would the T-accounts be affected?" By answering these questions, they can see how a transaction will affect the financial statements. In short, accountants and managers have found that they can think straighter if they visualize the transaction in terms of the balance sheet equation and debits and credits.

Running Balance Column

Exhibit 3-2 shows a popular ledger account format that adds an additional column to provide a *running balance*. Notice the similarity of the running balance format for the cash account and your chequebook. The debit column records deposits, the credit column records cheques written, and the balance column has an up-to-date cash balance. The running balance feature is easily achieved by computers.

Above all, note that the same postings to Cash (or any other pertinent accounts) are made regardless of the account format used: T-account (Exhibit 3-1) or running balance (Exhibit 3-2).

Exhibit 3-2

Ledger Account with
Running Balance
Column

			CASH			Account No. 100	
Date	Explanation	Journ. Ref.	Debit		Credit	Balance	
19X1							
12/31	(often blank because the explanation is already	1	400,000			400,000	
12/31	in the journal)	2	100,000			500,000	
19X2							
1/2		3			150,000	350,000	

■ ANALYZING TRANSACTIONS FOR THE JOURNAL AND LEDGER

Objective 3

Analyze transactions for journalizing and posting and explain the relationship of revenue and expenses to shareholders' equity.

As we have seen, transactions are analyzed mentally and then are journalized before being posted to the ledger. This process can now be extended to the Biwheels Company's transactions 4 through 13 as a continuation of the journal entries 1 through 3 in Exhibit 3-1.

4. Transaction: Acquired inventory on credit, $10,000.
   Analysis: The asset **Merchandise Inventory** is increased.
   The liability **Accounts Payable** is increased.
   Entry: In the journal (explanation omitted):

Merchandise inventory	10,000	
Accounts payable		10,000

Post to the ledger (postings are indicated by circled amounts):

Merchandise Inventory*			Accounts Payable		
(3)	150,000			(4)	10,000
(4)	10,000				

* If it is the only type of inventory account, it is often simply called Inventory.

simple entry An entry for a transaction that affects only two accounts.

Transaction 4, like transactions 1, 2, and 3, is a **simple entry** in that only the two accounts shown are affected by the transaction. Note that the balance sheet equation always remains in balance.

5. Transaction: Acquired store equipment for $4,000 cash plus $11,000 trade credit.
   Analysis: The asset **Cash** is decreased.
   The asset **Store Equipment** is increased.
   The liability **Accounts Payable** is increased.
   Entry: In the journal:

Store equipment	15,000	
Cash		4,000
Accounts payable		11,000

Post to the ledger:

Cash				Accounts Payable		
(1)	400,000	(3)	150,000		(4)	10,000
(2)	100,000	(5)	4,000		(5)	11,000

Store Equipment		
(5)	15,000	

compound entry An entry for a transaction that affects more than two accounts.

Transaction 5 is a **compound entry**, which means that more than two accounts are affected by a single transaction. Whether transactions are simple or compound, the total of all left-side entries always equals the totals of all right-side entries. The net effect is *always* to keep the accounting equation in balance:

Assets = Liabilities + Shareholders' Equity
15,000   4,000 = | 11,000

Helpful hint: When analyzing a transaction, initially pinpoint the effects (if any) on cash. Did cash increase or decrease? Then think of the effects on other accounts. In this way, you get off to the right start. Usually, it is much easier to identify the effects of a transaction on cash than to identify the effects on other accounts.

6. **Transaction:** Sold unneeded showcase to neighbour for $1,000 on open account.
   Analysis: The asset **Accounts Receivable** is increased.
   The asset **Store Equipment** is decreased.
   Entry: In the journal:
   Accounts receivable   1,000
       Store equipment   1,000

   Post to the ledger:

   Accounts Receivable
   (6)   1,000 |

   Store Equipment
   (5)   15,000 | (6)   1,000

In transaction 6, one asset goes up, and another asset goes down. No liability or shareholders' equity account is affected.

7. **Transaction:** Returned inventory to supplier for full credit, $800.
   Analysis: The asset **Merchandise Inventory** is decreased.
   The liability **Accounts Payable** is decreased.
   Entry: In the journal:
   Accounts payable   800
       Merchandise inventory   800

   Post to the ledger:

Merchandise Inventory			Accounts Payable		
(3)	150,000	(7) 800	(7) 800	(4)	10,000
(4)	10,000			(5)	11,000

8. **Transaction:** Paid cash to creditors, $4,000.
   Analysis: The asset **Cash** is decreased.
   The liability **Accounts Payable** is decreased.
   Entry: In the journal:
   Accounts payable   4,000
       Cash   4,000

   Post to the ledger:

Cash			Accounts Payable		
(1)	400,000	(3) 150,000	(7) 800	(4)	10,000
(2)	100,000	(5) 4,000	(8) 4,000	(5)	11,000
		(8) 4,000			

9. Transaction: Collected cash from debtors, $700.
Analysis: The asset **Cash** is increased.
The asset **Accounts Receivable** is decreased.
Entry: In the journal:

Cash	700	
Accounts receivable		700

Post to the ledger:

	Cash		
(1)	400,000	(3)	150,000
(2)	100,000	(5)	4,000
(9)	(700)	(8)	4,000

	Accounts Receivable		
(6)	1,000	(9)	(700)

Transactions 7, 8, and 9 are all simple entries. In transactions 7 and 8 an asset and a liability both go down. In transaction 9 one asset goes up while another asset goes down.

Revenue and Expense Transactions

Revenue and expense transactions deserve special attention because their relation to the balance sheet equation is less obvious. Focus on the balance sheet equation:

$$\text{Assets} = \text{Liabilities} + \text{Shareholders' equity} \tag{1}$$
$$\text{Assets} = \text{Liabilities} + (\text{Paid-in capital} + \text{Retained earnings}) \tag{2}$$

Recall from Chapter 2 that if we ignore dividends, retained earnings are merely the accumulated revenue less expenses. Therefore the T-accounts can be grouped as follows:

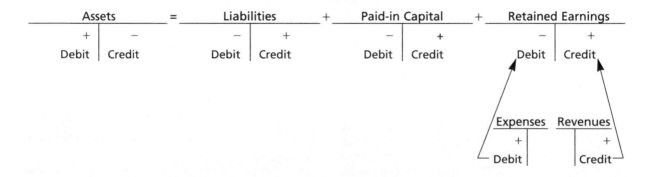

Assets have a left-hand balance; that is, debit entries increase the balance in an asset account. In contrast, liabilities, paid-in capital, and retained earnings have right-hand balances; credit entries increase their balances. Expense and Revenue accounts are part of Retained Earnings. You can think of them as separate compartments within the larger Retained Earnings account. The Revenue account collects items that increase retained earnings. Any credit to Revenue is essentially a credit to Retained Earnings; both revenue and retained earnings are increased by such a credit entry. The Expense account collects items that decrease retained earnings. A debit to Expense is essentially a debit to Retained Earnings. *While a debit entry increases expenses, it results in a decrease in retained earnings.*

Consider transactions 10a and 10b in detail:

10a. Transaction: Sales on credit, $160,000.

Analysis: The asset **Accounts Receivable** is increased.
The shareholders' equity **Sales Revenues** is increased.

Entry: In the journal:

Accounts receivable	160,000	
Sales revenues		160,000

Post to the ledger:

Accounts Receivable				Sales Revenues		
(6)	1,000	(9)	700		(10a)	160,000
(10a)	160,000					

The Sales Revenues account is increased by a credit, or right-side, entry in this transaction, essentially increasing the shareholders' equity account, Retained Earnings.

10b. Transaction: Cost of merchandise inventory sold, $100,000.

Analysis: The asset Merchandise Inventory is decreased.
The shareholders' equity is decreased by creating an expense account, **Cost of Goods Sold**, which is essentially a negative shareholders' equity account.

Entry: In the journal:

Cost of goods sold	100,000	
Merchandise inventory		100,000

Post to the ledger:

Merchandise Inventory				Cost of Goods Sold		
(3)	150,000	(7)	800	(10b)	100,000	
(4)	10,000	(10b)	100,000			

In this transaction, the expense account, Cost of Goods Sold, is increased by a debit, or left-side, entry. The effect is to decrease the shareholders' equity account, Retained Earnings.

Before proceeding, reflect on the logic illustrated by transactions 10a and 10b. Revenues increase shareholders' equity because the revenue accounts and the shareholders' equity accounts are right-side balance accounts. Expenses decrease shareholders' equity because expenses are left-side balance accounts. They are offsets to the normal right-side balances of shareholders' equity. Therefore *increases* in expenses are *decreases* in shareholders' equity. The following logic applies to the analysis of the $100,000 Cost of Goods Sold expense:

If only a lone shareholders' equity account is used:

Shareholders' Equity	
Decreases	Increases
(100,000)	

If two shareholders' equity accounts are used without a revenue or expense account:

Paid-in Capital		Retained Earnings	
Decreases	Increases	Decreases	Increases
		(100,000)	

If revenue and expense accounts are created that will eventually be summarized into a single net effect on retained income:

Expenses		Revenues	
Increases			Increases
(100,000)			

Revenue and expense accounts are really "little" shareholders' equity accounts. *That is, they are fundamentally a part of shareholders' equity.* The revenue and expense accounts are periodically summarized into one number, *net income,* which increases retained earnings (or *net loss,* which decreases retained earnings).

Exhibit 3-3 presents the rules of debit and credit and the normal balances of the accounts discussed in this section. It demonstrates the basic principles of the balance sheet equation and the double-entry accounting system:

Left side = Right side
Debit = Credit

Exhibit 3-3	Rules of Debit and Credit and Normal Balances of Accounts

Rules of Debit and Credit

ASSETS	=	LIABILITIES	+			SHAREHOLDERS' EQUITY	

Assets		=	Liabilities		+	Paid-in Capital		+	Retained Earnings	
+	−		−	+		−	+		−	+
Increase	Decrease		Decrease	Increase		Decrease	Increase		Decrease	Increase
Debit	Credit		Debit	Credit		Debit	Credit		Debit	Credit
Left	Right		Left	Right		Left	Right		Left	Right
Normal Bal.				Normal Bal.			Normal Bal.			Normal Bal.

Revenues	
−	+
Decrease	Increase
Debit	Credit
Left	Right
	Normal Bal.

Expenses	
+*	−
Increase	Decrease
Debit	Credit
Left	Right
Normal Bal.	

Normal Balances

	Debit	Credit
Assets	Debit	
Liabilities		Credit
Shareholders' Equity (overall)		Credit
Paid-in Capital		Credit
Revenues		Credit
Expenses	Debit	

* Remember that *increases* in expenses *decrease* retained earnings.

The exhibit also emphasizes that revenues increase shareholders' equity; hence they are recorded as credits. Because expenses decrease shareholders' equity, they are recorded as debits.

Note in Exhibit 3-3 that Retained Earnings is a balance sheet account. All *changes* in retained earnings between balance sheet dates could be recorded directly in the account. However, keeping revenues and expenses, which are changes in retained earnings resulting from operations, in separate accounts makes it easier to prepare an income statement. Revenues and expenses are summarized as net income (or net loss) on the income statement. In essence, the income statement provides the detailed explanation of how operations caused the retained earnings shown on the balance sheet to change during the period.

Prepaid Expenses and Amortization Transactions

Recall from Chapter 2 that prepaid expenses, such as prepaid rent, and amortization expenses relate to assets having a useful life that will expire some time in the future. Biwheels transactions 11, 12, and 13 demonstrate the analysis for journalizing and posting of prepaid rent expenses and amortization of store equipment.

11. Transaction: Paid rent for three months in advance, $6,000.
    Analysis: The asset **Cash** is decreased.
                 The asset **Prepaid Rent** is increased.
      Entry: In the journal:

Prepaid rent	6,000	
Cash		6,000

Post to the ledger:

Cash			
(1)	400,000	(3)	150,000
(2)	100,000	(5)	4,000
(9)	700	(8)	4,000
		(11)	(6,000)

Prepaid Rent		
(11)	(6,000)	

Transaction 11 represents the acquisition of the asset. It affects only asset accounts—Cash is decreased (credited) and Prepaid Rent is increased (debited). Transaction 12 represents the subsequent expiration of one-third of the asset as an expense.

12. Transaction: Recognized expiration of rental services, $2,000.
    Analysis: The asset **Prepaid Rent** is decreased.
                 The negative shareholders' equity **Rent Expense** is increased.
      Entry: In the journal:

Rent expense	2,000	
Prepaid rent		2,000

Post to the ledger:

Prepaid Rent					Rent Expense	
(11)	6,000	(12)	(2,000)	(12)	(2,000)	

Remember that in this transaction, the effect of the $2,000 increase in Rent Expense is a decrease in shareholders' equity on the balance sheet.

13. Transaction: Recognized amortization, $100.

Analysis: The asset-reduction account **Accumulated Amortization Store Equipment** is increased.

The negative shareholders' equity **Amortization Expense** is increased.

Entry: In the journal:

Amortization expense	100
Accumulated amortization store equipment	100

Post to the ledger:

Accumulated Amortization Store Equipment		Amortization Expense	
	(13) (100)	(13) (100)	

    In transaction 13, a new account, *Accumulated Amortization,* is opened. While it is described as an *asset-reduction* account in our analysis and corresponding journal entry, a more popular term is *contra account.* A **contra account** is a separate but related account that offsets or is a deduction from a companion account. A contra account has two distinguishing features: (1) it always has a companion account; and (2) it has the opposite balance of the companion account. In our illustration, accumulated amortization is a **contra asset** account because it is a contra account offsetting an asset. The asset and contra asset accounts on January 31, 19X2, are:

Asset:	Store equipment	$14,000
Contra asset:	Accumulated amortization, equipment	100
Net asset:	Book value	$13,900

    The **book value** or **net book value** or **carrying amount** or **carrying value** is defined as the balance of an account shown on the books, net of any contra accounts. In our example, the book value of Store Equipment is $13,900, the original acquisition cost less the contra account for accumulated amortization.

A Note on Accumulated Amortization[1]

The balance sheet distinguishes between the store equipment's original cost and its accumulated amortization. As the name implies, **accumulated amortization** (sometimes called **allowance for amortization**) is the cumulative sum of all amortization recognized since the date of acquisition of the particular assets described. Published balance sheets routinely report both the original cost and accumulated amortization.

    Why is there an Accumulated Amortization account? Why not reduce Store Equipment directly by $100? Conceptually, a direct reduction is indeed justified. However, accountants have traditionally preserved the original cost in the original asset account throughout the asset's useful life. Accountants can then readily refer to that account to learn the asset's initial cost. Such information may be sought for reports to management, government regulators, and tax authorities. Moreover the original $14,000 cost is the height of accuracy; it is a reliable, objective number. In contrast, the Accumulated Amortization is an *estimate,* the result of a calculation whose accuracy depends heavily on the accountant's less reliable prediction of an asset's useful life.

    In addition, users can estimate the average age of the assets by computing the percentage of the original cost that has been amortized. For example,

---

contra account A separate but related account that offsets or is a deduction from a companion account. An example is accumulated amortization.

contra asset A contra account that offsets an asset.

book value (net book value, carrying amount, carrying value) The balance of an account shown on the books, net of any contra accounts. For example, the book value of equipment is its acquisition cost minus accumulated amortization.

accumulated amortization (allowance for amortization) The cumulative sum of all amortization recognized since the date of acquisition of the particular assets described.

---

1. The term amortization is used in this book to be consistent with the *CICA Handbook,* s. 3060. It is synonymous with depreciation and depletion.

Microsoft has accumulated amortization of $314 million on an original cost of plant and equipment of $1,037 million, making it 30% amortized. Most of Microsoft's assets must be quite young, which is what would be expected for a fast-growing company. In contrast, the German diversified industrial company VIAG Aktiengesellschaft has accumulated amortization of DM 17.1 billion on an original cost of DM 24.5 billion (DM stands for the German currency deutsche marks). Therefore, its assets are $17.1 \div 24.5 = 70\%$ amortized.

Objective 4

Prepare journal entries and post them to the ledger.

■ RECORDING TRANSACTIONS IN THE JOURNAL AND LEDGER

Exhibit 3-4 shows the formal journal entries for Biwheels' transactions 4 through 13 as analyzed in the previous section. The posting reference (Post

Exhibit 3-4

General Journal of Biwheels Company

Date	Entry No.	Accounts and Explanation	Post Ref.	Debit	Credit
19X2	4	Merchandise inventory	130	10,000	
		Accounts payable	203		10,000
		Acquired inventory on credit.			
	5	Store Equipment	170	15,000	
		Cash	100		4,000
		Accounts payable	203		11,000
		Acquired store equipment for cash plus credit.			
		(This is an example of a *compound journal entry*, whereby more than two accounts are affected by the same transaction.)			
	6	Accounts receivable	120	1,000	
		Store equipment	170		1,000
		Sold store equipment to business neighbour.			
	7	Accounts payable	203	800	
		Merchandise inventory	130		800
		Returned some inventory to supplier.			
	8	Accounts payable	203	4,000	
		Cash	100		4,000
		Payments to creditors.			
	9	Cash	100	700	
		Accounts receivable	120		700
		Collections from debtors.			
	10a	Accounts receivable	120	160,000	
		Sales	500		160,000
		Sales to customers on credit.			
	10b	Cost of goods sold	600	100,000	
		Merchandise inventory	130		100,000
		To record the cost of inventory sold.			
	11	Prepaid rent	140	6,000	
		Cash	100		6,000
		Payment of rent in advance.			
	12	Rent expense	601	2,000	
		Prepaid rent	140		2,000
		Recognize expiration of rental service.			
	13	Amortization expense	602	100	
		Accumulated amortization, store equipment	170A		100
		Recognize amortization for January.			

Ref.) column uses the account numbers from the Biwheels chart of accounts given earlier in this chapter. These account numbers also appear on each account in the Biwheels general ledger.

Exhibit 3-5 shows the Biwheels general ledger in T-account form. Pause and trace each of the following journal entries to its posting in the general ledger:

1. Initial investment
2. Loan from bank
3. Acquire merchandise inventory for cash
4. Acquire merchandise inventory on credit
5. Acquire store equipment for cash plus credit
6. Sale of equipment on credit
7. Return of merchandise inventory for credit
8. Payments to creditors
9. Collections from debtors
10a. Sales on credit
10b. Cost of merchandise inventory sold
11. Pay rent in advance
12. Recognize expiration of rental services
13. Recognize amortization

It is customary *not* to use dollar signs in either the journal or the ledger. Note too that negative numbers are never used in the journal or the ledger; the effect on the account is conveyed by the side on which the number appears.

In the ledger the account balance may be kept as a running balance, or it may be updated from time to time as desired. There are many acceptable techniques for updating. Accountants' preferences vary. The double horizontal lines in Exhibit 3-5 mean that all postings above the double lines are summarized as a single balance immediately below the double lines. Therefore all amounts above the double lines should be ignored for purposes of computing the next updated balance. (Many accountants prefer to use single horizontal lines instead of the double lines used in this book.)

The accounts without double lines in Exhibit 3-5 contain a lone number. This number automatically serves also as the ending balance. For example, the Note Payable entry of $100,000 also serves as the ending balance for the account.

trial balance A list of all accounts with their balances.

Objective 5

Prepare a trial balance and understand its role relative to the income statement and balance sheet.

■ PREPARING THE TRIAL BALANCE

Once journal entries have been posted to the ledger, the next step in the process of recording transactions is the preparation of a **trial balance**. A trial balance is a list of all accounts with their balances. The word *trial* was well chosen; the list is prepared as a *test* or *check* before proceeding further. Thus the purpose of the trial balance is twofold: (1) to help check on accuracy of posting by proving whether the total debits equal the total credits, and (2) to establish a convenient summary of balances in all accounts for the preparation of formal financial statements. The trial balance is an internal report that helps accountants to prepare financial statements. The public sees only the published financial statements, not the trial balance.

Exhibit 3-5

General Ledger of
Biwheels Company

Assets				Liabilities and Shareholders' Equity		
(Increases on left, decreases on right)				*(Decreases on left, increases on right)*		

Assets
(Increases on left, decreases on right)

Cash — Account No. 100

(1)	400,000	(3)	150,000
(2)	100,000	(5)	4,000
(9)	700	(8)	4,000
		(11)	6,000
1/31 Bal. 336,700			

Accounts Receivable 120

(6)	1,000	(9)	700
(10a)	160,000		
1/31 Bal. 160,300			

Merchandise Inventory 130

(3)	150,000	(7)	800
(4)	10,000	(10b)	100,000
1/31 Bal. 59,200			

Prepaid Rent 140

(11)	6,000	(12)	2,000
1/31 Bal. 4,000			

Store Equipment 170

(5)	15,000	(6)	1,000
1/31 Bal. 14,000			

Accumulated Amortization, Store Equipment 170A

		(13)	100

Liabilities and Shareholders' Equity
(Decreases on left, increases on right)

Note Payable 202

		(2)	100,000

Accounts Payable 203

(7)	800	(4)	10,000
(8)	4,000	(5)	11,000
		1/31 Bal.	16,200

Paid-in Capital 300

		(1)	400,000

Retained Earnings 400

		1/31 Bal.	57,900*

Expense and Revenue Accounts

Cost of Goods Sold 600

(10b)	100,000		

Rent Expense 601

(12)	2,000		

Amortization Expense 602

(13)	100		

Sales Revenues 500

		(10a)	160,000

* The details of the revenue and expense accounts appear in the income statement. Their net effect is then transferred to a single account, Retained Earnings, in the balance sheet. In this case, $160,000 – $100,000 – $2,000 – $100 = $57,900. The procedures for accomplishing this transfer, called "closing the books," are explained in Chapter 5.

Note: An ending balance is shown on the side of the account with the larger total.

A trial balance may be taken at any time the accounts are up-to-date, for example, on January 2, 19X2, after the first three transactions of Biwheels:

Biwheels Company
Trial Balance
January 2, 19X2

Account Number	Account Title	Balance	
		Debit	Credit
100	Cash	$350,000	
130	Merchandise inventory	150,000	
202	Note payable		$100,000
300	Paid-in capital		$400,000
	Total	$500,000	$500,000

Obviously, the trial balance becomes more detailed (and more essential) when there are many more accounts.

Exhibit 3-6 shows the trial balance of the general ledger in Exhibit 3-5. As shown, the trial balance is normally prepared with the balance sheet accounts listed first, in the order of assets, liabilities, and shareholders' equity. These are followed by the income statement accounts, Revenues and Expenses. Note that the last shareholders' equity account listed, Retained Earnings, has no balance here because it was zero at the start of the period in our example. The revenues and expenses for the current period that are on the list constitute the change in retained earnings for the current period. When the accountant prepares a formal balance sheet, the revenue and expense accounts will be deleted and their net effect will be added to the Retained Earnings account.

Exhibit 3-6

Biwheels Company
Trial Balance
January 31, 19X2

	Debits	Credits
Cash	$336,700	
Accounts receivable	160,300	
Merchandise inventory	59,200	
Prepaid rent	4,000	
Store equipment	14,000	
Accumulated amortization, store equipment		$ 100
Note payable		100,000
Accounts payable		16,200
Paid-in capital		400,000
Retained earnings		0 *
Sales revenues		160,000
Cost of goods sold	100,000	
Rent expense	2,000	
Amortization expense	100	
Total	$676,300	$676,300

* Of course, if a Retained Earnings balance existed at the start of the accounting period, it would appear here. However, in our example Retained Earnings were zero at the start of the period.

As can be seen, the trial balance assures the accountant that the debits and credits are equal. It is also the springboard for the preparation of the balance sheet and the income statement, as shown in Exhibit 3-7. The income statement accounts are summarized later as a single number, net income, which then becomes part of Retained Earnings in the formal balance sheet.

Exhibit 3-7

Trial Balance, Balance Sheet, and Income Statement

Biwheels Company
Trial Balance
January 31, 19x2

	Debits	Credits
Cash	$336,700	
Accounts receivable	160,300	
Merchandise inventory	59,200	
Prepaid rent	4,000	
Store equipment	14,000	
Accumulated amortization store equipment		$ 100
Note payable		100,000
Accounts payable		16,200
Paid-in capital		400,000
Retained earnings		0
Sales revenues		160,000
Cost of goods sold	100,000	
Rent expense	2,000	
Amortization expense	100	
Total	$676,300	$676,300

Biwheels Company
Balance Sheet
January 31, 19X2

Assets			Liabilities and Shareholders' Equity		
Cash		$336,700	Liabilities:		
Accounts receivable		160,300	Note payable		$100,000
Merchandise			Accounts payable		16,200
inventory		59,200	Total liabilities		$116,200
Prepaid rent		4,000	Shareholders' equity:		
Store equipment	14,000		Paid-in capital	$400,000	
Less accumulated			Retained earnings	57,900	
amortization	100	13,900	Total shareholders' equity		457,900
Total assets		$574,100	Total liabilities and shareholders' equity		$574,100

Biwheels Company
Income Statement
For the Month Ended January 31, 19X2

Sales revenues		$160,000
Deduct expenses:		
Cost of goods sold	$100,000	
Rent	2,000	
Amortization	100	
Total expenses		102,000
Net income		57,900

While the trial balance helps alert the accountant to possible errors, a trial balance may balance even when there are recording errors. For example, a $10,000 cash receipt on account may erroneously be recorded as $1,000. Then both Cash and Accounts Receivable would be in error by offsetting amounts of $9,000. Another example would be the recording of a $10,000 cash receipt on account as a credit to Sales Revenues rather than as a credit reducing Accounts Receivable. Sales Revenues and Accounts Receivable would both be overstated by $10,000. Nevertheless, the trial balance would still show total debits equal to total credits.

■ EFFECTS OF ERRORS

Objective 6

Correct erroneous entries and describe how errors affect accounts.

When a journal entry contains an error, the entry can be erased or crossed out and corrected—if the error is discovered immediately. However, if the error is detected later, typically after posting to ledger accounts, the accountant makes a *correcting entry*, as distinguished from a correct entry. Consider the following examples:

1. A repair expense was erroneously debited to Equipment on December 27. The error is discovered on December 31:

CORRECT ENTRY		
12/27 Repair Expense	500	
Cash		500
ERRONEOUS ENTRY		
12/27 Equipment	500	
Cash		500
CORRECTING ENTRY		
12/31 Repair Expense	500	
Equipment		500

The correcting entry shows a credit to Equipment to cancel or offset the erroneous debit to Equipment. Moreover, the entry debits Repair Expense correctly. Notice that the credit to Cash was correct and therefore was not changed.

2. A collection on account was erroneously credited to Sales on November 2. The error is discovered on November 28:

CORRECT ENTRY		
11/2 Cash	3,000	
Accounts Receivable		3,000
ERRONEOUS ENTRY		
11/2 Cash	3,000	
Sales		3,000
CORRECTING ENTRY		
11/28 Sales	3,000	
Accounts Receivable		3,000

The debit to Sales in the correcting entry offsets the incorrect credit to Sales in the erroneous entry. The credit to Accounts Receivable in the correcting entry places the collected amount where it belongs. The debit to Cash is unaffected by the correcting entry.

Some Errors Are Counterbalanced

Accountants' errors can affect a variety of items, including revenues and expenses for a given period. Some errors are counterbalanced by offsetting errors in the ordinary bookkeeping process in the next period. Such errors misstate net income in both periods, but they only affect the balance sheet of the first period, not the second.

Consider a payment of $1,000 in December 19X1 for rent. Suppose this was for January 19X2's rent. Instead of recording it as prepaid rent, the payment was listed as Rent Expense:

INCORRECT ENTRY

December 19X1 Rent expense	1,000	
Cash		1,000
One month's rent.		

CORRECT ENTRY

December 19X1 Prepaid rent	1,000	
Cash		1,000
Payment for January 19X2's rent.		
January 19X2 Rent Expense	1,000	
Prepaid rent		1,000
Expiration of January's rent.		

The effects of this counterbalancing error would (1) overstate rent expense for the first year (which understates pretax income) and understate year-end assets by $1,000 and (2) understate rent expense for the second year (which overstates income by $1,000). These errors have no effect on the second year's ending assets. The *total* of the incorrect pretax incomes for the two years would be identical with the *total* of the correct pretax incomes for the two years. The retained income balance at the end of the second year would be correct on a pretax basis.

Some Errors Are Not Counterbalanced

Accountants' errors that are undetected can affect a variety of accounts. As we have just seen, some errors may be counterbalanced in the ordinary course of the next period's transactions. However, other errors may not be counterbalanced in the ordinary bookkeeping process. Until specific correcting entries are made, all subsequent balance sheets will be in error.

For example, overlooking an amortization expense of $2,000 in *one year only* (1) would overstate pretax income, assets, and retained income by $2,000 in that year, and (2) would continue to overstate assets and retained income on successive balance sheets for the life of the fixed asset. But observe that pretax income for each subsequent year would not be affected unless the same error were committed again.

■ INCOMPLETE RECORDS

Accountants must sometimes construct financial statements from incomplete data. For example, documents may be stolen, destroyed, or lost. T-accounts help organize an accountant's thinking and aid the discovery of unknown amounts. For example, suppose the proprietor of a local sports shop asks you to prepare an income statement for 19X5. She provides the following accurate but incomplete information:

List of customers who owe money:	
December 31, 19X4	$ 4,000
December 31, 19X5	6,000
Cash receipts from customers during 19X5	
appropriately credited to customers' accounts	280,000

You want to compute revenue (sales) on the accrual basis. Assume that all sales were made on account. Shortcuts may be available, but the following steps demonstrate a general approach to the reconstruction of incomplete accounts:

Step 1: Enter all known items into the key T-account. Knowledge of the usual components of such an account is essential. Let S equal sales on account. We know that credit sales are debited to Accounts Receivable:

Accounts Receivable			
Bal. 12/31/X4	4,000	Collections	280,000
Sales	S		
Total debits	(4,000+S)	Total credits	280,000
Bal. 12/31/X5	6,000		

Step 2: Find the unknown. Simple arithmetic will often suffice; however, the following solution illustrates the algebraic nature of the relationships in an asset T-account:

$$\text{Total debits} - \text{Total credits} = \text{Balance}$$
$$(4{,}000 + S) - \quad 280{,}000 = 6{,}000$$
$$S = 6{,}000 + 280{,}000 - 4{,}000$$
$$S = 282{,}000$$

Obviously, the analyses become more complicated if more entries have affected a particular account. Nevertheless, the key idea is to fill in the account with all known debits, credits, and balances. Then solve for the unknown.

■ DATA PROCESSING AND COMPUTERS

Data processing is a general term that usually means the totality of the procedures used to record, analyze, store, and report on chosen activities. An accounting system is a data-processing system. For instructional ease, most introductory accounting textbooks focus on the manual (pen-and-ink) methods that were once used in all businesses. Today almost all organizations use advanced technology, ranging from a simple cash register to bar-code scanners at grocery store checkouts to massive computer systems that automatically record and bill billions of telephone transactions per month.

Objective 8

Understand the significance of computers in data processing.

Amoco Corporation
www.amoco.com/
index.shtml

The physical forms of journals and ledgers are generally magnetic tape or disks or some other form of computer record, not paper. Nevertheless, whatever their form, journals and ledgers remain the backbone of accounting systems. Each transaction can be journalized by entering the appropriate account numbers and amounts into a computer. The computer then does the posting to the ledger. If managers desire, they can have a new balance sheet each day.

The microcomputer has enabled small organizations to process data more efficiently than ever. When you check out at a pharmacy or clothing store, the cash register often does more than just record a sale. It may also record a decrease in inventory. It may activate an order to a supplier if the inventory level is low. If a sale is on credit, the machine may check a customer's credit limit, update the accounts receivable, and eventually prepare monthly statements for mailing to the customer.

Automation has decreased data processing costs. Consider the oil companies. Amoco Oil Company once received 650,000 separate sales slips daily. But today most credit sales are recorded by computers reading the magnetic strips on credit cards. Many stations have the card-reading equipment built into the gasoline pumps, eliminating the need for sales clerks. Information about each credit sale is electronically submitted to a central computer which prepares all billing documents and financial statements. Millions of transactions are recorded automatically into the general journal without any paperwork or keyboard entry. Imagine the increase in accuracy in addition to the savings in time and money.

Computers Have Changed Accounting

Midway through your first experience of posting a pageful of journal entries to the ledger, you probably thought, "Couldn't a computer do this?" Yes, computers can and do post journal entries. Data entry and sorting were among the first large-scale uses of computers. Herman Hollerith, founder of one of the companies that eventually combined to form IBM, used punch cards and a forerunner of the computer to tabulate data as early as the 1890 U.S. census.

During World War II intricate calculations such as those used to design the atomic bomb at Los Alamos spawned development of electronic computers. Early computers primarily solved complex scientific calculations, such as the differential equations needed to guide a missile toward a moving airplane.

At first, computers were too expensive for routine business data processing and accounting. However, since 1950, the cost of computing has been cut in half approximately every three years. By the late 1970s, even some small businesses used computers. Doctors used them for billing; bowling alleys used them for tabulating league standings; and many small businesses did payrolls and general accounting on computers. But these computers were primitive by today's standards. They offered only 16 kilobytes of internal memory but nevertheless cost from $15,000 to $30,000.

By the mid-1990s a small business could buy a computer with more than 100 megabytes of memory for less than $1,000. The computing power that once filled a room can now easily be carried in a briefcase. Combined with the appropriate software, such a computer is capable of managing the accounting functions of the business. Because computers can now do the routine bookkeeping functions, some students wonder why they should study debits, credits, journals, and ledgers. It is useful to remember what has been said about computers from the beginning: The power of a computer depends on the knowledge and abilities of the operator. ■

Sources: S. Engelbourg, International Business Machines: A Business History (Arno Press, 1976); F. M. Fisher, J. W. McKie, and R. B. Mancke, IBM and the U.S. Data Processing Industry: An Economic History (Praeger, 1983); L. G. Tesler, "Networked Computing in the 1990s," Scientific American (September, 1991), p. 86.

■ MORE ON GENERALLY ACCEPTED ACCOUNTING PRINCIPLES

Basic concepts of accounting theory are too vast to consume in one gulp, so they are being introduced gradually as we proceed. Previous chapters discussed some basic concepts of accounting, such as entity, recognition, matching and cost recovery, and stable monetary unit. We now consider three other major ideas that are part of the body of generally accepted accounting principles: going concern, materiality, and cost-benefit.

Going Concern Convention

going concern convention (continuity convention) The assumption that in all ordinary situations an entity persists indefinitely.

The **going concern convention**, or **continuity convention**, is the assumption that in all ordinary situations an entity persists indefinitely. This notion implies that existing *resources*, such as plant assets, *will be used* to fulfill the general purposes of a continuing entity *rather than be sold* in tomorrow's real estate or equipment markets. It also implies that existing liabilities will be paid at maturity in an orderly manner.

For example, suppose some old specialized equipment has a book value (that is, original cost less accumulated amortization) of $10,000, a replacement cost of $12,000, and a realizable value of $7,000 on the used-equipment market. The going concern convention is often cited as the justification for adhering to the $10,000 book value (or acquisition cost less amortization) as the primary basis for valuing such an asset. Some critics believe that replacement cost ($12,000) or realizable values upon liquidation ($7,000) would be more informative. Defenders of using $10,000 as an appropriate asset valuation argue that a going concern will generally use the asset as originally intended to produce revenue over its useful life. Allocating historical cost over time provides an objective matching of revenue and expense. Other values are not as germane because replacement or disposal will not occur en masse as of the balance sheet date. Moreover, replacement costs and realizable values are less objective, less easily determined, and likely to be estimated differently by different parties. They do not arise from a completed, arms-length transaction.

The opposite view of this going concern, or continuity, convention is an immediate-liquidation assumption whereby all items on a balance sheet are valued at the amounts appropriate if the entity were to be liquidated in piecemeal fashion within a few days or months. This liquidation approach to valuation is usually used only when the probability is high that the company will be liquidated.

Materiality Convention

materiality convention The concept that states that a financial statement item is material if its omission or misstatement would tend to mislead the reader of the financial statements under consideration.

Because accounting is a practical art, the practitioner often tempers accounting reports by applying judgments about *materiality*. The **materiality convention** asserts that a financial statement item is *material* if its omission or misstatement would tend to mislead the reader of the financial statements under consideration.

Many acquisitions that should theoretically be recorded as assets are immediately written off as expenses because of their insignificance. For example, many corporations require the immediate write-off to expense of all outlays under a specified minimum such as $100, regardless of the useful life of the asset acquired. For example, coat hangers may last indefinitely but never appear in the balance sheet as assets. The resulting $100 understatement of assets and shareholders' equity is considered too trivial to worry about. In general, GAAP need not be applied to immaterial items. The FASB regularly includes the following statement in its standards: "The provisions of this statement need not be applied to immaterial items."

When is an item material? There will probably never be a universal, clear-cut answer. What is trivial to the Royal Bank may be material to Evelyn's Boutique. A working rule is that an item is material if its proper accounting would probably affect the decision of a knowledgeable party. In sum, materiality is an important convention. But it is difficult to use anything other than prudent judgment to tell whether an item is material.

Cost-Benefit Criterion

cost-benefit criterion As a system is changed, its expected additional benefits should exceed its expected additional costs.

Accounting systems vary in complexity, from the minimum crude records kept by a small business to satisfy government authorities to the sophisticated budgeting and feedback schemes that are at the heart of management planning and control in a huge, multinational corporation. The **cost-benefit criterion** means that as a system is changed, its expected additional benefits should exceed its expected additional costs. Often the benefits are difficult to measure, but this criterion at least implicitly underlies the decisions about the design and change of accounting systems. Reluctance to adopt suggestions for new ways of measuring financial position and performance is often due to the fact that the apparent benefits do not exceed the obvious costs of gathering and interpreting the information.

Room for Judgment

Accounting is commonly misunderstood to be a precise discipline that produces exact measurements of a company's financial position and performance. As a result, many individuals regard accountants as mechanical tabulators who grind out financial reports after processing an imposing amount of detail in accordance with stringent predetermined rules. Accountants do take methodical steps with masses of data, but their rules of measurement require judgment. As business practices evolve, new types of transactions and contracts must be incorporated into the accounts. Managers and accountants must make judgments, guided by the basic concepts, techniques, and conventions called generally accepted accounting principles. The basic concepts that guide these judgments will become clearer as these concepts are applied in future chapters.

Summary Problems for Your Review

Problem One

Do you agree with the following statements? Explain.

1. To charge an account means to credit it.
2. One person's debit is another person's credit.
3. A charge account may be credited.
4. My credit is my most valuable asset.

5. When I give credit, I debit my customer's account.

Solution to Problem One

Remember that in accounting, *debit* means left side and *credit* means right side.

1. No. *Charge* and *debit* and *left side* are synonyms.
2. Yes, in certain situations. The clearest example is probably the sale of merchandise on open account. The buyer's account payable would have a credit (right) balance, and the seller's account receivable would have a debit (left) balance.
3. Yes. When collections are received, Accounts Receivable is credited (right).
4. Note that "charge" as used in "charge account" is not a synonym for debit. As used in this statement, "my credit" refers to "my ability to borrow," not which side of a balance sheet is affected. "My ability to borrow" may indeed be a valuable right, but the accountant does not recognize that ability (as such) as an asset to be measured and reported in the balance sheet. When borrowing occurs, the borrower's assets are increased (debited, increased on the left side) and the liabilities are increased (credited, increased on the right side).
5. Yes. Accounts Receivable is debited (left). "Give credit" in this context means that the seller is allowing the customer to defer payment. The corresponding account payable on the customer's accounting records will be increased (credited, right).

Problem Two

The trial balance of Hassan Used Auto Co. on March 31, 19X1, follows:

	Balance	
Account Title	*Debit*	*Credit*
Cash	$ 10,000	
Accounts receivable	20,000	
Automobile inventory	100,000	
Accounts payable		$ 3,000
Notes payable		70,000
Hassan, owner's equity		57,000
Total	$130,000	$130,000

The Hassan business entity is not incorporated; it is a proprietorship. The equity account used here is Hassan, Owner's Equity; in practice, it is often called Hassan, Capital.

Hassan rented operating space and equipment on a month-to-month basis. During April, the business had the following summarized transactions:

a.   Hassan invested an additional $20,000 cash in the business.
b.   Collected $10,000 on accounts receivable.
c.   Paid $2,000 on accounts payable.
d.   Sold autos for $120,000 cash.
e.   Cost of autos sold was $70,000.

f. Replenished inventory for $60,000 cash.

g. Paid rent expense in cash, $14,000.

h. Paid utilities in cash, $1,000.

i. Paid selling expense in cash, $30,000.

j. Paid interest expense in cash, $1,000.

Required

1. Open the following T-accounts in the general ledger: cash; accounts receivable; automobile inventory; accounts payable; notes payable; Hassan, owner's equity; sales; cost of goods sold; rent expense; utilities expense; selling expense; and interest expense. Enter the March 31 balances in the appropriate accounts.
2. Journalize transactions *a–j* and post the entries to the ledger. Key entries by transaction letter.
3. Prepare the trial balance at April 30, 19X1.
4. Prepare an income statement for April. Ignore income taxes.

Solution to Problem Two

The solutions to requirements 1 through 4 are in Exhibits 3-8 through 3-11. The opening balances are placed in the appropriate accounts in Exhibit 3-9; the journal entries are prepared in Exhibit 3-8 and posted to the ledger in Exhibit 3-9; a trial balance is prepared in Exhibit 3-10; and the income statement is shown in Exhibit 3-11.

Exhibit 3-8

Hassan Used Auto Co.

General Journal

Entry	Accounts and Explanation	Post Ref.*	Debit	Credit
a.	Cash	✓	20,000	
	Hassan, owner's equity	✓		20,000
	Investment in business by Hassan.			
b.	Cash	✓	10,000	
	Accounts receivable	✓		10,000
	Collected cash on accounts.			
c.	Accounts payable	✓	2,000	
	Cash	✓		2,000
	Disbursed cash on accounts owed to others.			
d.	Cash	✓	120,000	
	Sales (or Sales Revenue)	✓		120,000
	Sales for cash.			
e.	Cost of goods sold	✓	70,000	
	Automobile inventory	✓		70,000
	Cost of inventory that was sold to customers.			
f.	Automobile inventory	✓	60,000	
	Cash	✓		60,000
	Replenished Inventory.			
g.	Rent expense	✓	14,000	
	Cash	✓		14,000
	Paid April rent.			

continued

Entry	Accounts and Explanation	Post Ref.*	Debit	Credit
h.	Utilities expense	✓	1,000	
	Cash	✓		1,000
	Paid April utilities.			
i.	Selling expense	✓	30,000	
	Cash	✓		30,000
	Paid April selling expenses.			
j.	Interest expense	✓	1,000	
	Cash	✓		1,000
	Paid April interest expense.			

* Ordinarily, account numbers are used to denote specific posting references. Otherwise check marks are used to indicate that the entry has been posted to the general ledger.

Exhibit 3-9

Hassan Used Auto Co.
General Ledger

Cash

Bal.*	10,000	(c)	2,000
(a)	20,000	(f)	60,000
(b)	10,000	(g)	14,000
(d)	120,000	(h)	1,000
	160,000	(i)	30,000
		(j)	1,000
			108,000†
Bal.	52,000		

Accounts Receivable

Bal.*	20,000	(b)	10,000
Bal.	10,000		

Automobile Inventory

Bal.*	100,000	(e)	70,000
(f)	60,000		
Bal.	90,000		

Accounts Payable

(c)	2,000	Bal.*	3,000
		Bal.	1,000

Notes Payable

		Bal.*	70,000

Cost of Goods Sold

(e)	70,000	

Selling Expense

(i)	30,000	

Utilities Expense

(h)	1,000	

Hassan, Owner's Equity

		Bal.*	57,000
		(a)	20,000
		Bal.	77,000

Sales

		(d)	120,000

Rent Expense

(g)	14,000	

Interest Expense

(j)	1,000	

* Balances denoted with an asterisk are as of March 31; balances without asterisks are as of April 30. A lone number in any account also serves as an ending balance.

† Subtotals are included in the Cash account. They are not an essential part of T-accounts. However, when an account contains many postings, subtotals ease the checking of arithmetic.

Exhibit 3-10

Hassan Used
Auto Co.
Trial Balance
April 30, 19X1

Account Title	Balance	
	Debit	Credit
Cash	$ 52,000	
Accounts receivable	10,000	
Automobile inventory	90,000	
Accounts payable		$ 1,000
Notes payable		70,000
Hassan, owner's equity		77,000
Sales		120,000
Cost of goods sold	70,000	
Rent expense	14,000	
Utilities expense	1,000	
Selling expense	30,000	
Interest expense	1,000	
Total	$268,000	$268,000

Exhibit 3-11

Hassan Used
Auto Co.
Income Statement
For the Month
Ended April 30, 19X1

Sales		$120,000
Deduct expenses:		
Cost of goods sold	$70,000	
Rent expense	14,000	
Utilities expense	1,000	
Selling expense	30,000	
Interest expense	1,000	116,000
Net Income		$ 4,000

Problem Three

A recent annual report of Kobe Steel, Ltd., one of the world's largest producers of iron and steel, showed (in billions of Japanese yen):

Property, plant, and equipment, at cost	¥2,062	
Accumulated amortization	1,051	¥1,011

Required

1. Open T-accounts for (a) Property, Plant, and Equipment, (b) Accumulated Amortization, and (c) Amortization Expense. Enter the above amounts therein.
2. Assume that during the ensuing month no additional property, plant, and equipment were acquired, but amortization expense of ¥80 billion was incurred. Prepare the journal entry, and post to the T-accounts.
3. Show how Kobe Steel would present its property, plant, and equipment accounts in its balance sheet after the journal entry in requirement 2.

Solution to Problem Three

1. Amounts are in billions of Japanese yen.

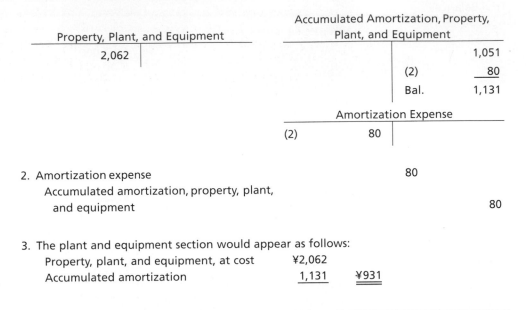

Property, Plant, and Equipment		Accumulated Amortization, Property, Plant, and Equipment	
2,062			1,051
		(2)	80
		Bal.	1,131

Amortization Expense	
(2) 80	

2. Amortization expense   80
     Accumulated amortization, property, plant,
        and equipment   80

3. The plant and equipment section would appear as follows:
     Property, plant, and equipment, at cost   ¥2,062
     Accumulated amortization   1,131   ¥931

Highlights to Remember

The accountant's recording process concentrates on the journal and the general ledger. The journal provides a chronological record of transactions, whereas the general ledger provides a dated summary of the effects of the transactions on all accounts, account by account. This book uses a simplified version of general ledger accounts called T-accounts. Accountants at all levels use T-accounts to help think through complex transactions.

Accountants use the terms *debit* and *credit* repeatedly. Remember that debit simply means "left side" and credit means "right side."

Journal entries are a convenient, simple way to analyze a transaction. Journal entries are always posted to the general ledger.

Revenues and expenses are essentially shareholders' equity accounts. Don't be confused by the fact that both assets and expenses normally have debit balances. Expenses have debit balances because they are reductions in shareholders' equity. In other words, expenses are a negative component of shareholders' equity.

Trial balances are internal reports that are used for detecting errors in the accounts and to aid in preparing financial statements. Trial balances that fail to balance are inevitably the result of careless or rushed journalizing or posting. The good news is that the out-of-balance condition lets you know that an error has been made.

Basic concepts in accounting are difficult to digest in one gulp. Therefore, they are introduced gradually in this book. Going concern, materiality, and cost-benefit are important concepts introduced in this chapter. All three concepts require accountants to exercise judgment.

Despite precautions, errors sometimes occur in accounting entries. Such errors should be corrected when discovered, adjusting account balances so that they equal the amounts that would have existed if the correct entry had been made.

T-accounts help organize thinking and aid in the discovery of unknown amounts. The key idea is to fill in the related accounts with all known debits, credits, and balances, and then solve for the unknown amounts.

Pause before proceeding. There is no shortcut to learning debits and credits. Learning occurs by solving homework problems. Whether such homework is satisfying depends largely on your approach. Before you prepare journal entries, think hard about the relationships among the accounts. The mechanics of the journal and the ledger then become much easier to understand.

Assignment Material

QUESTIONS

3-1. "Double entry means that amounts are shown in the journal and ledger." Do you agree? Explain.

3-2. "Increases in cash and shareholders' equity are shown on the right side of their respective accounts." Do you agree? Explain.

3-3. "Debit and credit are used as verbs, adjectives, or nouns." Give examples of how debit may be used in these three meanings.

3-4. Name three source documents for transactions.

3-5. "The ledger is the major book of original entry because it is more essential than the journal." Do you agree? Explain.

3-6. "Revenue and expense accounts are really little shareholders' equity accounts." Explain.

3-7. "Accumulated amortization is the total amortization expense for the year." Do you agree? Explain.

3-8. Give two synonyms for book value.

3-9. "A trial balance assumes that the amounts in the financial statements are correct." Do you agree? Explain.

3-10. "If debits equal credits in a trial balance, you can be assured that no errors were made." Do you agree? Explain.

3-11. "In double-entry accounting, errors are not a problem because they are self-correcting." Do you agree? Explain.

3-12. Are all data processing systems computerized? Explain.

3-13. "This idea implies that existing equipment will be used rather than sold in tomorrow's equipment markets." What is the name of this idea?

3-14. "What is trivial to Canadian Tire may be significant to Don's Hobby Shop." What idea is being described?

EXERCISES

3-15 Debits and Credits

For each of the following accounts, indicate whether it normally possesses a debit or a credit balance. Use *Dr.* or *Cr.*:

1. Sales
2. Accounts payable
3. Accounts receivable
4. Supplies expense
5. Supplies inventory
6. Retained earnings
7. Amortization expense
8. Dividends payable
9. Paid-in capital
10. Subscription revenue

3-16 Debits and Credits

Indicate for each of the following transactions whether the account *named in parentheses* is to be debited or credited:

1. Bought merchandise on account (Merchandise Inventory), $4,000.
2. Paid Fassi Associates $3,000 owed them (Accounts Payable).
3. Received cash from customers on accounts due (Accounts Receivable), $1,000.
4. Bought merchandise on open account (Accounts Payable), $5,000.
5. Sold merchandise (Merchandise Inventory), $1,000.
6. Borrowed money from a bank (Notes Payable), $10,000.

3-17 Debits and Credits

For the following transactions, indicate whether the accounts *in parentheses* are to be debited or credited. Use *Dr. or Cr.*:

1. Merchandise was sold on credit (Accounts Receivable).
2. Dividends were declared and paid in cash (Retained Earnings).
3. A county government received property taxes (Tax Revenue).
4. Wages were paid to employees (Wages Expense).
5. A newsstand sold magazines (Sales Revenue).
6. A three-year fire insurance policy was acquired (Prepaid Expenses).

3-18 True or False

Use *T* or *F* to indicate whether each of the following statements is true or false:

1. Repayments of bank loans should be charged to Notes Payable and credited to Cash.
2. Asset debits should be on the left and liability debits should be on the right.
3. Inventory purchases on account should be credited to Accounts Payable and debited to an expense account.
4. In general, all credit entries are recorded on the right side of accounts and represent decreases in the account balances.
5. Cash collections of accounts receivable should be recorded as debits to Cash and credits to Accounts Receivable.
6. Credit purchases of equipment should be debited to Equipment and charged to Accounts Payable.
7. In general, entries on the right side of asset accounts represent decreases in the account balances.
8. Increases in liability and revenue accounts should be recorded on the left side of the accounts.
9. Decreases in retained earnings are recorded as debits.
10. Both increases in assets and decreases in liabilities are recorded on the debit sides of accounts.
11. In some cases, increases in account balances are recorded on the right sides of accounts.

3-19 Matching Transaction Accounts

Listed here are a series of accounts that are numbered for identification. Accompanying this problem are columns in which you are to write the identification numbers of the accounts affected by the transactions described. The same account may be used in several answers. For each transaction, indicate which account(s) are to be debited and which are to be credited.

1. Cash
2. Accounts receivable
3. Inventory
4. Equipment
5. Accumulated amortization, equipment
6. Prepaid insurance
7. Accounts payable

8. Notes payable
9. Paid-in capital
10. Retained earnings
11. Sales revenues
12. Costs of goods sold
13. Operating expense

	Debit	Credit
(a) Purchased new equipment for cash plus a short-term note.	4	1, 8
(b) Made sales on credit. Inventory is accounted for as each sale is made.		
(c) Paid cash for salaries and wages for work done during the current fiscal period.		
(d) Collected cash from customers on account.		
(e) Paid some old trade bills with cash.		
(f) Purchased three-year insurance policy on credit.		
(g) Sold for cash some old equipment at cost.		
(h) Paid off note owed to bank.		
(i) Bought regular merchandise on credit.		
(j) Paid cash for inventory that arrived today.		
(k) In order to secure additional funds, 400 new shares of common stock were sold for cash.		
(l) Some insurance premiums have expired.		
(m) Recorded the entry for amortization on equipment for the current fiscal period.		
(n) Paid cash for ad in today's *Globe & Mail*.		

3-20 Journalizing and Posting

(Alternate is 3-21.) Prepare journal entries and post to T-accounts the following transactions of Renaldo's Catering Company:

a. Cash sales, $11,000.
b. Collections on accounts, $7,000.
c. Paid cash for wages, $3,000.
d. Acquired inventory on open account, $5,000.
e. Paid cash for janitorial services, $400.

3-21 Journalizing and Posting

(Alternate is 3-20.) Prepare journal entries and post to T-accounts the following transactions of Rita Rosen, Realtor:

a. Acquired office supplies of $1,000 on open account. Use a Supplies Inventory account.
b. Sold a house and collected a $9,000 commission on the sale. Use a Commissions Revenue account.
c. Paid cash of $700 to a local newspaper for current advertisements.
d. Paid $800 for a previous credit purchase of a desk.
e. Recorded office supplies used of $300.

3-22 Reconstruct Journal Entries

(Alternate is 3-23.) Reconstruct the journal entries (omit explanations) that resulted in the postings to the following T-accounts of a consulting firm:

Cash				Equipment		Revenue from Fees	
(a) 60,000	(b) 1,000		(c) 15,000				(d) 90,000
	(c) 5,000						

Accounts Receivable		Note Payable	
(d) 90,000			(c) 10,000

Supplies Inventory		Paid-in Capital		Supplies Expense	
(b) 1,000	(e) 300		(a) 60,000	(e) 300	

3-23 Reconstruct Journal Entries

(Alternate is 3-22.) Reconstruct the journal entries (omit explanations) that resulted in the postings to the following T-accounts of a small computer retailer:

Cash		Accounts Payable		Paid-in Capital	
(a) 40,000	(e) 30,000	(e) 30,000	(b) 90,000		(a) 40,000

Accounts Receivable	
(c) 100,000	

Inventory		Cost of Goods Sold		Sales	
(b) 90,000	(d) 57,000	(d) 57,000			(c) 100,000

3-24 Effects of Errors

The bookkeeper of Hyland Legal Services included the cost of a new computer, purchased on December 30 for $15,000 and to be paid in January, as an operating expense instead of as an addition to the proper asset account. What was the effect of this error ("no effect," "overstated," or "understated"?—use symbols *n, o,* or *u,* respectively) on:

1. Operating expenses for the year ended December 31		_____
2. Profit from operations for the year		_____
3. Retained earnings as of December 31 after the books are closed		_____
4. Total assets as of December 31		_____
5. Total liabilities as of December 31		_____

3-25 Effects of Errors

Assume Matheson Company is a going concern and analyze the effect of the following errors on the net profit figures for 19X1 and 19X2. Choose one of three answers: understated (*u*), overstated (*o*), or no effect (*n*). Problem *a* has been answered as an illustration.

a. EXAMPLE: Failure to adjust at end of 19X1 for prepaid rent that had expired during December 19X1. The remaining prepaid rent was charged in 19X2. 19X1: *o*; 19X2: *u*. (*Explanation*: In 19X1, expenses would be understated and profits overstated. This error would carry forward so that expenses in 19X2 would be overstated and profits understated.)

b. Omission of Amortization on Office Machines in 19X1 only. Correct amortization was taken in 19X2.

c. During 19X2 $300 of office supplies were purchased and debited to Office Supplies, an asset account. At the end of 19X2 only $100 worth of office supplies were left. No entry had recognized the use of $200 of office supplies during 19X2.

d. Machinery, cost price $500, bought in 19X1, was not entered in the books until paid for in 19X2. Ignore amortization; answer in terms of the specific error described.

e. Three months' rent, paid in advance in December 19X1, for the first quarter of 19X2 was debited directly to Rent Expense in 19X1. No prepaid rent was on the books at the end of 19X1.

PROBLEMS

3-26 Account Numbers, Journal, Ledger, Trial Balance
Journalize and post the entries required by the following transactions for Kowalski Construction Company. Prepare a trial balance, April 30, 19X6. Ignore interest. Use dates, posting references, and the following account numbers:

Cash	100	Note payable	130
Accounts receivable	101	Paid-in capital	140
Equipment	111	Retained earnings	150
Accumulated amortization, equipment	111A	Revenues	200
		Expenses	300, 301, etc.
Accounts payable	120		

- April 1, 19X6. The Kowalski Construction Company was formed with $95,000 cash upon the issuance of common stock.
- April 2. Equipment was acquired for $75,000. A cash down payment of $25,000 was made. In addition, a note for $50,000 was signed.
- April 3. Sales on credit to a local hotel, $2,200.
- April 3. Supplies acquired (and used) on open account, $200.
- April 3. Wages paid in cash, $600.
- April 30. Amortization expense for April, $1,000.

3-27 Account Numbers, T-Accounts, and Transaction Analysis
Consider the table (in thousands) at the top of page 120:

Kwality Printing
Trial Balance
December 31, 19X4

Account Number	Account Titles	Balance Debit	Balance Credit
10	Cash	$ 50	
20	Accounts receivable	115	
21	Note receivable	100	
30	Inventory	130	
40	Prepaid insurance	12	
70	Equipment	120	
70A	Accumulated amortization, equipment		$ 30
80	Accounts payable		135
100	Paid-in capital		60
110	Retained earnings		182
130	Sales		950
150	Cost of goods sold	550	
160	Wages expense	200	
170	Miscellaneous expense	80	
		$1,357	$1,357

The following information had not been considered before preparing the trial balance:

1. The note receivable was signed by a major customer. It is a three-month note dated November 1, 19X4. Interest earned during November and December was collected at 4 p.m. on December 31. The interest rate is 12% per year.
2. The Prepaid Insurance account reflects a one-year fire insurance policy acquired for cash on August 1, 19X4.
3. Amortization for 19X4 was $15,000.
4. Wages of $13,000 were paid in cash at 5 p.m. on December 31.

Required

1. Enter the December 31 balances in a general ledger. Number the accounts. Allow room for additional T-accounts.
2. Prepare the journal entries prompted by the additional information. Show amounts in thousands.
3. Post the journal entries to the ledger. Key your postings. Create logical new account numbers as necessary.
4. Prepare a new trial balance, December 31, 19X4.

3-28 Trial Balance Errors
Consider the trial balance (in thousands of dollars) at the top of page 121:

Delgado Auto Parts Store
Trial Balance for the Year Ended December 31, 19X7

Cash	$ 15	
Equipment	33	
Accumulated amortization, equipment	15	
Accounts payable	42	
Accounts receivable	15	
Prepaid insurance	1	
Prepaid rent		$ 4
Inventory	129	
Paid-in capital		12
Retained earnings		10
Cost of goods sold	500	
Wages expense	100	
Miscellaneous expenses	80	
Advertising expense		30
Sales		788
Note payable	40	
	$970	$844

Required   List and describe all the errors in the above trial balance. Be specific. On the basis of the available data, prepare a corrected trial balance.

3-29   Journal, Ledger, and Trial Balance
(Alternates are 3-31 through 3-35 and 3-39.) Appleton Bazaar is a retailer. The entity's balance sheet accounts had the following balances on October 31, 19X5:

Cash	$ 39,000	
Accounts receivable	90,000	
Inventory	10,000	
Prepaid rent	2,000	
Accounts payable		$ 25,000
Paid-in capital		100,000
Retained earnings		16,000
	$141,000	$141,000

Following is a summary of the transactions that occurred during November:

a.   Collections of accounts receivable, $85,000.
b.   Payments of accounts payable, $19,000.
c.   Acquisitions of inventory on open account, $80,000.
d.   Merchandise carried in inventory at a cost of $70,000 was sold on open account for $86,000.
e.   Recognition of rent expense for November, $1,000.
f.   Wages paid in cash for November, $8,000.
g.   Cash dividends declared and disbursed to shareholders on November 29, $15,000.

Required 1. Prepare journal entries (in thousands of dollars).
2. Enter beginning balances in T-accounts. Post the journal entries to T-accounts. Use the transaction letters to key your postings.
3. Prepare a trial balance, November 30, 19X5.
4. Explain why accounts payable increased by so much during November.

3-30   Financial Statements
Refer to problem 3-29. Prepare a balance sheet as of November 30, 19X5, and an income statement for the month of November. Prepare a statement of retained income. Prepare the income statement first.

3-31   Journal, Ledger, and Trial Balance
(Alternates are 3-29, 3-32 through 3-35 and 3-38.) The trial balance of Kim Appliance Co. on December 31, 19X4, follows:

| | Balance | |
Account Title	Debit	Credit
Cash	$ 25,000	
Accounts receivable	30,000	
Merchandise inventory	120,000	
Accounts payable		$ 35,000
Notes payable		80,000
Paid-in capital		29,000
Retained earnings		31,000
Total	$175,000	$175,000

Operating space and equipment are rented on a month-to-month basis. A summary of January transactions follows:

a. Collected $26,000 on accounts receivable.
b. Sold appliances for $70,000 cash and $40,000 on open account.
c. Cost of appliances sold was $60,000.
d. Paid $18,000 on accounts payable.
e. Replenished inventory for $63,000 on open account.
f. Paid selling expense in cash, $33,000.
g. Paid rent expense in cash, $7,000.
h. Paid interest expense in cash, $1,000.

Required 1. Open the appropriate T-accounts in the general ledger. In addition to the seven accounts listed in the trial balance of December 31, open accounts for Sales, Cost of Goods Sold, Selling Expense, Rent Expense, and Interest Expense. Enter the December 31 balances in the accounts.
2. Journalize transactions *a–h*. Post the entries to the ledger, keying by transaction letter.
3. Prepare a trial balance, January 31, 19X5.

3-32   Journal, Ledger, and Trial Balance
(Alternates are 3-29, 3-31, 3-33, 3-34, 3-37, and 3-38.) Jessica Howard owned and managed a franchise of Taco Tents, Inc. The accompanying trial balance existed on September 1, 19X5, the beginning of a fiscal year.

Howard's Taco Tent
Trial Balance
September 1, 19X5

Cash	$ 2,300	
Accounts receivable	25,200	
Merchandise inventory	77,800	
Prepaid rent	4,000	
Store equipment	21,000	
Accumulated amortization, store equipment		$ 5,750
Accounts payable		45,000
Paid-in capital		30,000
Retained earnings		49,550
	$130,300	$130,300

Summarized transactions for September were:

1. Acquisitions of merchandise inventory on account, $52,000.
2. Sales for cash, $39,300.
3. Payments to creditors, $29,000.
4. Sales on account, $38,000.
5. Advertising in newspapers, paid in cash, $3,000.
6. Cost of goods sold, $40,000.
7. Collections on account, $33,000.
8. Miscellaneous expenses paid in cash, $8,000.
9. Wages paid in cash, $9,000.
10. Entry for rent expense. (Rent was paid quarterly in advance, $6,000 per quarter. Payments were due on February 1, May 1, August 1, and November 1.)
11. Amortization of store equipment, $250.

Required

1. Enter the September 1 balances in a general ledger.
2. Prepare journal entries for each transaction.
3. Post the journal entries to the ledger. Key your postings.
4. Prepare an income statement for September and a balance sheet as of September 30, 19X5.

3-33   Journalizing, Posting, Trial Balance
(Alternates are 3-29, 3-31, 3-32, 3-34, 3-37, and 3-38.) Alou Gardens, a retailer of garden supplies and equipment, had the accompanying balance sheet accounts, December 31, 19X3:

Assets			Liabilities and Shareholders' Equity	
Cash		$ 20,000	Accounts payable*	$111,000
Accounts receivable		39,000	Paid-in capital	40,000
Inventory		131,000	Retained earnings	79,000
Prepaid rent		4,000		
Store equipment	$60,000			
Less: Accumulated amortization	24,000	36,000		
Total		$230,000	Total	$230,000

* For merchandise only.

Following is a summary of transactions that occurred during 19X4:

a. Purchases of merchandise inventory on open account, $550,000.
b. Sales, all on credit, $810,000.
c. Cost of merchandise sold to customers, $450,000.
d. On June 1, 19X4, borrowed $80,000 from a supplier. The note is payable at the end of 19X8. Interest is payable yearly on December 31 at a rate of 15% per annum.
e. Disbursed $25,000 for the rent of the store. Add to Prepaid Rent.
f. Disbursed $165,000 for wages through November.
g. Disbursed $76,000 for miscellaneous expenses such as utilities, advertising, and legal help. (Combined here to save space. Debit Miscellaneous expenses.)
h. On July 1, 19X4, lent $20,000 to the office manager. He signed a note that will mature on July 1, 19X5, together with interest at 10% per annum. Interest for 19X4 is due on December 31, 19X4.
i. Collections on accounts receivable, $690,000.
j. Payments on accounts payable $470,000.

The following entries were made on December 31, 19X4:

k. Previous rent payments applicable to 19X5 amounted to $3,000.
l. Amortization for 19X4 was $6,000.
m. Wages earned by employees during December were paid on December 31, $5,000.
n. Interest on the loan from the supplier was disbursed.
o. Interest on the loan made to the office manager was received.

Required
1. Prepare journal entries in thousands of dollars.
2. Post the entries to the ledger, keying your postings by transaction letter.
3. Prepare a trial balance, December 31, 19X4.

3-34 Transaction Analysis, Trial Balance
(Alternates are 3-29, 3-31, 3-32, 3-33, 3-37 and 3-38.) Tulalip Appliance Repair Service, Incorporated, had the accompanying trial balance on January 1, 19X5.

Cash	$ 5,000	
Accounts receivable	4,000	
Parts inventory	2,000	
Prepaid rent	2,000	
Trucks	36,000	
Equipment	8,000	
Accumulated amortization, trucks		$15,000
Accumulated amortization, equipment		5,000
Accounts payable		2,800
Paid-in capital		17,000
Retained earnings		17,200
Total	$57,000	$57,000

During January, the following summarized transactions occurred:

Jan 2 Collected accounts receivable, $3,000.
   3 Rendered services to customers for cash, $2,200 ($700 collected for parts, $1,500 for labour). Use two accounts, Parts Revenue and Labour Revenue.

3 Cost of parts used for services rendered, $300.

7 Paid legal expenses, $400 cash.

9 Acquired parts on open account, $900.

11 Paid cash for wages, $1,100.

13 Paid cash for truck repairs, $500.

15 Paid cash for utilities, $400.

19 Billed customer for services, $4,000 ($1,200 for parts and $2,800 for labour).

19 Cost of parts used for services rendered, $500.

24 Paid cash for wages, $1,300.

27 Paid cash on accounts payable, $1,500.

31 Rent expense for January, $1,000 (reduce Prepaid Rent).

31 Amortization for January: trucks, $600; equipment, $200.

31 Paid cash to local gas station for gasoline for trucks for January, $300.

31 Paid cash for wages, $900.

Required

1. Enter the January 1 balances in T-accounts. Leave room for additional accounts.
2. Record the transactions in the journal.
3. Post the journal entries to the T-accounts. Key your entries by date. (Note how keying by date is not as precise as by transaction number or letter. Why? Because there is usually more than one transaction on any given date.)
4. Prepare a trial balance, January 31, 19X5.

3-35 Preparation of Financial Statements from Trial Balance

Heart Technology, Inc., prepared a condensed trial balance in late June to be used in compiling financial statements for the six months ended June 30, 1994. The company, makes the Rotablator® system used in coronary care to clear clogged arteries. Production rates are about 60,000 systems per year. The trial balance follows (in thousands):

	Debits	Credits
Current assets	$56,964	
Property and equipment, net	14,760	
Intangible assets, net	2,416	
Other assets	51	
Current liabilities		$ 4,481
Long-term debt		0
Shareholders' equity*		69,195
Revenue		24,973
Cost of goods sold	11,364	
Research and development expenses	1,472	
Selling, general, and administrative expenses	10,047	
Interest income		925
Shareholder litigation settlement expense	2,500	
Total	$99,574	$99,574

*Includes *beginning* retained earnings.

Required

1. Prepare Heart Technology's income statement for the six months ended June 30, 1994.
2. Prepare Heart Technology's balance sheet as of June 30, 1994.

CRITICAL THINKING PROBLEM

3-36   Management Incentives, Financial Statements, and Ethics
Margarita Reynolds was controller of the St. Louis Electronic Components (SLEC) division of a major medical instruments company. On December 31, 1995, Reynolds prepared a preliminary income statement and compared it with the 1995 budget:

	Budget	Preliminary Actual
Sales revenues	$1,200	$1,600
Cost of goods sold	600	800
Gross margin	600	800
Other operating expenses	450	500
Operating income	$ 150	$ 300

The top managers of each division had a bonus plan that paid each a 10% bonus if operating income exceeded budgeted income by more than 20%. It was obvious to Reynolds that the SLEC division had easily exceeded the $180,000 of operating income needed for a bonus. In fact, she wondered if it wouldn't be desirable to reduce operating income this year—after all, the higher the income this year, the higher top management is likely to set the budget next year. Besides, if some of December's sales could just be held back and recorded in January, the division would have a running start on next year.

Reynolds had always been a team player, and she saw holding back sales as the best strategy for her team of managers. Therefore, she recorded only $1,500,000 of sales in 1995—the other $100,000 was recorded as January 1996 sales. Operating income for 1995 then became $250,000 and there was a head start of $50,000 on 1996's operating income.

Required   Comment on the ethical implications of Reynolds's decision.

COMPANY CASES

3-37   Transaction Analysis, Trial Balance
(Alternates are 3-29, 3-31 through 3-34, and 3-38.) McDonald's Corporation is a well-known fast-foods restaurant company. Examine the accompanying condensed trial balance at January 1, 1994, which is based on McDonald's annual report and actual terminology.

Cash	$ 186	
Accounts and notes receivable	315	
Inventories	43	
Prepaid expenses	119	
Property and equipment, at cost	13,459	
Other assets	1,291	
Accumulated depreciation		$ 3,378
Notes and accounts payable		589
Other liabilities		5,172
Paid-in capital		1,026
Retained earnings		5,248
Total	$15,413	$15,413

Consider the following assumed partial summary of transactions for 1994 (in millions):

a. Revenues in cash, company-owned restaurants, $2,200.

b. Revenues, on open account from franchised restaurants, $500. Set up a separate revenue account for these sales.

c. Inventories acquired on open account, $827.

d. Cost of the inventories sold, $820.

e. Depreciation, $226. (Debit Depreciation Expense.)

f. Paid rents and insurance premiums in cash in advance, $42. (Debit Prepaid Expenses.)

g. Prepaid expenses expired, $37. (Debit Operating Expenses.)

h. Paid other liabilities, $148.

i. Cash collections on receivables, $590.

j. Cash disbursements on notes and accounts payable, $747.

k. Paid interest expense in cash, $100.

l. Paid other expenses in cash, mostly payroll and advertising, $1,510. (Debit Operating Expenses.)

Required

1. Record the transactions in the journal.
2. Enter beginning balances in T-accounts. Post the journal entries to the T-accounts. Key your entries with the transaction letters used here.
3. Prepare a trial balance, December 31, 1994.

3-38   Transaction Analysis, Trial Balance

(Alternates are 3-29, and 3-31 through 3-37) Kellogg Company's major product line is ready-to-eat breakfast cereals. Examine the condensed trial balance below which is based on Kellogg's annual report at January 1, 1994 (in millions).

Kellogg Company
www.kelloggs.com/

Cash	$ 98.1	
Accounts receivable	536.8	
Inventories	403.1	
Prepaid expenses	121.6	
Property and equipment	4,272.5	
Other assets	309.1	
Accumulated depreciation		$1,504.1
Accounts payable		308.8
Other liabilities		2,214.9
Paid-in capital		149.6
Retained earnings		1,563.8
Total	$5,741.2	$5,741.2

Consider the following assumed partial summary of transactions for 1994 (in millions):

a. Acquired inventories for $1,700 on open account.

b. Sold inventories that cost $1,600 for $2,500 on open account.

c. Collected $2,550 on open account.

d. Disbursed $1,650 on open accounts payable.

e. Paid cash of $300 for advertising expenses. (Use an Operating Expenses account.)

f. Paid rent and insurance premiums in cash in advance, $20. (Use a Prepaid Expenses account.)

g. Prepaid expenses expired, $18. (Use an Operating Expenses account.)

h. Other liabilities paid in cash, $110.

i. Interest expense of $13 was paid in cash. (Use an Interest Expense account.)

j. Depreciation of $50 was recognized. (Use an Operating Expenses account.)

Required

1. Record the transactions in the journal.

2. Enter beginning balances in T-accounts. Post the journal entries to the T-accounts. Key your entries with the transaction letters used here.

3. Prepare a trial balance, December 31, 1994.

4. Explain why cash increased more than five-fold during 1994.

3-39   Reconstructing Journal Entries, Posting

NEC Corporation
www.nec.com/

NEC Corporation is a leading international supplier of electronic products, including computers. The NEC annual report at the end of the 1993 fiscal year included the following balance sheet items (in millions of Japanese yen):

Cash	¥397,715
Receivables	997,565
Prepaid expenses	49,256
Land	77,574
Accounts payable	738,329

Consider the following assumed transactions that occurred immediately subsequent to the balance sheet date (in millions of yen):

a. Collections from customers	¥940,000
b. Purchase of land for cash	20,000
c. Purchase of insurance policies on account	12,000
d. Disbursements to trade creditors	690,000

Required

1. Enter the five account balances in T-accounts.
2. Journalize each transaction.
3. Post the journal entries to T-accounts. Key each posting by transaction letter.

3-40   Reconstructing Journal Entries, Posting

Procter & Gamble
www.pg.com/

(Alternate is 3-41.) Procter & Gamble has many popular products, including Tide, Crest, Jif, and Prell. A partial income statement from its annual report for the 1993 fiscal year showed the following actual numbers, nomenclature, and format (in millions):

Income:	
Net sales	$ 30,433
Interest and other income	445
	30,878
Costs and expenses:	
Cost of products sold	17,683
Marketing, administrative, and other expenses	9,589
Interest expense	552
Other expenses	2,705
	30,529
Earnings before income taxes	$ 349

Required

1. Prepare six summary journal entries for the given data. Label your entries *a* through *f*. Omit explanations. For simplicity, assume that all transactions (except for cost of products sold) were for cash.
2. Post to a ledger for all affected accounts. Key your postings by transaction letter.
3. The company uses *income* as a heading for the first part of its income statement. Suggest a more descriptive term. Why is your term more descriptive?

3-41   Reconstructing Journal Entries, Posting
(Alternate is 3-40.) Corel Corporation has many popular products including Cheerios and Wheaties. A partial income statement from its annual report for the 1995 fiscal year showed the following actual numbers, nomenclature, and format (in thousands of $US):

Sales		$ 196,379
Cost and expenses:		
Cost of sales, exclusive of items below	$ 47,352	
Advertising	55,099	
Selling, general, and administrative expenses	40,292	
Research and development	27,232	
Depreciation and amortization expenses	9,468	
Foreign exchange expense	136	
Total costs and expenses		179,579
Income from operations		$ 16,800

Required

1. Prepare six summary journal entries for the given data. Label your entries *a* through *f*. Omit explanations. For simplicity, assume that all transactions (except for cost of sales and depreciation expense) were for cash.
2. Post to a ledger for all affected accounts. Key your postings by transaction letter.

3-42   Plant Assets and Accumulated Depreciation
Magna, an automotive parts company, had the following in its 1995 annual report (in millions):

Total property, plant, and equipment, at cost	$1,942.1
Accumulated Depreciation	739.2
Property, Plant, and Equipment, Net	$1,202.9

Required

1. Open T-accounts for (a) Property, Plant, and Equipment; (b) Accumulated Depreciation, Property, Plant, and Equipment; and (c) Depreciation Expense. Enter the above amounts into the T-accounts.
2. Assume that in 1996 no assets were purchased or sold. Depreciation expense for 1996 was $150 million. Prepare the journal entry, and post to the T-accounts.
3. Prepare the property, plant, and equipment section of Magna's balance sheet at the end of 1996.
4. Land comprises $105 million of Magna's property, plant, and equipment, and land is not depreciated. Comment on the age of the company's depreciable assets (that is, all property, plant, and equipment except land) at the end of 1996.

3-43 Hudson's Bay Company Annual Report

This problem helps to develop skill in recording transactions by using an actual company's account titles. Refer to the financial statements of the Hudson's Bay Company in Appendix A at the end of the book. Note the following summarized items from the income statement for the 1997 fiscal year (in thousands):

Revenues		$6,007,212
Cost of sales, operating, selling, and general and administrative expenses	$5,756,003	
Interest costs	108,505	5,864,508
Income before income taxes and unusual item		$ 142,704

Required

1. Prepare three summary journal entries for the given data. Use the Hudson's Bay Company account titles and label your entries *a* through *c*. Omit explanations. For simplicity, assume that all transactions (except for cost of sales) were for cash.
2. Post to a ledger for all affected accounts. Key your postings by transaction letter.

3-44 Annual Report Disclosure

Select the financial statements of any company of your choice.

Required

1. Prepare an income statement in the following format:

> Total sales (or revenues)
> Cost of goods sold
> Gross margin
> Other expenses
> Income before income taxes

Be sure that all revenues are included in the first line and that all expenses (except income taxes) are included in either Cost of goods sold or Other expenses.

2. Prepare three summary journal entries for the income statement data you prepared. Use the given account titles and label your entries *a*, *b*, and *c*. Omit explanations. For simplicity, assume that all "Other expenses" were paid in cash.
3. Post to a ledger for all affected accounts. Key your postings by transaction letter.

4

Accounting Adjustments and Financial Statement Preparation

Learning Objectives

After studying this chapter, you should be able to

1 Explain the meaning of explicit and implicit transactions, and tell why adjustments to the accounts are important.

2 Understand and make adjustments for the expiration of prepaid expenses.

3 Understand and make adjustments for the earning of unearned revenues.

4 Understand and make adjustments for the accrual of unrecorded expenses, including accrued wages, interest, and income taxes.

5 Understand and make adjustments for the accrual of unrecorded revenues.

6 Give the sequence of the final steps in the recording process and describe the relationship between cash flows and adjusting entries.

7 Prepare a classified balance sheet and use the current asset and current liability classifications to assess solvency.

8 Prepare single- and multiple-step income statements and use ratios based on income statement categories to assess profitability.

Before preparing financial statements, an accountant makes *adjusting entries* in the accounting records. This chapter describes these entries, why they are necessary, and how to make them. The chapter then discusses the preparation of balance sheets and income statements, with special attention to the format of each. Finally, it shows how to assess solvency using financial ratios based on balance sheet data and how to assess profitability using financial ratios based on income statement data.

Like Chapter 3, this chapter focuses on procedures and techniques rather than concepts. Remember, however, that the concept of double-entry, accrual accounting is the foundation of the procedures. You will understand better the procedures and techniques if you appreciate *why* they are being done.

Entities as large as IBM or Imperial Oil and as small as Mama's Mexican Cafe use accrual accounting and must make adjusting entries before preparing financial statements. Accountants in nonprofit as well as for-profit organizations, and accountants in France, Kenya, China, and every other country in the world, must be able to apply the procedures and techniques of this chapter. In addition, decision makers throughout the world must be able to understand and interpret the financial statements that are prepared.

■ ADJUSTMENTS TO THE ACCOUNTS

explicit transactions
Events such as cash receipts and disbursements, credit purchases, and credit sales that trigger nearly all day-to-day routine entries.

The majority of events in the life of a business entity are recorded by accountants when they occur. In addition, at the end of an accounting period, the accountant makes *adjustments* to the accounts. The need for these adjusting entries stems from the fact that some transactions are *implicit* rather than *explicit*.

Explicit transactions are events such as cash receipts and disbursements, credit purchases, and credit sales that trigger nearly all day-to-day routine entries. Recording of *explicit transactions* is straightforward. Entries for such transactions are supported by explicit evidence, usually in the form of miscellaneous source documents (for example, sales slips, purchase invoices, and employee payroll cheques). Note that some explicit transactions do not involve actual exchanges of goods and services between the entity and another party. For instance, the losses of assets from fire or theft are also explicit transactions even though no market exchange occurs.

implicit transactions
Events (such as the passage of time) that are temporarily ignored in day-to-day recording procedures and are recognized via end-of-period adjustments.

On the other hand, the events that trigger *implicit transactions* are not so obvious. **Implicit transactions** are events (such as the passage of time) that are temporarily ignored in day-to-day recording procedures and are recognized only at the end of an accounting period. For example, entries for amortization expense and expiration of prepaid rent are prepared at the end of an accounting period from special schedules or memoranda, not because an explicit event occurred.

adjustments (adjusting entries)
The key final process (before the computation of ending account balances) of assigning the financial effects of transactions to the appropriate time periods.

The accountant uses *adjustments* to record implicit transactions at the end of each reporting period. **Adjustments** (also called **adjusting entries**, *adjusting the books*, and *adjusting the accounts*) can be defined as the key final process (before the computation of ending account balances) of assigning the financial effects of implicit transactions to the appropriate time periods. Thus adjustments are made at periodic intervals, usually when the financial statements are about to be prepared.

accrue Accumulation of a receivable or payable during a given period even though no explicit transaction occurs.

Adjusting entries are at the heart of accrual accounting. **Accrue** means the accumulation of a receivable or payable during a given period even though no explicit transaction occurs. Examples of accruals are the wages of employees for partial payroll periods and the interest on borrowed money before the interest payment date. The receivables or payables grow as the clock ticks; as some services are continously acquired and used, so they are said to accrue (accumulate).

Adjustments help provide a complete and accurate measure of efforts, accomplishments, and financial position. They are an essential part of accrual accounting because they improve the *matching* of revenues and expenses to a particular period. For example, consider the $5 million annual contract of a baseball star, such as Ken Griffey, Jr., or Barry Bonds, for the 1996 season. If all $5 million is paid in cash in 1996, it is an obvious explicit transaction. But suppose only $2 million is paid in cash and $3 million is deferred until 1997 or later. The $2 million cash payment is an explicit transaction and is recorded as an expense when the payment is made. Since no explicit transaction for the $3 million occurs during the period, it is not routinely entered into the accounting record. However, since the entire $5 million contract was incurred for the benefit of the 1996 season, the $3 million deferred payment is an expense for 1996 that arises because of an implicit transaction for the period. Thus, at the end of the period, when the 1996 financial statements are being prepared, an adjustment is necessary to record the deferred $3 million payment as an expense and to record a $3 million liability for its payment.

Objective 1

Explain the meaning of explicit and implicit transactions, and tell why adjustments to the accounts are important.

The principal adjustments can be classified into four types:

I. Expiration of prepaid expenses
II. Realization (earning) of unearned revenues
III. Accrual of unrecorded expenses
IV. Accrual of unrecorded revenues

Each of the four will be explained in the following sections.

■ I. EXPIRATION OF PREPAID EXPENSES

Objective 2

Understand and make adjustments for the expiration of prepaid expenses.

Recall from previous chapters that some costs expire because of the passage of time. The adjustments to the accounts for the cost of these assets were illustrated in Chapter 2 by the recognition of monthly amortization expense and rent expense. The examples in Chapter 3 described the analysis of these transactions for entry into the journal and ledger. Thus we will not dwell on expiration of prepaid expenses here. Other examples of adjusting for asset expirations include the write-offs to expense of such assets as Office Supplies Inventory, Advertising Supplies Inventory, and Prepaid Fire Insurance. A characteristic of these items is that an explicit transaction in the past has created an asset and the implicit transaction adjusts the asset to its appropriate book value.

unearned revenue (deferred revenue, deferred credit) Revenue received and recorded before it is earned.

■ II. EARNING OF UNEARNED REVENUES

Just as some assets are acquired and then expire over time, some revenue is received and then earned over time. **Unearned revenue** (also called **deferred**

revenue or **deferred credit**) is revenue that is received and recorded before it is earned. That is, payment is received in exchange for a commitment to provide services (or goods) at a later date.

The analysis of adjusting entries for unearned revenue is easier to understand if we visualize the financial positions of both parties to a contract. For example, recall the Biwheels Company's January advance payment of $6,000 for three months' rent. Compare the financial impact on Biwheels Company with the impact on the owner of the property, who received the rental payment:

Objective 3

Understand and make adjustments for the earning of unearned revenues.

	Owner of Property (Landlord, Lessor)			Biwheels Company (Tenant, Lessee)		
	A =	L +	SE	A =	L +	SE
	Cash	Unearned Rent Revenue	Rent Revenue	Cash	Prepaid Rent	Rent Expense
(a) Explicit transaction (advance payment of three months' rent)	+6,000 =	+6,000		−6,000	+6,000 =	
(b) January adjustment (for one month's rent)	=	−2,000	+2,000		−2,000 =	−2,000
(c) February adjustment (for one month's rent)	=	−2,000	+2,000		−2,000 =	−2,000
(d) March adjustment (for one month's rent)	=	−2,000	+2,000		−2,000 =	−2,000

The journal entries for (a) and (b) follow:

OWNER (LANDLORD)

(a) Cash	6,000	
Unearned rent revenue		6,000
(b) Unearned rent revenue	2,000	
Rent revenue		2,000

BIWHEELS CO. (TENANT)

(a) Prepaid rent	6,000	
Cash		6,000
(b) Rent expense	2,000	
Prepaid rent		2,000

(Entries for (c) and (d) are the same as for (b).)

We are already familiar with the analysis from Biwheels' point of view. The $2,000 monthly entries for Biwheels are examples of the first type of adjustments, the expiration of prepaid expenses. From the viewpoint of the owner of the rental property, transaction *a* recognizes the receipt of unearned revenue. The balancing amount for the increase in cash is recorded as a *liability* because the lessor is obligated to deliver the rental services (or to refund the money if the services are not delivered). Sometimes this account is called Rent Collected in Advance, rather than Unearned Rent Revenue as in our example, but it is an unearned revenue type of liability account no matter what its label. That is, it is revenue collected in advance that has not yet been earned.

Franchises and Revenue Recognition

In a franchise arrangement, a central organization, such as McDonald's or the National Hockey League, sells the right to use the company name and company products to a franchisee. The franchisee also receives the benefit of centralized advertising, management assistance, and product development.

Franchising raises an interesting accounting problem. How does the central organization account for the franchise fees? At first glance, it might seem clear that such fees should be recorded as revenue. However, under accrual accounting, revenue should be recorded only after two conditions have been satisfied: (1) The "work" has been completed, and (2) Collectability of the fee is reasonably assured.

Jiffy Lube, a subsidiary of Pennzoil Company, is a franchiser of fast oil-change centres and provides an example of receipt of franchise fees before the related work is performed. Jiffy Lube sells its franchisees area development rights, which grant the franchisee the exclusive right to develop Jiffy Lube outlets in a certain area. In return for these rights, Jiffy Lube receives an upfront fee. Should Jiffy Lube record the fee as revenue? No, because Jiffy Lube's work is not done until the franchisee actually opens the outlets. In the interim, Jiffy Lube must report the fees as unearned revenue.

Porta-John, which acquires chemical toilets and sells the right to service the toilets to franchisees, illustrates the collectability condition. The franchisees agree to pay Porta-John an upfront fee. However, only 10% of the fee is collected in cash, and historically, franchisees have taken up to 10 years to pay the remainder of the fee. The fact is that many of the franchisees don't stick with the portable toilet business for very long, so the collectability of the total fee is quite uncertain. Accordingly, Porta-John is required to account for the fees using the cash basis, reporting revenue only as the franchise fees are actually received in cash. ■

Sources: Statistical Abstract of the United States: 1991, *U.S. Bureau of the Census, Table 1.368; K. Weisman and R. Khalaf, "Number Pumpers," Forbes (November 11, 1991), p. 110; P. Wang, "Claiming Tomorrow's Profits Today," Forbes (October 17, 1988), p. 78; Pennzoil 1993 Annual Report.*

Jiffy Lube
www.jiffylube.com/

Pennzoil Company
www.pennzoil.com/

Porta-John of America, Inc.
www.toilets.com/

Notice that transaction *a* does not affect shareholders' equity. The revenue is recognized (earned) when the adjusting entries are made in transactions *b*, *c*, and *d*. That is, as the liability Unearned Rent Revenue is decreased (debited), the shareholders' equity account Rent Revenue is increased (credited). The net effect is an increase in shareholders' equity at the time the revenue is recognized.

Adjustments I and II (p. 133) are really mirror images of each other. If one party to a contract has a prepaid expense, the other has an unearned revenue. A similar analysis could be conducted for, say, a three-year fire insurance policy or a three-year magazine subscription. The buyer recognizes a prepaid expense (asset) and uses adjustments to spread the initial cost to an expense account over the useful life of the services. In turn, the seller, such as a magazine publisher, must initially record its liability, Unearned Subscription Revenue, on receipt of payment for the three-year subscription. For example, the publisher, Thomson Corporation, showed a liability of over $810 million as of December 31, 1996, calling it Deferred Revenue. The deferred or unearned revenue is then systematically recognized as *earned* revenue when magazines and publications are delivered throughout the life of the subscription. The following diagrams show that explicit cash transactions in such situations are initially recorded as balance sheet items and are later transformed into income statement items via periodic adjustments:

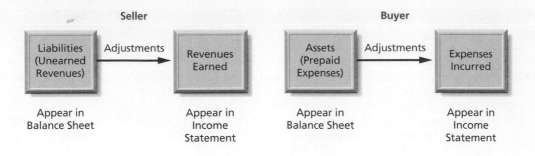

Seller

Liabilities (Unearned Revenues) — Adjustments → Revenues Earned

Appear in Balance Sheet   Appear in Income Statement

Buyer

Assets (Prepaid Expenses) — Adjustments → Expenses Incurred

Appear in Balance Sheet   Appear in Income Statement

Air Canada
www.aircanada.ca/

Unearned revenues are essentially advances from customers who have paid for goods or services to be delivered at a future date. For instance, airlines often require advance payments for special-fare tickets. Air Canada showed a balance of $209 million at December 31, 1993 in an unearned revenue account labelled Advance Ticket Sales.

Both the terms *unearned income* and *deferred income* are used; however revenue is a more accurate description than income. The latter is, strictly speaking, a difference, or "what's left over" after deducting appropriate expenses from revenue. When unearned revenue becomes earned, the expenses matched with the revenue are also recognized. Income is the amount by which the earned revenue exceeds the related cost of goods or services delivered to customers.

■ III. ACCRUAL OF UNRECORDED EXPENSES

It is awkward and unnecessary to make hourly, daily, or even weekly formal recordings in the accounts for many accrued expenses. The cost of such detailed recording would certainly exceed the benefits. Consequently, adjustments are made to bring each expense (and corresponding liability) account up-to-date just before the formal financial statements are prepared in order to match the expense to the period.

Accounting for Payment of Wages

Consider wages. Most companies pay their employees at predetermined times. Here is a sample calendar for January:

			January			
S	M	T	W	T	F	S
		1	2	3	4	5	6
7	8	9	10	11	12	13
14	15	16	17	18	19	20
21	22	23	24	25	26	27
28	29	30	31			

The Biwheels Company, for example, pays its employees each Friday for services rendered during that week. Thus, wages paid on January 26 are compensation for the week ended January 26. The cumulative total wages paid on the Fridays during January amount to $20,000, or $5,000 per five-day workweek, or $1,000 per day. Biwheels uses the popular method described in Chapter 3 to make routine entries for wage payments at the end of each week in January. At the end of January, the balance sheet shows the summarized amounts and their effect on the accounting equation:

	Assets A =	Liabilities L	+	Shareholders' Equity SE
	Cash			Wages Expense
(a) Routine entries for explicit transactions	−20,000 =			−20,000

Accounting for Accrual of Wages

Suppose the Biwheels accountant wishes to prepare financial statments at the end of January. In addition to the $20,000 actually paid to employees during the month, Biwheels owes $3,000 for employee services rendered during the last three days of the month. The employees will not be paid for these services until Friday, February 2. To ensure accurate financial statements for the month of January, adjustments must be made to account for the accrual of these unrecorded wages, which are owed but not paid in January. Transaction *a* shows the total of the routine entries in the journal for the explicit wage payments made to employees, and transaction *b* shows the entries for the accrued wages.

(a) Wages expense	20,000	
Cash		20,000
(b) Wages expense	3,000	
Accrued wages payable		3,000

The *total* effects of wages on the balance sheet equation for the month of January are as follows:

	A =	L	+	SE
	Cash	Accrued Wages Payable		Wages Expense
(a) Routine entries for explicit transactions	−20,000 =			20,000
(b) Adjustment for implicit transaction, the accrual of unrecorded wages	=	+3,000		− 3,000
Total effects	−20,000 =	+3,000		− 23,000

Entry **b** is the first example in this book that shows an expense that is offset by an increase in a liability instead of a decrease in an asset. On February 2, the liability will be paid off, together with the wages expense for February 1 and 2:

```
Wages expense (February 1 and 2) . . . . . . . . . . .    2,000
Accrued wages payable. . . . . . . . . . . . . . . . . .    3,000
     Cash . . . . . . . . . . . . . . . . . . . . . . . . . . . . .              5,000
(To record wages expense for February 1 and 2
and to pay wages for the week ended February 2.)
```

These entries clearly demonstrate the matching principle. The routine entries and the adjusting entries match the wage expenses to the periods in which they help generate revenues.

Accrual of Interest

Other examples of accrued expenses include sales commissions, property taxes, income taxes, and interest paid on borrowed money. *Interest* is "rent" paid for the use of money, just as rent is paid for the use of buildings. The interest accumulates (accrues) as time unfolds, regardless of when the actual cash for interest is paid.

Recall that Biwheels borrowed $100,000 on December 31, 19X1. Assume that the principal ($100,000) plus interest on the one-year loan is payable on December 31, 19X2. The interest rate is 9%. (Unless stated otherwise, quoted interest rates typically imply an interest rate *per year*.)

As of January 31, Biwheels has had the benefit of a $100,000 bank loan for one month. Biwheels owes the bank for these services (the use of money); the amount is $\frac{1}{12} \times 0.09 \times \$100,000 = \$750$. These money services costing $750 have been acquired *and* used up. Therefore, an adjusting entry is required for the month of January. Since the amount is not actually paid in January, it is a liability, Accrued Interest Payable. The adjustment is analyzed and recorded in a fashion similar to the adjustment for accrued wages:

	A =	L	+	SE
		Accrued Interest Payable		Interest Expense
Adjustment to accrue January interest not yet recorded	=	+750		−750

The adjusting journal entry is:

```
Interest expense. . . . . . . . . . . . . . . . . . . . . . . . .    750
     Accrued interest payable . . . . . . . . . . . . . .              750
```

If the adjusting entry is omitted, liabilities will be understated. At the end of January, Biwheels owes the bank $100,750, not $100,000. The adjusting entry matches the $750 interest expense with the period in which it occurred.

Accrual of Income Taxes

As income is generated, income tax expense should be accrued. Income taxes are worldwide, although rates and details differ from country to country and from province to province. Corporations in Canada are subject to federal and provincial corporate income taxes. For many public companies, the federal-plus-provincial income tax rates hover around 40% to 50%. For a small, Canadian-controlled private company the combined corporate tax rate is about 20% to 25%.

Various labels are used for income taxes on the income statement: *income tax expense, provision for income taxes*, and just plain *income taxes* are found most frequently. For multinational firms income tax expense may include tax obligations in every country in which they operate. Most companies show income taxes as a separate item just before net income. This arrangement is logical because income tax expense is based on income before taxes. For example, the Oshawa Group reported the following for their fiscal year 1996 ($millions):

Earnings before income taxes	$111.6
Income taxes	46.4
Net earnings	$65.2

PolyGram

www.media.philips.com/
polygram/PolyGram.html

PolyGram, Europe's leading recorded music company, has slightly different terminology but the same information (in millions of Netherlands guilders):

Income before taxes	NLG 927
Income taxes	(264)
Income after taxes	NLG 663

pretax income
Income before income taxes.

Income tax expenses are accrued each month (not just once a year) as pretax income is generated. **Pretax income** is a popular synonym for income before income taxes. The amount of the accrual for income taxes obviously depends on the amount of pretax income.

■ IV. ACCRUAL OF UNRECORDED REVENUES

Objective 5

Understand and make adjustments for the accrual of unrecorded revenues.

The accrual of unrecorded revenues is the mirror image of the accrual of unrecorded expenses. The adjusting entries show the recognition of revenues that have been earned but not yet shown in the accounts. According to the revenue recognition principle, then, revenues affect shareholders' equity in the period they are earned, not received.

Suppose First National Bank had loaned the $100,000 to Biwheels. As of January 31, First National Bank has earned $750 on the loan. The following tabulations show the mirror-image effect:

	First National Bank, as a Lender			Biwheels, as a Borrower		
	A	= L + SE		A=	L	+ SE
	Accrued Interest Receivable	*Interest Revenue*			*Accrued Interest Payable*	*Interest Expense*
January interest	+750	= +750		=	+750	−750

The adjusting journal entries are:

FIRST NATIONAL BANK (LENDER)

Accrued interest receivable.	750	
Interest revenue.		750

BIWHEELS (BORROWER)

Interest expense.	750	
Accrued interest payable.		750

Other examples of accrued revenues and receivables include "unbilled" fees. For example, lawyers, public accountants, physicians, and advertising agencies may earn hourly fees during a particular month but not send out bills to their clients until the completion of an entire contract or engagement. Under the accrual basis of accounting, such revenues should be recorded in the month in which they were earned rather than at a later time. Suppose a lawyer renders $10,000 of services during January that will not be billed until March 31. Before the lawyer's financial statements can be prepared for January, an adjustment for unrecorded revenue for the month is necessary:

	A	= L + SE
	Accrued (Unbilled) Fees Receivable	*Fee Revenue*
Adjustment for fees earned	+10,000	= +10,000

The adjusting journal entry is:

Accrued (unbilled) fees receivable.	10,000	
Fee revenue		10,000

Utilities often recognize unbilled revenues for services provided but not yet billed. For example, American Water Works Company, a utility that provides water supply services to more than 1.6 million customers in 625 communities in 20 states, includes more unbilled revenues than accounts receivable among its current assets:

Customer accounts receivable	$46,795,000
Unbilled revenues	57,298,000

■ THE ADJUSTING PROCESS IN PERSPECTIVE

Chapter 3 demonstrated the various steps in recording transactions:

These steps have a final aim: financial statements prepared on the accrual basis. To accomplish this goal, adjusting entries are needed to record implicit transactions, and the final steps in the process are divided further as follows:

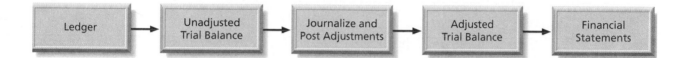

Each adjusting entry affects at least one income statement account—a revenue or an expense. The other side of the entry is a balance sheet account—an asset or a liability. No adjusting entry debits or credits cash. Why? Because cash transactions are explicit transactions that are routinely recorded as they happen. The end-of-period adjustment process is reserved for the implicit transactions that must be recognized by the accrual basis of accounting. Exhibit 4-1 summarizes the major adjusting entries.

Exhibit 4-1

Summary of
Adjusting Entries

Adjusting Entry	Type of Account Debited	Type of Account Credited
I. Expiration of prepaid expenses	Expense	Prepaid Expense, Accumulated Amortization
II. Realization (earning) of unearned revenues	Unearned Revenue	Revenue
III. Accrual of unrecorded expenses	Expense	Payable
IV. Accrual of unrecorded revenues	Receivable	Revenue

Objective 6

Give the sequence
of the final steps
in the recording
process and
describe the rela-
tionship between
cash flows and
adjusting entries.

Cash Flows and Adjusting Entries

Cash flows (that is, cash receipts and disbursements) may precede or follow the adjusting entry that recognizes the related revenue or expense. The accompanying diagrams underscore the basic differences between the cash flows and the accrual accounting entries.

Entries for adjustments I and II, expiration of prepaid expenses and real-ization (earning) of unearned revenues, are usually made *subsequent* to the cash flows. For example, the cash received or disbursed for rent had an *initial* impact on the balance sheet. The adjustment process was used to show the *later* impact on the income statement.

I. Expiration of Prepaid Expenses.

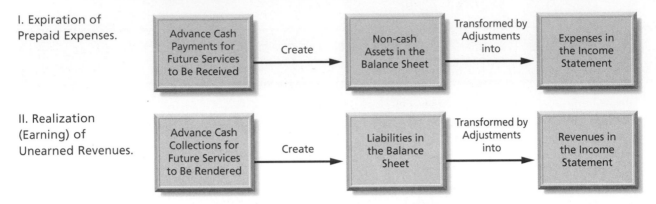

Entries for adjustments III and IV, accrual of unrecorded expenses and accrual of unrecorded revenues, are made *before* the related cash flows. The income statement is affected *before* the cash receipts and disbursements occur. The accounting entity must compute the amount of goods or services provided or received prior to any cash receipt or payment.

III. Accrual of Unrecorded Expenses.

IV. Accrual of Unrecorded Revenues.

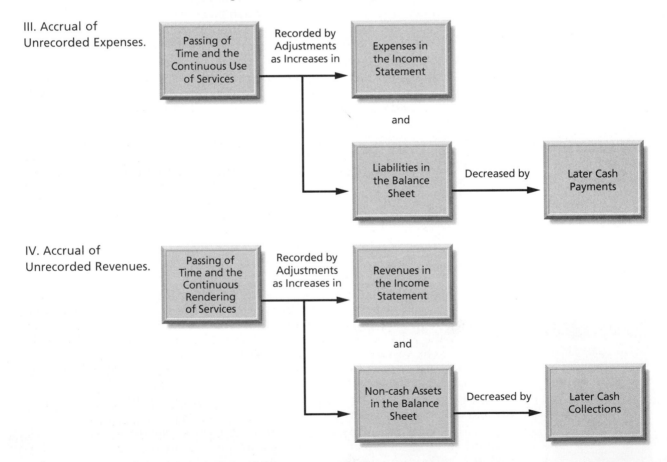

Summary Problem for Your Review

Problem One

Chan Audio Co. is a retailer of stereo equipment. Chan Audio has been in business one month. The company's *unadjusted* trial balance, January 31, 19X2, has the following accounts:

Cash	$ 71,700	
Accounts receivable	160,300	
Note receivable	40,000	
Merchandise inventory	250,200	
Prepaid rent	15,000	
Store equipment	114,900	
Note payable		$100,000
Accounts payable		117,100
Unearned rent revenue		3,000
Paid-in capital		400,000
Sales		160,000
Cost of goods sold	100,000	
Wages expense	28,000	
Total	$780,100	$780,100

Consider the following adjustments on January 31:

a. January amortization, $1,000.

b. On January 2, rent of $15,000 was paid in advance for the first quarter of 19X2, as shown by the debit balance in the Prepaid Rent account. Adjust for January rent.

c. Wages earned by employees during January but not paid as of January 31 were $3,750.

d. Chan borrowed $100,000 from the bank on January 1. This explicit transaction was recorded when the business began, as shown by the credit balance in the Note Payable account. The principal and 9% interest are to be paid one year later (January 1, 19X3). However, an adjustment is necessary now for the interest expense of $\frac{1}{12} \times 0.09 \times \$100,000 = \$750$ for January.

e. On January 1, a cash loan of $40,000 was made to a local supplier, as shown by the debit balance in the Note Receivable account. The promissory note stated that the loan is to be repaid one year later (January 1, 19X3), together with interest at 12% per annum. On January 31, an adjustment is needed to recognize the interest earned on the note receivable.

f. On January 15, a nearby corporation paid $3,000 cash to Chan Audio Co. as an advance rental for Chan's storage space and equipment to be used temporarily from January 15 to April 15 (three months). This $3,000 is the credit balance in the Unearned Revenue account. On January 31, an adjustment is needed to recognize the rent revenue earned for one-half month.

g. Income tax expense was accrued on January income at a rate of 50% of income before taxes.

Required

1. Enter the trial-balance amounts in the general ledger. Set up the new asset account, Accrued Interest Receivable, and the new asset-reduction account, the contra account, Accumulated Amortization, Store Equipment. Set up the following new

liability accounts: Accrued Wages Payable, Accrued Interest Payable, and Accrued Income Taxes Payable. Set up the following new expense and revenue accounts: Amortization Expense, Rent Expense, Interest Expense, Interest Revenue, Rent Revenue, and Income Tax Expense.

2. Journalize adjustments *a-g* and post the entries to the ledger. Key entries by transaction letter.
3. Prepare an adjusted trial balance as of January 31, 19X2.

Solution to Problem One

The solutions to requirements 1 through 3 are in Exhibits 4-2 below, 4-3 (p. 145), and 4-4 (p. 146). Accountants often refer to the final trial balance, Exhibit 4-4, as the adjusted trial balance. Why? Because all the necessary adjustments have been made, and the trial balance provides the data necessary for the formal financial statements.

Exhibit 4-2

Chan Audio Co.
Journal Entries

(a)	Amortization expense	1,000	
	Accumulated amortization, store equipment		1,000
	Amortization for January.		
(b)	Rent expense	5,000	
	Prepaid rent		5,000
	Rent expense for January.		
(c)	Wages expense	3,750	
	Accrued wages payable		3,750
	Wages earned but not paid.		
(d)	Interest expense	750	
	Accrued interest payable		750
	Interest for January.		
(e)	Accrued interest receivable	400	
	Interest revenue		400
	Interest earned for January:		
	$\frac{1}{2} \times \$40,000 \times .12 = \$400$.		
(f)	Unearned rent revenue	500	
	Rent revenue		500
	Rent earned for January. Rent per month is		
	$\$3,000 \div 3 = \$1,000$; for one-half month, \$500.		
(g)	Income tax expense	11,200	
	Accrued income taxes payable		11,200
	Income tax on January income:		
	$.50 \times [160,000 + 400 + 500 - 100,000 - 31,750 - 1,000 - 5,000 - 750]$		

■ CLASSIFIED BALANCE SHEET

classified balance sheet A balance sheet that groups the accounts into subcategories to help readers quickly gain a perspective on the company's financial position.

Accounts are listed on the balance sheet according to the major categories of assets, liabilities, and shareholders' equity as we have seen throughout this book thus far. A **classified balance sheet** groups the accounts into subcategories to help readers quickly gain a perspective on the company's financial position. The classifications help to draw attention to certain amounts or groups of accounts.

Assets are frequently classified into two groupings: current assets and long-term assets. Liabilities are similarly classified: current liabilities and long-term liabilities. In this section we concentrate on current assets and liabilities; long-term assets and liabilities are covered in detail in Chapters 9 and 10.

current assets
Cash plus assets that are expected to be converted to cash or sold or consumed during the next twelve months or within the normal operating cycle if longer than a year.

current liabilities
Liabilities that fall due within the coming year or within the normal operating cycle if longer than a year.

Current Assets and Liabilities

Current assets are cash plus assets that are expected to be converted to cash or sold or consumed during the next twelve months or within the normal operating cycle if longer than a year. Similarly, **current liabilities** are those liabilities that fall due within the coming year or within the normal operating cycle if longer than a year. (Long-term assets and liabilities are expected to affect cash at some time beyond a year, or beyond the length of the normal operating cycle if it is longer than a year.) Companies that build ships or construct buildings are examples of companies that may take more than a year to complete an operating cycle.

Exhibit 4-3

Chan Audio Co.
General Ledger

Assets	—	Liabilities + Shareholders' Equity
(Increases Left, Decreases Right)		
		(Decreases Left, Increases Right)

Cash	Note Payable	Paid-in Capital
Bal. 71,700	Bal. 100,000	Bal. 400,000

Accounts Receivable	Accounts Payable	Sales
Bal. 160,300	Bal. 117,100	Bal. 160,000

Note Receivable	Unearned Rent Revenue	Cost of Goods Sold
Bal. 40,000	(f) 500 │ Bal. 3,000	Bal. 100,000
	Bal. 2,500	

Merchandise Inventory		Wages Expense
Bal. 250,200	Accrued Wages Payable	Bal. 28,000
	(c) 3,750	(c) 3,750
Prepaid Rent		Bal. 31,750
Bal. 15,000 │ (b) 5,000	Accrued Interest Payable	
Bal. 10,000	(d) 750	Amortization Expense
		(a) 1,000
Store Equipment	Accrued Income Taxes Payable	Rent Expense
Bal. 114,900	(g) 11,200	(b) 5,000

Accumulated Amortization, Store Equipment		Interest Expense
(a) 1,000		(d) 750

Accrued Interest Receivable		Interest Revenue
(e) 400		(e) 400

		Rent Revenue
		(f) 500

		Income Tax Expense
		(g) 11,200

Objective 7

Prepare a classified balance sheet and use the current asset and current liability classifications to assess solvency.

Exhibit 4-5 shows the classified balance sheet for Chan Audio Company, which is prepared from the adjusted trial balance for the company (shown in Exhibit 4-4). On the balance sheet, the current asset accounts are generally listed in the order in which they will be converted to cash during the coming year. Thus, Cash is listed first (since it is already in the form of cash). Accounts Receivable are listed next since cash payments will be received within weeks or months. Note Receivable and Accrued Interest Receivable, which are listed as the third and fourth accounts, will be converted to cash by the end of the year. Nonmonetary assets, such as inventories and prepaid expenses (in this case, Merchandise Inventory and Prepaid Rent) are usually listed last in the current assets section of the balance sheet. As shown in Exhibit 4–5, current liability accounts are also listed in the order in which they will draw on, or decrease, cash during the coming year.

Exhibit 4-4

Chan Audio Co.

Adjusted Trial Balance January 31, 19X2

Account Title	Balance		
	Debit	Credit	
Cash	$ 71,700		
Accounts receivable	160,300		
Note receivable	40,000		
Merchandise inventory	250,200		
Prepaid rent	10,000		
Store equipment	114,900		
Accumulated amortization, store equipment		$ 1,000	Balance
Accrued interest receivable	400		Sheet
Note payable		100,000	Exhibit 4-5
Accounts payable		117,100	
Unearned rent revenue		2,500	
Accrued wages payable		3,750	
Accrued interest payable		750	
Accrued income taxes payable		11,200	
Paid-in capital		400,000	
Sales		160,000	
Cost of goods sold	100,000		
Wages expense	31,750		
Amortization expense	1,000		Income
Rent expense	5,000		Statement,
Interest expense	750		Exhibit 4-8
Interest revenue		400	
Rent revenue		500	
Income tax expense	11,200		
Total	$797,200	$797,200	

working capital
The excess of current assets over current liabilities.

The excess of current assets over current liabilities is known as **working capital.** In the case of the Chan Audio Company, the working capital on January 31, 19X2, is $297,300 ($532,600 – $235,300).

Exhibit 4-5 shows only one long-term asset, Store Equipment (and its related accumulated amortization) and no long-term liabilities. However, most balance sheets contain several long-term assets and at least one type of long-term debt.

The shareholders' equity is $400,000 of paid-in capital plus January net income of $11,200, or $411,200. Note that the $11,200 does not appear as a separate number in the adjusted trial balance (Exhibit 4-4). Instead the $11,200 is the net effect of all the balances in the revenue and expense accounts. The balance sheet condenses the $11,200 effect as retained earnings. (The next chapter will explain the journal entries necessary to achieve this effect.)

Current Ratio

solvency An entity's ability to meet its financial obligations as they become due.

current ratio (working capital ratio) Current assets divided by current liabilities.

The classifications of current assets and current liabilities can help readers of financial statements assess a business entity's **solvency**, which is its ability to meet its financial obligations as they become due. The **current ratio** (also called the **working capital ratio**), which is widely used to evaluate solvency, is found by dividing current assets by current liabilities. Chan Audio's current ratio, for example, is:

$$\text{Current ratio} = \frac{\text{Current assets}}{\text{Current liabilities}} = \frac{\$532,600}{\$235,300} = 2.3$$

Other things being equal, the higher the current ratio, the more assurance creditors have about being paid in full and on time. Conversely, a current ratio that is too high may indicate excessive holdings of cash, accounts receivable, or inventories. Analysts will compare a company's current ratio with those of past years and with those of similar companies to make judgments about the company's solvency.

An old rule of thumb was that the current ratio should be greater than 2.0. However, a better assessment can be made by comparing a company's current ratio with the extent to which cash receipts for sales are relatively certain and predictable. For example, the Oshawa Group operates grocery stores. As customers pay cash for groceries, it can operate with a current ratio of 1.6 at July 31, 1995. This is considerably lower than the current ratio of 3.5 for Andrés Wines at March 31, 1996.

Although the current ratio is widely used as a measure of short-term debt-paying ability, a budget (prediction) of cash receipts and disbursements is more useful. Whether cash is too low or too high really depends on the predictions of operating requirements over the coming months. Intelligent management calls for trying to invest any temporary excess cash to generate additional income.

Exhibit 4-5   Chan Audio Co. Balance Sheet, January 31, 19X2

Assets		Liabilities and Owners' Equity	
Current assets:		Current liabilities:	
Cash	$ 71,700	Note payable	$100,000
Accounts receivable	160,300	Accounts payable	117,100
Note receivable	40,000	Unearned rent revenue	2,500
Accrued interest receivable	400	Accrued wages payable	3,750
Merchandise inventory	250,200	Accrued interest payable	750
Prepaid rent	10,000	Accrued income taxes payable	11,200
Total current assets	$532,600	Total current liabilities	$235,300
			continued

Assets			Liabilities and Owners' Equity		
Long-term asset:			Shareholders' equity:		
Store equipment	$114,900		Paid-in capital	$400,000	
Accumulated			Retained earnings	11,200	411,200
amortization	1,000	113,900			
Total		$646,500	Total		$646,500

Managing Working Capital

The traditional view is that large amounts of working capital and high current ratios are good—they show that a company is likely to remain solvent. However, maintaining solvency is not as big a problem for most companies as generating profits. Large amounts of working capital may needlessly tie up funds that could profitably be used elsewhere in the company.

The main components of working capital for the typical company are accounts receivable plus inventories less accounts payable. In the 1990s building inventories and accounts receivable fell out of fashion. Each dollar not invested in working capital is a dollar of free cash available for investing in value-adding activities—activities that actually create and deliver products or services to customers. In addition, there is another downside to large accounts receivable or inventories. Receivables may grow because of increasing sales, but they can also zoom upward when collection of receivables slows down. Soaring inventories may mean increased ability to deliver orders on time; they may also mean that sales are not keeping up with production or that the company is incurring excessive storage and handling costs for inventory. Companies with large inventories may also lack the ability to adapt products quickly to customers' wishes.

You can see that there are mixed signals in measures such as working capital and current ratio. In the 1990s many companies have made a concerted effort to reduce working capital and hence lower their current ratios. For example, in the fiscal year ending May 1994, Campbell Soup reduced its working capital by $80 million. This meant that Campbell had an extra $80 million to invest in new products, corporate acquisitions, or whatever other opportunity presented itself. Another food company, Quaker Oats, reduced its working capital by $200 million, primarily by smoothing out its production runs. Instead of building inventories and then offering huge discounts to entice customers to

take delivery, Quaker now produces its cereals and other products just in time to ship them. Each product is produced once a week instead of once every six weeks or so. Of course, this requires more time resetting machines to produce a different product. By streamlining its procedures, one Quaker Oats factory spent only $20,000 a year on the extra machine setups compared with the annual savings of $500,000 from lowering inventories.

A measure of working capital that is increasingly popular is working capital per dollar of sales. The Fortune 500 firms have an average ratio of $.20 for every dollar of sales. Recent figures for Quaker Oats and Campbell Soup are $.07 and $.14, respectively.

Reduction of working capital is not just a North American phenomenon. Consider Wabco UK, the British auto products manufacturer. In the last five years, its working capital has gone from $13 million to a negative $154,000. Currently, payables exceed receivables by $2.35 million and inventories are only $2.2 million. How did it accomplish this? Partly by cutting cycle time—the time from receipt of an order to delivery of the product. For example, a vacuum pump that took three weeks to build in 1989 can now be built in six minutes. Wabco is also collecting receivables more quickly—42 days compared with 54 days five years ago.

Many companies have set a target of zero working capital and therefore a current ratio of 1.0. As these efforts prove to be successful, the rule of thumb of a desirable current ratio of 2.0 is being revised. Companies with twice as many current assets as current liabilities may be solvent but may lose out in the long run. Why? Because they may not be using their capital as profitably as possible. ■

Sources: Shawn Tully, "Raiding a Company's Hidden Cash," Fortune (August 22, 1994), p. 82-87; Campbell Soup, Annual Report, 1994; Quaker Oats, Annual Report, 1994.

Formats of Balance Sheets

The particular detail and format of balance sheets and other financial statements vary among companies. Yet, all balance sheets contain the same basic information, regardless of format. For example, consider the reproduction of the balance sheet of National Sea Products Limited, a company that harvests, procures, processes and markets fish and seafood, as shown in Exhibit 4-6. The format and classifications are those actually presented. Note the captions used for noncurrent items. Captions such as *fixed assets* and *long-term liabilities* might be used instead of noncurrent assets and noncurrent liabilities, respectively. Some accountants prefer to omit a general caption for noncurrent items when there are only one or two items within a specific class.

report format A classified balance sheet with the assets at the top.

account format A classified balance sheet with the assets at the left.

Exhibit 4-6 presents a classified balance sheet in the **report format** (assets at top) in contrast to the **account format** (assets at left) that has previously been illustrated (Exhibit 4-5). Either format is acceptable.

Exhibit 4-6

National Sea Products Limited
Balance Sheet
December 30, 1995
(in thousands)

Assets		
Current Assets:		
Cash	$	1,806
Accounts receivable		22,876
Inventories		47,184
Income taxes recoverable		102
Prepaid expenses		957
Total current assets		72,925
Fixed Assets:		
Property and equipment, at cost, less accumulated depreciation and amortization		63,055
Other noncurrent assets		9,998
Total Assets		$ 145,978
Liabilities and Shareholders' Equity		
Current Liabilities:		
Bank indebtedness	$	12,752
Accounts payable and accrued charges		33,174
Current portion of long-term liabilities		10,150
Total current liabilities		56,076
Long-term Liabilities:		
Long-term indebtedness		60,655
Deferred income taxes		1,074
Minority interest		910
Total noncurrent liabilities	$	62,639
Shareholders' Equity:		
Convertible income debenture		9,962
Share capital		24,546
Deficit		(7,492)
Foreign currency translation accounts		247
Total shareholders' equity		27,263
Total Liabilities and Shareholders' Equity		$ 145,978

British Petroleum Co.
www.bp.com

Some companies may use other formats. Exhibit 4-7 shows a condensed balance sheet for British Petroleum Company. Notice that fixed assets (that is, long-term assets) are listed before current assets. Current liabilities are deducted from current assets to give a direct measure of working capital (called *net current assets* by British Petroleum). Note that British Petroleum has negative working capital of £46 million. Today, zero or negative working capital is becoming more common as companies reduce their inventories and accounts receivable.

Exhibit 4-7

British Petroleum Company
Balance Sheet
December 31, 1993
(in millions)

Fixed assets		£22,706
Current assets	£8,311	
Current liabilities	8,357	
Net current assets		(46)
Total assets less current liabilities		£22,660
Long-term liabilities		12,912
Shareholders' interests		£ 9,748

■ INCOME STATEMENT

Most investors are vitally concerned about a company's ability to produce long-run earnings and dividends. In this regard, income statements are often considered much more important than balance sheets. Like the balance sheet, income statements may be prepared with subcategories that draw attention to certain accounts or groups of accounts.

Single- and Multiple-Step Income Statements

single-step income statement An income statement that groups all revenues together and then lists and deducts all expenses together without drawing any intermediate subtotals.

multiple-step income statement An income statement that contains one or more subtotals that highlight significant relationships.

gross profit (gross margin) The excess of sales revenue over the cost of the inventory that was sold.

operating income (operating profit) Gross profit less all operating expenses.

The adjusted trial balance for Chan Audio Company (Exhibit 4-4) provides the data for two formats of income statements shown in Exhibit 4-8. The statement in Part A of the exhibit is called a **single-step income statement** because it groups all revenues together (sales plus interest and rent revenues) and then lists and deducts all expenses together without drawing any intermediate subtotals.

Another major form of income statement is the **multiple-step income statement**. It contains one or more subtotals that highlight significant relationships. For example, Exhibit 4-8, Part B, shows a *gross profit* figure. **Gross profit** is defined as the excess of sales revenue over the cost of the inventory that was sold. It is also called **gross margin**.

The next section of the multiple-step statement usually contains a group of recurring expenses that are often labelled as operating expenses because they pertain to the firm's routine, ongoing operations. Examples are wages, rent, amortization, and various other expenses such as telephone, heat, and advertising. These operating expenses are deducted from the gross profit to obtain **operating income**, which is also called **operating profit**. Cost of goods sold could also be viewed as an operating expense because it is also deducted from sales

Objective 8

Prepare single- and multiple-step income statements and use ratios based on income statement categories to assess profitability.

revenue to obtain "operating income." However, because of its size and importance, it is usually deducted separately from sales revenue, as shown here.

The next grouping is usually called *other revenue and expense* (or *other income* or *other expense* or *nonoperating items* or some similar catchall title). These are not directly related to the mainstream of a firm's operations. The revenues are usually minor in relation to the revenues shown at the top of the income statement. The expenses are also minor, with one likely exception, interest expense.

Exhibit 4-8, Part A

Single-Step Income Statement
Chan Audio Co.

Income Statement for the Month Ended January 31, 19X2

Sales		$160,000
Rent revenue		500
Interest revenue		400
Total sales and other revenues		$160,900
Expenses:		
Cost of goods sold	$100,000	
Wages	31,750	
Amortization	1,000	
Rent	5,000	
Interest	750	
Income taxes	11,200	
Total expenses		149,700
Net income		$ 11,200

Exhibit 4-8, Part B

Multiple-Step Income Statement
Chan Audio Co.

Income Statement for the Month Ended January 31, 19X2

Sales		$160,000
Cost of goods sold		100,000
Gross profit		$ 60,000
Operating expenses:		
Wages	$ 31,750	
Amortization	1,000	
Rent	5,000	37,750
Operating income		$ 22,250
Other revenues and expenses:		
Rent revenue	$ 500	
Interest revenue	400	
Total other revenue	$ 900	
Deduct: Interest expense	750	150
Income before income taxes		$ 22,400
Income taxes (at 50%)		11,200
Net income		$ 11,200

Accountants have usually regarded interest revenue and interest expense as "other" items because they arise from lending and borrowing money—activities that are distinct from the ordinary selling of goods or services. Some companies make heavy use of debt, which causes high interest expenses, whereas other companies incur little debt and have low interest expenses. Because interest

Financial Statement Classification

The grouping of items in balance sheets and income statements is intended to emphasize the most important items and to highlight their relationships. For many firms, particularly retailers such as Mark's Work Wearhouse and manufacturers such as Corel, the relationship between sales and cost of goods sold is crucial and is thus highlighted as gross profit in a multiple-step income statement. However, gross profit is not the most significant relationship in all businesses. For example, how would a bank report cost of goods sold? Instead of gross profit, banks typically highlight the relationship between interest revenue (what the bank makes on its loans) and interest expense (what the bank pays to depositors). As the first two categories in its 1996 income statement, Bank of Montreal reported interest income of $10,671 million and interest expense of $6,881 million; the difference of $3,790 million was called *net interest income*.

Some firms find that the most useful format for the income statement is to group revenues and expenses by functional area. In its 1993 Income Statement, Walt Disney reported revenues and expenses for three areas: theme parks and resorts ($3,441 million revenue and $2,694 million expense), filmed entertainment ($3,673 million revenue and $3,051 million expense), and consumer products ($1,415 million revenue and $1,060 million expense).

The assets and liabilities in almost all balance sheets are separated into current and noncurrent categories. However, the arrangement of the categories can differ. Utilities typically list noncurrent assets before the current assets because the plant and equipment of a utility are far and away their most important assets. In 1995, the Island Telephone Company Limited, the Prince Edward Island telephone company, lists Net Telecommunications Property of $129,579 thousand before its Current Assets of $15,094 thousand and Other Assets of $7,272 thousand.

Most British firms show current liabilities as a subtraction from current assets. In its December 31, 1993 balance sheet, British Aerospace reported Net Current Assets of £2,323 million, consisting of current assets of £6,612 million minus current liabilities of £4,289 million. This arrangement highlights the fact that the acquisition of current assets is typically financed through current liabilities and that only the net amount, often called working capital, requires financing from long-term debt or equity sources. ■

Sources: Annual Reports of Mark's Work Wearhouse, Corel, Walt Disney, Bank of Montreal, Island Telephone Company Limited, and British Aerospace.

British Aerospace
www.bae.co.uk/

revenue and expense appear in a separate category, comparisons of operating income between years and between companies can be made easily.

Examples of Actual Income Statements

Exhibits 4-9 and 4-10 demonstrate how two different companies use assorted terminology and formats for their individual statements of income. Note that extremely condensed income statement information is provided in published reports (as opposed to the detail that is shown for internal use).

The Consumers Packaging Inc. income statement in Exhibit 4-9 uses a *multiple-step* format. The multiple-step format has subtotals to highlight significant relationships. In addition to net income, the format also presents two key measures of performance, gross margin and operating income.

Accountants use the label *net* to denote that some amounts have been deducted in computing the final result. Thus *other expenses, net* in the Consumers Packaging statement, means that some revenue items and some expense items have been combined into one number. In a statement of income, the term *net* is not ordinarily used to describe any subtotals of income that precede the final net income number.

Canadian Tire uses a *single-step* format for its income statement in Exhibit 4-10. Canadian Tire follows the single-step model and groups all revenues together and all expenses together without drawing subtotals within revenue and expense categories.

Gross Sales	$458,064
Sales deductions	25,270
Net sales	432,794
Cost of goods sold	298,884
Gross margin	133,910
Costs and expenses	
Distribution	31,920
Administration and selling	25,205
Depreciation	35,383
	92,508
Operating income	41,402
Interest and financial charges	15,231
Earnings from continuing operations	26,171
Gain from discontinued operations	—
Net earnings	$ 26,171

Gross operating revenue	$3,599,231
Operating expenses	
Cost of merchandise sold and all expenses	
except for the undernoted items	3,277,805
Interest	
Long-term debt	49,709
Short-term debt	14,488
Depreciation and amortization	60,325
Employee profit sharing plans	16,024
Total operating expenses	3,418,351
Operating earnings	180,880
Investment and interest income	4,735
Earnings from continuing operations before income taxes	185,615
Income taxes	
Current	89,316
Deferred	(18,470)
Total income taxes	70,846
Net earnings from continuing operations	114,769
Net loss from discontinued operations	(109,277)
Net earnings	$ 5,492

As Consumers shows, the term *costs and expenses* is sometimes found instead of just *expenses*. Expenses would be an adequate description. Why? Because the "costs" listed on the income statement are expired costs, such as cost of sales, and thus are really expenses of the current period.

profitability evaluation The assessment of the likelihood that a company will provide investors with a particular rate of return on their investment.

■ PROFITABILITY EVALUATION RATIOS

Income statements provide information useful for evaluating a company's profitability. In its ultimate sense, **profitability evaluation** is the assessment of the likelihood that a company will provide investors with a particular rate of return on their investment. Profitability measures are also useful decision-making tools for company managers. Profitability comparisons through time and within and among industries are thus used as a basis for predictions and decisions by both external and internal users of financial statements. Consider three of the most popular ratios for measuring profitability:

1. A ratio based on gross profit (sales revenues minus cost of goods sold) is particularly useful to a retailer in choosing a pricing strategy and in judging its results. This measure, the **gross profit percentage**, or **gross margin percentage**, is defined as gross profit divided by sales. The Chan Audio gross profit percentage for January was

gross profit percentage (gross margin percentage) Gross profit divided by sales.

$$\text{Gross profit percentage} = \text{Gross profit} \div \text{Sales}$$
$$= \$60,000 \div \$160,000$$
$$= 37.5\%$$

These relationships can also be presented as follows:

	Amount	Percentage
Sales	$160,000	100.0%
Cost of goods sold	100,000	62.5
Gross profit	$ 60,000	37.5%

Gross profit percentages vary greatly by industry. Software companies have high gross profit percentages—Cord's is 76% in 1995. Why? Because most costs are in research and development and sales and marketing, not in cost of goods sold. In contrast, retail companies have lower gross margin percentages because product costs are their main expense. For example, the gross profit percentage for Canadian Tire in 1994 is 9%.

2. A ratio based on a comparison of expenses and sales will be carefully followed by managers from month to month. The **return on sales ratio** shows the relationship of net income, the famous "bottom line," after all expenses have been deducted from all revenues, to sales revenue. Chan Audio's return on sales ratio is computed as follows:

return on sales ratio Net income divided by sales.

$$\text{Return on sales} = \text{Net income} \div \text{Sales}$$
$$= \$11,200 \div \$160,000$$
$$= 7\%$$

3. The **return on shareholders' equity ratio** also uses net income but compares it with invested capital (as measured by average shareholders' equity) instead of sales. This ratio is widely regarded as the ultimate measure of overall accomplishment. The calculation for Chan Audio is:

return on shareholders' equity ratio Net income divided by invested capital (measured by average shareholders' equity).

$$\text{Return on shareholders' equity} = \text{Net income} \div \text{Average shareholders' equity}$$
$$= \$11,200 \div 1/2 \text{ (January 1 balance, \$400,000 + January 31 balance, \$411,200)}$$
$$= \$11,200 \div \$405,600$$
$$= 2.8\% \text{ (for one month)}$$

Some recent examples of actual annual return on sales and return on shareholders' equity ratios are:

	Return on Sales	Return on Shareholders' Equity
Consumers Packaging	9%	24%
Nike	9%	22%
McDonald's	15%	17%
Bell Atlantic	11%	17%
Electrohome	4%	9%
British Petroleum (United Kingdom)	2%	6%
Nordstrom	4%	12%
Kobe Steel (Japan)	1%	3%

These three profitability ratios are being introduced at this early stage because they are so widely encountered. Chan Audio's 37.5% gross profit is relatively low compared with the usual 40% to 45% for the retail stereo industry. However, Chan Audio has maintained excellent expense control because its 7% return on sales and its 33.6% return on shareholders' equity (an annual rate of 2.8% × 12 = 33.6%) are higher than the 6% and 18% annual returns usually earned by the industry.

Statistical studies have shown that *profitability evaluation ratios* such as the three just discussed have higher power than *solvency determination ratios* (such as the current ratio) for predicting performance regarding *both* income and solvency. Later chapters study the uses and limitations of these and other ratios.

Summary Problem for Your Review

The first problem appeared earlier in the chapter, page 143.

Problem Two

Johnson & Johnson (maker of Tylenol, Band-Aids, and other products) uses a statement of earnings and retained earnings, as follows:

Johnson & Johnson
Statement of
Earnings and
Retained Earnings
(dollars in millions
except per share
figures)

Sales to customers	$14,138
Cost of products sold	4,791
Selling, distribution, and administrative expenses	5,771
Research expense	1,182
Interest income	(80)
Interest expense	126
Other expense	16
	11,806
Earnings before provision for taxes on income	2,332
Provision for taxes on income	545
Net earnings	1,787
Retained earnings at beginning of period	6,648
Cash dividends paid	(708)
Retained earnings at end of period	$ 7,727
Net earnings per share	$ 2.74

Johnson & Johnson
www.jnj.com

Prepare any necessary adjusting or correcting entries called for by the following situations *which were discovered at the end of the calendar year*. With respect to each situation, assume that no entries have been made regarding the situation other than those specifically described (i.e., no monthly adjustments have been made during the year). *Consider each situation separately*. These transactions were not necessarily conducted by one business firm. Amounts are in thousands of dollars. *Illustration:* Purchased new equipment for $100 cash, plus a $300 short-term note. The bookkeeper failed to record the transaction. The answer would appear as follows:

	Account		Amount	
	Debit	Credit	Debit	Credit
Illustration	13	1 & 15	400	100 & 300
a.				
b.				
c.				
etc.				

a. A $300 purchase of equipment on December 5 was erroneously debited to Accounts Payable. The credit was correctly made to Cash.

b. A business made several purchases of fuel oil. Some purchases ($800) were debited to Fuel Expense, while others ($1,100) were charged to an assets account. An oil gauge revealed $400 of fuel on hand at the end of the year. There was no fuel on hand at the beginning of the year.

c. On April 1, a business took out a fire insurance policy. The policy was for two years, and the premium paid was $400. It was debited to Insurance Expense on April 1.

d. On December 1, $400 was paid in advance to the landlord for four months' rent. The tenant debited Unexpired Rent for $400 on December 1. What adjustment is necessary on December 31 on the tenant's books?

e. Machinery is repaired and maintained by an outside maintenance company on an annual fee basis, payable in advance. The $240 fee was paid in advance on September 1 and charged to Repairs and Maintenance Expense. What adjustment is necessary on December 31?

f. On November 16, $800 of machinery was purchased. $200 cash was paid down and a ninety-day, 5% note payable was signed for the balance. The November 16 transaction was properly recorded. Prepare the adjustment for the interest.

g. A publisher sells subscriptions to magazines. Customers pay in advance. Receipts are originally credited to Unearned Subscription Revenue. On August 1, many one-year subscriptions were collected and recorded, amounting to $12,000.

h. On December 30, certain merchandise was purchased for $1,000 on open account. The bookkeeper debited Machinery and Equipment and credited Accounts Payable for $1,000. Prepare a correcting entry.

i. A 120-day, 7%, $7,500 cash loan was made to a customer on November 1. The November 1 transaction was recorded correctly.

PROBLEMS

4-28   Adjusting Entries

(Alternates are 4-30, 4-36, and 4-37.) Jennifer Blair, a professional accountant, had the following transactions (among others) during 19X2:

a. For accurate measurement of performance and position, Blair uses the accrual basis of accounting. On August 1, she acquired office supplies for $2,000. Office Supplies Inventory was increased, and Cash was decreased by $2,000 on Blair's books. On December 31, her inventory was $800.

b. On September 1, a client gave Blair a retainer fee of $48,000 cash for monthly services to be rendered over the following twelve months. Blair increased Cash and Unearned Fee Revenue.   *16,000*

c. Blair accepted an $8,000 note receivable from a client on October 1 for tax services. The note plus interest of 12% per year were due in six months. Blair increased Note Receivable and Fee Revenue by $8,000.

d. As of December 31, Blair had not recorded $400 of unpaid wages earned by her secretary during late December.

Required

For the year ended December 31, 19X2, prepare all adjustments called for by the above transactions. Assume that appropriate entries were routinely made for the explicit transactions described above. However, no adjustments have been made before December 31. For each adjustment, prepare an analysis in the same format used when the adjustment process was explained in the chapter (i.e., the balance sheet equation format). Also prepare the adjusting journal entry.

4-29   Multiple-Step Income Statement

(Alternate is 4-38.) From the following data, prepare a multiple-step income statement for the Redmond Company for the fiscal year ended May 31, 19X6 (in thousands except for percentage). *Hint*: see page 151.

Sales	$890	Cost of goods sold	$440
Interest expense	72	Amortization	30
Rent expense	52	Rent revenue	10
Interest revenue	14	Wages	200
Income tax rate	40%		

4-30   Four Major Adjustments

(Alternates are 4-28, 4-36, and 4-37.) Judith Noller, a lawyer, had the following transactions (among others) during 19X2, her initial year in practicing law:

a. On August 1, Noller leased office space for one year. The landlord (lessor) insisted on full payment in advance. Prepaid Rent was increased and Cash was decreased by $24,000 on Noller's books. Similarly, the landlord increased Cash and increased Unearned Rent Revenue.

b. On October 1, Noller received a retainer fee of $18,000 cash for services to be rendered to her client, a local trucking company, over the succeeding twelve months. Noller increased Cash and Unearned Fee Revenue. The trucking company increased Prepaid Expenses and decreased Cash.

c. As of December 31, Noller had not recorded $400 of unpaid wages earned by her secretary during late December.

d. During November and December, Noller rendered services to another client, a utility company. She had intended to bill the company for $5,400 services through December 31, but she decided to delay formal billing until late January when the case would probably be settled.

Required

1. For the year ended December 31, 19X2, prepare all adjustments called for by the above transactions. Assume that appropriate entries were routinely made for the explicit transactions described above. However, no adjustments have been made before December 31. For each adjustment, prepare an analysis in the same format as the adjustment process explained in the chapter (i.e., the balance sheet equation format). Prepare two adjustments for each transaction, one for Noller and one for the other party to the transaction. In part *c*, assume that the secretary uses the accrual basis for his personal entity.
2. For each transaction, prepare the journal entries for Judith Noller *and* the other entities involved.

4-31   Accounting for Dues
(Alternate is 4-32) The Pebble Island Golf Club provided the following data from its comparative balance sheets:

	December 31	
	19X3	*19X2*
Dues receivable	$90,000	$75,000
Unearned dues revenue	—	$30,000

The income statement for 19X3, which was prepared on the accrual basis, showed dues revenue earned of $720,000. No dues were collected in advance during 19X3.

Required

Prepare journal entries and post to T-accounts for the following:

1. Earning of dues collected in advance.
2. Billing of dues revenue during 19X3.
3. Collection of dues receivable in 19X3.

4-32   Accounting for Subscriptions
(Alternate is 4-31.) A French magazine company collects subscriptions in advance of delivery of its magazines. However, many magazines are delivered to magazine distributors (for newsstand sales), and these distributors are billed and pay later. The subscription revenue earned for the month of March on the accrual basis was FF200,000 (FF refers to the French franc). Other pertinent data were:

	March	
	31	*1*
Unearned subscription revenue	FF190,000	FF140,000
Accounts receivable	7,000	9,000

Required

Reconstruct the entries for March. Prepare journal entries and post to T-accounts for the following:

1. Collections of unearned subscription revenue of $140,000 prior to March 1.
2. Billing of accounts receivable (a) of $9,000 prior to March 1, and (b) of $80,000 during March. (Credit Revenue Earned)
3. Collections of cash during March and any other entries that are indicated by the given data.

4-33   Financial Statements and Adjustments

Marcella Wholesalers, Inc. has just completed its fourth year of business, 19X3. A set of financial statements was prepared by the principal shareholders' eldest child, a college student who is beginning the third week of an accounting course. Following is a list (in no systematic order) of the items appearing in the student's balance sheet, income statement, and statement of retained income:

Accounts receivable	$183,100	Advertising expense	$ 98,300
Note receivable	36,000	Merchandise inventory	201,900
Cash	99,300	Cost of goods sold	590,000
Paid-in capital	620,000	Unearned rent revenue	4,800
Building	300,000	Insurance expense	2,500
Accumulated amortization,		Unexpired insurance	2,300
building	20,000	Accounts payable	52,500
Land	169,200	Interest expense	600
Sales	936,800	Telephone expense	2,900
Salary expense	124,300	Notes payable	20,000
Retained earnings:		Net income	110,500
December 31,19X2	164,000	Miscellaneous expense	3,400
December 31,19X3	274,500	Maintenance expense	4,300

Assume that the statements in which these items appear are current and complete except for the following matters not taken into consideration by the student:

a. Salaries of $5,200 have been earned by employees for the last half of December 19X3. Payment by the company will be made on the next payday, January 2, 19X4.

b. Interest at 10% per annum on the note receivable has accrued for two months and is expected to be collected by the company when the note is due on January 31, 19X4.

c. Part of the building owned by the company was rented to a tenant on November 1, 19X3, for six months, payable in advance. This rent was collected in cash and is represented by the item labelled Unearned Rent Revenue.

d. Amortization on the building for 19X3 is $6,100.

e. Cash dividends of $60,000 were declared in December 19X3, payable in January 19X4.

f. Income tax at 40% applies to 19X3, all of which is to be paid in the early part of 19X4.

Required   Prepare the following corrected financial statements:

1. Multiple-step income statement for 19X3.
2. Statement of retained earnings for 19X3.
3. Classified balance sheet at December 31, 19X3. (Show appropriate support for the dollar amounts you compute.)

4-34   Mirror Side of Adjustments

Problem 4-28 described some Blair adjustments. Repeat the requirement for each adjustment as it would be made by the client in transactions *b* and *c* and by the secretary in transaction *d*. For our purposes here, assume that the secretary keeps personal books on the accrual basis.

CRITICAL THINKING PROBLEM

4-35   Adjusting Entries and Ethics

By definition, adjusting entries are not triggered by an explicit event. Therefore, accountants must initiate adjusting entries. For each of the following adjusting entries, discuss a potential unethical behaviour that an accountant or manager might undertake:

a. Recognition of expenses from the prepaid supplies account.

b. Recognition of revenue from the unearned revenue account.

c. Accrual of interest payable.

d. Accrual of fees receivable.

COMPANY
CASES

4-36   Four Major Adjustments
(Alternates are 4-28, 4-30, and 4-37.) Bombardier Inc. included the following items in its January 31, 1996 balance sheet (in millions):

Prepaid expenses (a current asset)	$31.8
Income taxes payable (a current liability)	51.4

Required

Analyze the impact of the following transactions on the financial position of Bombardier. Prepare your analysis in the same format as the adjustment process explained in the chapter. Also show adjusting journal entries.

1. On January 31, an adjustment of $3 million was made for the rentals of various retail outlets that had originally increased Prepaid Expenses but had expired.

2. During December 1995, Bombardier sold parts for $2 million cash to the Toronto Transit Commision, but delivery was not made until January 28. Unearned Revenue had been increased in December. No other adjustments have been made since. Prepare the adjustment on January 31.

3. Bombardier had lent cash to several of its independent retail dealers. As of January 31, the dealers owed $4 million of interest that had been unrecorded.

4. On January 31, Bombardier increased its accrual of income taxes by $21 million.

4-37   Four Major Adjustments
(Alternates are 4-28, 4-30, and 4-36.) Alaska Airlines had the following items in its balance sheet, December 30, 1995, the end of the fiscal year:

Inventories and supplies	$ 41,269,000
Prepaid expenses and other current assets	56,498,000
Air traffic liability	108,360,000
Accrued wages, vacation pay, and payroll taxes	40,192,000

A footnote stated: "Passenger ticket sales are recorded as revenue when the transportation is used. The value of unused tickets is included in current liabilities in the financial statements." The title of this current liability is Air Traffic Liability.
The income statement included:

Passenger revenues	$1,001,975,000
Wages and benefits expense	368,152,000

Required

Analyze the impact of the following assumed transactions on the financial position of Alaska. Prepare your analysis in the same format as the adjustment process explained in the chapter. Also show adjusting journal entries.

1. Rented a sales office in a Transamerica office building for one year, beginning December 1, 1995, for $18,000 cash.
2. On December 30, 1995, an adjustment was made for the rent in requirement 1.
3. Sold two charter flights to Apple Computer for $100,000 each. Cash of $200,000 was received in advance on November 20, 1995. The flights were for transporting marketing personnel to two business conventions in New York.

4. As the financial statements were being prepared on December 30, accountants for both Alaska and Apple Computer independently noted that the first charter flight had occurred in late December. The second would occur in early February. An adjustment was made on December 30.
5. Alaska had lent $2 million to Boeing. Interest of $160,000 was accrued on December 30.
6. Additional wages of $140,000 were accrued on December 30.

4-38 Budweiser Financial Statements

(Alternate is 4-29.) Anheuser-Busch (maker of Budweiser beer) is the largest beer producer in the United States. Some actual financial data and nomenclature from its 1993 annual report were (in millions):

Interest expense, net	$ 166	Cash dividends declared	$?
Sales	11,505	Other income	4
Gross profit	4,085	Net income	594
Operating income	1,212	Retained earnings:	
Other operating expenses	565	Beginning of year	5,795
Marketing, administrative,		End of year	6,023
and research expenses	?	Provision for income taxes	
Cost of products sold	?	(income tax expense)	456

Required

1. Prepare a combined multiple-step statement of income and retained earnings for the year ended December 31, 1993. *Hint*: see page 151.
2. Compute the percentage of gross profit on sales and the percentage of net income on sales.
3. The average shareholders' equity for the year was $4,438 million. What was the percentage of net income on average shareholders' equity?

4-39 Mirror Side of Adjustments

Problem 4-36 described some Bombardier adjustments. Repeat the requirements for each adjustment as it would be made by (1) landlords, (2) Toronto Transit Commission, (3) retail dealers, and (4) Canadian and foreign governments. Assume that all use accrual accounting.

4-40 Mirror Side of Adjustments

Problem 4-37 described some Alaska Airlines adjustments numbered 1 to 6. Repeat the requirements for each adjustment as it would be made by the other party in the transaction. Specifically, (1) and (2) Transamerica, (3) and (4) Apple Computer, (5) Boeing, and (6) employees. Assume that all use accrual accounting.

4-41 Journal Entries and Posting

Nike, Inc., has many well-known products, including footwear. The company's balance sheet included (in thousands):

	May 31	
	1993	**1992**
Prepaid expenses	$42,452	$32,977
Income taxes payable	17,150	42,422

Suppose that during the fiscal year ended May 31, 1993, $210,000,000 cash was disbursed and charged to Prepaid Expenses. Similarly, $254,772,000 was disbursed for income taxes and charged to Income Taxes Payable.

Required 1. Assume that the Prepaid Expenses account relates to outlays for miscellaneous operating expenses (for example, supplies, insurance, and short-term rentals). Prepare summary journal entries for (a) the disbursements and (b) the expenses for fiscal 1993. Post the entries to the T-accounts.
2. Assume that there were no other accounts related to income taxes. Prepare summary journal entries for (a) the disbursements and (b) the expenses for fiscal 1993. Post the entries to T-accounts.

4-42   Advance Service Contracts

Diebold, Incorporated, a manufacturer of automated teller machines (ATMs), showed the following balance sheet account:

	December 31	
	1993	*1992*
Deferred income	$45,001,000	$41,522,000

A footnote to the financial statements stated: "Deferred income is recognized for customer billings in advance of the period in which the service will be performed and is recognized in income on a straight-line basis over the contract period."

Required 1. Prepare summary journal entries for the creation in 1992 and subsequent earning in 1993 of the deferred income of $41,522,000. Use the following accounts: Accounts Receivable, Deferred Income, and Income from Advance Billings.
2. A one-year job contract was billed to Keystone Bank on January 1, 1993, for $36,000. Work began on January 1. The full amount was collected on February 15. Prepare all pertinent journal entries through February 28, 1993. ("Straight-line" means an equal amount per month.)

4-43   Journal Entries and Adjustments

Rogers Cantel Mobile Communication Inc. included the following footnote in its 1995 annual report:

Unearned revenue includes subscriber deposits and amounts received from subscribers related to services to be provided in future periods.

The income statements showed (in thousands of dollars):

	1995	1994
Revenue	$899,521	$750,420
Operating income	106,177	101,785

The balance sheet showed (in thousands of dollars):

	December 31	
	1995	*1994*
Accounts receivable	$131,932	$97,173
Unearned revenues	27,505	24,098

Required Prepare the adjusting journal entry for (a) the unearned revenue at the end of 1995 and (b) the eventual providing of services for the unearned revenues. Ignore income taxes.

4-44   Classified Balance Sheet and Current Ratio

Fisher Imaging Corporation is a high-technology company that produces x-ray imaging systems for the medical profession. Major products include minimally invasive systems for diagnosis and treatment of breast cancer, heart disease, and vascular disease. The company's balance sheet for December 31, 1993 contained the following items:

Property and equipment, net	4,526,575
Accrued salaries and wages	2,461,997
Cash	161,520
Other assets	8,046,411
Other noncurrent liabilities	1,535,779
Short-term bank loans	1,824,148
Inventories	19,131,834
Other current liabilities	6,344,662
Notes payable	8,169,702
Other current assets	3,084,997
Trade accounts payable	5,769,111
Trade accounts receivable	21,599,625
Long-term debt	?
Shareholders' equity	27,033,116

Required

1. Prepare a December 31, 1993 classified balance sheet for Fisher Imaging Corporation. Include the correct amount for long-term debt.
2. Compute the company's working capital and current ratio.
3. Comment on the company's current ratio. In 1991 the ratio was 1.5; in 1989 it was 1.6. The industry average is 2.0.
4. During 1993 Fisher Imaging increased its short-term borrowing from banks by $3.3 million. Suppose the company had not increased its short-term borrowing but had instead increased its long-term debt by $3.3 million. How would this have affected Fisher Imaging's current ratio? How would it have affected the company's solvency?

4-45 Multiple-Step Income Statement

Corel Corporation included the following data in its 1995 annual report (in thousands of US$):

Cost of sales	$47,352	Depreciation and amortization	$9,468
Advertising	55,099	Loss on foreign exchange	136
Selling, general and		Interest income	5,023
administrative	40,292	Income taxes	7,339
Research and development	27,232	Gross profit	149,027

Required   Prepare a multiple-step statement of income.

4-46 Single-Step Income Statement

A. T. Cross Company's best-known products are writing instruments such as ballpoint pens. The Cross 1992 annual report contained the following items (in thousands):

Interest and other income	$ 3,206	Selling, general, and	
Cost of goods sold	111,600	administrative expenses	$ 76,029
Provision for income taxes		Retained earnings at end	
(income tax expense)	5,191	of year	125,187
Sales	200,432	Cash dividends	21,648

Required

1. Prepare a combined single-step statement of income and retained earnings for the year.
2. Compute the percentage of gross profit on sales and the percentage of net income on sales.
3. The average shareholders' equity for the year was about $156 million. What was the percentage of net income on average shareholders' equity?
4. In 1990 the gross profit percentage was 46.6%, the percentage of net income to sales was 12.2%, and the return on average shareholders' equity was 6.9%. Comment on the changes between 1990 and 1992.

4-47   Retail Company Financial Statements

Kmart Corporation is one of the world's largest retailers. The 1993 annual report included the data shown below (in millions of dollars). Unless otherwise specified, the balance sheet amounts are the balances at the end of the 1993 fiscal year.

Sales	$38,124	Interest expense	$ 432
Cash dividends	455	Long-term debt	3,237
Merchandise inventories	8,752	Cash	611
Cost of merchandise sold	28,485	Selling & administrative expense	7,781
Paid-in capital	1,836	Accrued taxes payable	614
Accounts receivable	1,146	Accrued payroll and other current	
Retained earnings:		liabilities	1,332
Beginning of year	5,214	Provision for income taxes	485
End of year	5,700	Property & equipment, net	6,405
Notes payable	590	Other noncurrent assets	2,017
Accounts payable	2,959	Other noncurrent liabilities	2,663

Required

1. Prepare a combined multiple-step statement of income and retained earnings.
2. Prepare a classified balance sheet.
3. The average shareholders' equity for the year was about $7,213 million. What was the percentage of net income on average shareholders' equity?
4. Compute (a) gross profit percentage and (b) percentage of net income to sales.
5. Optional: Why might shareholders want to invest in a company with such a consistently low percentage of net income to sales?

4-48   Preparation of Financial Statements from Trial Balance

ConAgra, the Omaha company that produces consumer foods such as Armour and Swift meats, Banquet and Morton frozen foods, and Healthy Choice brands, prepared the following (slightly modified) trial balance as of May 29, 1994 (in millions), the end of the company's fiscal year:

	Debits	Credits
Cash and cash equivalents	$ 166.4	
Receivables	1,589.6	
Inventories	2,884.4	
Prepaid expenses	216.9	
Other current assets	286.0	
Property, plant, and equipment, at cost	4,150.4	
Accumulated depreciation, property, plant, and equipment		$ 1,564.1
Brands, trademarks, and goodwill, net	2,626.4	
Other assets	365.8	
Notes payable		419.0
Accounts payable		1,937.0
Accrued payroll		262.4
Advances on sales (deferred revenues)		914.9
Other current liabilities		1,219.5
Long-term debt		2,206.8
Other noncurrent liabilities		1,079.7

continued

Preferred stock		455.6
Common stock, $5 par value		1,263.6
Retained earnings		1,167.0
Additional paid in capital		304.9
Treasury and restricted stock*	764.3	
Net sales		23,512.2
Cost of goods sold	20,452.2	
Selling, administrative, and general expenses	2,091.0	
Interest expense	254.2	
Other income		5.2
Income taxes	282.9	
Cash dividends	181.4	
Total	$36,311.9	$36,311.9

*Part of shareholders' equity.

Required

1. Prepare ConAgra's income statement for the year ended May 29, 1994, using a multiple-step format.
2. Prepare ConAgra's income statement for the year ended May 29, 1994, using a single-step format. Which format for the income statement is more informative? Why?
3. Prepare ConAgra's classified balance sheet as of May 29, 1994.

4-49   Professional Football Income

Examine the accompanying condensed income statement of the Green Bay Packers, Inc. for a recent year.

Income:		
Regular season:		
Net receipts from home games	$ 3,223,803	
Out-of-town games	2,288,967	
Television and radio programs	14,322,244	$19,835,014
Preseason:		
Net receipts from preseason games	1,356,751	
Television and radio programs	355,032	1,711,783
Miscellaneous:		
Club allocation of league receipts	784,988	
Other income	511,516	1,296,504
Total income		22,843,301
Expenses:		
Salaries and other season expenses	16,243,729	
Training expense	725,079	
Overhead expense	4,744,336	
Severance pay	656,250	22,369,394
Income from operations		473,907
Interest income		1,203,281
Income before taxes		1,677,188
Provision for income taxes		167,000
Net income		$ 1,510,188

Required

1. Do you agree with the choice of terms in this statement? If not, suggest where a preferable label should be used.
2. Is this a single-step income statement? If not, which items would you shift to prepare a single-step statement?
3. Identify the major factors that affect the Packers' net income.

4-50   Hudson's Bay Company Annual Report

This problem uses an actual company's accounts to develop skill in preparing adjusting journal entries. Refer to the financial statements of the Hudson's Bay Company (Appendix A at the end of the book). Note the following balance sheet items:

	January 31 ($000's)	
	1997	1996
Prepaid expenses	$ 47,287	$ 60,067
Other accounts payable and accrued expenses	$407,124	$386,051

Suppose that during the 1997 fiscal year, $2,400,000,000 cash was disbursed and charged to Prepaid Expenses and $8,200,000,000 of other accounts payable and accrued expenses were paid.

Required

1. Assume that the Prepaid Expenses account relates to outlays for miscellaneous Operating Expenses (for example, supplies, insurance, and short–term rentals). Prepare summary journal entries for (a) the disbursements and (b) the expenses (for our purposes, debit Operating, Selling, and General and Administrative Expenses) for fiscal 1997. Post the entries to the T-accounts.
2. Prepare summary journal entries for (a) the disbursements and (b) the expenses related to the other accounts payable and accrued expenses for fiscal 1997. (For our purposes, debit Operating, Selling, and General and Administrative Expenses.) Post the entries to the T-accounts.

4-51.   Annual Report Disclosure

Select a company of your choice.

Required

1. Determine the amount of working capital and the current ratio for each of two year's reports.
2. Compare the current ratios. For which year does the company have the larger ratio, and what do the ratios tell you about the solvency of the company?
3. Compute the gross margin percentage, the return on sales, and the return on share-holders' equity for each year.
4. Compare the profitability of the company between the two years.

5

Accounting Cycle: Recording and Formal Presentation

Learning Objectives

After studying this chapter, you should be able to

1 Explain the accounting cycle and analyze transactions, including those that relate to the adjustments of the preceding period.

2 Analyze cash transactions used in the statement of changes in financial position.

3 Prepare closing entries for pertinent accounts.

4 Explain the role of auditors of financial statements.

5 Use a work sheet to prepare adjustments, financial statements, and closing entries (Appendix 5A).

6 Prepare adjustments when alternative recording methods are used for the related originating transactions (Appendix 5B).

7 Use special journals to process transactions (Appendix 5C).

This chapter describes the accounting cycle, which is the process of recording transactions from the beginning of a period to its end in order to produce the firm's financial statements. The chapter identifies the steps in the cycle and uses the transactions of an example company to review the techniques for recording data that will be used in the financial statements. The transactions necessary to close the books after the statements have been prepared are also demonstrated. Three chapter appendices provide more details on the processing of accounting data.

This chapter includes primarily a review of materials covered in Chapters 1 through 4 and the addition of some technical data-processing details. Therefore, some instructors may elect to omit it. Nevertheless, we recommend that any student who had difficulty with the processing of transactions in the earlier chapters pay particular attention to pages 180-188. In addition, students planning to become accountants and those who want a complete understanding of how financial statements are produced should learn the procedures for closing the books, as described on pages 190-194.

The major focus in this chapter is on how the recording process leads to the final output of the accounting cycle. The financial statements present a picture of the firm's financial standing. They show the efficiency of its operations and its ability to generate profits. The role of auditing, which is also discussed at the end of this chapter, is crucial in assuring readers that the financial statements fairly present the firm's results for the period.

Although accounting serves different purposes in different countries, the accounting cycle and double-entry bookkeeping are mainstays of accounting throughout the world. Socialist governments have tried to outlaw Western accounting methods (including double-entry systems) as capitalist. They have tried to develop "moneyless" bookkeeping systems. Nevertheless, accounting systems based on double-entry bookkeeping have always emerged as the preferred method for recording and reporting the economic events and transactions of an organization, regardless of the type of economic system employed. As many formerly socialist countries have moved to embrace capitalism, training in accounting and the development of reliable information for investors have emerged as high priorities.

■ THE ACCOUNTING CYCLE

accounting cycle
The multistage process by which accountants produce an entity's financial statements.

The **accounting cycle** is the multistage process by which accountants produce an entity's financial statements. Exhibit 5-1 shows the principal steps in the cycle.

As previous chapters have demonstrated, many transactions are journalized and posted to ledger accounts during the period of the cycle. At the end of the period, an *unadjusted* trial balance or a work sheet may be prepared to assist in the analysis of adjusting entries and corrections to the accounts. The adjusting entries are then journalized and posted, and an *adjusted* trial balance is prepared. Finally, the formal financial statements are prepared, and the books are closed for the period.

Objective 1

Explain the accounting cycle and analyze transactions, including those that relate to the adjustments of the preceding period.

A Practical Exercise in the Accounting Cycle

The financial statements of the Oxley Company, a retailer of nursery products for lawns and gardens, are used in this section and the following one to illustrate the principal steps in the accounting cycle. (Preparation of the optional work sheet is described in Appendix 5A.) Although many simplifying assumptions have been made, the Oxley Company illustration provides both a review of previous chapters and a sequential view of the accounting cycle in its entirety.

Exhibit 5-1

Steps in the Accounting Cycle

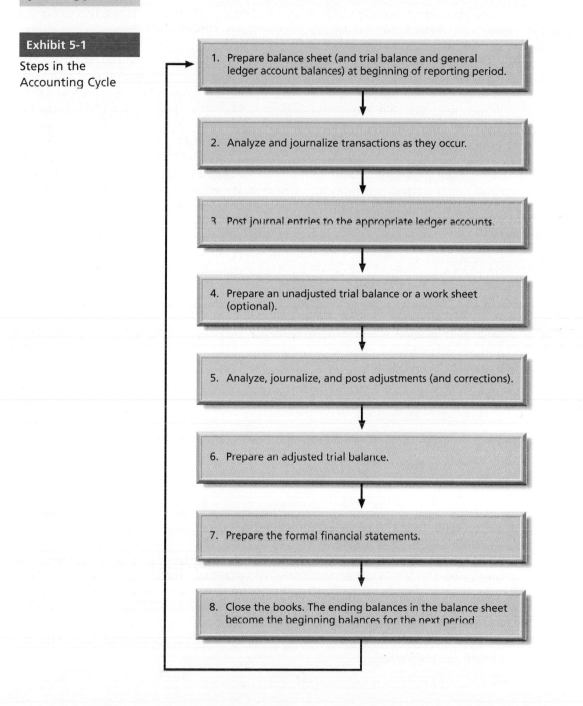

1. Prepare balance sheet (and trial balance and general ledger account balances) at beginning of reporting period.

2. Analyze and journalize transactions as they occur.

3. Post journal entries to the appropriate ledger accounts.

4. Prepare an unadjusted trial balance or a work sheet (optional).

5. Analyze, journalize, and post adjustments (and corrections).

6. Prepare an adjusted trial balance.

7. Prepare the formal financial statements.

8. Close the books. The ending balances in the balance sheet become the beginning balances for the next period.

comparative financial statements Statements that present data for two or more reporting periods.

Exhibits 5-2, 5-3, and 5-4 display Oxley Company's balance sheet, income statement, and statement of retained income, respectively. Oxley's accounting cycle is for a year, but it could occur monthly, quarterly, or for any other period as desired. The exhibits contain **comparative financial statements**, which present data for two or more reporting periods. Note that the most

Exhibit 5-2

**Oxley Company
Balance Sheet
(in thousands)**

		December 31		
Assets		**19X2**		**19X1**
Current assets:				
Cash		$150		$ 57
Accounts receivable		95		70
Accrued interest receivable		15		15
Inventory of merchandise		20		60
Prepaid rent		10		—
Total current assets		$290		$202
Long-term assets*				
Long-term note receivable		288		288
Equipment, at original cost	$200		$200	
Deduct: Accumulated amortization	120		80	
Equipment, net		80		120
Total assets		$658		$610
Liabilities and Shareholders' Equity				
Current liabilities:				
Accounts payable		$ 90		$ 65
Accrued wages payable		24		10
Accrued income taxes payable		16		12
Accrued interest payable		9		9
Unearned sales revenue		—		5
Note payable, current portion		80		—
Total current liabilities		$219		$101
Long-term note payable		40		120
Total liabilities		$259		$221
Shareholders' equity:				
Capital stock†		$102		$102
Retained earnings		297		287
Total shareholders' equity		$399		$389
Total liabilities and shareholders' equity		$658		$610

* This caption is frequently omitted. Instead the long-term note receivable, the equipment, and other categories are merely listed as separate items following the current assets.
† Details are often shown in a supplementary statement or in footnotes. In this case, there are 200,000 common shares outstanding: $.25 par per share, or 200,000 × $.25 = $50,000. Additional paid-in capital is $52,000, the total being the $102,000 shown here.

recent data are usually shown in the first column, as is the case with the Oxley Company data. In a series of years, the oldest data generally appear in the last column on the right. Publicly held corporations in the United States generally present comparative income statements for three periods and balance sheets for two periods.

Exhibit 5-3		For the Year Ended December 31, 19X2		For the Year Ended December 31, 19X1	
Oxley Company Statement of Income (in thousands except earnings per share)	Sales		$999		$800
	Cost of goods sold		399		336
	Gross profit (or gross margin)		$600		$464
	Operating expenses:				
	Wages	$214		$150	
	Rent	120		120	
	Miscellaneous	100		50	
	Amortization	40	474	40	360
	Operating income (or operating profit)		$126		$104
	Other revenue and expenses:				
	Interest revenue	$ 36		$ 36	
	Deduct: Interest expense	12	24	12	24
	Income before taxes		$150		$128
	Income tax expense		60		48
	Net income		$ 90		$ 80
	Earnings per common share*		$.45		$.40

* Dividends per share, $.40 and $.20, respectively. For publicly held companies, there is a requirement to show earnings per share on the face of the income statement, but it is not necessary to show dividends per share. Calculations of earnings per share: $90,000 ÷ 200,000 = $.45, and $80,000 ÷ 200,000 = $.40.

Consider the Oxley balance sheet for December 31, 19X1 as the start of our illustration of the accounting cycle. The following Oxley transactions, which are condensed here, occurred during 19X2 (amounts are in thousands):

a.   Acquired merchandise inventory on account, $359.
b.   Delivered merchandise to customers who had previously paid $5 in full in advance.
c.   Sales of merchandise (all on account and excluding transaction *b*) during 19X2 were $994.
d.   The cost of merchandise sold (including that in transaction *b*) during 19X2 was $399.
e.   Cash collected on account was $969.
f.   The note receivable was from a key industrial customer. The $288 principal is payable on August 1, 19X4. Interest of 12.5% per annum is collected each August 1 (to be computed).

Cash was disbursed as follows for

g.   Accounts payable, $334.

Exhibit 5-4

Oxley Company
Statement of
Retained Earnings
(in thousands)

	For the Year Ended December 31	
	19X2	19X1
Retained earnings, beginning of year	$287	$247
Add: Net income	90	80
Total	$377	$327
Deduct: Dividends declared	80	40
Retained earnings, end of year	$297	$287

h. Wages, $200, including the $10 accrued on December 31, 19X1.

i. Income taxes, $56, including the $12 accrued on December 31, 19X1.

j. Interest on note payable, including the $9 accrued on December 31, 19X1. Interest of 10% per annum on the $120 principal is paid each March 31 (to be computed).

k. Rent, $130 for 13 months, which was debited to Prepaid Rent.

l. Miscellaneous expenses, $100.

m. Dividends, $80. A separate account called Dividends Declared was created. For simplicity, assume that declaration and payment occurred on the same day.

No interim statements were prepared, so no adjusting entries were made until December 31, 19X2, when the following were recognized:

n. Accrual of interest receivable (to be computed, see item f).

o. The disbursements for rent included $10 paid on December 31, 19X2, pertaining to the month of January 19X3 (see item k).

p. Accrual of wages payable, $24.

q. Accrual of interest payable (to be computed, see item j).

r. Depreciation for 19X2, $40.

s. Two-thirds of the principal of the note payable is transferred to Note Payable, Current Portion, because two-thirds is due March 31, 19X3. The other third is payable on March 31, 19X5 (see item j).

t. Accrual of income taxes payable. The total income tax expense for 19X2 is 40% of the income before income taxes (to be computed).

Required

1. Prepare a general ledger in T-account form, entering the account balances as of December 31, 19X1. Provide space for additional accounts.

2. Analyze and journalize all transactions for 19X2, including the year-end adjustments.

3. Post the entries in requirement 2 to the T-accounts.

4. Prepare an adjusted trial balance as of December 31, 19X2. If it fails to balance, check to see that all items were posted to the correct sides of the accounts.

5. Prepare a multiple-step income statement for 19X2.

6. Prepare a statement of retained income for 19X2.

7. Prepare a comparative classified balance sheet for December 31, 19X1 and 19X2.

8. Prepare a statement of changes in financial position for 19X2.

9. Journalize and post the entries necessary to "close the books" for 19X2.

You are *urged* to try to solve requirements 1-4 on your own before examining the solution. The general ledger (requirements 1 and 3), illustrated in Exhibit 5-6, incorporates all of the 19X2 transactions including yearly transactions and adjusting entries. The general journal (requirement 2) is illustrated in

Exhibit 5-5. Note how the accounts are numbered. Posting and journalizing are keyed to facilitate cross-checking. The adjusted trial balance (requirement 4) is illustrated in Exhibit 5-7.

Requirements 5 through 7 were illustrated in Exhibits 5-2, 5-3, and 5-4. Requirements 8 and 9 are described later in this chapter, requirement 8 in the section on "Statement of Changes in Financial Position" and requirement 9 in the section entitled "Closing the Accounts."

Exhibit 5-5

Journal Entries

Date	Entry No.	Accounts and Explanation	Post Ref.	Debit	Credit
19X2				(in thousands of dollars)	
Dates are varied and are not entered in this illustration except for Dec. 31	a	Inventory of merchandise	130	359	
		Accounts payable	200		359
		Acquired inventory on account			
	b	Unearned sales revenue	237	5	
		Sales	320		5
		Delivery of merchandise to customers who had paid in advance			
	c	Accounts receivable	110	994	
		Sales	320		994
		Sales on account			
	d	Cost of goods sold	340	399	
		Inventory of merchandise	130		399
		To record the cost of inventory sold			
	e	Cash	100	969	
		Accounts receivable	110		969
		Collections from customers			
	f	Cash	100	36	
		Accrued interest receivable	111		15
		Interest revenue	330		21
		Collection of interest (12.5% of $288 = $36)			
	g	Accounts payable	200	334	
		Cash	100		334
		Payments to creditors			
	h	Accrued wages payable	210	10	
		Wages expense	350	190	
		Cash	100		200
		Payments of wages			
	i	Accrued income taxes payable	220	12	
		Income tax expense	395	44	
		Cash	100		56
		Payments of income taxes			
	j	Accrued interest payable	230	9	
		Interest expense	380	3	
		Cash	100		12
		Payment of interest (10% of $120)			
	k	Prepaid rent	140	130	
		Cash	100		130
		Disbursements for rent			

989
395.4

Exhibit 5-7

**Oxley Company
Adjusted Trial
Balance
December 31, 19X2
(in thousands)**

Cash	$ 150	
Accounts receivable	95	
Accrued interest receivable	15	
Inventory of merchandise	20	
Prepaid rent	10	
Long-term note receivable	288	
Equipment	200	
Accumulated amortization, equipment		$ 120
Accounts payable		90
Accrued wages payable		24
Accrued income taxes payable		16
Accrued interest payable		9
Note payable, current portion		80
Long-term note payable		40
Capital stock		102
Retained earnings, December 31, 19X1		287
Dividends declared	80	
Sales		999
Interest revenue		36
Cost of goods sold	399	
Wages expense	214	
Rent expense	120	
Miscellaneous expense	100	
Amortization expense	40	
Interest expense	12	
Income tax expense	60	
	$1,803	$1,803

Helpful hint: Entries for interest, wages, income taxes, and other accruals (for example, see *f, h, i,* and *j*) have a common theme: They relate to the adjustments of the preceding period. The explicit subsequent transaction involves a cash inflow or outflow. Part of each cash flow in this example relates to the accrual made at the end of 19X1. *Failure to remember the accruals may result in double-counting of expenses (or revenues).* A common error, for instance, would be to recognize the entire $12,000 disbursement for interest in entry *j* as an expense of 19X2, whereas $9,000 was already recognized as an expense in 19X1 and is properly charged in entry *j* to the liability account Accrued Interest Payable.

a. Transaction: Acquired merchandise inventory on account, $359.
Analysis: The asset **Inventory of Merchandise** is increased.
The liability **Accounts Payable** is increased.
Entry: In the journal (explanation omitted):

Inventory of merchandise	359	
Accounts payable		359

Post to the ledger (postings are indicated by the circled amounts):

Inventory of Merchandise				Accounts Payable	
Bal.	60		Bal.		65
(a)	(359)		(a)		(359)

b. Transaction: Delivered merchandise to customers who had previously paid $5.
Analysis: The liability **Unearned Sales Revenue** is decreased.
The shareholders' equity **Sales** is increased.
Entry: In the journal:

Unearned sales revenue	5	
Sales		5

Post to the ledger:

Unearned Sales Revenue				Sales	
(b)	(5)	Bal.	5	(b)	(5)

c. Transaction: Sales of merchandise on account, $994.
Analysis: The asset **Accounts Receivable** is increased.
The shareholders' equity **Sales** is increased.
Entry: In the journal:

Accounts receivable	994	
Sales		994

Post to the ledger:

Accounts Receivable				Sales	
Bal.	70			(b)	5
(c)	(994)			(c)	(994)

d. Transaction: The cost of merchandise sold, $399.
Analysis: The Asset **Inventory of Merchandise** is decreased.
The negative shareholders' equity **Cost of Goods Sold** is increased.
Recall that all expense accounts are reductions in shareholders' equity; thus expense accounts can be regarded as negative shareholders' equity.
Entry: In the journal:

Cost of goods sold	399	
Inventory of merchandise		399

Post to the ledger:

Inventory of Merchandise				Cost of Goods Sold		
Bal.	60	(d)	(399)	(d)	(399)	
(a)	359					

e. Transaction: Cash collected on account from customers, $969.

Analysis: The asset **Cash** is increased.

The asset **Accounts Receivable** is decreased.

Entry: In the journal:

Cash   969
   Accounts receivable   969

Post to the ledger:

Cash				Accounts Receivable		
Bal.	57			Bal.	70	(e) (969)
(e)	(969)			(c)	994	

f. Transaction: Collection of interest on August 1, 12.5% of $288 = $36.

Analysis: The asset **Cash** is increased.

The asset **Accrued Interest Receivable** is decreased.

The shareholders' equity **Interest Revenue** is increased.

Interest revenue earned is $36 \div 12 = \$3$ per month. Seven months $\times$ $3 = \$21$. The $15 decrease in Accrued Interest Receivable pertains to revenue earned during the preceding year.

Entry: In the journal:

Cash   36
   Accrued interest receivable   15
   Interest revenue   21

Post to the ledger:

Cash				Accrued Interest Receivable		
Bal.	57			Bal.	15	(f) (15)
(e)	969					
(f)	(36)					

				Interest Revenue		
					(f)	(21)

g. Transaction: Payments to trade creditors on account, $334.

Analysis: The asset **Cash** is decreased.

The liability **Accounts Payable** is decreased.

Entry: In the journal:

Accounts payable   334
   Cash   334

Post to the ledger:

Cash				Accounts Payable		
Bal.	57	(g)	(334)	(g) (334)	Bal.	65
(e)	969				(a)	359
(f)	36					

h. Transaction: Payments of wages, $200.

 Analysis: The asset **Cash** is decreased.

The liability **Accrued Wages Payable** is decreased. The negative share-holders' equity **Wages Expense** is increased. The Accrued Wages Payable was $10, as shown in the balance sheet in Exhibit 5-2.

 Entry: In the journal:

Accrued wages payable	10	
Wages expense	190	
Cash		200

Post to the ledger:

Cash					Accrued Wages Payable		
Bal.	57	(g)	334	(h)	(10)	Bal.	10
(e)	969	(h)	(200)				
(f)	36						

	Wages Expense	
(h)	(190)	

i. Transaction: Payments of income taxes, $56.

 Analysis: The asset **Cash** is decreased.
The liability **Accrued Income Taxes Payable** is decreased.
The negative shareholders' equity **Income Tax Expense** is increased. The payable was $12, as shown in the balance sheet in Exhibit 5-2.

 Entry: In the journal:

Accrued income taxes payable	12	
Income tax expense	44	
Cash		56

Post to the ledger:

Cash					Accrued Income Taxes Payable		
Bal.	57	(g)	334	(i)	(12)	Bal.	12
(e)	969	(h)	200				
(f)	36	(i)	(56)				

	Income Tax Expense	
(i)	(44)	

j. Transaction: Payment of interest on March 31, 10% of $120 = $12.

 Analysis: The asset **Cash** is decreased.
The liability **Accrued Interest Payable** is decreased. The negative shareholders' equity **Interest Expense** is increased. Interest expense is $12 ÷ 12 = $1 per month; three months × $1 = $3. The $9 decrease in Accrued Interest Payable pertains to interest expense during the preceding year.

 Entry: In the journal:

Accrued interest payable	9	
Interest expense	3	
Cash		12

Post to the ledger:

	Cash				Accrued Interest Payable		
Bal.	57	(g)	334	(j)	(9)	Bal.	9
(e)	969	(h)	200				
(f)	36	(i)	56				
		(j)	(12)				

	Interest Expense	
(j)	(3)	

k. Transaction: Payment of rent, $130.

Analysis: The asset **Cash** is decreased.

The asset **Prepaid Rent** is increased.

Entry: In the journal:

Prepaid rent	130	
Cash		130

Post to the ledger:

	Cash				Prepaid Rent	
Bal.	57	(g)	334	(k)	(130)	
(e)	969	(h)	200			
(f)	36	(i)	56			
		(j)	12			
		(k)	(130)			

l. Transaction: Payment of miscellaneous expenses, $100.

Analysis: The asset **Cash** is decreased.

The negative shareholders' equity **Miscellaneous Expenses** is increased.

Entry: In the journal:

Miscellaneous expenses	100	
Cash		100

Post to the ledger:

	Cash				Miscellaneous Expenses	
Bal.	57	(g)	334	(l)	(100)	
(e)	969	(h)	200			
(f)	36	(i)	56			
		(j)	12			
		(k)	130			
		(l)	(100)			

m. Transaction: Dividends declared and paid, $80.

Analysis: The asset **Cash** is decreased.

The negative shareholders' equity **Dividends Declared** (an offsetting account to Retained Earnings) is increased.

Entry: In the journal:

Dividends declared	80	
Cash		80

Post to the ledger:

Cash				Dividends Declared	
Bal.	57	(g)	334	(m)	⑧⓪
(e)	969	(h)	200		
(f)	36	(i)	56		
		(j)	12		
		(k)	130		
		(l)	100		
		(m)	⑧⓪		

n. Transaction: Accrual of interest receivable for 5 months × $3 = $15.
   Analysis: The asset **Accrued Interest Receivable** is increased.
   The shareholders' equity **Interest Revenue** is increased.
   Entry: In the journal:

Accrued interest receivable	15	
Interest revenue		15

Post to the ledger:

Accrued Interest Receivable				Interest Revenue	
Bal.	15	(f)	15	(f)	21
(n)	⑮			(n)	⑮

o. Transaction: Recognition of rent expense.
   Analysis: All prepaid rent has expired except for $10 for the month of January 19X3.
   The asset **Prepaid Rent** is decreased.
   The negative shareholders' equity **Rent Expense** is increased.
   Entry: In the journal:

Rent expense	120	
Prepaid rent		120

Post to the ledger:

Prepaid Rent				Rent Expense	
(k)	130	(o)	⑫⓪	(o)	⑫⓪

p. Transaction: Accrual of wages payable, $24.
   Analysis: The liability **Accrued Wages Payable** is increased.
   The negative shareholders' equity **Wages Expense** is increased.
   Entry: In the journal:

Wages expense	24	
Accrued wages payable		24

Post to the ledger:

Accrued Wages Payable				Wages Expense	
(h)	190	Bal.	10	(h)	190
		(p)	㉔	(p)	㉔

q. Transaction: Accrual of interest payable for 9 months × $1 = $9. (See transaction j.)
   Analysis: The liability **Accrued Interest Payable** is increased.
   The negative shareholders' equity **Interest Expense** is increased.
   Entry: In the journal:

Interest expense	9	
Accrued interest payable		9

Post to the ledger:

Accrued Interest Payable				Interest Expense	
(j)	9	Bal.	9	(j)	3
		(q)	⑨	(q)	⑨

r. Transaction: Amortization, $40.

     Analysis: The asset reduction account **Accumulated Amortization, Equipment** is increased.

                The negative shareholders' equity **Amortization Expense** is increased.

       Entry: In the journal:

Amortization expense	40	
Accumulated amortization, equipment		40

Post to the ledger:

Accumulated Amortization, Equipment			Amortization Expense	
	Bal.	80	(r)	㊵
	(r)	㊵		

s. Transaction: Reclassification of note payable ⅔ × $120 = $80.

     Analysis: The liability **Long-term Note Payable** is decreased.

                The liability **Note Payable, Current** portion is increased.

       Entry: In the journal:

Long-term note payable	80	
Note payable, current		80

Post to the ledger:

Long-term Note Payable				Note Payable, Current	
(s)	⑧⓪	Bal.	120	(s)	⑧⓪

t. Transaction: Income tax expense for the year. Income before taxes must be computed and then 40% thereof recognized as expense (.40 × $150 = $60). Moreover, the accrued liability must be accurate. Therefore, because $44 has already been paid for the current year and charged to expense (see transaction *i*), the amount remaining ($60 – $44 = $16) must be charged to expense.

     Analysis: The liability **Accrued Income Taxes Payable** is increased.

                The negative shareholders' equity **Income Tax Expense** is increased.

       Entry: In the journal:

Income tax expense	16	
Accrued income taxes payable		16

Post to the ledger:

Accrued Income Taxes Payable				Income Tax Expense	
(i)	12	Bal.	12	(i)	44
		(t)	⑯	(t)	⑯

A Note on Dividends Declared

A corporation must declare a dividend before paying it. The board of directors alone has the authority to declare a dividend. The corporation has no obligation to pay a dividend unless the board declares one; however, when declared, the dividend becomes a legal liability of the corporation.

The overall approach to accounting for cash dividends was explained in Chapter 2. As shown there, some companies reduce Retained Earnings directly when their board of directors declares dividends. However, as shown in transaction *m* in Exhibits 5-5 and 5-6, other companies prefer to use a separate "temporary" shareholders' equity account (Dividends Declared or simply Dividends) to compile the cumulative amounts of the dividends for a given year. Publicly held companies generally declare dividends quarterly. Internationally, many companies pay dividends twice a year.

Oxley's transaction *m* summarized the overall effect of $80,000 dividend payments throughout the year. In the real world, $20,000 would have been declared and paid quarterly. The declaration is usually made on one date, and the payment follows declaration by a few weeks. Oxley would have made the following entries for the first quarter, specific dates assumed:

February 10	Dividends declared..............................	20	
	Dividends payable.............................		20
	To record quarterly declaration of dividends.		
February 27	Dividends payable	20	
	Cash.......................................		20
	To record payment of dividends.		

Dividends Payable is a current liability. If a balance sheet is prepared between the date of declaration and the date of payment, Dividends Payable will be listed with the other current liabilities. For example, Magna International, the automotive parts manufacturer, declared $65.2 million in dividends in fiscal 1995.

Consider another example. The journal entry for a quarterly dividend recently declared by the H. J. Heinz Company would be:

Dividends declared	83,366,580	
Dividends payable		83,366,580
To record declaration of $.33 per share dividend on 252,626,000 shares.		

The Dividends Declared account will have a normal left-side balance. It represents a reduction in Retained Earnings and Shareholders' Equity.

Magna International
www.magnaint.com/Magna/

H.J. Heinz Company of Canada Ltd.
www.istar.ca/~hjheinz/

■ STATEMENT OF CHANGES IN FINANCIAL POSITION

Objective 2

Analyze cash transactions used in the statement of changes in financial position.

The emphasis so far in this chapter has been on the Oxley Company's balance sheet, income statement, and statement of retained income (Exhibits 5-2, 5-3, and 5-4) because they are prepared directly from the general ledger accounts. But we should not forget the other required financial statement, the *statement of changes in financial position*. It was described briefly in Chapter 2 and will be covered in more detail in Chapter 6.

The statement of changes in financial position provides details on the entries to the cash account. Oxley's transactions *e* through *m* affect cash, as shown in the Cash T-account in Exhibit 5-6. Therefore, these items are included in the statement of changes in financial position in Exhibit 5-8. Recall that the statement of changes in financial position classifies activities affecting cash into three categories: operating activities, investing activities, and financing activities. Eight of the nine items, all except payment of cash dividends, are operating activities. Payment of dividends is a financing activity because it provides a return to shareholders who supplied capital to the company. Oxley had no investment activities during 19X2. The items in Exhibit 5-8 explain why Oxley's cash increased by $93,000, from $57,000 to $150,000, during 19X2.

Exhibit 5-8		
Oxley Company Statement of Changes in Financial Position for the Year Ended December 31, 19X2 (in thousands)	CASH FLOWS FROM OPERATING ACTIVITIES	
	Cash collections from customers	$969
	Interest received	36
	Cash payments to suppliers	(334)
	Cash payments to employees	(200)
	Cash payments for income taxes	(56)
	Cash payments for interest	(12)
	Cash payments for rent	(130)
	Cash payments for miscellaneous expenses	(100)
	Net cash provided by operating activities	$173
	CASH FLOWS FROM INVESTING ACTIVITIES	
	None	
	CASH FLOWS FROM FINANCING ACTIVITIES	
	Cash dividends	$ (80)
	Net cash used by financing activities	$ (80)
	Net increase in cash	$ 93
	Cash balance, December 31, 19X1	57
	Cash balance, December 31, 19X2	$150

■ CLOSING THE ACCOUNTS

closing the books The final step taken in the accounting cycle to update retained earnings and facilitate the recording of the next year's transactions.

After preparing financial statements, accountants must get ledger accounts ready to record the next period's transactions. This process is called *closing the books*.

Transferring and Summarizing

closing entries Entries that transfer the revenues, expenses, and dividends declared balances from their respective accounts to the retained earnings account.

Closing the books is the final step taken in the accounting cycle to update retained earnings and facilitate the recording of the *next* year's transactions. This step is called *closing*, but *transferring and summarizing* or *clearing* are better labels. All balances in the "temporary" shareholders' equity accounts (revenue, expense, and dividends declared accounts) are summarized and transferred to a "permanent" shareholders' equity account, Retained Earnings. **Closing entries** transfer the revenues, expenses, and dividends declared balances from their respective accounts to the retained earnings account.

When the closing entries are completed, the revenue, expense, and dividends declared accounts have zero balances. Closing is a clerical procedure.

Objective 3

Prepare closing
entries for perti-
nent accounts.

It is devoid of any new accounting theory. Its main purpose is to set the revenue
and expense meters back to zero so that those accounts can be used afresh in the
new year. For instance, without the closing process the sales account of a business like Imperial Oil would continue to accumulate revenue, so that the balance
would be the sum of many years of sales rather than only one year of sales.

Exhibit 5-9 shows the closing (transferring) process for the Oxley Company.
How does the debit-credit process accomplish this summarizing and transferring?

Step 1. An Income Summary account, which has a life of one day (or an
instant), is typically created. As Exhibit 5-9 indicates, the Income Summary
account is a convenience. It facilitates an orderly sequence of events and helps auditors trace transactions through to their impact on the financial statements.
However, it is not absolutely necessary; many accountants prefer to accomplish the
entire closing process by a single (massive) compound entry to Retained Earnings.

Exhibit 5-9   General Effects of Closing the Accounts   (Data are from Exhibit 5-6, p. 181)

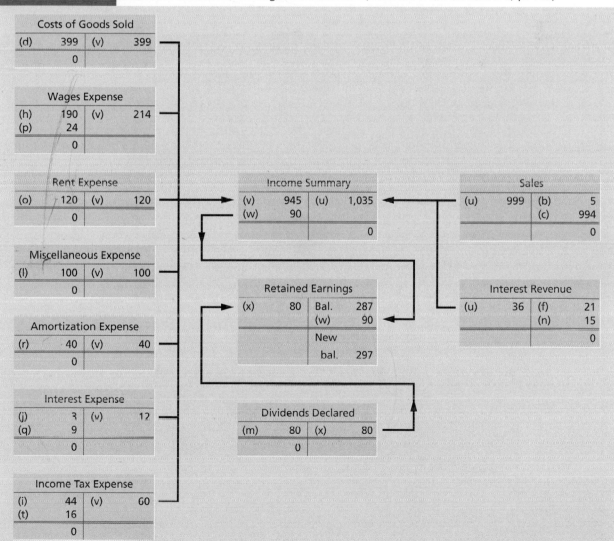

Step 2. The credit balances of the revenue accounts are debited to those accounts in entry *u* in Exhibit 5-9. The balances in Sales and Interest Revenues are now zero. They have been "closed." Their meters are back to zero, but their amounts have not vanished. Instead, the amounts now rest in aggregate form as a credit of $1,035 in Income Summary.

Step 3. The debit balances of the expense accounts are credited to each expense account, as shown in entry *v*. Their individual amounts also now reside in aggregate form as a debit of $945 in Income Summary.

Step 4. The net income is computed and transferred from Income Summary to its "permanent" home, Retained Earnings, as shown in entry *w*. Thereafter, the Income Summary account has a balance of zero.

Step 5. The Dividends Declared account is then closed directly to Retained Earnings, as shown in entry *x*. Note that the Income Summary account is not used for closing the Dividends account because dividends are *not* expenses and do *not* affect net income.

Chrysler Corp.
www.chrysler.com

How Long Does It Take to Close the Books?

If closing the books at the end of the fiscal year were merely a mechanical process, computers would have the job completed by the time the Rose Bowl started on January 1. However, because of the large amount of accounting judgment required, the process takes longer. Company accountants must decide what adjusting entries are necessary and also what estimates (about bad debts and amortization, for example) are appropriate. Then these judgments and estimates must be scrutinized by the independent auditors as part of their examination of the fairness of the financial statements.

After the year ends, the first piece of information provided to the public is typically a preliminary earnings announcement. Firms with shares listed on the major stock exchanges usually make a preliminary earnings announcement sometime in January or February. For middle- and large-sized firms, these announcements are published in the financial press. A selection of announcement dates for IBM and Chrysler are listed below:

	1993	1990	1980	1970
IBM	1/26/94	1/18/91	1/19/81	1/18/71
Chrysler	1/19/94	2/8/91	3/2/81	2/10/71

For most companies, the date of the preliminary earnings announcement is fairly constant year after year. In fact, market participants have come to expect earnings announcements for certain firms on certain dates. Late announcements are generally interpreted as bad news. It is no coincidence that Chrysler announced its 1980 earnings almost a month later than usual. Chrysler lost $1.71 billion in 1980. Since 1990 Chrysler has speeded up its closing of the books and is now reporting its earnings nearly three weeks earlier than it did before 1990.

Some time after the preliminary earnings announcement is made, the auditors finish their work and sign their audit opinion. IBM's independent audit report for 1993 is dated February 16, 1994, twenty-one days after its earnings announcement appeared in the *Wall Street Journal*. The final annual report is then compiled, printed, and mailed out to shareholders, analysts and the stock exchange. ■

Sources: Wall Street Journal Index, *1994, 1991, 1981, and 1971; A. E. Chambers and S. H. Penman, "Timeliness of Reporting and the Stock Price Reaction to Earnings Announcements,"* Journal of Accounting Research *(Spring 1984), pp. 21–47.*

At the end of Step 5, the Retained Earnings account has been brought up to date. The books (the journal and ledger) are now ready for a new year. Exhibit 5-9 presents zero balances for all temporary accounts. In essence, all revenue and expense meters have been set back to zero.

Detailed Analysis of Closing Transactions

Because the discussion of Exhibit 5-9 did not show formal journal entries recorded in the general journal, the following analysis gives the journal entries for the closing transactions:

u. Transaction: Clerical procedure of transferring the ending balances of revenue accounts to the Income Summary account.

Analysis: The shareholders' equity accounts **Sales** and **Interest Revenue** are decreased.
The shareholders' equity account **Income Summary** is increased.

Entry: In the journal:

Sales	999	
Interest revenue	36	
Income summary		1,035

To close the revenue accounts by transferring their ending balances to Income Summary.

Post to the ledger:

Sales					Income Summary		
(u)	(999)	(b)	5		(u)		(1,035)
		(c)	994				
			0				

Interest Revenue			
(u)	(36)	(f)	21
		(n)	15
			0

v. Transaction: Clerical procedure of transferring the ending balances of expense accounts to the Income Summary account.

Analysis: The negative shareholders' equity accounts **Cost of Goods Sold, Wages Expense**, etc., are decreased. The shareholders' equity account **Income Summary** is decreased.

Entry: In the journal:

Income summary	945	
Cost of goods sold		399
Wages expense		214
Rent expense		120
Miscellaneous expense		100
Amortization expense		40
Interest expense		12
Income tax expense		60

To close the expense accounts by transferring their ending balances to Income Summary.

Post to the ledger:

Cost of Goods Sold				Income Summary			
(d)	399	(v)	(399)	(v)	(945)	(u)	1,035
	0						

Rent Expense				Wages Expense			
(o)	120	(v)	(120)	(h)	190	(v)	(214)
				(p)	24		
	0				0		

Amortization Expense				Miscellaneous Expense			
(r)	40	(v)	(40)	(l)	100	(v)	(100)
	0				0		

Interest Expense				Income Tax Expense			
(j)	3	(v)	(12)	(i)	44	(v)	(60)
(q)	9			(t)	16		

w. Transaction: Clerical procedure of transferring the ending balance of Income Summary account to the Retained Income account.

Analysis: The shareholders' equity account **Income Summary** is decreased. The shareholders' equity account **Retained Earnings** is increased.

Entry: In the journal

Income summary	90	
Retained earnings		90

To close Income Summary by transferring
net income to Retained Earnings

Post to the ledger:

Income Summary				Retained Earnings			
(v)	945	(u)	1,035			Bal.	287
(w)	(90)					(w)	(90)
			0				

x. Transaction: Clerical procedure of transferring the ending balance of Dividends Declared to the Retained Earnings account.

Analysis: The negative shareholders' equity account **Dividends Declared** is decreased. The shareholders' equity account **Retained Earnings** is decreased

Entry: In the journal:

Retained Earnings	80	
Dividends declared		80

To close Dividends Declared by transferring
the ending balance to Retained Earnings.

Post to the ledger:

Dividends Declared				Retained Earnings			
(m)	80	(x)	(80)	(x)	(80)	Bal.	287
						(w)	90
	0					Bal.	297

Terminology of Types of Accounts

temporary accounts Accounts that are subjected to periodic closing, i.e., revenue, expense, and dividends declared accounts.

Accounts that are subjected to periodic closing are frequently called **temporary accounts**, as distinguished from *permanent accounts*. The temporary accounts are the revenues, expenses, and dividends declared. They are all really subparts of ownership equity. They are created to provide a detailed explanation for the changes in retained earnings from period to period. They are the ingredients of the income statement and the statement of retained earnings.

permanent accounts Balance sheet accounts.

In contrast, the **permanent accounts** are the balance sheet accounts. The word *permanent* may be misleading. After all, the balances of permanent accounts fluctuate. Moreover, some permanent accounts come and go. For example, unearned sales revenue appears on Oxley's balance sheet of December 31, 19X1, but not on December 31, 19X2.

Computers and the Accounting Cycle

Computer software can do all the steps in the accounting cycle except generate the numbers for initial journal entries and for many adjusting entries. Many computer systems produce paper output that looks much like the examples of journals and ledgers in this book. Computers eliminate the drudgery of posting, writing and rewriting, and adding and subtracting. Best of all, they make no mathematical errors and can be programmed to check for many other common errors.

Computer systems have made many time-honoured manual accounting methods obsolete. For example, the entire "closing the books" process, including the use of Income Summary accounts, was designed in large part to control clerical errors. But computers do not make such errors. Furthermore, an ordinary journal is unnecessary if a computer can indefinitely store the effects of accounting transactions in its memory and print an analysis of any transaction upon command.

■ AUDITING THE FINANCIAL STATEMENTS

Objective 4

Explain the role of auditors of financial statements.

It is management's responsibility to carry out the steps in the accounting cycle (see Exhibit 5-1, page 175) and produce formal financial statements. If the company's stock is traded in the capital markets, statements must then be published as part of the company's annual report and submitted to the appropriate provincial securities commission. Because managers have a personal stake in the results reported in financial statements, shareholders, creditors, government officials, and other external users often want assurance that the financial statements fairly present the company's financial results. Indeed, managers also want to assure the public that the statements are not misleading. Why? So that investors and creditors are willing to buy stock or lend the company money when it needs additional capital. Therefore, it is in everyone's interest to hire an **auditor**, who provides an independent examination of financial statements.

auditor An accountant who provides an independent examination of the financial statements.

In Canada, auditors are not government officials but professionals who are licensed to attest to the accuracy of financial statements. Most countries have an auditing profession and rules for evaluating financial disclosures by management. However, in the newly emerging countries of the former USSR the independent auditing profession is less established. Why? Because under the Communist system there was no external ownership that required assurance as to the reliability of financial reports.

What does the auditor do? Certainly an auditor cannot check every transaction recorded in the accounting system; the costs would surely exceed the benefits. But by systematically checking a sample of transactions and by studying the system that records and stores transaction data and prepares statements from the data, the auditor forms an opinion about whether the financial statements "present fairly" the financial position and results of the period. In the United Kingdom, the auditors use the words "give a true and fair view" instead of "present fairly," but the effect is the same. The opinion, an example of which is in Chapter 1, is published with the financial statements.

Because auditors examine only a sample of transactions, they cannot provide 100% assurance that financial statements are accurate. Furthermore, although auditors technically are hired by the board of directors, they work closely with management and might be unduly influenced by management's position. To guard against this, auditors must meet high technical and ethical standards. Auditors are valuable only if the public has a high regard for their competence and integrity, so they are careful to protect their reputations. To assure the public that an audit is thorough, auditors follow standard audit procedures developed by the Canadian Institute of Chartered Accountants (CICA) and others, and they make sure the statements conform to GAAP as determined primarily by the CICA.

Auditing is a costly but valuable service. An audit might cost a small nonprofit organization only a few hundred dollars, but major corporations pay millions of dollars. For example, the annual audit fee for huge companies like Ford and General Motors can exceed $4 million. But without the assurance provided by auditors, widespread trading in the stock of companies would be severely curtailed.

Summary Problems for Your Review

Problem One

Review the transactions for the Oxley Company during 19X2. Suppose wages expense accrued but unpaid at the end of 19X2 were $34 instead of $24. What numbers would be changed on the income statement for 19X2 and on the balance sheet, December 31, 19X2? What would be the new numbers? The financial statements are on pages 176-178.

Solution to Problem One

Income Statement Items	For the Year Ended December 31, 19X2	
	As in Exhibit 5-3	Revised
Wages expense	$214	$224
Total operating expenses	474	484
Operating income	126	116
Income before income taxes	150	140
Income tax expense (at 40%)	60	56
Net income	90	84

| | December 31, 19X2 | |
Balance Sheet Accounts	As in Exhibit 5-2	Revised
Accrued wages payable	$ 24	$ 34
Accrued income taxes payable	16	12
Retained earnings	297	291

Note the effects on the year-end balance sheet. Retained earnings would be decreased by $6, and total liabilities would be increased by a net of $6. Accrued wages payable increase by $10, but accrued income taxes payable decrease by $4 (40% of the $10 decrease in income before taxes).

Problem Two

Coca-Cola Company
www.cocacola.com/

The balance sheet of Coca-Cola Bottling Co. showed Accrued Interest of $11,042,000 under current liabilities at the beginning of a recent year. Interest payments of $31,928,000 were disbursed during the year. Prepare the journal entry that summarizes those disbursements.

Solution to Problem Two

Accrued interest	11,042,000	
Interest expense	20,886,000	
Cash		31,928,000

To record disbursements for interest; interest expense is $31,928,000 less $11,042,000, or $20,886,000.

The nomenclature used here illustrates why beginners in accounting should be alert to how the account description is used by a particular entity. That is, the term *Accrued Interest* is basically unclear. Does it mean *receivable* or *payable*? The answer is obvious in the annual report of Coca-Cola because the account is classified as a current liability. But some other company may use the same term, *Accrued Interest*, to describe a receivable. Hence, for clarity this textbook generally uses *accrued interest receivable* or *accrued interest payable* rather than *accrued interest* alone.

Highlights to Remember

The accounting cycle refers to the recording process that leads from the initial recording of transactions to the ending financial statements. In addition to recording explicit transactions as they occur, the accounting cycle includes making adjustments for implicit transactions. It is especially important to recognize how adjustments for implicit transactions in the preceding period affect the proper accounting in the current period for related explicit transactions. For example, if wages are accrued at the end of the prior period, the first payroll of the current period will eliminate that payable.

Moving to a new accounting period is aided by closing the books, which is a clerical procedure that transfers balances for revenues and expenses into retained income and gets the books ready for the start of a new accounting cycle.

Although closing the books and preparing financial statements complete the accounting cycle, auditors often examine the statements before they are released to the public. An audit adds credibility to the statements.

Appendix 5A: The Work Sheet

Purpose of Work Sheet

work sheet (working paper) A columnar approach to moving from a trial balance to the finished financial statements.

The body of this chapter described the rudiments of the accounting cycle. This appendix explores the cycle in more detail by explaining a favourite tool of the accountant. The **work sheet** (also called a **working paper**) is a columnar approach to moving from a trial balance to the finished financial statements. It provides an orderly means for (1) preparing adjusting entries, (2) computing net income, (3) preparing the formal financial statements, and (4) closing the books.

Although a work sheet is not essential to obtaining financial statements, it is a valuable informal device for bringing everything together in a single place, especially when there are numerous accounts and year-end adjustments. It helps assure the accountant that potential errors and overlooked adjustments will be discovered.

For learning purposes, the work sheet is usually prepared with a pencil. However, as already mentioned, accountants typically use electronic spreadsheets for work sheets, as discussed at the end of this appendix.

Steps in Preparation

Objective 5

Use a work sheet to prepare adjustments, financial statements, and closing entries.

Because the work sheet is an informal tool, there is no unique way of preparing it. However, a typical work sheet is illustrated in Exhibit 5-10. A step-by-step description of its preparation follows.

1. The accountant initially prepares an "unadjusted" trial balance as the first pair of columns in the work sheet. Then adjusting entries are listed in the second pair of columns. This provides a systematic and convenient way of reviewing the unadjusted trial balance together with the adjustments to make sure that nothing is overlooked.

The numbers in the first pair of columns come from the balances in the general ledger in Exhibit 5-6 *after* the last entry for the period's explicit transactions (entry *m*) but *before* the first entry for the end-of-period adjustments (entry *n*). This preparation of the unadjusted trial balance provides a check on the general accuracy of the ledger *before* adjustments are entered. Thus it provides an early chance to catch errors. As students and practicing accountants will testify, frequent use of self-checks as detailed work proceeds inevitably saves time. Few accounting tasks are more maddening than trying to trace an error discovered at a final stage back through a maze of interrelated journal entries and ledgers.

Concentrate on the first pair of columns, the Unadjusted Trial Balance. Many accounts are listed in their appropriate locations even though they have zero balances (for example, Accrued Wages Payable). Why? Because through experience the accountant knows that such accounts are almost always affected by the adjustment process. Listing all the accounts can help avoid overlooking required adjustments. However, inasmuch as the work sheet is an informal document, some accountants prefer first to list only the accounts with balances and later to list the additional accounts (below the $1,699 total in this illustration) when adjustments are made.

2. The second pair of columns is used for preparing the adjusting entries *n* through *t*. These columns are also totalled as a check on accuracy.

3. After the adjustments have been made, the third pair of columns represents the net effects of the first pair plus the second pair. That is, the unadjusted trial balance plus the adjustments equals the adjusted trial balance. Note how check after check is built into the work sheet.

4. The fourth pair of columns provides an income statement; the fifth pair, a statement of retained income; the sixth pair, a balance sheet. By tracing the numbers in those columns to the formal statements in Exhibits 5-2, 5-3, and 5-4 (pp. 176-178), you can readily see how a work sheet aids the preparation of the formal statements.

The Income Statement columns are sometimes used to compute income before taxes and the income tax expense for the year. That is why income tax expense appears below the subtotals. The net income amount is then transferred to the fifth pair of columns for the statement of retained income. Again, as in every pair, the columns are totalled to check accuracy.

The Income Statement and the Retained Earnings columns often guide the preparation of closing entries. Note how the Income Statement columns contain all the details necessary for the closing process; indeed, you can visualize the pair as a detailed Income Summary T-account used for closing. Similarly, the Retained Earnings columns can be visualized as the Retained Earnings T-account.

The final step is to move the ending balance of Retained Earnings from the fifth pair of columns to the sixth pair, the Balance Sheet columns.

The detailed sequence for the fourth, fifth, and sixth pairs of columns follows:

a.   Add each of the two Income Statement columns and calculate the difference, as follows:

Credit column total (revenues)	$1,035
Debit column total (expenses)	885
Income before income taxes	$ 150

b.   Compute the income tax expense, which is .40 × $150 = $60. Extend the $60 on the Income Tax Expense line as a debit in the Income Statement columns. Net income amounts to $150 − $60 = $90.

c.   Add "net income" to the list of account titles. Place the $90 amount in the Income Statement debit column and in the Statement of Retained Earnings credit column. Note that this is akin to the closing journal entry that transfers net income from Income Summary to Retained Income.

d.   Add each of the two Income Statement columns to see that the totals are equal.

e.   Add the two Statement of Retained Earnings columns and calculate the difference, as follows:

Credit column total (beginning balance of retained earnings plus net income for the period)	$377
Debit column total (dividends declared)	80
Retained earnings balance, December 31, 19X2	$297

Exhibit 5-10   Oxley Company Work Sheet for the Year Ended December 31, 19X2

Accounts Titles (in thousands of dollars)	Unadjusted Trial Balance Debit	Credit	Adjustments Debit	Credit	Adjusted Trial Balance Debit	Credit	Income Statement Debit	Credit	Statement of Retained Earnings Debit	Credit	Balance Sheet Debit	Credit
Cash	150				150						150	
Accounts receivable	95				95						95	
Accrued interest receivable			(n) 15		15						15	
Inventory of merchandise	20				20						20	
Prepaid rent	130			(o) 120	10						10	
Long-term note receivable	288				288						288	
Equipment	200				200						200	
Accumulated amortization, equipment		80		(r) 40		120						120
Accounts payable		90				90						90
Accrued wages payable				(p) 24		24						24
Accrued income taxes payable				(t) 16		16						16
Accrued interest payable				(q) 9		9						9
Note payable–current portion				(s) 80		80						80
Long-term note payable		120	(s) 80			40						40
Paid-in capital		102				102						102
Retained earnings, December 31, 19X1		287				287				287		
Dividends declared	80				80				80			
Sales		999				999		999				
Interest revenue		21		(n) 15		36		36				
Cost of goods sold	399				399		399					
Wages expense	190		(p) 24		214		214					
Rent expense			(o) 120		120		120					
Miscellaneous expense	100				100		100					
Amortization expense			(r) 40		40		40					
Interest expense	3		(q) 9		12		12					
							885	1035				
Income tax expense	44		(t) 16		60		60					
	1699	1699	304	304	1803	1803						
Net income							90			90		
							1035	1035		377		
Retained earnings, December 31, 19X2									297			297
									377	377	778	778

(n) Accrual of interest receivable, $15   (o) Rent expense, $120   (p) Accrual of wages, $24   (q) Accrual of interest payable, $9   (r) Amortization expense, $40
(s) Reclassification of note, $80   (t) Income tax expense, .40 x $150 income before income taxes = $60. Adjustment for accrued portion is $16.

f. Add "retained earnings, December 31, 19X2," to the list of account titles. Place the $297 amount in the Statement of Retained Earnings, debit column and in the Balance Sheet credit column.

g. Add each of the two Statement of Retained Earnings columns to see that the totals are equal.

h. Add each of the two Balance Sheet columns to see that the totals are equal. When they are equal, the accountant is ready to prepare the formal statements. When they are not equal, the accountant seldom smiles. He or she faces the labour of rechecking the preceding steps in reverse order to find the errors.

Flexibility of Uses

Ponder the work sheet in its entirety. It is a clever means of summarizing masses of interrelated data. Accountants often use the work sheet to prepare monthly and quarterly financial statements. Adjustments may be necessary for preparing these interim statements, but the accountant may not wish to enter adjustments formally in the journal and ledger each month. For example, suppose the work sheet in Exhibit 5-10 were for January 19X2. Adjustments entered on the work sheet as shown would not be made in the journals and ledgers. Formal interim financial statements can be prepared without the books being cluttered by the elaborate adjusting and closing entries each month.

Electronic Spreadsheet

Exhibit 5-11 shows the work sheet from Exhibit 5-10 as it would be prepared using an electronic spreadsheet. An Excel spreadsheet was used, but the format would be basically the same with Lotus 1-2-3, QuatroPro, or any other spreadsheet. Note that the spreadsheet contains columns that are labelled with letters and rows that are labelled with numbers. After the spreadsheet is set up, the accountant must simply enter in the cells the first four columns of numbers, and the computer will prepare the rest. The general procedure for using the spreadsheet follows:

1. List the accounts.

2. Enter the trial balance amount of each account as shown in the columns *B* and *C* of Exhibit 5-11.

3. Enter the adjustment amounts in columns *E* and *G*; if desired, you can key the entries to the corresponding journal entries by entering the appropriate letter in column *D* or *F*, as was done in the example.

4. Program the spreadsheet to calculate the adjusted trial balance amounts and place them in columns *H* and *I*. For example, the adjusted trial balance amount for prepaid rent is in cell *I19* and is calculated as follows:

$$H9 = B9 + E9 - G9$$

For a credit-balance account, consider the long-term note payable, cell I18:

$$I18 = C18 - E18 + G18$$

5. Program the spreadsheet to place the amount from the adjusted trial balance into the correct financial statement column. Rows 5 through 19 are placed in the appropriate (debit or credit) column of the balance sheet, rows 20 and 21 in the statement of retained earnings, and rows 22 through 29 and 31 in the income statement.

6. Program the spreadsheet to compute column totals. Be sure that the total debits equal the total credits in each pair of columns. (Note that subtotals are computed in columns *J*, *K*, *L*, and *M*. Such subtotals are handy but are not necessary.)

Major advantages of the electronic spreadsheet include the following:

1. The format is stored and can be used repeatedly. This avoids laborious writing of column heads and account titles.

2. Revisions of the basic format are easy.

3. Mathematical computations and placements of each account are achieved via computer. Speed and accuracy are maximized. Drudgery is minimized.

4. "What if" analysis is easily conducted. For example, suppose a manager wants to know the effects of various contemplated expense or revenue transactions on the income statement and balance sheet. Electronic spreadsheets can answer such questions instantly.

Appendix 5B: Variety in Data Processing and in Journalizing

This appendix stresses that there are many appropriate data-processing paths to the same objectives. The focus should be on the final product, not on whether one path is theoretically better than other paths. For example, should we use manual or computer methods? Should we use one pattern of journal entries or another? The answers to the questions of data-processing alternatives are inherently tied to the *overall* costs and benefits of the possible competing systems in a *specific* organization. What is good for Alcan Aluminium Limited is probably not good for Sophia's Pizza House, and vice versa.

Variety in Recording Assets

Objective 6

Prepare adjustments when alternative recording methods are used for the related originating transactions.

Oxley Company's entries for rent (see entries *k* and *o* reproduced below from our chapter illustration) exemplify how accountants might adopt different patterns for journalizing:

Entry	As in Chapter: All Asset Now; Recognize Expense Later		Alternative: All Expense Now; Recognize Asset Later	
k. Cash payment	Prepaid rent 130 Cash	130	Rent expense 130 Cash	130
o. End-of-period adjustment	Rent expense 120 Prepaid rent	120	Prepaid rent 10 Rent expense	10

Is one choice better than another? Both produce the same final account balances. However, from a strict theory point of view, the method used in the chapter is superior because of its straightforward recognition that all acquisitions of goods and services are assets that expire and become expenses later. Under this method, entry *k* regards all acquisitions as assets, and entry *o* writes off the prepayments that have expired. Good theory often also makes good

Exhibit 5-11 Oxley Company Work Sheet for the Year Ended December 31, 19X2

Account titles	Unadjusted Trial Balance Debit	Unadjusted Trial Balance Credit	Adjustments Debit	Adjustments Credit	Adjusted Trial Balance Debit	Adjusted Trial Balance Credit	Income Statement Debit	Income Statement Credit	Statement of Retained Earnings Debit	Statement of Retained Earnings Credit	Balance Sheet Debit	Balance Sheet Credit
(in thousands of dollars)												
Cash	150				150						150	
Accounts receivable	95				95						95	
Accrued interest receivable			(n) 15		15						15	
Inventory of merchandise	20				20						20	
Prepaid rent	130			(o) 120	10						10	
Long-term note receivable	288				288						288	
Equipment	200				200						200	
Accumulated amortization, equipment		80		(r) 40		120						120
Accounts payable		90				90						90
Accrued wages payable				(p) 24		24						24
Accrued income taxes payable				(t) 16		16						16
Accrued interest payable				(q) 9		9						9
Note payable–current portion				(s) 80		80						80
Long-term note payable		120	(s) 80			40						40
Paid-in capital		102				102						102
Retained earnings, December 31, 19X1		287				287				287		
Dividend declared	80				80				80			
Sales		999				999		999				
Interest revenue		21		(n) 15		36		36				
Cost of goods sold	399				399		399					
Wages expense	190		(p) 24		214		214					
Rent expense			(o) 120		120		120					
Miscellaneous expense	100				100		100					
Amortization expense			(r) 40		40		40					
Interest expense	3		(q) 9		12		12					
							885	1035				
Income tax expense	44		(t) 16		60		60					
	1699	1699	304	304	1803	1803						
Net income							90			90		
							1035	1035		377		
Retained earnings, December 31, 19X2									297			297
									377	377	778	778

practice. For example, it is often easier to review asset accounts to determine what should be expensed than it is to review expense accounts to determine what should not have been expensed.

The alternative is to record as expenses such items as rent (or insurance premiums or office supplies) when cash is disbursed (or when a liability such as accounts payable is created) upon their acquisition, as entry *k* illustrates. Adjustments such as entry *o* are made at the end of the reporting period to reduce the expenses that would otherwise be overstated and to increase the assets for the unused part of the prepayments. This alternative is frequently encountered in practice.

Either alternative is acceptable. The accountant should choose the easier one. By far the most important point is that any of the alternatives, properly applied, will lead to the same answers—the correct expense and the correct ending asset balance.

Variety in Recording Liabilities

As in the recording of assets, alternative recordings of liabilities are acceptable, provided that they ultimately result in the proper ending balances for the expense and liability accounts. Consider the entries for income taxes:

Entry	As in Chapter: Pay Old Liability and Recognize Expense; Recognize More Expense Later			Alternative: Recognize Expense Now; Adjust to Get Correct Balances Later	
i. Cash payment	Accrued income taxes payable	12		Income tax expense	56	
	Income tax expense	44		Cash		56
	Cash		56			
t. End-of-period adjustment	Income tax expense	16		Income tax expense	4	
	Accrued income taxes payable		16	Accrued income taxes payable		4

The chapter entries *i* and *t* followed the most theoretically defensible position. Entry *i* recognized that $12 of the $56 disbursement pertained to the liability carried over from the preceding period. Entry *t* recognized that the year-end liability arising from the current period was $16.

In the alternative, all disbursements are initially recorded as expenses. The Canadian government does not want to wait until after the end of the year to get its income taxes. Interim payments of estimated income taxes must be made and are frequently debited to income tax expense before the exact amount of the annual income tax expense is computed. At year-end (entry *t*), the income tax of $60 is computed, and the additional expense of $60 – $56 = $4 is charged. The accrued income taxes payable becomes the bèginning balance of $12 plus the addition of $4, or $16 in total.

Temporarily Incorrect Balances

The major lesson of this appendix deserves emphasis. For sensible reasons governing day-to-day recording procedures, accountants may routinely debit expense for the *full amount* when cash changes hands. This may result in temporarily incorrect balances in a number of accounts throughout a reporting period. However, the accountant is aware that such a condition is commonplace. Adjustments become necessary to achieve the correct balances for the reporting period.

The justification for such "full amount" approaches centres on costs and benefits. On a day-to-day basis, an accountant or a clerk or a computer does not have to be concerned with remembering whether routine cash flows really affect past accruals. Instead, all receipts or disbursements are handled in *identical fashion* throughout the year. To the extent that such routines (used by, say, a computer or a lower-level clerk) cause temporary errors in accruals, the year-end adjustments (prepared by, say, a higher-level accountant) produce the necessary corrections.

Reversing Entries

reversing entries
Entries that switch back all debits and credits made in a related preceding adjusting entry.

Reversing entries are sometimes used to cope with the proper accounting for accruals. As the name implies, **reversing entries** switch back all debits and credits made in a related preceding adjusting entry. To illustrate their effect, compare the pattern of journal entries illustrated in the chapter with the pattern of reversing entries that would be employed, as shown in Exhibit 5-12. The adjustments (and the closing entries, not shown) would be identical whether reversing entries are used or not. The differences occur only for the routine journalizing during the following year, 19X3, as Exhibit 5-12 demonstrates.

Some accountants favour using reversing entries because they or their clerks or their computers do not have to be concerned with whether a later routine cash disbursement (or receipt) applies to any accrued liabilities (or assets) that were recognized at the end of the preceding period. So reversing entries are creatures of practical data processing, especially in manual systems. They have no theoretical merit, and, with the widespread use of computers, their use is diminishing.

Appendix 5C: Processing Data Using Special Journals

Objective 7

Use special journals to process transactions.

Elsewhere in this textbook, the only book of original entry is a general journal. This appendix describes the use of special journals in addition to a general journal. This material is important to anyone who wants to know the details about how an accounting system processes data.

special journals
Journals used to record particular types of voluminous transactions; examples are the sales journal and the cash receipts journal.

Chapters 4 and 5 use the general journal as the basic step in data processing. However, in all but the smallest accounting systems, *special journals* (or procedures akin to special journals) are used in addition to the general journal. **Special journals** are used to record particular types of recurring voluminous transactions. We will discuss two special journals, the sales journal and the cash receipts journal. These two special journals illustrate how special journals aid data processing. In practice you will find many other special journals including a purchases journal, cash disbursements journal, sales returns and allowances journal, and purchase returns and allowances journal.

Exhibit 5-12

	Without Reversing Entries: the Pattern Illustrated in Chapter	With Reversing Entries

Adjustment December 31, 19X2 **Entry *p* from the chapter example.**	Wages expense 24
	   Accrued wages payable 24
		Wages expense 24
		   Accrued wages payable 24

Books closed for 19X2 (Entries would be identical and therefore are not shown here. The key point is that, under either approach, closing the books brings the balance in Wages Expense to zero at the start of 19X3.)

| **Reversal** January 2, 19X3. | None | Accrued wages payable 24
   Wages expense 24 |
| **Disbursements during 19X3** (assumed a total of 210). | Accrued wages payable 24
Wages expense 186
   Cash 210 | Wages expense 210
   Cash 210 |

Postings during 19X3

Without Reversing Entries:

Accrued Wages Payable		Wages Expense
24	Bal. 24	186

With Reversing Entries:

Accrued Wages Payable		Wages Expense
24	Bal. 24	210	24

Every accounting system has a general journal, whether kept in pen and ink or on computer tape or disk. But a general journal is not an efficient device for recording numerous repetitive transactions. How would you enjoy using a general journal to debit Accounts Receivable and credit Sales for each credit sale made in a Wal-Mart store on a busy Saturday? Moreover, how would you like to post each journal entry to the general ledger accounts for accounts receivable and sales? Not only would the work be long, tedious, and dull, but it would be outrageously expensive.

As we will see, all entries in each specialized journal have common features. Combining multiple similar transactions allows us to post only the totals and provides speed, efficiency, and economy of data processing.

Sales Journal

The sales journal in Exhibit 5-13 is probably better called a *credit sales journal* because it includes only credit sales, cash sales being recorded in the cash receipts journal. If a general journal were used for these five credit sales transactions, five separate entries debiting Accounts Receivable and crediting Sales would be required. In addition, five separate postings would be made to these accounts in the general ledger. Obviously, if five thousand sales occurred in June, journalizing and posting each individual transaction would become oppressive.

Consider the details in Exhibit 5-13. As each sale is entered, the accountant debits the *subsidiary* ledger account for the particular customer. The invoice reference provides a trail to any underlying details of the sale. A check mark is put in the Post column as each amount is posted to the individual subsidiary accounts.

The general ledger accounts, Accounts Receivable and Sales, are not written out as entries are being made in the sales journal. The dollar amount is entered once, not twice, for each sale. Column totals are posted to the general ledger periodically, usually at the end of the month. Posting the $6,400 total directly to the two accounts eliminates the need for a journal entry, but it has the same effect as if the following general journal entry were made:

	POST	AMOUNTS	
Accounts receivable........	4	6,400	
Sales..............	88		6,400

Of course, the direct posting from the sales journal eliminates having the above general journal entry.

The sum of the balances in the subsidiary ledger must agree with the Accounts Receivable account in the general ledger. When there is a subsidiary ledger, its corresponding summary account in the general ledger is often called a control account. The existence of a subsidiary ledger for a particular general ledger account is often denoted by adding the word *control* to the latter's title—for example, Accounts Receivable Control.

Cash Receipts Journal

Special journals may have a single money column, as in the sales journal just illustrated, or they may have several columns, as Exhibit 5-14 demonstrates. The number of columns depends on the frequency of transactions affecting

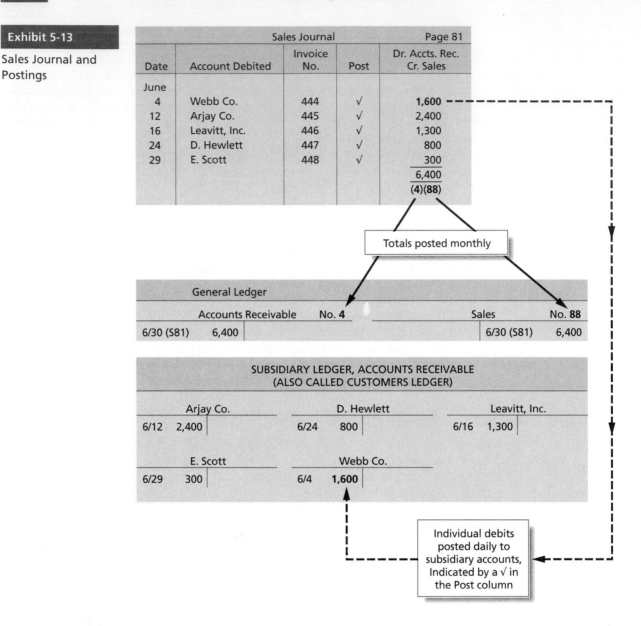

Exhibit 5-13

Sales Journal and Postings

particular accounts. Moreover, as the cash receipts journal in Exhibit 5-14 shows, the most frequently affected columns might be placed at the far right—regardless of whether the amounts therein are debits or credits. The important point about debits and credits is that they are ultimately entered on the correct sides of the *ledger* accounts, even though the format of some special *journals* places debit columns on the right-hand side of the page.

Cash sales and collections on accounts receivable are the two most common types of cash receipts, so special columns are formed for Cash, Sales, and Accounts Receivable. The amounts of the cash sales are entered in the Cash and Sales columns. The amounts of the collections on accounts are entered in the

Exhibit 5-14   Cash Receipts Journal and Postings

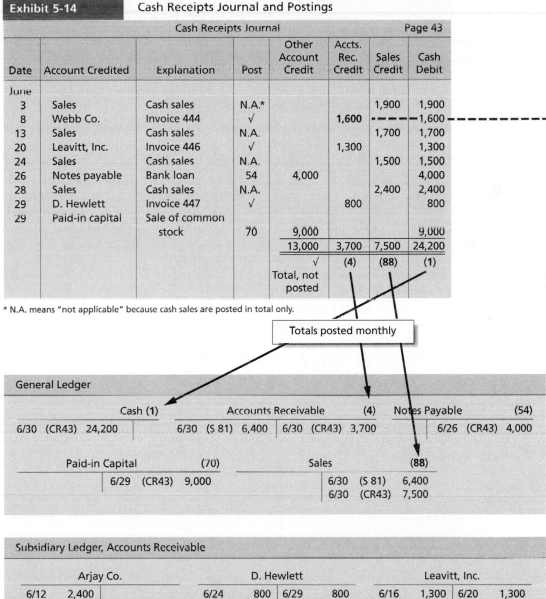

	Cash Receipts Journal						Page 43
Date	Account Credited	Explanation	Post	Other Account Credit	Accts. Rec. Credit	Sales Credit	Cash Debit
June							
3	Sales	Cash sales	N.A.*			1,900	1,900
8	Webb Co.	Invoice 444	√		1,600		1,600
13	Sales	Cash sales	N.A.			1,700	1,700
20	Leavitt, Inc.	Invoice 446	√		1,300		1,300
24	Sales	Cash sales	N.A.			1,500	1,500
26	Notes payable	Bank loan	54	4,000			4,000
28	Sales	Cash sales	N.A.			2,400	2,400
29	D. Hewlett	Invoice 447	√		800		800
29	Paid-in capital	Sale of common stock	70	9,000			9,000
				13,000	3,700	7,500	24,200
				√ Total, not posted	(4)	(88)	(1)

* N.A. means "not applicable" because cash sales are posted in total only.

Totals posted monthly

General Ledger

Cash (1)			Accounts Receivable	(4)	Notes Payable		(54)
6/30 (CR43) 24,200		6/30 (S 81) 6,400	6/30 (CR43) 3,700			6/26 (CR43) 4,000	

Paid-in Capital	(70)	Sales		(88)
	6/29 (CR43) 9,000		6/30 (S 81) 6,400	
			6/30 (CR43) 7,500	

Subsidiary Ledger, Accounts Receivable

Arjay Co.		D. Hewlett			Leavitt, Inc.		
6/12 2,400		6/24 800	6/29 800		6/16 1,300	6/20 1,300	

E. Scott		Webb Co.		
6/29 300		6/4 1,600	6/8 **1,600**	

Individual credits posted daily to subsidiary accounts, indicated by a √ in the Post column

Cash and Accounts Receivable columns. This specialized approach replaces the need for countless repetitions of the following familiar entries that would otherwise have to be made in the general journal:

```
Cash ....................................    xx
      Sales .........................         xx

Cash ...................................    xx
      Accounts receivable ..............        xx
```

Infrequent cash receipts, such as those illustrated for the bank loan and the sale of common stock, are entered in the Cash and the Other Accounts columns.

The columns are totalled (accountants say *footed*) at the end of each month to make sure that the total debits equal the total credits: 13,000 + 3,700 + 7,500 = 24,200. Then the totals of each column are posted to the indicated accounts in the general ledger. Of course, the Other Accounts total is not posted. Instead, the individual amounts therein are posted to the relevant individual general ledger accounts. The account numbers (54 and 70) are placed in the Post column as evidence that the postings have been made. The illustrated general ledger accounts now contain postings from the cash receipts journal and those made previously from the sales journal.

The only subsidiary ledger in this illustration is for Accounts Receivable. The postings from the cash receipts journal are made in the same manner as those from the sales journal. A principal internal control feature is illustrated by the monthly schedule of the individual customer balances. The sum should agree with the general ledger balance, June 30:

Arjay Co.	$2,400
E. Scott	300
Balance, subsidiary ledger	$2,700
Balance, Accounts Receivable in general ledger	$2,700

Assignment Material

QUESTIONS

5-1. How many years are usually covered by the comparative income statements and balance sheets of publicly held corporations?

5-2. "It's a several-stage process by which accountants produce an entity's financial statements for a specific period of time." What is the term that describes the process?

5-3. What is the purpose of a Dividends Declared account?

5-4. "A corporation has no obligation to pay a dividend on its common stock." Do you agree? Explain.

5-5. A company declared a dividend of $100,000. Using a Dividends Declared account, prepare a journal entry for the transaction.

5-6. "Cash dividends that are payable are a part of shareholders' equity." Do you agree? Explain.

5-7. "Dividends Declared has a normal left-side balance. It represents a reduction in Retained Earnings and Shareholders' Equity." Do you agree? Explain.

5-8. "Closing is a clerical procedure. It is devoid of any new accounting theory." Do you agree? Explain.

5-9. "Net assets are always equal to shareholders' equity." Do you agree? Explain.

5-10. "Closing the books might better be called clearing the revenue and expense accounts." Do you agree? Explain.

5-11. "The word *permanent* to describe balance sheet accounts is misleading." Explain.

5-12. "If it were up to management, there would be no auditors." Do you agree? Explain.

5-13. Why do auditors protect their reputations so carefully?

5-14. Appendix 5A. Why are work sheets used?

5-15. Appendix 5A. "Preparing a work sheet using an electronic spreadsheet is more trouble than it is worth." Do you agree? Explain.

5-16. Appendix 5B. "Variety in recording accounting transactions is unacceptable diversity." Do you agree? Explain.

5-17. Appendix 5B. "Liabilities can have temporary debit balances." Explain.

5-18. Appendix 5C. Name two common special journals, and briefly describe the types of entries to each.

EXERCISES

5-19 Journal Entry Explanations

Prepare possible explanations for the following journal entries:

a.	Accounts receivable	4,000	
	Sales		4,000
b.	Cash	3,000	
	Accounts receivable		3,000
c.	Accrued wages payable	2,500	
	Wages expense	400	
	Cash		2,900
d.	Long-term note payable	1,800	
	Notes payable, current		1,200
	Cash		600
e.	Unearned sales revenue	1,500	
	Sales		1,500
f.	Dividend payable	300	
	Cash		300

5-20 Effects of Adjustments of Preceding Period

The Big Pine Boat Company had the following balances as of December 31, 19X5:

Unearned sales revenue	$100,000
Accrued interest receivable	120,000
Accrued wages payable	190,000

During early 19X6, cash was collected for interest of $170,000. Cash was disbursed for wages of $900,000. Total sales of $700,000 included $100,000 of deliveries to all customers who had made advance payments during 19X5.

Required Set up T-accounts and prepare the journal entries for the 19X6 transactions described. Post to the T-accounts.

5-21 Closing the Accounts

The following accounts show their final balances before closing and their closing entries (in thousands). Prepare the closing journal entries that were evidently made. What is the balance in Retained Earnings after closing?

Cost of Goods Sold		Dividends Declared		Other Revenues	
500	500	70	70	40	40

Income Summary		Sales		Retained Earnings	
840	930	890	890	70	500
90					90

Other Expenses	
340	340

5-22   Dividends

On March 10, Liverpool Music Company declared dividends of £.25 per share for each of the 100,000 shares outstanding. Payment was made on March 31. (£ is the symbol for British pounds.)

Required   Prepare journal entries pertaining to dividends in March. Include appropriate dates and explanations.

5-23   Income Versus Cash Flow

Pedro's Equipment sells farm implements. January 19X6 was a slow month. The only sale was one tractor, sold for $30,000 with a $15,000 cash down payment and $15,000 due in six months. The tractor was purchased for inventory in 19X5 for $18,000 cash. January's operating expenses were $9,000; $7,000 was paid in cash and $2,000 was amortization.

Required
1. Compute net income for January. Ignore taxes.
2. Compute net cash flows from operating activities for January.
3. Why do the amounts in requirements 1 and 2 differ?

PROBLEMS

5-24   Journalize, Post, and Prepare Trial Balance

Consider the trial balance at June 25, 19X5 for Limacher Software Consultants, Inc., shown at the top of the next page.

The following additional information pertains to June 29 and 30, which is the end of Limacher's fiscal year (amounts in thousands):

a. Wages incurred but unpaid, $12.

b. One-third of the prepaid insurance had expired. (Increase Miscellaneous Expenses.)

c. The note is payable on July 31. It is a 16%, seven-month note. Principal and interest are payable at maturity.

d. Amortization expense for the fiscal year is $10.

e. Billed clients for $15.

f. Paid the liability for dividends.

g. Unbilled revenue as of June 30, based on time logged on various client projects, was $60. (Increase Unbilled Client Receivables.)

h. Half the prepaid trade association dues had expired. (Increase Miscellaneous Expenses.)

i. Received $14 cash advance from a client for services to be rendered after June 30.

j. Income tax rate was 35%.

	Debit	Credit
Cash	$ 38	
Accounts receivable	95	
Unbilled client receivables	—	
Prepaid trade association dues	6	
Prepaid insurance	3	
Equipment	59	
Accumulated amortization, equipment		$ 8
Accounts payable		21
Note payable		75
Accrued interest payable (on note)		5
Dividends payable		10
Accrued wages payable		—
Accrued income taxes payable		—
Unearned fee revenue		—
Paid-in capital		50
Retained earnings		20
Dividends declared	10	
Fee revenue		840
Rent expense	21	
Wages expense	400	
Amortization expense	—	
Miscellaneous expense	362	
Interest expense	5	
Income tax expense	30	
Total	$1,029	$1,029

Required

1. After posting the above balances to T-accounts, analyze and journalize all entries arising from the above information.
2. Post the journal entries to T-accounts. Use check marks as posting references in the journal.
3. Prepare an adjusted trial balance, June 30, 19X5.

5-25   Closing Entries

(Alternates are 5-26, 5-47, and 5-48.) Limacher Software Consultants, Inc., had the following accounts included in an adjusted trial balance, June 30, 19X5 (in thousands):

Retained earnings	$ 20	Rent expense	$ 21	Miscellaneous	
Dividends		Wages expense	412	expenses	$366
declared	10	Amortization		Interest expense	6
Fee revenue	915	expense	10	Income tax	
				expense	35

Required

After posting the above balances to T-accounts, journalize and post the entries necessary to close the books. Number your entries as 1, 2, etc. What is the balance in Retained Earnings after closing?

5-26   Closing Entries

(Alternates are 5-25, 5-47, and 5-48.) Post the following balances to T-accounts. Then, journalize and post the entries required to close the books (in thousands):

Retained earnings		Wages expense	$300
(before closing entries)	$245	Miscellaneous	
Sales	890	expenses	40
Interest revenue	30	Income tax expense	15
Cost of goods sold	500	Dividends declared	30

What is the balance in Retained Income after closing entries?

5-27   Adjustments and Closing

Consider the accompanying Soderstrom Company unadjusted trial balance at December 31, 19X2 (in thousands).

	Debit	Credit
Cash	$ 32	
Accounts receivable	89	
Notes receivable	50	
Merchandise inventory	120	
Prepaid rent	12	
Equipment	95	
Accumulated amortization, equipment		$ 25
Accounts payable		132
Paid-in capital		100
Retained earnings		66
Sales		990
Cost of goods sold	570	
Wages expense	200	
Miscellaneous expense	120	
Income tax expense	25	
Total	$1,313	$1,313

The following additional information is not reflected in the trial balance (amounts are in thousands):

a. Interest accrued on notes receivable, $5.

b. Amortization, $9.

c. Wages accrued but unpaid, $7.

d. Utilities accrued but unpaid, $4. (Increase Miscellaneous Expenses.)

e. Rent expired, $5.

f. Dividend declared but unpaid, $14. Use a Dividends Declared account, which is really just an offset to Retained Earnings.

g. A cash receipt of $2 from a credit customer was credited erroneously to Accounts Payable, so a correction must be made.

h. Additional income tax expense must be accrued. The income tax rate is 40% of pre-tax income. Compute the additional tax after computing the effects of the above adjustments to revenue and expense accounts.

Required

1. After posting the above balances to T-accounts, analyze and journalize all entries arising from the descriptions in *a* through *h* above. Use new accounts as necessary.
2. Post your journal entries to T-accounts. Use check marks as posting references in the journal.
3. Prepare an adjusted trial balance, December 31, 19X2. Allow space for four columns, placing your numbers for this requirement in the first pair of columns.
4. Prepare and post the closing journal entries to T-accounts. Key the entries as *i*, *j*, etc.
5. Prepare a postclosing trial balance by placing the appropriate numbers in the second pair of columns in your answer to requirement 3 above.

5-28   Prepare Financial Statements

Consider the accompanying Soccer Specialties, Inc. adjusted trial balance at December 31, 19X5 (in thousands).

	Debit	Credit
Accounts payable		$ 85
Accounts receivable	$ 65	
Accrued income taxes payable		10
Accrued interest payable (due annually)		4
Accrued wages payable		20
Accumulated amortization, building		70
Accumulated amortization, equipment		47
Building	130	
Cash	68	
Cost of goods sold	488	
Dividends declared	11	
Equipment	70	
Income tax expense	20	
Interest expense	6	
Inventory	120	
Long-term note payable (due in 19X8)		50
Other operating expenses	110	
Paid-in capital		110
Prepaid insurance	2	
Retained earnings		34
Sales		960
Wages expense	300	
Total	$1,390	$1,390

Required

1. Prepare a multiple-step income statement.
2. Prepare a statement of retained earnings .
3. Prepare a classified balance sheet.
4. Compute the working capital and the current ratio.

5-29   Income and Cash Flows

Following are the summarized transactions of Dr. Rose Francisco, a dentist, for 19X7, her first year in practice:

1. Acquired equipment and furniture for $60,000 cash. Amortization expense for 19X7 is $10,000.

2. Fees collected, $85,000. These fees included $3,000 paid in advance by some patients on December 31, 19X7.

3. Rent is paid at the rate of $500 monthly, payable on the twenty-fifth of each month for the following month. Total disbursements during 19X7 for rent were $6,500.

4. Fees billed but uncollected, December 31, 19X7, $15,000.

5. Utilities expense paid in cash, $600. Additional utility bills unpaid at December 31, 19X7, $100.

6. Salaries expense of dental assistant and secretary, $15,000 paid in cash. In addition, $2,000 was earned but unpaid on December 31, 19X7.

Required

1. Prepare an income statement and a statement of changes in financial position provided by operating activities. Ignore taxes.

2. Compare operating income with net cash provided by operating activities. Which basis do you prefer as a measure of Dr. Francisco's performance? Why?

5-30   Prepare Income Statement and Balance Sheet

Nancy Yamaguchi runs a small consulting-engineering firm that specializes in designing and overseeing the installation of environmental-control systems. However, even though she is the president, she has had no formal training in management. She has been in business one year and has prepared the following income statement for her fiscal year ended June 30, 19X4:

Fees collected in cash		$455,000
Expenses paid in cash except for amortization:		
Rent	$ 12,500	
Utilities	10,000	
Wages	150,000	
President's salary	46,000	
Office supplies	14,000	
Travel	40,000	
Miscellaneous	80,000	
Amortization	10,000	$362,500
Operating income		$ 92,500

Yamaguchi realized that the entire $50,000 cost of equipment acquired on July 1, 19X3 should not be an expense of one year. She predicted a useful life of five years, a terminal value of zero, and deducted $10,000 as amortization for the first year.

Yamaguchi is thinking about future needs for her expanding business. For example, although she now uses rented space in an office building, she is considering buying a small building. She showed her income statement to a local banker, who reacted: "Nancy, this statement may suffice for filing income tax forms, but the bank will not consider any long-term financing until it receives a balance sheet and income statement prepared on the accrual basis of accounting. Moreover, the statements must be subjected to an audit by an independent certified public accountant."

As a professional auditor, you are asked to audit her records and fulfill the bank's request.

The following data have been gathered:

1. On July 1, 19X3, Yamaguchi invested $25,000 cash, and two friends each invested $2,000 cash in the firm in return for capital stock.

2. Yamaguchi acquired $50,000 of equipment on July 1, 19X3. A down payment of $20,000 cash was made. A $30,000 two-year note bearing an annual interest rate of 15% was signed. Principal plus interest were both payable at maturity.

3. On June 30, 19X4, clients owed Yamaguchi $95,000 on open accounts.

4. Salaries are paid on the fifteenth of every month. As business expanded throughout the fiscal year, additional employees were hired. The total payroll paid on June 15, 19X4, including the president's monthly salary of $4,000, was $40,000.

5. Rent was paid in advance on the fifteenth of every month. An initial payment of $1,500 covered July 1, 19X3–August 15, 19X3. Payments of $1,000 monthly were paid beginning August 15, 19X3.

6. Office Supplies on hand on June 30, 19X4, were $5,000.

7. On April 1, 19X4, a local oil refinery gave Yamaguchi a retainer fee of $40,000 cash in exchange for twelve months of consulting services beginning at that date.

Required

1. Using the accrual basis of accounting, prepare an income statement for the fiscal year. Submit supporting computations properly labelled.

2. Prepare a balance sheet, dated June 30, 19X4. Assume that the cash balance is $111,500.

5-31   Prepare Statement of Changes in Financial Position

Refer to the preceding problem. Prepare a statement of changes in financial position that proves that the ending cash balance is indeed $111,500. Label your analysis fully. Note that interest payments are operating cash flows. Explain why net income differs from net cash provided by operating activities.

5-32   Summarized Corporate Annual Report

Inspect an annual report of a publicly held corporation. (Your instructor will give more specific instructions regarding how to obtain access to such reports at your school.) Read the report. The report will contain many details not covered in your study to date. Nevertheless, you will see the general picture portrayed by the balance sheet, income statement, and other statements. Complete the following. If the item is not reported by the corporation, write "not available."

1. Name of company.
2. Location of corporate headquarters.
3. Principal products or services.
4. Main geographic area of activity.
5. Name and title of chief executive officer (CEO).
6. Ending date of latest operating year reported.
7. Indicate the terms (if any) used instead of (a) balance sheet, (b) income statement, (c) retained earnings, (d) shareholders' equity, (e) revenues, (f) expenses.
8. Total assets.
9. Total liabilities.
10. Total shareholders' equity.
11. Total revenues (you may need to compute this).
12. Total expenses (you may need to compute this).
13. Net income (see above and subtract item 12 from item 11, then check the result with reported net income).
14. Total cash dividends declared.
15. Earnings per share of common stock (EPS).
16. Annual dividends per share of common stock.
17. Market in which stock is traded (see *The Globe and Mail*, *Financial Post* or local newspapers).
18. Latest market price of common stock (see *The Globe and Mail*, *Financial Post* or local newspapers).
19. Price-earnings ratio (compute or see *The Globe and Mail*, *Financial Post* or local newspapers).

20. Dividend yield (compute or see *The Globe and Mail, Financial Post,* or local newspapers).

21. Dividend-payout ratio (you may need to compute this).

22. Name of independent professional accountants.

23. Did they certify that all amounts were correct? If not, what did they say? (Do not simply copy the actual wording; be brief.)

24. Total number of shareholders (if provided).

25. Total number of employees (if provided).

26. Total number of shares of common stock outstanding.

27. Common shareholders' equity per share (book value per share).

28. Comparative statistics (financial and operating data) were reported for how many years?

29. Give very briefly your general impression of this report (for example, quality, scope, usefulness, format, readability, interest to you, etc.).

5-33   Comprehensive Review

This is a comprehensive review of Chapters 1 through 5. Mallard Clothing, a retail corporation, had the following postclosing trial balance, December 31, 19X4 (in thousands of dollars):

Account Number	Name of Account	Dr.	Cr.
10	Cash	30	
20	Accounts receivable	91	
34	Notes receivable, current	100	
35	Accrued interest receivable	16	
40	Merchandise inventory	160	
52	Prepaid fire insurance	3	
62	Notes receivable, long-term	100	
74	Equipment	120	
74A	Accumulated amortization, equipment		76
100	Accounts payable		90
111	Accrued wages payable		8
123	Accrued income taxes payable		4
137	Unearned sales revenue		10
200	Paid-in capital		110
230	Retained earnings		322
		620	620

The following summarized transactions (in thousands of dollars) occurred during 19X5:

a. Merchandise inventory purchased on open account was $480.

b. Total sales were $890, of which 80% were on credit.

c. The sales in *b* were exclusive of the deliveries of goods to customers who had paid in advance as of December 31, 19X4. All of those goods ordered in advance were indeed delivered during 19X5.

d. The cost of goods sold for 19X5, including those in *c*, was $440.

e. Collections from credit customers were $682.

f. The notes receivable are from a major supplier of belts. Interest for twelve months on all notes was collected on May 1. The rate is 12% per annum. The accounting system provides for cash collections of interest to be credited first to existing accrued interest receivable carried over from the preceding period.

g. The principal of the current notes receivable was collected on May 1, 19X5. The principal of the remaining notes is payable on May 1, 19X6 (see entry *r*).

h. As of December 31, 19X5, customers had made a total of $7 in advance cash payments for "layaway" plans and for merchandise not yet in stock. These payments were exclusive of any other transactions described above.

Cash disbursements were:

i. To trade creditors, $470.

j. To employees for wages, $193. The accounting system for wages is to debit any existing accrued payables first and debit any remainder of a disbursement to expense.

k. For miscellaneous expenses such as store rents, advertising, utilities, and supplies, which were all paid in cash, $189. (These items are combined here to reduce the detailed recording of items that are basically accounted for alike.)

l. For new equipment acquired on July 1, 19X5, $74.

m. To the insurance company for a new three-year fire insurance policy effective September 1, 19X5, $36 (rates had increased). Prepayments of expenses are routinely debited to asset accounts.

n. To the federal and provincial governments for income taxes, $19. Income tax expense was debited for $15 of the $19. (For your general information, most businesses must pay income taxes regularly throughout the year.)

o. The board of directors declared cash dividends of $26 on December 15 to shareholders of record, January 5, and to be paid on January 21, 19X6. (Note that this is not a cash disbursement until payment has been made.) Debit Dividends Declared, which is really just an offset to Retained Earnings.

The following adjustments were made on December 31, 19X5:

p. For the interest on notes receivable.

q. For insurance. The prepaid insurance of December 31, 19X4 had expired too.

r. For reclassification of the notes receivable.

s. For amortization. Amortization expense for 19X5 was $30.

t. Wages earned but unpaid, December 31, 19X5, $15.

u. Total income tax expense for 19X5 is $20, computed as 40% of pretax income of $50. (Note that part of the 19X5 tax expense has already been recorded and paid, as indicated in transaction *n*.)

Required

1. After posting the opening balances to T-accounts, analyze and journalize all transactions, including adjustments, for 19X5.
2. Post all journal entries to T-accounts. Be painstaking as you post. Use the given account numbers as posting references. For accounts not in the trial balance of December 31, 19X4, use check marks as posting references instead.
3. Prepare a trial balance, December 31, 19X5.
4. Prepare a multiple-step income statement for 19X5.
5. Prepare a statement of retained income for 19X5.
6. Prepare classified comparative balance sheets for December 31, 19X4 and 19X5. Classify the prepaid insurance, December 31, 19X4, as a current asset even though a portion thereof might justifiably be classified as a long-term asset.
7. Journalize and post the entries necessary to "close the books" for 19X5.

5-34   Work Sheet

Study Appendix 5A. Refer to the preceding problem. Examine the accompanying unadjusted trial balance that includes the results of transactions *a* through *o* (in thousands).

Required

1. Prepare a twelve-column work sheet, using the unadjusted trial balance as the first pair of columns. Add pairs of columns for adjustments, adjusted trial balance, income statement, statement of retained earnings, and balance sheet. When entering the unadjusted trial balance on the work sheet, allow space for new accounts as follows: two spaces after Accounts Receivable, two spaces after Accounts Payable, and three spaces between Miscellaneous Expense and Income Tax Expense.
2. Enter the adjustments for transactions *p* through *u*.
3. Complete the work sheet. Check the accuracy of your work by comparing the work sheet results with the formal financial statements prepared in the solution to Problem 5-33.

Mallard Clothing
Unadjusted Trial
Balance

Account Title	Debit	Credit
Cash	$ 40	
Accounts receivable	121	
Merchandise inventory	200	
Prepaid fire insurance	39	
Notes receivable, long-term portion	100	
Equipment	194	
Accumulated amortization, equipment		$ 76
Accounts payable		100
Dividends payable		26
Unearned sales revenue		7
Paid-in capital		110
Retained earnings		322
Dividends declared	26	
Sales		900
Interest revenue		8
Cost of goods sold	440	
Wages expense	185	
Miscellaneous expense	189	
Income tax expense	15	
Total	$1,549	$1,549

5-35   Work Sheet

Study Appendix 5A. An unadjusted trial balance for Gonzales Sporting Goods is on the accompanying work sheet on page 221. The following additional information is available.

a. Wages earned but unpaid, $2,050.

b. Adjustment for prepaid rent. Rent was paid quarterly in advance, $9,000 per quarter. Payments were due on January 1, April 1, July 1, and October 1.

c. The store equipment originally cost $16,800 on February 1, 19X1. It is being amortized on a straight-line basis over seven years with zero expected terminal value.

d. The note payable is based on a one-year loan of $20,000. The note is dated November 1, 19X1. Principal plus 12% interest is payable at maturity.

e. Income taxes are to be accrued. The applicable income tax rate is 30%.

Required   Enter the adjustments and complete the work sheet.

5-36   Work Sheet

Study Appendix 5A. Refer to problem 5-24. Prepare a complete work sheet, including pairs of columns for unadjusted trial balance, adjustments and other entries, adjusted

Gonzales Sporting Goods   Work Sheet for the Month Ended February 28, 19X2

Account Title	Unadjusted Trial Balance		Adjustments		Adjusted Trial Balance		Income Statement		Statement of Retained Earnings		Balance Sheet	
	Debit	Credit	Debit	Credit	Debit	Credit	Debit	Credit	Debit	Credit	Debit	Credit
Cash	24800											
Accounts receivable	56000											
Merchandise inventory	112000											
Prepaid rent	6000											
Store equipment	16800											
Accumulated amortization, equip.		2400										
Accounts payable		62000										
Note payable		20000										
Accrued interest payable		750										
Paid-in capital		50000										
Retained earnings		45250										
Sales		80200										
Cost of goods sold	50000											
Advertising expense	4000											
Wages expense	11000											
Miscellaneous expenses	10000											
	270600	270600										

trial balance, income statement, and statement of retained earnings, and balance sheet for Limacher Software Consultants, Inc.

5-37   Work Sheet

Study Appendix 5A. Refer to problem 5-27. Prepare a complete work sheet, including pairs of columns for unadjusted trial balance, adjustments and other entries, adjusted trial balance, income statement, and statement of retained earnings, and balance sheet for Soderstrom Company. If you did not solve Problem 5-27, prepare closing journal entries now.

5-38   Alternative Analyses of Transactions

(Alternate is 5-39.) Study Appendix 5B. Consider the following balances, December 31, 19X1:

Accrued interest receivable	$ 8,000
Prepaid rent	12,000
Accrued wages payable	16,000

During 19X2, $24,000 cash was received for interest for one year on a long-term note of $200,000. Interest was due yearly on September 1. In addition, half the principal of the note was paid on September 1, 19X2.

During 19X2, cash disbursements of $78,000 were made for rent. The rent was payable, $18,000 quarterly in advance on March 1, June 1, September 1, and December 1. The rent was raised to $24,000 quarterly beginning December 1, 19X2.

During 19X2, $800,000 was disbursed for wages. The ending balance of accrued wages payable, December 31, 19X2, was $26,000.

In responding to the requirement for journal entries, use the following format:

Explanation of Entry	Requirement 1		Requirement 2	
	(in thousands of dollars)			
Summary cash receipts or disbursements	Journal entry		Journal entry	
End-of-period adjustments	Journal entry		Journal entry	

Example: Paid insurance of $40,000	Prepaid insurance
	  Cash
		40
		
			Insurance expense
			  Cash
				40

		40		40

Adjustment so that ending balance of prepaid insurance is $30,000	Insurance expense
	  Prepaid insurance
		10
		
			Prepaid insurance
			  Insurance expense
				30

		10		30

Required

1. Assume that the accounting system provides for the appropriate portions of the above cash collections and cash disbursements to be applied to any balances of accruals and prepayments carried over from the preceding period. Given the above data, prepare summary journal entries, including the adjusting entries, for 19X2. Post the entries to T-accounts. Do not prepare the entry for the repayment of the principal on the note.

2. Assume that the accounting system regards all the above cash collections and cash disbursements as revenues or expenses. Adjustments are then made at the end of each year to recognize the appropriate accruals and prepayments. Given the above data, prepare summary journal entries, including the adjusting entries for 19X2. Post the entries to T-accounts.

3. Which set of data-processing procedures do you prefer, those in requirement 1 or those in requirement 2? Explain.

5-39 Alternate Analyses of Transactions

(Alternate is 5-38.) Study Appendix 5B. Consider the following balances, December 31, 19X4 (in thousands of dollars):

Accrued interest receivable	$16
Prepaid fire insurance	3
Accrued wages payable	8

The accounting system provides for cash collections of interest to be credited first to any existing accrued interest receivable carried over from the preceding period. Cash collections for interest during 19X5 were $26. Label this as entry *f*.

The accounting system for wages is to debit any existing accrued payables first and debit any remainder of the disbursement to expense. Cash disbursements for wages during 19X5 were $193. Label this as entry *i*.

Prepayments of expenses are routinely debited to asset accounts. A cash disbursement for a three-year insurance policy, effective September 1, 19X5, was $36. Label this as entry *l*.

Required

1. Prepare T-accounts for Accrued Interest Receivable, Interest Revenue, Prepaid Fire Insurance, Insurance Expense, Accrued Wages Payable, and Wages Expense. Post the opening balances therein, December 31, 19X4. Journalize and post the above entries *f*, *i*, and *l* to the appropriate accounts. (At the same time, you may wish to use a Cash T-account to complete the postings. However, the Cash T-account is not required for purposes of this problem.)

2. The following correct balances were applicable at the end of 19X5:

Accrued interest receivable	$10
Prepaid fire insurance	?
Accrued wages payable	15

Journalize and post the adjusting entries, December 31, 19X5. Label them as *o*, *p*, and *s*. Assume that the prepaid insurance of December 31, 19X4, expired during 19X5.

3. Assume the same data as in requirements 1 and 2. However, suppose the following summarized journal entries had been made during 19X5:

Entry	Accounts and Explanation	Post Ref.	Debit (in thousands of dollars)	Credit (in thousands of dollars)
f	Cash	✓	26	
	Interest revenue	✓		26
	Collection of interest.			
i	Wages expense	✓	193	
	Cash	✓		193
	Payments of wages.			
l	Insurance expense	✓	36	
	Cash	✓		36
	Payment of insurance.			

Given these revised entries *f*, *i*, and *l*, prepare alternate adjusting journal entries *o*, *p*, and *s*, December 31, 19X5. Post the entries to a new set of T-accounts having the same opening balances given in the first paragraph of this problem. How do the ending balances in the accounts affected by the adjustments compare with the ending balances in the same accounts in requirement 2?

4. Which set of data-processing procedures do you prefer for interest, wages, and insurance, those in requirements 1 and 2 or those in requirement 3? Explain.

5-40   Special Journals

(Alternate is 5-41.) Study Appendix 5C. The Cambridge Trading Company uses a sales journal, a cash receipts journal, and a general journal. It has a general ledger and subsidiary ledgers for accounts receivable. For simplicity, only a few transactions of each kind are illustrated in the accompanying list of transactions. Moreover, the beginning balances of the pertinent accounts are not given, nor are they necessary for the purposes of this problem. The currency is British pounds, £.

The numbers of some pertinent accounts are:

Cash	No. 10
Accounts receivable	30
Allowance for bad debts	32
Notes payable	75
Paid-in capital	80
Sales	90
Bad debts expense	99

Consider the following list of transactions.

July	Description	Invoice Date	Invoice No.	Terms	Cheque No.	Amount
2	Cash sales	—	—	—	—	£ 2,000
3	Credit sales to Major	—	319	n30	—	1,200
8	Collection of Invoice 319	—	—	—	—	1,200
10	Credit sale to Ramakrishnan	—	320	n30	—	2,800
13	Cash sales	—	—	—	—	1,900
16	Credit sale to Haynes	—	321	n30	—	1,800
20	Collection of Invoice 321	—	—	—	—	1,800
23	Credit sale to Cyert	—	322	n30	—	900
24	Cash sales	—	—	—	—	2,000
26	Borrowed from bank, 60-day loan	—	—	—	—	5,000
28	Cash sales	—	—	—	—	2,500
29	Credit sale to Holford	—	323	n30	—	600
31	Sale of additional common stock for cash	—	—	—	—	10,000
31	Addition to allowance for uncollectible accounts	—	—	—	—	100

Required

1. Journalize the transactions for July, using the appropriate journals.
2. Post the effects of the transactions to the general and subsidiary ledgers. Show posting details such as dates and account numbers.
3. Prepare a listing of the accounts receivable subsidiary ledger balances. Make sure that the total agrees with the related general ledger account.

5-41 Special Journals

(Alternate is 5-40.) Study Appendix 5C. Huang Company, a wholesaler of luggage, uses a general journal and two special journals with amount columns as shown:

- General journal: two columns, debit and credit
- Sales journal: single amount column
- Cash receipts journal: debit columns for Cash and for Sales Discounts; credit columns for Sales, Accounts Receivable, and Other Accounts

The general-ledger accounts needed for this problem are included in the table following with their account numbers and June 1, 19X1, balances, if any:

Cash (10)	$ 5,000	
Accounts receivable (25)	18,000	
Office supplies (40)	2,000	
Office equipment (44)	21,000	
Accounts payable (84)		12,000
Notes payable (88)		
Sales (142)		
Sales returns and allowances (143)		
Sales discounts (144)		
Purchases (162)		
Purchase returns and allowances (163)		
Purchase discounts (164)		
All other accounts (300)	46,000	80,000
Total	$92,000	$92,000

The subsidiary ledger accounts needed and their June 1 balances, if any, are:

Accounts Receivable
Stratton Co.
Davey & Ramos
Maxson's, Inc.
Joy Bros., $18,000 debit balance

Required

1. Set up journals and ledgers, entering beginning account balances, if any.
2. Enter the transactions described below in the appropriate journals.
3. Post amounts from all journals to T accounts, showing details: dates, account numbers, and posting references.
4. Take a trial balance of the general ledger at June 30.
5. Prepare a schedule for the accounts receivable subsidiary ledger to prove its agreement with the controlling account at June 30.

Transactions

June 4	Cash sales of merchandise, $1,800.
6	Sold merchandise to Stratton Co., $9,000; terms 2/10, n/30; invoice number 1063.
10	Sold merchandise to Davey & Ramos, $12,000; terms 2/10, n/30; invoice number 1064.
*12	Purchased office equipment from Langley Co., $5,400; terms n/30.
14	Received cash to settle Stratton Co. invoice 1063, less 2% cash discount. (Use only one line for this entry in the cash receipts journal.)
15	Sold merchandise to Maxson's, Inc., $15,000; terms 2/10, n/30; invoice number 1065.
21	Borrowed $18,000 for ninety days from First National Bank at 15% interest to be paid at due date of note.
*24	Issued credit memo number 88 for $600 to Davey & Ramos for unsatisfactory merchandise sold June 10.

* These transactions are to be entered in the general journal. Be sure to post the debit and credit amounts for receivables to the subsidiary ledger accounts as well as to the related control accounts.

CRITICAL THINKING PROBLEM

5-42 External Auditors and Ethics

Managers (with the help of staff accountants) prepare the financial statements, which are then examined by external auditors. Compare and contrast the types of ethical responsibilities of external auditors with those of managers and staff accountants.

COMPANY CASES

5-43 Effects of Adjustments of Preceding Period

(Alternates are 5-44 and 5-45.) The Thomson Corporation showed the following actual balances and descriptions in its balance sheet, December 31, 1996:

Current liabilities:	
Accounts payable	$1,398,000
Deferred revenue	810,000

Suppose the company also showed Interest Receivable of $55,000.

During early 1997, assume the following: $85,200 was collected for interest; cash of $5,200,000 was disbursed for accounts payable; and deliveries of $640,000 were made of the company's publications that had been subscribed to and fully collected before 1997.

Required

Set up T-accounts and prepare the journal entries for the 1997 transactions. Post to the T-accounts.

5-44 Effects of Adjustments of Preceding Period

Rogers Cantel Mobile Communications reported the following balances in its annual report at December 31, 1995.

Rogers Cantel Mobile Communications
www.rogers.com/RCI/

Accounts receivable	$131,932
Accounts payable	231,316
Unearned revenue	27,505

Assume that during early 1996, accounts receivable of $125,000 was collected in cash. Cash of $280,000 was disbursed for accounts payable. Deliveries of $25,000 were made of services that had been subscribed to and fully collected before 1996.

Required Set up T-accounts and prepare the journal entries for the 1996 transactions. Post to the T-accounts.

5-45 Journal Entries

(Alternates are 5-43 and 5-44.) Delta Air Lines, Inc., had the following three actual balance sheet items in its 1993 annual report (in thousands):

Maintenance and operating supplies	$ 90,593
Air traffic liability	1,189,883
Accrued rent	200,471

A footnote stated: "Passenger ticket sales are recorded as revenue when the transportation is provided. The value of unused tickets is included in current liabilities as air traffic liability." Therefore air traffic liability is an unearned revenue account.

Required Set up T-accounts and prepare journal entries and postings for the following transactions that occurred subsequent to the date of the balance sheet in the 1993 annual report. All numbers are in thousands.

1. Use of $70,000 of maintenance and operating supplies.
2. Sales of $900,000 of tickets in advance of air travel. (Increase Cash.)
3. Revenues of $4,440,000 including $1,200,000 of transportation provided for passengers who paid in advance.
4. Additional accruals of rent payable, $180,000.
5. Payments of rent, $187,041.

Indicate the balances in Maintenance and Operating Supplies, Air Traffic Liability, and Accrued Rent after posting for the five transactions.

5-46 Journal Entries

Cincinnati Bell, Inc. provides communications services, mainly telephone services, in parts of Ohio, Kentucky, and Indiana. Its total revenues for a recent year were $1,089,637,000. Its balance sheets showed:

	End of Year	Beginning of Year
Advance billing and customers' deposits	$31,553,000	$26,464,000

To save space, annual reports often combine accounts. In this instance, Advance Billing is really one account, an unearned revenue account. For example, customers typically are billed for their basic monthly phone charges in advance of the service rendered.

Customers' Deposits is another account. For example, a new customer may be required to make a security deposit of $300. When the customer terminates the service, the deposit is usually returned in cash.

Required Post all entries to three T-accounts. (Use Cash, Advance Billing and Customers' Deposits, and Operating Revenues.)

1. Prepare a summary journal entry to show how the $26,464,000 was initially recorded.

2. (a) During the year, additional amounts of advance billings and deposits amounted to $17 million. (b) Moreover, $3 million of customers' deposits was returned in cash to customers. Prepare summary journal entries for these events.

3. At the end of the year, prepare the necessary adjusting journal entry to obtain the balance given for the year.

5-47 Closing Entries

(Alternates are 5-25, 5-26, and 5-48.) National Sea Products is a prominent processor of fish and seafood located in eastern Canada. The actual balances and descriptions that follow pertain to the 1995 fiscal year and are in thousands of dollars:

Sales	$254,234	Other expenses	$10,206
Cost of sales	185,205	Income taxes	851
Selling, general and administrative expenses	52,397	Cash dividends	106
		Retained earnings (deficit), beginning of year	(102,753)

Required   After posting the balances to T-accounts, journalize and post the entries required to close the books. What is the balance in Retained Earnings after closing entries?

5-48 Closing Entries

(Alternates are 5-25, 5-26, and 5-47.) In addition to ketchup, pickles, and other products with the Heinz brand name, H. J. Heinz Company produces foods with the brands Ore-Ida, StarKist, and Weight Watchers. The accompanying actual balances and descriptions pertain to a recent year and are in millions of dollars.

Retained earnings, beginning of year	$3,356	Selling, general, and administrative expenses	$1,597
Sales	7,047	Interest and other expenses, net	146
Cost of products sold	4,382	Provision for income taxes	319
		Cash dividends	326

Required   After posting the balances to T-accounts, journalize and post the entries required to close the books. What is the balance in Retained Earnings after closing entries?

5-49 Financial Statements

Mitsubishi Kasei Corporation, Japan's premier diversified chemical company, has annual sales of more than $12 billion. The company's 1993 annual report included the items listed below (in billions of yen). The balance sheet items included here are the amounts at March 31, 1993, unless otherwise indicated.

Property, plant, and equipment, original cost	¥1,327
Accumulated amortization	848
Net sales	1,181
Interest expense	36
Interest income	11

continued

Bank loans payable	288
Retained earnings, March 31, 1992	82
Common stock	108
Cost of sales	930
Provision for income taxes	9
Marketable securities	99
Accrued income taxes	5
Long-term debt	404
Additional paid-in capital	106
Selling, general, and administrative expenses	217
Dividends declared	12
Inventories	160
Prepaid expenses	23
Other income	6
Accounts payable	247
Accounts receivable	360
Other current liabilities	49
Accrued expenses	47
Other liabilities (noncurrent)	85
Cash and time deposits	101
Other assets (noncurrent)	193

Required

1. Prepare a combined multi-step statement of income and retained earnings.
2. Prepare the classified balance sheet as of the end of the year.
3. Compute the working capital and the current ratio.

5-50   Preparation of Financial Statements from Trial Balance

Apple Computer, Inc., prepared the following (slightly modified) trial balance as of September 30, 1994 (in millions), the end of the company's fiscal year:

	Debits	Credits
Cash and cash equivalents	$ 1,204	
Short-term investments	54	
Accounts receivable	1,581	
Inventories	1,088	
Prepaid income taxes	293	
Other current assets	256	
Property, plant, and equipment, at cost	1,452	
Accumulated depreciation and amortization		$ 785
Other assets	159	
Notes payable		292
Accounts payable		882
Accrued compensation and employee benefits		137
Accrued marketing and distribution expenses		178
Other current liabilities		455
Long-term debt		304
Deferred income taxes		671

continued

Common stock, no par value		298
Retained earnings		1,831
Net sales		9,189
Cost of sales	6,845	
Research and development expenses	565	
Selling, general, and administrative expenses	1,384	
Other operating expenses (revenues)		127
Interest and other expenses, net	22	
Provision for income taxes	190	
Cash dividends	56	
Total	$15,149	$15,149

Required

1. Prepare Apple Computer's income statement for the year ended September 30, 1994.
2. Prepare Apple Computer's balance sheet as of September 30, 1994.

5-51 Hudson's Bay Company Annual Report

Refer to the financial statements of the Hudson's Bay Company in Appendix A. This problem will familiarize you with some of the accounts of this actual company.

Required

1. Which balance sheet format does the Hudson's Bay Company use, the account format or the report format?
2. Name the company's largest current asset and current liability.
3. How much were total current assets and total current liabilities at January 31, 1997? What is the current ratio at January 31, 1997?
4. What was the original cost of the Property, plant, and equipment assets on January 31, 1997? What was the book value of the Property, plant, and equipment assets at January 31, 1997?

5-52 Annual Report Disclosure

Select any company of your choice and examine the most recent financial statements, focusing on the balance sheet.

Required

1. Identify the company's auditor. What is the auditor's role in relation to the financial statements?
2. Name the company's largest current asset and the largest current liability.
3. How much were total current assets and total current liabilities at the most recent balance sheet date? What was the current ratio at that date?
4. What was the original cost of the Property, plant, and equipment assets at the most recent balance sheet date? What was the book value of the Property, plant, and equipment assets at that date?

6

Statement of Changes in Financial Position

Learning Objectives

After studying this chapter, you should be able to

1   Explain the concept of the statement of changes in financial position.

2   Classify activities affecting cash as operating, investing, or financing activities.

3   Prepare a statement of changes in financial position using the direct method.

4   Calculate cash flows from operations using the indirect method.

5   Explain how amortization affects cash flows provided by operating activities.

6   Describe several reconciling items between net income and cash provided by operating activities.

7   Explain treatment of gains and losses from fixed asset sales and debt extinguishments in the statement of changes in financial position (Appendix 6A).

8   Use the T-account approach to prepare the statement of changes in financial position (Appendix 6B).

This chapter provides a detailed look at the statement of changes in financial position and the information it provides to readers of financial statements. We discuss how and why cash flows are classified into three categories: operating, financing, and investing. The statement of changes in financial position may be *structured* in either the direct or indirect method, both of which are presented in the chapter. Some companies use the balance sheet approach, as presented in the chapter, to *prepare* the statement of changes in financial position. Others use the T-account approach, which is presented in Appendix 6B.

The accrual basis of accounting is the primary means of presenting financial position (balance sheet) and operating performance (income statement). But investors and managers are also concerned about an entity's ability to generate cash and to meet forthcoming obligations. Several large businesses have failed in the recent past because they did not produce enough cash to meet their obligations. Examples include Consumers Distributing and Olympia & York. The statement of changes in financial position is intended to enable investors to identify such risks in advance and to aid managers in avoiding the disastrous outcomes often associated with insufficient cash.

Until the 1980s, only the income statement and balance sheet were required in Canada. In 1985, a third statement, which presented year-to-year changes in financial position on a cash basis, became required. In many other countries a statement like the statement of changes in financial position is required, but the definitions and the structure of the statement differ widely. Moreover, in some countries, including Japan, Austria, India, and Uruguay, no such statement is common.

■ OVERVIEW OF STATEMENT OF CHANGES IN FINANCIAL POSITION

Purposes of Statement

Objective 1

Explain the concept of the statement of changes in financial position.

Rampant inflation in the late 1970s and early 1980s engendered many criticisms of the traditional accrual measures of income and financial position. One response has been a more intense focus on the effects of activities on cash. The CICA reacted to this change in focus by requiring the statement of changes in financial position as a basic financial statement.

A *statement of changes in financial position* reports the cash receipts and cash payments of an entity during a period. It explains the causes for the changes in cash by providing information about operating, financing, and investing activities. The statement of changes in financial position is a basic financial statement in corporate annual reports.

Why is a statement of changes in financial position useful? Because:

1. It shows the relationship of net income to changes in cash balances. Cash balances can decline despite positive net income and vice versa.
2. It reports past cash flows as an aid to
   a. Predicting future cash flows.
   b. Evaluating management's generation and use of cash.
   c. Determining a company's ability to pay interest and dividends and to pay debts when they are due.
3. It identifies changes in the mix of productive assets.

Balance sheets show the status of an entity at a day in time. In contrast, statements of changes in financial position, income statements, and statements of

Post-mortem Finds Evidence of Questionable Accounting

A probe into the collapse of Coopérants Mutual Life Insurance Society has found evidence of irregular accounting practices, questionable financial deals and inadequate disclosure to regulators.

Coopérants, once a sprawling Montreal-based financial conglomerate with 2,400 employees and $3-billion in assets, hid a deepening financial crisis from nearly everyone through the use of unrealized "paper profits" and irregular accounting practices, according to a post-mortem report by accounting firm Poissant Thibault Thorne. Poissant Thibault was commissioned to look into the collapse by liquidators Raymond Chabot Fafard Gagnon Inc. Quebec Superior Court ordered the report made available to creditors earlier this month.

Officials of both the liquidator and an insurance industry bailout fund confirmed yesterday that they are considering suing officers, directors, auditors and actuaries involved in the failure of the company. Its liquidation in January was the first for a Canadian life insurance company.

The company's financial statements were so out of whack with reality that it reported profits in 1988 and 1989 that should have been losses and dramatically understated a massive 1990 loss, according to the report, which runs to three volumes and more than 300 pages.

Poissant Thibault said the insurer's real losses in 1990, 1989 and 1988 were $90.1-million, $22.1-million and $12.5-million. Reports sent to regulators and thousands of policy holders instead showed a $31-million loss in 1990 and profits of $3-million and $7-million in the two previous years....

According to the report, Coopérants had exhausted its financial resources by the end of 1987, but chose to artificially prop itself up with paper profits.

In 1988, for example, it created Groupe Coopérants Inc. and reported a $29.5-million gain by selling several of its own subsidiaries to the new company. The gain was unjustified, Poissant Thibault said.

By 1990, its problems were snowballing. In a report to top executives and directors, Coopérants chairman Paul Dolan said the company had failed to meet its own performance targets for seven consecutive quarters and had been losing money for the past three years.

Mr. Dolan's comments were never reflected in the company's financial statements. Poissant Thibault said the profits shown in its financial statements did not reflect the financial state of the company and its 30-odd subsidiaries. ■

Source: Barrie McKenna, "Coopérants crisis hidden, probe concludes," The Globe and Mail, *(December 16, 1992, p. B1, 15). Reprinted with permission from The Globe and Mail.*

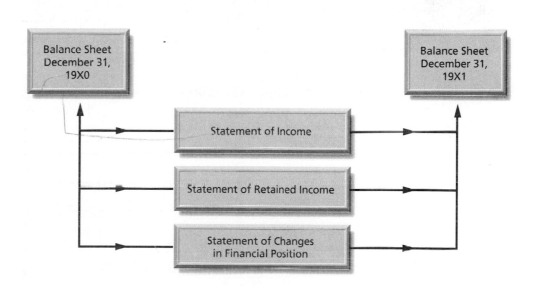

retained income cover periods of time; they provide the explanations of why the balance sheet items have changed. This linkage is depicted in the diagram above:

The statement of changes in financial position explains where cash came from during a period and where it was spent. The statement of changes in financial position usually explains changes in cash and cash equivalents. *Cash equivalents* are highly liquid short-term investments that can easily be converted into cash with little delay. Examples include money market funds and treasury bills. They are usually temporary investments of excess cash, and they can readily be converted into cash as obligations become due. Hereafter, when we refer to cash, we mean both cash and cash equivalents.

Readers of financial statements want information on a firm's activities in two primary areas: its operating management and its financial management. **Operating management** is largely concerned with the major day-to-day activities that generate revenues and expenses. The income statement, prepared on an accrual basis, is the primary statement used in assessing operating management.

Financial management is largely concerned with where to get cash (*financing activities*) and how to use cash (*investing activities*). For example, financial managers decide about the issuance or retirement of long-term debt or additional capital stock and about how to invest the capital raised. The statement of changes in financial position reports the results of both financial management and operating management. It includes three categories of activities: operating activities, investing activities, and financing activities.

Typical Activities Affecting Cash

The following are typical activities in statements of changes in financial position:

OPERATING ACTIVITIES

Cash Inflows	*Cash Outflows*
Collections from customers	Cash payments to suppliers
Interest and dividends collected	Cash payments to employees
Other operating receipts	Interest and taxes paid
	Other operating cash payments

INVESTING ACTIVITIES

Cash Inflows	*Cash Outflows*
Sale of property, plant, and equipment	Purchase of property, plant, and equipment
Sale of securities that are not cash equivalents	Purchase of securities that are not cash equivalents
Receipt of loan repayments	Making loans

FINANCING ACTIVITIES

Cash Inflows	*Cash Outflows*
Borrowing cash from creditors	Repayment of amounts borrowed
Issuing equity securities	Repurchase of equity shares (including the purchase of treasury stock)
Issuing debt securities	Payment of dividends

As the lists of activities indicate, **operating activities** are generally transactions that affect the income statement. For example, sales are linked to collections from customers, and wage expenses are closely tied to cash payments to employees. **Investing activities** involve (1) providing and collecting cash as a lender or as an

operating management Is mainly concerned with the major day-to-day activities that generate revenues and expenses.

financial management Is mainly concerned with where to get cash and how to use cash for the benefit of the entity.

Objective 2

Classify activities affecting cash as operating, investing, or financing activities.

operating activities Transactions that affect the income statement.

investing activities Activities that involve (1) providing and collecting cash as a lender or as an owner of securities and (2) acquiring and disposing of plant, property, equipment, and other long-term productive assets.

financing activities
In the statement of changes in financial position, obtaining resources as a borrower or issuer of securities and repaying creditors and owners.

owner of securities and (2) acquiring and disposing of plant, property, equipment, and other long-term productive assets. **Financing activities** involve obtaining resources as a borrower or issuer of securities and repaying creditors and owners. Note that the two parties to a transaction treat it differently in the statement of changes in financial position. When stock is issued for cash to an investor, the issuer treats it as a financing activity and the investor treats it as an investing activity.

Exhibit 6-1

APT Company
Financial Statements

Balance Sheets for the Years Ended December 31

Assets	19X1	19X0	Liabilities and Shareholders' Equity	19X1	19X0
Cash	$1,200	$ 4,000	Accounts payable	$ 200	$ 200
Supplies	600	400	Shareholders'		
Computer	2,000	0	equity	3,600	4,200
Total assets	$3,800	$4,400	Total Liab. and SE	$3,800	$4,400

Income Statement for the Year Ended December 31, 19X1

Sales		$35,000
Wages	$20,000	
Depreciation	1,000	
Supplies	3,000	24,000
Net income		$11,000

Statement of Changes in Financial Position for the Year Ended December 31, 19X1

CASH FLOWS FROM OPERATING ACTIVITIES:	
Collections from customers	$ 35,000
Payments to employees	(20,000)
Payments to suppliers	(3,200)
Net cash provided by operating activities	11,800
CASH FLOWS FROM INVESTING ACTIVITIES:	
Cash investment in computer	(3,000)
Net cash used for investing activities	(3,000)
CASH FLOWS FROM FINANCING ACTIVITIES:	
Cash dividend payments	(11,600)
Net cash used for financing activities	(11,600)
Decrease in cash	$ (2,800)
Cash balance December 31, 19X0	4,000
Cash balance December 31, 19X1	$ 1,200

As a concrete example, consider the operating and financial management activities of the APT Company. The APT Company provides daily cleaning services for homes. Exhibit 6-1 displays its financial statements. APT pays all wages in cash daily, and all revenues are collected in cash daily. If these were the only transactions affecting income, net income would equal cash provided by operations. But APT owns a computer, and amortization on the computer is allocated to the income statement over the computer's anticipated three-year life. Since amortization does not involve a cash flow, it appears on the income statement as an expense but does not affect cash provided by operations.

Cleaning supplies are purchased for cash periodically, but the supplies are not necessarily paid for upon delivery. Moreover, supplies are kept in inventory to be used as needed, so all the supplies acquired are not immediately used. The income statement reports the $3,000 of supplies *used* during the period, while the statement of changes in financial position reports the $3,200 of supplies *paid for* during the period.

In comparing the income statement and cash flows from operations, you can see that the only differences are for supplies and amortization. The APT Company has only one investing activity, the purchase of a computer, and one financing activity, the payment of cash dividends.

Approaches to Calculating the Cash Flow from Operating Activities

cash flows from operating activities The first major section of the statement of changes in financial position. It shows the cash effects of transactions that affect the income statement.

direct method In a statement of changes in financial position, the method that calculates net cash provided by operating activities as collections minus operating disbursements.

indirect method In a statement of changes in financial position, the method that adjusts the accrual net income to reflect only cash receipts and outlays.

Two approaches can be used to compute **cash flow from operating activities** (or operations), the first major section of the statement of changes in financial position, which shows the cash effects of transactions affecting the income statement. Computing it as collections less operating disbursements is called the **direct method**. This is the method illustrated for APT. Adjusting the accrual net income to reflect only cash receipts and outlays is called the **indirect method**.

Under the direct method, we identify only the cash part of each item in the income statement. Since amortization does not use cash, it is not part of the calculation. For APT we had only to do a calculation for supplies. By examining the balance sheet, we see that supplies inventory rose from $400 to $600. This suggests we bought more than we used, so cost of supplies in the income statement was smaller than purchases. But did we pay for what we bought? Yes, we paid for exactly the quantity purchased during the year because the Accounts Payable balance remained unchanged. Whatever the increases to the account were for new purchases, the decreases for payments were identical. So if we paid for all we bought, and we bought $200 more than we sold, we must have paid for $3,200. Therefore, net cash provided by operating activities must be cash sales of $35,000 less $20,000 in cash wages and $3,200 cash paid for supplies for a net of $11,800, as shown in Exhibit 6-1.

Alternatively, cash flow from operations can be calculated by the *indirect* method. The income statement provides an accrual-based net income of $11,000, and we can simply adjust it for the accrual elements that are different from the cash outlays. We deducted $1,000 of amortization to calculate net income, but amortization involved no cash, so let's add it back to get $12,000 ($11,000 plus $1,000). In addition we know we spent $200 more on supplies than we used, so let's subtract that $200 as an operating use of cash that does not appear in net income. By adjusting net income, we again calculate $11,800 ($11,000 + $1,000 − $200).

While some may prefer the direct method because it shows operating cash receipts and payments in a way that is easier for investors to understand, the indirect method is more common. The two approaches are shown below:

APT Company
Cash Flow from
Operating Activities

	Direct Method		Indirect Method	
Collections from customers		$35,000	Net earnings	$11,000
Payments to employees	$20,000		Add amortization*	1,000
Payments to suppliers	3,200	23,200	Deduct supplies†	(200)
Net cash provided by operating activities		$11,800		$11,800

*Amortization was deducted to compute net earnings but did not involve a cash flow.
†Payments for supplies exceeded the amount charged as expense.

TRANSACTIONS AFFECTING CASH FLOWS FROM ALL SOURCES

The APT Company was an intentionally simplified illustration that gave us a first look at the principles behind the statement of changes in financial position. Now we will enlarge our scope.

Activities Affecting Cash

Exhibit 6-2 summarizes the effects of most major transactions on cash. The zeros in the "change in cash" column indicate that the transaction has no effect on cash. Examples are sales and purchases on account and even the accrual recording of cost of goods sold. Cash flow emphasizes the flow of cash to and from customers and suppliers; accrual accounting emphasizes the flow of goods and services.

Exhibit 6-2

Analysis of Effects of Transactions on Cash

Type of Transaction	Change in Cash
OPERATING ACTIVITIES:	
Sales of goods and services for cash	+
Sales of goods and services on credit	0
Receive dividends or interest	+
Collection of accounts receivable	+
Recognize cost of goods sold	0
Purchase inventory for cash	−
Purchase inventory on credit	0
Pay trade accounts payable	−
Accrue operating expenses	0
Pay operating expenses	−
Accrue taxes	0
Pay taxes	−
Accrue interest	0
Pay interest	−
Prepay expenses for cash	−
Write off prepaid expenses	0
Charge depreciation or amortization	0
INVESTING ACTIVITIES:	
Purchase fixed assets for cash	−
Purchase fixed assets by issuing debt	0
Sell fixed assets	+
Purchase securities that are not cash equivalents	−
Sell securities that are not cash equivalents	+
Make a loan	−
FINANCING ACTIVITIES:	
Increase long-term or short-term debt	+
Reduce long-term or short-term debt	−
Sell common or preferred shares	+
Repurchase and retire common or preferred shares	−
Purchase treasury stock	−
Pay dividends	−
Convert debt to common stock	0
Reclassify long-term debt to short-term debt	0

With regard to interest and dividend payments, each company may classify either or both as operating or financing activities, depending upon their own assessment of their circumstances.

Cash Flow and Earnings

cash flow Usually refers to net cash provided by operating activities.

A focal point of the statement of changes in financial position is the net cash flow from operating activities. Frequently, this is called simply **cash flow**. The importance of cash flow has been stressed by Harold Williams, the former chairman of the Securities and Exchange Commission, quoted in *Forbes*: "If I had to make a forced choice between having earnings information and having cash flow information, today I would take cash flow information." Fortunately, we do not have to make a choice. Cash flow and income both convey useful information about an entity.

In prior years, some companies stressed a cash-flow-per-share-from-operations figure and provided it in addition to the required earnings-per-share figure. But net cash flow from operating activities gives an incomplete picture of management performance. Why? Because it ignores noncash expenses that are just as important as cash expenses for judging overall company performance. Moreover, a reported cash-flow-per-share says nothing about the cash needed for replacement and expansion of facilities. Thus, the entire per-share cash flow from operations may not be available for cash dividends. Because it gives an incomplete picture, a cash-flow-per-share figure can be quite misleading.

Both cash flow and accrual earnings data are useful. As Professor Loyd Heath said, "Asking which one is better, cash flow or earnings, is like asking which shoe is more useful, your right or your left?"

■ THE ECO-BAG COMPANY—A MORE-DETAILED EXAMPLE

Consider the Eco-Bag Company, whose financial statements are shown in Exhibit 6-3. The statement of changes in financial position is prepared using the direct method.

Because the statement of changes in financial position explains the *causes* for the change in cash, the first step is always to compute the amount of the change (which represents the net *effect*):

Cash, December 31, 19X1	$ 25,000
Cash, December 31, 19X2	16,000
Net decrease in cash	$ 9,000

Eco-Bag Company's statement illustrates how this information is often shown at the bottom of a statement of changes in financial position. The beginning cash balance is added to the net change to compute the ending cash balance. Another common practice is to place the beginning cash balance at the top of the statement and the ending cash balance at the bottom. However, there is no requirement that beginning and ending cash balances be shown explicitly in the statement of changes in financial position. Showing only the net change is sufficient.

When business expansion occurs, as in this case, and where there is a strong cash position at the outset, cash often declines. Why? Because cash is usually needed for investment in various business assets required for expansion, including investment in accounts receivable and inventories.

Eco-Bag Company's statement gives a direct picture of where cash came from and where it went. In this instance, the excess of cash outflows over cash inflows reduced cash by $9,000. Without the statement of changes in financial position, the readers of the annual report would have to conduct their own analyses of the beginning and ending balance sheets, the income statement, and the statement of retained income to grasp the impact of financial management decisions.

Most important, this illustration demonstrates how a firm may simultaneously (1) have a significant amount of net income, as computed by accountants on the accrual basis, and yet (2) have a decline in cash that could become severe. Indeed, many growing businesses are desperate for cash even though reported net income zooms upward.

Exhibit 6-3

Eco-Bag Company
Balance Sheet as of
December 31
(in thousands)

Assets			Liabilities and Shareholders' Equity		
	19X2	19X1		19X2	19X1
Current assets:			Current liabilities:		
			Accounts payable	$ 74	$ 6
Cash	$ 16	$ 25	Wages and		
Accounts receivable	45	25	salaries payable	25	4
Inventory	100	60			
Total current assets	161	110	Total current liabilities	99	10
Fixed assets, gross	581	330	Long-term debt	125	5
Accum. amortization	(101)	(110)	Shareholders' equity	417	315
Net	480	220			
			Total liabilities and		
Total assets	$641	$330	shareholders' equity	$641	$330

Eco-Bag Company
Statement of Income
for the Year Ended
December 31, 19X2
(in thousands)

Sales		$200
Cost and expenses:		
Cost of goods sold	$100	
Wages and salaries	36	
Amortization	17	
Interest	4	
Total costs and expenses		$157
Income before income taxes		43
Income taxes		20
Net income		$ 23

Eco-Bag Company
Statement of
Changes in Financial
Position
for the Year Ended
December 31, 19X2
(in thousands)

CASH FLOWS FROM OPERATING ACTIVITIES:		
Cash collections from customers		$180
Cash payments:		
To suppliers	$ 72	
To employees	15	
For interest	4	
For taxes	20	
Total cash payments		(111)
Net cash provided by operating activities		$ 69
CASH FLOWS FROM INVESTING ACTIVITIES:		
Purchases of fixed assets	$(287)	
Proceeds from sale of fixed assets	10	
Net cash used by investing activities		(277)
CASH FLOWS FROM FINANCING ACTIVITIES:		
Proceeds from issue of long-term debt	$ 120	
Proceeds from issue of common stock	98	
Dividends paid	(19)	
Net cash provided by financing activities		199
Net decrease in cash		$ (9)
Cash, December 31, 19X1		25
Cash, December 31, 19X2		$ 16

■ PREPARING A STATEMENT OF CHANGES IN FINANCIAL POSITION—THE DIRECT METHOD

Changes in the Balance Sheet Equation

Objective 3

Prepare a statement of changes in financial position using the direct method.

Accountants use various techniques for preparing a statement of changes in financial position. The balance sheet approach is frequently used, but accountants may also use work sheets or T-accounts (described in Appendix 6B). The balance sheet provides the conceptual framework underlying all financial statements, including the statement of changes in financial position. The equation can be rearranged as follows:

$$\text{Assets} = \text{Liabilities} + \text{Shareholders' equity}$$
$$\text{Cash} + \text{Noncash assets} = \text{Liabilities} + \text{Shareholders' equity}$$
$$\text{Cash} = \text{Liabilities} + \text{Shareholders' equity} - \text{Noncash Assets}$$
$$\text{Cash} = \text{L} + \text{SE} - \text{NCA}$$

Any change (Δ) in cash must be accompanied by a change in one or more items on the right side to keep the equation in balance:

$$\Delta \text{ Cash} = \Delta \text{ L} + \Delta \text{ SE} - \Delta \text{ NCA}$$

Therefore:

$$\text{Change in cash} = \text{Change in all noncash accounts}$$

or

$$\text{What happened to cash} = \text{Why it happened}$$

The statement of changes in financial position focuses on the changes in the noncash accounts as a way of explaining how and why the level of cash has gone up or down during a given period. Thus, the major changes in the accounts on the right side of the equation appear in the statement of changes in financial position as *causes* of the change in cash. The left side of the equation measures the net *effect* of the change in cash.

Consider the following summary of 19X2 transactions for the Eco-Bag Company. In practice, this summary might be produced by a careful review of the general ledger accounts to combine similar transactions that occurred during the year. Those involving cash have an asterisk (*):

1. Sales on credit, $200,000.
*2. Collections of accounts receivable, $180,000.
3. Recognition of cost of goods sold, $100,000.
4. Purchases of inventory on account, $140,000.
*5. Payments of trade accounts payable, $72,000.
6. Recognition of wages expense, $36,000.
*7. Payments of wages, $15,000.
*8. Recognition of interest accrued and paid, $4,000.
*9. Recognition and payment of income taxes, $20,000.
10. Recognition of amortization expense, $17,000.
*11. Acquisition of fixed assets for cash, $287,000.
*12. Sale of fixed assets at book value, $10,000.
*13. Issuance of long-term debt, $120,000.
*14. Issuance of common stock, $98,000.
*15. Declaration and payment of dividends, $19,000.

Exhibit 6-4 applies the balance sheet equation to the Eco-Bag Company data. We can see, step by step, how the statement of changes in financial position in Exhibit 6-3 is based on the same theoretical foundation that underlies the other financial statements.

When statements become complicated, accountants prefer to use work sheets or T-accounts to help their analysis. In any event, the totals in the tabulation of Exhibit 6-4 show that all transactions affecting cash have been accounted for. The $9,000 decrease in cash is explained by the changes in the liability, shareholders' equity, and noncash asset accounts. Each noncash account can be analyzed in detail if desired.

Computing Cash Flows from Operating Activities

The first major section in Eco-Bag Company's statement of changes in financial position (Exhibit 6-3) is *cash flows from operating activities*. The section might also be called *cash flow from operations, cash provided by operations*, or, if operating activities decrease cash, *cash used for operations*.

Collections from sales to customers are almost always the major operating activity that increases cash. Correspondingly, disbursements for purchases of goods to be sold and operating expenses are almost always the major operating cash outflows. The excess of collections over disbursements is the net cash provided by operating activities. In Exhibit 6-3, collections of $180,000 minus the $111,000 of operating disbursements equals net cash provided by operating activities, $69,000.

5-4

tual
Foundation: The
Balance Sheet
Equation (in thou-
sands of dollars)

	Δ Cash	=	Δ L	+ Δ SE	– Δ NCA
Operating activities:					
1. Sales on credit		=		+200	– (+200)
*2. Cash collections from customers	+180	=			– (– 180)
3. Cost of goods sold		=		–100	– (– 100)
4. Inventory purchases on account		=	+140		– (+140)
*5. Payments to suppliers	– 72	=	– 72		
6. Wages and salaries expense		=	+ 36	– 36	
*7. Payments to employees	– 15	=	– 15		
*8. Interest expense paid	– 4	=		– 4	
*9. Income taxes paid	– 20	=		– 20	
Net cash provided by operating activities, a subtotal	69				
Expenses not requiring cash:					
10. Amortization		=		– 17	– (– 17)
Net income, a subtotal				+ 23	
Investing activities:					
*11. Acquire fixed assets	–287	=			– (+287)
*12. Dispose of fixed assets	+ 10	=			– (– 10)
Financing activities:					
*13. Issue long-term debt	+120	=	+120		
*14. Issue common stock	+ 98	=		+ 98	
*15. Pay dividends	– 19	=		– 19	
Net changes	– 9	=	+209	+102	– (+320)

Working from Income Statement Amounts to Cash Amounts

Many accountants build the statement of changes in financial position from the *changes* in balance sheet items, a few additional facts, and a familiarity with the typical causes of changes in cash. For instance, for convenience the $180,000 amount of cash collections from Eco-Bag Company customers for 19X2 was given in our example. However, most accounting systems do not provide such a balance. Therefore, accountants often compute the collections by beginning with the sales revenue shown on the income statement (an amount calculated using the accrual basis) and adding a decrease (or deducting an increase) in the accounts receivable balance. A detailed analysis of collections and other operating items follows.

a. Eco-Bag Company recognized $200,000 of revenue in 19X2, but because accounts receivable increased by $20,000, only $180,000 was collected from customers:

Sales	$200,000
+ Beginning accounts receivable	25,000
Potential collections	$225,000
– Ending accounts receivable	45,000
Cash collections from customers	$180,000

or

Sales	$200,000
Decrease (increase) in accounts receivable	(20,000)
Cash collections from customers	$180,000

Note that a decrease in accounts receivable means that collections exceeded sales. Conversely, an increase in accounts receivable means sales exceeded collections.

b. The difference between the $100,000 cost of goods sold and the $72,000 cash payment to suppliers is accounted for by changes in inventory *and* accounts payable. The $40,000 increase in inventory indicates that purchases exceeded the cost of goods sold by $40,000:

Ending inventory	$100,000
+ Cost of goods sold	100,000
Inventory to account for	$200,000
– Beginning inventory	(60,000)
Purchases of inventory	$ 140,000

Although purchases were $140,000, payments to suppliers were only $72,000. Why? Because trade accounts payable increased by $68,000, from $6,000 to $74,000:

Beginning trade accounts payable	$ 6,000
+ Purchases	140,000
Total amount to be paid	$ 146,000
– Ending trade accounts payable	(74,000)
Accounts paid in cash	$ 72,000

The effects of inventory and trade accounts payable can be combined as follows:

Cost of goods sold	$ 100,000
Increase (decrease) in inventory	40,000
Decrease (increase) in trade accounts payable	(68,000)
Payments to suppliers	$ 72,000

c. Cash payments to employees were only $15,000 because the wages and salaries expense of $36,000 was offset by a $21,000 increase in wages and salaries payable:

Beginning wages and salaries payable	$ 4,000
+ Wages and salaries expense	36,000
Total to be paid	$ 40,000
– Ending wages and salaries payable	(25,000)
Cash payments to employees	$ 15,000

or

Wages and salaries expense	$ 36,000
Decrease (increase) in wages and salaries payable	(21,000)
Cash payments to employees	$15,000

d. Notice that both interest payable and income taxes payable were zero at the beginning and at the end of 19X2. Therefore the entire $4,000 interest expense and the $20,000 income tax expense were paid in cash in 19X2.

Comparsion of Income Statement and Statement of Changes in Financial Position

Accrual-based measures of revenue and expense are reported in the income statement. Most of these are naturally linked to related asset or liability accounts and the cash effects of the revenue and expense transactions are moderated by changes in their related asset or liability accounts. The indirect method adjusts accrual-based values for changes in account balances. The following illustration emphasizes the process.

Exhibit 6-5

Comparison of Net Income and Net Cash Provided by Operating Activities

Panel I.   THE GENERAL CASE: Common Adjustments to Convert Income Statement Amounts to Cash Flow Amounts

Income Statement Amount	Related Noncash Asset	Related Liability
Sales revenue	Accounts receivable	Unearned revenue
Cost of goods sold	Merchandise inventory	Accounts payable
Wage expense	Prepaid wages	Wages payable
Rent expense	Prepaid rent	Rent Payable
Insurance expense	Prepaid insurance	Insurance payable
Depreciation expense	Plant, property, or equipment	
Amortization expense	Intangible asset	

Panel II.   THE ECO–BAG COMPANY EXAMPLE

Income Statement		Asset Change	Liability Change	Statement of Changes in Financial Position
		− Increases +Decreases	+ Increases −Decreases	
Sales revenue	$200,000	$ (20,000)		= $180,000
Cost of goods sold	(100,000)	(40,000)	$68,000	= (72,000)
Wage and salary expense	(36,000)		21,000	= (15,000)
Interest expense	(4,000)			= (4,000)
Income taxes	(20,000)			= (20,000)
Amortization	(17,000)	17,000		
Net income	$ 23,000	$ (43,000)	$89,000	$ 69,000

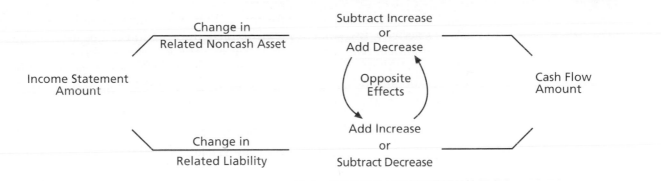

Note that liability changes have opposite effects from asset changes. Each revenue or expense account has a related asset and/or liability account, some examples of which are shown in Panel I of Exhibit 6-5.

Panel II of Exhibit 6-5 summarizes the application of this concept to the details of the Eco-Bag Company. For example, the $20,000 increase in accounts receivable indicates that not all of the sales were collected, so sales revenue is reduced from $200,000 to $180,000, the actual cash collected. Similarly, the $40,000 increase in inventory indicates that we might have paid for more goods than we sold, an additional use of cash. This effect is offset by the increase in accounts payable of $68,000. We delayed the use of cash by increasing our trade credit.

Computing Cash Flows from Investing and Financing Activities

cash flow from investing activities
The second major section of the statement of changes in financial position describing purchase or sale of plant, property, equipment, and other long-lived assets.

The second and third major sections of the statement of changes in financial position are **cash flows from investing activities** and **cash flows from financing activities.** The former lists cash flows from the purchase or sale of plant, property, equipment, and other long-lived assets. The latter shows cash flows to and from providers of capital. If the necessary information regarding these cash flows is not directly available, accountants analyze *changes* in all balance sheet items *except* cash. The following rules pertain:

- *Increases in cash (cash inflows)*
    Increases in liabilities or shareholders' equity
    Decreases in noncash assets
- *Decreases in cash (cash outflows)*
    Decreases in liabilities or shareholders' equity
    Increases in noncash assets

cash flows from financing activities
The third major section of the statement of changes in financial position describing flows to and from providers of capital.

Consider Eco-Bag Company's balance sheet (Exhibit 6-3). All noncash *current* assets and *current* liabilities of the company were affected only by operating activities. Three *noncurrent* accounts—(a) fixed assets, (b) long-term debt, and (c) shareholders' equity—affect the cash flows from investing activities ($277,000 outflow) and financing activities ($199,000 inflow), respectively.

a. Net fixed assets increased by $260,000 in 19X2, as you can see by examining the balance sheet in Exhibit 6-3. Three items usually explain changes in net fixed assets: (1) assets acquired, (2) asset dispositions, and (3) amortization expense for the period. Therefore:

Increase in net plant assets = Acquisitions – Disposals – Amortization expense

Preparing the cash flow from investing activities requires some knowledge of the year's activity. But sometimes incomplete information can be used to figure out the unknown part. For example, you might know the increase in net plant assets, acquisitions of new fixed assets, and amortization expense without knowing about Eco-Bag Company's asset disposals. The book value of disposals could be computed from the above equation:

$$\$260{,}000 = \$287{,}000 - \text{Disposals} - \$17{,}000$$
$$\text{Disposals} = \$287{,}000 - \$17{,}000 - \$260{,}000$$
$$\text{Disposals} = \$10{,}000$$

Eco-Bag Company received exactly the book value for the assets sold. (Appendix 6A discusses disposals for more or less than book value.) If the amount of disposals were known, but either acquisitions or amortization expense were unknown, the missing item could be determined by applying this same equation. Both asset acquisitions and asset disposals are *investing activities* that affect cash.

b. Long-term debt increased by $\$125{,}000 - \$5{,}000 = \$120{,}000$. Long-term debt was issued, a *financing activity* that increased cash.

c. The $102,000 increase in shareholders' equity can be explained by three factors: (1) issuance of capital stock, (2) net income (or loss), and (3) dividends. Therefore:

Increase in shareholders' equity = New issuance + Net income − Dividends

Suppose data about the issuance of new capital stock had not been provided:

$$\$102{,}000 = \text{New issuance} + \$23{,}000 - \$19{,}000$$
$$\text{New issuance} = \$102{,}000 - \$23{,}000 + \$19{,}000$$
$$\text{New issuance} = \$98{,}000, \text{ an inflow of cash}$$

Both the issuance of new shares and the payment of cash dividends are *financing activities* that affect cash.

Reexamine the statement of changes in financial position in Exhibit 6-3. The asset acquisitions and disposals from paragraph **a** are listed with cash flows from investing activities, and the effects of debt and equity issues and dividend payments from paragraphs **b** and **c** are shown with cash flows from financing activities.

Noncash Investing and Financing Activities

Major investment and financing activities that do not affect cash must be reported in a schedule that accompanies the statement of changes in financial position. In our example, Eco-Bag Company did not have any noncash investing or financing activities. But suppose Eco-Bag Company had the following such activities:

1. Acquired a $14,000 fixed asset by issuing common stock.
2. Acquired a small building by signing a mortgage payable for $97,000.
3. Long-term debt of $35,000 was converted to common stock.

Cash Flows, or Does It?

Although investors make important economic decisions on the basis of the so-called bottom line, one *Forbes* writer claims that earnings numbers reported by companies have become "virtually worthless" as a measure of what is really happening inside a company. In support of this claim the writer cited the case of Prime Motor Inns, the world's second-largest hotel operator, which reported earnings of $77 million on revenues of $410 million for 1989. That is a return on sales (net income ÷ revenues) of nearly 19%. Moreover, revenues increased by nearly 11% from the preceding year. Despite its impressive earnings performance, Prime lacked the cash to meet its obligations. Prime filed for bankruptcy in September 1990. Under bankruptcy protection, a firm's obligations to its creditors are frozen as management figures out how to pay its creditors. How can a firm with $77 million in earnings file for bankruptcy about a year later?

Much of Prime's reported earnings in 1989 arose from *selling* hotels. When outside financing for the hotel sales became harder to obtain, Prime financed the sales itself by accepting notes and mortgages receivable from the buyer. Hotel sales cannot continue forever, and when the seller finances the transaction, the reported gain may exceed the cash received. In the same year that Prime reported a net income of $77 million, an astute analyst would have noted that Prime had a net cash *outflow* from operations of $15 million, compared with the net cash inflow of $58 million in the previous year.

On July 31, 1992, the plan of reorganization became effective. Prime entered bankruptcy with 141 hotels and emerged half as large, with 75 hotels and a new name, Prime Hospitality Corporation. The new company kept its great stock symbol, "PDQ," and investors who bought the new shares for about $1.50 when the reorganization occurred have done well. In May of 1995, the price was $9.63. On the other hand, the shareholders who bought

the old company for $35 per share in 1989 watched their investment fall to under $1 in one year.

Another writer for the *Financial Post* also reported a scenario which questions the usefulness of reported financial information. Livent produces and stages live stage shows such as *Phantom of the Opera, Joseph and the Amazing Technicolor Dreamcoat*, and *Kiss*. These productions require substantial pre-production costs, which can be financed through a variety of means. The accounting for these cash flows is problematic such that Livent reported two sets of financial data for the first quarter ending March 31, 1995. To the Securities and Exchange Commission total assets were $154.0 million, revenues $57.3 million and cash from operations $1.7 million. However, to its shareholders, Livent reported total assets of $152.6 million, revenues of $49.6 million and negative cash from operations of (663,269). These differences in reported cash results for the same events would seem to question accounting practices.

An analysis of the statement of changes in financial position *in conjunction* with the earnings statement provides a complete perspective on the company's operating results. The value of this statement to investors is becoming more widely understood. ■

Sources: "Cash Flow Statements Should Be of Help in Diagnosing the Health of a Company," Financial Times *(February 21, 1992); Dana Wechsler Linden, "Lies of the Bottom Line,"* Forbes *(November 12, 1990), p. 106; John R. Dorfman, "Stock Analysts Increase Focus on Cash Flow,"* Wall Street Journal *(February 14, 1987), p. 35; Prime Motor Inns, Inc.,* 1989 Annual Report; *Prime Hospitality Corporation,* 1993 annual report, *NYSE Stock Reports, February 1991 and 1995; Philip Mathias, "Livent's Accounting May Puzzle the Experts,"* Financial Post *(September 23, 1995).*

Prime Hospitality Corp.
biz.yahoo.com/p/p/
pdq.html

These items affect the balance sheet equation as follows:

Δ Cash = Δ L		+ Δ SE		−	ΔNCA
1. 0 =		+$14,000	Increase Common Stock	− (+$14,000)	Increase Fixed Asset
2. 0 = +$97,000	Increase Mortgage payable			− (+$97,000)	Increase Building
3. 0 = −$35,000	Decrease Long-term Debt	+$35,000	Increase Common Stock		

None of these transactions affects cash, and therefore none belongs in a statement of changes in financial position. On the other hand, each transaction is almost identical to one involving cash flows. For example, a company might accomplish the first by issuing common stock for $14,000 cash and immediately using the cash to purchase the fixed asset. Because of the similarities between these noncash transactions and ones involving cash, readers of statements of changes in financial position should be informed of such noncash activities. Therefore such items must be included in a separate schedule accompanying the statement of changes in financial position. Eco-Bag Company's schedule for these additional transactions would be:

Schedule of noncash investing and financing activities:	
Common stock issued to acquire fixed asset	$14,000
Mortgage payable for acquisition of building	$97,000
Common stock issued on conversion of long-term debt	$35,000

■ PREPARING A STATEMENT OF CHANGES IN FINANCIAL POSITION—THE INDIRECT METHOD

Objective 4

Calculate cash flows from operations using the indirect method.

The Eco-Bag Company statement of changes in financial position in Exhibit 6-3 used the direct method to compute net cash provided by operating activities. The alternative, and often more convenient, *indirect method* of computing cash flows from operating activities reconciles net income to the net cash provided by operating activities. It also shows the link between the income statement and the statement of changes in financial position.

Using the direct method, the cash flow effect of each operating activity is calculated by adjusting the income statement amounts for changes in related asset and liability accounts. Simply stated, the indirect method considers the same changes in related asset and liability accounts but shows their effects directly on the net income number, rather than on the individual revenue and expense items that comprise net income.

Reconciliation of Net Income to Net Cash Provided by Operations

In the indirect method, the statement begins with net income. Then additions or deductions are made for changes in related asset or liability accounts, that is, for items that affect net income and net cash flow differently. Using the numbers in our Eco-Bag Company example, Exhibit 6-6 shows the reconciliation. As we saw in Exhibit 6-5, net cash provided by operating activities exceeds net income by $46,000. If a company uses the direct method, it is common to report a reconciliation such as Exhibit 6-6 as a *supporting schedule* to the statement of changes in financial position.

Consider the logic applied in the reconciliation in Exhibit 6-6:

1. Amortization is added back to net income because it was deducted in the computation of net income. To calculate cash provided by operations, the amortization of $17,000 would not have been subtracted. Why? Because it used no cash. Since it *was* subtracted in computing net income, it must now be added back to income to get cash from operations. The addback simply cancels the earlier deduction.

2. Increases in noncash current assets such as receivables and inventory result in less cash flow from operations. For instance, suppose the $20,000 increase in receivables was a result of credit sales made near the end of the year. The $20,000 sales figure would be included in the computation of net income, but the $20,000 would not have increased cash flow from operations. Therefore the reconciliation deducts the $20,000 from the net income to help pinpoint the effects on cash.

Exhibit 6-6		
Eco-Bag Company Reconciliation of Net Income to Net Cash Provided by Operating Activities (in thousands)		

Net income		$23
Adjustments to reconcile net income to net cash provided by operating activities:		
Amortization	$ 17	
Net increase in accounts receivable	(20)	
Net increase in inventory	(40)	
Net increase in accounts payable	68	
Net increase in wages and salaries payable	21	
Total additions and deductions		46
Net cash provided by operating activities		$69

3. Increases in current liabilities such as accounts payable and wages payable result in more cash flow from operations. For instance, suppose the $21,000 increase in wages payable was attributable to wages earned near the end of the year, but not yet paid in cash. The $21,000 wages expense would be deducted in computing net income, but the $21,000 would not yet have decreased cash flow from operations. Therefore the reconciliation adds the $21,000 to net income to offset the deduction and thereby show the effect on cash.

The general rules for additions and deductions to adjust net income using the indirect method are identical to those for adjusting the line items of the income statement under the direct method. We focus on current assets and liabilities because they are most often tied to operations.

Changes in Noncash Current Assets	**Changes in Noncash Current Liabilities**
deduct increases	add increases
add decreases	deduct decreases
Examples: Accounts Receivable Inventory	Examples: Accounts Payable Wages Payable

A final step is to reconcile for gains and losses that are included in net income but arise from investing or financing activities (in contrast to operating activities). Examples, which are explained in Appendix 6A, are:

- Add loss (or deduct gain) from sale of fixed assets
- Add loss (or deduct gain) on extinguishment of debt

Objective 5

Explain how amortization affects cash flows provided by operating activities.

Role of Amortization

The most crucial aspect of a statement of changes in financial position prepared by the indirect method is how amortization and other expenses that do not require cash relate to the flow of cash. The way amortization affects the indirect calculation of cash flow has led to widespread misunderstanding of the role of amortization in financial reporting, so let us examine this point in detail.

Amortization is an allocation of historical cost to expense and does not entail a current outflow of cash. Consider again the calculation of Eco-Bag Company's cash flows in Exhibit 6-5. Why is the $17,000 of amortization added to net income to compute cash flow? Simply to cancel its deduction in calculating net income. Unfortunately, use of the indirect method may at first glance create an erroneous impression that amortization is added because it, by itself, is a source of cash. If that were really true, a corporation could merely double or triple its bookkeeping entry for amortization expense when cash was badly needed! What would happen? Cash provided by operations would be unaffected. Suppose amortization for Eco-Bag Company is doubled:

	With Amortization of $17,000	With Amortization of $34,000
Sales	$200,000	$ 200,000
All expenses except amortization (including income taxes)*	(160,000)	(160,000)
Amortization	(17,000)	(34,000)
Net income	$ 23,000	$ 6,000
Nonamortization adjustments †	29,000	29,000
Add amortization	17,000	34,000
Net cash provided by operating activities	$ 69,000	$ 69,000

* $100,000 + $36,000 + $4,000 + $20,000 = $160,000
† From Exhibit 6-6, $(20,000) + $(40,000) + $68,000 + $21,000 = $29,000

The doubling affects amortization and net income, but it has no direct influence on cash provided by operations, which, of course, still amounts to $69,000. (For additional discussion, see Chapter 9, page 388, the section called "Amortization and Cash Flows." The effects of amortization on income tax outflows are explained there.)

Reconciliation Items

We have seen that net income rarely coincides with net cash provided by operating activities. Consequently, many necessary additions or deductions are commonly shown to reconcile net income to net cash provided by operating activities, as explained earlier for amortization and changes in noncash current assets and current liabilities.

Objective 6

Describe several
reconciling items
between net
income and cash
provided by operat-
ing activities.

Some other additions and deductions are listed below. Chapter references
are shown in parentheses for readers who want to study the nature of the items
in more depth:

ADD CHARGES AGAINST INCOME (EXPENSES) NOT REQUIRING CASH	DEDUCT CREDITS TO INCOME (REVENUES) NOT PROVIDING CASH
Amortization (Chapter 9)	Amortization of premium on bonds payable (Chapter 10)
Depletion (Chapter 9)	Extraordinary and nonoperating gains (Chapter 13)
Amortization of long-lived assets such as patents, copyrights, and goodwill (Chapter 9)	
Amortization of discount on bonds payable (Chapter 10)	
Extraordinary and nonoperating losses (Chapter 13)	

Nike's Statement of Changes in Financial Position

Nike, Inc.
www.nike.com

Exhibit 6-7 contains a statement of changes in financial position for Nike, Inc.,
maker of running shoes and other athletic clothing and equipment. Other publicly held corporations may include more details, but the general format of the
statement of changes in financial position is similar to that shown. Note that
Nike uses the indirect method in the body of the statement of changes in financial position to report the cash flows from operating activities. Most companies
use this format.

Most of the items in Exhibit 6-7 have been discussed earlier in the chapter, but
one deserves mention here. Proceeds from exercise of options is *cash received* from
issuance of shares to executives as part of a stock option compensation plan.

Summary Problems for Your Review

Problem One

The Buretta Company has prepared the data in Exhibit 6-8.

In December 19X2, Buretta paid $54 million cash for a new building acquired to
accommodate an expansion of operations. This was financed partly by a new issue of
long-term debt for $40 million cash. During 19X2, the company also sold fixed assets for
$5 million cash, which was equal to their book value. All sales and purchases of mer-
chandise were on credit.

Because the net income of $4 million was the highest in the company's history,
Alice Buretta, the Chairperson of the Board, was perplexed by the company's
extremely low cash balance.

Exhibit 6-7

Nike, Inc.
Consolidated
Statement of
Changes in Financial
Position for the Year
Ended May 31, 1994
(in thousands)

Cash provided (used) by operations:	
Net income	$298,794
Income charges (credits) not affecting cash:	
Amortization	64,531
Deferred income taxes and purchased tax benefits	(23,876)
Other non-current liabilities	(3,588)
Other, including amortization	8,067
Changes in certain working capital components:	
Decrease (increase) in inventory	160,823
Decrease (increase) in accounts receivable	23,979
Decrease (increase) in other current assets	6,888
Increase (decrease) in accounts payable, accrued liabilities and income taxes payable	40,845
Cash provided by operations	576,463
Cash provided (used) by investing activities:	
Additions to property, plant, and equipment	(95,266)
Disposals of property, plant, and equipment	12,650
Acquisition of subsidiaries:	
Goodwill	(2,185)
Net assets acquired	(1,367)
Additions to other non-current assets	(5,450)
Cash used by investing activities	(91,618)
Cash provided (used) by financing activities:	
Additions to long-term debt	6,044
Reductions in long-term debt including current portion	(56,986)
Decrease in notes payable	(2,939)
Proceeds from exercise of options	4,288
Repurchase of stock	(140,104)
Dividends—common and preferred	(60,282)
Cash used by financing activities	(249,979)
Effect of exchange rate changes on cash	(7,334)
Net increase in cash and equivalents	227,532
Cash and equivalents, beginning of year	291,284
Cash and equivalents, end of year	$518,816

Required

1. Prepare a statement of changes in financial position from the Buretta data in Exhibit 6-8 on the next page. Ignore income taxes. You may wish to use Exhibit 6-3 (p. 239) as a guide. Use the direct method for reporting cash flows from operating activities.
2. Prepare a supporting schedule that reconciles net income to net cash provided by operating activities.
3. What is revealed by the statement of changes in financial position? Does it help you reduce Alice Buretta's puzzlement? Why?

Exhibit 6-8

Buretta Co.

Income Statement and Statement of Retained Earnings for the Year Ended December 31, 19X2 (in millions)

Sales		$ 100
Less cost of goods sold:		
Inventory, December 31, 19X1	$ 15	
Purchases	105	
Cost of goods available for sale	$120	
Inventory, December 31, 19X2	47	73
Gross profit		$ 27
Less other expenses:		
General expenses	$ 8	
Amortization	8	
Property taxes	4	
Interest expense	3	23
Net income		$ 4
Retained earnings, December 31, 19X1		7
Total		$ 11
Dividends		1
Retained earnings, December 31, 19X2		$ 10

Trial Balances

	December 31 (in millions)		Increase (Decrease)
	19X2	19X1	
Debits			
Cash	$ 1	$ 20	$(19)
Accounts receivable	20	5	15
Inventory	47	15	32
Prepaid general expenses	3	2	1
Fixed assets, net	91	50	41
	$162	$92	$ 70
Credits			
Accounts payable for merchandise	$ 39	$ 14	$ 25
Accrued property tax payable	3	1	2
Long-term debt	40	—	40
Capital stock	70	70	—
Retained earnings	10	7	3
	$162	$92	$ 70

Solution to Problem One

1. See Exhibit 6-9. Cash flows from operating activities were computed as follows (in millions):

Sales	$ 100
Less increase in accounts receivable	(15)
Cash collections from customers	$ 85
Cost of goods sold	$ 73
Plus increase in inventory	32
Purchases	$105
Less increase in accounts payable	(25)
Cash paid to suppliers	$ 80
General expenses	$ 8
Plus increase in prepaid general expenses	1
Cash payment for general expenses	$ 9
Cash paid for interest	$ 3
Property taxes	$ 4
Less increase in accrued property tax payable	(2)
Cash paid for property taxes	$ 2

Exhibit 6-9

Buretta Company Statement of Changes in Financial Position for the Year Ended December 31, 19X2 (in millions)

CASH FLOWS FROM OPERATING ACTIVITIES:		
Cash collections from customers		$ 85
Cash payments:		
Cash paid to suppliers	$ (80)	
General expenses	(9)	
Interest paid	(3)	
Property taxes	(2)	(94)
Net cash used by operating activities		$ (9)
CASH FLOWS FROM INVESTING ACTIVITIES:		
Purchase of fixed assets (building)	$ (54)	
Proceeds from sale of fixed assets	5	
Net cash used by investing activities		(49)
CASH FLOWS FROM FINANCING ACTIVITIES:		
Long-term debt issued	$ 40	
Dividends paid	(1)	
Net cash provided by financing activities		39
Net decrease in cash		$ (19)
Cash balance, December 31, 19X1		20
Cash balance, December 31, 19X2		$ 1

Exhibit 6-10

Supporting Schedule to Statement of Changes in Financial Position. Reconciliation of Net Income to Net Cash Provided by Operating Activities for the Year Ended December 31, 19X2 (in millions)

Net income (from income statement)	$ 4
Adjustments to reconcile net income to net cash provided by operating activities:	
Add: Amortization, which was deducted in the computation of net income but does not decrease cash	8
Deduct: Increase in accounts receivable	(15)
Deduct: Increase in inventory	(32)
Deduct: Increase in prepaid general expenses	(1)
Add: Increase in accounts payable	25
Add: Increase in accrued property tax payable	2
Net cash used by operating activities	$ (9)

2. Exhibit 6-10 reconciles net income to net cash provided by operating activities.
3. The statement of changes in financial position shows where cash has come from and where it has gone. Operations used $9 million of cash. Why? The statement in Exhibit 6-9, which uses the direct method, shows the result clearly: $94 million in cash paid for operating activities exceeded $85 million in cash received from customers. The indirect method, in Exhibit 6-10, shows why, in a profitable year, operating cash flow could be negative. The three largest items differentiating net income from cash flow are changes in inventory, accounts receivable, and accounts payable. Sales during the period were not collected in full. Indeed, accounts receivable rose sharply, by $15 million, a 300% increase. Similarly, cash was committed to inventory growth, although much of that growth was financed by increased accounts payable. In summary, large increases in accounts receivable ($15 million) and inventory ($32 million), plus a $1 million increase in prepaid expenses, used $48 million of cash. In contrast, only $39 million (that is, $4 + $8 + $25 + $2 million) was generated.

Investing activities also consumed cash because $54 million was invested in a building, and only $5 million was received from sales of fixed assets. Financing activities generated $39 million cash, which was $19 million less than the $58 million used by operating and investing activities.

Alice Buretta should no longer be puzzled. The statement of changes in financial position shows clearly that cash payments exceeded receipts by $19 million. However, she may still be concerned about the depletion of cash. Either operations must be changed so that they do not require so much cash, or investment must be curtailed, or more long-term debt or ownership equity must be raised. Otherwise Buretta Company will soon run out of cash.

Problem Two

To understand how cash flow and net income vary during the life cycle of a business, consider the following example that portrays the four-year life of a short-lived merchandising company, Trend-2000. The first year the entrepreneurs bought twice as much as they sold because they were building their base inventory levels. Trend-2000 suppliers offered payment terms that resulted in 80% of each year's purchases being paid during that year and 20% in the next year. Sales were for cash with a 100% markup on cost. Selling activities were constant over the life of the business and were paid in cash. At the end of the fourth year the suppliers were paid in full and all of the inventory was sold. Use the following summary results to prepare four income statements and statements of changes in financial position from operations for Trend-2000, one for each year of its life.

	Year 1	Year 2	Year 3	Year 4
Purchases	2,000 units	1,500 units	1,500 units	1,000 units
$1 each	$2,000	$1,500	$1,500	$1,000
Sales	1,000 units	1,500 units	2,000 units	1,500 units
$2 each	$2,000	$3,000	$4,000	$3,000
Cost of sales	$1,000	$1,500	$2,000	$1,500
Selling expense	$1,000	$1,000	$1,000	$1,000
Merchandise payments*	$1,600	$1,600	$1,500	$1,300

*.8×2,000 = 1,600; (.2×2,000) + (.8×1,500) = 1,600; (.2×1,500) + (.8×1,500) = 1,500; (.2×1,500) + (1.0×1,000) = 1,300

Solution to Problem Two

	Year 1	Year 2	Year 3	Year 4	Total
Income statement					
Sales	$2,000	$3,000	$4,000	$3,000	$12,000
Cost of sales	1,000	1,500	2,000	1,500	6,000
Selling expenses	1,000	1,000	1,000	1,000	4,000
Net income	$ 0	$ 500	$1,000	$ 500	$ 2,000
Cash flows from Operations: Direct method					
Collections	$2,000	$3,000	$4,000	$3,000	$12,000
Payments on account	1,600	1,600	1,500	1,300	6,000
Payments for selling efforts	1,000	1,000	1,000	1,000	4,000
Cash flow from operations	$ (600)	$ 400	$1,500	$ 700	$ 2,000
Cash flows from Operations: Indirect method					
Net income	$ 0	$ 500	$1,000	$ 500	$ 2,000
– Increase in inventory	(1,000)				(1,000)
+Decrease in inventory			500	500	1,000
+Increase in accounts payable	400				400
– Decrease in accounts payable		(100)		(300)	(400)
	$ (600)	$ 400	$1,500	$ 700	$ 2,000

Balance Sheet Accounts at the end of:	Year 1	Year 2	Year 3	Year 4	
Merchandise inventory	$1,000	$1,000	$ 500	$ 0	
Accounts payable	$ 400	$ 300	$ 300	$ 0	

This problem illustrates the difference between accrual-based earnings and cash flows. Observe that significant cash outflows occur for operations during the first year as payments to acquire inventory far exceed collections from customers. In fact, it is not until the third year that cash flow from operations exceeds net earnings for the year.

Highlights to Remember

The statement of changes in financial position focuses on the changes in cash and the activities that cause those changes. Accrual-based net income is a useful number, but we also ask, How did our cash position change? How much of the change in cash was caused by operating activities? By investing activities such as buying another company or new plant and equipment? By financing activities such as borrowing from a bank, issuing bonds, or paying dividends to shareholders?

The direct method of calculating net cash provided by operations requires that we restate each income element. We convert revenue to cash collected from customers, cost of goods sold to cash paid to suppliers, and so on. These cash items are then combined directly to yield cash from operations. The more common method in practice is the indirect method, which starts with net income and adjusts it for the differences, typically account by account, between accrual income and operating cash flow. Both methods yield the same result.

Under the indirect method, amortization is added to net income because it is an expense not requiring the use of cash. In addition to amortization, other items affect the reconciliation of net income to cash from operations. Examples covered in the text through Chapter 6 include depletion, amortization of bond premium and discount, and amortization of goodwill.

Appendix 6A: More on the Statement of Changes in Financial Position

Objective 7

Explain treatment of gains and losses from fixed asset sales and debt extinguishments in the statement of changes in financial position.

This appendix describes two common items that affect the statement of changes in financial position. One need not be familiar with these items to have a basic understanding of the statement. However, the items occur frequently in the statements of changes in financial position of major corporations. Some instructors may wish to assign one but not both of the following sections. Each section independently introduces an item for Eco-Bag Company that was not considered in the chapter.

For purposes of this appendix, we will assume that Eco-Bag Company is concerned with preparing a supporting schedule that reconciles net income to net cash provided by operating activities. For simplicity, we will also assume that none of the changes introduced in this appendix affects income taxes.

Gain or Loss on Disposal of Fixed Assets

In the chapter, the Eco-Bag Company sold fixed assets for their book value of $10,000. More often a fixed asset is sold for an amount that differs from its book value. Suppose the fixed assets sold by Eco-Bag Company for $10,000 had a book value of $6,000 (original cost = $36,000; accumulated amortization = $30,000). Therefore net income would be $27,000, comprising the $23,000 shown in Exhibit 6-3 (p. 239) plus a $4,000 gain on disposal of fixed assets. (Recall that we are assuming no tax effect.)

Consider first the disposal's effects on cash and income using the balance sheet equation:

$$\Delta \text{ Cash} = \Delta \text{ L} + \Delta \text{ SE} - \Delta \text{ NCA}$$

$$\text{Proceeds} = \qquad \text{Gain} - (-\text{Book value})$$

$$\$10,000 = \qquad \$4,000 - (-\$6,000)$$

The book value does not affect cash. The statement of changes in financial position again contains the following item under investing activities:

Proceeds from sale of fixed assets $10,000

The body of the statement of changes in financial position under the direct method, in the section "Cash flows from operating activities," would not include any gains (or losses) from the disposal of fixed assets. However, consider Exhibit 6-6, p. 249, which reconciles net income to net cash provided by operating activities. The new net income of $27,000, which is the starting point of the reconciliation, already includes the $4,000 gain. To avoid double count-ing (that is, showing inflows of $4,000 in operating activities and $10,000 in investing activities), Eco-Bag Company must deduct from net income the $4,000 gain on disposal:

Net income	$27,000
Plus adjustments in Exhibit 6-6	46,000
Less gain on disposal of fixed assets	(4,000)
Net cash provided by operating activities	$69,000

Losses on the disposal of assets would be treated similarly except that they would be added back to net income. Suppose the book value of the fixed assets sold by Eco-Bag Company was $17,000, creating a $7,000 loss on disposal and net income of $16,000. The reconciliation would show:

Net income	$16,000
Plus adjustments in Exhibit 6-6	46,000
Plus loss on disposal of assets	7,000
Net cash provided by operating activities	$69,000

Losses and gains on disposal are essentially nonoperating items that are included in net income. As such, their effect must be removed from net income when it is reconciled to net cash flow provided by operating activities.

Gain or Loss on Extinguishment of Debt

Issuing and retiring debt are financing activities. Any gain or loss on extinguish-ment of debt must be removed from net income in a reconciliation schedule. Suppose Eco-Bag Company paid $37,000 to retire long-term debt with a book value of $34,000, generating a $3,000 loss on extinguishment of debt. Net income would be $23,000 − $3,000 = $20,000. The balance sheet equation would show:

$$\Delta \text{ Cash} = \quad \Delta \text{ L} \quad + \quad \Delta \text{ SE} - \Delta \text{ NCA}$$

$$-\text{Payment} = -\text{Book value} \quad -\text{Loss}$$

$$-\$37,000 = -\$34,000 \quad -\$3,000$$

The $3,000 loss would be added back to net income to determine net cash provided by operating activities:

Net income	$20,000
Plus adjustments in Exhibit 6-6	46,000
Plus loss on retirement of debt	3,000
Net cash provided by operating activities	$69,000

The entire *payment* for debt retirement would be listed among the financ-ing activities:

Proceeds from issue of long-term debt	$120,000
Payment to retire long-term debt	(37,000)
Proceeds from issue of common stock	98,000
Dividends paid	(19,000)
Net cash provided by financing activities	$162,000

Appendix 6B: T-Account Approach to Statement of Changes in Financial Position

Objective 8

Use the T-account approach to prepare the statement of changes in financial position.

Many statements of changes in financial position can be prepared by using the steps described in the body of the chapter. However, as the facts become complicated, a T-account approach deserves serious consideration. When constructing any statement of changes in financial position, we know that the increases and decreases of cash must total to the change in cash during the year. The T-account approach is simply a methodical procedure for being sure all items are identified.

To illustrate this approach, we will again use the Eco-Bag Company data from Exhibit 6-3. We will also use three facts disclosed earlier: Eco-Bag Company sold assets for their $10,000 book value, paid dividends of $19,000, and issued $98,000 in new stock. Exhibit 6-11 shows the T-accounts that represent the final result that will be obtained when we are finished.

T-Accounts and the Direct Method

This appendix shows how the direct method can be used with T-accounts. The T-accounts are reproduced in Exhibit 6-11. For the direct method, reasonably complete re-creations of the summary journal entries for the year are required. The journal entries are shown below, keyed to the entries in Exhibit 6-11. Those involving cash have an asterisk (*).

The T-account approach displayed in Exhibit 6-11 is merely another way of applying the balance sheet equation described in the body of the chapter:

Δ Cash	=	Δ Current liabilities	+	Δ Long-term liabilities	+	Δ Shareholders' equity	−	Δ Noncash current assets	−	Δ Fixed assets, net
Δ Cash	=	Δ Accounts and wages payable	+	Δ Long-term debt	+	Δ Shareholders' equity	−	Δ Accounts receivable and inventory	−	Δ Fixed assets, net
9		68		120		102		20		260
		21						40		
		89						60		

$$-9 = 89 + 120 + 102 - 60 - 260$$

1. Sales on credit:
    Accounts receivable   200
            Sales   200

*2   Collection of accounts receivable:
    Cash   180
            Accounts receivable   180

3. Recognition of cost of goods sold:
    Cost of goods sold   100
            Inventory   100

4. Purchases of inventory on credit:
    Inventory   140
            Trade accounts payable   140

*5. Payment of trade accounts payable:
    Trade accounts payable   72
            Cash   72

6. Recognition of wages and salaries expense:
    Wages and salaries expense   36
            Wages and salaries payable   36

*7. Payment of wages and salaries:
    Wages and salaries payable   15
            Cash   15

*8. Recognition of interest accrued and paid:
    Interest expense   4
            Cash   4

*9. Recognition and payment of income taxes:
    Income tax expense   20
            Cash   20

10. Recognition of amortization expense:
    Amortization expense   17
            Fixed assets, net   17

*11. Acquisition of fixed assets for cash:
    Fixed assets, net   287
            Cash   287

*12. Sale of fixed assets at book value:
    Cash   10
            Fixed assets, net   10

*13. Issuance of long-term debt:
    Cash   120
            Long-term debt   120

*14. Issuance of common stock:
    Cash   98
            Shareholders' equity   98

*15. Declaration and payment of dividends:
    Dividends declared and paid   19
            Cash   19

Again, we focus on the *changes* in the noncash accounts to explain why cash *changed*.

The summarized transactions for 19X2 entered in the Cash account are the basis for the preparation of the formal statement of changes in financial position, as can be seen by comparing the cash account from Exhibit 6-11 with the statement of changes in financial position in Exhibit 6-3 (p. 240).

Exhibit 6-11

Eco-Bag Company
T-Account Approach
Using Direct Method
Statement of Cash
Flows
for the Year Ended
December 31, 19X2
(in thousands)

Cash

Bal. 12/31/X1	25	

Operating Activities

2. Collection of accounts receivable	180	5. Pay accounts payable	72
		7. Pay wages and salaries	15
		8. Pay interest	4
		9. Pay taxes	20

Investing Activities

12. Disposal of fixed assets	10	11. Acquisition of fixed assets	287

Financing Activities

13. Issue long-term debt	120	15. Pay dividends	19
14. Issue common stock	98		
Total debits	408	Total credits	417
		Net decrease	9
Bal. 12/31/X2	16		

Accounts Receivable

Bal. 12/31/X1	25		
1. Sales	200	2. Collections	180
Net increase	20		
Bal. 12/31/X2	45		

Accounts Payable

		Bal. 12/31/X1	6
5. Payments	72	4. Purchases	140
		Net increase	68
		Bal. 12/31/X2	74

Inventory

Bal. 12/31/X1	60		
4. Purchases	140	2. Cost of goods sold	100
Net increase	40		
Bal. 12/31/X2	100		

Wages and Salaries Payable

		Bal. 12/31/X1	4
7. Payments	15	6. Accruals	36
		Net increase	21
		Bal. 12/31/X2	25

Fixed Assets, Net

Bal. 12/31/X1	220		
11. Acquisition	287	10. Amortization	17
		12. Disposals	10
Net increase	260		
Bal. 12/31/X2	480		

Long-Term Debt

		Bal. 12/31/X1	5
		13. New issue	120
		Bal. 12/31/X2	125

Shareholders' Equity

		Bal. 12/31/X1	315
3. Cost of goods sold	100	1. Sales	200
6. Wages	36	14. New issue	98
8. Interest	4		
9. Income taxes	20		
10. Amortization	17		
15. Dividends	19		
Total debits	196	Total credits	298
		Net increase	102
		Bal. 12/31/X2	417

Assignment Material

Special note: The following exercises and problems can be solved without reading beyond page 248, the end of "Preparing a Statement of Changes in Financial Position: The Direct Method": 6-28 through 6-31, 6-34, 6-37, 6-40, 6-42, 6-49, 6-53, 6-57, 6-58, 6-61.

QUESTIONS

6-1. "The statement of changes in financial position is an optional statement included by most companies in their annual reports." Do you agree? Explain.

6-2. What are the purposes of a statement of changes in financial position?

6-3. Distinguish between *operating management* and *financial management*.

6-4. Define *cash equivalents*.

6-5. What three types of activities are summarized in the statement of changes in financial position?

6-6. Name four major operating activities included in a statement of changes in financial position.

6-7. Name three major investing activities included in a statement of changes in financial position.

6-8. Name three major financing activities included in a statement of changes in financial position.

6-9. Where does interest received or paid appear on the statement of changes in financial position?

6-10. Why is there usually a difference between the cash collections from customers and sales revenue in a period's financial statements?

6-11. What are the two major ways of computing net cash provided by operating activities?

6-12. Demonstrate how the fundamental balance sheet equation can be recast to focus on cash.

6-13. The indirect method for reporting cash flows from operating activities can create an erroneous impression about noncash expenses (such as amortization). What is the impression, and why is it erroneous?

6-14. An investor's newsletter had the following item: "The company expects increased cash flow in 1996 because amortization charges will be substantially greater than they were in 1995." Comment.

6-15. "Net losses mean drains on cash." Do you agree? Explain.

6-16. "Amortization is an integral part of a statement of changes in financial position." Do you agree? Explain.

6-17. "Cash flow per share can be downright misleading." Why?

6-18. XYZ Company's only transaction in 19X1 was the sale of a fixed asset for cash of $20,000. The income statement included only "Gain on sale of fixed asset, $5,000." Correct the following statement of changes in financial position:

Cash flows from operating activities:	
Gain on sale of fixed asset	$ 5,000
Cash flows from investing activities:	
Proceeds from sale of fixed asset	20,000
Total increase in cash	$25,000

6-19. Why are noncash investing and financing activities listed on a separate schedule accompanying the statement of changes in financial position?

6-20. The Lawrence Company sold fixed assets with a book value of $5,000 and recorded a $4,000 gain. How should this be reported on a statement of changes in financial position? (Appendix 6A).

6-21. A company acquired a fixed asset in exchange for common stock. Explain how this transaction should be shown, if at all, in the statement of changes in financial position. Why is your suggested treatment appropriate?

6-22. A company operated at a profit for the year, but cash flow from operations was negative. Why might this occur? What industry or industries might find this a common occurrence?

6-23. Suppose a company paid off a $1 million short-term loan to one bank with the proceeds from an identical loan from another bank. The change in the short-term debt account would be zero. Should anything appear in the statement of changes in financial position? Explain.

6-24. Suppose the loan in the preceding question was renewed at the same bank. Does this change the answer? Explain.

6-25. Do all changes in current assets and liabilities affect cash flows from operations? If not, give an example of an account that does not.

6-26. Suppose an auto company introduced a five-year, 50,000-kilometre warranty plan to replace the old two-year, 20,000-kilometre plan. Would this be likely to require an adjustment to cash flow from operations under the indirect method?

6-27. A company operated at a loss for the year, but cash flow from operations was positive. Why might this occur? What industry or industries might find this a common occurrence?

EXERCISES

6-28   Cash Received from Customers

Good Foods, Inc., had sales of $730,000 during 19X1, 80% of them on credit and 20% for cash. During the year, accounts receivable increased from $65,000 to $75,000, an increase of $10,000. What amount of cash was received from customers during 19X1?

6-29   Cash Paid to Suppliers

Cost of goods sold for Good Foods, Inc., during 19X1 was $480,000. Beginning inventory was $105,000, and ending inventory was $125,000. Beginning trade accounts payable were $24,000, and ending trade accounts payable were $44,000. What amount of cash was paid to suppliers?

6-30   Cash Paid to Employees

Good Foods, Inc., reported wage and salary expenses of $250,000 on its 19X1 income statement. It reported cash paid to employees of $215,000 on its statement of changes in financial position. The beginning balance of accrued wages and salaries payable was $20,000. What was the ending balance in accrued wages and salaries payable? Ignore payroll taxes.

6-31   Simple Cash Flows from Operating Activities

Beatty and Associates provides accounting and consulting services. In 19X2, net income was $185,000 on revenues of $470,000 and expenses of $285,000. The only noncash expense was amortization of $30,000. The company has no inventory. Accounts receivable increased by $5,000 during 19X2, and accounts payable and salaries payable were unchanged.

Required   Prepare a statement of cash flows from operating activities. Use the direct method. Omit supporting schedules.

6-32   Net Income and Cash Flow

Refer to Problem 6-31. Prepare a schedule that reconciles net income to net cash flow from operating activities.

6-33   Book Value of Asset Disposals

The UPtown Broadcasting Company reported net fixed assets of $47 million at December 31, 19X5, and $53 million at December 31, 19X6. During 19X6, the company purchased fixed assets for $10 million and had $3 million of amortization. Compute the book value of the fixed asset disposals during 19X6.

6-34   Financing Activities

During 19X3, the Bremen Shipping Company refinanced its long-term debt. It spent DM 175,000 to retire long-term debt due in 2 years and issued DM 200,000 of 15-year bonds at par. DM signifies deutsche mark, the German monetary unit. It then bought and retired common shares for cash of DM 35,000. Interest expense for 19X3 was DM 22,000, of which DM 20,000 was paid in cash; the other DM 2,000 was still payable at the end of the year. Dividends declared and paid during the year were DM 10,000.

Required   Prepare a statement of changes in financial position from financing activities.

6-35   Amortization and Cash Flows

(Alternate is 6-39.) Aballo Company had sales of $970,000, all received in cash. Total operating expenses were $650,000. All except amortization were paid in cash. Amortization of $90,000 was included in the $650,000 of operating expenses. Ignore income taxes.

Required   1. Compute net income and net cash provided by operating activities.
2. Assume that amortization is tripled. Compute net income and net cash provided by operating activities.

6-36   Loss on Disposal of Equipment

Study Appendix 6A. The Lynnwood Insurance Company sold a computer. It had purchased the computer five years ago for $100,000, and accumulated amortization at the time of sale was $70,000.

Required

1. Suppose Lynnwood received $30,000 cash for the computer. How would the sale be shown on the statement of changes in financial position?
2. Suppose Lynnwood received $20,000 for the computer. How would the sale be shown on the statement of changes in financial position (including the schedule reconciling net income and net cash provided by operating activities)?
3. Redo requirement 2 assuming cash received was $50,000.

PROBLEMS

6-37   Prepare a Statement of Changes in Financial Position, Direct Method

(Alternate is 6-40.) Fix-it, Inc., is a chain of retail hardware stores. Its cash balance on December 31, 19X6, was $55 thousand, and net income for 19X7 was $414 thousand. Its 19X7 transactions affecting income or cash were (in thousands):

a. Sales of $1,600, all on credit. Cash collections from customers, $1,500.
b. The cost of items sold, $800. Purchases of inventory totalled $850; inventory and accounts payable were affected accordingly.
c. Cash payments on trade accounts payable, $825.
d. Salaries and wages: accrued, $190; paid in cash, $200.
e. Amortization, $45.
f. Interest expense, all paid in cash, $11.
g. Other expenses, all paid in cash, $100.
h. Income taxes accrued, $40; income taxes paid in cash, $35.
i. Bought plant and facilities for $435 cash.
j. Issued long-term debt for $110 cash.
k. Paid cash dividends of $39.

Required   Prepare a statement of changes in financial position using the direct method for reporting cash flows from operating activities. Omit supporting schedules.

6-38   Reconcile Net Income and Net Cash Provided by Operating Activities

(Alternate is 6-41.) Refer to Problem 6-37. Prepare a supporting schedule that reconciles net income to net cash provided by operating activities.

6-39   Amortization and Cash Flows

(Alternate is 6-35.) The following condensed income statement and reconciliation schedule are from the annual report of Vinales Company (in millions):

Sales	$484
Expenses	460
Net income	$ 24

Reconciliation Schedule of Net Income to Net Cash Provided by Operating Activities

Net income	$ 24
Add noncash expenses:	
Amortization	25
Deduct net increase in noncash operating working capital	(17)
Net cash provided by operating activities	$ 32

A shareholder has suggested that the company switch to a more accelerated amortization method on its annual report to shareholders. He maintains that this will increase the cash flow provided by operating activities. According to his calculations, using accelerated methods would increase amortization to $45 million, an increase of $20 million; net cash flow from operating activities would then be $52 million.

Required

1. Suppose Vinales Company adopts the accelerated amortization method proposed. Compute net income and net cash flow from operating activities. Ignore income taxes.
2. Use your answer to requirement 1 to prepare a response to the shareholder.

6-40   Prepare a Statement of Changes in Financial Position

(Alternate is 6-37.) Nakata Importers is a wholesaler of Asian goods. By the end of 19X0, the company's cash balance had dropped to $20 thousand, despite net income of $254 thousand in 19X0. Its transactions affecting income or cash in 19X0 were (in thousands):

a. Sales were $2,510, all on credit. Cash collections from customers were $2,413.
b. The cost of items sold was $1,599.   1599
c. Inventory increased by $56.
d. Cash payments on trade accounts payable were $1,653.
e. Payments to employees were $305; accrued wages payable decreased by $24.
f. Other operating expenses, all paid in cash, were $94.
g. Interest expense, all paid in cash, was $26.
h. Income tax expense was $105; cash payments for income taxes were $108.
i. Amortization was $151.
j. A warehouse was acquired for $540 cash.
k. Sold equipment for $37; original cost was $196, accumulated amortization was $159.
l. Received $28 for issue of common stock.
m. Retired long-term debt for $25 cash.
n. Paid cash dividends of $88.

Required

Prepare a statement of changes in financial position using the direct method for reporting cash flows from operating activities. Omit supporting schedules.

6-41   Reconcile Net Income and Net Cash Provided by Operating Activities

(Alternate is 6-38.) Refer to Problem 6-40. Prepare a supporting schedule to the statement of changes in financial position that reconciles net income to net cash provided by operating activities.

6-42   Prepare Statement of Changes in Financial Position from Income Statement and Balance Sheet

(Alternate is 6-49.) During 19X4, the Riley Software company declared and paid cash dividends of $10 thousand. Late in the year, the company bought new personal computers for its staff for a cash cost of $125 thousand, financed partly by its first issue of long-term debt. Interest on the debt is payable annually. Several old computers were sold for cash equal to their aggregate book value of $5 thousand. Taxes are paid in cash as incurred. The following data are in thousands:

Income Statement
for the Year Ended
December 31, 19X4

Sales		$316
Cost of sales		154
Gross margin		162
Salaries	$ 82	
Amortization	40	
Cash operating expenses	15	
interest	2	139
Income before taxes		23

continued

Income taxes		8
Net income		$ 15

Balance Sheets

	December 31		Increase (Decrease)
	19X4	**19X3**	
Assets			
Cash and cash equivalents	$ 97	$ 5	$ 92
Accounts receivable	40	95	(55)
Inventories	57	62	(5)
Total current assets	194	162	32
Fixed assets, net	190	110	80
Total assets	$384	$272	$112
Liabilities and Shareholders' Equity			
Accounts payable	$ 21	$ 16	$ 5
Interest payable	2	—	2
Long-term debt	100	—	100
Paid-in capital	220	220	—
Retained earnings	41	36	5
Total liabilities and shareholders' equity	$384	$272	$112

(handwritten annotations: "source use" next to Cash/Accounts receivable; "source source" next to Accounts payable; "11/07" in left margin)

Required

Prepare a statement of changes in financial position. Use the direct method for reporting cash flows from operating activities. Omit supporting schedules.

6-43   Indirect Method: Reconciliation Schedule in Body of Statement
Refer to Problem 6-42. Prepare a statement of changes in financial position that includes a reconciliation of net income to net cash provided by operating activities in the body of the statement.

6-44   Cash Flows, Indirect Method
The Edgardo Company has the following balance sheet data (in millions):

	December 31				December 31		
	19X7	**19X6**	**Change**		**19X7**	**19X6**	**Change**
Current assets:				Current liabilities (detailed)	$105	$ 30	$ 75
Cash	$ 13	$ 25	$(12)				
Receivables, net	50	15	35	Long-term debt	150	—	150
Inventories	100	50	50	Shareholders' equity	208	160	48
Total current assets	$163	$ 90	$ 73				
Plant assets (net of accumulated amortization)	300	100	200				
				Total liabilities and shareholders' equity	$463	$190	$273
Total assets	$463	$190	$273				

Net income for 19X7 was $60 million. Net cash inflow from operating activities was $80 million. Cash dividends paid were $12 million. Amortization was $30 million. Fixed assets were purchased for $230 million, $150 million of which was financed via the issuance of long-term debt outright for cash.

Edgardo Freytes, the President and majority shareholder of Edgardo, was a superb operating executive. He was imaginative and aggressive in marketing and ingenious and creative in production. But he had little patience with financial matters. After examining the most recent balance sheet and income statement, he muttered, "We've enjoyed ten years of steady growth; 19X7 was our most profitable ever. Despite such profitability, we're in the worst cash position in our history. Just look at those current liabilities in relation to our available cash! This whole picture of the more you make, the poorer you get, just does not make sense. These statements must be cockeyed."

Required

1. Prepare a statement of changes in financial position using the indirect method. Include a schedule reconciling net income to net cash provided by operating activities in the body of the statement.

2. Using the statement of changes in financial position and other information, write a short memorandum to Freytes, explaining why there is such a squeeze on cash.

6-45 Prepare Statement of Changes in Financial Position

The Friedlander Company has assembled the accompanying (a) balance sheets and (b) income statement and reconciliation of retained earnings for December 31, 19X9 (in millions).

	19X9	19X8	Change
Assets:			
Cash	$ 10	$ 25	$(15)
Accounts receivable	40	28	12
Inventory	70	50	20
Prepaid general expenses	4	3	1
Plant assets, net	202	150	52
	$326	$256	$ 70
Liabilities and Shareholders' Equity:			
Accounts payable for merchandise	$ 74	$ 60	$ 14
Accrued tax payable	3	2	1
Long-term debt	50	—	50
Capital stock	100	100	—
Retained earnings	99	94	5
	$326	$256	$ 70

Sales		$250
Less cost of goods sold:		
Inventory, Dec. 31, 19X8	$ 50	
Purchases	160	
Cost of goods available for sale	$210	
Inventory, Dec. 31, 19X9	70	140
Gross profit		$110
Less other expenses:		
General expense	$ 51	
Amortization	40	
Taxes	10	101
Net income		$ 9
Dividends		4
Net income of the period retained		$ 5
Retained earnings, Dec. 31, 19X8		94
Retained earnings, Dec. 31, 19X9		$ 99

On December 30, 19X9, Friedlander paid $98 million in cash to acquire a new plant to expand operations. This was partly financed by an issue of long-term debt for $50 million in cash. Plant assets were sold for their book value of $6 million during 19X9. Because net income was $9 million, the highest in the company's history, Sidney Friedlander, the Chief Executive Officer, was distressed by the company's extremely low cash balance.

Required

1. Prepare a statement of changes in financial position using the direct method for reporting cash flows from operating activities. You may wish to use Exhibit 6-3, page 240, as a guide.
2. Prepare a schedule that reconciles net income to net cash provided by operating activities.
3. What is revealed by the statement of changes in financial position? Does it help you reduce Mr. Friedlander's distress? Why? Briefly explain to Mr. Friedlander why cash has decreased even though net income was $9 million.

6-46   Balance Sheet Equation
Refer to Problem 6-45, requirement 1. Support your financial statement by using a form of the balance sheet equation. Step by step, show in equation form how each item in the statement of changes in financial position affects cash.

6-47   Noncash Investing and Financing Activities
The Aaron Amusement Company operates a chain of video-game arcades. Among Aaron's activities in 19X7 were:

1. Traded four old video games to another amusement company for one new "Flightime" game. The old games could have been sold for a total of $9,000 cash.
2. Paid off $50,000 of long-term debt by paying $30,000 cash and signing a $20,000 six-month note payable.
3. Issued debt for $75,000 cash, all of which was used to purchase new games for its Northwest Arcade.
4. Purchased the building in which one of its arcades was located by assuming the $120,000 mortgage on the building and paying $15,000 cash.
5. Debtholders converted $66,000 of debt to common stock.
6. Refinanced debt by paying cash to buy back an old issue at its call price of $21,000 and issued new debt at a lower interest rate for $21,000.

Required   Prepare a schedule of noncash investing and financing activities to accompany a statement of changes in financial position.

6-48   Comprehensive Statement of Changes in Financial Position
During the past 30 years, Cascade Toys, Inc. has grown from a single-location specialty toy store into a chain of stores selling a wide range of children's products. Its activities in 19X7 included the following:

a. Purchased 40% of the stock of Quebec Toy Company for $3,846,000 cash.
b. Issued $1,906,000 in long-term debt; $850,000 of the proceeds was used to retire debt that became due in 19X7 and was listed on the books at $900,000.
c. Property, plant, and equipment were purchased for $1,986,000 cash, and property with a book value of $576,000 was sold for $500,000 cash.
d. A note payable was signed for the purchase of new equipment; the obligation was listed at $516,000.

e. Executives exercised stock options for 8,000 shares of common stock, paying cash of $166,000.

f. On December 30, 19X7, bought Sanchez Musical Instruments Company by issuing common stock with a market value of $297,000.

g. Issued common stock for $3,000,000 cash.

h. Withdrew $800,000 cash from a money market fund that was considered a cash equivalent.

i. Bought $249,000 of treasury stock to hold for future exercise of stock options.

j. Long-term debt of $960,000 was converted to common stock.

k. Selected results for the year:

Net income	$ 679,000
Amortization	615,000
Increase in inventory	72,000
Decrease in accounts receivable	13,000
Increase in accounts and wages payable	7,000
Increase in taxes payable	25,000
Interest expense	144,000
Increase in accrued interest payable	15,000
Sales	9,739,000
Cash dividends received from investments	159,000
Cash paid to suppliers and employees	8,074,000
Cash dividends paid	240,000
Cash paid for taxes	400,000

Required   Prepare a statement of changes in financial position for 19X7 using the direct method. Include a schedule that reconciles net income to net cash provided by operating activities. Also include a schedule of noncash investing and financing activities.

6-49 Prepare Statement of Changes in Financial Position from Income Statement and Balance Sheet

(Alternate is 6-42.) Crevice Company had the following income statement and balance sheet items at December 31, 19X8 (in thousands):

Sales	$ 870
Cost of goods sold	(510)
Gross margin	$ 360
Operating expenses	(210)
Amortization	(60)
Interest	(10)
Income before taxes	$ 80
Income taxes	(25)
Net income	$ 55
Cash dividends paid	(35)
Total increase in retained earnings	$ 20

Balance Sheets

	December 31		Increase (Decrease)
	19X8	**19X7**	
Assets			
Cash	$ 20	$ 60	$ (40)
Accounts receivable	240	150	90
Inventories	450	350	100
Total current assets	$ 710	$560	$ 150
Fixed assets, gross	$ 890	$715	$175
Accumulated amortization	(570)	(550)	(20)
Fixed assets, net	$ 320	$165	$ 155
Total assets	$1,030	$725	$305
Liabilities and Shareholders' Equity			
Trade accounts payable	$ 520	$300	$220
Long-term debt	245	180	65
Shareholders' equity	265	245	20
Total liabilities and shareholders' equity	$1,030	$725	$305

During 19X8, Crevice purchased fixed assets for $415,000 cash and sold fixed assets for their book value of $200,000. Operating expenses, interest, and taxes were paid in cash. No long-term debt was retired.

Required

Prepare a statement of changes in financial position. Use the direct method for reporting cash flows from operating activities. Omit supporting schedules.

6-50 T-Account Approach
Study Appendix 6B. Refer to the facts concerning the Buretta Company's "Summary Problem for Your Review" in the chapter (p. 251). Prepare a set of T-accounts that supports the statement of changes in financial position shown in Exhibit 6-9 (p. 254). Use Exhibit 6-11 (p. 261) as a guide. Key your postings by number.

6-51 T-Account Approach
Study Appendix 6B. Refer to the facts concerning the Friedlander Company in Problem 6-45. Prepare a set of T-accounts that supports the statement of changes in financial position. Use Exhibit 6-11 (p. 261) as a guide. Key your postings by number.

CRITICAL THINKING PROBLEM

6-52 Interpretation of the Statement of Changes in Financial Position and Ethics
Megasoft was a successful developer of personal computer software in the early 1990s. The company's peak year was 1992. Since then, both sales and profits have fallen. The following information is from the company's 1994 annual report (in thousands):

	1994	1993	1992
Net income	$1,500	$4,500	$7,500
Accounts receivable (end of year)	900	1,800	6,000
Inventory (end of year)	1,050	2,100	2,850
Net cash provided by operations	675	1,050	2,250
Capital expenditures	900	1,050	1,350
Proceeds from sales of fixed assets	2,700	1,500	2,250
Net gain on sales of fixed assets plus net extraordinary gains	2,250	1,800	2,400

Megasoft
media.megasoft.com/

During 1995, $9 million of short-term loans became due. Megasoft paid off only $2.25 million and was able to extend the terms on the other $6.75 million. Accounts payable continued at a very low level in 1995, and the company maintained a large investment in corporate equity securities, enough to generate $450,000 of dividends received in 1995. Megasoft neither paid dividends nor issued stock or bonds in 1995. Its December 31, 1995, Statement of Changes in Financial Position (in thousands) was as follows:

Cash flows from operating activities:		
Net income	$ 1,050	
Adjustments to reconcile net income to net cash provided by operating activities:		
Amortization	600	
Net decrease in accounts receivable	150	
Net decrease in inventory	225	
Investment revenue from equity investments, less $900 of dividends received	(600)	
Gains on sales of fixed assets	(2,100)	
Extraordinary loss on building fire	1,200	
Net cash provided by operating activities		$ 525
Cash flows from investing activities:		
Purchase of fixed assets	$ (600)	
Insurance proceeds on building fire	3,000	
Sale of plant assets	3,750	
Purchase of corporate equity securities	(2,250)	
Net cash provided by investing activities		3,900
Cash flows from financing activities:		
Principal payments on short-term debt to banks	$(2,250)	
Purchase of treasury stock	(900)	
Net cash used for financing activities		(3,150)
Net increase in cash		1,275
Cash, December 31, 1994		1,800
Cash, December 31, 1995		$ 3,075

Required

1. Interpret the Statement of Changes in Financial Position for Megasoft.
2. Describe any ethical issues relating to the strategy and financial disclosures of Megasoft.

COMPANY CASES

6-53   Identify Operating, Investing, and Financing Activities
The items listed below were found on the 1996 statement of changes in financial position of the Oshawa Group. For each item, indicate which section of the statement should contain the item—the operating, investing, or financing section. Also indicate whether the Oshawa Group uses the direct or indirect method for reporting cash flows from operating activities.

a. Proceeds from sale of real estate
b. Net earnings
c. Long-term debt issued

    d. Purchase of fixed assets

    e. Issue of Class A shares

    f. Proceeds from sale of real estate

    g. Decrease in working capital

    h. Disposal of fixed assets

    i. Depreciation and amortization

6-54   Cash Provided by Operations

Kellogg Company is the world's leading producer of ready-to-eat cereal products and manufactures numerous other food products. In 1994, net sales of $6.5 billion represented a 4% increase over 1993 and produced a 3.6% earnings increase to $705.4 million. To calculate net earnings, Kellogg recorded $256.1 million in amortization and other items of revenue and expense not requiring cash reduced cash flow from operations by $51.5 million. Dividends of $313.6 million were paid during 1994. Among the changes in balance sheet accounts during 1994 were (in millions):

Accounts receivable	$ 27.7	increase
Inventories	6.8	decrease
Accrued liabilities	57.4	increase
Other current assets	5.4	increase
Accounts payable	25.7	increase

Required   Compute the net cash provided by operating activities using the indirect method.

6-55   Cash Flows from Operating Activities, Indirect Method

Deere & Company
www.deere.com

Deere & Company's 1994 annual report indicates that it "manufactures, distributes, and finances a full range of agricultural equipment; a broad range of industrial equipment for construction, forestry, and public works; and a variety of lawn and grounds care equipment." During 1994, Deere & Company earned $603.6 million on revenues of approximately $7.6 billion. The following summarized information relates to Deere's statement of changes in financial position:

	(millions of dollars)
Provision for amortization	$292.8
Principal payments on long-term borrowing	590.7
Proceeds from long-term borrowing	188.5
Other noncash operating expenses	13.6
Decrease in accounts receivable	147.8
Decrease in inventories	164.5
Other increases in cash from operations due to changes in current assets and liabilities	121.1
Purchases of property and equipment	228.1
Dividends paid	171.8

Required   Compute the net cash provided by operating activities. All of the information necessary for that task is provided, together with some information related to other elements of the statement of changes in financial position. Note that the format does not include parentheses to differentiate elements that increase cash from those that (decrease) cash, but the distinction should be clear from the captions.

6-56   Cash Flows from Financing Activities

Eli Lilly and Company is a global, research-based corporation that develops, manufactures, and markets pharmaceuticals, medical instruments, diagnostic products, and agricultural products. Its 1994 sales exceeded $6 billion. Lilly's 1994 statement of changes in financial position included the following items, among others:

Dividends paid	$ (700.4)
Repurchase of common stock	(25.8)
Additions to property and equipment	(633.5)
Depreciation and amortization	398.3
Stock issuances	19.8
Decrease in short-term borrowings	(152.7)
Additions to investments	(1,001.7)
Net income	(480.2)
Additions to long-term debt	383.8
Reductions of long-term debt	(39.8)

Required   Prepare the section "Cash flows from financing activities" from Eli Lilly's 1994 annual report. All items necessary for that section appear above. Some items from other sections have been omitted.

6-57   Statement of Changes in Financial Position, Indirect Method

Andrés Wines Ltd. had cash and cash equivalents of $4,181,059 at the beginning of the year starting April 1, 1995. The following items are on the company's statement of changes in financial position for the year:

Net earnings for the year	5,420,131
Issue of Class A shares	262,508
Acquisition of minority interest in subsidiary company	(198,303)
Additions to fixed assets	(3,285,035)
Dividends paid	(2,693,573)
Decrease in noncash working capital items	153,610
Depreciation and amortization	2,182,052
Deferred income taxes (treat in the same manner as the depreciation and amortization)	1,274,000

Required   Prepare a statement of changes in financial position for Andrés Wines using the indirect method. Include the balance of cash and cash equivalents at year end.

6-58   Cash Flows from Investing Activities

Kmart is one of the world's largest retailers offering both discount store and specialty store retailing. For the year ended January 30, 1995, Kmart reported sales of $34,313 million with net earnings of $296 million. The Statement of Changes in Financial Position for the fiscal year ended January 30, 1995, included the following elements:

Kmart
www.kmart.com

	(millions)
Divestiture of subsidiary (net)	$ 590
Sale of interest in subsidiary	896
Net income	296

continued

Acquisitions of other companies	(12)
Proceeds from issuance of long-term debt	66
Proceeds from sale of assets	945
Depreciation and amortization	724
(Increase) decrease in inventories	(716)
Reduction in long-term debt	(717)
Reduction in capital lease obligations	(124)
Other investing uses of cash—net	(12)
Capital expenditures—owned property	(1,247)

Required   Prepare the section "Cash flows from investing activities" for Kmart for the year ended January 30, 1995. All items necessary are among those listed in this problem.

6-59   Reconcile Net Income and Net Cash Provided by Operating Activities
Refer to Problem 6-58. Identify the elements in the list that would be part of a schedule reconciling net income to cash provided by operating activities. List at least two items that are missing from the list.

6-60   Statement of Changes in Financial Position, Direct and Indirect Methods
Nordstrom, Inc., the fashion retailer, had the following income statement for the year ended January 31 (in thousands):

Net sales		$2,893,904
Costs and expenses:		
Cost of sales	$2,000,250	
Selling, general, and administrative	747,770	
Interest	52,228	
Less: Other income	(84,660)	
Total costs and expenses		2,715,588
Earnings before income taxes		$ 178,316
Income taxes		62,500
Net earnings		$ 115,816

The company's net cash provided by operating activities, prepared using the indirect method, was:

Net earnings	$115,816
Adjustments to reconcile net earnings to net cash provided by operating activities:	
Amortization	85,615
Changes in:	
Accounts receivable	(39,234)
Merchandise inventories	(28,368)
Prepaid expenses	(20,018)
Accounts payable	8,928
Accrued salaries and wages	24,982
Accrued interest	(963)
Other accrued expenses	6,551
Income taxes payable	(5,182)
Net cash provided by operating activities	$148,127

Required

Prepare a statement showing the net cash provided by operating activities using the direct method. Assume that all "other income" was received in cash and that prepaid expenses and accrued salaries and wages and other accrued expenses relate to selling, general, and administrative expenses.

6-61 Statement of Changes in Financial Position, Direct Method, for a Utility
The Columbia Gas System had operating revenues of $2.4 billion from providing gas services ranging from exploration and production to pipeline transmission to final distribution to users. The company's statement of changes in financial position contained the following items (some have been slightly summarized):

	(in millions)
Issuance of common stock	$ 225.3
Retirement of long-term debt	(71.7)
Dividends paid	(103.9)
Cash received from customers	2,829.8
Other operating cash receipts	161.2
Capital expenditures	(600.1)
Issuance of long-term debt	204.5
Other financing activities—net	86.0
Cash paid to suppliers	(1,319.2)
Interest paid	(172.5)
Taxes paid	(256.3)
Other investments—net	(166.3)
Cash paid to employees and for their benefit	(445.2)
Other operating cash payments	(377.7)

Required

1. Prepare the statement of changes in financial position for Columbia Gas using the direct method. Omit the schedule reconciling net income to net cash provided by operating activities.
2. Discuss the relation between operating cash flow and investing and financing needs.

6-62 Interpreting the Statement of Changes in Financial Position
The Kellogg Company statement of changes in financial position appears in Exhibit 6-12.

Required

Use that statement to answer two questions. Does Kellogg generate sufficient cash flow from operations to cover ongoing investing activities and pay dividends to its shareholders? How has Kellogg changed its debt-equity ratio during the period 1992 to 1994?

Exhibit 6-12 Kellogg Company and Subsidiaries Consolidated Statement of Changes in Financial Position Years ended December 31	(millions)	1994	1993	1992
	Operating activities			
	Net earnings	$705.4	$680.7	$431.2
	Items in net earnings not requiring (providing) cash:			
	Cumulative effect of accounting change			251.6
	Amortization	256.1	265.2	231.5
	Pre-tax gain on sale of subsidiaries	(26.7)	(65.9)	(58.5)
	Deferred income taxes	24.5	(22.3)	.1
	Other	(49.3)	11.9	34.7
	Change in operating assets and liabilities:			
	Accounts receivable	(27.7)	(17.7)	(99.1)

continued

(millions)	1994	1993	1992
Operating activities			
Inventories	6.8	13.3	(15.3)
Other current assets	(5.4)	(32.3)	(.9)
Accounts payable	25.7	(5.0)	24.0
Accrued liabilities	57.4	(27.7)	(57.4)
Net cash provided from operating activities	966.8	800.2	741.9
Investing activities			
Additions to properties	(354.3)	(449.7)	(473.6)
Proceeds from sale of subsidiaries	95.5	95.6	115.0
Property disposals	15.6	19.0	18.8
Other	7.8	(25.1)	(10.6)
Net cash used in investing activities	(235.4)	(360.2)	(350.4)
Financing activities			
Net borrowings of notes payable	(111.9)	176.7	21.6
Issuance of long-term debt	200.0	208.3	311.7
Reduction of long-term debt	(2.9)	(1.7)	(270.2)
Issuance of common stock	2.3	2.9	13.4
Common stock repurchases	(327.3)	(548.1)	(224.1)
Cash dividends	(313.6)	(305.2)	(286.4)
Other	(6.1)	2.9	11.4
Net cash used in financing activities	(559.5)	(464.2)	(422.6)
Effect of exchange rate changes on cash	(3.7)	(4.0)	(20.6)
Increase (decrease) in cash and temporary investments	168.2	(28.2)	(51.7)
Cash and temporary investments at beginning of year	98.1	126.3	178.0
Cash and temporary investments at end of year	$266.3	$ 98.1	$126.3

6-63 Cash Flows from Operating Activities

Boise Cascade Corporation, the forest products company with headquarters in Boise, Idaho, reported net income of over $75 million. The following data are condensed from the company's income statement and balance sheet (in thousands):

Revenues:	
Sales	$ 4,184,560
Costs and expenses:	
Nonamortization expenses (summarized)	(3,737,780)
Amortization	(212,890)
Income from operations	233,890
Interest expense	(116,620)
Interest income	4,130
Income before income taxes	121,400
Income tax provision	46,130
Net income	$ 75,270

		Increase (Decrease)
Current assets:		
Cash	$ 19,781	$ 66
Short-term investments	6,165	639
Receivables	412,558	(9,010)
Inventories	484,972	60,533
Other	74,107	13,038
Total current assets	$997,583	$ 65,266
Current liabilities:		
Current portion of long-term debt	$136,731	$ 106,341
Income taxes payable	140	(4,133)
Notes payable	40,000	40,000
Accounts payable	344,384	(47,158)
Accrued liabilities:		
Compensation and benefits	99,530	(14,552)
Interest payable	38,460	(1,611)
Other	99,127	1,261
Total current liabilities	$758,372	$ 80,148

You have determined that other current assets are all operating items, as are other accrued liabilities. Short-term investments are cash equivalents. Amortization is the only noncash expense. Interest income is all in cash.

Required
1. Prepare a statement of changes in financial position from operating activities. Use the direct method that begins with cash collections from customers.
2. Reconcile net income to net cash provided by operating activities. (*Hint*: The cash outflow for nonamortization expense is an aggregation of more specific outflows. There is no way to break the total amount into its component parts.)

6-64   Prepare Statement of Changes in Financial Position, Indirect Method

The income statement and balance sheets in Exhibit 6-14 (p. 279) are from a recent annual report of Data I/O, a world leader in developing and marketing computer-aided engineering tools. (The statements are slightly modified to avoid items beyond the scope of this text.) Assume the following information about activities in 19X8:

a. Amortization on fixed assets was $3,427,000, which is included in operating expenses.

b. Fixed assets were sold for their book value of $2,186,000; fixed assets were acquired at a cost of $2,351,000.

c. Common stock was purchased for $16,064,000 and retired. Additional common stock was issued for stock options.

d. No notes payable were retired.

Required Prepare a 19X8 statement of changes in financial position for Data I/O. Use the indirect method in the body of the statement for reporting cash flows from operating activities.

6-65   Miscellaneous Cash Flow Questions

McDonald's Corporation is a well-known provider of food services around the world. McDonald's statement of changes in financial position for 1994 is reproduced with a few slight modifications and omissions as Exhibit 6-13. Use that statement and the additional information provided to answer the following questions:

1. In the Financing activities section, all parentheses for 1994 have been removed. Which numbers should be put in parentheses?

2. In the Investing activities section, all parentheses for 1994 have been removed. Which numbers should be put in parentheses?

3. Estimate the interest expense that was originally deducted in the income statement if interest paid was $323.9 million.

4. The 1994 values for the change in cash and cash equivalents and for beginning and end-of-year balances have been omitted and replaced with the letters *a*, *b*, and *c*. Provide the proper values for these three missing numbers.

5. Retained earnings at December 31, 1993, were $7,612.6 million. Calculate the retained earnings balance at December 31, 1994.

6. Comment on the relation between cash flow from operations and cash used for investing activities.

7. What do you conclude about changes in McDonald's debt-to-equity ratio during this period?

| Exhibit 6-13 | McDonald's Corporation | Consolidated Statement of Changes in Financial Position |

(In millions of dollars)	Years ended December 31, 1994	1993
Operating activities		
Net income	$ 1,224.4	$ 1,082.5
Adjustments to reconcile to cash provided by operations		
Depreciation and amortization	628.6	568.4
Deferred income taxes	(5.6)	52.4
Changes in operating working capital items		
Accounts receivable increase	(51.6)	(48.3)
Inventories, prepaid expenses and other current assets (increase) decrease	(15.0)	(9.6)
Accounts payable increase	105.4	45.4
Accrued interest payable decrease	(25.5)	(5.1)
Taxes and other liabilities increase (decrease)	95.2	26.5
Other–net	(29.7)	(32.4)
Cash provided by operations	1,926.2	1,679.8
Investing activities		
Property and equipment expenditures	1,538.6	(1,316.9)
Sales of restaurant businesses	151.5	114.2
Purchases of restaurant businesses	133.8	(64.2)
Notes receivable additions	15.1	(33.1)
Property sales	66.0	61.6
Notes receivable reductions	56.7	75.7
Other	92.6	(55.3)
Cash used for investing activities	1,505.9	(1,218.0)
Financing activities		
Net short-term borrowings	521.7	(8.9)
Long-term financing issuances	260.9	1,241.0
Long-term financing repayments	536.9	(1,185.9)
Treasury stock purchases	495.6	(620.1)
Common and preferred stock dividends	215.7	(201.2)
Other	39.4	62.6
Cash used for financing activities	426.2	(712.5)
Cash and equivalents increase (decrease)	a	(250.7)
Cash and equivalents at beginning of year	b	436.5
Cash and equivalents at end of year	$ c	$ 185.8

6-66 Statement of Changes in Financial Position, Indirect Method
Star Data Systems Inc. is a leading supplier of online, real-time financial information services and systems in Canada. At May 31, 1994, its bank indebtedness was $478 (thousands). Its Statement of Changes in Financial Position for the next year showed the following items (some have been slightly amended):

	(in thousands)
Net income for the year	$4,742
Proceeds from term loans	2,608
Net purchases of fixed assets	(8,260)
Net assets purchased on acquisition of another company	(2,633)
Proceeds from other financing activities	2,930
Depreciation and amortization	4,381
Increase in non-cash working capital balances relating to operations	(2,072)

Required Prepare Star Data System's statement of changes in financial position in proper format, using the indirect method.

6-67 T-Account Approach
Study Appendix 6B. Refer to the facts concerning Data I/O, Problem 6-64. Prepare a set of T-accounts that supports the statement of changes in financial position. Use the direct method for computing net cash flow from operating activities. (This differs from the requirements of 6-64, which asked you to use the indirect method.) Key your postings by number. Use Exhibit 6-11 (p. 261) as a guide. Assume that all sales are on open credit.

Exhibit 6-14

Data I/O
Income Statement at
December 31, 19X8
(in thousands)

Net sales	$ 65,117
Cost of goods sold	(26,825)
	38,292
Operating expenses	(31,714)
Earnings before taxes on income	6,578
Taxes on income	(1,973)
Net earnings	$ 4,605

Balance Sheets at
December 31
(in thousands)

Assets	19X8	19X7	Increase (Decrease)
Current Assets:			
Cash and cash equivalents	$20,344	$27,014	$ (6,670)
Trade accounts receivable, less allowance for doubtful accounts	14,811	13,796	1,015
Inventories	6,433	6,664	(231)
Prepaid operating expenses	1,317	4,602	(3,285)
Total current assets	42,905	52,076	(9,171)
Fixed assets, gross	34,608	38,091	(3,483)
Accumulated amortization	(15,344)	(15,565)	221
Net fixed assets	19,264	22,526	(3,262)
Total assets	$62,169	$74,602	$(12,433)

Liabilities and Shareholders' Equity	19X8	19X7	Increase (Decrease)
Current Liabilities:			
Trade accounts payable	$ 2,185	$ 3,173	$ (988)
Accrued operating expenses	9,084	10,004	(920)
Income taxes payable	1,600	1,160	440
Notes payable	1,052	974	78
Total current liabilities	13,921	15,311	(1,390)
Shareholders' equity:			
Common stock, authorized, 30,000,000 shares; issued and outstanding, 6,530,496 and 8,649,672 shares	17,647	33,295	(15,648)
Retained earnings	30,601	25,996	4,605
Total shareholders' equity	48,248	59,291	(11,043)
Total liabilities and shareholders' equity	$62,169	$74,602	$(12,433)

6-68   Hudson's Bay Company Annual Report
Refer to the financial statements contained in Appendix A at the end of the book.

Required

1. Generally, companies have operating cash flow in excess of net earnings because of noncash expenses such as amortization. In 1996, Hudson's Bay Company's net cash inflow from operating activities was almost the same as earnings before income taxes which in 1997 was over three times earnings. What was the primary cause of this relation?
2. Hudson's Bay Company uses the indirect format for its statement of changes in financial position. Calculate the amount it would show as cash collections from customers using the direct method.

6-69   Annual Report Disclosure
Select a company of your choice and review its annual report.

Required

1. Determine whether cash flow from operations is stable through time.
2. Relate cash flow from operations to investing and dividend payment needs.
3. Compare cash flow from operations to net income. Explain why they differ.

MAJOR ELEMENTS OF FINANCIAL STATEMENTS

7

Sales Revenue, Cash, and Accounts Receivable

Learning Objectives

After studying this chapter, you should be able to

1 Determine the proper time to record a particular revenue item on the income statement.

2 Explain how to account for sales returns and allowances, sales discounts, and bank credit card sales.

3 Explain why cash is important and how it is managed.

4 Explain how uncollectible accounts affect the valuation of accounts receivable.

5 Estimate bad debts expense under the allowance method using (a) percentage of sales, (b) percentage of ending accounts receivable, and (c) aging of accounts.

6 Understand techniques for assessing the level of accounts receivable.

7 Describe the accounting for temporary investments. (Appendix 7)

8 Contrast the equity and cost methods of accounting for investments. (Appendix 7)

9 Explain the preparation of consolidated financial statements.

In this chapter we consider sales revenue and related current assets. Combining these topics in one chapter stresses their interrelated character. When sales are recognized in the income statement, a corresponding change occurs in the firm's asset composition. The firm receives either cash or the promise of cash. Income statement and balance sheet effects are intertwined.

The creation and delivery of a product or service occur in very different ways in different industries. When a barber cuts hair and receives payment there is little uncertainty about when the service is complete and when the revenue is earned. Other transactions are not so well defined, and the accountant's task is to determine when transactions are sufficiently complete to warrant the recording of sales revenue.

A related question is, How much revenue should be recognized? Or stated another way, How valuable is the customer's promise to pay? Suppose you sold a $5,000 oriental rug to a local realtor who promised to pay you in five monthly payments of $1,000. Two months later, after receiving the second cheque, you read in the paper that the realtor had declared personal bankruptcy and was not expected to be able to repay his debts. How can we report this transaction to capture the economic reality of what happened? Such issues occupy our attention in this chapter.

■ RECOGNITION OF SALES REVENUE

Objective 1

Determine the proper time to record a particular revenue item on the income statement.

Why is the timing of revenue recognition important? Because it is critical to the measurement of net income. Under the *matching principle*, described in Chapter 2, the cost of the items sold is reported in the same period in which revenue is recognized. Net income is the excess of revenues over the cost of goods sold and related expenses.

Managers often receive higher salaries or greater bonuses for increasing sales and net income. Therefore, they prefer to recognize sales revenue as soon as possible. Owners and potential investors, on the other hand, want to be sure the economic benefits of the sale are guaranteed before recognizing revenue. Because of these different perspectives, accountants must carefully assess when revenue should be recognized.

Chapter 2 described the principles that accountants use to determine when revenue is recognized in the financial statements. Under *cash-basis accounting*, accountants recognize revenue when cash is collected for sales of goods and services. Under *accrual-basis accounting*, however, recognition of revenue requires a two-pronged test: (1) goods or services must be delivered to the customers (that is, the revenue is *earned*); and (2) cash or an asset virtually assured of being converted into cash must be received (that is, the revenue is *realized*).

Most revenue is recognized at the point of sale. Suppose you buy a compact disc at a local music store. Both revenue recognition tests are generally met at the time of purchase. You receive the merchandise and the store receives cash, a cheque, or a credit card slip. Because both cheques and credit card slips are readily converted to cash, the store can recognize revenue at the point of sale regardless of which of these three methods of payment you use.

Sometimes the two revenue recognition tests are not met at the same time. In such cases, revenue is generally recognized only when both tests are met.

Consider magazine subscriptions. The *realization* test is met when the publisher receives cash. However, revenues are not *earned* until magazines are delivered. Therefore revenue recognition is delayed until the time of delivery.

Sometimes accountants must exercise judgment in deciding when the recognition criteria are met. For example, accounting for long-term contracts might require such judgment. Suppose an engineering firm signs a $40 million contract with the government to produce a major bridge. The contract is signed, and work begins on January 2, 19X1. The completion date is December 31, 19X4. Payment will be made upon completion of the bridge. The engineering firm expects to complete one-fourth of the project each year. When should the $40 million of revenue be recorded on the income statement?

The most common answer is that one-fourth of the revenue is *earned* each year, so $10 million of the revenue should be recognized annually. Generally, payments on contracts with the government or with major corporations are reasonably certain. Therefore, revenues on such contracts are recognized as the work is performed. Because collection from the government is virtually certain, realization can be said to occur because the work has been performed and the government has an obligation. For other customers, where payment on the contract is uncertain, the *realization* test may not be met until the product is delivered and a bill is sent. In such a case, all revenues might be recognized at completion of the project.

As another example, consider a land developer with a three-hundred-hectare tract of bare land that is being subdivided and sold in one-hectare vacation lots. The sales office has a scale model showing each lot as being "available" or "sold." It also shows the (future) municipal park, (future) paved roads and sidewalks, (future) community building, (future) swimming pool, and so on. A customer who likes the model, the $5,000 price for a lot, and the payments of $20 per month (for a very long time) signs a contract, making the minimum down payment of $50.

Is this transaction a sale? The developer might think so. He or she cashes the $50 deposit and records "sold" on the scale model. The developer believes that other customers, impressed by the rapid sale, might be more inclined to buy.

What can go wrong in this type of situation? Financially distressed customers can walk away from their deposits and payment contracts. The developer can fail to complete the promised amenities, and existing lot owners can sue for refunds or completion. Given these conditions and others that can prevent fulfillment of the contract by either the customer or the seller, recognition of the sale based on a small deposit is not sound practice. Creditors, potential investors in the development company, or buyers of lots can be misled by financial statements that treat sales contracts with minimal down payments as completed sales.

■ MEASUREMENT OF SALES REVENUE

Cash and Credit Sales

After deciding when revenue is to be recognized, the accountant must determine *how much* revenue to record. In other words, how should accountants measure revenue? Ordinarily, accountants approximate the *net realizable value*

Objective 2

Explain how to account for sales returns and allowances, sales discounts, and bank credit card sales.

of the asset inflow from the customer. That is, the revenue is measured in terms of the present cash equivalent value of the asset received.

Revenue is recorded equal to the asset received:

```
Cash . . . . . . . . . . . . . . . . . . . . . . . . . . . . .    xxx
     Sales revenue  . . . . . . . . . . . . . . . .           xxx
OR
Accounts receivable  . . . . . . . . . . . . . . .    xxx
     Sales revenue  . . . . . . . . . . . . . . . .          xxx
```

Notice that a cash sale increases Sales Revenue, an income statement account, and increases Cash, a balance sheet account. A credit sale on open account is recorded much like a cash sale except that the balance sheet account Accounts Receivable is increased instead of Cash.

In fact, the realizable value of a credit sale is often less than that of a cash sale. Why? Because some accounts receivable may never be collected. Adjustments for uncollectible accounts are discussed later in this chapter in the "Credit Sales and Accounts Receivable" section beginning on page 290.

Merchandise Returns and Allowances

sales returns (purchase returns)
Products returned by the customer.

Suppose revenue is recognized at the point of sale, but later the customer decides to return the merchandise. He or she may be unhappy with the product for many reasons, including colour, size, style, quality, or simply changing of the mind. The supplier (vendor) calls these **sales returns**; the customer calls them **purchase returns**. Such merchandise returns are minor for manufacturers and wholesalers but are major for retail department stores. For instance, returns of 12% of gross sales are not abnormal for major department stores.

sales allowance (purchase allowance)
Reduction of the selling price (the original price previously agreed upon).

Or suppose that instead of returning the merchandise, the customer demands a reduction of the selling price (the original price previously agreed upon). For example, a customer may complain about finding scratches on a household appliance or about buying a toaster for $40 on Wednesday and seeing the same item for sale in the same store or elsewhere for $35 on Thursday. Such complaints are often settled by the seller's granting a **sales allowance**, which is essentially a reduction of the selling price. The buyer calls such a price reduction a **purchase allowance**.

gross sales Total sales revenue before deducting sales returns and allowances.

Gross sales revenue equal to the sales price must be decreased by the amount of the returns and allowances to give the **net sales**. But instead of directly reducing the revenue (or sales) account, managers of retail stores typically use a contra account, Sales Returns and Allowances, which combines both returns and allowances in a single account. Managers use a contra account so they can watch changes in the level of returns and allowances. For instance, a change in the percentage of returns in fashion merchandise may give early signals about changes in customer tastes. Similarly, a buyer of fashion or fad merchandise may want to keep track of purchase returns to help assess the quality of products and services of various suppliers.

net sales Total sales revenue reduced by sales returns and allowances.

Consider an example of how to account for sales and sales returns and allowances. Suppose a Bay Department Store has $900,000 gross sales on credit and $80,000 sales returns and allowances. The analysis of transactions would show:

	A	=	L +	SE	
Credit sales on open account	+900,000 [Increase Accounts Receivable]	=		+900,000 [Increase Sales]	
Returns and allowances	-80,000 [Decrease Accounts Receivable]	=		-80,000 [Increase Sales Returns and Allowances]	

The journal entries (without explanations) are:

Accounts receivable   900,000
　　　Sales . . . .　　　　　　900,000

Sales returns and allowances   80,000
　　　Accounts receivable . . . .　　　　　　80,000

The income statement would begin:

Gross sales	$900,000
Deduct: Sales returns and allowances	80,000
Net sales	$820,000
or	
Sales, net of $80,000 returns and allowances	$820,000

Discounts from Selling Prices

trade discounts
Reductions to the gross selling price for a particular class of customers to arrive at the actual selling price (invoice price).

There are two major types of sales discounts: *trade* and *cash*. **Trade discounts** apply one or more reductions to the gross selling price for a particular class of customers in accordance with a company's management policies. These discounts are price concessions or ways of quoting the actual prices that are charged to various customers. An example is a discount for large-volume purchases. The seller might offer no discount on the first $10,000 of merchandise per year but a 2% discount on the next $10,000 and 3% on all sales to a customer in excess of $20,000.

Companies set trade discount terms for various reasons. If common in the industry, the seller may offer trade discounts to be competitive. Discounts may also be used to encourage certain customer behaviour. For example, manufacturers with seasonal products (gardening supplies, snow shovels, fans, Christmas gifts, and so on) might offer price discounts on early orders and deliveries to smooth out production throughout the year and minimize the cost of storing the inventory. The gross sales revenue recognized from a trade discount sale is the price received after deducting the discount.

cash discounts
Reductions of invoice prices awarded for prompt payment.

In contrast to trade discounts, **cash discounts** are rewards for prompt payment. The terms of the discount may be quoted in various ways on the invoice:

Credit Terms	Meaning
n/30	The full billed price (net price) is due on the thirtieth day after the invoice date.
1/5, n/30	A 1% discount can be taken for payment within five days of the invoice date; otherwise the full billed price is due in thirty days.
15 E.O.M.	The full price is due within fifteen days after the end-of-the-month of sale. An invoice dated December 20 is due January 15.

Consider an example. A manufacturer sells $30,000 of toys to Kmart, a retailer, on terms 2/10, n/60. Therefore, Kmart may remit $30,000 less a cash discount of 0.02 × $30,000, or $30,000 – $600 = $29,400, if payment is made within ten days after the invoice date. Otherwise the full $30,000 is due in sixty days.

Cash discounts entice prompt payment and reduce the manufacturer's need for cash. Early collection also reduces the risk of bad debts. Favourable credit terms with attractive cash discounts are also a way to compete with other sellers. That is, if one seller grants such terms, competitors tend to do likewise.

Should cash discounts be taken by purchasers? The answer is usually yes, but the decision depends on the relative costs of interest. Suppose Kmart decides not to pay the $30,000 invoice for sixty days. It has the use of $29,400 for an extra fifty days (60 – 10) for an "interest" payment of $600. Based on a 365-day year, that is an effective interest rate of approximately:

$$\frac{\$600}{\$29,400} = \begin{array}{l}\text{2.04\% for 50 days, or 14.9\% for 365 days (14.9\% is 2.04\%} \\ \text{multiplied by 365 ÷ 50, or 7.3 periods of 50 days each)}\end{array}$$

Most well-managed companies, such as Kmart, can usually obtain funds for less than 14.9% interest per annum, so their accounting systems are designed to take advantage of all cash discounts automatically. However, some retailers pass up the discounts. Why? Because they have trouble getting loans or other financing at interest rates lower than the annual rates implied by the cash discount terms offered by their suppliers. Usage of cash discounts varies through time and from one industry to another. You may be familiar with some gas stations that offer a lower price for cash payment, while other stations do not.

Accounting for Net Sales Revenue

Cash discounts and sales returns and allowances are recorded as deductions from Gross Sales. Consequently, a detailed income statement will often contain:

Gross sales		xxx
Deduct:		
Sales returns and allowances	x	
Cash discounts on sales	x	xxx
Net sales		xxx

Reports to shareholders often omit details and show only net revenues. For example, when Mitel Corporation shows "Revenues... $588,800" on its income statement, the number refers to its *net* revenues. Note also that in some countries outside Canada, the word **turnover** is used as a synonym for *sales* or *revenues*. British Petroleum began its income statement with "Turnover... £ 34,950,000,000."

turnover A synonym for sales or revenues in many countries outside Canada.

An important feature of the income statement is the fact that returns, allowances, and discounts are offsets to gross sales. Management may design an accounting system to use one account, Sales, or several accounts, as shown above. If only one account is used, all returns, allowances, and cash discounts are direct decreases to the sales account. If a separate account is used for cash discounts on sales, the following analysis is made, using the numbers in our Kmart example:

	A	= L +	SE
1. Sell at terms of 2/10,n/60	+30,000 [Increase Accounts Receivable]	=	+30,000 [Increase Sales]

Followed by either 2 or 3

2. Either collect $29,400 ($30,000 less 2%)	+29,400 [Increase Cash]		−600 Increase Cash Discounts on Sales
	−30,000 [Decrease Accounts Receivable]	=	

or

3. collect $30,000	+30,000 [Increase Cash]		(no effect)
	−30,000 [Decrease Accounts Receivable]	=	

The journal entries follow: *a.S.*

1. Accounts receivable	. . . .	30,000	
Sales	. . . .		30,000
2. Cash	. . . .	29,400	
Cash discounts on sales	. . . .	600	
Accounts receivable	. . . .		30,000
OR			
3. Cash	. . . .	30,000	
Accounts receivable	. . . .		30,000

Visa
www.visa.com

American Express
www.americanexpress.com

MasterCard
www.mastercard.com/

Recording Bank Card Charges

Cash discounts also occur when retailers accept bank cards such as Visa or MasterCard or similar cards, such as American Express, Carte Blanche, or

Diner's Club. Retailers do so for three major reasons: (1) to attract credit customers who would otherwise shop elsewhere, (2) to get cash immediately rather than wait for customers to pay in due course, and (3) to avoid the cost of keeping track of many customers' accounts.

Retailers can deposit VISA slips in their bank accounts daily (just like cash). But this service costs money, and this cost must be included in the calculations to determine net sales revenue. Service charges for bank cards are usually from 1% to 3% of gross sales, although large-volume retailers bear less cost as a percentage of sales. For example, JC Penney had an arrangement whereby it paid 4.3 cents per transaction plus 1.08% of the gross sales using bank cards.

With the 3% rate, credit sales of $10,000 will result in cash of only $10,000 – 0.03 ($10,000), or $10,000 – $300, or $9,700. The $300 amount may be separately tabulated for management control purposes:

JC Penney
www.jcpenney.com/

	A	= L	+	SE
				+10,000 ⌈Increase Sales⌉
Sales using Visa	+9,700 ⌈Increase Cash⌉	=		
				−300 Increase Cash Discounts for Bank Cards

Cash	9,700	
Cash discounts for bank cards	300	
Sales		10,000

■ CASH

Objective 3

Explain why cash is important and how it is managed.

Revenue is generally accompanied by an increase in either cash or accounts receivable. This section discusses cash, and the next discusses accounts receivable.

Cash has the same meaning to organizations that it does to individuals. Cash encompasses all the items that are accepted for deposit by a bank, notably paper money and coins, money orders, and cheques. Banks do not accept postage stamps (which are really prepaid expenses), notes receivable, or post-dated cheques as cash. Indeed, although deposits are often credited to the accounts of bank customers on the date received, the bank may not provide cash for a cheque until it "clears" through the banking system. If the cheque fails to clear because its writer has insufficient funds, its amount is deducted from the depositor's account.

cash equivalents
Highly liquid short-term investments that can easily be converted into cash.

Many companies combine cash and *cash equivalents* on their balance sheets. **Cash equivalents** are highly liquid short-term investments that can easily be converted into cash with little delay. For example, the 1994 balance sheet of Chrysler begins with "Cash and equivalents. . . $5,145 million." Chrysler describes its cash equivalents as "highly liquid investments with a maturity of three months or less at the date of purchase." Examples of cash equivalents include money market funds and treasury bills.

Compensating Balances

Sometimes the entire cash balance in a bank account is not available for unrestricted use. Banks frequently require companies to maintain **compensating balances**, which are required minimum balances on deposit to compensate the bank for providing loans. The size of the minimum balance often depends on either the amount borrowed or the amount of credit available, or both.

Compensating balances increase the effective interest rate paid by the borrower. When borrowing $100,000 at 10% per year, annual interest will be $10,000. With a 10% compensating balance, the borrower can use only $90,000 of the loan, raising the effective interest rate on the usable funds to 11.1% ($10,000 ÷ $90,000).

Management of Cash

Cash is usually a small portion of the total assets of a company. Yet, managers spend much time managing cash. Why? For many reasons. First, although the cash balance may be small at any one time, the flow of cash can be enormous. Weekly receipts and disbursements of cash may be many times as large as the cash balance. Second, because cash is the most liquid asset, it is enticing to thieves and embezzlers. Safeguards are necessary. Third, adequate cash is essential to the smooth functioning of operations. Managers must carefully plan for the acquisition and use of cash. Finally, cash itself does not earn income, so it is important not to hold excess cash.

Most organizations have detailed, well-specified procedures for receiving, recording, and disbursing cash. Cash is usually placed in a bank account, and the company's books are periodically reconciled with the bank's records. To **reconcile a bank statement** means to verify that the bank balance and the accounting records are consistent. The two balances are rarely identical. A company accountant records a deposit when made and a payment when the cheque is written. The bank, however, may receive or record the deposit several days after the accountant recorded it because of postal delay, deposit on a bank holiday or weekend, and so on. The bank may also process a cheque days, weeks, or even months after it was issued.

In addition to reconciling the bank balance, other internal control procedures (discussed in Chapter 12) are set up to safeguard cash. Briefly, the major procedures include the following:

1. The individuals who receive cash do not also disburse cash.
2. The individuals who handle cash cannot access accounting records.
3. Cash receipts are immediately recorded and deposited and are not used directly to make payments.
4. Disbursements are made by serially numbered cheques, only upon proper authorization by someone other than the person writing the cheque.
5. Bank accounts are reconciled monthly.

Why are such controls necessary? Consider a person who handles cash and makes entries into the accounting records. That person could take cash and cover it up by making the following entry in the books:

Operating expenses xxx
Cash xxx

Besides guarding against dishonest actions, the procedures help ensure accurate accounting records. Suppose a cheque is written but not recorded in the books. Without serially numbered cheques, there would be no way of discovering the error before receiving a bank statement showing that the cheque was paid. But if cheques are numbered, an unrecorded check can be identified, and such errors can be discovered early.

■ CREDIT SALES AND ACCOUNTS RECEIVABLE

accounts receivable (trade receivables, receivables) Amounts owed to a company by customers as a result of delivering goods or services and extending credit in the ordinary course of business.

Credit sales on open account increase **accounts receivable**, which are amounts owed to the company by its customers as a result of delivering goods or services and extending credit for these goods or services. Accounts receivable, sometimes called **trade receivables** or simply **receivables**, should be distinguished from deposits, accruals, notes, and other assets not arising out of everyday sales.

Uncollectible Accounts

uncollectible accounts (bad debts) Receivables determined to be uncollectible because debtors are unable or unwilling to pay their debts.

bad debts expense The cost of granting credit that arises from uncollectible accounts.

Granting credit entails cost and benefits. One *cost* is **uncollectible accounts** or **bad debts**, receivables that some credit customers are either unable or unwilling to pay. Accountants often label this major cost as **bad debts expense**. Another cost is administration and collection. The *benefit* is the boost in sales and profit that would otherwise be lost if credit were not extended. That is, many potential customers would not buy if credit were unavailable.

The extent of nonpayment of debts varies. It often depends on the credit risks that managers are willing to accept. For instance, many small retail establishments will accept a higher level of risk than larger stores such as Sears. The extent of a nonpayment can also depend on the industry. The problem of uncollectible accounts is especially difficult in a privatized health-care industry. For example, the Bayfront Medical Center of St. Petersburg, Florida, suffered bad debts equal to 21% of gross revenue. Some hospitals and physicians hire a collection agency for a fee that is based on collections attained, while others attempt to collect their own delinquent accounts rather than pay the collection agency fee.

Deciding When and How to Grant Credit

Objective 4

Explain how uncollectible accounts affect the valuation of accounts receivable.

Competition and industry practice affect whether and how companies offer credit. Offering credit involves costs such as credit administration and uncollectible accounts. Companies offer credit only when the additional earnings on credit sales exceed these costs. Suppose bad debts are 5% of credit sales, administrative costs of a credit department are $5,000 per year, and $20,000 of credit sales (with earnings of $8,000 before credit costs) are achieved. Assume that

Concern Over Accounting and Lending Practices

The regulators had problems with **Standard Trust Co.'s** accounting and mortgage lending practices in 1989, more than a year before investors had any inkling that the company would end up insolvent.

The federal Office of the Superintendent of Financial Institutions repeatedly warned Standard Trust officials that its accounting was aggressive and that it had taken on too many risky loans, according to documents filed in the Ontario Court's General Division.

The superintendent's office told Standard Trust officials to stop recognizing income on delinquent mortgage loans and to change the makeup of its loan portfolio. But its warnings were ignored.

Donald Macpherson, deputy superintendent of OSFI, said in a letter in September, 1989, to Brian O'Malley, who resigned as chief executive of Standard late last year, that he was reiterating his concerns.

The letter, dealing with OSFI's review of Standard's 1988 financial statements and filed in court, says the regulators were urging the company to comply with their guidelines by having less risky residential mortgage loans make up a higher percentage of its loan portfolio.

But the company argued that if it were forced to meet the guidelines, it would be increasingly difficult for it to make a profit because of competitive conditions in the market.

"The guidelines are intended to be indications of prudent lending policies and we would urge you to meet them," Mr. Macpherson wrote.

When OSFI reviewed the 1989 financial statements, it found that the company was continuing to recognize income on delinquent loans and that the number of loans in arrears had increased, said Keith Bell, director of OSFI's registration and investigation division, in an affidavit.

Officials from OSFI began examining the company last June and forced it to have its midyear financial statements audited. In July, the company provided its first hint to the public that things were not as rosy as it had said. The audit, released in November, transformed a profit of $5-million into a loss of $50-million for the six months ended June 30, 1990.

That loss has more than doubled to $102-million for the entire 1990 calendar year, according to draft audited financial statements filed in the courts, but not previously made public. Included in the loss is a provision of $96-million to cover non-performing loans. The losses have wiped out shareholders' equity, leaving the company with a deficit of $31-million.

Other documents filed in the courts reveal OSFI's reasons for wanting to close Standard's 37 loan and trust branches. The government seized its $1.4-billion in assets on April 18 after creditors moved to place its parent, Standard Trustco Ltd., into bankruptcy.

Michael Mackenzie, Superintendent of Financial Institutions, says in a report to the Minister of Finance that he was seeking the go-ahead to seize the assets because the company had no capital, creditors had rejected a proposed bailout by Laurentian Bank of Canada and the Canadian Imperial Bank of Commerce had stopped processing cheques drawn on customer accounts at the trust company.

The trust company's precarious financial condition apparently made CIBC uneasy long before the regulators padlocked the doors.

The bank wanted to stop acting as Standard Trust's clearing agent as early as last November and only stayed on with the help of a $17-million guarantee provided by Canada Deposit Insurance Corp., according to Mr. Bell's affidavit.

Like most small trust companies, Standard had to use the services of a large bank to process its cheques and to be able to do business.

Around that time, a business plan prepared by chartered accountants Deloitte & Touche for the company indicated that Standard would lose $2.5-million a month from December, 1990 "for an indeterminate length of time."

Source: Karen Howlett, "Standard Trust warned in 1989," The Globe and Mail (May 9, 1991). Reprinted with permission of The Globe and Mail.

none of the credit sales would have been made without granting credit. The earnings of $8,000 exceeds the credit costs of $6,000 (5% × $20,000 + $5,000), so offering credit is worthwhile.

■ MEASUREMENT OF UNCOLLECTIBLE ACCOUNTS

Suppose Compuport has credit sales of $100,000 (two hundred customers averaging $500 each) during 19X1. Collections during 19X1 were $60,000. The December 31, 19X1 accounts receivable of $40,000 includes the accounts of eighty different customers who have not yet paid for their 19X1 purchases:

Customer	Amount Owed
1. Jones	$ 1,400
2. Slade	125
42. Monterro	600
79. Weinberg	700
80. Porras	11
Total receivables	$40,000

How should Compuport account for this situation? There are two basic ways: the specific write-off method and the allowance method.

Specific Write-off Method

specific write-off method This method of accounting for bad debt losses assumes all sales are fully collectible until proved otherwise.

A company that rarely experiences a bad debt might use the **specific write-off method**, which assumes that all sales are fully collectible until proved otherwise. When a specific customer account is identified as uncollectible, the account receivable is reduced. Because no specific customer's account is deemed to be uncollectible at the end of 19X1, the December 31, 19X1 Compuport balance sheet would show an Account Receivable of $40,000.

Now assume that during the second year, 19X2, the retailer identifies Jones and Monterro as customers who are not expected to pay. When the chances of collection from specific customers become dim, the amounts in the *particular* accounts are written down and the *bad debts expense* is recognized:

Bad debts expense	2,000	
Accounts receivable, Jones		1,400
Accounts receivable, Monterro		600

Effects of the specific write-off method on the balance sheet equation in 19X1 and 19X2 are (ignoring the collections of accounts receivable):

Specific Write-off Method	A	= L +	SE
19X1 Sales	+100,000 [Increase Accounts Receivable]	=	+100,000 [Increase Sales]

continued

Specific Write-off Method	A	= L +	SE
19X2 Write-off	−2,000 [Decrease Accounts Receivable]	=	2,000 [Increase Bad Debts Expense]

The specific write-off method has been criticized justifiably because it fails to apply the matching principle of accrual accounting. The $2,000 bad debts expense in 19X2 is related to (or caused by) the $100,000 of 19X1 sales. Matching requires recognition of the bad debts expense at the same time as the related revenue, that is, in 19X1, not 19X2. The specific write-off method produces two errors. First, 19X1 income is overstated by $2,000 because no bad debts expense is charged. Second, 19X2 income is understated by $2,000. Why? Because 19X1's bad debts expense of $2,000 is charged in 19X2. Compare the specific write-off method with a correct matching of revenue and expense:

	Specific Write-off Method: Matching Violated		Matching Applied Correctly	
	19X1	19X2	19X1	19X2
Sales revenue	100,000	0	100,000	0
Bad debts expense	0	2,000	2,000	0

allowance method
Method of accounting for bad debt losses using estimates of the amount of sales that will ultimately be uncollectible and a contra asset account, allowance for doubtful accounts.

The principal arguments in favour of the specific write-off method are based on cost-benefit and materiality. The method is simple. Moreover, no great error in measurement of income occurs if amounts of bad debts are small and similar from one year to the next.

Allowance Method   C S -

allowance for uncollectible accounts (allowance for doubtful accounts, allowance for bad debts, reserve for doubtful accounts)
A contra asset account that offsets total receivables by an estimated amount that will probably not be collected.

Most accountants oppose the specific write-off method because it violates the matching principle. An alternate method makes use of an estimate of uncollectible accounts that can be better matched to the related revenue. Suppose that Compuport knows from experience that 2% of sales is never collected. Therefore 2% × $100,000 = $2,000 of the 19X1 sales can be estimated to be uncollectible. However, the exact customer accounts that will not be collected are unknown at December 31, 19X1. (Of course, all $2,000 must be among the $40,000 of accounts receivable because the other $60,000 has already been collected.) Bad debts expense can be recognized in 19X1, before the specific uncollectible accounts are identified, by using the **allowance method**, which has two basic elements: (1) an *estimate* of the amount of sales that will ultimately be uncollectible and (2) a *contra account*, which records the estimate and is deducted from the accounts receivable. The contra account is usually called **allowance for uncollectible accounts** (or **allowance for doubtful accounts, allowance for bad debts,** or **reserve for doubtful accounts**). It measures the amount of receivables estimated to be uncollectible from as yet unidentified customers. The effects of the allowance method on the balance sheet equation follow:

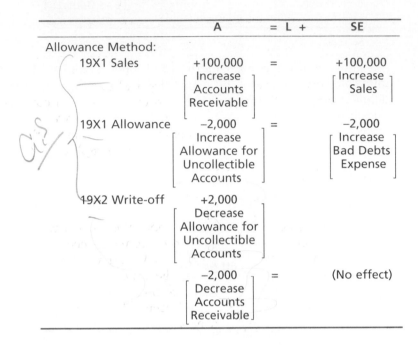

	A	= L +	SE
Allowance Method:			
19X1 Sales	+100,000	=	+100,000
	[Increase Accounts Receivable]		[Increase Sales]
19X1 Allowance	–2,000	=	–2,000
	[Increase Allowance for Uncollectible Accounts]		[Increase Bad Debts Expense]
19X2 Write-off	+2,000		
	[Decrease Allowance for Uncollectible Accounts]		
	–2,000	=	(No effect)
	[Decrease Accounts Receivable]		

The associated journal entries are:

19X1 Sales	Accounts receivable	100,000	
	Sales		100,000
19X1 Allowances	Bad debts expense	2,000	
	Allowance for uncollectible accounts ...		2,000
19X2 Write-offs	Allowance for uncollectible accounts	2,000	
	Accounts receivable, Jones		1,400
	Accounts receivable, Monterro		600

Objective 5

Estimate bad debts expense under the allowance method using (a) percentage of sales, (b) percentage of ending accounts receivable, and (c) aging of accounts.

The principal argument in favour of the allowance method is its superiority in measuring accrual accounting income in any given year. That is, the $2,000 of 19X1 sales that is estimated never to be collected should be recorded in 19X1, the period in which the $100,000 sales revenue is recognized.

The allowance method results in the following presentation in the Compuport balance sheet, December 31, 19X1:

Accounts receivable	$40,000
Less: Allowance for uncollectible accounts	2,000
Net accounts receivable	$38,000

Other formats for presenting the allowance method on recent balance sheets of actual companies include the following; however, in Canada many companies do not report the allowance for uncollectible accounts.

	1995
Mitel Corporation (in millions):	
Accounts receivable,	
less allowance: $7.2	$ 128.5
Moore Corporation Limited (in millions):	
Accounts receivable	
less allowance for doubtful accounts: $13.9	$ 477.0

Allowance methods are based on historical experience and assume the current year is similar to prior years in terms of economic circumstances (growth versus recession, interest rate levels, and so on) and in terms of customer composition. Estimates are revised when conditions change. For example, if a local employer closed or drastically reduced employment, Compuport might increase expected bad debts.

Applying the Allowance Method Using a Percentage of Sales

percentage of sales method An approach to estimating bad debts expense and uncollectible accounts based on the historical relations between credit sales and uncollectibles.

A contra asset account is created under the allowance method because of the inability to write down a specific customer's account at the time bad debts expense is recognized. A **percentage of sales method** based on historical relations between credit sales and uncollectibles is one method used to estimate the amount recorded in this contra account. In our example, at the end of 19X1 the retailer has $40,000 in Accounts Receivable. On the basis of experience, a bad debts expense is recognized at a rate of 2% of total credit sales, or 0.02 × $100,000, or $2,000.

Visualize the relationship between the general ledger item Accounts Receivable and its supporting detail (which is a form of supporting ledger, called a *subsidiary ledger*) on December 31, 19X1. The sum of the balances of all the customer accounts in the subsidiary ledger must equal the accounts receivable balance in the general ledger.

Compuport General Ledger, December 31, 19X1

* Total of these individual customer accounts must equal $40,000.

In 19X2, after exhausting all practical means of collection, the retailer judges the Jones and Monterro accounts to be uncollectible. Recording the $2,000 write-off for Jones and Monterro in 19X2 has the following effect:

Compuport General Ledger, December 31, 19X1

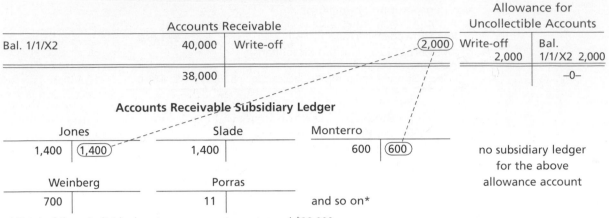

* Total of these individual customer accounts must equal $38,000.

Convince yourself that the ultimate write-off has no effect on total assets:

	Before Write-off	After Write-off
Accounts receivable	$40,000	$38,000
Allowance for uncollectible accounts	2,000	—
Book value (net realizable value)	$38,000	$38,000

Applying the Allowance Method Using a Percentage of Accounts Receivable

percentage of accounts receivable method An approach to estimating bad debts expense and uncollectible accounts at year end using the historical relations of uncollectibles to accounts receivable.

Like the percentage of sales method, the **percentage of accounts receivable method** uses historical experience, but the estimate of uncollectible accounts is based on the historical relations of uncollectibles to year-end gross accounts receivable, not sales.

The additions to the Allowance for Bad Debts are calculated to achieve a desired balance in the Allowance account. This addition to the allowance equals the Bad Debts Expense, as shown below. Consider the historical experience in the following table:

	Accounts Receivable at End of Year	Bad Debts Deemed Uncollectible and Written Off
19X1	$100,000	$ 3,500
19X2	80,000	2,450
19X3	90,000	2,550
19X4	110,000	4,100
19X5	120,000	5,600
19X6	112,000	2,200
Six-year total	$612,000	$20,400
Average (divide by 6)	$102,000	$ 3,400
Average percentage not collected = 3,400 ÷ 102,000 = 3.33%		

At the end of 19X7, assume the accounts receivable balance is $115,000. The 19X7 addition to the Allowance for Bad Debts is computed as follows:

1. Divide average bad debt losses of $3,400 by average ending accounts receivable of $102,000 to calculate average percentage not collected of 3.33%.
2. Apply the percentage not collected to the ending Accounts Receivable balance for 19X7 to determine the balance that should be in the Allowance account at the end of the year: 3.33% × $115,000 receivables at the end of 19X6 is $3,833.
3. Prepare an adjusting entry to bring the Allowance to the appropriate amount. Suppose the books show a $700 credit balance in the Allowance account at the end of 19X7. Then the adjusting entry for 19X7 is $3,833 – $700, or $3,133 to record the Bad Debts expense. The journal entry is:

Bad debts expense	3,133	
Allowance for bad debts		3,133
To bring the Allowance to the level		
justified by bad debt experience during		
the past six years.		

The percentage of accounts receivable method differs from the percentage of sales method in two ways: (1) the percentage is based on the ending accounts receivable balance rather than on sales, and (2) the dollar amount calculated using the percentage is the appropriate *ending balance* in the allowance account, not the amount added to the account for the year.

Applying the Allowance Method Using the Aging of Accounts Receivable

aging of accounts receivable An analysis of the elements of individual accounts receivable according to the time elapsed after the dates of billing.

A refinement of the percentage of accounts receivable approach is the **aging of accounts receivable** method, which considers the composition of the end-of-year accounts receivable. As time elapses after the sale, ultimate collection becomes less likely. The seller may send the buyer a late notice thirty days after the sale, a second reminder after sixty days, make a phone call after ninety days, and place the account with a collection agency after 120 days. Companies that analyze the age of their accounts receivable for credit management purposes naturally incorporate this evidence into estimates of the allowance for uncollectibles. For example, the $115,000 balance in Accounts Receivable on December 31, 19X7, might be aged as follows:

Name	Total	1–30 Days	31–60 Days	61–90 Days	Over 90 Days
Oxwall Tools	$ 20,000	$20,000			
Cambridge Castings	10,000	10,000			
Estee	20,000	15,000	$ 5,000		
Western Pipe	22,000		12,000	$10,000	
Ceilcote	4,000			3,000	$1,000
Other accounts (each detailed)	39,000	27,000	8,000	2,000	2,000
Total	$115,000	$72,000	$25,000	$15,000	$3,000
Historical bad debt percentages		0.1%	1%	5%	90%
Bad debt allowance to be provided	$ 3,772 =	$ 72 +	$ 250 +	$ 750 +	$2,700

This aging schedule produces a different target balance for the Allowance account than the percentage of accounts receivable method did: $3,772 versus $3,833. Also, the journal entry is slightly different. Given the same $700 credit balance in the Allowance account, the journal entry to record the Bad Debts Expense is $3,772 – $700, or $3,072:

Bad debts expense	$3,072	
Allowance for uncollectible accounts . . .		$3,072
To bring the Allowance to the level justified by		
prior experience using the aging method.		

Whether the percentage of sales, percentage of accounts receivable, or aging method is used to estimate bad debts expense and the Allowance for Uncollectible Accounts, the subsequent accounting for write-offs is the same—a decrease in Accounts Receivable and a decrease in the allowance for Uncollectible Accounts.

Bad Debt Recoveries

bad debt recoveries
Accounts receivable that were written off as uncollectible but then were collected at a later date.

A few accounts will be written off as uncollectible, but then collection occurs at a later date. When such **bad debt recoveries** occur, the write-off should be reversed, and the collection handled as a normal receipt on account. In this way, a company will be better able to keep track of the customer's true payment history. Return to the Compuport example and assume that Monterro's account for $600 is written off in February 19X2 and collected in October 19X2. The following journal entries produce a complete record of the transactions in Monterro's individual accounts receivable account.

Feb. 19X2	Allowance for uncollectible accounts	600	
	Accounts receivable		600
	To write off uncollectible account of		
	Monterro, a specific customer.		
Oct. 19X2	Accounts receivable	600	
	Allowance for uncollectible accounts		600
	To reverse February 19X2 write-off of		
	account of Monterro.		
	Cash	600	
	Accounts receivable		600
	To record the collection on account.		

Note that these 19X2 entries have no effect on the level of bad debt expense in 19X1. At the end of 19X1, journal entries created bad debt expense based on the expected level of uncollectibles. Briefly, in 19X2 Compuport thought that Monterro would be a nonpaying customer. This was not ultimately the case, and the records now reflect Monterro's payment.

■ ASSESSING THE LEVEL OF ACCOUNTS RECEIVABLE

accounts receivable turnover Credit sales divided by average accounts receivable.

Management and financial analysts assess the firm's ability to *control* accounts receivable. Can the firm generate sales without excessive growth in receivables? One measure of this ability is the **accounts receivable turnover**, which is calculated by dividing the credit sales by the average accounts receivable for the period during which the sales were made:

Objective 6

Understand techniques for assessing the level of accounts receivable.

$$\text{Accounts receivable turnover} = \frac{\text{Credit sales}}{\text{Average accounts receivable}}$$

Suppose credit sales (or sales on account) in 19X2 were $1 million and beginning and ending accounts receivable were $115,000 and $112,000 respectively.

$$\text{Accounts receivable turnover} = \frac{1,000,000}{0.5\,(115,000 + 112,000)} = 8.81$$

Credit managers, bank loan officers, and auditors evaluate trends in this ratio. They may compare it with ratios of similar-sized companies in the industry. Reductions in the accounts receivable turnover are generally unwelcome.

Alternatively, receivables can be assessed in terms of how long it takes to collect them. Here, the **days to collect accounts receivable,** or **average collection period,** is calculated by dividing 365 by the accounts receivable turnover. For our example:

days to collect accounts receivable (average collection period) 365 divided by accounts receivable turnover.

$$\begin{aligned}\text{Days to collect} \atop \text{accounts receivable} &= \frac{365 \text{ days}}{\text{Accounts receivable turnover}} \\[6pt] &= \frac{365 \text{ days}}{8.81} \\[6pt] &= 41.4 \text{ days}\end{aligned}$$

The following illustrates the variability in accounts receivable turnover levels among industries.

Industry	Median Levels	
	Accounts Receivable Turnover	Days to Collect Accounts Receivable
Automobile Retailer	57.7	6.3
Department Stores	33.1	11.0
Furniture Retailer	17.2	21.2
Jewellery Retailer	6.9	52.9
Management Consulting Firms	5.4	67.6

Source: Robert Morris Associates, *Annual Statement Studies for 1994.*

The high accounts receivable turnovers for automobile retailers and department stores correspond to the way customers finance purchases. For automobiles, customers generally finance through banks or through the credit arms of the automobile manufacturer. For department stores, credit is increasingly obtained via national credit cards such as Visa and MasterCard. In both industries the seller receives cash quickly. The other three industries more frequently involve direct granting of credit by the selling firm.

Summary Problems for Your Review

Problem One

Hector Lopez, marketing manager for Fireplace Distributors, sold twelve woodstoves to Woodside Condominiums, Inc. The sales contract was signed on April 27, 19X1. The list price of each wood stove was $1,200, but a 5% quantity discount was allowed. The wood-stoves were to be delivered on May 10, and a cash discount of 2% of the amount owed was offered if payment were made by June 10. Fireplace Distributors delivered the woodstoves as promised and received the proper payment on June 9.

Required

1. How much revenue should be recognized in April? in May? in June? Explain.
2. Suppose Fireplace Distributors has a separate account titled "Cash Discounts on Sales." What journal entries would be made on June 9 when the cash payment is received?
3. Suppose Fireplace Distributors has another account titled "Sales Returns and Allowances." Suppose further that one of the woodstoves had a scratch, and Fireplace Distributors allowed Woodside to deduct $100 from the total amount due. What journal entries would be made on June 9 when the cash payment is received?

Solution to Problem One

1. Revenue of $13,680 (12 × $1,200 less a 5% quantity discount of $720) would be recognized in May and none in April or June. The key is whether the revenue is earned and the asset received from the buyer is realized. The revenue is not earned until the merchandise is delivered; therefore revenue cannot be recognized in April. Provided that Woodside Condominiums has a good credit rating, the receipt of cash is reasonably ensured before the cash is actually received. Therefore recognition of revenue need not be delayed until June. On May 10 both revenue recognition tests were met, and the revenue would be recorded on May's income statement.

2. The original revenue recorded was $13,680. The 2% cash discount is 2% × $13,680 = $273.60. Therefore the cash payment is $13,680 − $273.60 = $13,406.40:

Cash	13,406.40	
Cash discounts on sales	273.60	
Accounts receivable		13,680.00

3. The only difference from requirement 2 is a $100 smaller cash payment, a $100 debit to sales returns and allowances and a 2% discount on $13,580 = $271.60:

Cash	13,308.40	
Cash discounts on sales	271.60	
Sales returns and allowances	100.00	
Accounts receivable		13,680.00

Problem Two

H. J. Heinz Company sells many popular food products, including its best-selling Heinz ketchup. Its balance sheet showed the following (in thousands):

	April 27,1994	April 28,1993
Receivables	$827,908	$995,234
Less allowance for doubtful accounts	15,407	16,299
	$812,501	$978,935

Required

Suppose a large grocery chain that owed Heinz $2 million announced bankruptcy on April 28, 1994. Heinz decided that chances for collection were virtually zero. The account was immediately written off. Show the balances as of April 28, 1994, after the write-off. Explain the effect of the write-off on income for the year beginning April 28, 1994.

Solution to Problem Two

Receivables ($827,908 − $2,000)	$825,908
Less allowance for doubtful accounts ($15,407 − $2,000)	13,407
	$812,501

Because Heinz has an account labelled allowance for doubtful accounts, it must use the allowance method. The write-off will not affect the *net* carrying amount of the receivables, which is still $812,501,000. Moreover, the income will be unaffected. Why? Because the estimated expense has already been recognized in prior periods. Under the allowance method, net assets and income are affected when the estimation process occurs, not when the write-off happens.

HIGHLIGHTS TO REMEMBER

Revenue is generally recognized when two tests are met: (1) the revenue is earned, and (2) the asset received in return is realized. Most often, revenue is recognized at the point of sale, when the product is delivered to the customer. In offering products for sale many special practices produce differences between the list price at which a product is offered and the final price which a customer is charged. The term *net sales* represents the final proceeds to the seller—gross sales less offsetting amounts for returns, allowances, and cash discounts.

Sales made for cash are the most easily recorded and valued. However, cash creates a number of procedural problems for the firm. Protecting cash from theft or loss, adequately planning for the availability of cash as needed, and reconciling the firm's accounting records with the bank's records were introduced in this chapter.

Potential uncollectible accounts reduce the amount of accounts receivable reported on the balance sheet. Reporting the uncollectible portion of credit sales requires estimates that may be based on a percentage of sales, a percentage of accounts receivable, or an aging of accounts receivable. These estimates permit the financial statements to (1) properly reflect asset levels on the balance sheet, and (2) properly match bad debts expense with revenue on the income statement.

Companies and analysts use ratios to assess the level of accounts receivable. The accounts receivable turnover ratio and the days to collect accounts receivable both relate the average dollar value of accounts receivable to the level of sales activity during the year. Comparisons with other companies in the same industry or examination of a particular company over time draw attention to unusual circumstances and possible problems.

Appendix 7: Intercorporate Investments

■ AN OVERVIEW OF CORPORATE INVESTMENTS

As noted earlier, when a firm has an excess of cash, sound management dictates that the cash be invested rather than remain idle in the company's chequing account. Corporations frequently make both short- and long-term investments in securities issued by other corporations.

In many instances, companies invest in debt securities issued by governments, banks, or other corporations. Both short-term and long-term debt investments in securities are common. In addition to debt securities, companies also invest in other corporations' equity securities. These investments are typically long-term investments, and when they are large enough, they allow the investing company varying degrees of control over the company issuing the securities. The links among corporations created by such investments are common and arise from various motivations. After companies create intercorporate linkages, the accountant must develop ways to report on the financial results of these complicated entities.

All investments made by companies are classified on a balance sheet according to *purpose* or *intention*. An investment should be carried as a current asset if it is a short-term investment. Other investments are classified as non-current assets and usually appear as either (1) a separate *investments* category between current assets and property, plant, and equipment, or (2) a part of *other* assets below the plant assets category.

temporary (short-term) investment A temporary investment in marketable securities of otherwise idle cash.

marketable securities Any notes, bonds, or stocks that can readily be sold via public markets. The term is often used as a synonym for temporary investments.

■ TEMPORARY (SHORT-TERM) INVESTMENTS

As its name implies, **a temporary or short-term investment** is a temporary investment in marketable securities of otherwise idle cash. **Marketable securities** are notes, bonds, or stocks that can be readily sold. The short-term *investment portfolio* (total of securities owned) usually consists of *short-term debt securities* and *short-term equity securities*. The investments are highly liquid (easily convertible into cash) and have stable prices.

Ordinarily, temporary investments are expected to be completely converted into cash within a year after the balance sheet date. But some companies hold part of their portfolio of investments beyond a twelve-month period. Nevertheless, these investments are still classified as current assets if management intends to convert them into cash *when needed*. The key point is that conversion to cash is immediately available at the option of management.

Objective 7

Describe the accounting for temporary investments.

Some companies use the term *marketable securities* to describe their temporary investments. Cash equivalents, discussed in Chapter 6, are usually marketable securities that mature quickly and are repaid by the issuer. Strictly speaking, marketable securities may be held as *either* temporary investments or long-term investments. Thus 100 shares of BCE common stock may be held as a temporary investment by one company and another 100 shares may be held as a long-term investment by a second company. Consequently, this book will not use the term *marketable securities* as a synonym for the more descriptive term *temporary investments*, a term which includes the intention of the owner.

short-term debt securities Largely notes and bonds with maturities of one year or less.

Short-Term Securities

Short-term debt securities consist largely of notes and bonds with maturities of one year or less. They represent interest-bearing debt of businesses and governments. Investors purchase debt securities to gain the interest income.

certificates of deposit Short-term obligations of banks.

commercial paper Short-term notes payable issued by large corporations with top credit ratings.

Treasury bills Interest-bearing notes, bonds, and bills issued by the federal government.

short-term equity securities Capital stock in other corporations held with the intention to liquidate within one year as needed.

Typically, debt security investments include short-term obligations of banks, called **certificates of deposit,** and **commercial paper**, which consists of short-term notes payable issued by large corporations with top credit ratings. **Treasury bills** refer to interest-bearing notes, bonds, and bills issued by the federal government. These debt securities may be held until maturity or may be resold in securities markets.

The investor's balance sheet shows temporary investments immediately after cash. These securities are initially recorded at cost. Because their market values are reliable and readily observable, when those market values differ from cost there is a requirement to write them down to their market value. Interest income from short-term debt securities is recognized as it accrues.

Short-term equity securities consist of capital stock (shares of ownership) in other corporations. Equity securities are regularly bought and sold on the public stock exchanges. If the investing firm intends to sell the equity securities it holds within one year or within its normal operating cycle, then the securities are considered a temporary investment.

When marketable securities are held in a trading category or as available-for-sale, they are carried in the financial statements using the lower-of-cost and market method (LCM). Under the LCM method, the reported asset values in the balance sheet are recorded at the lower of their original or market value in total for the entire portfolio of marketable securities. For temporary securities, the changes in balances appear as unrecognized gains or losses in the income statement.

Suppose a portfolio cost $50 million and had the following market values at the end of four subsequent periods (in millions):

	End of Period			
	1	2	3	4
Assumed market value	50	45	47	54
Balance Sheet Presentation				
Temporary investment at cost	50	50	50	50
Valuation adjustment to market	0	(5)	(3)	0
Carrying value	50	45	47	50
For Trading securities:				
Income Statement Presentation				
Unrealized gain (loss) on changes in market	0	(5)	2	3

The tabulation shows the results for four periods. Most companies will present the LCM value directly as a single line on the balance sheet. The valuation adjustment is shown to provide a linkage to cost and to emphasize that the balance can be decreased or increased with changes in market value, but never higher than cost.

The journal entries for the securities for periods 2, 3, and 4 would appear as follows, without explanations:

Period	Trading Securitites		
2	Unrealized loss	5	
	Marketable Securities		5
3	Marketable Securities	2	
	Unrealized gain..............		2
4	Marketable Securities	3	
	Unrealized gain..............		3

■ THE COST AND EQUITY METHODS FOR INTERCORPORATE INVESTMENTS

Long-term investments in the equity securities of one company are frequently made by another company. The investor's accounting depends on the relationship between the "investor" and the "investee." The question is, How much can the investor influence the operations of the investee? For example, the holder of a small number of shares in a company's stock is a passive investor and follows the **cost method,** whereby the investment is carried at cost and dividends are recorded as income when received. This type of investor cannot affect how the company invests its money, conducts its business, or declares and pays its dividends.

As an investor acquires more substantial holdings of a company's shares, the ability to influence the company changes. A shareholder with 2% or 3% ownership will have little difficulty making appointments to speak with management. Once the investor has "significant influence," a term that GAAP rather arbitrarily defines as about 20% ownership, the cost method no longer adequately reflects the economic relationship between the potentially *active investor* and the investee (or **affiliated company**). In Canada, such an investor must use the **equity method,** which accounts for the investment at acquisition cost adjusted for the investor's share of dividends and earnings or losses of the investee subsequent to the date of investment. Accordingly, the carrying amount of the investment is increased by the investor's share of the investee's earnings. The carrying amount is reduced by dividends received from the investee and by the investor's share of investee's losses. The equity method is generally used for a 20% through 50% interest, because such a level of ownership is regarded as a presumption that the investor has the ability to exert significant influence, whereas the cost method is generally used to account for interests of less than 20%. The treatment of an interest in excess of 50% is based on the belief that the investor has control. See the following section entitled "Consolidated Financial Statements."

cost method
Accounting for an investment carried at cost and dividends received recorded as revenues.

affiliated company
A company that has 20% to 50% of its voting shares owned by another company.

equity method
Accounting for an investment at acquisition cost adjusted for the investor's share of dividends and earnings or losses of the investee subsequent to the date of investment.

Suppose Buyit invests $80 million in each of two companies, Passiveco and Influential. Influential has a total market value of $200 million, earnings of $30 million, and pays dividends of $10 million. Passiveco has a total market value of $800 million, earnings of $120 million, and pays dividends of $40 million. Buyit owns 40% of Influential and accounts for that investment using the equity method. Buyit owns only 10% of Passiveco and uses the cost method in its accounting.

To compare the methods, consider how Buyit's balance sheet equation is affected differently by investee earnings and dividends, as follows:

	Cost Method–Passiveco				Equity Method–Influential			
	A		=	L + SE	A		=	L + SE
	Cash	Investments		Liab.	SE	Cash	Investments	Liab.	SE
1. Acquisition	−80	+80	=			−80	+80	=	
2. a. Net income of Passiveco	No entry and no effect								
b. Net income of Influential							+12	=	+12
3. a. Dividends from Passiveco	+ 4		=		+4			=	
b. Dividends from Influential						+ 4	− 4		
Effects for year	−76	+80	=		+4	−76	+88	=	+12

Passiveco: Under the cost method, the investment account is unaffected. The dividend increases the cash amount by $4 million. Dividend revenue increases shareholders' equity by $4 million.

Influential: Under the equity method, the investment account has a net increase of $8 million for the year. The dividend increases the cash account by $4 million. Investment revenue increases shareholders' equity by $12 million.

The following journal entries accompany the above table:

Cost Method-Passiveco			Equity Method-Influential		
1. Investment in Passiveco	80		1. Investment in Influential	80	
Cash...................		80	Cash		80
2. No entry			2. Investment in Influential	12	
			Investment revenue*		12
3. Cash	4		3. Cash	4	
Dividend revenue†		4	Investment in Influential. ...		4

* Frequently called "equity in earnings of affiliated companies."
† Frequently called "dividend income."

Under the equity method, income is recognized by Buyit as it is earned by Influential rather than when dividends are received. Cash dividends from Influential do not affect net income; they increase Cash and decrease the Investment balance. In a sense, Buyit's claim on Influential grows by its share of Influential's net income. The dividend is a partial liquidation of Buyit's "claim." The receipt of a dividend is similar to the collection of an account receivable. The revenue from a sale of merchandise on account is recognized when the receivable is created; to include the collection also as revenue would be double-counting. Similarly, it would be double-counting to include the $4 million of dividends as income after the $12 million of income is already recognized as it is earned.

The major justification for using the equity method instead of the cost method is that it more appropriately recognizes increases or decreases in the economic resources that the investor can influence. The reported net income of an equity investor is affected by its share of net income or net loss recognized by the investor. Unlike the cost method, the reported net income of the "equity" investor is not affected by the dividend policies of the investee, over which the investor might have significant influence.

Equity Affiliates and the Statement of Changes in Financial Position

A company with equity affiliates may use the direct method or the indirect method to prepare its statement of changes in financial position. If the *direct method* is used, no special problem arises because only the cash received from the affiliate as a dividend appears. However, if the *indirect method* is used, net earnings is increased by the investor's share of its affiliates' earnings or is decreased by its share of the affiliates' loss. We must adjust reported income to reflect cash flow from operations. Suppose the investor had net income of $7.6 million, including equity in earnings of an affiliate of $2.5 million, and received $1.3 in dividends from the affiliate. Cash flow is $1.3 million. Since net earnings includes $2.5 million, the indirect method must adjust net earnings by $2.5 – $1.3 = $1.2, the amount of the equity in earnings that was not received in cash.

■ CONSOLIDATED FINANCIAL STATEMENTS

parent company A company owning more than 50% of the voting shares of another company, called the subsidiary company.

subsidiary A corporation owned or controlled by a parent company through the ownership of more than 50% of the voting stock.

consolidated statements Combinations of the financial positions and earnings reports of the parent company with those of various subsidiaries into an overall report as a single entity.

Canadian companies with substantial ownership of other companies constitute a single overall economic unit that is composed of two or more separate legal entities. This is almost always a parent-subsidiary relationship where one corporation (the **parent company**) owns more than 50% of the outstanding voting shares of another corporation (the **subsidiary**).

Why have subsidiaries? Why not have the corporation take the form of a single legal entity? The reasons include limiting the liabilities in a risky venture, saving income taxes, conforming with government regulations with respect to a part of the business, doing business in a foreign country, and expanding in an orderly way. For example, there are often tax advantages in acquiring the capital stock of a going concern rather than its individual assets.

Consolidated statements combine the financial positions and earnings reports of the parent company with those of various subsidiaries into an overall report as if they were a single entity. The aim is to give the readers a better perspective than they could obtain by examining separate reports of individual companies.

Consolidated statements have been common in North America since the turn of the century, when interconnected corporate entities first began to appear in the form of "holding companies," a parent with many subsidiaries. J. P. Morgan's U.S. Steel, formed in 1901, is a classic example. As this economic form spread to Great Britain and the Netherlands, so also did consolidated accounting begin to spread. However, all countries did not embrace it. As recently as 1977, consolidated accounts were rare in Japan. In 1977, the law was changed, and now both "parent-only" and consolidated statements are publicly available although the consolidated statements are generally released later. Some countries in Europe, for example Switzerland, have been slow to adopt consolidation, but in the 1992 culmination of the EEC, the Seventh Company Law Directive required full implementation of consolidation by EEC members of the European Community. Similarly, the International Accounting Standards Committee has encouraged this trend since 1976.

Objective 9

Explain the preparation of consolidated financial statements.

The Acquisition

To illustrate the concept of consolidated financial statements, consider two companies: the parent (P) and a subsidiary (S). Initially, they are separate companies with assets of $650 million and $400 million, respectively. P acquires all of the stock of S by purchasing the shares from their current owners for $213 million paid in cash. Exhibit 7-1 shows the two companies before and after this transaction. Figures in this and subsequent tables are in millions.

This purchase transaction is a simple exchange of one asset for another from P's perspective. In terms of the balance sheet equation, cash declines by $213 million and the asset account, Investment in S, increases by the same amount. *The subsidiary S is entirely unaffected from an accounting standpoint*, although it now has one centralized owner with unquestionable control over all economic decisions S may make in the future. In this example, the purchase price and the "Investment in S" equal the shareholders' equity of the acquired company. The preparation of consolidated statements in situations where these two amounts differ is discussed later, in the section entitled "Accounting for Goodwill."

Note that the $213 million is paid to the *former owners* of S as private investors. The $213 million is *not* an addition to the existing assets and shareholders' equity of S. *That is, the books of S are unaffected by P's investment and P's subsequent accounting thereof.* S is not dissolved; it lives on as a separate legal entity but with a new owner, P.

Exhibit 7-1		Before Purchase		After Purchase	
Before and After the		S	P	S	P
Acquisition Parent (P)					
Buys Subsidiary (S)	Cash	$100	$300	$100	$ 87
	Net Plant	300	350	300	350
	Investment in S				213
	Total Assets	$400	$650	$400	$650
	Accounts Payable	$187	$100	$187	$100
	Bonds Payable	—	100	—	100
	Shareholders' Equity	213	450	213	450
	Total Liabilities and SE	$400	$650	$400	$650

The following journal entry occurs:

P Books		
Investment in S	213	
Cash		213

S Books
No entry

Each legal entity has its individual set of books; the consolidated entity does not keep a separate set of books. Instead, working papers are used to prepare the consolidated statements.

Consider a consolidated balance sheet prepared immediately after the acquisition. The consolidated statement shows the details of all assets and liabilities of both the parent and the subsidiary. The Investment in S account on P's books is the evidence of an ownership interest, which is held by P but is really composed of all the assets and liabilities of S. The consolidated statements cannot show both the evidence of interest *plus* the detailed underlying assets and liabilities. So this double-counting is avoided by eliminating the reciprocal evidence of ownership present in two places: (a) the Investment in S on P's books and (b) the Shareholders' Equity on S's books:

Entity	Types of Records
P	Parent books
+ S	Subsidiary books
= Preliminary consolidated report	No separate books, but periodically P and S assets and liabilities are added together via work sheets
− E	"Eliminating entries" remove double-counting and appear on a consolidating worksheet, not on the books of P or S
= Consolidated report to investors	

On the work sheet for consolidating the balance sheet, the entry to eliminate the double-counting of ownership interest in journal format is:

Shareholders' equity (on S books)   213
         Investment in S (on P books)   213

Separately, after the purchase, P has assets of $650 and S has assets of $400 but when we consolidate and eliminate the double-counting the consolidated assets are $213 less, $837. The consolidated result, expressed in terms of the accounting equation, is:

	Assets			=	Liabilities	+	Shareholders' Equity
	Investment in S	+	Cash and Other Assets	=	Accounts Payable, etc.	+	Shareholders' Equity
P's accounts, Jan. 1:							
Before acquisition			650	=	200	+	450
Acquisition of S	+213		−213	=			
S's accounts, Jan. 1			400	=	187	+	213
Intercompany eliminations	−213			=			−213
Consolidated, Jan. 1	0	+	837	=	387	+	450

After Acquisition

After the initial acquisition, P accounts for its long-term investment in S by the same equity method used to account for an unconsolidated ownership interest of

20% through 50%. Suppose S has a net income of $50 million for the subsequent year (Year 1). If the parent company P were reporting alone using the equity method, it would account for the net income of its subsidiary by increasing its Investment in S account and its Shareholders' Equity account (in the form of Retained Earnings) by 100% of $50 million.

The income statements for the year are (numbers in millions assumed):

	P	S	Consolidated
Sales	$900	$300	$1,200
Expenses	800	250	1,050
Operating income	$100	$ 50	$ 150
Investment revenue*	50	—	
Net income	$150	$ 50	

*Pro-rata share (100%) of subsidiary net income.

P's parent-company-only income statement would show its own sales and expenses plus its pro-rata share of S's net income (as the equity method requires). The journal entry on P's books is:

Investment in S   50
       Investment revenue*   50
* Or "equity in net income of subsidiary."

After this year's result is recorded by P, the entry to eliminate the Investment in S on the work sheet used for consolidating the balance sheets is $213 + $50 = $263.

Reflect on the changes in P's accounts, S's accounts, and the consolidated accounts (in millions of dollars):

	Assets			=	Liabilities +		Shareholders' Equity
	Investment in S	+	Cash and Other Assets	=	Accounts Payable, etc.	+	Shareholders' Equity
P's accounts:							
Beginning of year	+213	+	437	=	200	+	450
Operating income			+100	=			+100*
Share of S income	+50			=			+50*
End of year	263	+	537	=	200	+	600
S's accounts:							
Beginning of year			400	–	187	+	+213
Net income			+50	=			+50*
End of year			450	=	187	+	263
Intercompany eliminations	–263			=			–263
Consolidated, end of year	0	+	987	=	387	+	600

* Changes in the retained income portion of shareholders' equity.

Review at this point to see that consolidated statements are the summation of the individual accounts of two or more separate legal entities. They are prepared periodically via work sheets. *The consolidated entity does not have a separate continuous set of books like the legal entities.* Moreover, a consolidated income statement is merely the summation of the revenue and expenses of the separate legal entities being consolidated after eliminating double-counting. The income statement for P shows the same $150 million net income as the consolidated income statement. The difference is that P's "parent-only" income statement shows its 100% share of S as a single $50 million item, whereas the consolidated income statement combines the detailed revenue and expense items for P and S.

Intercompany Eliminations

When two companies are consolidated, the accountant carefully avoids double-counting. In many cases the parent and subsidiary do business together. Suppose S charges P $12 for products that cost S $10, and the sale is made on credit. The following journal entries are made:

P's Records			S's Records		
Merchandise Inventory	12		Accounts Receivable	12	
Accounts Payable		12	Sales Revenue		12
			Cost of Goods Sold	10	
			Merchandise Inventory		10

But has anything happened economically? Not really. As far as the consolidated entity is concerned the product is just moved from one location to another. If P paid cash to S, the cash just shifts from "one pocket to another." So this transaction is not an important one from the perspective of the consolidated company and should be eliminated. It is important that each separate legal entity keep track of its transactions, but the accountant can undo these intercompany transactions when the consolidation is done. The accountant needs to eliminate the intercompany receivable and payable, eliminate the costs and revenues, and be sure the inventory is carried at its cost to the consolidated company, $10. The following consolidation journal entries are used in the work sheet consolidation process to accomplish that.

Accounts Payable (P)	12	
Accounts Receivable (S)		12
Sales Revenue (S)	12	
Cost of Goods Sold (S)		10
Merchandise Inventory (P)		2

The parenthetical letters show whose records contain the account balances. But remember, these entries *are not* recorded on the individual records of either company, only in the consolidation work sheet.

Non-controlling Interests

Our example of the consolidation of P and S assumes that P purchased 100% of S. This is often not true. One company can control another with just 51% of the shares. The owners of the remaining 49% have claims that are called *non-controlling interests*. **Non-controlling interests** represent the rights of non-majority shareholders in the assets and earnings of a company that is consolidated into the accounts of its major shareholder.

non-controlling interests The outside shareholders' interests, as opposed to the parent's interests, in a subsidiary corporation.

To make this idea more concrete, assume that our parent company (P) bought 90% of S. The next table, using the basic figures of the previous example, shows the overall approach to a consolidated balance sheet immediately after the acquisition. P's 90% of S cost 0.90 × $213, or $192 million. The minority interest is 10%, or $21 million. (All dollar amounts are rounded to the nearest million.)

	Assets			=	Liabilities +		Shareholders' Equity		
	Investment in S	+	Cash and Other Assets	=	Accounts Payable, etc.	+	Minority Interest	+	Shareholders' Equity
P's accounts, Jan. 1:									
Before acquisition			650	=	200			+	450
Acquisition of 90% of S	+192		−192	=					
S's accounts, Jan. 1:			400	=	187			+	213
Intercompany eliminations	−192			=			+21		−213
Consolidated, Jan. 1	0	+	858	=	387	+	21	+	450

Again, suppose S has a net income of $50 million for the year. The same basic procedures are followed by P and by S regardless of whether S is 100% owned or 90% owned. However, the presence of a minority interest changes the *consolidated* income statement slightly, as follows:

	P	S	Consolidated
Sales	$900	$300	$1,200
Expenses	800	250	1,050
Operating income	$100	$ 50	$ 150
Investment Revenue*	45	—	
Net income	$145	$ 50	
Minority interest (10%) in subsidiary's net income			5
Net income to consolidated entity			$ 145

*Pro-rata share (90%) of subsidiary net income.

Consolidated balance sheets at the end of the year would also be affected, as follows:

	Assets			=	Liabilities +		Shareholders' Equity	
	Investment in S	+	*Cash and Other Assets*	=	*Accounts Payable, etc.*	+	*Minority Interest* +	*Shareholders' Equity*
P's accounts:								
Beginning of year, before acquisition			650	=	200		+	450
Acquisition	192		−192	=				
Operating income			+100	=				+100
Share of S income	+45			=				+45
End of year	237	+	558	=	200		+	595
S's accounts:								
Beginning of year			400	=	187		+	213
Net income			+50	=				+50
End of year		+	450	=	187		+	263
Intercompany eliminations	−237			=			+26*	−263
Consolidated, end of year	0	+	1,008	=	387	+	26*	+	595

* Beginning minority interest plus minority interest in net income: 21 + .10(50) = 21 + 5 = 26.

As indicated in the table, the eliminating entry on the work sheet used for consolidating the balance sheet is:

Shareholders' equity (on S books)	263	
Investment in S (on P books)		237
Minority interest (on consolidated statements)		26

Thus the minority interest can be regarded as identifying the interests of those shareholders who own the 10% of the *subsidiary* shareholders' equity that is not eliminated by consolidation.

Accounting for Goodwill

The example in the previous section on consolidated financial statements assumed that the acquisition cost of Company S by Company P was equal to the *book value* of Company S. However, the total purchase price paid by P often exceeds the book values of the assets acquired. In fact, the purchase price also often exceeds the sum of the fair market values (current values) of the identifiable individual assets less the liabilities. Such excess of purchase price over fair market value is called *goodwill* or *purchased goodwill* or, more accurately, *excess of cost over fair value of net identifiable assets of businesses acquired.*

To see the impact of goodwill on the consolidated statements, refer to our initial example on consolidations, in which there was an acquisition of a 100% interest in S by P for $213 million. Suppose the price were $40 million higher, or a total of $253 million cash. For simplicity, assume that the fair values of the individual assets of S are equal to their book values. The balance sheets immediately after the acquisition are:

	Assets		=	Liabilities	+	Shareholders' Equity
	Investment in S	+ *Cash and Other Assets*	=	*Accounts Payable, etc.*	+	*Shareholders' Equity*
P's accounts:						
Before acquisition		650	=	200	+	450
Acquisition	+253	−253	=			
S's accounts		400	=	187	+	213
Intercompany eliminations	−213		=			−213
Consolidated	40*	+ 797	=	387	+	450

* The $40 million "goodwill" would appear in the consolidated balance sheet as a separate intangible asset account. It is often shown as the final item in a listing of assets. It is usually amortized in a straight-line manner as an expense in the consolidated income statement over a span of no greater than forty years.

As suggested in the table, the eliminating entry on the work sheet for consolidating the balance sheet is:

```
Shareholders' equity (on S books) . . . . . . . . . . .   213
Goodwill (on consolidated balance sheet) . . . . .    40
    Investment in S (on P books)                             253
```

Fair Values of Individual Assets

If the book values of the individual assets of S are *not* equal to their fair values, the usual procedures are:

1. S continues as a going concern and keeps its accounts on the same basis as before.
2. P records its investment at its acquisition cost (the agreed purchase price).
3. For consolidated reporting purposes, the excess of the acquisition cost over the book values of S is identified with the individual assets, item by item. (In effect, they are revalued at the current market prices prevailing when P acquired S.) Any *remaining* excess that cannot be identified is labelled as purchased goodwill.

Suppose the fair value of the other assets of S (e.g., machinery and equipment) exceeded their book value by $30 million in our example. The balance sheets immediately after acquisition would be the same as above. In consolidation, the $40 million goodwill would now be only $10 million. The remaining $30 million would appear in the consolidated balance sheet as an integral part of the other assets. That is, the S equipment would be shown at $30 million higher in the consolidated balance sheet than the carrying amount on S's books. Similarly, the amortization expense on the consolidated income statement would be higher. For instance, if the equipment had five years of useful life remaining, the straight-line depreciation would be $30 million ÷ 5, or $6 million higher per year.

As in the preceding tabulation, the $10 million goodwill would appear in the consolidated balance sheet as a separate intangible asset account. The eliminating entry on the working papers for consolidating the balance sheet is:

```
Shareholders' equity (on S books) . . . . . . . . . . .   213
Equipment (on consolidated balance sheet) . . .     30
Goodwill (on consolidated balance sheet) . . . . .    10
    Investment in S (on P books) . . . . . . . . . .         253
```

Amortization of Goodwill

Most long-lived assets other than land are depreciated or amortized over the period during which they benefit the firm. What about goodwill? Over what period does it benefit the firm? Does it have perpetual life? On the one hand, we might claim that reputations persist a long while. But they do so because the company continues to advertise, to produce a quality product, and to satisfy its customers.

How do accountants reflect this limited life in financial statements? Historically, international practice has ranged from recent British practice, which permitted immediate write-off of goodwill against shareholders' equity, to U.S. practice prior to 1970, which treated goodwill as infinitely lived. Notice that in both cases net income was unaffected by the presence of goodwill. Current Canadian GAAP requires that goodwill purchased after 1970 be amortized as an expense against net income over the period benefited, not to exceed forty years. The forty-year maximum is arbitrary and reflects the negotiated nature of many accounting principles. People could live with that flexibility. Amortization periods vary around the world. Germany and Japan require amortization over no more than five years, Australia limits the amortization period to twenty years, while Canada, the United States, and the United Kingdom allow periods as long as forty years.

Managers, investors, and accountants tend to be uncomfortable about the presence of goodwill on the balance sheet. Somehow it is regarded as an inferior asset even though management decided that it was valuable enough to warrant a total outlay in excess of the total current value of the individual assets. As a practical matter, many accountants feel that the income-producing factors of goodwill are unlikely to have a value in perpetuity even though expenditures may be aimed at maintaining their value. Nevertheless, the generally accepted accounting principles do not permit the lump-sum write-off of goodwill upon acquisition.

Assignment Material

QUESTIONS

7-1. Describe the two alternatives for the timing of revenue recognition on a $50 million long-term government contract with work spread evenly over five years. Which method do you prefer? Explain.

7-2. Why is the realizable value of a credit sale often less than that of a cash sale?

7-3. Distinguish between a *sales allowance* and a *purchase allowance*.

7-4. Distinguish between a *cash discount* and a *trade discount*.

7-5. "Trade discounts should not be recorded by the accountant." Do you agree? Explain.

7-6. "Retailers who accept Visa or MasterCard are foolish because they do not receive the full price for merchandise they sell." Comment.

7-7. Describe and give two examples of *cash equivalents*.

7-8. "A compensating balance essentially increases the interest rate on money borrowed." Explain.

7-9. "Cash is only 3% of our total assets. Therefore we should not waste time designing systems to manage cash. We should use our time on matters that have a better chance of affecting our profits." Do you agree? Explain.

7-10. The Personal Fitness Therapy Clinic uses the allowance method in accounting for bad debts. A journal entry was made for writing off the accounts of Jane Jensen, Eunice Belmont, and Samuel Maze:

Bad debts expense 14,321
    Accounts receivable 14,321

Do you agree with this entry? If not, show the correct entry and the correcting entry.

7-11. Distinguish between the allowance method and the specific write-off method for bad debts.

7-12. "The Allowance for Uncollectible Accounts account has no subsidiary ledger, but the Accounts Receivable account does." Explain.

7-13. Z Company received a $100 cash payment from a customer and immediately deposited the cash in a bank account. Z Company *debited* its Cash account, but the bank statement showed the deposit as a *credit*. Explain.

7-14. "The cash balance on a company's books should always equal the cash balance shown by its bank." Do you agree? Explain.

7-15. How can a credit balance arise in an Accounts Receivable subsidiary ledger? How should it be accounted for?

7-16. "Under the allowance method, there are three popular ways to estimate the bad debts expense for a particular year." Name the three.

7-17. What is meant by "aging of accounts"?

7-18. Describe why a write-off of a bad debt should be reversed if collection occurs at a later date.

7-19. What is the relationship between the average collection period and the accounts receivable turnover?

7-20. Distinguish between the percentage of sales approach to applying the allowance method and the aging of accounts receivable approach.

7-21. How can a debit balance arise in the allowance for bad debts account?

7-22. What is the cost-benefit relationship in deciding whether or not to offer credit to customers? Whether or not to accept bank credit cards?

7-23. You are opening a new department store and setting policy on merchandise returns. Would you grant cash refunds or store credit only? Would you require receipts? Would you base the refund on the price at which the transaction occurred or on the selling price when the return occurred?

7-24. What are the advantages of accepting bank credit cards rather than having your own, store-specific credit card?

7-25. If a company accepts bank credit cards, why might they accept specific cards rather than all of them? For example, some retailers accept Visa and MasterCard, but not American Express or Diner's Club, while the exact opposite is true for some restaurants.

7-26. It is common in sub shops and pizza parlours around a university campus to find signs that say "Your purchase is free if the clerk does not give you a receipt" or "Two free lunches if your receipt has a red star." What is management trying to accomplish with these free offers?

EXERCISES

7-27   Revenue Recognition, Cash Discounts, and Returns

Campus Bookstore ordered 1,000 copies of an introductory economics textbook from Prentice Hall on July 17, 19X0. The books were delivered on August 12, at which time a bill was sent requesting payment of $40 per book. However, a 2% discount was allowed if Prentice Hall received payment by September 12. Campus Bookstore sent the proper payment, which was received by Prentice Hall on September 10. On December 18 Campus Bookstore returned 60 books to Prentice Hall for a full cash refund.

Required

1. Prepare the journal entries (if any) for Prentice Hall on (a) July 17, (b) August 12, (c) September 10, and (d) December 18. Include appropriate explanations.
2. Suppose this was the only sales transaction in 19X0. Prepare the revenue section of Prentice Hall's income statement.

7-28   Revenue Recognition

Godoy Logging Company hired Atencio Construction Co. to build a new bridge across the Gray River. The bridge would extend a logging road into a new stand of timber. The contract called for a payment of $10 million upon completion of the bridge. Work was begun in 19X0 and completed in 19X2. Total costs were:

19X0	$2 million
19X1	2 million
19X2	3 million
Total	$7 million

Required

1. Suppose the accountant for Atencio Construction Co. judged that Godoy Logging might not be able to pay the $10 million. Still, the chance of a $3 million profit makes the contract attractive enough to sign. How much revenue would you recognize each year?
2. Suppose Godoy Logging is a subsidiary of a major wood-products company. Therefore receipt of payment on the contract is reasonably certain. How much revenue would you recognize each year?

7-29   Compensating Balances

Pegasus Company borrowed $100,000 from First Bank at 9% interest. The loan agreement stated that a compensating balance of $10,000 must be kept in the Pegasus chequing account at First Bank. The total Pegasus cash balance rose to $45,000 as a result.

Required

1. How much usable cash did Pegasus Company receive for its $100,000 loan?
2. What was the real interest rate paid by Pegasus?
3. Prepare a footnote for the annual report of Pegasus Company explaining the compensating balance.

7-30   Sales Returns and Discounts

Atlantic Electronics Wholesalers had gross sales of $700,000 during the month of March. Sales returns and allowances were $50,000. Cash discounts granted were $22,000.

Required

Prepare an analysis of the impact of these transactions on the balance sheet equation. Also show the journal entries. Prepare a detailed presentation of the revenue section of the income statement.

7-31   Gross and Net Sales

Sausilito, Inc. reported the following in 19X0 (in thousands):

Net sales	$520
Cash discounts on sales	20
Sales returns and allowances	35

Required

1. Prepare the revenue section of the 19X0 income statement.
2. Prepare journal entries for (a) initial revenue recognition for 19X0 sales, (b) sales returns and allowances, and (c) collection of accounts receivable. Assume that all sales were on credit and all accounts receivable for 19X0 sales were collected in 19X0. Omit explanations.

7-32   Cash Discounts Transactions

AV Wholesalers sells on terms of 2/10, n/30. It sold equipment to Beaulieu Retailers for $200,000 on open account on January 10. Payment (net of cash discount) was received on January 19. Using the equation framework, analyze the two transactions for AV. Also prepare journal entries.

7-33   Entries for Cash Discounts and Returns on Sales

The Niagara Wine Company is a wholesaler of wine that sells on credit terms of 2/10, n/30. Consider the following transactions:

June 9 Sales on credit to Riordan Wines, $20,000.
June 11 Sales on credit to Marty's Restaurants, $12,000.
June 18 Collected from Riordan Wines.
June 26 Accepted the return of six cases from Marty's, $1,000.
July 10 Collected from Marty's.
July 12 Riordan returned some defective wine that she had acquired on June 9 for $100. Niagara issued a cash refund immediately.

: COMPUTERS, INC.

NCE SHEET

TS

ENT ASSETS:

CASH AND CASH EQUIV	1204
SHORT-TERM INVESTMENTS	54
ACCOUNTS RECEIVABLES	1581
INVENTORIES	1088
PREPAID INCOME TAXES	293
OTHER CURRENTS ASSETS	256
TOTAL CURRENT ASSETS	4476

:

AT COST	1452
ACCUMULATED DEP AND AMORT	785
NET PPE	667
HER ASSETS	159
OTAL ASSETS	5302

ABILITIES AND SHARHOLDER'S EQUITY

URRENT LIABILITIES:

NOTES PAYABLE	292
ACCOUNTS PAYABLE	882
ACCR EMP COMP & BENEFITS	137
ACCRUED MARKETING AND DIS EXPENSE	178
OTHER CURRENT LIABILITIES	455
TOTAL CURRENT LIABILITIES	1944
LONG TERM DEBT	304
DEFERRED INCOME TAXES	671

SHAREHOLDER'S EQUITY:

COMMON STOCK	298
RETAINED EARNINGS	2085
TOTAL SHAREHOLDERS' EQUITY	2383
	5302

RILEY SOFTWARE COMPANY

STATEMENT OF CHANGES IN FINANCIAL POSITION

FOR THE YEAR ENDED DECEMBER 31, 1990

(IN THOUSANDS)

CASH FLOWS FROM OPERATING ACTIVITIES:

CASH COLLECTIONS FROM CUSTOMERS		371
CASH PAYMENTS:	-144	
TO SUPPLIERS	-82	
TO EMPLOYEES	-15	
FOR OTHER EXPENSES	-8	
FOR INCOME TAXES		
CASH DISBURSED FOR OP. ACT		-249
NET CASH PROVIDED BY OPERATING ACTVITIES		122

CASH FLOWS FROM INVESTING ACTIVITIES:

PURCHASE OF PERSONAL COMPUTERS	-125	
PROCEEDS FROM SALE OF OLD COMPUTERS	5	
NET CASH USED FOR INVESTING ACTIVITIES		-120

CASH FLOWS FROM FINANCING ACTIVITIES:

NEW ISSUE OF LONG TERM DEBT	100	
PAYMENT OF DIVIDENDS	-10	
NET INCREASE IN CASH		90
BALANCE, CASH AND CASH EQUIV, DEC 31, 1993		92
BALANCE, CASH AND CASH EQUIV, DEC 31, 1994		5
		97

MALLARD CLOTHING

INCOME STATEMENT

FOR THE YEAR ENDED DEC 31, 19X5

(IN THOUSANDS)

SALES		900
COST OF GOODS SOLD		400
GROSS MARGIN		460
OPERATING EXPENSES:		
WAGES	200	
MISC EX	189	
INSURANCE	7	
AMORTIZATION	30	
TOTAL OPERATING EX		426
OPERATING INCOME		34
OTHER REVENUE: INTEREST		16
INCOME BEFORE INCOME TAXES		50
INCOME TAX EXPENSE		20
NET INCOME		30

MALLARD CLOTHING

STATEMENT OF RETAINED EARNINGS

FOR THE YEAR ENDED DEC 31, 19X5

(IN THOUSANDS)

RETAINED EARNINGS, DEC 31, 19X4	322
ADD: NET INCOME FOR 19X5	30
TOTAL	352
DEDUCT: DIVIDENDS DECLARED	26
RETAINED EARNINGS, DEC 31, 19X5	326

Required   Prepare journal entries for these transactions. Omit explanations. Assume that the full appropriate amounts were exchanged.

7-34   Credit Terms, Discounts, and Annual Interest Rates

As the struggling owner of a new Thai restaurant, you suffer from a habitual shortage of cash. Yesterday the following invoices arrived:

Vendor	Face Amount	Terms
Val Produce	$ 600	n/30
Rose Exterminators	90	EOM
Top Meat Supply	500	15,EOM
John's Fisheries	1,000	1/10, n/30
Garcia Equipment	2,000	2/10, n/30

Required
1. Write out the exact meaning of each of the terms.
2. You can borrow cash from the local bank on a ten-, twenty-, or thirty-day note bearing an annual interest rate of 16%. Should you borrow to take advantage of the cash discounts offered by the last two vendors? Why? Show computations. For interest rate computations, assume a 360-day year.

7-35   Accounting for Credit Cards

The Byard Clothing Store has extended credit to customers on open account. Its average experience for each of the past three years has been:

	Cash	Credit	Total
Sales	$500,000	$300,000	$800,000
Bad debts expense	—	6,000	6,000
Administrative expense	—	10,000	10,000

Cynthia Byard is considering whether to accept bank cards (e.g., Visa, MasterCard). She has resisted because she does not want to bear the cost of the service, which would be 5% of gross sales.

The representative of Visa claims that the availability of bank cards would have increased overall sales by at least 10%. However, regardless of the level of sales, the new mix of the sales would be 50% bank card and 50% cash.

Required
1. How would a bank card sale of $200 affect the accounting equation? Where would the discount appear on the income statement?
2. Should Byard adopt the bank card if sales do not increase? Base your answer solely on the sparse facts given here.
3. Repeat requirement 2, but assume that total sales would increase 10%.

7-36   Trade-Ins Versus Discounts

Many provinces base their sales tax on gross sales less any discount. Trade-in allowances are not discounts, so they are not deducted from the sales price for sales tax purposes. Suppose Sven Gustafson has decided to trade in his old car for a new one with a list price of $20,000. He will pay cash of $12,000 plus sales tax. If he had not traded in a car, the dealer would have offered a discount of 15% of the list price. The sales tax is 8%.

Required   How much of the $8,000 price reduction should be called a discount? How much a trade-in? Mr. Gustafson wants to pay as little sales tax as legally possible.

7-37   Uncollectible Accounts

During 19X2, the Saskatoon Paint Store had credit sales of $800,000. The store manager expects that 2% of the credit sales will never be collected, although no accounts are written off until ten assorted steps have been taken to attain collection. The ten steps require a minimum of fourteen months.

Assume that during 19X3, specific customers are identified who are never expected to pay $14,000 that they owe from the sales of 19X2. All ten collection steps have been completed.

Required
1. Show the impact on the balance sheet equation of the above transactions in 19X2 and 19X3 under (a) the specific write-off method and (b) the allowance method. Which method do you prefer? Why?
2. Prepare journal entries for both methods. Omit explanations.

7-38   Bad Debts

Prepare all journal entries regarding the following data. Consider the following balances of a chain of back therapy clinics, December 31, 19X1: Receivables from patients, $200,000; and Allowance for Doubtful Receivables, $50,000. During 19X2, total billings to individual patients, excluding the billings to third-party payers such as Blue Cross and Medicare, were $3 million. Past experience indicated that 20% of such individual billings would ultimately be uncollectible. Write-offs of receivables during 19X2 were $590,000.

7-39   Bad Debt Allowance

Holtz Appliance had sales of $1,000,000 during 19X2, including $600,000 of sales on credit. Balances on December 31, 19X1 were Accounts Receivable, $45,000; and Allowance for Bad Debts, $4,000. Data for 19X2: Collections on accounts receivable were $530,000. Bad debts expense was estimated at 2% of credit sales, as in previous years. Write-offs of bad debts during 19X2 were $11,000.

Required
1. Prepare journal entries regarding the above information for 19X2.
2. Show the ending balances of the balance sheet accounts, December 31, 19X2.
3. Based on the given data, what questions seem worth raising with Ingrid Holtz, the president of the store?

7-40   Bad Debt Recoveries

Cayuga Department Store has many accounts receivable. The Cayuga balance sheet, December 31, 19X1, showed Accounts Receivable, $950,000 and Allowance for Uncollectible Accounts, $40,000. In early 19X2, write-offs of customer accounts of $30,000 were made. In late 19X2, a customer, whose $3,000 debt had been written off earlier, won a $1 million sweepstakes cash prize. She immediately remitted $3,000 to Cayuga. The store welcomed her money and her return to a high credit standing. Prepare the journal entries for the $30,000 write-off in early 19X2 and the $3,000 receipt in late 19X2.

7-41   Subsidiary Ledger

An appliance store makes credit sales of $800,000 in 19X4 to a thousand customers: Schumacher, $4,000; Cerruti, $7,000; others, $789,000. Total collections during 19X4 were $700,000 including $4,000 from Cerruti, but nothing was collected from Schumacher. At the end of 19X4 an allowance for uncollectible accounts was provided of 3% of credit sales.

Required
1. Set up appropriate general ledger accounts plus a subsidiary ledger for Accounts Receivable. The subsidiary ledger should consist of two individual accounts plus a third account called Others. Post the entries for 19X4. Prepare a statement of the ending balances of the individual accounts receivable to show that they reconcile with the general ledger account.
2. On March 24, 19X5, the Schumacher account was written off. Post the entries.

7-42   Trading Securities

Study Appendix 7. The Martinez Company has a portfolio of trading securities consisting of common and preferred stocks. The portfolio cost $160 million on January 1. The market values of the portfolio were (in millions): March 31, $150; June 30, $138; September 30, $152; and December 31, $168.

Required

1. Prepare a tabulation showing the balance sheet presentations and income statement presentations for interim reporting purposes.
2. Show the journal entries for quarters 1, 2, 3, and 4.

7-43   Cost Method or Equity Method

Study Appendix 7. Fred's Outdoors acquired 25% of the voting stock of Steve's Snowshoes for $40 million cash. In Year 1, Steve's had a net income of $32 million and paid a cash dividend of $20 million.

Required

1. Using the equity and the cost methods, show the effects of the three transactions on the accounts of Fred's Outdoors. Use the balance sheet equation format. Also show the accompanying journal entries. Assume constant market value for Steve's.
2. Which method, equity or cost, would Fred's use to account for its investment in Steve's? Explain.

7-44   Equity Method

Study Appendix 7. Company X acquired 30% of the voting stock of company Y for $90 million cash. In Year 1, Y had a net income of $50 million and paid cash dividends of $20 million.

Required

Prepare a tabulation that uses the equity method of accounting for X's investment in Y. Show the effects on the balance sheet equation. What is the year-end balance in the Investment in Y account under the equity method?

PROBLEMS

7-45   Aging of Accounts

Consider the following analysis of Accounts Receivable, February 28, 19X1:

Name of Customer	Total	Remarks
White Nurseries	$ 20,000	50% over 90 days, 50% 61–90 days
Michael's Landscaping	8,000	75% 31–60 days, 25% under 30 days
Shoven Garden Supply	10,000	60% 61–90 days, 40% 31–60 days
Bonner Perennial Farm	16,000	all under 30 days
Hjortshoj Florists	4,000	25% 61–90 days, 75% 1–30 days
Other accounts (each detailed)	80,000	50% 1–30 days, 30% 31–60 days, 15% 61–90 days, 5% over 90 days
Total	$138,000	

7-64   Annual Report

Select a company's annual report of your choice.

Required   Calculate the accounts receivable turnover and days to collect accounts receivable for the company for two years and comment on the results.

8

Valuing Inventories, Cost of Goods Sold, and Gross Profit

Learning Objectives

After studying this chapter, you should be able to

1. Explain the importance of inventory in measuring profitability.

2. Explain and illustrate the differences between perpetual and periodic inventory systems.

3. Identify the items included in the cost of merchandise acquired.

4. Explain the four principal inventory valuation methods and their effect on measurement of assets and net income.

5. Understand the reasons for choosing and using the inventory methods.

6. Explain the meaning of holding gains and inventory profits.

7. Explain why the lower-of-cost-and-market method is used to value inventories.

8. Show the effects of inventory errors on financial statements.

9. Explain the uses of the gross profit percentage and inventory turnover measures.

This chapter introduces the details involved in assigning value to inventories and calculating the cost of goods sold. These important measures are used to determine a firm's gross profits. Since a firm's goal is profitable sales, we need effective accounting techniques to measure profitability. This chapter covers the methods and procedures for valuing inventory on the balance sheet and for recording costs of goods sold on the income statement. As in prior chapters, the chapter also presents ratios to assess the profitability of the firm and the effective management of inventory levels.

This chapter continues to link the preparation of the income statement and the balance sheet. When inventory is acquired it initially appears on the balance sheet as an asset. Under the matching principle, when revenue is recognized, the cost of the sale is also recognized. Thus, when a sale occurs, the costs of the inventory become an expense, cost of goods sold, in the income statement. The chapter also explains how different inventory valuation techniques affect financial statements.

The accounting procedures discussed in this chapter are responses to a reporting need encountered in every nation of the world. While the dominant practices differ slightly from country to country, the issues remain. Even within a country, many different procedures are encountered. Thus, the reader of financial statements must understand alternative practices in order to compare intelligently the economic performance of different firms.

■ GROSS PROFIT AND COST OF GOODS SOLD

Objective 1

Explain the importance of inventory in measuring profitability.

For firms that purchase and resell merchandise, a beginning guide to assessing profitability is *gross profit* (also called *profit margin* or *gross margin*), which is defined as the difference between sales revenues and the costs of the goods sold. These calculations rely on the value of the firms' inventories, which are goods that are being held for resale.

Sales revenue must cover the cost of goods sold and provide a gross profit sufficient to cover all other costs, including research and development, selling and marketing, administration, and so on. As illustrated in Exhibit 8-1, prior to sale, items held for sale are reported as inventory, a current asset in the balance sheet. When the goods are sold, the costs of the inventory become an expense, Cost of Goods Sold, in the income statement. This expense is deducted from Net Sales to determine Gross Profit, and additional expenses are deducted from Gross Profit to determine Net Income.

The Basic Concept of Inventory Accounting

The key to calculating the cost of goods sold is accounting for inventory. Conceptually, the process is very simple. Suppose Christina sells T-shirts. Periodically, she orders many shirts of various sizes and colours. They sell, she orders more, and her business operating cycle continues. After a year, to evaluate her success, Christina prepares financial statements. To calculate the value of inventory on hand, she obtains a *physical count* of inventory items remaining at year end. She then develops a **cost valuation**, which assigns a specific value from the historical cost records to each item in ending inventory. With 100 shirts remaining at a cost of $5.00 each, Christina's total ending inventory is $500. Suppose she had no shirts at the beginning of the year, and total

cost valuation
Process of assigning specific historical costs to items counted in the physical inventory.

purchases for the year were $26,000. Her cost of goods sold is $25,500 ($26,000 of available shirts minus $500 of unsold shirts).

In practice, the process is not this simple. Complexity arises from many sources. The following sections describe alternate techniques for measuring inventories and how they differ.

Exhibit 8-1

Merchandising Company (Retailer or Wholesaler)

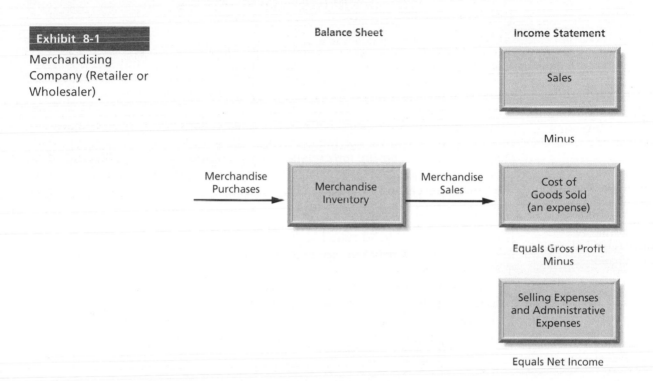

■ PERPETUAL AND PERIODIC INVENTORY SYSTEMS

perpetual inventory system A system that keeps a running, continuous record that tracks inventories and the cost of goods sold on a day-to-day basis.

There are two fundamental ways of keeping inventory records for merchandise: perpetual and periodic. The **perpetual inventory system** (which has been assumed in previous chapters) keeps a running, continuous record that tracks inventories and the cost of goods sold on a day-to-day basis. Such a record helps managers control inventory levels and prepare interim financial statements. Nonetheless, physical inventory counts should be taken at least once a year to check on the accuracy of the clerical records.

Previous chapters have described the inventory cycle as follows:

		A	=	L	+	SE
a. Purchase	+	Increase Merchandise Inventory	= +	Increase Accounts Payable		
b. Sale	+	Increase Accounts Receivable	=		+	Increase Sales Revenue
Cost of inventory sold	−	Decrease Inventory	=		−	Increase Cost of Goods Sold

In the perpetual inventory system, the journal entries are:

a. When inventory is purchased:

Merchandise inventory	xxx	
Accounts payable		xxx

b. When inventory is sold:

Accounts receivable (or cash)	xxx	
Sales revenue		xxx
Cost of goods sold	xxx	
Inventory		xxx

Thus, in the perpetual inventory system, the sale and the inventory reduction are recorded simultaneously.

periodic inventory system The system in which the cost of goods sold is computed periodically by relying solely on physical counts without keeping day-to-day records of units sold or on hand.

The **periodic inventory system,** conversely, does *not* involve a day-to-day record of inventories or of the cost of goods sold. Instead the cost of goods sold and an updated inventory balance are computed only at the end of an accounting period, when a physical count of inventory is taken. The cost of the goods purchased is accumulated by recording the individual purchase transactions throughout any given reporting period, such as a year. The accountant computes the cost of goods sold by subtracting the ending inventories (determined by physical count) from the sum of the opening inventory and purchases. Christina applied the periodic inventory method to her T-shirt business.

While the cost of goods sold under the perpetual system is computed instantaneously as goods are sold, under the periodic system, the computation is delayed:

$$\underbrace{\text{Beginning inventory} + \text{Purchases}}_{\text{Goods available for sale}} - \underbrace{\text{Ending inventory}}_{\text{Inventory left over}} = \underbrace{\text{Cost of goods sold}}_{\text{Cost of goods sold}}$$

cost of goods available for sale Sum of beginning inventory plus current year purchases.

The periodic system computes cost of goods sold as a *residual amount*. First, the beginning inventory is added to the purchases to obtain the total **cost of goods available for sale.** Then the ending inventory is counted, and its cost is deducted from the cost of goods available for sale to obtain the cost of goods sold.

Exhibit 8-2

Inventory Systems

Periodic System		Perpetual System	
Beginning inventories (by physical count)	xxx	Cost of goods sold (kept on a day-to-day basis rather than being determined periodically)*	xxx
Add: Purchases	xxx		
Cost of goods available for sale	xxx		
Less: Ending inventories (by physical count)	xxx		
Cost of goods sold	xxx		

* Such a condensed figure does not preclude the presentation of a supplementary schedule similar to that on the left.

Comparison of Systems

Objective 2

Explain and illustrate the differences between perpetual and periodic inventory systems.

Exhibit 8-2 compares the perpetual and periodic inventory systems. For annual financial statements, the two methods give equivalent results. Historically, the perpetual system has been used for low-volume, high-value items. The periodic system has been preferred for high-volume, low-value, and mixed-value inventory operations. The more expensive and cumbersome perpetual system was typically implemented when it gave significant managerial information to aid in pricing or ordering. Sometimes it improved control over loss and theft of inventory. Computerized inventory systems and optical scanning equipment at checkout counters have made implementation of perpetual inventory systems less costly.

The perpetual system does not eliminate the need for a physical count and valuation of the inventory. While the perpetual system captures information about goods purchased and sold, the physical inventory allows management to delete from inventory goods that are damaged or obsolete. It also reveals disagreements between perpetual records and the physical count that may arise from **inventory shrinkage.** Inventory shrinkage refers to theft, breakage, and loss, which are substantial factors in some businesses.

inventory shrinkage Difference between (a) the value of inventory that would occur if there were no theft, breakage, or losses of inventory and (b) the value of inventory when it is physically counted.

If the physical count differs from the perpetual inventory amount, the following result might be obtained:

Perpetual inventory record:	Part 1F68X	142 units @ $20	$2,840
Physical count:	Part 1F68X	125 units @ $20	$2,500

Seventeen units (142 units – 125 units) have disappeared without being charged as cost of goods sold. The journal entry to adjust inventory from $2,840 to $2,500 is:

Inventory shrinkage	340	
Merchandise inventory		340

To adjust the ending inventory to its balance per physical count.

In summary, the perpetual system is more accurate in providing timely information, but it is more costly. The periodic system is less accurate, especially for monthly or quarterly statements. It is less costly because there is no day-to-day processing regarding cost of goods sold. However, if theft or the accumulation of obsolete merchandise is likely, periodic systems often prove to be more expensive in the long run.

Physical Inventory

physical count The process of counting all the items in inventory at a moment in time.

Good inventory control procedures require a **physical count** of each item being held in inventory at least annually in both periodic and perpetual inventory systems. The physical count is an imposing, time-consuming, and expensive process. You may have seen "closed for inventory" signs. To simplify counting and valuation, firms often choose fiscal accounting periods so that the year ends when inventories are low. For example, some department chains have late January year ends, which follow the holiday season.

The physical inventory is so important to income determination that external auditors usually observe the client's physical count and confirm the

Gross sales			$1,740
Deduct: Sales returns and allowances		$ 70	
Cash discounts on sales		100	170
Net sales			$1,570
Deduct: Cost of goods sold:			
Merchandise inventory, December 31, 19X1		$ 100	
Purchases (gross)	$960		
Deduct: Purchase returns and allowances	$75		
Cash discounts on purchases	5	80	
Net purchases		$880	
Add: Freight in		30	
Total cost of merchandise acquired		910	
Cost of goods available for sale		$1,010	
Deduct: Merchandise inventory,			
December 31, 19X2		140	
Cost of goods sold			870
Gross profit			$ 700

While management may find such detail valuable, summary information is much more common in the annual report to shareholders:

Net Sales	$1,570
Cost of Goods Sold	870
Gross Profit	$ 700

■ COMPARING ACCOUNTING PROCEDURES FOR PERIODIC AND PERPETUAL INVENTORY SYSTEMS

A Detailed Example

GoodEarth Products, Inc. has a balance of $100,000 in merchandise inventory at the beginning of 19X2 (December 31, 19X1). A summary of transactions for 19X2 follows:

a. Purchases	$990,000
b. Purchase returns and allowances	80,000

Net purchases were therefore $990,000 less $80,000, or $910,000. The physical count of the ending inventory for 19X2 led to a cost valuation of $140,000. Note how these figures can be used to compute the $870,000 cost of goods sold:

$$\begin{array}{ccccc} \text{Beginning inventory} & + \text{ Net purchases} & - & \text{Ending inventory} & = & \text{Cost of goods sold} \\ \$100,000 & + \ \$910,000 & & - \ \$140,000 & = & \$870,000 \end{array}$$

$$\begin{array}{ccccc} \text{Cost of goods available for sale} & - & \text{Cost of goods left over} & = & \text{Cost of goods sold} \\ \$1,010,000 & & - \ \$140,000 & = & \$870,000 \end{array}$$

The periodic and perpetual procedures would record these transactions differently. As Exhibit 8-3 shows, the perpetual system entails directly increasing the Inventory account by the $990,000 purchases (entry *a*) and decreasing it by the $80,000 in returns and allowances (entry *b*) and the $870,000 cost of goods sold (entry *C*). The Cost of Goods Sold account would be increased daily as sales are made. In a nutshell, these entries should be familiar. The only new aspect here is the purchase returns and allowances, which directly reduce the Inventory account. Although no purchase (cash) discounts are illustrated, their treatment would parallel purchase returns and allowances.

Before proceeding, reflect on how the perpetual system in Exhibit 8-3 creates the ending inventory of $140,000.

GoodEarth Products, Inc. General Ledger at December 31, 19X2 (amounts in thousands) Perpetual Inventory

Inventory				Cost of Goods Sold			
Balance 12/31/X1	100	(b)	80	(c)	870	(d3)	870
(a)	990	(c)	870				
Balance 12/31/X2	140						

The periodic system is called "periodic" because neither the Cost of Goods Sold account nor the Inventory account is computed on a daily basis. Moreover, Purchases and Purchase Returns and Allowances are accounted for in a separate account, as entries *a* and *b* indicate. Entries *d1* and *d2* at the bottom of Exhibit 8-3 show the eventual periodic calculation of cost of goods sold in the Cost of Goods Sold Account.

Exhibit 8-3	Comparison of Perpetual and Periodic Inventory Entries (amounts in thousands)

	Perpetual Records			Periodic Records		
a. Gross purchases:	Inventory	990		Purchases	990	
	Accounts payable ...		990	Accounts payable		990
b. Returns and allowances:	Accounts payable	80		Accounts payable	80	
	Inventory		80	Purchase returns and allowances		80
c. As goods are sold:	Cost of goods sold	870		No entry		
	Inventory		870			
d. At the end of the accounting period.	d1. } No entry d2. }			d1. Cost of goods sold ...	1,010	
				Purchase returns and allowances	80	
				Purchases		990
				Inventory		100
				d2. Inventory	140	
				Cost of goods sold		140
	d3. Income summary	870		d3. Income summary	870	
	Cost of goods sold ..		870	Cost of goods sold		870

Entry *d1* transfers the beginning inventory balance, purchases, and purchase returns and allowances, totalling $1,010,000, to cost of goods sold. This provides the cost of goods available for sale, the first step in calculating cost of goods sold.

Next, the ending inventory is physically counted and its cost is computed. Entry *d2* recognizes the $140,000 ending inventory and reduces the $1,010,000 cost of goods available for sale by $140,000 to obtain a final cost of goods sold of $870,000. All of these details can be shown in the cost of goods sold section of the income statement. However, published income statements usually include only a single cost of goods sold number.

The periodic system may seem awkward when compared with the perpetual system. The beginning inventory and cost of goods sold accounts are untouched until the end of the period. However, the periodic system avoids the costly process of calculating the cost of goods sold for each sale.

GoodEarth Products, Inc.
General Ledger at December 31, 19X2 (amounts in thousands)
Periodic Inventory

Inventory					Cost of Goods Sold			
Balance,				(d1)	1,010	(d2)	140
12/31/X1	100	(d1)	100			(d3)	870
(d2)	140						
Balance,							
12/31/X2	140						

As shown in entry *d3*, the cost of goods sold is closed to Income Summary under either method.

Note that the periodic method produces the same final balances in Inventory and Income Summary as the perpetual method. However, as entries *d1* and *d2* demonstrate, the cost of goods sold is computed at the end of the year; consequently, the related journal entries and postings are made then.

Note that in the perpetual system, the Inventory and Cost of Goods Sold account balances are always up to date, without special action by the accountant. In contrast, under the periodic system, more accounts are in use and information is simply being accumulated. No balance appears in the Cost of Goods Sold account until the company prepares financial statements and uses an adjusting journal entry to state inventory balances and cost of goods sold properly.

■ PRINCIPAL INVENTORY VALUATION METHODS

Objective 4

Explain the four principal inventory valuation methods and their effect on measurement of assets and net income.

Each period, accountants must divide the cost of beginning inventory and merchandise acquired between cost of goods sold and cost of items remaining in ending inventory. Under a perpetual system, a cost must be assigned to each item sold. Under a periodic system, the costs of the items remaining in ending inventory must be measured. Regardless of the inventory system, costs of individual items must be determined by some inventory valuation method. Four principal inventory valuation methods have been generally accepted in Canada: specific identification, FIFO, LIFO, and weighted-average. Each will be explained and compared in this section.

If unit prices and costs did not fluctuate, all inventory methods would show identical results. But prices change, and these changes raise central issues regarding cost of goods sold (income measurement) and inventories (asset measurement). As a simple example of the valuation method choices facing management, consider Emilio, a new vendor of a cola drink at the fairgrounds, who begins the week with no inventory. He buys one can on Monday for 30 cents; a second can on Tuesday for 40 cents; and a third can on Wednesday for 56 cents. He then sells one can on Thursday for 90 cents. What is his gross profit? His ending inventory? Answer these questions in your own mind before reading on.

Four Major Methods

Panel I of Exhibit 8-4 provides a first glimpse of the nature of the four generally accepted methods for inventory valuation. As the exhibit shows, Emilio's choice of an inventory method can significantly affect the amount reported as cost of goods sold (and hence gross profit and net income) and ending inventory. Note, for example, that three different gross profit margins may occur under the specific identification method. FIFO yields a 60 cent profit, while LIFO yields only a 34 cent profit.

specific identification method This inventory method concentrates on the physical tracing of the particular items sold.

1. Specific identification method. This method concentrates on the *physical* linking of the *particular* items sold. Suppose Emilio could tell which can of cola was purchased on each day. If he reached for the Monday can instead of the Wednesday can, the *specific identification* method would show different results. Thus Panel I of Exhibit 8-4 indicates that gross profit for operations of Monday through Thursday could be 60 cents, 50 cents, or 34 cents, depending on the particular can handed to the customer. Emilio could choose which can to sell and affect reported results by doing so.

first-in, first-out (FIFO) This method of accounting for inventory assumes that the units acquired earliest are used or sold first.

2. First-in, first-out (FIFO). This method assumes that the stock acquired earliest is sold (used up) first. It does not track the physical flow of individual items except by coincidence. Thus the Monday can of cola is deemed to have been sold regardless of the actual can delivered. In times of rising prices, FIFO usually shows the *largest* gross profit (60 cents in Panel I of Exhibit 8-4).

last-in, first-out (LIFO) This inventory method assumes that the units acquired most recently are used or sold first.

3. Last-in, first-out (LIFO). This method assumes that the stock acquired most recently is sold (used up) first. Thus the Wednesday can of cola is deemed to have been sold regardless of the actual can delivered. In times of rising prices, LIFO generally shows the lowest gross profit (34 cents in Panel I of Exhibit 8-4).

weighted-average cost This inventory method computes a unit cost by dividing the total acquisition cost of all items available for sale by the number of units available for sale.

4. Weighted-average cost. This method computes a unit cost by dividing the total acquisition cost of all items available for sale by the number of units available for sale. Exhibit 8-4 shows the calculations Emilio would make. The weighted-average method usually produces a gross profit somewhere between that obtained under FIFO and that under LIFO (48 cents as compared with 60 cents and 34 cents in Panel I of Exhibit 8-4).

| Exhibit 8-4 | **Emilio's Cola Sales**   Comparison of Inventory Methods (all monetary amounts are in cents) | | | | | |

	(1) Specific Identification			(2)	(3)	(4) Weighted Average
	(1A)	(1B)	(1C)	FIFO	LIFO	
Panel I						
Income Statement for the Period Monday through Thursday						
Sales	90	90	90	90	90	90
Deduct cost of goods sold:						
1 30¢ (Monday) unit	30			30		
1 40¢ (Tuesday) unit		40				
1 56¢ (Wednesday) unit			56		56	
1 weighted-average unit [(30 + 40 + 56) ÷ 3 = 42]						42
Gross profit for Monday through Thursday	60	50	34	60	34	48
Thursday's ending inventory, 2 units:						
Monday unit @ 30¢		30	30		30	
Tuesday unit @ 40¢	40		40	40	40	
Wednesday unit @ 56¢	56	56		56		
Weighted-average units @ 42¢						84
Total ending inventory on Thursday	96	86	70	96	70	84
Panel II						
Income Statement for Friday						
Sales, 2 units @ 90¢	180	180	180	180	180	180
Cost of goods sold (Thursday ending inventory from above)	96	86	70	96	70	84
Gross profit, Friday only	84	94	110	84	110	96
Panel III						
Gross profit for full week						
Monday through Thursday (Panel 1)	60	50	34	60	34	48
Friday (Panel II)	84	94	110	84	110	96
Total gross profit	144	144	144	144	144	144

Inventory Methods and the Matching Principle

Under the matching principle, we must link the cost of goods sold with the sales revenue generated when the product is delivered to a customer. What is challenging is to *measure* cost of goods sold. Panel I of Exhibit 8-4 identifies four measurement methods—specific identification, FIFO, LIFO, and weighted-average cost—each with both strengths and weaknesses.

Think of these methods as expressions of how Emilio might physically store and sell his cola. He could mark each can with its cost and record that cost as cost of goods sold when the can was handed to a customer. Specific identification captures this procedure. He could put each new can, as it is acquired, into the top of a cooler. At each customer purchase, the top can is the one sold. LIFO reflects this procedure. In contrast, each new can could be placed at the back of the cooler to chill and the oldest, coldest can sold first. FIFO captures this physical flow. If the cans are mixed together, the weighted-average method is a rough approximation of what Emilio knows about the cost of each can sold.

Because the physical flow of products has little importance to the financial success of most businesses, the accounting profession has concluded that companies may choose any of the four methods to record cost of goods sold. Since the method is not linked to the physical flow of merchandise, inventory methods are often referred to as *cost flow assumptions*. For example, when we decide that the cost of the first inventory item purchased will be matched with the sales revenue from the first item sold to calculate the gross profit from the sale, we are adopting the FIFO cost flow assumption.

Suppose Emilio sells his remaining inventory on Friday and enters a more attractive business. Panel II of Exhibit 8-4 shows Friday's gross profit. Panel III of Exhibit 8-4 shows that the *cumulative* gross profit over the life of Emilio's business would be the same $1.44 under any of the inventory methods. What makes the choice of method important is our having to match particular costs to particular periods *during* the life of the business in order to prepare financial statements and evaluate performance.

The Consistency Convention

consistency
Conformity from period to period with unchanging policies and procedures.

While companies have broad latitude in choosing their inventory cost flow assumption, they are expected to use the chosen method consistently over time. **Consistency** refers to the use of the same accounting policies by one company from one accounting period to the next accounting period. Interpreting financial performance over time involves comparing the results of different periods. If accounting methods for inventory were changed often, meaningful comparisons over time would be impossible. Exhibit 8-4 illustrates the extreme difference that the choice of inventory method produces for Emilio's reported gross profits in different periods.

Occasionally a change in market conditions or other circumstances may justify a change in inventory method, and a firm may change method. But the firm is required to note the change in its financial statements, and the auditor will also refer to the change in the audit opinion so that financial statement readers are alerted to the possible effects of the change on their analysis.

■ CHOOSING AND USING INVENTORY METHODS

Objective 5

Understand the reasons for choosing and using the inventory methods.

The four inventory methods have different benefits and drawbacks. Among the issues facing management when choosing a method are such questions as: Which method provides the highest reported net income? Which method provides management the most flexibility in affecting reported earnings? How do the methods affect income tax obligations? Which methods are inexpensive to apply? Which method provides an inventory valuation that approximates the actual value of the inventory?

Consider the link between cost of goods sold and the valuation of ending inventory. Emilio's three cola cans had a total cost of goods available for sale of $1.26. At the end of the period, this $1.26 must be allocated either to cans sold or to cans in ending inventory. The higher the cost of goods sold, the lower the ending inventory. Exhibit 8-5 illustrates that interdependence. At one extreme, FIFO treats the 30 cent cost of the first can acquired as cost of goods sold and 96 cents as ending inventory. At the other extreme, LIFO treats the 56 cent cost of the last can acquired as cost of goods sold and 70 cents as ending inventory.

Before considering each method in detail, one other general relation is worth studying. Note from columns 2 and 3 of Exhibit 8-4 that during this period of rising prices, FIFO yields higher inventory *and* higher gross profit than LIFO. This result is consistent with the accounting equation that requires that A = L + SE. If inventory is higher under FIFO (higher assets) and the equation is to balance, either liabilities or shareholders' equity must also be higher. Higher gross profit under FIFO implies higher net income and higher shareholder's equity (SE in the equation). Note that nothing in our choice of methods would affect accounts payable. We record each new inventory purchase at its cost and recognize a liability in that amount in the same way under all of these methods.

Exhibit 8-5	
Emilio's Cola Sales Diagram of Inventory Methods (data are from Panel I, Exhibit 8-4; monetary amounts are in cents)	

Beginning inventory	+	Merchandise purchases	=	Cost of goods available for sale
0	+	126	=	126

Cost of goods available for sale	−	Cost of goods sold	=	Ending inventory
		30		96	
126	−	[or 40 or 56]	=	[or 86 or 70]	Specific identification
1 @ 30 1 @ 40 1 @ 56					
126	−	30	=	96	FIFO
126	−	56	=	70	LIFO
126	−	42	=	84	Weighted average

Specific Identification

The specific identification method, which uses physical observation or the labelling of items in stock with individual numbers or codes, is easy and economically justifiable for relatively expensive low-volume merchandise like custom artwork, diamond jewellery, and automobiles. However, most organizations have vast segments of inventories that are too numerous and insufficiently valuable per unit to warrant such individualized attention. Since the cost of goods sold is determined by the specific item handed to the customer, this method permits managers to manipulate income and inventory values by filling a sales order from a number of physically equivalent items with different historical costs.

FIFO

FIFO (First In, First Out) is sometimes referred to as LISH (Last In, Still Here). When the first costs represent goods sold, the last costs represent goods still on hand. By using the latest costs to measure the ending inventory, FIFO tends to provide inventory valuations that closely approximate the actual market value of the inventory at the balance sheet date. In addition, in periods of rising prices, FIFO leads to higher net income. Higher reported incomes may favourably affect investor attitudes toward the company. Similarly, higher reported incomes may lead to higher salaries, higher bonuses, or higher status for the management of the company. Unlike specific identification, FIFO specifies the order in which acquisition costs will become cost of goods sold, so management cannot affect income by choosing to sell one identical item rather than another.

LIFO

While FIFO associates the most recent costs with inventories, LIFO (Last In, First Out) treats the most recent costs as costs of goods sold. LIFO provides an income statement perspective in the sense that net income measured using LIFO combines current sales prices and current acquisition costs. *In a period of rising prices and constant or growing inventories, LIFO yields lower net income.* In Canada, LIFO is not allowed under the Income Tax Act for income tax purposes; thus its use is limited. However, in the United States, the lower net income is an important feature of LIFO, because in the United States LIFO is an acceptable inventory accounting method for income tax purposes. When lower income is reported to the tax authorities, lower taxes are paid, so it is not surprising that almost two thirds of U.S. corporations use LIFO for at least some of their inventories. (The Internal Revenue Code requires that if LIFO is used for tax purposes, it must also be used for financial reporting purposes.)

During a recent period of higher inflation, the *Wall Street Journal* reported that many small firms changed from FIFO to LIFO. As an example, Chicago Heights Steel Co. "boosted cash by 5% to 10% by lowering income taxes when it switched to LIFO." When Becton Dickinson and Company changed to LIFO, its annual report stated that its "change to the LIFO method... for both financial reporting and income tax purposes resulted in improved cash flow due to lower income taxes paid." Indeed, some observers maintain that executives are guilty of serious mismanagement by not adopting LIFO when FIFO produces significantly higher taxable income.

In a study by the American Institute of Certified Public Accountants, fewer than 25% of the respondents in the following industries used LIFO: electronics, business equipment, ship building, and railway equipment. If tax benefits are so important, why doesn't everyone use LIFO? Recall that LIFO yields lower net income and lower taxes *in a period of rising prices and constant or growing inventories.* One answer is that some industries don't face rising prices. For such industries, FIFO yields lower net income and lower taxes. In electronics, for example, technology has consistently driven prices down. Think back to two decades of constant reductions in prices for radios, stereo systems, clocks, and watches. The situation is similar for business equipment such as word processors and computers. With ship building and railway equipment, specific identification is an appropriate method since each unit is large and expensive.

LIFO does permit management to influence reported income by the *timing of purchases* of inventory items. Consider Emilio's case. Suppose that acquisition prices increase from 56 cents on Wednesday to 68 cents on Thursday, the day of the sale of the one unit. How is net income affected if one more unit is acquired on Thursday? Under LIFO, cost of goods sold would change to 68 cents, and profit would fall by 12 cents. In contrast, FIFO cost of goods sold and gross profit would be unchanged.

American Institute of Certified Public Accountants

www.rutgers.edu/ Accounting/raw/aicpa/ home.htm

	LIFO		FIFO	
	As in Exhibit 8-4	If One More Unit Acquired	As in Exhibit 8-4	If One More Unit Acquired
Sales	90¢	90¢	90¢	90¢
Cost of goods sold	56¢	68¢	30¢	30¢
Gross profit	34¢	22¢	60¢	60¢
Ending inventory:				
First layer, Monday	30¢	30¢		
Second layer, Tuesday	40¢	40¢	40¢	40¢
Third layer, Wednesday		56¢	56¢	56¢
Fourth layer, Thursday				68¢
	70¢	126¢	96¢	164¢

Weighted Average

Exhibit 8-4 illustrates that the weighted average costing method produces less extreme results than either LIFO or FIFO relative to both the income statement and the balance sheet. The weighted average is also subject to minimal manipulation by management action. The term *weighted* average can be better understood by assuming Emilio bought two cans rather than one on Monday at 30 cents each. To get the weighted average, we must consider not only the price paid, but also the number purchased as follows:

$$\text{Weighted average} = \text{Cost of goods available for sale} \div \text{Units available for sale}$$

$$\text{Weighted average} = [(2 \times 30¢) + (1 \times 40¢) + (1 \times 56¢)] \div 4$$

$$= 156¢ \div 4$$

$$= 39¢$$

Objective 6
Explain the meaning of holding gains and inventory profits.

replacement cost
The cost at which an inventory item could be acquired today.

holding gain (inventory profit)
Increase in the replacement cost or other measure of current value of the inventory held during the current period.

Holding Gains and Inventory Profits

LIFO's income statement orientation provides a reasonable economic interpretation of operating performance in inflationary periods. Consider Emilio. For him to be as well off after selling the can of cola as he was before, he must be able to replace it with the proceeds from his sale. If he must spend 56 cents to replace the can that was sold, we might call 56 cents the **replacement cost** of the inventory. The 26 cent difference between the historical cost of, say, 30 cents (the Monday can) and 56 cents (the Wednesday replacement cost) is called a **holding gain**. This holding gain is sometimes called an **inventory profit**. Because LIFO matches recent acquisition costs with sales revenue, LIFO cost of goods sold typically offers a close approximation to replacement cost, and reported net income rarely contains significant holding gains. The LIFO profit is 90 − 56 = 34 cents. In contrast, recall that using FIFO, Emilio reports a profit of 60 cents (90 cents − 30 cents). This profit contains two parts, the economic profit of 34 cents calculated as sales price less replacement costs, plus the inventory profit or holding gain of 26 cents that arose because the value of the inventory item rose with the passage of time.

■ LOWER-OF-COST-AND-MARKET METHOD

lower-of-cost-and-market method (LCM) The superimposition of a market-price test on an inventory cost method

Under the **lower-of-cost-and-market method (LCM)**, a market-price test is run on an inventory costing method. The *current market price* is compared with *historical cost* derived under one of the four primary methods: specific identification, FIFO, LIFO, or average. The lower of the two—current market value or historical cost— is conservatively selected as the basis for the valuation of goods at a specific inventory date. When market value is lower and is used for valuing the ending inventory, the effect is to increase the amount reported as cost of goods sold.

conservatism Selecting the methods of measurement that yield lower net income, lower assets, and lower shareholders' equity in the early years.

LCM is an example of conservatism. **Conservatism** means selecting methods of measurement that yield lower net income, lower assets, and lower shareholders' equity. Conservatism was illustrated in accounts receivable with the use of an allowance for bad debts. We estimated and recorded losses on uncollectible accounts before they were certain. With inventories, conservatism dictates the use of the LCM method.

Conservatism has been criticized as being inherently inconsistent. If replacement market prices are sufficiently objective and verifiable to substitute for cost when market prices are declining, why are they not sufficient to use when market values are rising? Accountants reply by saying that erring in the direction of conservatism usually has less severe economic consequences than erring in the direction of overstating assets and net income. The accountant's conservatism balances management's optimism. Management prepares the financial statements. The conservatism principle moderates management's human tendency to hope for, and expect, the best.

Objective 7

Explain why the lower-of-cost-and-market method is used to value inventories.

Defining Market Price

Bombardier
www.bombardier.com

Under GAAP, the definition of *market price* is vague. For our purposes we will think of it as the *replacement cost* (or net realizable value, or net realizable value less normal profit margin) of the inventory item—that is, the cost that would be incurred to buy the inventory item today. For example, Bombardier values its inventories at "the lower of cost and replacement cost or net realizable value" and The Oshawa Group values its inventories at "the lower of cost and net realizable values less normal profit margins." Implicit in the method is the assumption that when replacement costs decline in the wholesale market, so do the retail selling prices. Consider the following example. The Ripley Company has 100 units in its ending FIFO inventory on December 31, 19X1. Its gross profit for 19X1 has been tentatively computed as follows:

Sales	$2,180
Cost of goods available for sale	$1,980
Ending inventory of 100 units, at cost	$ 790
Cost of goods sold	$1,190
Gross profit	$ 990

write-down A reduction in carrying value to below cost in response to a decline in value.

Assume a sudden decline in market prices during the final week of December from $7.90 per unit to $4 per unit. If the lower market price is indicative of lower ultimate sales prices, an inventory **write-down** of ($7.90 – $4.00) ×100 units, or $390, is in order. A write-down is a reduction in carrying value to below cost in response to a decline in value. The required journal entry is:

```
Loss on write-down of inventory (or cost of goods          390
   sold) ........................................
          Inventory ...............................          390
   To write down inventory from $790 cost to
   $400 market value.
```

The write-down of inventories increases cost of goods sold by $390. Therefore reported income for 19X1 would be lowered by $390:

	Before $390 Write-Down	After $390 Write-Down	Difference
Sales	$2,180	$2,180	
Cost of goods available	$1,980	$1,980	
Ending inventory	790	400	– $390
Cost of goods sold	$1,190	$1,580	+ $390
Gross profit	$ 990	$ 600	– $390

The theory states that of the $790 historical cost, $390 is considered to have expired during 19X1 because the cost cannot be justifiably carried forward to the future as an asset. Furthermore, the decision to purchase was made during 19X1, and the fluctuation in the replacement market price occurred during the same period. This decline in price caused the inventory to lose some value, some revenue-producing power, because the decline in replacement cost generally corresponds to a decline in selling price.

If *selling prices* are not likely to fall, the revenue-producing power of the inventory will be maintained and no write-down would be justified. In sum, if predicted selling prices would be *unaffected* by the fact that current replacement costs are below the carrying cost of the inventory, do nothing. If predicted selling prices would be lower, use replacement cost.

If a write-down occurs, the new $4 per unit replacement cost valuation becomes, for accounting purposes, the unexpired cost of the inventory. Thus, if replacement prices subsequently rise to $8 per unit in January 19X2, no restoration of the December write-down will be permitted. In short, the lower-of-cost-and-market method would regard the December 31 $4 cost as the "new historical cost" of the inventory. Historical cost is the ceiling for valuation under generally accepted accounting principles.

Conservatism in Action

Compared with a pure cost method, the lower-of-cost-and-market method reports less net income in the period of decline in market value of the inventory and more net income in the period of sale. More generally, cumulative net income (the sum of all net income amounts from the inception of the firm to the present date) is never lower and is usually higher under the strict cost method. The lower-of-cost-and-market method affects how much income is reported in each year but not the total income over the company's life. Exhibit 8-6 underscores this point. Suppose the Ripley Company goes out of business in early 19X2. That is, no more units are acquired. There are no sales in 19X2 except for the disposal of the inventory in question at $8 per unit (100 × $8 = $800). Neither combined gross profit nor combined net income for the two periods will be affected by the LCM method, as the bottom of Exhibit 8-6 reveals.

Exhibit 8-6

The Ripley Company
Effects of Lower-of-Cost-and-Market

	Cost Method		Lower-of-Cost-and-Market Method	
	19X1	*19X2*	*19X1*	*19X2*
Sales	$2,180	$800	$2,180	$800
Cost of goods available	$1,980	$790	$1,980	$400
Ending inventory	790	—	400*	—
Cost of goods sold	$1,190	$790	$1,580	$400
Gross profit	$ 990	$ 10	$ 600	$400

Combined gross profit for two years:
  Cost method: $990 + $10 = $1,000
  Lower-of-cost-and-market method: $600 + $400 = $1,000

* The inventory is shown here after being written down by $390, from $790 to $400. For internal purposes, many accountants prefer to show the write-down separately, presenting a gross profit before write-down of inventory, the write-down, and a gross profit after write-down.

This example shows that conservatism can be a double-edged sword in the sense that net income in a current year will be hurt by a write-down of inventory (or any asset), and net income in a future year will be helped by the amount of the write-down. As Exhibit 8-6 illustrates, 19X2 income is $390 higher because of the $390 write-down of 19X1.

A full-blown lower-of-cost-and-market method is rarely encountered in practice. Why? Because it is expensive to get the correct replacement costs of hundreds or thousands of different products in inventory. Still, auditors definitely feel that the costs of inventories should be fully recoverable from future revenues. Therefore, auditors inevitably make market-price tests of a representative sample of the ending inventories. In particular, auditors want to write down the subclasses of inventory that are obsolete, shopworn, or otherwise of only nominal value.

Objective 8

Show the effects of inventory errors on financial statements.

■ EFFECTS OF INVENTORY ERRORS

Inventory errors can arise from many sources. Examples are wrong physical counts (possibly because goods that are in receiving or shipping areas instead of the inventory stockroom were omitted when physical counts were made) and clerical errors.

An undiscovered inventory error usually affects two reporting periods. It is counterbalanced by the ordinary accounting process in the next period. That is, the error affects income by identical offsetting amounts. An undiscovered inventory error affects the balance sheet at the end of the first period but not at the end of the second. For example, suppose ending inventory in 19X7 is understated by $10,000 because of errors in the physical count. The year's cost of goods sold would be overstated, pretax income understated, assets understated, and retained earnings understated.

These effects are easier to understand when a complete illustration is studied. Consider the following income statements (all numbers are in thousands), which assume ending 19X7 inventory is reported to be $10 too low.

19X7	Correct Reporting		Incorrect Reporting*		Effects of Errors
Sales		$980		$980	
Deduct: Cost of goods sold:					
Beginning inventory	$100		$100		
Purchases	500		500		
Cost of goods available for sale	$600		$600		
Deduct: Ending inventory	70		60		Understated by $10
Cost of goods sold		530		540	Overstated by $10
Gross profit		$450		$440	Understated by $10
Other expenses		250		250	
Income before income taxes		$200		$190	Understated by $10
Income tax expense at 40%		80		76	Understated by $4
Net income		$120		$114	Understated by $6
Ending balance sheet items:					
Inventory		$70		$60	Understated by $10
Retained earnings includes current net income of		120		114	Understated by $6
Income tax liability†		80		76	Understated by $4

* Because of error in ending inventory.
† For simplicity, assume that the entire income tax expense for the year will not be paid until the succeeding year. Therefore, the ending liability will equal the income tax expense.

Think about the effects of the uncorrected error on the following year, 19X8. The beginning inventory will be $60,000 rather than the correct $70,000. Therefore *all* the errors in 19X7 will be offset by counterbalancing errors in 19X8. Thus the retained earnings at the end of 19X8 would show a cumulative effect of zero. This is because the net income in 19X7 would be understated by $6,000, but the net income in 19X8 would be overstated by $6,000.

The point to stress is that the ending inventory of one period is also the beginning inventory of the succeeding period. Assume that the operations during 19X8 are a duplication of those of 19X7 except that the ending inventory is correctly counted as $40,000. Note the role of the error in the beginning inventory.

19X8	Correct Reporting		Incorrect Reporting*		Effects of Errors
Sales		$980		$980	
Deduct: Cost of goods sold:					
Beginning inventory	$ 70		$ 60		Understated by $10
Purchases	500		500		
Cost of goods available for sale	$ 570		$ 560		Understated by $10
Deduct: Ending inventory	40		40		
Cost of goods sold		530		520	Understated by $10
Gross profit		$ 450		$ 460	Overstated by $10
Other expenses		250		250	
Income before income taxes		$ 200		$ 210	Overstated by $10
Income tax expense at 40%		80		84	Overstated by $4
Net income		$120		$126	Overstated by $6
Ending balance sheet items:					
Inventory		$ 40		$ 40	Correct
Retained earnings includes:					
Net income of previous year		120		114	Counterbalanced and
Net income of current year		120		126	thus now correct in total
Two-year total		240		240	
Income tax liability:					
End of previous year		80		76	Counterbalanced and
End of current year		80		84	thus now correct in total†
Two-year total		160		160	

* Because of error in beginning inventory.
† The $84 really consists of the $4 that pertains to income of the previous year plus $80 that pertains to income of the current year.

The complete illustration shows the full detail of the inventory error, but we can use the accounting equation to develop our intuition. A useful generalization is: If ending inventory is understated, retained earnings is understated. If ending inventory is overstated, retained earnings is overstated. These relations are clear from the accounting equation. The presence of taxes means only that the effects need to be considered in two parts. Understated inventory implies overstated cost of goods sold and therefore lower current-year income and lower taxes. The shortcut analysis follows:

	A	=	L	+	SE
	Inventory		Income Tax Liability		Retained Earnings
Effects of error	$10,000 understated	=	$4,000 understated	+	$6,000 understated*

* Cost of goods overstated	$10,000
Pretax income understated	$10,000
Income taxes understated	4,000
Net income, which is included in ending retained earnings, understated	$ 6,000

■ THE IMPORTANCE OF GROSS PROFITS

As we have seen, gross profits are the result of sales revenue less the cost of goods sold as determined by one of the accounting methods for inventory valuation. Management and investors are intensely interested in gross profit and its changes. Will gross profits be large enough to cover operating expenses and produce a net income?

Gross Profit Percentage

Objective 9

Explain the uses of the gross profit percentage and inventory turnover measures.

Gross profit is often expressed as a percentage of sales. Consider the following information on a past year for a typical Safeway grocery store:

	Amount	Percentage
Sales	$10,000,000	100%
Net cost of goods sold	7,500,000	75%
Gross profit	$ 2,500,000	25%

The *gross profit percentage*—gross profit divided by sales—here is 25%. The following illustrates the extent to which gross profit percentages vary among industries.

Industry	Gross Profit (%)
Auto retailers	12.3
Auto manufacturers	17.6
Jewellery retailers	47.6
Grocery retailers	22.6
Grocery wholesalers	16.1
Drug manufacturers	40.8

Source: Robert Morris Associates, *Financial Statement Studies for 1994.*

wholesaler An intermediary that sells inventory items to retailers.

retailer A company that sells items directly to the final users, individuals.

The gross profit percentages range from a low of 12.3% to a high of 47.6%. Several patterns are evident. **Wholesalers** sell in larger quantity and incur fewer selling costs because they sell to other companies rather than individuals. As a result of competition and high volumes, they have smaller gross profit percentages than **retailers**. Retailers sell directly to individuals. Among retailers, jewellers have twice the gross profits of grocers because of expensive inventory and extensive personal selling. High gross profit percentages for drug manufacturers derive from patent protection and the need for substantial research and development outlays (up to 15% of sales). In contrast, auto manufacturers face more direct competition and earn lower gross profit percentages.

Estimating Intraperiod Gross Profit and Inventory

Exact ending inventory balances are not usually available for monthly or quarterly reports. The physical count required for an exact inventory count and accurate cost of goods sold calculation is too costly to obtain other than for year-end annual statements and reports. Interim reports thus use estimates derived from percentage or ratio methods. When the actual ending inventory is unavailable for monthly and quarterly financial statements, the gross profit percentage is often used to estimate the amount.

For example, assume that past sales of Tip Top Variety Store have usually resulted in a gross profit percentage of 25%. (Unless otherwise stated, any gross profit percentage given is based on net sales, not cost.) The accountant would estimate gross profit to be 25% of sales. If the monthly sales are $800,000, the cost of goods sold can be estimated as follows:

$$\text{Sales} - \text{Cost of goods sold} = \text{Gross profit}$$
$$S - CGS = GP$$
$$\$800,000 - CGS = 0.25 \times \$800,000 = \$200,000$$
$$CGS = \$600,000$$

If we know Tip Top's beginning inventory is $30,000 and purchases are $605,000, we can estimate ending inventory to be $35,000 as follows:

$$\text{Beginning inventory} + \text{Purchases} - \text{Ending Inventory} = CGS$$
$$BI + P - EI = CGS$$
$$\$30,000 + \$605,000 - EI = \$600,000$$
$$EI = \$35,000$$

In retailing, profit margins may be expressed as "markups" on cost. When an item costing $60 is sold for $80 it is a 25% profit margin as defined in this accounting text, but marketing professionals might call it a 33⅓% markup on cost ($20 markup ÷ $60 cost).

Gross Profit Percentage and Turnover

inventory turnover
The cost of goods sold divided by the average inventory held during the period.

Retailers often attempt to increase total profits by increasing sales levels. They lower prices and hope to increase their gross profits by selling their inventories more quickly, replenishing, selling again, and so forth. Managers speak of improving their **inventory turnover**, which is defined as cost of goods sold divided by the average inventory held during a given period. Average inventory is usually the sum of beginning inventory and ending inventory divided by 2. For the Tip Top Variety Store, the average inventory is ($30,000 + $35,000) ÷ 2 = $32,500. The inventory turnover is computed as follows:

$$\text{Turnover} = \text{Cost of goods sold} \div \text{Average inventory}$$
$$= \$600,000 \div \$32,500 = 18.5$$

Suppose the inventory sells twice as quickly if prices are lowered. With a 5% reduction in sales price, sales revenue on the current level of business drops from $800,000 to (0.95 × $800,000), or $760,000. But twice as many units are sold, so total revenue becomes 2 × $760,000, or $1,520,000. How profitable is Tip Top? Cost of goods sold doubles from $600,000 to $1,200,000. Total gross profit is $320,000. The inventory turnover doubles: $1,200,000 divided by $32,500 (the unchanged average inventory) is 36.9. However, the gross profit percentage falls from 25% to 21% ($320,000 divided by $1,520,000).

Is the company better off? Maybe. Certainly, in the current month gross profit has risen. However, strategic questions remain. *Is this new sales level maintainable?* For some products, when prices fall, consumers sharply increase purchases and stockpile the extras for later consumption. There is little increase in underlying demand, just a shift of future purchases to the present.

Another strategic question is, *What will the competition do?* If Tip Top's increased sales came at a competitor's expense, the competitor's response may be a similar decrease in prices. The competition might recover most of its old customers, with each buying a little more at the new price than at the old. But the whole market would see, not a doubling of sales, but perhaps a 20% sales growth. Tip Top would be worse off in the aggregate; the 20% growth would not cover the 5% price reduction.

Exhibit 8-7 illustrates two principles. Panel A shows that if a firm can increase inventory turnover while maintaining a constant gross profit percentage, it should do so. However, as shown in panel B, if the increased inventory turnover results from a decrease in sales price, the gross margin percentage may fall. The desirability of the change depends on whether the sales gain could offset the decreased margin. In the Tip Top Variety Store example, when a 5% price reduction produces a 20% increase in units sold, the new gross margin of $192,000 is still less than the initial $200,000. Dropping the price is not justified even though the inventory turnover rises to 22.2 from 18.5. However, at a 50% increase in sales volume, the new gross margin of $240,000 exceeds the original $200,000.

Exhibit 8-7

Tip Top Variety Store
Effects of Increased Inventory Turnover (in thousands)

| | | | Unit Sales Increase | |
Panel A	Original	20%	50%	100%
No change in sales price				
Sales	$ 800	$ 960	$1,200	$ 1,600
Cost of goods sold (75%)	600	720	900	1,200
Gross margin (25%)	$ 200	$ 240	$ 300	$ 400
Inventory turnover	18.5	22.2	27.7	36.9
Panel B				
5% reduction in sales price				
Sales (95% of above)	$ 760	$ 912	$1,140	$ 1,520
Cost of goods sold (as above)	600	720	900	1,200
Gross margin (21% of sales)	$ 160	$ 192	$ 240	$ 320
Inventory turnover (as above)	18.5	22.2	27.7	36.9

The industry variability in gross margin percentages referred to earlier is also reflected in inventory turnover percentages.

Industry	Gross Profit (%)	Inventory Turnover
Grocery wholesalers	16.1	14.7
Grocery retailers	22.6	16.9
Drug manufacturers	40.8	3.3
Jewellery retailers	47.6	1.4

Source: Robert Morris Associates, *Financial Statement Studies for 1994.*

The data are ordered from lowest gross profit percentage to highest for the industries displayed. There is a tendency for the inventory turnovers to move in the opposite direction.

When ratios are being calculated it is important to keep the accounting methods in mind. Consider the following data for Ford Motor Company:

Ford Motor Company
($ in millions)

	1994 Inventory			Cost of Goods Sold
	Beginning	*Ending*	*Average*	
LIFO	$5,538	$6,487	$6,012.5	$96,180
LIFO Reserve	1,342	1,383	1,362.5	
FIFO	$6,880	$7,870	$7,375.0	$96,139

Ford Motor Company
www.ford.com

Using reported LIFO results for Ford Motor Company, we can calculate the inventory turnover and gross profit percentages (sales of $107,137 million) to be:

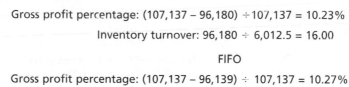

LIFO

Gross profit percentage: (107,137 – 96,180) ÷ 107,137 = 10.23%

Inventory turnover: 96,180 ÷ 6,012.5 = 16.00

FIFO

Gross profit percentage: (107,137 – 96,139) ÷ 107,137 = 10.27%

Inventory turnover: 96,139 ÷ 7,375.0 = 13.04

LIFO tends to *decrease* the gross profit percentage and to *increase* the inventory turnover relative to FIFO. Why? Because, under LIFO, cost of goods sold is usually greater and inventory values are lower.

Gross Profit Tests

Revenue Canada
www.revcan.ca/

Auditors, including those from Revenue Canada, use the gross profit percentage to help satisfy themselves about the accuracy of records. For example, Revenue Canada compiles gross profit percentages by types of retail establishment. If a company shows an unusually low percentage compared with similar companies, Revenue Canada auditors may suspect that the taxpayer has failed to record all cash sales. Similarly, managers watch changes in gross profit percentages to judge operating profitability and to monitor how well employee theft and shoplifting are being controlled.

Suppose a Revenue Canada auditor, a manager, or an outside auditor had gathered the following data for a particular jewellery company for the past three years (in millions):

	19X3	19X2	19X1
Net sales	$350	$300	$300
Cost of goods sold	210	150	150
Gross profit	$140	$150	$150
Gross profit percentage	40%	50%	50%

gross profit test
The comparing of gross profit percentages to detect any phenomenon worth investigating.

These data illustrate a **gross profit test** whereby the gross profit percentages are compared to detect any phenomenon worth investigating. Obviously, the decline in the percentage might be attributable to many factors. Possible explanations include the following:

1. Competition has intensified, resulting in intensive price wars that reduced selling prices.

2. The mix of goods sold has shifted so that, for instance, the $350 million of sales in 19X3 is composed of relatively more products bearing lower gross margins (e.g., more costume jewellery bearing low margins and less diamond jewellery bearing high margins).

3. Shoplifting or embezzling has soared out of control. For example, a manager may be pocketing and not recording cash sales of $70 million. After all, sales in 19X3 would have been $210 × 2 = $420 million if the past 50% margin had been maintained.

Reports to Shareholders

The importance of gross profits to investors is demonstrated in the following example based on a quarterly report to shareholders of Superscope, Inc., a manufacturer and distributor of stereophonic equipment that encountered rocky times. The following condensed income statement was presented for a three-month period (in thousands):

	Current Year	Previous Year
Net sales	$ 40,000	$40,200
Cost and expenses:		
Cost of sales	33,100	28,200
Selling, general, and administrative	11,200	9,900
Interest	2,000	1,200
Total costs and expenses	46,300	39,300
Income (loss) before income tax provision (benefit)	(6,300)	900
Income tax provision (benefit)	(3,000)	200
Net income (loss)	$ (3,300)	$ 700

Although the statement does not show the amount of gross profit, the gross profit percentages can readily be computed as ($40,000 – $33,100) ÷ $40,000 = 17% and ($40,200 – $28,200) ÷ $40,200 = 30%. To show how seriously these percentages are considered, the chairman's letter to shareholders began as follows:

> I shall attempt herein to provide you with a candid analysis of the Company's present condition, the steps we have instituted to overcome current adversities, and the potential which we believe can, in due course, be realized by the Company's realistic positive determination to regain profitability.

In the second quarter the Company's gross profit margins decreased to 17% compared to 30% in the corresponding quarter of a year ago. For the first six months gross profit margins were 22%, down from 31% for the corresponding period of a year ago.

Essentially, the gross profits and consequential operating losses in the second quarter, as reflected in the condensed financial statements appearing in this report, resulted from lower than anticipated sales volume and from the following second quarter factors: liquidation of our entire citizens band inventory; increases in dealer cash discounts and sales incentive expenses; gross margin reductions resulting from sales of slow moving models at less than normal prices; and markdown of slow moving inventory on hand to a realistic net realizable market value.

Summary Problems for Your Review

Problem One

Examine Exhibit 8-8. The company uses the periodic inventory system. Using these facts, prepare a columnar comparison of income statements for the year ended December 31, 19X2. Compare the FIFO, LIFO, and weighted-average inventory methods. Assume that other expenses are $1,000. The income tax rate is 40%.

Exhibit 8-8

Facts for Summary Problem One

	Purchases	Sales	Inventory
December 31, 19X1			200 @ $5 = $1,000
January 25	170@ $6 = $1,020		
January 29		150*	
May 28	190@ $7 = $1,330		
June 7		230*	
November 20	150@ $8 = $1,200		
December 15		100*	
Total	510 $3,550	480*	
December 31, 19X2			230 @ ?

* Selling prices were $9, $11, and $13, respectively, providing total sales of:

			Summary of costs:	
	150 @ $ 9 = $1,350	Beginning inventory	$ 1,000
	230 @ $11 = $2,530	Purchases	$ 3,550
	100 @ $13 = $1,300	Cost of goods available	
Total sales	480 $5,180	for sale	$4,550

Exhibit 8-9		Comparison of Inventory Methods for the Year Ended December 31, 19X2		

	FIFO		LIFO	Weighted Average
Sales, 480 units		$5,180	$5,180	$5,180
Deduct cost of goods sold:				
Beginning inventory, 200 @ $5		$1,000	$1,000	$1,000
Purchases, 510 units (from Exhibit 8-8)*		3,550	3,550	3,550
Available for sale, 710 units †		$4,550	$4,550	$4,550
Ending inventory, 230 units ‡				
150 @ $8	$1,200			
80 @ $7	560	1,760		
or				
200 @ $5			$1,000	
30 @ $6			180 1,180	
or				
230 @ $6.408		———	———	1,474
Cost of goods sold, 480 units		2,790	3,370	3,076
Gross profit		$2,390	$1,810	$2,104
Other expenses		1,000	1,000	1,000
Income before income taxes		$1,390	$ 810	$1,104
Income taxes at 40%		556	324	442
Net income		$ 834	$ 486	$ 662

*Always equal across all three methods.

†These amounts will not be equal in general across the three methods because beginning inventories will generally be different. They are equal here only because beginning inventories were assumed to be equal.

‡Under FIFO, the ending inventory is composed of the last purchases plus the second-last purchases, and so forth, until the costs of 230 units are compiled. Under LIFO, the ending inventory is composed of the beginning inventory plus the earliest purchases of the current year until the costs of 230 units are compiled. Under weighted average, the ending inventory and cost of goods sold are accumulations based on a unit cost. The latter is the cost of goods available for sale divided by the number of units available for sale: $4,550 ÷ 710 = $6.408.

Solution to Problem One

See Exhibit 8-9.

Problem Two

"When prices are rising, FIFO results in fool's profits because more resources are needed to maintain operations than previously." Do you agree? Explain.

Solution to Problem Two

The merit of this position depends on the concept of income favoured. LIFO gives a better measure of "distributable" income than FIFO. Recall the Emilio's Cola Sales example in the chapter (Exhibit 8-4, p. 340). The gross profit under FIFO was 60 cents, and under LIFO it was 34 cents. The 60¢ – 34¢ = 26¢ difference is a fool's profit because it must be reinvested to maintain the same inventory level as previously. It arises from a profit on holding inventory as prices change rather than from buying at wholesale and selling at retail. Therefore the 26 cents cannot be distributed as a cash dividend without reducing the current level of operations.

Problem Three

Fay's Incorporated operates about 260 super drugstores in the Northeast and 321 stores in total, including a chain of discount auto supply stores and 29 Paper Cutter stores. Some results for fiscal 1994 were (in thousands):

Sales	$919,719
Cost of merchandise sold	649,078
Net earnings	5,223
Beginning merchandise inventory	137,896
Ending merchandise inventory	153,627

Required

1. Calculate the 1994 gross profit and gross profit percentage for Fay's Incorporated.
2. Calculate the inventory turnover ratio.
3. What gross profit would have been reported if inventory turnover in 1994 had been 7, the gross profit percentage calculated in requirement 1 had been achieved, and the level of inventory was unchanged?

Solution to Problem Three

1. Gross profit = Sales – Cost of merchandise sold

    = $919,719 – $649,078

    = $270,641

   Gross profit percentage = Gross profit ÷ Sales

    = $270,641 ÷ $919,719

    = 29.4%

2. Inventory turnover = Cost of merchandise sold ÷ Average merchandise inventory

    = $649,078 ÷ [($137,896 + $153,627) ÷ 2]

    = $649,078 ÷ $145,762

    = 4.45

3. Cost of merchandise sold = Inventory turnover × Average merchandise inventory

    = 7 × $145,762

    = $1,020,334

   Gross profit percentage = (Sales – Cost of merchandise sold) ÷ Sales

    29.4% = (S – $1,020,334) ÷ S

    0.294 × S = S – $1,020,334

    S – (0.294 × S) = $1,020,334

    S × (1 – 0.294) = $1,020,334

    S = $1,020,334 ÷ (1 – 0.294)

    S = $1,445,232

   Gross profit = Sales – Cost of merchandise sold

    = $1,445,232 – $1,020,334

    = $424,898

The increase in inventory turnover from 4.45 to 7.0 would raise gross profit from $270,641 to $424,898.

Problem 4

At the end of 19X1, a $1,000 error was made in the physical inventory so that the inventory value was understated. The error went undetected. The subsequent inventory at the end of 19X2 was done correctly. Assess the effect of this error on income before tax, taxes, net income, and retained earnings for 19X1 and 19X2, assuming a 40% tax rate.

Solution to Problem 4

First calculate the effect on Cost of Goods Sold.

	19X1	19X2
Beginning Inventory	ok	too low
Purchases	ok	ok
Goods available for sale	ok	too low
Ending Inventory	too low	ok
Cost of goods sold	too high	too low

Note that 19X1 Ending Inventory becomes 19X2 Beginning Inventory, reversing the effects on Cost of Goods Sold.

The 19X1 Cost of Goods Sold being too high causes 19X1 income before tax to be too low by $1,000. Therefore, taxes will be too low by .40 × $1,000 = $400 and net income will be too low by $600, causing retained income to be too low by $600 also.

In 19X2 the effects reverse and by year's end retained income is correctly stated.

Highlights to Remember

Inventory accounting involves allocating the cost of goods available for sale between cost of goods sold and ending inventory as of the balance sheet date. Under the *perpetual* system, this allocation occurs continually; cost of goods sold is recorded for each sale. Under the *periodic* system, the allocation occurs via an adjusting entry at year end. A physical inventory is conducted under either system. The goods on hand are counted, and a cost is calculated for each item from purchase records. The cost of an item of inventory includes not only the purchase price but also inward transportation costs.

Under the *periodic* system the physical inventory is the basis for the year-end adjusting entry to recognize cost of goods sold. Under the perpetual system the physical inventory is used to confirm the accounting records. Differences, if any, lead to adjustments to cost of goods sold and ending inventory. Adjustments reflect inventory shrinkage due to theft, spoilage, damage, and so on, or to accounting errors in the perpetual records.

Valuation of inventories involves the assignment of specific historical costs of acquisition either to units sold or to units on hand. Four major inventory valuation methods are in use: specific identification, weighted average, FIFO, and LIFO. When prices are rising and inventories are constant or growing, less income is shown by LIFO than by FIFO. LIFO liquidation refers to the relatively higher profits generated under LIFO when reductions in inventory levels cause older, lower inventory costs to be used in calculating cost of goods sold. Notice that even with declining inventories, with rising costs the *cumulative* income is always less under LIFO than FIFO because the inventory valuation is less and the cumulative cost of goods sold is higher.

Conservatism leads to the lower-of-cost-and-market method, which treats cost as the maximum value of inventory. Inventory is reduced to replacement cost (with a corresponding increase in cost of goods sold) when acquisition prices fall below historical cost levels.

The nature of accrual accounting for inventories creates a self-correcting quality to errors in counting or valuing the ending inventory. This occurs because the ending inventory in one period becomes the beginning inventory of the subsequent period.

Financial analysts and managers use gross profit percentages as a measure of profitability and inventory turnover as a measure of efficient asset use. These measures are compared with prior levels to examine trends and with current levels of other industry members to assess relative performance.

Appendix 8: Inventory in a Manufacturing Environment

In the chapter, inventory accounting is covered from the viewpoint of a wholesaler or retailer, companies that acquire their inventory by purchase from another company. When a company *manufactures* products, the cost of inventory is a combination of the acquisition cost of raw material, the wages paid to workers who combine the raw materials into finished products, and an allocation of the costs of space, energy, and equipment used by the workers as they transform the various elements into a finished product.

Consider how costs are accumulated in a manufacturing environment for Packit, a company that makes backpacks. The raw materials are heavy fabric, glue, and thread. The transformation occurs when workers use cutters to make the panels that other workers sew and glue together. The costs of manufacture include amortization on the manufacturing building, amortization on the sewing machines and cutters, and utilities to support the effort in the form of heat, power, and light. The finished goods are backpacks.

The accounting process is easiest to understand when calculating the cost of a complete year of production. In the example below, 100,000 backpacks are produced during Packit's first year at a total cost of $800,000, providing a cost per backpack of $8.00 each ($800,000 ÷ 100,000 units). At year end, if all have been sold, the financial statements would include $800,000 in cost of goods sold.

Calculation of cost of manufacturing for a year's production of 100,000 backpacks:

Beginning inventory	—
Fabric purchased and used	$200,000
Wages paid to workers	300,000
Thread and glue used	50,000
Amortization on building and equipment	220,000
Utilities	30,000
Total Costs to Manufacture	$800,000
Cost per backpack ($800,000 ÷ 100,000)	$8.00

In the above example, all of the materials acquired during the year are transformed into finished products before year end and sold. In fact, if we take a snapshot of the typical backpack manufacturer at year end we would observe bolts of fabric, spools of thread and gallons of glue waiting to be put into production. We call these items held for use in the manufacturing of a product

raw material inventory Includes the cost of materials held for use in the manufacturing of a product.

work in process inventory Includes the cost incurred for partially completed items, including raw materials, labour, and other costs.

finished goods inventory The accumulated costs of manufacture for goods that are complete and ready for sale.

raw material inventory. In addition we would also observe fabric already cut but not assembled and some partially completed backpacks.

We refer to the material, labour and other costs accumulated for partially completed items as **work in process inventory**. When manufacture is complete and the goods are ready to deliver to customers, the inventory is called **finished goods inventory**. The accounting system for managing these costs is illustrated in Exhibit 8-10 for the second year of production of our backpack manufacturer. During this second year 120,000 backpacks are completed and 110,000 are sold. Some remain in the assembly process at year end, and unused fabric thread and glue are held in preparation for future production.

The schematic in Exhibit 8-10 captures the production process. You might think of each of the accounts as corresponding to a physical reality. The raw material is stored in a locked room, ready for use. The work-in-process is located in the production room and as it is finished it is physically transferred to a storage site. When goods are sold they are removed from that storage site and are given to the customer in exchange for cash or an account receivable. Raw materials, work-in-process, and finished goods are all forms of inventory and appear on the balance sheet as current assets. They are simply in different stages of completion. The act of sale converts the asset into an expense to be reported on the income statement. At year end, Packit will show total inventory on its year 2 balance sheet of $126,000, as follows:

Raw Materials Inventory	$ 25,000
Work in Process Inventory	22,000
Finished Goods Inventory	79,000
Total Inventory	$126,000

Exhibit 8-10

Packit Company Accounting for Manufacturing Costs

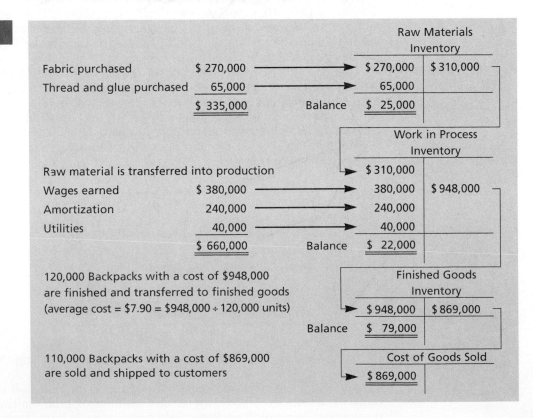

			Raw Materials Inventory	
Fabric purchased	$ 270,000	→	$ 270,000	$ 310,000
Thread and glue purchased	65,000	→	65,000	
	$ 335,000	Balance	$ 25,000	

			Work in Process Inventory	
Raw material is transferred into production		→	$ 310,000	
Wages earned	$ 380,000	→	380,000	$ 948,000
Amortization	240,000	→	240,000	
Utilities	40,000	→	40,000	
	$ 660,000	Balance	$ 22,000	

120,000 Backpacks with a cost of $948,000 are finished and transferred to finished goods (average cost = $7.90 = $948,000 ÷ 120,000 units)

		Finished Goods Inventory	
→	$ 948,000	$ 869,000
Balance	$ 79,000	

110,000 Backpacks with a cost of $869,000 are sold and shipped to customers

	Cost of Goods Sold
→	$ 869,000

The summary journal entries to record these events for year 2 would be:

Purchase of raw material:

Raw material inventory	335,000	
Accounts payable		335,000

Production activity:

Work in process inventory	310,000	
Raw materials inventory		310,000
Work in process inventory	660,000	
Wages payable		380,000
Accumulated amortization		240,000
Utilities payable		40,000

Completion of production:

Finished goods inventory	869,000	
Work in process inventory		869,000

Assignment Material

QUESTIONS

8-1. "There are two major steps in accounting for inventories at year end." What are they?

8-2. Distinguish between *F.O.B. destination* and *F.O.B. shipping point*.

8-3. "Freight out should be classified as a direct offset to sales, not as an expense." Do you agree? Explain.

8-4. What are the two phases of accounting for a sales transaction?

8-5. Distinguish between the *perpetual* and *periodic* inventory systems.

8-6. "An advantage of the perpetual inventory system is that a physical count of inventory is unnecessary. The periodic method requires a physical count to compute cost of goods sold." Do you agree? Explain.

8-7. Name the four inventory cost flow assumptions or valuation methods that are generally accepted. Give a brief phrase describing each.

8-8. What is *consistency*, and why is it an important accounting principle?

8-9. "An inventory profit is a fictitious profit." Do you agree? Explain.

8-10. LIFO produces absurd inventory valuations. Why?

8-11. "Purchases of inventory at the end of a fiscal period can have a direct effect on income under LIFO." Do you agree? Explain.

8-12. "There is a single dominant reason why more and more U.S. companies have adopted LIFO." What is the reason?

8-13. "Conservatism always results in lower reported profits." Do you agree? Explain.

8-14. "Accountants have traditionally favoured taking some losses but no gains before an asset is exchanged." What is this tradition or convention called?

8-15. What does *market* mean in inventory accounting?

8-16. "The lower-of-cost-and-market method is inherently inconsistent." Do you agree? Explain.

8-17. Express the cost of goods sold section of the income statement as an equation.

8-18. "Gross profit percentages help in the preparation of interim financial statements." Explain.

8-19. "Inventory errors are counterbalancing." Explain.

8-20. If a company uses a FIFO cost flow assumption, will it report the same cost of goods sold using the periodic inventory method that it reports using the perpetual method? Why or why not?

8-21. Assume that the physical level of inventory is constant at the beginning and end of year and that the cost of inventory items is rising. Which will produce a higher ending inventory value, LIFO or FIFO?

8-22. Will LIFO or FIFO produce higher cost of goods sold during a period of *falling* prices? Explain.

8-23. Which of the following items would a company be likely to account for using a perpetual inventory system and the specific identification inventory method?

a. Corporate jet aircraft
b. Large sailboats
c. Pencils
d. Diamond rings
e. Timex watches
f. Automobiles
g. Books
h. Compact discs

EXERCISES

8-24   Gross Profit Section

Given the following, prepare a detailed gross profit section for Ramon's Jewellery Wholesalers for the year ended December 31, 19X1 (in thousands):

Cash discounts on purchases	$ 6		Cash discounts on sales	$ 5
Sales returns and allowances	40		Purchase returns and allowances	27
Gross purchases	650			
Merchandise inventory, December 31, 19X0	103		Merchandise inventory, December 31, 19X1	180
Gross profit	360		Freight in	50

8-25   Gross Margin Computations and Inventory Costs

On January 15, 19X4, Ruth Burton valued her inventory at cost, $40,000. Her statements are based on the calendar year, so you find it necessary to establish an inventory figure as of January 1, 19X4. You find that from January 2 to January 15, sales were $71,000; sales returns, $2,100; goods purchased and placed in stock, $54,000; goods removed from stock and returned to suppliers, $2,000; freight in, $500. Calculate the inventory cost as of January 1, assuming that goods are priced to provide a 23% gross profit.

8-26   Journal Entries

Castellon Inc. had sales of $24 million during the year. The goods cost Castellon $16 million. Give the journal entry or entries at the time of sale under the perpetual and the periodic inventory systems.

8-27   Valuing Inventory and Cost of Goods Sold

Hurman Ltd. had the following inventory transactions during the month of January.

1/1 beginning inventory,	4,000 units @ $2.00	$ 8,000
week 1, purchases	2,000 units @ $2.10	4,200
week 2, purchases	3,000 units @ $2.20	6,600
week 3, purchases	1,000 units @ $2.30	2,300
week 4, purchases	1,000 units @ $2.40	2,400

On January 31, a count of the ending inventory was completed, and 5,500 units were on hand. Using the periodic inventory system, calculate the cost of goods sold and ending inventory using LIFO, FIFO, and weighted-average inventory methods.

8-28   Entries for Purchase Transactions

The Vanhonacker Company is a Swiss wholesaler of small giftware. Its unit of currency is the Swiss franc (Sfr.). Vanhonacker uses a periodic inventory system. Prepare journal entries for the following summarized transactions (omit explanations):

Aug. 2 Purchased merchandise, Sfr. 300,000, terms 2/10, n/45.

Aug. 3 Paid cash for freight in, Sfr. 10,000.

Aug. 7 Vanhonacker complained about some defects in the merchandise acquired on August 2. The supplier hand-delivered a credit memo granting an allowance of Sfr. 20,000.

Aug. 11 Cash disbursement to settle purchase of August 2.

8-29   Cost of Inventory Acquired

On July 5, Solanski Company purchased on account a shipment of sheet steel from Halifax Steel Co. The invoice price was $160,000, F.O.B. shipping point. Shipping cost from the steel mill to Solanski's plant was $12,000. When inspecting the shipment, Neisha, the Solanski receiving clerk, found several flaws in the steel. Neisha informed Halifax's sales representative of the flaws, and after some negotiation, Halifax granted an allowance of $16,000.

To encourage prompt payment, Halifax grants a 2% cash discount to customers who pay their accounts within thirty days of billing. Solanski paid the proper amount on August 1.

Required

1. Compute the total cost of the sheet steel acquired.
2. Prepare the journal entries for the transaction. Omit explanations.

8-30   Entries for Periodic and Perpetual Systems

Viteri Co. had an inventory of $250,000, December 31, 19X1. Data for 19X2 follow:

Gross purchases	$960,000
Cost of goods sold	920,000
Inventory, December 31, 19X2	200,000
Purchase returns and allowances	90,000

Required

Using the data, prepare comparative journal entries, including closing entries, for a perpetual and a periodic inventory system.

8-31   Entries for Purchase Transactions

Winbush Landscape Wholesalers uses a periodic inventory system. Prepare journal entries for the following summarized transactions for 19X2 (omit explanations). For simplicity, assume that the beginning and ending balances in accounts payable were zero.

1. Purchases (all using trade credit), $900,000.
2. Purchase returns and allowances, $60,000.
3. Freight in, $72,000 paid in cash.
4. Cash discounts on purchases, $10,000.

8-32   Closing Entries, Periodic Inventory System

Refer to the data in the preceding problem. Inventories were: December 31, 19X1, $81,000; December 31, 19X2, $130,000. Sales were $1,300,000. Prepare the closing journal entries, December 31, 19X2. Omit explanations.

8-33   Closing Entries, Periodic Inventory System

Consider the following data taken from the adjusted trial balance of the Silva Company, December 31, 19X3 (in millions):

Purchases	$125	Sales	$244
Sales returns and allowances	5	Purchase returns and	
Freight in	14	allowances	6
Cash discounts on purchases	1	Cash discounts on sales	8
Inventory (beginning of year)	25	Other expenses	80

Required Prepare the closing journal entries. The ending inventory was $30 million.

8-34   Reconstruction of Transaction

Apple Computer, Inc. produces the well-known Macintosh computer. Consider the following account balances (in thousands):

	September 30	
	1994	1993
Inventories	$355,473	$475,377

Required The purchases of inventories during the 1994 fiscal year were $2,486,319,000. The income statement had an item "cost of sales." Compute its amount.

8-35   Reconstruction of Records

An earthquake caused heavy damage to the Bebop Record Store on May 3, 19X1. All the merchandise was destroyed. Some accounting data are missing. In conjunction with an insurance investigation, you have been asked to estimate the cost of the inventory destroyed. The following data for 19X1 are available:

Cash discounts on purchases	$ 1,000	Inventory, December 31, 19X0	$ 19,000
Gross sales	140,000	Purchase returns and allowances	4,000
Sales returns and allowances	12,000	Inward transportation	3,000
Gross purchases	80,000	Gross profit percentage on net sales	45%

8-36   Cost of Inventory Destroyed by Fire

E. Ravelo requires an estimate of the cost of merchandise lost by fire on March 9. Merchandise inventory on January 1 was $70,000. Purchases since January 1 were $190,000; freight in, $28,000; purchase returns and allowances, $10,000. Sales are made at a gross margin of 20% of *sales* and totalled $200,000 up to March 9. What was the cost of the merchandise destroyed?

8-37   Inventory Shortage

An accounting clerk of the Bettis Company absconded with cash and a truck full of the entire electronic merchandise on May 14, 19X2. The following data have been compiled:

Beginning inventory, January 1	$ 80,000
Sales to May 14, 19X2	280,000
Average gross profit rate	25%
Purchases to May 14, 19X2	180,000

Required Compute the estimated cost of the missing merchandise.

8-38   Inventory Errors

At the end of his first business year, Irving counted and priced the inventory. A few very high-value items were hidden in a dark corner of the storage shelves and Irving understated his 19X5 inventory by $10,000. His business financial statements and his tax return were affected. Assume a 40% tax rate.

Required

1. Calculate the effect on taxable income, taxes, net income, and retained earnings for 19X5.
2. Repeat requirement 1 for 19X6, assuming the 19X6 ending inventory is correctly calculated.

8-39 Decision about Pricing

Rivera Jewellers, Inc., a retail jewellery store, had gross profits of $880,000 on sales of $1,600,000 in 19X3. Average inventory was $720,000.

Required

1. Compute inventory turnover.
2. Jaime Rivera is considering whether to become a "discount" jeweller. For example, Jaime believes that a cut of 20% in average selling prices would have increased turnover to 1.5 times per year. Beginning and ending inventory would be unchanged. Suppose Jaime's beliefs are valid. Would the gross profit in 19X3 have improved? Show computations.

8-40 LIFO and FIFO

The inventory of the Childers Chat Company on June 30 shows 1,000 tonnes at $9 per tonne. A physical inventory on July 31 shows a total of 1,200 tonnes on hand. Revenue from sales of gravel for July totals $98,000. The following purchases were made during July:

July 8	5,000 tonnes @ $10 per tonne
July 13	1,000 tonnes @ $11 per tonne
July 22	1,100 tonnes @ $12 per tonne

Required

1. Compute the inventory cost as of July 31, using (a) LIFO and (b) FIFO.
2. Compute the gross profit, using each method.

8-41 Lower-of-cost-and-market

(Alternate is 8-68.) Saeki Company uses the inventory method "lower-of-cost-and-market." There were no sales or purchases during the periods indicated, although selling prices generally fluctuated in the same directions as replacement costs. At what amount would you value merchandise on the dates listed below?

	Invoice Cost	Replacement Cost
December 31, 19X1	$200,000	$180,000
April 30, 19X2	200,000	190,000
August 31, 19X2	200,000	220,000
December 31, 19X2	200,000	165,000

8-42 Profitability and Turnover

Dano's Garden Supply began 19X1 with inventory of $170,000. Dano's 19X1 sales were $800,000, purchases of inventory totalled $680,000, and ending inventory was $230,000.

Required

1. Prepare a statement of gross profit for 19X1
2. What was Dano's inventory turnover?

PROBLEMS

8-43 Detailed Income Statement

(Alternate is 8-62.) Following are accounts taken from the adjusted trial balance of the Myrick Building Supply Company, December 31, 19X5. The company uses the periodic inventory system. Prepare a detailed income statement for 19X5. All amounts are in thousands:

Sales salaries and commissions	$160	Freight in	$ 50
Inventory, December 31, 19X4	200	Miscellaneous expenses	13
Allowance for bad debts	14	Sales	1,080
Rent expense, office space	10	Bad debts expense	8
Gross purchases	600	Cash discounts on purchases	15
Amortization expense, office equipment	3	Inventory, December 31, 19X5	325
		Office salaries	60
Cash discounts on sales	10	Rent expense, selling space	90
Advertising expense	40	Income tax expense	44
Purchase returns and allowances	40	Sales returns and allowances	50
		Office supplies used	6
Delivery expense	20	Amortization expenses, trucks, and store fixtures	29

8-44 Perpetual Inventory Calculations

Park Electric is a wholesaler for commercial builders. The company uses a perpetual inventory system and a FIFO cost-flow assumption. The data concerning QuiteQuiet Switches for the year 19X2 follows:

	Purchased	Sold	Balance
December 31, 19X1			110 @ $5 = $550
February 10, 19X2	80 @ $6 = $ 480		
April 14		60	
May 9	110 @ $7 = $ 770		
July 14		120	
October 21	100 @ $8 = $ 800		
November 12		80	
Total	290 $2,050	260	

Required   Calculate the ending balance in units and dollars.

8-45 Gross Profit and Turnover

Retailers closely watch a number of financial ratios, including the gross profit (gross margin) percentage and inventory turnover. Suppose the results for the furniture department in a large store in a given year were:

Sales	$3,000,000
Cost of goods sold	1,800,000
Gross profit	$1,200,000
Beginning inventory	$ 650,000
Ending inventory	$ 550,000

Required   1. Compute the gross profit percentage and the inventory turnover.
2. Suppose the retailer is able to maintain a reduced inventory of $450,000 throughout the succeeding year. What inventory turnover would have to be obtained to achieve the same $1,200,000 gross profit? Assume that the gross profit percentage is unchanged.

3. Suppose the retailer maintains inventory at the $450,000 level throughout the succeeding year but cannot increase the inventory turnover from the level in requirement 1. What gross profit percentage would have to be obtained to achieve the same total gross profit?

4. Suppose the average inventory of $600,000 is maintained. Compute the total gross profit in the succeeding year if there is

   a. A 10% increase of the gross profit *percentage* (that is, 10% of the percentage, not an additional ten percentage points) and a 10% decrease of the inventory turnover; or

   b. A 10% decrease of the gross profit percentage and a 10% increase of the inventory turnover.

5. Why do retailers find the above types of ratios helpful?

8-46   Comparison of Inventory Methods

(Alternates are 8-63 and 8-65.) The Caen Co. is a wholesaler for commercial builders. The company uses a periodic inventory system. The data concerning Airvent Grill RD8 for the year 19X2 follow:

	Purchases		Sold	Balance
December 31, 19X1				110 @ $5 = $550
February 10, 19X2	80 @ $6 =	$480		
April 14			60	
May 9	120 @ $7 =	$840		
July 14			120	
October 21	100 @ $8 =	$800		
November 12			80	
Total	300	$2,120	260	
December 31, 19X2				150 @ ?

The sales during 19X2 were made at the following selling prices:

60 @ $8 =	$ 480
120 @ 10 =	1,200
80 @ 11 =	880
260	$2,560

Required

1. Prepare a comparative statement of gross profit for the year ended December 31, 19X2, using FIFO, LIFO, and weighted-average inventory methods.

2. By how much would income taxes differ if Caen used LIFO instead of FIFO for Airvent Grill RD8? Assume a 40% income tax rate. Also assume that LIFO is acceptable for income tax purposes.

8-47   Effects of Late Purchases

(Alternates are 8-64 and 8-66.) Refer to the preceding problem. Suppose 100 extra units had been acquired on December 30 for $8 each, a total of $800. How would net income and income taxes have been affected under FIFO? under LIFO? Show a tabulated comparison.

8-48   LIFO, FIFO, and Lower-of-cost-and-market

DRP Company began business on March 15, 19X0. The following are DRP's purchases of inventory:

March 17	100 units @ $10	$1,000
April 19	50 units @ $12	600
May 14	100 units @ $13	1,300
Total		$2,900

On May 25, 140 units were sold, leaving inventory of 110 units. DRP Company's accountant was preparing a balance sheet for June 1, at which time the replacement cost of the inventory was $12 per unit.

Required

1. Suppose DRP Company uses LIFO, without applying lower-of-cost-and-market. Compute the June 1 inventory amount.
2. Suppose DRP Company uses lower-of-LIFO-cost-or-market. Compute the June 1 inventory amount.
3. Suppose DRP Company uses FIFO, without applying lower-of-cost-and-market. Compute the June 1 inventory amount.
4. Suppose DRP Company uses lower-of-FIFO-cost-or-market. Compute the June 1 inventory amount.

8-49 Inventory Errors
(Alternate is 8-56.) The following data are from the 19X1 income statement of the Woolen Carpet Stores (in thousands):

Sales		$1,600
Deduct Cost of goods sold:		
Beginning inventory	$ 390	
Purchases	720	
Cost of goods available for sale	$1,110	
Deduct: Ending inventory	370	
Cost of goods sold		740
Gross profit		$ 860
Other expenses		610
Income before income taxes		$ 250
Income tax expense at 40%		100
Net income		$ 150

The ending inventory was overstated by $30,000 because of errors in the physical count. The income tax rate was 40% in 19X1 and 19X2.

Required

1. Which items in the income statement are incorrect? By how much? Use *O* for overstated, *U* for understated, and *N* for not affected. Complete the following tabulation:

	19X1	19X2
Beginning inventory	N	O $30
Ending inventory	?	?
Cost of goods sold	?	?
Gross margin	?	?
Income before income taxes	?	?
Income tax expense	?	?
Net income	?	?

2. What is the dollar effect of the inventory error on retained income at the end of 19X1? at the end of 19X2?

8-50   LIFO, FIFO, Prices Rising and Falling

The Romero Company has a periodic inventory system. Inventory on December 31, 19X1 consisted of 10,000 units @ $10 = $100,000. Purchases during 19X2 were 13,000 units. Sales were 12,000 units for sales revenue of $20 per unit.

Required

Prepare a four-column comparative statement of gross margin for 19X2:

1. Assume purchases were at $12 per unit. Assume FIFO and then LIFO.
2. Assume purchases were at $8 per unit. Assume FIFO and then LIFO.
3. Assume an income tax rate of 40%. Suppose all transactions were for cash. Which inventory method in requirement 1 would result in more cash for Romero Company? by how much? Assume that LIFO is acceptable for income tax purposes.
4. Repeat requirement 3. Which inventory method in requirement 2 would result in more cash for Romero Company? by how much?

8-51   LIFO, FIFO, Cash Effects

In 19X2, Inverness Company had sales revenue of £ 370,000 for a line of woolen scarves. The company uses a periodic inventory system. Pertinent data for 19X2 included:

Inventory, December 31, 19X1	14,000 units @ £ 6	£ 84,000
January purchases	20,000 units @ £ 7	140,000
July purchases	32,000 units @ £ 8	256,000
Sales for the year	30,000 units	

Required

1. Prepare a statement of gross margin for 19X2. Use two columns, one assuming LIFO and one assuming FIFO.
2. Assume a 40% income tax rate. Suppose all transactions were for cash. Which inventory method would result in more cash for Inverness Company? by how much? Assume that LIFO is acceptable for income tax purposes.

8-52   FIFO and LIFO

Two companies, the LIFO Company and the FIFO Company, are in the scrap metal warehousing business as arch competitors. They are about the same size and in 19X1 coincidentally encountered seemingly identical operating situations. Only their inventory accounting systems differed.

Their beginning inventory was 10,000 tonnes; it cost $50 per tonne. During the year, each company purchased 50,000 tonnes at the following prices:

- 20,000 @ $60 on March 17
- 30,000 @ $70 on October 5

Each company sold 45,000 tonnes at average prices of $100 per tonne. Other expenses in addition to cost of goods sold but excluding income taxes were $650,000. The income tax rate is 40%.

Required

1. Compute net income for the year for both companies. Assume that each of their inventory valuation approaches is acceptable for income tax purposes. Show your calculations.
2. As a manager, which method would you prefer? Why? Explain fully. Include your estimate of the overall effect of these events on the cash balances of each company, assuming that all transactions during 19X1 were direct receipts or disbursements of cash.

8-53 Effects of LIFO and FIFO

The GHS Company is starting in business on December 31, 19X0. In each *half year*, from 19X1 through 19X4, it expects to purchase 1,000 units and sell 500 units for the amounts listed below. In 19X5 it expects to purchase no units and sell 4,000 units for the amount indicated in the following table:

	19X1	19X2	19X3	19X4	19X5
Purchases:					
First 6 months	$ 2,000	$ 4,000	$ 6,000	$ 6,000	0
Second 6 months	4,000	9,000	6,000	8,000	0
Total	$ 6,000	$13,000	$12,000	$14,000	0
Sales (at selling price)	$10,000	$10,000	$10,000	$10,000	$40,000

Assume that there are no costs or expenses other than those shown above. The tax rate is 40%, and taxes for each year are payable on December 31 of each year. GHS Company is trying to decide whether to use periodic FIFO or LIFO throughout the five-year period. Assume that LIFO is acceptable for income tax purposes.

Required

1. What was net income under FIFO for each of the five years? under LIFO? Show calculations.
2. Explain briefly which method, LIFO or FIFO, seems more advantageous, and why.

8-54 Effects of LIFO on Purchase Decisions

The Bihan Corporation is nearing the end of its first year in business. The following purchases of its single product have been made:

	Units	Unit Price	Total Cost
January	1,000	$10	$ 10,000
March	1,000	10	10,000
May	1,000	11	11,000
July	1,000	13	13,000
September	1,000	14	14,000
December	4,000	15	60,000
	9,000		$118,000

Sales for the year will be 5,000 units for $120,000. Expenses other than cost of goods sold will be $20,000.

The president is undecided about whether to adopt FIFO or LIFO for income tax purposes as either method is acceptable for income tax purposes in Bihan's country of business. The company has ample storage space for up to 7,000 units of inventory. Inventory prices are expected to stay at $15 per unit for the next few months.

Required

1. What would be the net income before taxes, the income taxes, and the net income after taxes for the year under (a) FIFO and (b) LIFO? Income tax rates are 30% on the first $25,000 of net taxable income and 50% on the excess.
2. If the company sells its year-end inventory in Year 2 @ $24 per unit and goes out of business, what would be the net income before taxes, the income taxes, and the net income after taxes under (a) FIFO and (b) LIFO? Assume that other expenses in Year 2 are $20,000.

3. Repeat requirements 1 and 2, assuming that the 4,000 units @ $15 purchased in December were not purchased until January of the second year. Generalize on the effect on net income of the timing of purchases under FIFO and LIFO.

8-55   Changing Quantities

Consider the following data for the year 19X2:

	Units	Unit Cost
Beginning inventory	2	*
Purchases:	3	24
	3	28
Ending inventory	2	†

* FIFO, $20; LIFO, $16.
† To be computed.

Required

1. Prepare a comparative table computing the cost of goods sold, using columns for FIFO and LIFO. In a final column, show (a) the difference between FIFO and LIFO inventories (the LIFO reserve) at the beginning of the year and at the end of the year, and (b) how the *change* in this amount explains the difference in cost of goods sold.
2. Repeat requirement 1, except assume that the ending inventory consisted of (a) three units, (b) zero units.
3. In your own words, explain why, for a given year, the increase in the LIFO reserve measures the amount by which cost of goods sold is higher under LIFO than FIFO.

8-56   Inventory Errors, Three Years

(Alternate is 8-49.) The Rohm Company had the accompanying data for three successive years (in millions):

	19X3	19X2	19X1
Sales	$200	$160	$175
Deduct Cost of goods sold:			
Beginning inventory	15	25	40
Purchases	135	100	90
Cost of goods available for sale	150	125	130
Ending inventory	30	15	25
Cost of goods sold	120	110	105
Gross profit	80	50	70
Other expenses	70	30	30
Income before income taxes	10	20	40
Income tax expense at 40%	4	8	16
Net income	$ 6	$ 12	$ 24

In early 19X4, a team of internal auditors discovered that the ending inventory for 19X1 had been overstated by $20 million. Furthermore, the ending inventory for 19X3 had been understated by $10 million. The ending inventory for December 31, 19X2 was correct.

Required

1. Which items in the income statement are incorrect? by how much? Prepare a tabulation covering each of the three years.
2. Is the amount of retained income correct at the end of 19X1, 19X2, and 19X3? If it is erroneous, indicate the amount and whether it is overstated (O) or understated (U).

8-57 Review of Chapters 1-8. Adjusting and Correcting Entries
Examine the accompanying Unadjusted Trial Balance for Mantle Cloak Company as of December 31, 19X2.

Account	Debit	Credit
1. Cash	$ 5,000	
2. Note receivable	1,000	
3. Accounts receivable	10,300	
4. Allowance for bad debts		$ 300
5. Inventory balance, as of January 1, 19X2	20,000	
6. Unexpired insurance	600	
7. Office supplies on hand	400	
8. Unexpired rent		
9. Equipment	4,000	
10. Accumulated amortization, equipment		500
11. Accounts payable		10,000
12. Long-term 8% mortgage payable		3,000
13. Accrued interest payable		
14. Accrued wages payable		
15. Mantle capital		18,500
16. Sales		130,000
17. Sales returns	1,000	
18. Cash discounts on sales	1,000	
19. Purchases	81,000	
20. Purchase returns		1,000
21. Wages	22,000	
22. Rent and heat	10,000	
23. Bad debts expense		
24. Other operating expenses	7,000	
25. Supplies expense		
26. Insurance expense		
27. Amortization		
28. Interest expense		
	$163,300	$163,300

For each of the following items 1 through 12 prepare the necessary entries. Select only from the accounts listed in the Trial Balance. The same account may be used in several answers. Answer by using account *numbers* and indicating the dollar amounts of debits and credits. For example, item 1 would call for a debit to Cash (1) for $200, a debit to Equipment (9) for $300, and a credit to Mantle Capital (15) for $500. (*Note*: The accounts that carry no balances are listed in the table for your convenience in making adjustments. All accounts needed to answer the questions are included.)

Required

1. On December 30, the owner invested $200 in cash plus equipment valued at $300. The bookkeeper has not recorded the transaction.
2. It is estimated that the Allowance for Bad Debts should be *increased* by an amount equal to 0.5% of 19X2 gross sales.
3. A correct entry was made, early in December, for $500 worth of goods sold to a customer on open account. The customer returned these goods on December 29. The bookkeeper has made no entry for the latter transaction, although a credit memo was issued, December 31.

4. Unexpired insurance was $450 on December 31, 19X2.

5. The interest on the mortgage is payable yearly on January 2. (Adjust for a *full year's* interest. Do not refine the arithmetic for one or two days' interest.)

6. There was a $1,000 payroll robbery on December 15. Wages had been debited for $1,000 and Cash credited for $1,000 for the original payroll. A substitute payroll was made up on December 16, Wages again debited for $1,000, and Cash again credited for $1,000. However, the loss was covered by insurance. On December 20, the insurance company remitted $1,000, and the Mantle bookkeeper debited Cash and credited Sales.

7. The equipment cost is being allocated to operations on the basis of an estimated useful life of ten years and no residual value.

8. Mantle withdrew $500 in cash on December 31. The bookkeeper has not recorded the transaction.

9. A $400 rental charge for January 19X3 was paid in cash to the DiMaggio Realty Company on December 31. The Mantle Company bookkeeper did not record the transaction.

10. Wages of salesclerks earned, but not paid, amount to $100.

11. A physical count of the office supplies revealed that there is a balance of $250 on hand as of December 31, 19X2.

12. On December 20, a customer paid the Mantle Company $980 for a $1,000 invoice, deducting a 2% discount. The bookkeeper made the appropriate entries. On December 30, Mr. Mantle discovered that the customer should have paid the full $1,000 because the discount period had expired on December 17. He sent the customer another invoice for the extra $20. The bookkeeper has not recorded the last transaction.

8-58   LIFO, FIFO, Purchase Decisions, and Earnings Per Share

Pete's Pots, a company with one million shares of common stock outstanding, had the following transactions during 19X1, its first year in business:

Sales:	1,000,000 units @ $5
Purchases:	800,000 units @ $2
	300,000 units @ $3

The current income tax rate is a flat 50%; the rate next year is expected to be 40%.

It is December 20 and Pete, the president, is trying to decide whether to buy the 600,000 units he needs for inventory now or early next year. The current price is $4 per unit. Prices on inventory are expected to remain stable; in any event, no decline in prices is anticipated.

Pete has not chosen an inventory method as yet, but will pick either LIFO or FIFO. Both are acceptable for income tax purposes.

Other expenses for the year will be $1.4 million.

Required

1. Using LIFO, prepare a comparative income statement assuming the 600,000 units (a) are not purchased, (b) are purchased. The statement should end with reported earnings per share.

2. Repeat requirement 1, using FIFO.

3. Comment on the above results. Which method should Pete choose? Why? Be specific.

4. Suppose that in Year 2 the tax rate drops to 40%, prices remain stable, 1 million units are sold @ $5, enough units are purchased at $4 so that the ending inventory will be 700,000 units, and other expenses are reduced to $800,000.

   a. Prepare a comparative income statement for the second year showing the impact of each of the four alternatives on net income and earnings per share for the second year.

   b. Explain any differences in net income that you encounter among the four alternatives.

   c. Why is there a difference in ending inventory values under LIFO even though the same amount of physical inventory is in stock?

    d. What is the total cash outflow for income taxes for the two years together under the four alternatives?

    e. Would you change your answer in requirement 3 now that you have completed requirement 4? Why?

8-59 Lower-of-cost-and-market

(Alternate is 8-41.) Automatic Camera Corporation's annual report stated: "Inventories are valued on a first-in, first-out basis at the lower-of-cost-and-market value." Assume that severe price competition in 19X5 necessitated a write-down on December 31 for a class of camera inventories with a cost of $11 million. The appropriate valuation at market was deemed to be $8 million.

    Suppose the product line was terminated in early 19X6 and the remaining inventory was sold for $8 million.

Required

1. Assume that sales of this line of camera for 19X5 were $19 million and cost of goods sold was $14 million. Prepare a statement of gross margin for 19X5 and 19X6. Show the results under a strict FIFO cost method in the first two columns and under a lower-of-FIFO-cost-and-market method in the next two columns.
2. Assume that Automatic Camera did not discontinue the product line. Instead a new marketing campaign spurred market demand. Replacement cost of the cameras in the December 31 inventory was $9 million on January 31, 19X6. What inventory valuation would be appropriate if the inventory of December 31, 19X5, was still held on January 31, 19X6?

8-60 Manufacturing Costs

Study Appendix 8. Erik made custom T-shirts for himself and his friends for years before trying to treat his work seriously as a business. January 1, 19X1, he decided to become more serious. He bought some screening equipment for $5,000 that he figured was good for 10,000 screenings. He decided to use units of production amortization. He acquired 2,000 shirts for $4,000 and rented a studio for $500 per month. During the month he paid an assistant $1,600 and together they created three designs, screened 1,500 shirts, and sold 1,200 at $8 each. At month end, there were 500 shirts unused, 300 finished shirts ready for sale, and Erik was trying to figure out how he was doing.

Required

1. Calculate the cost of goods sold and the value of ending inventory (including raw material and finished goods).
2. Prepare an income statement for Erik's first month of operations. Assume a 30% tax rate.

COMPANY CASES

8-61 Reconstruction of Transactions

Consider the following account balances of Mark's Work Wearhouse, a clothing retail chain, (in thousands):

	January 26 1996	January 28 1995
Inventories	$44,619	$36,788

Required

The income statement for the fiscal year included the item "cost of sales" of $124,781. Compute the net cost of the acquisition of inventory for the 1996 fiscal year.

8-62   Detailed Income Statement

(Alternate is 8-43.) Hartmarx Corporation is a clothing company with many retail outlets, including Country Miss and Kuppenheimer. The company's annual report contained the following actual data for the year ended November 30, 19X1 (in thousands):

Net sales	$1,310,126
Cost of goods sold	806,237
Selling, administrative, and occupancy expenses	492,147
Other expenses (net)	106,552
Profit (or loss) before tax	$ (94,810)

The balance sheets included the following actual data (in thousands of dollars):

	November 30	
	19X1	19X0
Allowance for doubtful accounts	$ 13,980	$ 12,755
Inventories	409,599	473,999

Consider the following additional assumed data (in thousands of dollars):

Bad debts expense	$ 5,400	Freight in	$ 32,000
Gross purchases	737,837	Advertising expense	29,000
Cash discounts on sales	10,000	Sales returns and allowances	35,000
Sales salaries and compensation	279,747	Amortization expense	26,000
Purchase returns and allowances	24,000	Cash discounts on purchases	4,000
		Rent expense	100,000
Freight out	52,000	Miscellaneous other expenses (net)	106,552

Required   Prepare a detailed multistep income statement that ends with profit (or loss) before tax. You need not subclassify the selling, administrative, and occupancy expenses into three separate categories.

8-63 Comparison of Inventory Methods

(Alternates are 8-46 and 8-65.) Unisys Corporation is a producer of computer-based information systems. The following actual data and descriptions are from the company's fiscal 1993 annual report (in millions):

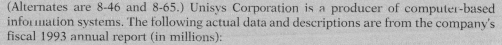

Unisys Corp.
www.unisys.com/

	December 31	
	1993	1992
Inventories	$753.9	$873.8

A footnote states: "Inventories are valued at the lower of cost or market. Cost is determined principally on the first-in, first-out method."

The income statement for the fiscal year ended December 31, 1993 included (in millions):

Net revenue from sales, service, and maintenance	$7,742.5
Cost of products sold, service, and maintenance	4,844.3

Assume that Unisys used the periodic inventory system. Suppose a division of Unisys had the accompanying data regarding the use of its computer parts that it acquires and resells to customers for maintaining equipment (dollars are *not* in millions):

	Units	Total
Inventory (December 31, 1993)	100	$ 400
Purchase (February 20, 1994)	200	1,000
Sales, March 17, 1994 (at $9 per unit)	150	
Purchase (June 25, 1994)	160	960
Sales, November 7, 1994 (at $10 per unit)	160	

Required

1. For these computer parts only, prepare a tabulation of the cost of goods sold section of the income statement for the year ended December 31, 1994. Support your computations. Round totals to the nearest dollar. Show your tabulation for four different inventory methods: (a) FIFO, (b) LIFO, (c) weighted-average, and (d) specific identification.

   For requirement *d*, assume that the purchase of February 20 was identified with the sale of March 17. Also assume that the purchase of June 25 was identified with the sale of November 7; the additional units sold were identified with the beginning inventory.

2. By how much would income taxes differ if Unisys used (a) LIFO instead of FIFO for this inventory item? (b) LIFO instead of weighted-average? Assume a 40% tax rate. Assume that LIFO is acceptable for income tax purposes.

8-64 Effects of Late Purchases

(Alternates are 8-47 and 8-66.) Refer to the preceding problem. Suppose Unisys acquired 60 extra units @ $7 each on December 29, 1994, a total of $420. How would gross profit and income taxes be affected under FIFO? That is, compare FIFO results before and after the purchase of 60 extra units. Under LIFO? That is, compare LIFO results before and after the purchase of 60 extra units. Show computations and explain.

8-65 Comparison of Inventory Methods

(Alternates are 8-46 and 8-63.) Texas Instruments is a major producer of semiconductors and other electrical and electronic products. Semiconductors are especially vulnerable to price fluctuations. The following actual data and descriptions are from the company's annual report (in millions):

Texas Instruments
www.ti.com

	December 31	
	1994	1993
Inventories	$882	$822

Texas Instruments uses a variety of inventory methods, but for this problem assume that only FIFO is used.

Net revenues for the fiscal year ended December 31, 1994 were $10,315 million. Cost of revenues was $7,471 million.

Assume that Texas Instruments had the accompanying data regarding one of its semiconductors. Assume a periodic inventory system.

	In	Out	Balance
December 31, 1993			80 @ $5 = 400
February 25, 1994	50 @ $6 = $ 300		
March 29		60* @ ?	
May 28	80 @ $7 = $ 560		
June 7		90* @ ?	
November 20	90 @ $8 = $ 720		
December 15		50* @ ?	
Total	220 $1,580	200	
December 31, 1994			100 @ ?

* Selling prices were $9, $11, and $13, respectively:

60	@ $ 9 =	$ 540
90	@ 11 =	990
50	@ 13 =	650
Total sales	200	$2,180

Summary of costs to account for:

Beginning inventory	$ 400
Purchases	1,580
Cost of goods available for sale	$1,980
Other expenses for this product	$ 500
Income tax rate, 40%	

Required

1. Prepare a comparative income statement for the 1994 fiscal year for the product in question. Use the FIFO, LIFO, and weighted-average inventory methods.
2. By how much would income taxes have differed if Texas Instruments had used LIFO instead of FIFO for this product? Assume that LIFO is acceptable for income tax purposes.
3. Suppose Texas Instruments had used the specific identification method. Compute the gross margin (or gross profit) if the ending inventory had consisted of (a) 90 units @ $8, and 10 units @ $7; and (b) 60 units @ $5, and 40 units @ $8.

8-66   Effects of Late Purchases

(Alternates are 8-47 and 8-64.) Refer to the preceding problem. Suppose Texas Instruments had acquired 50 extra units @ $8 each on December 30, 1994, a total of $400. How would income before income taxes have been affected under FIFO? That is, compare FIFO results before and after the purchase of 50 extra units. Under LIFO? That is, compare LIFO results before and after the purchase of 50 extra units. Show computations and explain.

8-67   Inventory Errors

IBM had inventories of $8.3 billion at December 31, 1993 and $9.2 billion one year earlier.

Required

1. Suppose the beginning inventory for fiscal 1993 had been overstated by $50 million because of errors in physical counts. Which items in the financial statements would be incorrect? By how much? Use O for overstated, U for understated, and N for not affected. Assume a 40% tax rate.

	Effect on Fiscal Year	
	1993	**1992**
Beginning inventory	O by $50	N
Ending inventory	?	?
Cost of sales	?	?
Gross profit	?	?
Income before taxes on income	?	?
Taxes on income	?	?
Net income	?	?

2. What is the dollar effect of the inventory error on retained earnings at the end of fiscal 1992? 1993?

8-68   Comparison of Gross Profit Percentages and Inventory Turnover
Dofasco and Stelco are competitors in the steel manufacturing industry. The gross margin for each company and average inventory appear below for the indicated years (both have December year ends).

Dofasco

	1996	**1995**	**1994**
	(in millions)		
Sales	2,942	2,636	2,425
Cost of sales	2,317	2,047	1,936
Gross profit	625	589	489
Average inventory	734	687	592

Stelco

	1996	**1995**	**1994**
	(in millions)		
Sales	2,941	2,926	2,916
Cost of Sales	2,480	2,369	2,388
Gross profit	461	557	528
Average inventory	582	528	475

Required   Calculate gross profit percentages and inventory turnovers for 1994, 1995, and 1996 for each company and compare them. What trends do you observe? Which company appears to perform better? To what extent do their different performances seem to relate to their relative positions in the retail market?

8-69   Hudson's Bay Company Annual Report
Refer to the Hudson's Bay Company financial statements in Appendix A.

Required   **1.** Assume that the Hudson's Bay Company cost of sales in 1997 was $4,800,000,000. Compute the amount of merchandise inventory purchased during fiscal 1997. (Hint: Use the inventory T-account.)
2. Compute the 1997 inventory turnover for the Hudson's Bay Company.
3. Calculate the operating profit margin percentage during 1996 and 1997 for each of the Bay and Zellers. Comment on any changes and differences.

8-70   Annual Report Disclosure
Select a company's annual report of your choice.

Required   **1.** Identify the inventory accounting method used.
2. Calculate gross profit percentages and inventory turnovers for any two years reported. Comment on any trends.

9 Long-Lived Assets and Amortization

Learning Objectives

After studying this chapter, you should be able to

1 Distinguish between tangible and intangible assets, and explain how the costs of each are charged.

2 Measure the acquisition cost of tangible assets such as land, buildings, and equipment.

3 Compute amortization for buildings and equipment using various amortization methods.

4 Differentiate financial statement amortization from income tax capital cost allowance.

5 Explain how amortization does not affect cash flow.

6 Discuss changes in estimates and timing of acquisition.

7 Distinguish expenses from expenditures that should be capitalized.

8 Compute gains and losses on disposal of fixed assets.

9 Explain how to account for depletion of natural resources.

10 Describe how to account for various intangible assets.

This chapter shows how to account for long-lived assets. It discusses the differences in accounting for various kinds of assets—land, buildings and equipment, natural resources, and intangible assets. The main issue is when to charge the cost of a long-lived asset as an expense on the income statement. For example, if an asset lasts ten years, how much of its cost should be assigned to each of the ten years it is used?

Long-lived assets are especially significant for companies with large capital investments. Consider the plant and equipment in the balance sheets of the following companies (in millions):

Imperial Oil
www.imperialoil.ca/

Company	Total Assets	Plant and Equipment	
		Total	*Percentage*
Bank of Montreal	$169,832	$1,867	17%
Imperial Oil	12,052	8,170	68
Canadian Tire	2,669	972	36

Imperial Oil invests heavily in plant and equipment. Canadian Tire, like many retailers, has more investment in inventories than in long-lived assets. Finally, banks such as Bank of Montreal have primarily financial assets and relatively minor plant and equipment.

Much of this chapter focuses on amortization (depreciation)—both understanding the nature of amortization and learning about the various amortization methods. Companies in Canada freely choose amortization methods. In contrast, in countries such as Japan, Germany, and France, amortization methods are specified by government (tax) authorities.

long-lived assets
Resources that are held for an extended time, such as land, buildings, equipment, natural resources, and patents.

tangible assets (fixed assets, capital assets)
Physical items that can be seen and touched, such as land, natural resources, buildings, and equipment.

intangible assets
Rights or economic benefits, such as franchises, patents, trademarks, copyrights, and goodwill, that are not physical in nature.

■ OVERVIEW OF LONG-LIVED ASSETS

Most business entities hold such major assets as land, buildings, equipment, natural resources, and patents. These resources are described as **long-lived assets** because they provide benefits for an extended time. These assets facilitate the production and sale of goods or services to customers. They are not available for sale in the ordinary course of business. Thus a delivery truck is a long-lived asset for nearly all companies. However, a truck dealer would regard trucks as merchandise inventory.

Tangible and Intangible Assets

Long-lived assets are often divided into tangible and intangible categories. **Tangible assets** (also called **fixed assets** or **capital assets**) are physical items that can be seen and touched. Examples are land, natural resources, buildings, and equipment. In contrast, **intangible assets** are rights or economic benefits, such as franchises, patents, trademarks, copyrights, and goodwill that are not physical in nature.

Land is unique in that it does not wear out or become obsolete. Therefore, it is reported in the financial records at its historical cost. Other long-lived assets may be used up, worn out, or become obsolete, so accountants charge their historical cost to expense over the period of time during which the firm

Balance Sheet	Income Statement
Land ————————————▶	—
Buildings and equipment ——————▶	Amortization or Depreciation
Natural resources ———————▶	Depletion
Intangible assets (for example, franchises or patents) ——▶	Amortization

amortization The systematic reduction of a lump-sum amount. When referring to long-lived assets, it usually means the allocation of the costs of such assets to the periods that benefit from these assets.

depletion The process of allocating the cost of natural resources to the period in which the resources are used.

benefits from their use. The word **amortization** is the general term that means the systematic reduction of a lump-sum amount and it might be used to describe any allocation of the acquisition cost of long-lived assets to the time periods of their use. In practice different words are used to describe the allocation of costs over time. For tangible assets such as buildings, machinery, and equipment, the allocation is frequently called amortization. For natural resources the allocation is called **depletion**. By convention, *amortization* is typically used to refer to the allocation of the costs of intangible assets to the periods that benefit from these assets. These terms are summarized in Exhibit 9-1.

Companies maintain carefully detailed records of their long-lived assets and of the accumulated depreciation, depletion and amortization of those assets over time. However, when the financial results are reported to shareholders, only summary totals are shown for large classes of assets and all of the accumulated depreciation, depletion, and amortization is typically shown in one total. An example of the reporting of long-lived assets is shown in the following excerpt from Magna's annual report:

Magna International Inc.
Fixed Assets
(in millions)

	1995	1994
Land	$ 105.0	$ 80.6
Buildings	370.5	252.4
Machinery and equipment	1,466.6	1,201.4
	1,942.1	1,534.4
Accumulated depreciation	739.2	608.8
	1,202.9	925.6
Deferred preproduction costs [net		14.4
of accumulated amortization]	$1,202.9	$ 940.0

■ ACQUISITION COST OF TANGIBLE ASSETS

The acquisition cost of all long-lived assets is their cash-equivalent purchase price, including incidental costs required to obtain title, to transport the asset, and to prepare it for use.

Land

The acquisition cost of land includes charges to the purchaser for the cost of land surveys, legal fees, title fees, realtors' commissions, transfer taxes, and even the demolition costs of old structures that might be torn down to get the land ready for its intended use. Under historical-cost accounting, land is carried indefinitely at its original cost. After many years of persistent inflation, its carrying amount is likely to be far below its current market value.

Should land acquired and held since 1936 be placed on a 1996 balance sheet at cost expressed in 1936 dollars? Accountants do exactly that. For example, Weyerhaeuser lists 5.9 million acres of land at $125 million (only $21 per acre). Critics of the basic historical-cost framework of accounting claim that some type of accounting for inflation should be mandatory. Inflation adjustment is common in many countries where double-digit inflation rates are the norm.

Buildings and Equipment

Unlike land, buildings and equipment wear out or become obsolete. In other words, the services provided by buildings and equipment are consumed. Amortization recognizes the consumption of these services. The cost of buildings, plant, and equipment should include all costs of acquisition and preparation for use. Consider the following example for some used packaging equipment:

Invoice price, gross	$100,000
Deduct 2% cash discount for payment within 30 days	2,000
Invoice price, net	$ 98,000
Provincial sales tax at 8% of $98,000	7,840
Transportation costs	3,000
Installation costs	8,000
Repair costs prior to use	7,000
Total acquisition cost	$123,840

capitalized A cost that is added to an asset account, as distinguished from being expensed immediately.

The $123,840 would be the total *capitalized cost* added to the Equipment account. A cost is described as being **capitalized** when it is added to an asset account, as distinguished from being "expensed" immediately. Note that ordinary repair costs incurred *after* equipment is being used are expensed.

Under GAAP, interest cost is usually an expense. However, interest on expenditures during an extended construction period should be added to the acquisition cost of the fixed asset under construction. Suppose a $2 million plant were constructed over two years. If no construction payments were made before the plant was completed, no interest would be capitalized. However, suppose $1 million were paid at the end of the first year, and $1 million at completion. Assume the interest rate on recent borrowing was 12%. Interest of $1,000,000 × 0.12 = $120,000 would be part of the capitalized cost of the plant.

basket purchase The acquisition of two or more types of assets for a lump-sum cost.

Frequently, companies acquire more than one type of long-lived asset for a single overall outlay. For instance, suppose a company acquires land and a building for $1 million. The acquisition of two or more types of assets for a lump-sum cost is sometimes called a **basket purchase**. How much of the $1 million should the company allocate to land and how much to the building? Invariably, the cost is allocated in proportion to some estimate of relative sales value for the land and the building as separate items. For example, if an appraiser indicates that the market value of the land is $480,000 and of the building $720,000, the cost would be allocated as follows:

	(1) Appraised Value	(2) Weighting	(3) Total Cost To Allocate	(2) × (3) Allocated Costs
Land	$ 480,000	480/1,200 (or 40%)	$1,000,000	$ 400,000
Building	720,000	720/1,200 (or 60%)	1,000,000	600,000
Total	$1,200,000			$1,000,000

Objective 3

Compute amortization for buildings and equipment using various amortization methods.

Allocating a basket purchase cost to the individual assets can significantly affect future reported income if the useful lives of various assets differ. In our example, if less cost is allocated to the land, more cost is allocated to the building, which is depreciable. In turn, amortization expenses are higher, operating income is lower, and fewer income taxes are paid. Within the bounds of the law, tax-conscious managers load as much cost as possible on depreciable assets rather than on land.

■ AMORTIZATION (DEPRECIATION) METHODS

Amortization is a key factor distinguishing accrual accounting from cash-basis accounting. Suppose a long-lived asset is purchased for cash. Cash-basis accounting would recognize the entire cost of the asset when it is purchased. In contrast, accrual accounting allocates the cost in the form of amortization over the periods the asset is used.

depreciable value
The amount of the acquisition cost to be allocated as amortization over the total useful life of an asset. It is the difference between the total acquisition cost and the predicted residual value.

Equipment and similar long-lived assets are initially recorded at *cost*. The major accounting difficulties centre on the choice of a pattern of amortization—that is, the allocation of the original cost to the particular periods that benefit from the use of assets. Amortization is frequently misunderstood. It is *not* a process of *valuation*. In everyday use, we might say that an auto depreciates in value, meaning a decrease in its current market value. But to an accountant, amortization or depreciation is *not* a technique for approximating current values such as replacement costs or resale values. It is simply *cost allocation*.

The amount of the acquisition cost to be allocated over the total useful life of the asset as amortization is the **depreciable value**. It is the difference between the total acquisition cost and the predicted *residual value*. The **residual value** is the amount received from disposal of a long-lived asset at the end of its useful life. Synonyms for residual value are **terminal value**, **disposal value**, **salvage value**, and **scrap value**.

residual value (terminal value, disposal value, salvage value, scrap value)
The amount received from disposal of a long-lived asset at the end of its useful life.

useful life (economic life) The time period over which an asset is amortized.

Amortization allocates the depreciable value to the income statement during the **useful life** (or **economic life**) of the asset. The useful life, the time period over which an asset is amortized, is determined as the shorter of the physical life of the asset before it wears out or the economic life of the asset before it is obsolete. Given the rapidly increasing speed and decreasing cost of computers in recent times, most companies replace them long before they wear out. That is, their economic life is shorter than their physical life. Sometimes an asset's life is measured directly in terms of the benefit it provides rather than the time period over which it is used. For example, the useful life of a truck might be measured as the total kilometres to be driven. This might be 100,000 or 200,000 kilometres. If a truck were purchased for $500,000, the amortization would be $.50 per mile if it was expected to last 100,000 kilometres with no salvage value.

amortization schedule The listing of amortization amounts for each year of an asset's useful life.

A list of amortization amounts for each year of an asset's useful life is called an **amortization schedule**. We will use the following symbols and amounts to compare various amortization schedules:

Symbols	Amounts for Illustration
Let	
C = total acquisition cost on December 31, 19X2	$41,000
R = residual value	$ 1,000
n = useful life (in years or kilometres)	4 years; 200,000 kilometres
D = amount of amortization (or depreciation)	Various

Straight-Line Depreciation

straight-line depreciation A method that spreads the depreciable value evenly over the useful life of an asset.

Straight-line depreciation spreads the depreciable value evenly over the useful life of an asset. It is by far the most popular method for corporate reporting to shareholders. It is used by almost 90% of major companies for at least part of their fixed assets, and 50% use it exclusively.

Exhibit 9-2 shows how the asset would be displayed in the balance sheet if a straight-line method of amortization were used. The annual amortization expense that would appear on the income statement is:

$$\text{Amortization expense} = \frac{\text{Acquisition cost} - \text{Residual value}}{\text{Years of useful life}}$$

$$= \frac{C - R}{n}$$

$$= \frac{\$41,000 - \$1,000}{4} = \$10,000 \text{ per year}$$

Amortization Based on Units

unit depreciation A method based on units of service when physical wear and tear is the dominating influence on the useful life of the asset.

When physical wear and tear is the dominating influence on the useful life of the asset, accountants often base amortization on *units of service* or *units of production* rather than on the units of time (years) so commonly used. Amortization based on units of service is called **unit depreciation**. Suppose the asset in our example were a large truck with a useful life of 200,000 kilometres. Amortization computed on a kilometres basis is:

$$D = \frac{C - R}{n}$$

$$= \frac{\$41,000 - \$1,000}{200,000 \text{ kilometres}}$$

$$= \$.20 \text{ per kilometre}$$

For some assets, such as transportation equipment, this amortization pattern may have more logical appeal than the straight-line method. However, the unit depreciation method is not widely used, probably for two major reasons:

1. Straight-line depreciation frequently produces approximately the same yearly amortization amounts.
2. Straight-line depreciation is easier because the entire amortization schedule can be set at the time of acquisition, and detailed records of units of service are not necessary.

Exhibit 9-2
Straight Line
Depreciation
Schedule

| | Balances at End of Year | | | |
	1	2	3	4
Plant and equipment (at original acquisition cost)	$41,000	$41,000	$41,000	$41,000
Less: Accumulated amortization (the portion of original cost that has already been charged to operations as expense)	10,000	20,000	30,000	40,000
Net book value (the portion of original cost that will be charged to future operations as expense)	$31,000	$21,000	$11,000	$ 1,000

A commonly encountered example of unit depreciation relates to the use of mining equipment. Instead of writing such costs off on a time basis, most mining companies depreciate the equipment costs at a rate per tonne of minerals extracted.

Double-Declining-Balance Depreciation

Any pattern of amortization that writes off depreciable costs more quickly than the ordinary straight-line method based on expected useful life is called **accelerated depreciation**. Although an infinite number of accelerated amortization methods are possible, the most popular form of accelerated amortization is the **double-declining-balance (DDB)** method, which is also referred to as declining-balance depreciation. DDB is computed as follows:

1. Compute a rate by dividing 100% by the years of useful life. This result is the straight-line rate. Then double the rate.[1] In our example, the straight-line rate is 100% ÷ 4 years = 25%. The DDB rate would be 2 × 25%, or 50%.
2. To compute the amortization for any year, ignore the residual value and multiply the beginning book value for the year by the DDB rate.

accelerated depreciation Any amortization method that writes off depreciable costs more quickly than the ordinary straight-line method based on expected useful life.

double-declining-balance depreciation (DDB) The most popular form of accelerated amortization. It is computed by doubling the straight-line rate and multiplying the resulting DDB rate by the beginning book value.

The DDB method can be illustrated as follows:

$$\text{DDB rate} = 2 \times (100\% \div n)$$
$$\text{DDB rate, 4-year life} = 2 \times (100\% \div 4) = 50\%$$
$$\text{DDB depreciation} = \text{DDB rate} \times \text{Beginning book value}$$

For year 1: D = .50 ($41,000)
= $20,500
For year 2: D = .50 ($41,000 − $20,500)
= $10,250
For year 3: D = .50 [$41,000 − ($20,500 + $10,250)]
= $5,125
For year 4: D = .50 [$41,000 − ($35,875)]
= $2,563

Cumulative 3-year total = $35,875

[1] *Double*-declining-balance requires doubling the rate. Other declining-balance methods use other multiples. For instance, 150% declining-balance requires the straight-line rate to be multiplied by 1.5.

regardless of actual use. Further, suppose the benefit from using an asset is the same each period. The matching principle would require that the cost be spread equally to all periods.

Proponents of accelerated amortization for shareholder reporting maintain that it is the more conservative option. They also point out that the full cost of using an asset includes amortization *plus* repairs and maintenance. They claim that accelerated methods record high amortization charges initially when repair and maintenance costs are low. Then amortization charges fall as repair and mainte- nance costs rise, keeping the full cost of using the asset relatively stable over its life.

■ AMORTIZATION AND CASH FLOW

Objective 5

Explain how amor- tization does not affect cash flow.

Too often, the relationships between amortization expense, income tax expense, cash, and accumulated amortization are confused. For example, the business press frequently contains misleading quotations such as "... we're look- ing for financing $3.75 billion. Of that, about 60% will be recovered in depreci- ation and amortization." As another example, consider a *Business Week* news report concerning an airline company: "And with a hefty boost from amortiza- tion and the sale of $6 million worth of property, its cash balance rose by $10 million in the year's first quarter."

These statements imply that amortization somehow generates cash. It does not. Amortization simply allocates the original cost of an asset to the periods in which the asset is used, nothing more and nothing less. Accumulated amortization is a summation of the amounts of the original cost already written off to expense in prior periods. Thus accumulated amortization is *not* a pile of cash waiting to be used.

Effects of Amortization on Cash

To illustrate that amortization does not generate cash, consider Acme Service Company, which began business with cash and common stock equity of $100,000. On the same day, equipment was acquired for $40,000 cash. The equipment had an expected four-year life and zero predicted residual value. The first year's oper- ations generated cash sales of $103,000 and cash operating expenses of $53,000. These facts are depicted visually below, and in Exhibit 9-4. Straight-line deprecia- tion in Panel I is ¼ × $40,000 = $10,000. Accelerated depreciation (double- declining-balance) in Panel II for the first year is 2 × 25% × $40,000 = $20,000.

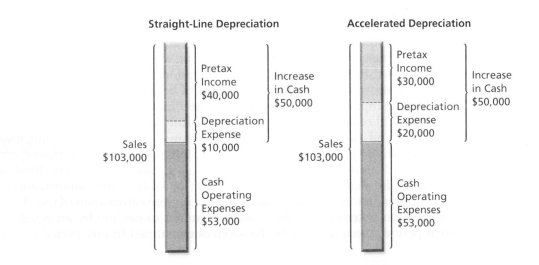

Exhibit 9-4 Acme Service Company   Analysis of Transactions (in thousands of dollars)

	A			= L	+ SE	
	Cash	+ Equipment	− Accumulated Depreciation	= Liabilities	+ Paid-in Capital	+ Retained Earnings
Panel I. STRAIGHT-LINE DEPRECIATION						
Initial investment	+ 100			=	+ 100	
Acquisition	− 40	+ 40		=		
Cash sales	+ 103			=		+ 103 Sales
Cash operating expenses	− 53			=		− 53 Expense
Depreciation, Year 1			− 10	=		− 10 Expense
Ia. Bal. Dec. 31 before taxes	+ 110	+ 40	− 10	=	+ 100	+ 40
Income taxes (40% of 30)	− 12			=		− 12 Expense
Ib. Bal. Dec. 31 after taxes	+ 98	+ 40	− 10	=	+ 100	+ 28
Panel II. ACCELERATED DEPRECIATION						
Initial investment	+ 100			=	+ 100	
Acquisition	− 40	+ 40		=		
Cash sales	+ 103			=		+ 103 Sales
Cash operating expenses	− 53			=		− 53 Expense
Depreciation, Year 1			− 20	=		− 20 Expense
IIa. Bal. Dec. 31 before taxes	+ 110	+ 40	− 20	=	+ 100	+ 30
Income taxes (40% of 30)	− 12			=		− 12 Expense
IIb. Bal. Dec. 31 after taxes	+ 98	+ 40	− 20	=	+ 100	+ 18
Panel III. SUMMARY						
BEFORE TAX BALANCES, DEC 31						
Line Ia. Straight Line	+ 110	+ 40	− 10		+ 100	+ 40
Line IIa. Accelerated	+ 110	+ 40	−	20	+ 100	+ 30
Change	0	0	− 10		0	− 10
AFTER TAX BALANCES, DEC 31						
Line Ib. Straight Line	+ 98	+ 40	− 10		+ 100	+ 28
Line IIb. Accelerated	+ 98	+ 40	− 20		+ 100	+ 18
Change	+ 0	0	− 10		0	− 10

Focus first on the December 31 balances before taxes in Exhibit 9-4, denoted Ia. and IIa. Comparing the before-tax amounts stresses the role of amortization expense most vividly. At year end, the cash balance *before taxes* is $110,000, regardless of the amortization method used. Before taxes, changes in the amortization method affect only the accumulated amortization and retained earnings accounts. The before-tax ending cash balances are completely unaffected. Panel III shows the before-tax equality of cash in summary form.

Consider next the effect of amortization on the before-tax income statement. The relevant amounts are in the last column of Exhibit 9-4, but the first two columns of Exhibit 9-5 present the same numbers in a more useful format. The cash provided by operations before income taxes is $50,000, regardless of the amortization method used. Pretax income under straight-line differs from that under accelerated amortization only because of differences in the noncash amortization expense.

Suppose amortization were $40,000. Before reading on, compute the pretax income and increase in cash. You should have obtained pretax income of only $10,000. However, the increase in cash remains at $50,000. Why? Because cash received from sales is $103,000 and cash expenses are $53,000, leaving $50,000 cash provided by operations.

	Income Statement and Statement of Changes in Financial Position for the Year Ended December 31, 19X1			
Exhibit 9-5	**Acme Service Company** (in thousands)			
	Before Taxes		**After Taxes**	
	Straight- Line Depreciation	*Accelerated Depreciation*	*Straight- Line Depreciation*	*Accelerated Depreciation*
Panel I. INCOME STATEMENT				
Sales	$103	$103	$103	$103
Operating expenses	53	53	53	53
Depreciation expense	10	20	10	20
Pretax income	40	30	40	30
Income tax expense (40% of 30)	—	—	12	12
Net income	$ 40	$ 30	$ 28	$ 18
Panel II. STATEMENT OF CHANGES IN FINANCIAL POSITION				
Cash collections	$103	$103	$103	$103
Cash operating expenses	53	53	53	53
Cash tax payments	—	—	12	12
Cash provided by operations*	$ 50	$ 50	$ 38	$ 38

* Sometimes called cash flow from operations or just cash flow. But it is usually simply called cash provided by operations, which is typically defined as cash collected on sales (a) less all operating expenses requiring cash and (b) less income taxes.

Effects of Amortization on Income Taxes

As accounting amortization is not deductible for income tax purposes, but capital cost allowance is allowed, the amount of amortization has no effect on taxable income. The amount of income taxes that a company must pay in cash is dependent upon taxable income. Thus the amortization method has no effect on income taxes and the cash payments.

Assume that capital cost allowance is 20, the same as for accelerated depreciation, then taxable income would be 30 and income taxes would be 12 for each depreciation method. Thus, from the first column of Exhibit 9-4, or the last two columns of Exhibit 9-5, we see that the cash balances are the same under either amortization method.

OTHER FACTORS AFFECTING AMORTIZATION

Changes in Amortization Estimates

Objective 6

Discuss changes in estimates and timing of acquisition.

Actual useful lives and residual values are seldom exactly equal to their predicted amounts. If the differences are material, how should we adjust the affected accounts? Consider the example of the $41,000 asset with a $1,000 residual value. Use the straight-line method. Suppose it is the beginning of Year 3. The firm's economists and engineers have altered their expectations; the asset's new expected useful life is five instead of four years. Moreover, the new expected residual value is $3,000 instead of $1,000. There are two ways to incorporate this new information into the amortization schedules, the *prospective* and *retroactive* methods.

Amortization Calculation	Original	Retroactive (Adjust Past)	Prospective (Change Future)
Cost	$41,000	$41,000	$41,000
Useful life	4 years	5 years	5 years
Residual value	$ 1,000	$ 3,000	$ 3,000
Straight-line depreciation per year:			
Old, $40,000 ÷ 4	$10,000		
New, retroactively*		$ 7,600	
New, prospectively			
First 2 years			$10,000
Last 3 years			$ 6,000

*($41,000 – $3,000) ÷ 5 = $7,600

These modifications to predictions are "changes in accounting estimates." GAAP requires that they be accounted for "prospectively" rather than "retroactively," in the sense that the records through Year 2 would not be adjusted. Instead, the *remaining* depreciable amount would be written off over the new *remaining* useful life:

Book value at end of Year 2 (beginning of Year 3): Cost less accumulated amortization	$41,000 – 2 ($10,000) = $21,000
Revised residual value	3,000
Revised depreciable amount	$18,000
Divide by remaining useful life in years, ÷ 3	
New straight-line depreciation per year	$ 6,000

Critics of the foregoing "prospective" method assert that it misstates the yearly amortization throughout the entire life of the asset. That is, amortization in early years is overstated and in later years is understated. This can be illustrated by comparing the prospective method in our example with the retroactive method (which uses perfect hindsight):

Year	Original	Prospective Method	Retroactive Method
1	$10,000	$10,000	$ 7,600
2	10,000	10,000	7,600
3	10,000	6,000	7,600
4	10,000	6,000	7,600
5	—	6,000	7,600
	$40,000	$38,000	$38,000

Although the retroactive method correctly matches expenses and revenues, it requires restating the accounts of prior periods, a procedure that many accountants oppose. The critics argue that the past accounting was as accurate as possible given the knowledge then existing. They fear that users of financial reports would be confused by frequent restatement and would lose confidence in financial statements that were often "corrected" after being issued. Therefore, GAAP requires that "a change in estimate should not be accounted for by restating amounts reported in financial statements of prior periods."

Amortization for Parts of a Year

Assets are rarely acquired exactly at the start of a year or a month. To simplify recordkeeping, various assumptions are made about amortization within the year. Each assumption must be reasonable and be consistently applied. For example, one of two methods might be used to determine when certain specified assets are placed in service:

1. *Half-year convention.* Treat all assets placed in service during the year as if they had been placed in service at the year's midpoint.
2. *Modified half-year convention.* Treat each asset placed in service during the first half of a year as if it had been placed in service on the first day of that year. Treat each asset placed in service during the last half of the year as if it had been placed in service on the first day of the *following* year.
3. *Monthly.* Record amortization for the portion of year in service using the number of months divided by 12 as a portion of a full-year of amortization expense.

Suppose our $41,000 asset had been acquired on October 1, 19X1, and DDB depreciation method was used. As shown on page 385, the amortization for the first year of use would be $20,500 and for the second year would be $10,250. Assume that the company's fiscal year and calendar year are the same and that amortization is to be included for the full month of October. The amortization schedule could appear as follows (in thousands of dollars):

Asset Year	Modified DDB Amortization from Page 385	Allocation to Each Calendar Year				
		19X1	19X2	19X3	19X4	19X5
1	20,500	5,125*	15,375†			
2	10,250		2,563	7,687		
3	5,125			1,281	3,844	
4	4,125				1,031	3,094
	40,000	5,125	17,938	8,968	4,875	3,094

* 3/12 of Year 1's amortization affects 19X1
† 9/12 of Year 1's amortization affects 19X2

For interim reporting, yearly amortization is usually spread uniformly *within* a given fiscal year (an equal amount for each month), regardless of whether straight-line or accelerated depreciation is used to compute the total amount for the year. The monthly statements in October, November, and December, 19X1 would each have amortization expense of $5,125 ÷ 3 = $1,708. In turn, the monthly statements of 19X2 would each have amortization expense of $17,938 ÷ 12 = $1,495.

■ EXPENSES VERSUS EXPENDITURES

expenditures The purchases of goods or services, whether for cash or on credit.

Expenditures are defined by accountants as the purchases of goods or services, whether for cash or on credit. Asset-related expenditures that are expected to benefit more than the current accounting year are *capitalized* (that is, added to an asset account) and are sometimes called *capital expenditures*. Such capital expenditures generally add new fixed assets or increase the capacity, efficiency, or useful life of an existing fixed asset. Expenditures deemed to have a life of one year or less are charged as *expenses* in the current year.

All expenditures eventually become expenses. Expenditures benefiting the current period are matched with current revenues and therefore become expenses in the current period. Expenditures that are capitalized benefit *future* revenues, and they are charged as expenses over future periods.

The Decision to Capitalize

Objective 7

Distinguish expenses from expenditures that should be capitalized.

The decision whether to capitalize an expenditure is often subjective. Auditors from both the public accounting firms and the income tax authorities regularly investigate whether a given outlay should be capitalized or expensed. For example, is an engine repair properly classified as an asset or an expense? The public accountant (who tends to prefer conservatism) is usually on the alert for any tendencies to understate current expenses through the unjustified charging of a repair to an asset account. In contrast, the income tax auditor is looking for the unjustified charging to an expense account (which provides an immediate income tax deduction).

Wherever doubt exists, there is a general tendency in practice to charge an expense rather than an asset account for repairs, parts, and similar items. First, many of these expenditures are minor, so the cost-benefit test of recordkeeping (the concept of materiality) justifies such action. Setting up an asset account and an amortization schedule is not worth the cost. For instance, many companies have a policy of charging to expense all expenditures that are less than a specified minimum such as $100, $500, or $1,000. Second, there is the temptation of an immediate deduction for income tax purposes (if, indeed, the deductions are allowable as reasonable expenses).

To Capitalize or Not to Capitalize

Late in the afternoon on St. Patrick's Day, 1992, Chambers Development Company, a rapidly growing waste-management firm, announced that it was changing the way it accounted for certain costs associated with landfill development. Instead of capitalizing indirect costs associated with landfill projects and listing them with the assets on the balance sheet, Chambers announced that it would follow industry practice and report those expenditures as expenses of the period in which they were incurred. The change had the effect of reducing reported income for 1991 from $49.9 million to $1.5 million.

To some observers, an accounting decision such as what to capitalize and what to charge immediately to expense is not very interesting. However, shareholders of Chambers Development soon became extremely interested. Chambers Development's stock price dropped from $30.50 to $11.50 the day after the announcement, a fall of 62%.

Chambers Development's management defended the change, maintaining that the capitalization in previous years had been warranted because Chambers had been a company in development. Now as an operating company, expensing seemed appropriate. At issue were costs such as the salaries of executives for that portion of their time spent on developing new landfills. Also in question were the company's costs related to the public relations and legal aspects of the landfills. The firm's auditor approved both the previous method and the change. In fact, speculation arose that the auditor *forced* the change because the amount of capitalized development costs had become so large that the amounts did not realistically represent costs that would be recovered in the future. Therefore the costs did not qualify as assets.

There is no easy answer as to what should be capitalized. Chambers spent millions to gain landfill permits, and there certainly is value to such permits. However, many accountants favour a conservative approach that recognizes all questionable items as expenses as soon as possible. The one thing that is clear is that decisions to capitalize expenditures can greatly affect shareholders. ∎

Source: G. Stern and L. P. Cohen, "Chambers Development Switches Accounting Plan," Wall Street Journal (March 19, 1992), p. B4.

Repairs and Maintenance Versus Capital Improvements

Repairs and maintenance costs are necessary to maintain a fixed asset in operating condition. The costs of repairs and maintenance are usually compiled in a single account and are regarded as expenses of the current period. *Repairs* are sometimes distinguished from *maintenance* as follows. *Repairs* include the occasional costs of restoring a fixed asset to its ordinary operating condition after breakdowns, accidents, or damage. *Maintenance* includes the routine recurring costs of oiling, polishing, painting, and adjusting. However, accountants spend little effort distinguishing between repairs and maintenance expenditures since both are period costs.

improvement (betterment, capital improvement) An expenditure that is intended to add to the future benefits from an existing fixed asset.

On the other hand, an **improvement** (sometimes called a **betterment** or a **capital improvement**) is an expenditure that is intended to add to the future benefits from an existing fixed asset by decreasing its operating cost, increasing its rate of output, or prolonging its useful life. An improvement differs from repairs and maintenance because the latter helps ensure a level of current benefits but does not enlarge the expected future benefits. Improvements are generally *capitalized*. Examples of capital improvements or betterments include the rehabilitation of an apartment house that will allow increased rents and the rebuilding of a packaging machine that increases its speed or extends its useful life.

In Exhibit 9-2 (p. 385), suppose that at the start of Year 3 a major overhaul costing $7,000 occurred. If this is judged to extend the useful life from four to five years, the required accounting would be:

1. Increase the book value of the asset (now $41,000 – $20,000 = $21,000) by $7,000. This is usually done by adding the $7,000 to Equipment.[2]

2. Assume straight-line depreciation. Revise the amortization schedule so that the new unexpired cost is spread over the remaining three years, as follows:

	Original Amortization Schedule		Revised Amortization Schedule	
	Year	Amount	Year	Amount
	1	$10,000	1	$10,000
	2	10,000	2	10,000
	3	10,000	3	9,000*
	4	10,000	4	9,000
			5	9,000
Accumulated amortization		$40,000		$47,000†

* New depreciable amount is [($41,000 – $20,000 + $7,000) – $1,000 residual value] = $27,000. New amortization expense is $27,000 divided by remaining useful life of 3 years, or $9,000 per year.

† Recapitulation:

Original cost	$41,000
Major overhaul	7,000
	48,000
Less residual	1,000
Depreciable cost	$47,000

■ GAINS AND LOSSES ON SALES OF FIXED ASSETS

Objective 8

Compute gains and losses on disposal of fixed assets.

Gains or losses on the disposal of property, plant, and equipment are inevitable. They are usually measured in a cash sale by the difference between the cash received and the net book value (net carrying amount) of the asset given up.[3]

Recording Gains and Losses

Suppose the equipment in Exhibit 9-2 (p. 385) were sold at the end of Year 2 for $27,000. The sale would have the following effects:

[2] A few accountants prefer to debit Accumulated Depreciation instead of Equipment. They argue that a portion of past depreciation is being "reversed" or "made good" by the improvement or betterment. Both accounting approaches increase the net book value of the equipment and increase subsequent depreciation by identical amounts.

[3] When an old asset is traded for a similar new asset, the new asset is valued at its cash-equivalent value (trade-in value) for purposes of computing gain or loss. For example, consider the trade-in of a five-year-old truck for a new truck. The cash-equivalent value of the old truck is the difference between the cash cost of the new truck without the trade-in and the cash paid with the trade-in. The trading of assets can become complex and is explained in advanced accounting texts.

A			= L + SE
+$27,000 −	$41,000 +	$20,000 =	+ $6,000
⎡ Increase ⎤ ⎣ Cash ⎦	⎡ Decrease ⎤ ⎣ Equipment ⎦	⎡ Decrease ⎤ ⎢ Accumulated ⎥ ⎣ Amortization ⎦	⎡ Increase ⎤ ⎢ Gain on ⎥ ⎢ Sale of ⎥ ⎣ Equipment ⎦

Note that the disposal of the equipment requires the removal of its carrying amount or book value, which appears in *two* accounts, not one. Therefore *both* the Accumulated Amortization account and the Equipment account are affected when dispositions occur.

If the selling price were $17,000 rather than $27,000:

+$17,000 −	$41,000 +	$20,000 =	−$4,000
⎡ Increase ⎤ ⎣ Cash ⎦	⎡ Decrease ⎤ ⎣ Equipment ⎦	⎡ Decrease ⎤ ⎢ Accumulated ⎥ ⎣ Amortization ⎦	⎡ Increase ⎤ ⎢ Loss on ⎥ ⎢ Sale of ⎥ ⎣ Equipment ⎦

The T-account presentations and journal entries are in Exhibit 9-6. Note especially that the disposal of the equipment necessitates the removal of the original cost of the equipment *and* the accompanying accumulated amortization. Of course, the net effect is to eliminate the $21,000 carrying amount of the equipment (cost of $41,000 less accumulated amortization of $20,000).

Exhibit 9-6	Journal and Ledger Entries Gain or Loss on Sale of Equipment (in thousands of dollars)

Sale at $27,000:

			Cash	Equipment	Gain on Sale of Equipment
			27	* 41 | 41	| 6
Cash	27				
Accumulated amortization	20			Accumulated Amortization, Equipment	
Equipment		41		20 | * 20	
Gain on sale of equipment		6			

Sale at $17,000:

			Cash	Equipment	Loss on Sale of Equipment
			17	* 41 | 41	4
Cash	17				
Accumulated amortization	20			Accumulated Amortization, Equipment	
Loss on sale of equipment	4			20 | * 20	
Equipment		41			

*Beginning balance

Income Statement Presentation

AT&T
www.att.com/

W.R. Grace & Co.
www.arch1.com/
product/grace/
graces.htm

In most instances, gains or losses on disposition of plant assets are not significant, so they are buried as a part of "other income" on the income statement and are not separately identified. For example, W. R. Grace & Co. includes an item on its income statement immediately after sales labelled "Dividends, interest, and other income." AT&T shows "Other income, net (Note D)" on a separate line after operating income in a recent annual report. Note D lists Gains (loss) on sale of fixed assets, $9.0 million, out of a total of $251.8 million of net other income.

When Gain on Sale of Equipment is shown as a separate item on an income statement, it is usually shown as a part of "other income" or some similar category. In single-step income statements, the gain is shown at the top along with other revenue items. For example:

Revenue:	
Sales of products	$xxx
Interest income (or interest revenue)	x
Other income: Gain on sale of equipment	x
Total sales and other income	$xxx

When a multiple-step income statement is used, the gain (or loss) is usually excluded from the computation of major profit categories such as gross profit or operating profit. Therefore, the gain or loss appears in some type of "other income" or nonoperating income section in the lower part of the income statement. For example, Coca-Cola Enterprises Inc. showed a $59.3 million "Gain on sale of operations" as one of four items in the category labelled "Nonoperating income (deductions)."

■ DEPLETION OF NATURAL RESOURCES

Objective 9

Explain how to account for depletion of natural resources.

Natural resources such as minerals, oil, and timber are sometimes called *wasting assets*. *Depletion* is the accounting measure of the gradual exhaustion of the original resources acquired. Depletion differs from amortization because depletion narrowly focuses on a physical phenomenon while amortization focuses more broadly on any reduction of the economic value of a fixed asset, including physical deterioration and obsolescence.

The costs of natural resources are usually classified as fixed assets. However, the investment in natural resources can be likened to a lump-sum acquisition of massive quantities of inventories under the ground (iron ore) or above the ground (timber). Depletion expense is the measure of that portion of this "long-term inventory" that is used up in a particular period. For example, a coal mine may cost $20 million and originally contain an estimated one million tonnes. The depletion rate would be $20 million ÷ 1 million tonnes = $20 per tonne. If 100,000 tonnes were mined during the first year, the depletion would be 100,000 × $20, or $2 million for that year; if 150,000 tonnes were mined the second year, depletion would be 150,000 × $20, or $3 million; and so forth.

As the above example shows, depletion is measured on a units-of-production basis. The annual depletion may be accounted for as a direct reduction of the mining asset, or it may be accumulated in a separate contra account similar to accumulated amortization.

Another example is timber. Boise Cascade Corporation, a large producer of forest products, describes its approach to depletion as follows:

Boise Cascade Corp.
www.bc.com/

> Timber and timberlands are shown at cost, less the cost of company timber harvested. Costs of company timber harvested and amortization of logging roads are determined on the basis of timber removals at rates based on the estimated volume of recoverable timber and are credited to the respective asset accounts.

The "cost of company timber harvested" is Boise Cascade's synonym for "depletion" of timber.

■ AMORTIZATION OF INTANGIBLE ASSETS

Objective 10

Describe how to account for various intangible assets.

Intangible assets are a class of long-lived assets that are not physical in nature. They are rights to expected benefits deriving from their acquisition and continued possession. Examples of intangible assets are *patents, copyrights, franchises,* and *goodwill.*

Intangible assets are accounted for in the same way as plant and equipment. That is, the acquisition costs are capitalized as assets and are then amortized over estimated useful lives. Because of obsolescence, the *economic lives* of intangible assets tend to be shorter than their *legal lives*.

An intangible asset is shown on a company's balance sheet only if the rights to some benefit are *purchased*. Equally valuable assets may be created by internal expenditures, but they are not recognized as assets. For example, suppose Pfizer spent $5 million to internally develop and patent a new drug. Pfizer would charge $5 million to expense; no asset would be recognized. In contrast, if Pfizer paid $5 million to another company for their patent on an identical drug, Pfizer would record the $5 million as an intangible asset. The difference in treatment acknowledges that it is difficult for management to honestly and objectively value the results of its internal research and development efforts, while an independent transaction between separate companies realistically measures the value.

Examples of Intangible Assets

patents Grants by the federal government to an inventor, bestowing the exclusive right to produce and sell the invention.

Patents are grants by the federal government to an inventor, bestowing the exclusive right to produce and sell the invention. Suppose a company acquires such a patent from the inventor for $170,000. Suppose further that because of fast-changing technology, the *economic life* (the expected useful life) of the patent is only five years. The amortization would be $170,000 ÷ 5 = $34,000 per year.

The write-offs of intangible assets are usually made via direct reductions of the accounts in question. Thus accounts such as Accumulated Amortization of Patents are rarely found. Furthermore, the residual values of intangible assets are nearly always zero.

Balance sheets seldom contain a separate line for patents or for any other single intangible asset. Patents are usually lumped with other items in a category labelled "intangible assets" or simply "other assets." A footnote often provides details.

copyrights Exclusive rights to reproduce and sell a book, musical composition, film, or similar products.

Copyrights are exclusive rights to reproduce and sell a book, musical composition, film, or similar products. These rights are issued by the federal government and provide protection to a company. The original costs of obtaining copyrights from the government are nominal, but a company may pay a large sum to purchase an existing asset from the owner. For example, a publisher of paperback books will pay the author of a popular novel in excess of a million dollars for his or her copyright. The economic lives of such assets may be no longer than two or three years, so amortization occurs accordingly.

trademarks Distinctive identifications of a manufactured product or of a service taking the form of a name, a sign, a slogan, a logo, or an emblem.

Trademarks are distinctive identifications of a manufactured product or of a service taking the form of a name, a sign, a slogan, a logo, or an emblem. An example is an emblem for Coca-Cola. Trademarks, trade names, trade brands, secret formulas, and similar items are property rights with economic lives depending on their length of use. For shareholder-reporting purposes, their costs are amortized over their useful lives, but for no longer than 40 years.

Remember that trademarks are recorded as intangible assets only if they are purchased. Companies like Coca-Cola, who have spent millions of advertising dollars creating public awareness of their brands, show no intangible asset, even though their trademark may be extremely valuable.

If a company has trademarks or other intangible assets that cease to have value, they should be immediately written off as an expense. For example, Brown-Forman Corporation had $60 million of intangible assets associated with the brand California Cooler when it decided the assets no longer provided future benefits. The $60 million expense reduced the company's income before taxes from $218 million to $158 million.

franchises (licences) Privileges granted by a government, manufacturer, or distributor to sell a product or service in accordance with specified conditions.

Franchises and **licences** are privileges granted by a government, manufacturer, or distributor to sell a product or service in accordance with specified conditions. An example is the franchise of a baseball team or the franchise of a local owner of a Holiday Inn. The lengths of the franchises vary from one year to perpetuity. Again, the acquisition costs of franchises and licences are amortized over their economic lives rather than their legal lives.

goodwill The excess of the cost of an acquired company over the sum of the fair market value of its identifiable individual assets less the liabilities.

Goodwill is defined as the excess of the cost of an acquired company over the sum of the fair market values of its identifiable individual assets less the liabilities. For example, General Motors (GM) acquired Hughes Aircraft for $5 billion but could assign only $1 billion to various identifiable assets such as receivables, plant, and patents less liabilities assumed by GM; the remainder, $4 billion, is goodwill. Identifiable intangible assets, such as franchises and patents, may be acquired singly, but goodwill cannot be acquired separately from a related business. This excess of the purchase price over the fair market value is called "goodwill" or "purchased goodwill" or, more accurately, "excess of cost over fair value of net identifiable assets of businesses acquired."

The accounting for goodwill illustrates how an *exchange* transaction is a basic concept of accounting. After all, there are many owners who could obtain a premium price for their companies. But such goodwill is *never* recorded. Only the goodwill arising from an *actual acquisition* with arm's-length bargaining is shown as an asset on the purchaser's records.

For shareholder-reporting purposes, goodwill must be amortized, generally in a straight-line manner, over the periods benefited. The maximum amortization period is forty years. The minimum amortization period is not specified by GAAP, but a lump-sum write-off on acquisition is forbidden.

Research and Development

In general, research and development (R&D) expenditures are expensed. However, as companies invest in R&D with the expectation of earning a return on this investment, GAAP in Canada permits the capitalization of the development expenditure portion if certain conditions exist. Essentially the future value to be realized from the developed product or service must be greater than its capitalized value from the development expenditures.

Practice varies internationally. For example, in the United States R&D expenditures are expensed, while in Korea and India R&D expenditures are capitalized and later amortized. Even in the United States there is an exception to the immediate expensing of all research and development costs. The costs of developing computer software to be sold or leased should be expensed only until the *technological feasibility* of the product is established. Thereafter, software production costs should be capitalized and amortized over the estimated economic life of the product.

Software development costs can be significant. Consider BMC Software, a Texas-based maker of software to support IBM mainframe systems. It began capitalizing software development costs in fiscal 1987, and in 1991 such costs were 36% of the company's noncurrent assets. During fiscal 1991, costs of $5,043,000 were capitalized, compared with only $1,388,000 of amortization. If all these costs had been expensed, income before taxes would have been $5,043,000 – $1,388,000 = $3,655,000 lower:

BMC Software Inc.
www.bmc.com/

BMC Software	With Capitalization of Software Development Costs	Without Capitalization of Software Development Costs
Income before software development costs	$19,045,000	$19,045,000
Amortization of software development costs	1,388,000	
Software development cost expense		5,043,000
Income before taxes	$17,657,000	$14,002,000
	Difference = $3,655,000	

This phenomenon continues as long as the rate of new software development continues to grow. By 1994, BMC's rate of new development levelled off. In that year, $4,771,000 amortization of previously capitalized software exactly equalled the 1994 software development cost. The consolidated balance sheet reported software costs as follows:

	1994	1993
Software development costs, net of accumulated amortization of $14,519 and $9,748.	$14,750	$14,750

Amortization of Leaseholds and Leasehold Improvements

Leaseholds and *leasehold improvements* are frequently classified with plant assets although they are technically intangible assets. The lessee owns the right to use the leased items, not the items themselves.

A **leasehold** is the right to use a fixed asset (such as a building or some portion thereof) for a specified period of time beyond one year. A **leasehold improvement** incurred by a lessee (tenant) can take various forms. Examples are the installation of new fixtures, panels, walls, and air-conditioning equipment that are not permitted to be removed from the premises when a lease expires.

The costs of leases and leasehold improvements are amortized over the life of the lease, even if the physical life of the leasehold improvement is longer. The straight-line method is used almost exclusively, probably because accelerated methods have not been permitted for income tax purposes. For more on leases, see Appendix 10B, page 456.

Amortization of Deferred Charges

Sometimes prepaid expenses are lumped with *deferred charges* as a single amount, *prepaid expenses and deferred charges*, that appears on the balance sheet at the bottom of the current asset classification or at the bottom of all the assets as an "other asset." **Deferred charges** are like prepaid expenses, but they have longer-term benefits. For example, the costs of relocating a mass of employees to a different geographical area, or the costs of rearranging an assembly line or developing new markets, may be carried forward as deferred charges and written off as expense over a three- to five-year period. This procedure is often described as the amortization of deferred charges.

Another example of deferred charges is *incorporation costs*, which include certain types of expenditures made in forming a corporation: fees for legal and accounting services, promotional costs for the sale of corporate securities, and the printing costs of stock certificates. These costs theoretically benefit the corporation indefinitely, but they are usually amortized for shareholder purposes.

Conservatism and Inconsistencies

The attitude of the regulatory bodies toward accounting for intangible assets has become increasingly conservative. Conservatism produces inconsistencies between the accounting for tangible and intangible long-lived assets. Provocative and knotty theoretical issues arise because accountants sometimes overlook the underlying reality of future economic benefits. Their preoccupation with physical evidence often results in the expensing of outlays that should be treated as assets. Thus, expenditures for research, advertising, employee training, and the like are generally expensed, although it seems clear that in an economic sense such expenditures represent expected future benefits.

The difficulty of measuring future benefits is the reason usually advanced for expensing these items. GAAP requires that *internal* research, advertising, and other such costs be written off to expense as incurred. In contrast, purchases of patents, trademarks, and similar intangibles that were incurred outside the firm are recorded as assets.

---

leasehold The right to use a fixed asset for a specified period of time, typically beyond one year.

leasehold improvement Investments by a lessee in items that are not permitted to be removed from the premises when a lease expires, such as installation of new fixtures, panels, walls, and air-conditioning equipment.

deferred charges Similar to prepaid expenses, but longer-term benefits.

In summary, accounting practice for intangible assets is not consistent. An annual report of Omark Industries exemplifies this inconsistency: "Costs of internally developed patents, trademarks, and formulas are charged to current operations. Costs of purchased patents, trademarks, and formulas are amortized over their legal or economic lives."

Cost Allocations Impact Revenues

Long-distance competitors are in peril because of the way Canadian telephone companies are able to allocate hundreds of millions of dollars worth of costs under regulatory rules, a lawyer for **Unitel Communications Inc.** says.

The critique of telecommunications accounting rules emerged during a crucial two-day exchange at a federal regulatory proceeding on the future of telecommunications.

Relying on a foot-high stack of documents, Michael Ryan, Unitel's vice-president of law, assailed what he called the telephone companies' exploitation of those rules during his cross-examination of a panel of vice-presidents from the Stentor consortium of Canada's nine largest telephone companies.

The Canadian Radio-television and Telecommunications Commission is conducting a marathon proceeding aimed at revamping all of its telecommunications rules to respond to competition....

Mr. Ryan said flaws in the cost rules, exploited by the phone companies, force customers and competitors to subsidize the phone companies' long-distance business.

The so-called "phase three" cost rules were adopted by the CRTC almost a decade ago and allocate phone company costs to several different categories in order to set subscriber rates.

But they are critical for two other reasons.

First, the 1985 rules are used to determine the contribution fee long-distance competitors must pay to the phone companies. That charge compensates the phone companies for their reduced long-distance surpluses, profits that provide subsidies to keep the price of their money-losing local service low.

And the second, the phase three rules are an integral part of a Stentor proposal to deregulate prices in the $7.5-billion-a-year long-distance business.

Acceptance of Stentor's rate proposal would entrench current cost distortions and allow the phone companies to accelerate the long-distance price war, Mr. Ryan said.

The three most important cost categories are local, toll (or long-distance) and access.

The access category is comprised of network-related costs that do not vary with use and produce no revenue. Phone companies recoup access costs from their own long-distance surplus and through contribution charges from competitors.

But Mr. Ryan said the telephone companies have inflated the access category with costs that should be included in their long-distance category. That means, he charged, that they have underestimated the costs of long-distance, to the detriment of competitors.

Mr. Ryan gave two dramatic examples.

His revelation that Stentor has allocated the $120-million cost of its alliance with U.S. long-distance carrier MCI Communications Corp. to the access category drew an admission from the Stentor panel that those costs should be allocated to the long-distance category.

Mr. Ryan also produced phone company accounting manuals that show how the costs of their giant switching computers are assigned to the access category, rather than to a specific category related to use.

A Unitel analysis of the costs of one kind of switch in **Bell Canada's** territory alone documents how the phone companies' use of the phase three rules have boosted their access costs by $460-million.

But George Hariton, a Bell Canada assistant vice-president of engineering economics, defended the accounting on the grounds that the costs of new switching computers do not vary with use. He said the CRTC cost rules allow non-usage-sensitive costs to be allocated to the access category....

Inflation of the access category with costs from the long-distance category has two adverse effects on competitors, Mr. Ryan said.

It increases the contribution charges competitors must pay because these contributions must in part defray the phone companies' access costs. The phone company shift also reduces their long-distance costs, allowing them to justify further price reductions to the CRTC.

"It means long-distance competitors are subsidizing the telephone companies to compete against them," Mr. Ryan said. ∎

Source: Lawrence Surtees, "Unitel accuses phone firms of exploiting accounting laws," The Globe and Mail, (November 22, 1993). Reprinted with permission of The Globe and Mail.

Summary Problems for Your Review

Problem One

"The net book value of plant assets is the amount that would be spent today for their replacement." Do you agree? Explain.

Solution to Problem One

Net book value of the plant assets is the result of deducting accumulated amortization from original cost. It is a result of cost allocation, not valuation. This process does not attempt to reflect all the technological and economic events that may affect replacement value. Consequently, there is little assurance that net book value will approximate replacement cost.

Problem Two

"Accumulated amortization provides cash for the replacement of fixed assets." Do you agree with this quotation from a business magazine? Explain.

Solution to Problem Two

Accumulated amortization is a contra asset. It is the amount of the asset already used up and in no way represents a direct stockpile of cash for replacement.

Problem Three

Refer to Exhibit 9-3 (p. 387). Suppose the predicted residual value had been $5,000 instead of $1,000.

1. Compute amortization for each of the first two years using straight-line and double-declining-balance methods.
2. Assume that DDB amortization is used and that the equipment is sold for $20,000 cash at the end of the second year. Compute the gain or loss on the sale. Show the effects of the sale in T-accounts for the equipment and accumulated amortization. Where and how would the sale appear in the income statement?
3. Assume that straight-line depreciation is used and that the equipment is sold for $20,000 cash at the end of the second year. Compute the gain or loss on the sale. Compare this amount to the gain or loss computed in the previous question.

Solution to Problem Three

1.

	Straight-Line Amortization $=\dfrac{C-R}{n}$	DDB Amortization $= \text{Rate}* \times$ (Beginning Book Value)
Year 1	$36,000/4 = $9,000	.50 ($41,000) = $20,500
Year 2	$36,000/4 = $9,000	.50 ($41,000 − $20,500) = $10,250

* Rate = 2(100% ÷ n) = 2(100% ÷ 4) = 50%

2.

Revenue	$20,000
Expense: Net book value of equipment sold is	
$41,000 – ($20,500 + $10,250), or	
$41,000 – $30,750 =	10,250
Gain on sale of equipment	$ 9,750

The effect of removing the book value is a $10,250 decrease in assets. Note that the effect of a *decrease* in Accumulated Amortization (by itself) is an *increase* in assets:

Equipment			
Acquisition cost	41,000	Cost of equipment sold	41,000

Accumulated Amortization, Equipment			
Accumulated amortization		Amortization for:	
on equipment sold	30,750	Year 1	20,500
		Year 2	10,250
			30,750

The $9,750 gain is usually shown as a separate item on the income statement as Gain on Sale of Equipment or Gain on Disposal of Equipment.

3.

Revenue	$20,000
Expense:	
$41,000 – ($9,000 + $9,000)	23,000
Loss on sale of equipment	$ 3,000

There is a loss of $3,000 instead of a gain of $9,750 because the book value is $12,750 higher. The amount of gains or losses on disposed-of equipment depends on the amortization method used.

Highlights to Remember

Long-lived assets are either tangible—physical in nature—or intangible—rights or benefits that are not physical. Depreciation, depletion, and amortization are similar concepts, providing for systematic write-offs of the acquisition costs of long-lived assets over their useful lives. Depletion usually refers to natural resources, amortization and depreciation to other tangible assets, and amortization to intangible assets. The acquisition cost includes both the purchase price and all incidental costs necessary to get the asset ready for use.

Land is not amortized; it remains on the books at acquisition cost. Buildings and equipment can be amortized using the straight-line method, units of production method, or an accelerated method, such as double-declining balance.

Financial reports to shareholders often differ from the reports to tax authorities. Keeping two sets of records to satisfy these two purposes is necessary, not illegal or immoral.

Amortization does not provide cash. Customers provide cash. Amortization is not deductible for income tax purposes.

Expenditures can be capitalized or expensed. Expenditures with benefits extending beyond the current year should be capitalized—other expenditures should be expensed.

When fixed assets are sold, the difference between the amount received from the sale and the book value of the asset is a gain or loss, which is generally included with "other income" on the income statement.

Intangible assets, such as patents, trademarks, or goodwill, are shown on the balance sheet if they were purchased. However, equally valuable items that were generated by internal expenditures are not recorded as assets.

Assignment Material

QUESTIONS

9-1. Distinguish between *tangible* and *intangible* assets.

9-2. Distinguish between *amortization*, *depreciation*, and *depletion*.

9-3. "The cash discount on the purchase of equipment is income to the buyer during the year of acquisition." Do you agree? Explain.

9-4. "When an expenditure is capitalized, shareholders' equity is credited." Do you agree? Explain.

9-5. "Accumulated amortization is a sum of cash being accumulated for the replacement of fixed assets." Do you agree? Explain.

9-6. "The accounting process of amortization is allocation, not valuation." Explain.

9-7. "Keeping two sets of books is immoral." Do you agree? Explain.

9-8. Compare the choice between straight-line and accelerated depreciation with the choice between FIFO and LIFO. Give at least one similarity and one difference.

9-9. "Most of the money we'll spend this year for replacing our equipment will be generated by amortization." Do you agree? Explain.

9-10. Criticize: "Amortization is the loss in value of a fixed asset over a given span of time."

9-11. "Accelerated depreciation saves cash but shows lower net income." Explain.

9-12. "Changes in accounting estimates should be reported prospectively rather than retroactively." Explain.

9-13. The manager of a division reported to the president of the company: "Now that our major capital improvements are finished, the division's expenses will be much lower." Is this really what he means to say? Explain.

9-14. "The gain on sale of equipment should be reported fully on the income statement." Explain what the complete reporting would include.

9-15. Name and describe four kinds of intangible assets.

9-16. Explain how goodwill is computed.

9-17. "Internally acquired patents are accounted for differently than externally acquired patents." Explain the difference.

9-18. "Goodwill may have nothing to do with the personality of the manager or employees." Do you agree? Explain.

9-19. "Accountants sometimes are too concerned with physical objects." Explain.

9-20. "Accounting for research and development is more conservative than it was before 1975." Explain.

EXERCISES

9-21 Computing Acquisition Costs

From the following data, calculate the cost to be added to the Land account and the Building account of St. Mary's Hospital.

On January 1, 19X9, the hospital acquired a twenty-hectare parcel of land immediately adjacent to its existing facilities. The land included a warehouse, parking lots, and driveways. The hospital paid $500,000 cash and also gave a note for $2 million, payable at $200,000 per year plus interest of 10% on the outstanding balance.

The warehouse was demolished at a cash cost of $250,000 so that it could be replaced by a new hospital building. The construction of the building required a cash down payment of $3 million plus a mortgage note of $7 million. The mortgage was payable at $400,000 per year plus interest of 10% on the outstanding balance.

Required   Prepare journal entries (without explanations) to record the above transactions.

9-22 Acquisition Equipment

A company acquired some used computer equipment. Installation costs were $7,000. Repair costs prior to use were $10,000. The purchasing manager's salary is $47,000 per annum and he spent one month evaluating equipment and completing the transaction. The invoice price was $400,000. The seller paid its salesman a commission of 4% and offered the buyer a cash discount of 2% if the invoice were paid within sixty days. Freight costs were $4,400, paid by the agency. Repairs during the first year of use were $9,000.

Required   Compute the total capitalized cost to be added to the Equipment account. The seller was paid within sixty days.

9-23 Basket Purchase

On February 21, 19X2, FastLube, an auto service chain, acquired an existing building and land for $720,000 from a local gas station that had failed. The tax assessor had placed an assessed valuation on January 1, 19X2, as follows:

Land	$220,000
Building	380,000
Total	$600,000

Required   How much of the $720,000 purchase price should be attributed to the building? Why?

9-24 Journal Entries for Amortization

(Alternates are 9-46 and 9-47.) On January 1, 19X1, the Marcos Company acquired 10 assembly robots for $660,000 cash. The robots had an expected useful life of ten years and an expected terminal scrap value of $60,000. Straight-line amortization was used.

Required   1. Set up T-accounts and prepare the journal entries for the acquisition and for the first annual amortization charge. Post to T-accounts.
2. One of the robots with an original cost of $66,000 on January 1, 19X1, and an expected terminal scrap value of $6,000 was sold for $40,000 cash on December 31, 19X3. Prepare the journal entry for the sale.
3. Refer to requirement 2. Suppose the robot had been sold for $55,000 cash instead of $40,000. Prepare the journal entry for the sale.

9-25 Simple Amortization Computations

A company acquired the following assets:
- a. Conveyor, five-year useful life, $38,000 cost, straight-line method, $3,000 residual value.
- b. Truck, three-year useful life, $18,000 cost, DDB method, $1,500 residual value.

Required   Compute the first three years of amortization.

9-26 Amortization on a Group of Assets

Horwath Company has just purchased the assets of a division of Sportsgear, Inc. for $4.3 million. Of the purchase price, $1.8 million was allocated to assets that will be amortized on a straight-line basis over a useful life of six years (assume no residual value). Another $800,000 was for special production machinery that will be amortized on a DDB basis over a useful life of five years. A total of $300,000 was for land. The remainder was goodwill, which Horwath will amortize by the straight-line method over forty years.

Required Compute the total amortization expense generated by the acquired assets for each of the first two years.

9-27   Units-of-Production Method

The Rockland Transport Company has many trucks that are kept for a useful life of 300,000 kilometres. Amortization is computed on a kilometre basis. Suppose a new truck is purchased for $97,000 cash. Its expected residual value is $7,000. Its kilometres driven during Year 1 is 60,000 and during Year 2 is 90,000.

Required
1. What is the amortization expense for each of the two years?
2. Compute the gain or loss if the truck is sold for $55,000 at the end of Year 2.

9-28   Fundamental Amortization Approaches

(Alternates are 9-30 and 9-31.) Consolidated Freight acquired some new trucks for $1 million. Their predicted useful life is five years, and predicted residual value is $100,000.

Required Prepare an amortization schedule similar to Exhibit 9-3, page 387, comparing straight-line and double-declining-balance.

9-29   Units-of-Production, Straight-Line, and DDB

Northern Mining Company buys special drills for $440,000 each. Each drill can extract about 100,000 tonnes of ore, after which it has a $40,000 residual value. One such drill was bought in early January, 19X1. Projected tonnage figures for the drill are 40,000 tonnes in 19X1, 40,000 tonnes in 19X2, and 20,000 tonnes in 19X3. Northern is considering units-of-production, straight-line, or double-declining-balance depreciation for the drill.

Required Compute amortization for each year under each of the three methods.

9-30   Comparison of Popular Amortization Methods

(Alternates are 9-28 and 9-31.) Elm Lumber Company acquired a machine for $32,000 with an expected useful life of five years and a $2,000 expected residual value. Prepare a tabular comparison (similar to Exhibit 9-3, p. 387) of the annual amortization and book value for each year under straight-line and double-declining-balance depreciation.

9-31   Fundamental Amortization Policies

(Alternates are 9-28 and 9-30.) The Mailing Services department of Bank of North America acquired some new package-handling equipment for $380,000. The equipment's predicted useful life is eight years and predicted residual value is $28,000.

Required Prepare an amortization schedule similar to Exhibit 9-3 (p. 387), comparing straight-line and double-declining-balance. Show all amounts in thousands of dollars (rounded to the nearest thousand). Limit the schedule to each of the first three years of useful life. Show the amortization for each year and the book value at the end of each year.

9-32   Changes in Amortization Estimates

Cascade Company acquired equipment for $50,000 with an expected useful life of five years and a $5,000 expected residual value. Straight-line depreciation was adopted. Suppose it is the end of Year 3. The company's engineers have altered their expectations; the equipment's new expected useful life is six instead of five years. Furthermore, the expected residual value is $2,000 instead of $5,000.

Required
1. Using the "prospective" method, compute the new annual straight-line depreciation.
2. Critics of the "prospective" method favour using the "retroactive" method instead. Prepare a table comparing annual amortization throughout the eight-year life using the prospective method and the retroactive method. Which method do you favour? Why?

9-33   Capital Expenditures

Consider the following transactions:

a.   Paid principal on building mortgage.

b. Paid cash dividends.
c. Paid plumbers for repair of leaky faucets.
d. Acquired new air-conditioning system for the building.
e. Replaced smashed front door (not covered by insurance).
f. Paid travel expenses of sales personnel.
g. Acquired building for a down payment plus a mortgage payable.
h. Paid interest on building mortgage.
i. Paid custodial wages.
j. Paid security guard wages.

Required   Answer by letter:
1. Indicate which transactions are capital expenditures.
2. Indicate which transactions are expenses in the current year.

9-34   Capital Expenditures

Consider each of the following transactions. For each one, indicate whether it is a capital expenditure (C) or an expense in the current year (E).

a. Paid for a tune-up on one of the autos in the company's fleet.
b. Paid a consultant to advise on marketing strategy.
c. Installed new lighting fixtures in a leased building.
d. Paid for routine maintenance on equipment.
e. Acquired a patent for $50,000.
f. Paid for overhaul of machinery that extends its useful life.
g. Developed a patentable product by paying for research and development.
h. Paid organization costs to incorporate a new company.

9-35   Amortization for Parts of Year

Rubanko Company acquired material-handling equipment on April 2, 19X1 for $280,000 cash. Its expected useful life was five years, and its expected residual value was $40,000. The double-declining balance method of amortization was adopted. Prepare a schedule of amortization for the first three calendar years of use. Show the total amount of amortization for each calendar year affected.

9-36   Repairs and Improvements

Harui Grain Company acquired harvesting equipment for $88,000 with an expected useful life of five years and an $8,000 expected residual value. Straight-line amortization was used. During its fourth year of service, expenditures related to the equipment were as follows:

1. Oiling and greasing, $200.
2. Replacing belts and hoses, $450.
3. Major overhaul during the final week of the year, including the replacement of an engine. The useful life of the equipment was extended from five to seven years. The cost was $20,000. The residual value is now expected to be $11,000 instead of $8,000.

Required   Indicate in words how each of the three items would affect the income statement and the balance sheet. Prepare a tabulation that compares the original amortization schedule with the revised amortization schedule.

9-37   Disposal of Equipment

Tompkins Community Hospital's Convenient Care Centre acquired x-ray equipment for $35,000 with an expected useful life of five years and a $5,000 expected residual value. Straight-line depreciation was used. The equipment was sold at the end of the fourth year for $16,000 cash.

Required

1. Compute the gain or loss on the sale. Show the effects of the sale on the balance sheet equation, identifying all specific accounts by name. Where and how would the sale appear on the income statement?
2. (a) Show the journal entries for the transaction in requirement 1. (b) Repeat 2a, assuming that the cash sales price was $7,000 instead of $16,000.

9-38 Gain or Loss on Sales of Fixed Assets

Ontime Delivery Company purchased a van in early 19X1 for $30,000. It was being amortized on a straight-line basis over its useful life of five years. Estimated residual value was $5,000. The van was sold in early 19X3 after two years of amortization had been recognized.

Required

1. Suppose Ontime received $22,000 for the van. Compute the gain or loss on the sale. Prepare the journal entries for the sale of the van.
2. Suppose Ontime received $15,000 for the van. Compute the gain or loss on the sale. Prepare the journal entries for the sale of the van.

9-39 Depletion

A zinc mine contains an estimated 900,000 tonnes of zinc ore. The mine cost $13.5 million. The tonnage mined during 19X4, the first year of operations, was 120,000 tonnes.

Required

1. What was the depletion for 19X4?
2. Suppose that in January 19X5 it was discovered that the mine originally contained 1 million tonnes. What was the estimated depletion for 19X5, assuming that 100,000 tonnes were mined?

9-40 Various Intangible Assets

Consider the following:

1. On December 29, 19X1, a publisher acquires the copyright for a book by Robert Ludlum for $2 million. Most sales of this book are expected to take place uniformly during 19X2 and 19X3. What will be the amortization for 19X2?
2. On January 4, 19X1, Company X acquires Company Y for $45 million and can assign only $35 million to identifiable individual assets. What is the minimum amount of amortization of the goodwill for 19X1? Could the entire amount be written off in 19X1? Why?
3. In 19X1, Company C spent $10 million in its research department, which resulted in new valuable patents. In December 19X1, Company D paid $10 million to an outside inventor for some valuable new patents. How would the income statements for 19X1 for each company be affected? How would the balance sheets as of December 31, 19X1 be affected?
4. On December 28, 19X8, Scholes Company purchased a patent for a calculator for $360,000. The patent has ten years of its legal life remaining. Technology changes fast, so Scholes expects the patent to be worthless in five years. What will be the amortization for 19X9?

PROBLEMS

9-41 Amortization, Income Tax, and Cash Flow

(Alternate is 9-56.) Morales Metal Products Co. had the following balances, among others, at the end of December 19X1: Cash, $300,000; Equipment, $400,000; Accumulated Amortization, $100,000. Total revenues (all in cash) were $900,000. Cash operating expenses were $600,000. Straight-line depreciation expense was $50,000. If accelerated depreciation had been used, amortization expense would have been $80,000.

Required

1. Assume zero income taxes. Fill in the blanks in the accompanying table. Show the amounts in thousands.
2. Repeat requirement 1, but assume an income tax rate of 40%. Assume also that Morales can use the same amortization method for reporting to shareholders and to income tax authorities.

3. Compare your answers to requirements 1 and 2. Does amortization provide cash? Explain as precisely as possible.
4. Assume that Morales had used straight-line depreciation for reporting to shareholders and to income tax authorities. Indicate the change (increase or decrease and amount) in the following balances if Morales had used accelerated depreciation instead of straight-line: Cash, Accumulated Amortization, Operating Income, Income Tax Expense, and Retained Income.
5. Refer to requirement 1. Suppose amortization were tripled under both straight-line and accelerated methods. How would cash be affected? Be specific.

Table for Problem 9-41
(amounts in thousands)

	1. Zero Income Taxes		2. 40% Income Taxes	
	Straight-Line Depreciation	*Accelerated Depreciation*	*Straight-Line Depreciation*	*Accelerated Depreciation*
Revenues	$	$	$	$
Cash operating expenses				
Cash provided by operations before income taxes				
Depreciation expense				
Operating income				
Income tax expense				
Net income	$	$	$	$
Supplementary analysis:				
Cash provided by operations before income taxes	$	$	$	$
Income tax payments				
Net cash provided by operations	$	$	$	$

9-42   Depreciation, Income Taxes, and Cash Flow

Mr. Kuhlmann, president of the Bremen Shipping Company, read a newspaper story that stated: "The Frankfurt Steel Company had a cash flow last year of 1,500,000 DM, consisting of 1,000,000 DM of net income plus 500,000 DM of depreciation. New plant facilities helped the cash flow, because depreciation was 25 percent higher than in the preceding year." "Cash flow" is frequently used as a synonym for "cash provided by operations," which, in turn, is cash revenue less cash operating expenses and income taxes. (DM stands for Deutschmark, the German unit of currency.)

Kuhlmann was encouraged by the quotation because Bremen Shipping Company had just acquired a vast amount of new transportation equipment. These acquisitions had placed a severe financial strain on the company. Kuhlmann was heartened because he thought that the added cash flow from the depreciation of the new equipment should ease the financial pressures on the company.

The income before income taxes of the Bremen Shipping Company last year (19X2) was 200,000 DM. Depreciation was 200,000 DM; it will also be 200,000 DM on the old equipment in 19X3.

Revenue in 19X2 was 2.1 million DM (all in cash), and operating expenses other than depreciation were 1.7 million DM (all in cash).

In 19X3, the new equipment is expected to help increase revenue by 1 million DM. However, operating expenses other than depreciation will increase by 800,000 DM.

Required

1. Suppose amortization on the new equipment for financial reporting purposes is 100,000 DM. What would be the "cash flow" from operations (cash provided by operations) for 19X3? Show computations. Ignore income taxes.

2. Repeat requirement 1, assuming that the depreciation on the new equipment is 50,000 DM. Ignore income taxes.

3. Assume an income tax rate of 40%. (a) Repeat requirement 1; (b) repeat requirement 2. Assume that the same amount of depreciation is shown for tax purposes and for financial reporting purposes.

4. In your own words, state as accurately as possible the effects on "cash flow" of depreciation. Comment on requirements 1, 2, and 3 above in order to bring out your points. This is a more important requirement than requirements 1, 2, and 3.

9-43   Disposal of Equipment

(Alternate is 9-59.) Western Airlines acquired a new Boeing 727-100 airplane for $26 million. Its expected residual value was $6 million. The company's annual report indicated that straight-line depreciation was used based on an estimated service life of ten years. In addition, the company stated: "The cost and related accumulated depreciation of assets sold or retired are removed from the appropriate accounts, and gain or loss, if any, is recognized in Other Income (Expense)."

Required

Show all amounts in millions of dollars.

1. Assume that the equipment is sold at the end of the sixth year for $15 million cash. Compute the gain or loss on the sale. Show the effects of the sale on the balance sheet equation, identifying all specific accounts by name. Where and how would the sale appear on the income statement?

2. (a) Show the journal entries for the transaction in requirement 1. (b) Repeat 2a, assuming that the cash sales price was $9 million instead of $15 million.

9-44   Deferred Charges

Simmons Airlines, Inc. was a regional carrier. Consider the following item under "Other assets" in its annual report:

	19X7	19X6
Deferred development costs, net of amortization (19X7, $329,000; 19X6, $285,000)	$385,000	$514,000

A footnote to the annual report stated: "Deferred development and preoperating costs: Costs related to the introduction of new types of aircraft are deferred and depreciated over five years."

Required

1. Suppose no new deferred development or preoperating costs were recorded during 19X7. Calculate the amount of deferred development costs amortized during 19X7.

2. Suppose Simmons took delivery of new Boeing 737s halfway through 19X8 and incurred $42,000 of training costs associated with the introduction of the new aircraft. Show the journal entries for recording these costs (assume that payment was in cash) and for recognizing depreciation at the end of the year.

CRITICAL THINKING PROBLEM

9-45   Meaning of Book Value

Sanchez Company purchased an office building twenty years ago for $1.2 million, $400,000 of which was attributable to land. The mortgage has been fully paid. The current balance sheet follows:

Required

1. Assume that some new cars are acquired on October 1, 1995 for $120 million. The useful life is one year. Expected residual values are $84 million. Prepare a summary journal entry for depreciation for 1995. The fiscal year ends on December 31.

2. Prepare a summary journal entry for depreciation for the first six months of 1996.

3. Assume that the automobiles are sold for $96 million cash on October 1, 1996. Prepare the journal entry for the sale. Automobiles are considered "revenue earning equipment."

4. What is the total depreciation expense for 1996? If the $96 million proceeds could have been predicted exactly when the cars were originally acquired, what would depreciation expense have been in 1995? In 1996? Explain.

9-58   Change in Service Life

An annual report of TWA contained the following footnote:

> Note 2. *Change in accounting estimate.* TWA extended the estimated useful lives of Boeing 727-100 aircraft from principally sixteen years to principally twenty years. As a result, depreciation and amortization expense was decreased by $9,000,000.

The TWA annual report also contained the following data: depreciation, $235,518,000; net income, $42,233,000.

The cost of the 727-100 aircraft subject to depreciation was $800 million. Residual values were predicted to be 10% of acquisition cost.

Required

Assume a combined federal and state income tax rate of 46% throughout all parts of these requirements.

1. Was the effect of the change in estimated useful life a material difference? Explain, including computations.

2. The same year's annual report of Delta Air Lines contained the following footnote:

> Depreciation—Substantially all of the flight equipment is being depreciated on a straight-line basis to residual values (10% of cost) over a 10-year period from dates placed in service.

   The Delta annual report also contained the following data: depreciation, $220,979,000; net income, $146,474,000. Suppose Delta had used a twenty-year life instead of a ten-year life. Assume a 46% applicable income tax rate. Compute the new depreciation and net income.

3. Suppose TWA had used a ten-year life instead of a twenty-year life on its 727-100 equipment. Compute the new depreciation and net income. For purposes of this requirement, assume that the equipment cost $800 million and has been in service one year and that reported net income based on a twenty-year life was $42,233,000.

9-59   Disposal of Property and Equipment

(Alternate is 9-43.) Rockwell International is an advanced technology company operating primarily in aerospace and electronics. The company's annual report indicted that both accelerated and straight-line depreciation were used for its property and equipment. In addition, the annual report said: "Gains or losses on property transactions are recorded in income in the period of sale or retirement."

Rockwell received $27.9 million for property that it sold.

Required

1. Assume that the total property in question was originally acquired for $150 million and that the $27.9 million was received in cash. There was a gain of $8.5 million on the sale. Compute the accumulated depreciation on the property and equipment sold. Show the effects of the sale on the balance sheet equation, identifying all specific accounts by name.

2. For this requirement, round your entries to the nearest tenth of a million dollars. (a) Show the journal entries and postings to T-accounts for the transaction in requirement 1. (b) Repeat 2a, assuming that the cash sales price was $17.9 million cash instead of $27.9 million.

9-60   Disposal of Equipment

Airline Executive reported on an airline as follows:

> Lufthansa's highly successful policy of rolling over entire fleets in roughly ten years—before the aircraft have outlived their usefulness—got started in a "spectacular" way when seven first-generation 747s were sold.
>
> The 747s were bought six to nine years earlier for $22–28 million each and sold for about the same price.

Required

1. Assume an average original cost of $25 million each, an average original expected useful life of ten years, a $2.5 million expected residual value, and an average actual life of eight years before disposal. Use straight-line depreciation. Compute the total gain or loss on the sale of the seven planes.

2. Prepare a summary journal entry for the sale.

9-61   Hudson's Bay Company Annual Report

Refer to the financial statements of the Hudson's Bay Company in Appendix A. The Hudson's Bay Company uses straight-line depreciation for most of its assets, as explained in Note 1. Amortization expense was $132,252,000 in fiscal 1997. For purposes of this problem, assume that all revenues and expenses, except amortization, are for cash. Therefore cash expenses for fiscal 1997 were $6,007,212,000 − 5,864,508,000 = 192,704,000.

Required

1. Assume the Hudson's Bay Company had used declining-balance instead of straight-line, and amortization expense was $139,777,000 instead of $132,252,000. Assume zero income taxes. Fill in the blanks in the table on the next page (in thousands of dollars).

2. Repeat requirement 1, but assume an income tax rate of 40.0%.

3. Compare your answers to requirements 1 and 2. Does amortization provide cash? Explain as precisely as possible.

9-62   Annual Report Disclosure

Select a company's annual report of your choice.

Required

1. Identify the amortization methods used by the company.

2. Calculate gross and net plant, property, and equipment as a percentage of total assets for the company.

3. Do the notes disclose any unusual practices with regard to long-lived assets?

Hudson's Bay Company
(amounts in thousands)

	1. Zero Income Taxes		2. 40% Income Taxes	
	Straight-Line Depreciation	*DDB Depreciation*	*Straight-Line Depreciation*	*DDB Depreciation*
Revenues	$	$	$	$
Cash expenses				
Cash provided before income taxes				
Depreciation expense				
Income before income taxes				
Income taxes				
Net income	$	$	$	$
Supplementary analysis:				
Cash provided before income taxes	$	$	$	$
Income taxes				
Net cash provided	$	$	$	$

10 Liabilities and Interest

Learning Objectives

After studying this chapter, you should be able to

1 Provide a perspective on why information about liabilities is so important to readers of financial statements.

2 Explain the accounting for current liabilities.

3 Describe the contractual nature of various long-term liabilities.

4 Use present value techniques in valuing long-term liabilities.

5 Value and account for bond issues over their entire life.

6 Explain the nature of pensions and other postretirement benefits.

7 Define contingent liabilities and explain why they are often disclosed by footnote rather than in the statements themselves.

8 Apply ratio analysis to assessing the debt levels of an entity.

9 Compute and interpret present and future values (Appendix 10A).

10 Describe, value, and account for long-term lease transactions (Appendix 10B).

11 Understand the concept of deferred income taxes (Appendix 10C).

This chapter considers the very broad categories of economic obligations that accountants classify as liabilities. It describes many kinds of liabilities and how they are reported. The accounting for common liabilities—such as the responsibility to repay a loan or to compensate an employee—is presented in more detail here than in earlier chapters. In addition, the fundamentals of compound interest are used as the basis for measuring and reporting long-term liabilities. These compound interest principles are applied to various types of bond issues, to the accounting for leases, and to obligations for pensions and other employee benefits. The chapter also describes the disclosure of potential liabilities, such as the obligations that *may* arise if a lawsuit against an entity is concluded in favour of the plaintiff.

The chapter closes with a consideration of the common ratios analysts use to evaluate the level of a firm's indebtedness. When individuals seek to buy a car or a house, lenders assess the buyer's financial position carefully and pay special attention to the size of the down payment the buyer will make. The larger the down payment, the more "equity" the borrower has in the purchase, and the more comfortable the lender is in making the loan. Similarly, potential investors in the common stock or bonds of a company carefully evaluate the amount of debt the company has relative to the amount of shareholders' equity to assess the potential risk of their investment. Thus, a major element of generally accepted accounting principles is the careful definition of what constitutes a liability and how best to disclose the liability to readers of financial statements.

Dow Corning was sued for several millions of dollars by customers claiming injury from the silicon gel implants the company manufactured. Is there a liability involved? When should it be recognized? Accountants have decided the answer depends on details about the case, the level of insurance coverage, and other factors. We consider this case in more detail in a boxed discussion.

Dow Corning
www.corning.com/

■ LIABILITIES IN PERSPECTIVE

Objective 1

Provide a perspective on why information about liabilities is so important to readers of financial statements.

Liabilities, as defined in previous chapters, are one entity's obligations to pay cash or to provide goods and services to other entities. Liabilities include wages due to employees, payables to suppliers, taxes to the government, interest and principal due to lenders, and so on. Ordinarily, these obligations arise from some transaction with an outside party such as a supplier, a lending institution, or an employee. However, obligations also arise from the imposition of taxes or the loss of a lawsuit.

Investors, financial analysts, management, and creditors consider existing liabilities of the firm when valuing the firm's common stock, when evaluating a new loan to the company, and in numerous other decisions. When companies show signs of excessive debt or of an inability to meet existing obligations, problems emerge. Suppliers who normally sell on credit may refuse to ship new items or may ship only C.O.D. (collect on delivery). Lenders may refuse to provide new loans. Customers worried about the reliability of warranties and product service may prefer to buy elsewhere. Valued employees concerned about promotion prospects may seek greener pastures. As problems multiply, conditions can worsen quickly.

When the debt burden is so heavy that the company cannot pay, the creditors can pursue legal channels to collect the debt. Depending on the type of obligation, creditors may be able to force sale of specific assets, take over the board of directors, or force the company out of business. Readers of financial statements are very concerned about debt levels, and the preparers of financial statements are careful to disclose fully the company's liabilities.

The actual example of a balance sheet presentation of liabilities, shown in Exhibit 10-1, is from the annual report of The Timberland Company. Timberland manufactures and markets footwear, apparel, and accessories.

Consistent with common practice, Timberland classifies liabilities as either current or long-term, which helps financial statement readers interpret the immediacy of the company's obligations. **Long-term liabilities** are obligations that fall due more than one year beyond the balance sheet date. *Current liabilities* are obligations that fall due within the coming year or within the normal operating cycle if longer than a year. Some long-term obligations are paid gradually, in yearly or monthly installments. As the Timberland example illustrates, the current portion of the company's long-term obligations is included as a part of its current liabilities.

Accounts payable are amounts owed to suppliers who extended credit for purchases on open account. These open account purchases from trade creditors are ordinarily supported by signatures on purchase orders or similar business documents. *Notes payable* are short-term loans backed by formal promissory notes held by a bank or by business creditors.

long-term liabilities
Obligations that fall due beyond one year from the balance sheet date.

Exhibit 10-1

The Timberland Company
Liabilities Section of Balance Sheet
(in thousands)

	December 31	
	1994	1993
Current liabilities		
Notes payable	$ 22,513	$ 10,061
Current maturities of long-term obligations	8,048	682
Accounts payable	37,035	32,526
Accrued expenses		
Payroll and related	6,038	8,873
Interest and other	24,459	9,609
Taxes	9,029	3,672
Total current liabilities	107,122	65,423
Long-term obligations, less current maturities	206,767	90,809
Total liabilities	$313,889	$156,232

As explained in earlier chapters, the accrual basis of accounting recognizes expenses as they pertain to the operations of a given time period regardless of when they are paid in cash. In the general ledger, separate accounts are maintained for liabilities such as wages, salaries, commissions, interest, and similar items. A report to shareholders may combine these liabilities and show them as a single current liability labelled *accrued liabilities* or *accrued expenses payable*. Sometimes the adjective *accrued* is deleted so that these liabilities are labelled simply taxes payable, wages payable, and so on. Similarly, the term *accrued* may be used and *payable* may be deleted.

Conceptually, a liability is best measured as the amount of cash required to discharge the obligation. For current liabilities, the accounting process is straightforward and the measurement is relatively easy. Accounting for these current obligations is considered before turning to the more difficult task of measuring and reporting long-term obligations.

■ ACCOUNTING FOR CURRENT LIABILITIES

Some current liabilities are recorded automatically as a result of a transaction with an outside entity, such as a lender or supplier. Other liabilities are recorded with an adjusting journal entry to acknowledge an obligation arising over time, such as interest or wages. In this section, accounting for various current liabilities is discussed in detail.

Accounts Payable

As defined in Chapter 1, *accounts payable* (or *trade accounts payable*) are obligations resulting from purchasing goods and services on credit. They are amounts owed to suppliers. Disbursements for accounts payable tend to be voluminous and repetitive. Therefore, special data-processing and internal control systems are usually designed for these transactions. Most companies show accounts payable as a separate line under current liabilities on their balance sheet. However, a few combine accounts payable with accrued liabilities.

Notes Payable

promissory note
A written promise to repay principal plus interest at specific future dates.

Obligations represented by a promissory note given by the borrower to the creditor are called *notes payable*. A **promissory note** is a written promise to repay principal plus interest at specific future dates. Most notes are payable to banks.

Only notes that are payable within the next year are shown as current liabilities; others are long-term liabilities. Some companies combine notes payable with other short-term obligations in a single account. For example, Chevron includes the current portion of long-term debt with notes payable in an account called *short-term debt*. Pfizer, a pharmaceutical company, calls a similar account *short-term borrowings*.

line of credit An agreement with a bank to provide automatically short-term loans up to some preestablished maximum.

Notes payable often result from **lines of credit**, which are agreements with a bank to provide automatically short-term loans up to some preestablished maximum. In the notes to the 1990 financial statements, Timberland disclosed various lines of credit totalling $55 million. At December 31, 1990, $12 million had actually been borrowed. Between 1990 and 1994 Timberland grew to rely more heavily on long-term debt, and on December 15, 1994, Timberland terminated its credit lines.

Pfizer
www.pfizer.com/

Accrued Employee Compensation

The accrual process is described in Chapter 4. Expenses that have been incurred and recognized on the income statement but not yet paid are *accrued liabilities*.

Employee-related liabilities account for a large part of most companies' accrued liabilities. In fact, a majority of companies have a separate current-liability account for such items, with a label such as *salaries, wages, and commissions payable*. Timberland follows this practice by separately stating "Payroll and Related" accrued liabilities.

Estimating Litigation Liabilities

L ate in the 1980s a company was confronting substantial accusations from patients who were dissatisfied with silicone implants made by the company and surgically installed for reconstructive or cosmetic purposes. The accusations became lawsuits over time, and the company was confronted with a significant product liability. What should be disclosed? How much was the liability? How many cases would there be? How much would be involved in financial settlements? What portion of these costs would be covered by insurance companies?

In 1995, the answers to these questions remain uncertain. Notice that the questions posed are financial accounting questions. There are significant philosophical issues about responsibility for the safety of products. There are equally important questions about how to determine scientifically what is safe. While these are important social questions, our immediate concern is about what constitutes a liability. How should companies measure their obligations, disclose the nature of the obligations, and record these amounts in financial statements?

The company, Dow Corning, Inc., has worked on this problem for almost a decade. In the late 1980s the issue was disclosure. There were not yet many cases in the courts, and there was little experience concerning how they would be resolved. Significant product liability insurance policies with multiple carriers would mitigate the direct cost to the company. So for several years the financial statements disclosed the litigation in some detail, but the balance sheet and income statement did not show specific numbers.

It is instructive to examine the last five years. In 1991, the company recorded $25 million of pretax costs, and in 1992, another $69 million. Remember that each of these was intended to be a best estimate of future costs to be incurred. The product was produced and delivered years before. Production ceased in 1992. The United States Food and Drug Administration (FDA) asked producers to suspend the sale and use of the product pending further investigation. Dow Corning did so, and shortly thereafter announced it would not resume production.

But the amounts provided through 1992 were woefully inadequate. In 1993, Dow Corning recorded another pretax charge of $640 million. Combined with expected insurance coverage exceeding $600 million, the total exceeded $1.2 billion. Dow Corning and other manufacturers joined together to structure a settlement that would assure plaintiffs of reasonable compensation, minimize legal costs, and allow the companies to survive. The deal required an agreement between the plaintiffs, the companies, and the insurance carriers. In late 1994, agreement seemed close. Dow Corning provided another pretax charge of $241 million. Combined with additional expected insurance costs the amounts set aside for injured parties approached $2 billion from Dow Corning and another similar amount from other manufacturers. There were over 19,000 pending lawsuits on this product.

In May of 1995, Dow Corning declared bankruptcy. They indicated that too many plaintiffs were unwilling to agree to the settlement. This changes the whole situation and leaves the final outcome very much in doubt. As this book is printed and used, the final outcome of the case will develop. However, the facts to date demonstrate the difficulty of predicting the cost of litigation. An initial extimate of $25 million was too low, by a big margin. ■

Source: Corning 1994 Annual Report.

Chapter 4 described compensation to employees in an elementary way. We assumed that an employee earned, say, $100 per week and, in turn, received $100 in cash on payday. In actuality, however, the complexities of payroll accounting can be awesome. First, employers must *withhold* some employee earnings and pay them instead to the government, insurance companies, labour unions, charitable organizations, and so forth.

For example, consider the withholding of income taxes, Canada Pension Plan (CPP) contributions, and Employment Insurance (EI) contributions. Assume a $100,000 monthly payroll and, for simplicity, assume that the only amounts withheld are $15,000 for income taxes, $3,000 for CPP, and $4,000 for EI. The withholdings are not additional employer costs. They are part of the employee wages and salaries that are payable to third parties. The journal entry for this $100,000 payroll is:

```
Compensation expense  . . . . . . . . . . . . .   100,000
        Salaries and wages payable  . . . . . .              78,000
        Income tax withholding payable  . .                  15,000
        CPP and EI payable  . . . . . . . . . . . .           7,000
```

A second complication is the existence of payroll deductions and fringe benefits. These are employee-related costs *in addition* to salaries and wages. *Payroll deductions* are amounts paid to the government for items such as the employee's portion of Canada Pension Plan, Employment Insurance, and Workers' Compensation. *Fringe benefits* include employee pensions, life and health insurance, and vacation pay. Liabilities are accrued for each of these costs. If they have not yet been paid at the balance sheet date, they are included among the current liabilities.

For example, employers commonly contribute to the employee's medical and drug benefits and the employee might also pay a portion of gross wages into a pension fund. This would generate the following journal entry.

```
Employee Pension Benefit Expense  . . . . .   17,000
        Medical Benefits Payable  . . . . . . . . .           7,000
        Pension Liability Payable  . . . . . . . . .         10,000
```

Income Taxes Payable

A corporation must pay income taxes as a percentage of its earnings. (To review the basic accounting for income taxes, see Chapter 5.) Corporations make periodic installment payments based on their estimated tax for the year. Therefore, the accrued liability for income taxes at year-end is generally much smaller than the annual income tax expense.

To illustrate, suppose a corporation has an estimated taxable income of $100 million for the calendar year 19X0. At a 40% tax rate, the company's estimated taxes for the year are $40 million. Installment payments must be made on a monthly basis to pay the estimated tax liability of $40 million.

The final income tax return must be filed and payment must be made within six months after the year-end. Suppose the actual taxable income is $110 million instead of the estimated $100 million. The corporation must pay the $4 million additional tax on the additional $10 million of taxable income. The accrued liability on December 31, 19X0 would be $4,000,000, and the journal entry would be the following at the company's year-end:

```
Income taxes expense  . . . . . . . . . . . . . . .   4,000
        Income taxes payable  . . . . . . . . . . .           4,000
```

Current Portion of Long-Term Debt

A company's long-term debt often includes some payments due within a year that should be reclassified as current liabilities. The journal entry for recognizing the current portion of long-term debt reclassifies a noncurrent liability as a current liability. Using the Timberland illustration in Exhibit 10-1, the reclassification journal entry for 1994 would be:

```
Long-term obligations  . . . . . . . . . . . . . . . . . . . . . . .   8,048
        Current portion of long-term obligations  . . .               8,048
```

Sales Tax

When retailers collect sales taxes, either provincial sales taxes (PST) or the federal Goods and Services Tax (GST), they are agents of the provincial or federal government. For example, suppose a 7% sales tax is levied on sales of $10,000. The total collected from the customer must be $10,000 + $700, or $10,700. The impact on the entity is:

A	=	L	+	SE
+ 10,700	=	+ 700		+ 10,000
⌈ Increase Cash ⌉ or Accounts Receivable		⌈ Increase ⌉ Sales Tax Payable		⌈ Increase ⌉ Sales

The sales tax payable appears on the balance sheet as a liability until the taxes are paid to the government. The sales shown on the income statement would be $10,000, not $10,700. The sales tax never affects the income statement. The $700 received for taxes affects the current liability account Sales Tax Payable and is shown on the balance sheet until it is paid to the government. The journal entries (without explanations) are:

```
Cash or accounts receivable  ...........   10,700
        Sales  .....................              10,000
        Sales tax payable .............                 700
Sales tax payable ...................      700
        Cash .........................                 700
```

Product Warranties

Some current liabilities are not measured with the same degree of certainty as the previous examples. A noteworthy example is the liability arising from product guarantees and warranties. If warranty obligations are material, they must be accrued when products are sold because the obligation arises then, not when the actual services are performed. Ford describes its accounting as follows: "Anticipated costs related to product warranty are accrued at the time of sale."

The *estimated* warranty expenses are typically based on past experience for replacing or remedying defective products. Although the estimates should be close, they are rarely precisely correct. Therefore, any differences between the estimated and actual results are usually added to or subtracted from the current warranty expense account as additional information unfolds. The accounting entry at the time of sale is:

```
        Warranty expense .....................     600,000
                Liability for warranties (or some similar title)    600,000
        To record the estimated liability for warranties
        arising from current sales. The provision is 3%
        of current sales of $20 million, or $600,000.
```

When a warranty claim arises, an entry such as the following is made:

```
Liability for warranties .....................      1,000
    Cash, accounts payable, accrued wages payable,
    and similar accounts ................                    1,000

To record the acquisition of supplies,
outside services, and employee services to
satisfy claims for repairs.
```

If the estimate for warranty expense is accurate, the entries for all claims will total about $600,000.

Returnable Deposits

Customers occasionally make money deposits that are to be returned in full, sometimes with interest and sometimes not. Well-known examples of returnable deposits are those with banks and similar financial institutions. Savings deposits are *interest-bearing deposits*, on which an explicit rate of interest is paid. In contrast, many chequing deposits do not bear interest and are thus interest-free or *non-interest-bearing deposits*. Other examples of deposits include those for returnable containers such as soft-drink bottles, oil drums, or beer kegs. Moreover, many lessors (landlords) require damage deposits that are to be returned in full if specified conditions are met by their lessees (tenants).

Companies that receive deposits view them as a form of payable, although the word *payable* may not be a part of their specific labelling. The accounting entries by the *recipients* of deposits have the following basic pattern (numbers assumed in thousands of dollars):

	Interest-Bearing		Non-Interest-Bearing	
1. Deposit	Cash	100	Cash	100
	Deposits (payable)	100	Deposits (payable)	100
2. Interest recognized	Interest expense	9	No entry	
	Deposits	9		
3. Deposit returned	Deposits	109	Deposits	100
	Cash	109	Cash	100

The account Deposits is a current liability of the company receiving the deposit. Ordinarily the recipient of the cash deposit may use the cash for investment purposes from the date of deposit to the date of its return to the depositor. For example, banks lend the cash deposited by some customers to other customers in order to earn interest revenue.

Unearned Revenue

Chapter 4 explained that revenue collected in advance is usually a current liability. The seller either must deliver the product or service or is obligated to make a full refund. Examples include lease rentals, magazine subscriptions, insurance premiums, advance airline or theatre ticket sales, and advance repair service contracts.

The accounting entries follow (in dollars):

Cash	100,000	
Unearned sales revenue		100,000
To record advance collections from customers.		
Unearned sales revenue	100,000	
Sales		100,000
To record sales revenue when products are		
delivered to customers who paid in advance.		

Unearned revenues are also called *revenues collected in advance*. These advance collections are also referred to as *deferred credits*. Why? Because, as the second entry shows, the ultimate accounting entry is a "credit" to revenue, but such an entry has been deferred to a later accounting period.

■ LONG-TERM LIABILITIES

How do accountants measure the value of obligations that are not due for at least a year? Such measurement must recognize the "time value of money." A dollar to be paid (or received) in the future is not worth as much as a dollar today. For example, suppose a company owes $105, due in one year. It can put $100 in a savings account that pays 5% interest. In one year, the original $100 plus the $5 interest earned can be used to pay the $105 obligation. Satisfying the $105 obligation took only 100 of today's dollars. Therefore a current balance sheet should include an obligation of $100, not $105.

To understand the accounting for long-term liabilities, you need to understand the principles of *compound interest* and related terms such as *future value* and *present value*. If you do not already have a thorough understanding of these items, carefully study Appendix 10A before reading further. You can test your understanding by solving Summary Problems Three and Four on pages 450 to 451.

Nature of Long-Term Liabilities

Objective 3

Describe the contractual nature of various long-term liabilities.

Long-term liabilities are generally recorded at the present value of all future payments, discounted at the market interest rate in effect when the liability was incurred. Consider a loan for a new car. Michelle Young graduated from college and wishes to buy a $14,000 car on January 1, 19X0. She has only $4,000 cash. She borrows $10,000 at 10% interest, agreeing to pay $3,154.71 each December 31 from 19X0 through 19X3. (Normally payments would be made monthly, but for simplicity we assume annual payments.) The loan is illustrated in Exhibit 10-2.

Michelle's total payments are 4 × $3,154.71 = $12,618.84. However, the *present value* of the payments at 10% is only 3.1699 × $3,154.71 = $10,000. (The 3.1699 factor is from the four-year row and 10% column of Table 3, page 460). What is the proper measure of her liability at January 1, 19X0? It is $10,000, the *present value* of the future payments, not the total of those payments. Most contracts would allow her to repay the amount borrowed without penalty at any time, so in a literal sense she could give the lender $10,000 on January 1, 19X0 and discharge her liability.

| Exhibit 10-2 | | Analysis of Car Loan | | | |

Year	(1) Beginning Liability	(2) Interest @ 10% (1) × 0.10	(3) End-of-Year Cash Payment	(4) Reduction of Principal (3) – (2)	(5) Ending Liability (1) – (4)
19X0	$10,000.00	$1,000.00	$3,154.71	$2,154.71	$7,845.29
19X1	7,845.29	784.53	3,154.71	2,370.18	5,475.11
19X2	5,475.11	547.51	3,154.71	2,607.20	2,867.91
19X3	2,867.91	286.79	3,154.71	2,867.92	– 0.01*

* Rounding error; should be 0.

private placement A process whereby notes are issued by corporations when money is borrowed from a few sources, not from the general public.

bonds Formal certificates of indebtedness that are typically accompanied by (1) a promise to pay interest in cash at a specified annual rate plus (2) a promise to pay the principal at a specific maturity date.

nominal interest rate (contractual rate, coupon rate, stated rate) A contractual rate of interest paid on bonds.

face amount (par value) The principal as indicated on the certificates of bonds or other debt instruments.

mortgage bond A form of long-term debt that is secured by the pledge of specific property.

Several types of obligations are classified as long-term liabilities. Notes and bonds are most common. Corporations issue notes when money is borrowed from a few sources. These issues are known as **private placements** because they are not held or traded among the general public. Instead, the creditors are financial institutions such as insurance companies or pension funds.

Corporations have heavy demands for borrowed capital, so they often borrow from the general public by issuing bonds. **Bonds** are formal certificates of indebtedness that typically represent (1) a promise to pay interest in cash at a specified annual rate (often called the **nominal interest rate, contractual rate, coupon rate,** or **stated rate**) plus (2) a promise to pay the principal (often called the **face amount** or **par value**) at a specific maturity date. The interest is usually paid every six months. Fundamentally, bonds are individual promissory notes issued to many lenders.

Pension and lease obligations are also long-term liabilities that are recorded at the present value of future payments. The CICA has decided that both are appropriately listed as liabilities and has provided specific rules for their measurement.

Mortgage Bonds and Debentures

Different lenders have different priority claims in collecting their money. As described below, mortgage bondholders have high priority claims on specific firm assets, while subordinated claims have lower priority claims on assets. A **mortgage bond** is a form of long-term debt that is secured by the pledge of specific property. In case of default, these bondholders can sell the pledged property to satisfy their claims. Moreover, the holders of mortgage bonds have a further unsecured claim on the corporation if the proceeds from the pledged property are insufficient.

In contrast, a **debenture** is a debt security with a general claim against the *total* assets, rather than a particular asset. Suppose a company defaults and is liquidated to repay the creditors. *Liquidation* means converting assets to cash and terminating outside claims. A debenture bond is secured on the general assets of the company and would rank behind any secured creditors but before unsecured creditors. To clarify these ideas, suppose a liquidated company had a single asset, a building, that was sold for $110,000 cash. The balance sheet immediately after liquidation is:

Assets		Equities	
Cash	$110,000	Accounts payable	$ 50,000
		First-mortgage bonds payable	80,000
		Subordinated debentures payable	40,000
		Total liabilities	170,000
		Shareholders' equity (negative)	(60,000)
Total assets	$110,000	Total equities	$110,000

debenture A debt security with a general claim against all assets rather than a specific claim against particular assets.

subordinated debentures Debt securities whose holders have claims against only the assets that remain after the claims of certain secured creditors are satisfied.

unsubordinated debenture A bond that is unsecured by specific pledged assets, giving its owner a general claim with a priority like an account payable.

The mortgage bondholders, having a direct claim on the building, will be paid in full ($80,000). The debenture holders, assuming they are subordinated only to the mortgage, will receive the balance of $30,000 in settlement of their claim ($0.75 on the dollar). The unsecured creditors which normally include trade creditors, would receive nothing.

A *mortgage bond*, which has a specific lien on particular assets, is an inherently safer investment than the company's *debentures*, which have no specific lien on any asset. However, the relative attractiveness of specific bonds depends *primarily* on the credit worthiness of the issuer. Thus, IBM can issue billions of dollars of debentures at relatively low interest rates when compared with the mortgage bonds that might be issued by real estate companies.

Bond Provisions

Bonds typically have a par value of $1,000, but they are quoted in terms of *percentages of par*. Some bonds are traded on the public stock exchanges. Examples of daily quotations follow:

Issuer	Coupon	Maturity	Price	Yield	$Change
Bell Canada*	8.80	17 Aug. 05	111.922	6.891	−0.039
Bombardier	6.40	22 Dec. 06	95.543	7.042	−0.018
Westcoast Energy	7.30	18 Dec. 06	94.600	7.767	+0.022

* The price of one $1,000 bond is 111.922%% of $1,000 = $1119.22

current yield Annual interest payments divided by the current price of a bond.

trust indenture A contract whereby the issuing corporation of a bond promises a trustee that it will abide by stated provisions.

protective covenant (covenant) A provision stated in a bond, usually to protect the bondholders' interests.

Bell Canada's bonds carrying an 8.8% coupon rate and maturing in August 17, 2005 closed at a price of $1,119.22 (111.922% of $1,000) at the end of the day. The **current yield** is calculated as the annual interest divided by the current price, or 7.863%. The yield to maturity is the current yield less the premium/discount over/below par value divided by the length of time until maturity. For Bell Canada this yield is 6.891%. The closing price was down $.39 from that of the previous day.

An issue of bonds is usually accompanied by a **trust indenture** whereby the issuing corporation promises a *trustee* (usually a bank or trust company) that it will abide by stated provisions, often called **protective covenants** or simply **covenants**. The indenture is designed primarily to protect the safety of the bondholders. The provisions pertain to payments of principal and interest, sales of pledged property, restrictions on dividends, and like matters. The trustee's major function is to represent the collective claims and concerns of the bondholders.

For example, MacMillan Bloedel, the large forest products company, indicated in a recent annual report that "*trust indentures* securing the company's debentures contain provisions limiting the amount of indebtedness the company can incur." Gordon Jewelry Corporation, a major jewellery company, mentioned many constraints in a recent annual report: "The note agreement contains restrictive *covenants* regarding the nature of the business, liabilities, financial ratios, indebtedness, liens, investments, leases, company stock, mergers, and dispositions."

Bonds issued by industrial corporations are normally **registered instruments**, which means that the interest and maturity payments are made to a specific owner. In contrast, bonds issued a number of years ago were normally **unregistered,** or **bearer instruments,** which means that the interest is paid to the individual who presents the interest *coupons* attached to the bond to the bank. Similarly, the principal is paid to the individual who presents the bond at the maturity date. Bearer instruments are like cash; they are more vulnerable to theft than are registered bonds.

Callable, Sinking Fund, and Convertible Bonds

Some bonds are **callable**, which means that they are subject to redemption before maturity at the option of the issuer. Typically, the call is at a redemption price in excess of par. The excess over par is referred to as a **call premium**. A bond issued in 1995 with a 2015 maturity date might be callable any time after 2010. Then it may be subject to call for an initial price in 2010 of 105 (105% of par), in 2011 of 104, in 2012 of 103, and so on. The call premium declines from $50 per $1,000 bond to $40 in 2011 and so on.

Sinking fund bonds require the issuer to make annual payments into a sinking fund. A **sinking fund** is cash or securities segregated for meeting obligations on bonded debt. It is an asset that is usually classified as part of an asset category called "investments" or "other assets." The sinking fund helps assure the bondholders that sufficient cash will be accumulated to repay the principal at maturity.

Convertible bonds are those bonds that may, at the holder's option, be exchanged for other securities. The conversion is usually for a predetermined number of common shares of the issuing company. Because of the conversion feature, convertible bondholders are willing to accept a lower interest rate than on a similar bond without the conversion privilege.

Most companies have an assortment of long-term debt, including a variety of bonds payable. There are too many types of bonds to discuss exhaustively here. Textbooks on corporate finance contain detailed descriptions. The body of the balance sheet usually summarizes such debt on one line. In contrast, the details in the footnotes can occupy an entire page.

---

registered instrument Bonds that require the interest and maturity payments to be made to specific owners.

unregistered instrument (bearer instrument) Bonds requiring interest to be paid to the individual who presents the interest coupons attached to the bond.

callable bonds Bonds subject to redemption before maturity at the option of the issuer.

call premium The amount by which the redemption price exceeds par.

sinking fund bonds Bonds with indentures that require the issuer to make annual payments to a sinking fund.

sinking fund Cash or securities segregated for meeting obligations on bonded debt.

convertible bonds Bonds that may, at the holder's option, be exchanged for other securities.

■ ACCOUNTING FOR BOND TRANSACTIONS

Market Valuation of Bonds

underwriters A group of investment bankers that buys an entire bond or stock issue from a corporation and then sells the bonds to the general investing public.

premium on bonds The excess of the proceeds over the face amount of a bond.

discount on bonds The excess of face amount over the proceeds upon issuance of a bond.

yield to maturity (market rate, effective interest rate) The interest rate that equates market price at a particular date to the present value of principal and interest.

Bonds are typically sold through a syndicate (special group) of investment bankers called **underwriters.** That is, the syndicate buys the entire issue from the corporation, thus guaranteeing that the company will obtain all of its desired funds. In turn, the syndicate sells the bonds to the general investing public.

A company's board of directors sets the stated or nominal interest rate. The investment banker who manages the underwriting syndicate provides advice. The nominal rate is usually set as close to the current market rate as possible. Many factors affect this rate, notably general economic conditions, industry conditions, risks of the use of the proceeds, and specific features of the bonds (examples include callability, sinking fund, convertibility). On the day of issuance, the proceeds to the issuer may be above par or below par, depending on market conditions. If the proceeds are above par, the bonds have been sold at a **premium;** if the proceeds are below par, the bonds are sold at a **discount.** Therefore the **yield to maturity (market rate, effective interest rate)**—the rate of interest demanded by investors in a bond—frequently differs from the *nominal interest rate.* The interest paid in cash, usually semiannually, is determined by the nominal rate, not the effective rate. The yield to maturity is the interest rate at which all contractual cash flows for interest and principal have a present value equal to the market price at a particular date.

Note that issuing bonds at a discount does not mean that the credit-worthiness of the issuer is especially bad, nor does issuing bonds at a premium mean that credit-worthiness is especially good. Discounts and premiums are determined by market forces that fluctuate from day to day and by the choice of the nominal rate of interest, relative to the then-current market rate of interest for bonds of similar risk.

A typical bond consists of a promise to pay interest every six months until maturity and a promise to pay a lump sum at maturity. Suppose a two-year $1,000 bond is issued that bears a nominal interest rate of 10%. Consider how the investor would value the bond, using the tables on pages 458-60.

Exhibit 10-3 shows how the bond would be valued, using three different interest rates. Note that:

1. Although the quoted bond rates imply a rate per annum, the bond markets do not mean that rate literally. Thus a 10% bond really pays 5% interest each semiannual period. A two-year bond has four periods, a ten-year bond has twenty periods, and so on.

2. The *higher* the effective (or market) rate of interest, the *lower* the present value.

3. When the market interest rate equals the coupon rate of 10%, the bond is worth $1,000. We say such a bond is issued at *par.*

4. When the market interest rate of 12% exceeds the 10% coupon rate, the bond sells at a discount (i.e., for less than par).

5. When the market interest rate of 8% is less than the coupon rate, the bond sells at a premium (i.e., for more than par).

Chrysler Bonds: 1982–1993

Some people may think of bonds as boring investments that provide semiannual interest payments until the eventual repayment of the original principal. What these people fail to realize is that the resale value of a bond may rise and fall substantially over its life as market conditions change. Large changes in value may accompany general changes in interest rates or changes in the specific circumstances of the issuing firm.

During October 1973, Chrysler issued 8% bonds with principal value of $1,000 maturing in 1998. The bonds were sold at $1,000 because the market rate of interest on equivalent risk bonds was also 8% per year.

What was the market price of Chrysler's bonds ten years after issuance, in October 1982? October 1983–93? Implicitly, investors calculate the price they are willing to pay for Chrysler's bonds using the market interest rate for bonds of equivalent risk at that time and the number of periods until maturity. At October 1982, Chrysler's bonds matured in sixteen years, or in thirty-two periods of half a year, and the market interest rate for bonds of equivalent risk was 17.6%, or 8.8% per half-year. The market value of the bonds can be calculated as the present value of the $40 interest payments made every half-year ($1,000 × 8% × 1/2 = $40) and the present value of the $1,000 principal payment at maturity:

Interest:	PV of $40 per period for 32 periods at 8.8% per period	=	$423.96
Principal:	PV of $1,000 at maturity in 32 periods at 8.8% per period	=	67.28
Market Value:		=	$491.24

The historical market value of Chrysler's bonds can be found in past issues of *Moody's Bond Record*. Moody's provides bond ratings that measure the likelihood that the issuer will be able to pay back the debt. They range from Aaa (highest) to Baa (middle) to C (lowest). When the Chrysler bonds were issued in 1973, Moody's assigned them an A rating. The table below shows the market value and bond rating in October for 1973 and 1982–93. Notice that in 1982 the price of the bonds fell to $491.24. Why? One reason is that Chrysler bonds became riskier, as indicated by the fall in Moody's rating from A to Caa. During the next year, Chrysler's condition improved significantly, its bond rating rose, and owners of these bonds earned a return of 50% including interest and appreciation. ■

Market Value of Chrysler 8% Bonds Due 1998

Date	Market Value	*Moody's* Rating
Oct. 1973	$1,000.00	A
$\int$	$\int$	$\int$
Oct. 1982	491.24	Caa
Oct. 1983	665.00	B2
Oct. 1984	621.25	Ba2
Oct. 1985	753.75	Baa3
Oct. 1986	922.50	Baa3
Oct. 1987	840.00	Baa1
Oct. 1988	912.50	Baa1
Oct. 1990	750.00	Baa3
Oct. 1991	680.00	Ba3
Oct. 1992	968.75	B1
Oct. 1993	1,021.25	Baa3

Source: Moody's Bond Record, 1982–1993.

Exhibit 10-3   Computation of Market Value of Bonds (in dollars)

	Present Value Factor	Total Present Value	Sketch of Cash Flows by Period				
			0	1	2	3	4
Valuation at 10% per year, or 5% per half-year:							
Principal, 4-period line, Table 2 .8227 × $1,000 = $822.70	.8227	822.70					1,000
Interest, 4-period line, Table 3 3.5460 × $50 = $177.30	3.5460	177.30		50	50	50	50
Total		1,000.00					
Valuation at 12% per year, or 6% per half-year:							
Principal	.7921	792.10					1,000
Interest	3.4651	173.25		50	50	50	50
Total		965.35					
Valuation at 8% per year, or 4% per half-year:							
Principal	.8548	854.80					1,000
Interest	3.6299	181.50		50	50	50	50
Total		1,036.30					

Bonds Issued at Par

Objective 5

Value and account for bond issues over their entire life.

Suppose that on December 31, 1996, a company issued 10,000 two-year, 10% debentures, at par. Therefore, the proceeds of the sale were equal to the face amount of 10,000 × $1,000 = $10 million. Exhibit 10-4 shows how the issuer would account for the bonds throughout their life, assuming that they are held to maturity. Because the bonds were issued at par, the interest expense equals the amount of the interest payments, 5% × $10 million = $500,000 each six months. The interest expense and the cash payments for interest each totals $2,000,000 over the four semiannual periods. The journal entries for the issue follow:

1. Cash 10,000,000
      Bonds payable 10,000,000
   To record proceeds upon issuance of 10% bonds maturing on December 31, 1998.

2. Interest expense 500,000
      Cash 500,000
   To record payment of interest each six-month period.

3. Bonds payable 10,000,000
      Cash 10,000,000
   To record payment of maturity value of bonds and their retirement.

The issuer's balance sheet at December 31, 1996, and December 31, 1997 (at the end of the first year, after paying semiannual interest) shows:

Bonds payable, 10% due December 31, 1998	$10,000,000

	A	=	L	+	SE
			Bonds		
	Cash		**Payable**		**Retained Earnings**
Issuer's records					
1. Issuance	+10,000	=	+10,000		
2. Semiannual interest (repeated twice a year for two years)	−500	=			−500 [Increase Interest Expense]
3. Maturity value (final payment)	−10,000	=	−10,000		
Bond-related totals (total of 4 semiannual payments)	− 2,000		0		−2,000

Bonds Issued at a Discount

Suppose the 10,000 bonds described in the preceding section are issued at a discount when annual market interest rates are 12%. Proceeds of the sale are 10,000 × $965.35 = $9,653,500, which reflects an effective interest rate of 6% per semiannual period, as shown in Exhibit 10-3. Therefore, a discount of $10,000,000 − $9,653,500 = $346,500 is recognized at issuance. The discount is the excess of the face amount over the proceeds. The company has use of only $9,653,500, not $10,000,000. The journal entry at issue is:

```
Cash ........................    9,653,500
Discount on bonds payable  .......    346,500
        Bonds payable .............              10,000,000
```

The discount on bonds payable is a *contra account*. It is deducted from bonds payable. The bonds payable account usually shows the face amount, and the difference between bonds payable and discount on bonds payable is the net *carrying amount* or net liability:

Issuer's Balance Sheet	December 31, 1996
Bonds payable, 10% due December 31, 1998	$10,000,000
Deduct: Discount on bonds payable	346,500
Net liability	$ 9,653,500

For bonds issued at a discount, interest takes two forms, semiannual cash outlays of 5% × $10 million = $500,000 plus an extra lump-sum cash payment of $346,500 at maturity (total payment of $10,000,000 at maturity when only $9,653,500 was actually borrowed). The extra $346,500 is another cost of using

discount amortization The spreading of bond discount over the life of the bonds as expense.

the proceeds over the four semiannual periods. It should be spread over all four periods, not simply charged at maturity. The spreading of the discount over the life of the bonds is called **discount amortization.**

How much of the $346,500 should be amortized each semiannual period? A simple alternative is *straight-line depreciation*:

Cash interest payment, 0.05 × $10,000,000	$500,000
Amortization of discount, $346,500 : 4 periods	86,625
Total semiannual interest expense	$586,625

The discount is used as an adjustment of nominal interest to obtain the real interest. Notice that the amortization of bond discount increases the interest expense of the issuer. The straight-line depreciation is simple, but it is conceptually flawed because it implies a different effective interest rate each period.

During the first six months, the implied interest rate would be 6.08% ($586,625 interest expense divided by proceeds or carrying value of $9,653,500). The $86,625 of amortized discount would increase the carrying value or book value of the debt to $9,740,125 in the second six months yielding an implied interest rate of 6.02% ($586,625 ÷ $9,740,125).

effective-interest amortization (compound interest method) An amortization method that uses a constant interest rate.

A preferred amortization method that uses a constant interest rate is **effective-interest amortization,** also called the **compound interest method.** The key to effective-interest amortization is that each period bears an interest expense equal to the carrying value of the debt (the net liability or the face amount less unamortized discount), multiplied by the market interest rate in effect when the bond was issued. The product is the *effective-interest amount*. The difference between the effective-interest amount and the cash interest payment is the amount of discount amortized for the period.

Consider our example with a market rate of 12% (or 6% each semiannual period) when the bond was issued. The effective-interest amortization schedule is shown in Exhibit 10-5. Notice that the discount amortized is not the same amount each period.

The balance sheet disclosure of the bond payable is the ending net liability calculated as the difference between the face or par value and the unamortized discount. Thus, at June 30, 1997, the balance sheet would reflect a liability of $9,732,707. The calculation might be shown on the balance sheet or in the footnotes as:

Issuer's Balance Sheets	12/31/96	6/30/97	12/31/97	6/30/98	12/31/98[*]
Bonds payable, 10% due 12/31/98	$10,000,000	$10,000,000	$10,000,000	$10,000,000	$10,000,000
Deduct: Unamortized discount	346,500	267,293	183,334	94,337	—
Net liability	$ 9,653,500	$ 9,732,707	$ 9,816,666	$ 9,905,663	$10,000,000

[*]Before payment at maturity.

Exhibit 10-5 shows the complete worksheet and journal entries for the effective-interest method of amortizing the bond discount. Be sure you understand this important exhibit before proceeding further. Note that the interest expense each period is the market rate of interest at issue times the carrying value or book value of the bond. (See column (2) of Exhibit 10-5.) This value changes each semiannual period. The cash payment is a constant $500,000 calculated as one-half the coupon rate (10% ÷ 2) times the par value ($10,000,000).

Exhibit 10-5				Effective-Interest Amortization of Bond Discount			
	(1)	**(2)**	**(3)**	**(4)**	**Ending Liability**		
For Six Months Ended	**Beginning Net Liability**	**Effective Interest* @ 6%****	**Nominal Interest† @ 5%**	**Discount Amortized (2) – (3)**	*Face Amount*	*Unamortized Discount*	*Ending Net Liability*
12/31/96	—	—	—	—	$10,000,000	$346,500	$ 9,653,500
6/30/97	$9,653,500	$579,207	$500,000	$79,207	10,000,000	267,293++	9,732,707
12/31/97	9,732,707	583,959	500,000	83,959	10,000,000	183,334	9,816,666
6/30/98	9,816,666	588,997	500,000	88,997	10,000,000	94,337	9,905,663
12/31/98	9,905,663	594,337	500,000	94,337	10,000,000	0	10,000,000

* Market interest rate when issued times beginning net liability, column (1).
** To avoid rounding errors, an unrounded actual effective rate slightly under 6% was used. The table used to calculate the proceeds of the issue has too few significant digits to calculate the exact present value of a number as large as $10 million. The more exact issue price would be $9,653,489.
† Nominal (coupon interest) rate times par value (face value), for six months.
++ $346,500 – $79,207 = $267,293; $267,293 – $83,959 = $183,334; etc.

Journal entries:
Discount
Amortization (without explanations)

12/31/96	1.	Cash	9,653,500	
		Discount on bonds payable	346,500	
		Bonds payable		10,000,000
6/30/97	2.	Interest expense	579,207	
		Discount on bonds payable		79,207
		Cash		500,000
12/31/97		Interest expense	583,959	
		Discount on bonds payable		83,959
		Cash		500,000
6/30/98		Interest expense	588,997	
		Discount on bonds payable		88,997
		Cash		500,000
12/31/98		Interest expense	594,337	
		Discount on bonds payable		94,337
		Cash		500,000
12/31/98	3.	Bonds payable	10,000,000	
		Cash		10,000,000

Exhibit 10-6		A	=		L	+	SE
Effective-Interest Amortization of Bond Discount (rounded to thousands of dollars)		Cash	Bonds Payable	Discount on Bonds Payable			Retained Earnings
	Issuer's records:						
	1. Issuance	19,654	+10,000	−346	Increase Discount		
	2. Semiannual interest Six months ended:						
	6/30/97	−500		+79			−579
	12/31/97	−500		+84	Decrease Discount		−584	Increase Interest Expense
	6/30/98	−500		+89			−589
	12/31/98	−500		+94			594
	3. Maturity value (final payment)	−10,000	−10,000	0			
	Bond-related totals	− 2,346	0	0			−2,346

Bonds Issued at a Premium

Accounting for bonds issued at a premium is not difficult after you have mastered bond discounts. The differences are reversed from discount bonds:

1. The cash proceeds *exceed* the face amount.
2. The amount of the contra account Premium on Bonds Payable is *added* to the face amount to determine the net liability reported in the balance sheet.
3. The amortization of bond premium *decreases* the interest expense.

To illustrate, suppose the 10,000 bonds described earlier were issued when annual market interest rates were 8% (and semiannual rates 4%). Proceeds would be 10,000 × $1,036.30 = $10,363,000 as shown in Exhibit 10-3. Exhibits 10-7 and 10-8 show how the effective-interest method is applied to the bond premium. The key concept remains the same as for amortization of bond discount: The interest expense equals the net liability multiplied by the market interest rate in effect when the bond was issued. Balance sheets show the net liability calculated as the face amount plus unamortized premium. The premium reduces to zero over the life of the bond:

Issuer's Balance Sheets	12/31/96	6/30/97	12/31/97	6/30/98	12/31/98[*]
Bonds payable, 10% due 12/31/98	$10,000,000	$10,000,000	$10,000,000	$10,000,000	$10,000,000
Add: Premium on bonds payable	363,000	277,517	188,615	96,157	0
Net liability	$10,363,000	$10,277,517	$10,188,615	$10,096,157	$10,000,000

*Before payment at maturity.

Journal entries:
Premium
Amortization
(without
explanations)

12/31/96	1.	Cash	10,363,000	
		Premium on bonds payable ...		363,000
		Bonds payable		$10,000,000
6/30/97	2.	Interest expense	414,517	
		Premium on bonds payable	85,483	
		Cash		500,000
12/31/97		Interest expense	411,098	
		Premium on bonds payable	88,902	
		Cash		500,000
6/30/98		Interest expense	407,542	
		Premium on bonds payable	92,458	
		Cash		500,000
12/31/98		Interest expense	403,843	
		Premium on bonds payable	96,157	
		Cash		500,000
12/31/98	3.	Bonds payable	10,000,000	
		Cash		10,000,000

Exhibit 10-7	Effective-Interest Amortization of Bond Premium

	(1)	(2)	(3)	(4)	Ending Liability		
For Six Months Ended	**Beginning Net Liability**	**Effective Interest*** **@ 4%****	**Nominal Interest†** **@ 5%**	**Premium Amortized** **(3) – (2)**	*Face Amount*	*Unamortized Premium*	*Ending Net Liability*
12/31/96	—	—	—	—	$10,000,000	$363,000	$10,363,000
6/30/97	$10,363,000	$414,517	$500,000	$85,483	10,000,000	277,517‡	10,277,517
12/31/97	10,277,517	411,098	500,000	88,902	10,000,000	188,615	10,188,615
6/30/98	10,188,615	407,542	500,000	92,458	10,000,000	96,157	10,096,157
12/31/98	10,096,157	403,843	500,000	96,157	10,000,000	0	10,000,000

* Market interest rate when issued times beginning net liability, column (1).
** To avoid rounding errors, an unrounded actual effective rate slightly under 4% was used.
† Nominal (coupon interest) rate times par value (face values), for six months.
‡ $363,000 – $85,483 = $277,517; $277,517 – $88,902 = $188,615; etc.

Early Extinguishment

Investors often dispose of bonds before maturity by selling them to other investors. Such a sale does not affect the issuer's books. However, the issuer may redeem its *own* bonds by purchases on the open market or by exercising its call option. Gains or losses on these early extinguishments of debt are computed in the usual manner. That is, the difference between the cash paid and the net carrying amount of the bonds (face, less unamortized discount or plus unamortized premium) is the gain or loss.

Consider the bonds issued at a discount and described in Exhibit 10-5. Suppose the issuer purchases all of its bonds on the open market for 96 on December 31, 1997 (after all interest payments and amortization were recorded for 1997):

Carrying amount:		
Face or par value	$10,000,000	
Deduct: Unamortized discount on bonds*	183,334	$ 9,816,666
Cash required, 96% of $10,000,000		9,600,000
Difference, gain on early extinguishment of debt		$ 216,666

* See Exhibit 10-5, page 438. Of the original $346,500 discount, $79,207 + $83,959 = $163,166 has been amortized, leaving $183,334 of the discount unamortized.

Exhibit 10-8

Effective-Interest Amortization of Bond Premium (rounded to thousands of dollars)

	A	=	L		+	SE
	Cash	Bonds Payable	Premium on Bonds Payable			Retained Earnings
Issuer's records:						
1. Issuance	+10,363	+10,000	363	[Increase Premium]		
2. Semiannual interest Six months ended:						
6/30/97	−500		−85			−415 [Increase
12/31/97	−500		−89	[Decrease		−411 Interest
6/30/98	−500		−92	Premium]		−408 Expense]
12/31/98	−500		−96			−404
3. Maturity value (final payment)	−10,000	−10,000				
Bond-related totals	− 1,637	0	1*			− 1,638*

* Rounding error; should equal 0 and 1637.

Exhibit 10-9 presents an analysis of the transaction (rounded to thousands of dollars). The $216,666 gain on extinguishment of debt would be shown on an income statement below operating income as a separate classification called an extraordinary item. The journal entry on December 31, 1997 is:

```
Bond payable . . . . . . . . . . . . . . . . . . . . .   10,000,000
    Discount on bonds payable . . . . . . .                 183,334
    Gain on early extinguishment of debt                    216,666
    Cash . . . . . . . . . . . . . . . . . . . . . .       9,600,000
To record open-market acquisition of
entire issue of 10% bonds at 96.
```

Exhibit 10-9

Analysis of Early Extinguishment of Debt on Issuer's Records (in thousands of dollars)

	A	=	L		+	SE	
	Cash	Bonds Payable	Discount on Bonds Payable			Retained Earnings	
Redemption, December 31, 1997	−9,600	= −10,000	+183	[Decrease Discount]	+217	[Gain on Early Extinguishment]	

Bonds Sold between Interest Dates

Bond interest payments are typically made semiannually. Suppose the company in our example had its $10 million, 10% bonds printed and ready for issuance on

December 31, 1996, but then market conditions delayed issuance of the bonds. On January 31, 1997, one month after the originally planned issuance date, the bonds were issued at par. The indenture requires the payment of $500,000 interest every six months, beginning June 30, 1997.

Bonds sold between interest dates command the market price *plus accrued interest*. Thus, the market quotations you see for bonds *always* mean that the investor must pay an extra amount for any *unearned* interest to be received at the next interest payment date. In our example, the price to be paid is:

Market price of bonds at 100 on 1/31/97	$10,000,000
Accrued interest, 0.10 × $10,000,000 × ½	83,333
Market price plus accrued interest	$10,083,333

Note that the $500,000 interest payment due on June 30, 1997 is spread over the first six months of 1997 by the straight-line method, that is, with an equal amount to each month.

Exhibit 10-10 presents an analysis of these transactions (rounded to thousands of dollars). Note that the interest expense for the first half of 1997 is properly measured as $500,000 − $83,333 = $416,667, pertaining to only five months that the money was actually in use. The journal entries follow:

1/31/97 Cash	$10,083,333	
Bonds payable		$10,000,000
Accrued interest payable		83,333
6/30/97 Accrued interest payable	83,333	
Interest expense	416,667	
Cash		500,000

Exhibit 10-10	A	=	L		+	SE
Analysis of Bonds Sold between Interest Dates (in thousands of dollars)	Cash		Bonds Payable	Accrued Interest Payable		Retained Earnings
Issuance, 1/31/97	+10,083	=	+10,000	+83		
Interest payment, 6/30/97	−500	=		−83		−417 ⎡Increase Interest Expense⎤

Obviously, the analysis of transactions can be made more complicated by combining the acquisitions of bonds between interest dates with discounts and premiums. However, these are mechanical details that do not involve any new accounting concepts.

Non-Interest-Bearing Notes and Bonds

Some notes and bonds do not bear explicit interest. Instead, they contain a promise to pay a lump sum at a specified date. An example is *zero coupon bonds*. To call such notes *non-interest-bearing* is misleading. These instruments cannot be marketed at face value. The investor demands interest revenue. Therefore, the investor pays less than the face value. The investor discounts the maturity value, using the market rate of interest for notes having similar terms and risks. The discount is amortized, or systematically reduced, as interest over the life of the note.

Banks often discount both long-term and short-term notes when making loans. Consider a two-year, non-interest-bearing, $10,000 face-value note issued on

December 31, 1995, when semiannual market interest rates were 5%. In exchange for a promise to pay $10,000 on December 31, 1997, the bank provides the borrower with cash equal to the present value (PV) of the $10,000 payment:

PV of $1.00 from Table 2, page 459, 5% column, 4-period row = 0.8227

PV of $10,000 note = $10,000 × 0.8227 = $8,227

implicit interest (imputed interest) An interest expense that is not explicitly recognized in a loan agreement.

imputed interest rate The market interest rate that equates the proceeds from a loan with the present value of the loan payments.

The note has no specific interest payments. However, there is **implicit interest** (or **imputed interest**), which is an interest expense that is not explicitly recognized in a loan agreement. The imputed interest amount is based on an **imputed interest rate,** which is the market rate that equates the proceeds with the present value of the loan payments.

In this example, the $10,000 payment on December 31, 1997 will consist of $8,227 repayment of principal and $1,773 ($10,000 – $8,227) of imputed interest. At issue, the note is shown on the borrower's balance sheet as follows:

Note payable, due December 31, 1997	$10,000
Deduct: Discount on note payable	1,773
Net liability	$ 8,227

Exhibit 10-11 shows how interest expense is recognized for each semiannual period. Each amortization of discount decreases the discount account and increases the net carrying amount.

The appropriate journal entries follow:

```
12/31/95 Cash ......................... 8,227
            Discount on note payable ..........   1,773
                Note payable .................          $10,000
 6/30/96 Interest expense ...................   411
                Discount on note payable .......            411
12/31/96 Interest expense ...................   432
                Discount on note payable ........          432
 6/30/97 Interest expense ...................   454
                Discount on note payable ........          454
12/31/97 Interest expense ...................   476
                Discount on note payable ........          476
            Note payable ...................... 10,000
                Cash ........................        10,000
```

Exhibit 10-11

Analysis of Transactions of Borrower, Discounted Notes

	A =	L		+	SE
	Cash	Notes Payable	Discount on Notes Payable		Retained Earnings
Proceeds of loan	+ 8,227	+10,000	–1,773 [Increase Discount]		
Semiannual amortization					
Six months ended:					
6/30/1996			+411		–411
12/31/1996			+432 [Decrease Discount]		–432 [Increase Interest Expense]
6/30/1997			+454		–454
12/31/1997			+476		–476
Payment of note	–10,000	–10,000			
Bond-Related Totals	– 1,773	0	0		–1773

■ PENSIONS AND OTHER POSTRETIREMENT BENEFITS

pensions Payments to former employees after they retire.

other postretirement benefits Benefits provided to retired workers in addition to a pension, such as life and health insurance.

Most large companies continue to pay retired employees after they stop working. Such payments are commonly called **pensions**. In addition, retirees often continue to receive health insurance, life insurance, or other employee benefits, which are commonly called **other postretirement benefits.** The details of how these are accounted for are complex and are therefore covered in more advanced courses. However, the concepts are important and are dealt with briefly here.

Accrual accounting matches expenses with the associated revenue. Since the worker "earns" the right to postretirement payments during the working years, accrual accounting requires recognition of the growing liability for future payments as the years pass. Imagine a firm with a forty-five-year-old employee. The employee has worked for twenty years earning $50,000 per year. She will receive a pension of $25,000 per year after retirement at age 65. The firm has a liability, and using present value concepts, we can calculate it. Assume an interest rate of 10% and a life expectancy of 20 years after retirement. The employee will collect a twenty-year annuity, which will have a present value of $212,840 (8.5136 from Table 3, p. 460, times $25,000) at retirement. Today, twenty years before retirement, the present value is $31,628 (0.1486 from Table 2 times $212,840).

Estimating this number requires estimates of life expectancy, future work lives, ages at retirement, and levels of future pension payments to retirees. The formal calculations are normally done by actuaries, specialists at making such predictions. In addition the firm must choose an interest rate for calculating the present value. The liabilities can be very large.

Suppose a company's current pension expense is $100,000, $90,000 of which is paid in cash to a pension fund. The accounting for pensions has the following fundamental framework:

	A	=	L	+	SE	
			Accrued Pensions			
	Cash		Payable		Retained Earnings	
Current pension expense	−90,000	=	+10,000		−100,000	⎡Increase⎤ Pension ⎣Expense⎦

The journal entry would be:

Pension expense	100,000	
Cash		90,000
Accrued pensions payable		10,000
To record pension expense for the year.		

The expense of life insurance, health insurance, and similar benefits paid for retirees is conceptually similar to pensions. Therefore, a liability equal to the present value of expected payments should be recorded. Increases in the liability will be recognized as a current expense.

Suppose the present value of obligations for other postretirement benefits is $100,000 at the beginning of 19X1 and $120,000 at the end of the year. The summary journal entry for 19X1 is:

Other postretirement benefits expense	$20,000	
Accrued postretirement benefits payable		$20,000

The balance sheets thus include the following:

	December 31,	
	19X1	19X0
Long-Term Liabilities: Other postretirement benefits	$120,000	$100,000

In the international context, practice varies widely regarding pensions and other postretirement benefits. Variations arise in part from differences in business practices. For example, many countries provide a portion of retirement income through individual savings or through tax-supported government transfers akin to the Canadian Pension Plan system. When company-sponsored pensions are modest or nonexistent, there is no material information to be reported. In approximately half of the forty-four countries examined in a recent survey, it was common practice for pensions to be managed by an independent outside trustee with *funding* from the sponsoring company through periodic payments to the trustee. Prior to the 1970s, it was very common for companies to go out of business and for their current and future retirees to be left without pensions. Today, outside trustees maintain financial assets and manage the pension fund on behalf of the workers. This separate fund complicates accounting disclosure somewhat but provides substantial security to employees that their future pensions claims will be honoured.

■ CONTINGENT LIABILITIES

contingent liability
A potential liability that depends on a future event arising out of a past transaction.

A **contingent liability** is a *potential* (possible) liability that depends on a *future* event arising out of a *past* transaction. Sometimes it has a definite amount. For instance, a company may guarantee the payment on a related company's note payable. This means that the guarantor will pay if, and only if, the primary borrower fails to pay. Such a note is the liability of the primary borrower and the contingent liability of the guarantor.

More often, a contingent liability has an indefinite amount. A common example is a lawsuit. Many companies have lawsuits pending against them. These are possible obligations of indefinite amounts.

Some companies show contingent liabilities on the balance sheet. Most often they are listed after long-term liabilities but before shareholders' equity. Consumers Packaging Inc. is a leading designer and producer of high quality glass containers with sales of $458 million in 1995. Its 1995 annual report provided the following footnote:

Objective 7

Define contingent liabilities and explain why they are often disclosed by footnote rather than in the statements themselves.

Contingency

An environmental audit has determined that the cost of remediation at certain plants acquired in 1989 ranges from $4,200,000 to $10,000,000. Under the terms of the acquisition agreement, these costs are the responsibility of the seller; however, any amounts not paid by the seller may become a liability of the Company. As the likelihood of such an occurrence is undeterminable, the Company has not made any provision for such costs in these financial statements.

IBM
www.ibm.com

Footnote disclosure of lawsuits is very common. The result of such *litigation* is extremely hard to estimate. Some years ago IBM lost a multimillion-dollar lawsuit for patent violation. On appeal, the verdict was reversed, and IBM ended up collecting damages from the plaintiff. Another example of uncertainty is the case of Eagle Picher, a company subject to extensive product liability claims over asbestos. The company initially estimated its costs to settle existing and future claims at $270 million and recorded them in the financial statements as an expense, with a related liability. Later it became apparent that the earlier estimate was substantially in error, and the asbestos liability was increased by $544 million.

To recapitulate, there are definite liabilities either of definite amounts (accounts payable) or of estimated amounts (product warranties). There are also contingent liabilities either of definite amounts (guaranteeing a note) or of estimated amounts (income tax dispute with Revenue Canada).

■ DEBT RATIOS AND INTEREST-COVERAGE RATIOS

Commonly encountered ratios for assessing a firm's debt load include:

Objective 8

Apply ratio analysis to assessing the debt levels of an entity.

$$\text{Debt-to-equity ratio} = \frac{\text{Total liabilities}}{\text{Total shareholders' equity}}$$

$$\text{Long-term-debt-to-total-capital ratio} = \frac{\text{Total long-term debt}}{\text{Total shareholders' equity} + \text{long-term debt}}$$

$$\text{Debt-to-total-assets ratio} = \frac{\text{Total liabilities}}{\text{Total assets}}$$

$$\text{Interest-coverage ratio} = \frac{\text{Pretax income} + \text{interest expense}}{\text{Interest expense}}$$

Note that the first three ratios are alternate ways of expressing the same thing: What part of the firm's resources is obtained by borrowing and what part is invested by the owners. Many other definitions of debt ratios exist. The interest coverage ratio measures the firm's ability to meet its interest obligation.

The debt burden varies greatly from firm to firm and industry to industry. For example, retailing companies, utilities, and transportation companies tend to have debt of more than 60% of their assets. Computer companies and textile firms have debt levels of about 45% of assets.

Debt-to-equity ratios that were thought to be too high a few years ago are becoming commonplace today. The average debt-to-total-assets ratio for major industrial companies grew from about 35% in 1960 to nearly 60% in the 1990s.

Many high debt-to-equity ratios result from leveraged buyouts (LBOs). In an LBO, a buyer takes over a company using the company's assets as collateral to borrow the money necessary for the buyout. For example, management might borrow against the firm's assets and use the proceeds to buy back all the outstanding stock.

The purchase of RJR Nabisco by Kohlberg Kravis Roberts was a $25 billion LBO. The resulting company had debt of $23 billion and equity of $7 billion for a debt-to-equity ratio of 23 to 7, or about 3.3 to 1. The debt-to-total-assets percentage was 23 ÷ 30 = 77%. Henry Kravis was quoted in *Fortune* that this debt-to-equity ratio was low compared with other LBOs: "We've rarely bought a company with a ratio that low.... It's usually 10 or 12 to 1. Others have gone as high as 25 to 1."

The following ratios demonstrate the variation among industries and among countries:

Company	Industry	Country	Debt-Total Capital	Interest-Coverage
Stelco	Steel	Canada	44%	4
Rogers Cantel	Cell Phones	Canada	108%	1
Andrés Wines	Winery	Canada	18%	31
RJR Nabisco	Tobacco	USA	76%	1
IBM	Computers	USA	24%	7
Eli Lilly	Drugs	USA	5%	33
Glaxo Holdings	Drugs	UK	1%	30
Exxon	Oil	USA	19%	8
Royal Dutch	Oil	Holland	9%	10
Repsol	Oil	Spain	6%	5
Ford	Autos	USA	66%	1
Volvo	Autos	Sweden	17%	1
Toyota	Autos	Japan	22%	8

Moody's
www.moodys.com/

Standard & Poor's Corp.
www.stockinfo.
standardpoor.com/

Moody's and Standard & Poor's Corporation (S&P) rates bonds issued by corporations according to their credit-worthiness. High proportions of debt and low interest-coverage ratios usually lead to lower bond ratings. Why? Because they imply less ability to meet bond obligations and hence more risk for bondholders.

Investors use bond ratings to evaluate the bond's price. Lower ratings lead to lower prices and, therefore, higher yields on the bond. As of 1991 and 1995, the average yields for industrial bonds rated by S&P were as follows, by rating category:

Rating	AAA	AA	A	BBB	BB	B
Yield 1991	8.67	9.22	9.67	10.03	11.78	14.17
Yield 1995	7.82	7.85	8.44	8.78	9.69	11.38

Note that in each year the yields rise uniformly as the ratings decrease. Interest rates have fallen significantly during the early 1990s. To assign the ratings, S&P often interviews management in addition to analyzing financial data. AAA bonds have the lowest debt ratios and the highest interest-coverage ratios, as you would expect. Investors will pay more (accept a lower yield) for debt issued by the least risky companies.

In assessing the riskiness of a company's securities, analysts rely heavily on the debt level. In Canada, debt obligations are legally enforceable, and many examples exist in which creditors have forced a company to liquidate in order to pay interest or to repay principal. But financial analysis must be adapted to the realities facing the specific companies. In Japan, for example, debt ratios tend to be much higher than in Canada. This difference partly reflects banking practices. Japanese banks lend very large sums to the biggest and most creditworthy corporations. While the transaction has the form of debt, it tends to be part of a very long-term relationship between bank and customer. The banks end up with long-term rights that look somewhat like the rights of a Canadian shareholder.

Summary Problems for Your Review

Problem One

Suppose that on December 31, 1996 CanCo. issued $12 million of ten-year, 10% debentures. Assume that the annual market interest rate at issuance was 10%.

Required

1. Compute the proceeds from issuing the debentures.
2. Prepare an analysis of the following items: (a) issuance of the debentures; (b) the first two semiannual interest payments; and (c) the payment of the maturity value. Use the balance sheet equation (similar to Exhibit 10-4, p. 436). Round to the nearest thousand dollars.
3. Prepare journal entries for the items in requirement 2.

Solution to Problem One

1. Because the market interest rate and the nominal rate are both 10%, the proceeds equal the face amount of $12 million. This can also be computed as the present value (PV) of the twenty $600,000 interest payments and the $12 million maturity value at 5% per semiannual period:

PV of interest payments: 12.4622 × $600,000	$ 7,477,320
PV of maturity value: .3769 × $12,000,000	4,522,800
Total proceeds (exceeds $12 million due to rounding error)	$12,000,120

2. See Exhibit 10-12.

3.

12/31/96:	Cash	12,000,000	
	Bonds payable		12,000,000
6/30/97:	Interest expense	600,000	
	Cash		600,000
12/31/97:	Interest expense	600,000	
	Cash		600,000
12/31/97:	Bonds payable	12,000,000	
	Cash		12,000,000

Exhibit 10-12

Analysis of CanCo's
Bond Transactions:
Problem One
(rounded to thou-
sands of dollars)

	A	=	L	+	SE	
	Cash		Bonds Payable		Retained Earnings	
CanCo's records:						
1. Issuance	12,000		12,000			
2. Semiannual interest						
Six months ended:						Increase
6/30/97	−600				−600	Interest
12/31/97	−600				−600	Expense
3. Maturity value						
(final payment)	12,000		−12,000			
Bond-related totals*	−12,000		0		−12,000	

* Totals after all 20 interest payments and payment at maturity (20 × 600).

Problem Two

Suppose that on December 31, 1996, CanCo issued $12 million of ten-year, 10% deben-
tures. Assume that the annual market interest rate at issuance was 14%.

Required

1. Compute the proceeds from issuing the debentures.
2. Prepare an analysis of the following items: (a) issuance of the debentures; (b) the
first two semiannual interest payments; and (c) the payment of the maturity value.
Use the balance sheet equation (similar to Exhibit 10-6, p. 439). Round to the nearest thousand dollars. Use a bond discount account.
3. Prepare journal entries for the items in requirement 2. Use a bond discount account.

Solution to Problem Two

1. Because the market interest rate exceeds the nominal rate, the proceeds will be less than
the face amount. This can be computed as the present value (PV) of the twenty $600,000
interest payments and the $12 million maturity value at 7% per semiannual period:

PV of interest payments: 10.5940 × $600,000	$6,356,400
PV of maturity value: 0.2584 × $12,000,000	3,100,800
Total proceeds	$9,457,200

2. See Exhibit 10-13.

3.

12/31/96:	Cash	9,457,200	
	Discount on bonds payable	2,542,800	
	Bonds payable		12,000,000
6/30/97:	Interest expense	662,004	
	Discount on bonds payable		62,004
	Cash		600,000
12/31/97:	Interest expense	666,344	
	Discount on bonds payable		66,344
	Cash		600,000
12/31/97:	Bonds payable	12,000,000	
	Cash		12,000,000

Exhibit 10-13

Analysis of Canco's
Bond Transactions:
Problem Two
(rounded to thousands of dollars)

	A =		L		+	SE	
	Cash	Bonds Payable	Discount on Bonds Payable			Retained Earnings	
Canco's records:							
1. Issuance	+9,457	+12,000	−2,543	[Increase Discount]			
2. Semiannual interest							
Six months ended:							
6/30/97	−600		+62	[Decrease Discount]		−662*	[Increase Interest Expense]
12/31/97	−600		+66			−666*	
3. Maturity value							
(final payment)	−12,000	−12,000					
Bond-related totals†	−14,543	0	0			−14,543	

* 7% × 9,457 = 662; 7% × (9,457 + 66) = 666.
† Totals after payment at maturity and all 20 entries for discount amortization and interest payments are made.

Problem Three

Xerox Corporation plans to enter some new communications business. The company expects to accumulate sufficient cash from its new operations to pay a lump sum of $200 million to Mutual Insurance Company at the end of five years. Mutual will lend money on a promissory note now, will take no payments until the end of five years, and desires 12% interest compounded annually.

Required

1. How much money will Mutual lend Xerox?
2. Prepare journal entries for Xerox at the inception of the loan and at the end of each of the first two years.

Solution to Problem Three

The initial step in solving present value problems focuses on a basic question, Which table should I use? No computations should be made until you are convinced that you are using the correct table.

1. Use Table 2. The $200 million is a future amount. Its present value is

$$PV = \$200,000,000 \times \frac{1}{(1 + 0.12)^5}$$

The conversion factor, $1/(1 + 0.12)^5$, is in row 5 and the 12% column. It is 0.5674.

$$PV = \$200,000,000 \times 0.5674 = \$113,480,000$$

2.

Cash	113,480,000	
Long-term note payable (or long-term debt) ...		113,480,000
To record borrowing that is payable in a lump sum at the end of five years at 12% interest compounded annually.		
Interest expense	13,617,600	
Long-term note payable		13,617,600
To record interest expense and corresponding accumulation of principal at the end of the first year: 0.12 × $113,480,000 = $13,617,600.		

Interest expense	15,251,712	
Long-term note payable		15,251,712

To record interest expense and corresponding
accumulation of principal at the end of the
second year: 0.12 × ($113,480,000 + $13,617,600).

Reflect on the entries for interest. Note how the interest expense becomes larger if no interest payments are made from year to year. This mounting interest expense occurs because the unpaid interest is being added to the principal to form a new higher principal each year.

Problem Four

Refer to the preceding problem. Suppose Xerox and Mutual agree on a 12% interest rate compounded annually. However, Xerox will pay a *total* of $200 million in the form of $40 million annual payments at the end of *each* of the next five years. How much money will Mutual lend Xerox?

Solution to Problem Four

Use Table 3. The $40 million is a uniform periodic payment at the end of a series of years. Therefore it is an annuity. Its present value is:

$$PV_A = \text{Annual payment} \times \text{Present value factor}$$

$$= \$40 \text{ million} \times \text{Present value factor for 5 years at 12\%}$$

$$= \$40 \text{ million} \times 3.6048$$

$$= \$144,192,000$$

In particular, note that Mutual is willing to lend more than in Problem Four even though the interest rate is the same. Why? Because Mutual will get its money back more quickly.

Highlights to Remember

Liabilities are recognized obligations to pay money or to provide goods or services. An entity's liability level is important to analysts because unpaid liabilities may produce difficulties ranging from an inability to raise additional capital to forced liquidation. To help assess debt levels, financial statements typically separate liabilities requiring payment within one year as *current liabilities*. Accounting for current liabilities is a straightforward extension of procedures covered in earlier chapters. Transactions are recorded as they occur, and accruals at the end of a period capture incomplete transactions such as accruing interest, wages, utilities, or taxes.

Long-term liabilities are more complex contracts that convey many rights and responsibilities over long periods of time. When contracts require multiple cash payments over time, present value techniques are used to determine the value of these future payments as of the current time period.

Bonds, a common long-term liability, are originally recorded at the amount received from investors at issue. This equals the present value of all of their future payments as of the issue date, calculated at the market rate of interest.

During the life of the bond, interest expense is recognized each period equal to the market rate at issue times the carrying value.

Pensions and other postretirement benefits involve long-term obligations to make future payments in retirement to current employees. Under the matching principle, companies report the expense of these benefits during the employees' active working years.

Contingent liabilities are uncertain in amount and timing of payment. Examples include lawsuits, contract disputes, possible losses on multiyear contracts, and environmental liabilities. Footnote disclosure is used to alert interested parties to the uncertain, unmeasurable future possibilities.

Debt ratios and interest-coverage ratios are two measures used to evaluate the level of a company's indebtedness. The more debt a company has, the more problems it will face if cash flow is inadequate to meet liabilities as they fall due.

Appendix 10A: Compound Interest, Future Value, and Present Value

Objective 9

Compute and interpret present and future values.

For the borrower, interest is the cost of using money. It is the rental charge for cash, just as rental charges are often made for the use of automobiles or boats. For the investor, *interest* is the return on investment or the fee for lending money. Contracts that bear interest have many forms, from simple short-term promissory notes to multimillion-dollar issues of long-term notes often called bonds. Commonly encountered terms include

- **Principal:** the amount invested, borrowed, or used on which interest accrues
- **Interest:** the rental charge for the use of principal

interest rate The percentage applied to a principal amount to calculate the interest charged.

interest period The time period over which the interest rate applies.

simple interest For any period, interest rate multiplied by an unchanging principal amount.

compound interest For any period, interest rate multiplied by a changing principal amount. The unpaid interest is added to the principal to become the principal for the new period.

Calculation of the amount of interest depends on the **interest rate**—a specified percentage of the principal—and the **interest period**—the time period over which this interest rate is applied.

Simple interest is calculated by multiplying an interest rate by an unchanging principal amount. Simple interest is rarely encountered in North American financial practice. In contrast, **compound interest** is calculated by multiplying an interest rate by a principal amount that is changed each interest period by the previously accumulated (unpaid) interest. The accumulated interest is added to the principal to become the principal for the new period.

Future Value

Consider an example. Suppose Christina's T-shirt business has $10,000 in cash that is not needed at this moment. Rather than hold the $10,000 in her business chequing account, which does not pay interest, she can deposit $10,000 in a financial institution that pays 10% interest per annum, compounded annually. She plans to let the amount accumulate for three years before withdrawing the full balance of the deposit. The amount accumulated in the account, including principal and interest, is called the **future value.**

Compound interest provides interest on interest. That is, the principal changes from period to period. Interest in year 1 is paid on $10,000: 10% × $10,000 = $1,000. If the interest is not withdrawn, the principal for year 2 includes the intial

future value The amount accumulated, including principal and interest.

$10,000 deposit plus the $1,000 of interest earned in the first year, $11,000. Interest in year 2 is paid on the $11,000: 10% × $11,000 = $1,100. The future value of the deposit at the end of three years with compound interest would be $13,310·

	Principal	Compound Interest	Balance End of Year
Year 1	$10,000	$10,000 × 10 = $1,000	$11,000
Year 2	11,000	11,000 × 10 = 1,100	12,100
Year 3	12,100	12,100 × 10 = 1,210	13,310

More generally, suppose you invest S dollars for two periods and earn interest at an interest rate i. After one period, the investment would be increased by the interest earned, Si. You would have $S + $Si = $S(1 + i)$. In the second period you would again earn interest ($i[S(1 + i)]$). After two periods you would have :

$$[S(1 + i)] + (i[S(1 + i)]) = S(1 + i)(1 + i) = S(1 + i)^2$$

The general formula for computing the future value (FV) of S dollars n years hence at interest rate i is

$$FV = S(1 + i)^n$$

In general, n refers to the number of periods the funds are invested. Periods can be years, months, days, or any other time period. However, the interest rate must be consistent with the time period. That is, if n refers to days, i must be expressed as X% *per day*.

The "force" of compound interest can be staggering. For example:

Compound Interest	Future Values at End of		
	10 Years	20 Years	40 Years
$10,000 × (1.10)^{10} = $10,000 × 2.5937 =	$25,937		
$10,000 × (1.10)^{20} = $10,000 × 6.7275 =		$67,275	
$10,000 × (1.10)^{40} = $10,000 × 45.2593 =			$452,593

Hand calculations of compound interest can quickly become burdensome. Therefore, compound interest tables have been constructed to ease computations. Table 1, page 458, shows the future values of $1 for various periods and interest rates. In the table each number is the solution to the expression $(1 + i)^n$. The value of i is given in the column heading. The value of n is given in the row label for number of periods. Notice that the three-year, 10% future value factor is 1.3310 (the third row, seventh column). This number is calculated as $(1 + 0.10)^3$.

Suppose you want to know how much $800 will grow to if left in the bank for nine years at 8% interest. Multiply $800 by $(1 + 0.08)^9$. The value for $(1 + .08)^9$ is found in the nine-year row and 8% column of Table 1.

$$800 × 1.9990 = $1,599.20$$

The factors in the tables in this appendix are rounded to four decimal places. The examples in this text use these rounded factors. If you use tables with different rounding, or if you use a hand calculator or personal computer, your answers may differ from those given because of a small rounding error.

Present Value

present value The value today of a future cash inflow or outflow.

Accountants generally use *present values* rather than future values to record long-term liabilities. The **present value** is the value today of a future cash inflow or outflow.

Suppose you invest $1.00 today. As shown in the discussion of future values, the $1.00 will grow to $1.06 in one year at 6% interest; that is, $1 \times 1.06 = $1.06. At the end of the second year its value is ($1 x 1.06) \times 1.06 = $1 \times (1.06)^2 = $1.1236. In general, $1.00 grows to $(1 + i)^n$ in n years at $i\%$ interest.

We know how to calculate the future value (FV) of S dollars invested at a known interest rate i for n periods. We can reverse the process to calculate the present value when we know the future value. If

$$FV = S (1 + i)^n$$

then the present value (PV) is S, or

$$S = \frac{FV}{(1 + i)^n}$$

If $1.00 is to be received in one year, it is worth $1 \div 1.06 = $0.9434 today. Suppose you invest $0.9434 today. In one year you will have $0.9434 \times 1.06 = $1.00. Thus $0.9434 is the *present value* of $1.00 a year hence at 6%. If the dollar will be received in two years, its present value is $1.00 \div (1.06)^2 = $0.8900. If $0.89 is invested today, it will grow to $1.00 at the end of two years. The general formula for the present value (PV) of a future value (FV) to be received or paid in n periods at an interest rate of $i\%$ per period is

$$PV = \frac{FV}{(1 + i)^n} = FV \times \frac{1}{(1 + i)^n}$$

discount rates The interest rates used in determining present values.

Table 2 gives factors for $1/(1 + i)^n$ (which is the present value of $1.00) at various interest rates (often called **discount rates**) over several different periods. Present values are also called *discounted* values, and the process of finding the present value is *discounting*. You can think of this as discounting (decreasing) the value of a future cash inflow or outflow. Why is the value discounted? Because the cash is to be received or paid in the future, not today.

Assume that a prominent city is issuing a three-year non-interest-bearing note payable that promises to pay a lump sum of $1,000 exactly three years from now. You desire a rate of return of exactly 6%, compounded annually. How much would you be willing to pay now for the three-year note? The situation is sketched as follows:

End of Year	0	1	2	3
	Present Value			Future Value
	? ◄———————			$1,000

The factor in the Period 3 row and 6% column of Table 2 is 0.8396. The present value of the $1,000 payment is $1,000 × 0.8396 = $839.60. You would be willing to pay $839.60 for the $1,000 to be received in three years.

Suppose interest is compounded semiannually rather than annually. How much would you be willing to pay? The three years become six interest payment periods. The rate per period is half the annual rate, or 6% : 2 = 3%. The factor in the Period 6 row and 3% column of Table 2 is 0.8375. You would be willing to pay $1,000 × 0.8375, or only $837.50 rather than $839.60.

As a further check on your understanding, review the earlier example of compound interest. Suppose the financial institution promised to pay $13,310 at the end of three years. How much would you be willing to deposit at time zero if you desired a 10% rate of return compounded annually? Using Table 2, the Period 3 row and the 10% column show a factor of 0.7513. Multiply this factor by the future amount and round to the nearest dollar:

$$PV = 0.7513 \times \$13,310 = \$10,000$$

Pause for a moment. Use Table 2 to obtain the present values of

1. $1,600, @ 20%, to be received at the end of 20 years.
2. $8,300, @ 10%, to be received at the end of 12 years.
3. $8,000, @ 4%, to be received at the end of 4 years.

Answers

1. $1,600 (0.0261) = $41.76.
2. $8,300 (0.3186) = $2,644.38.
3. $8,000 (0.8548) = $6,838.40.

Present Value of an Ordinary Annuity

annuity Equal cash flows to take place during successive periods of equal length.

An ordinary **annuity** is a series of equal cash flows to take place at the end of successive periods of equal length. Its present value is denoted PV_A. Assume that you buy a non-interest-bearing *serial note* from a municipality that promises to pay $1,000 at the end of *each* of three years. How much should you be willing to pay if you desire a rate of return of 6%, compounded annually?

You could solve this problem using Table 2. First, find the present value of each payment, and then add the present values as in Exhibit 10-14. You would be willing to pay $943.40 for the first payment, $890.00 for the second, and $839.60 for the third, a total of $2,673.00.

Exhibit 10-14

End of Year	6% PV Factor	Present Value	0	1	2	3
1st payment:	.9434	$ 943.40 ←	$1,000			
2nd payment:	.8900	890.00 ←		$1,000		
3rd payment:	.8396	839.60 ←				$1,000
		$2,673.00				

Since each cash payment is $1,000 with equal one-year periods between them, Table 3 provides a shortcut method. The present value in Exhibit 10-14 can be expressed as

$$PV_A = (\$1,000 \times .9434) + (\$1,000 \times .8900) + (\$1,000 \times .8396)$$
$$= \$1,000 \, (.9434 + .8900 + .8396)$$
$$= \$1,000 \, (2.6730)$$
$$= \$2,673.00$$

The three terms in brackets are the first three numbers from the 6% column of Table 2, and their sum is in the third row of the 6% column of Table 3: 0.9434 + 0.8900 + 0.8396 = 2.6730.

This shortcut is especially valuable if the cash payments or receipts extend over many periods. Consider an annual cash payment of $1,000 for 20 years at 6%. The present value, calculated from Table 3, is $1,000 × 11.4699 = $11,469.90. To use Table 2 for this calculation, you would perform twenty multiplications and then add the twenty products.

The factors in Table 3 can be calculated using the following general formula:

$$PV_A = \frac{1}{i} \left[1 - \frac{1}{(1 + i)^n} \right]$$

Applied to our illustration:

$$PV_A = \frac{1}{0.06} \, (1 - 0.83962) = \frac{0.16038}{0.06} = 2.6730$$

Use Table 3 to obtain the present values of the following ordinary annuities:

1. $1,600 to be received at the end of each year for 20 years, assuming interest at 20%.
2. $8,300 to be received at the end of each year for 12 years, assuming interest at 10%.
3. $8,000 to be received at the end of each year for 4 years, assuming interest at 4%.

Answers

1. $1,600 (4.8696) = $ 7,791.36.
2. $8,300 (6.8137) = $56,553.71.
3. $8,000 (3.6299) = $29,039.20.

In particular, note that the higher the interest rate, the lower the present value. Why? Because, at a higher interest rate, you would need to invest less now to obtain the same future value.

Appendix 10B: Accounting for Leases

lease A contract whereby an owner (lessor) grants the use of property to a second party (lessee) for rental payments.

Leasing is a big business. Any asset imaginable, from television sets to jumbo aircraft to buildings, can be acquired via a *lease* contract. A **lease** is a contract whereby an owner (lessor) grants the use of property to a second party (lessee) in exchange for rental payments. This discussion focuses on leasing from the lessee's point of view.

Leasing is important from an accounting perspective because lease contracts create both property rights and financial obligations for the lessee. Sometimes it becomes difficult to distinguish the economic characteristics of a lease contract from the rights conveyed by ownership of the property.

Objective 10

Describe, value, and account for long-term lease transactions.

The CICA asserted that many noncancelable leases are substantially equivalent to purchases in that the lessee has obtained similar risks and benefits to the asset being purchased. The lessee has full use of the asset and a legal obligation to make payments, the same as if money were borrowed and the asset purchased.

Operating and Capital Leases

Leases are divided into two major kinds: capital leases and operating leases. **Capital leases** (or **financing leases**) transfer substantially all the risks and benefits of ownership to the lessee. They are equivalent to installment sale and purchase transactions. The asset must be recorded essentially as having been sold by the lessor and having been purchased by the lessee.

All other leases are **operating leases**. Examples are telephones rented by the month and rooms rented by the day, week, or month. Operating leases are accounted for as ordinary rent expenses; no balance sheet accounts are affected by operating leases.

Consider a simple example to see how the accounting differs for operating and capital leases. Suppose the Bestick Company can acquire a truck that has a useful life of four years and no residual value under either of the following conditions:

capital lease (financing lease) A lease that transfers substantially all the risks and benefits of ownership to the lessee.

operating lease A lease that should be accounted for by the lessee as ordinary rent expenses.

Buy Outright	or	Capital Lease
Cash outlays, $50,000 Borrow $50,000 cash to be repaid in four equal installments at 12% interest compounded annually		Rental of $16,462 per year, payable at the end of each of four years

There is no basic difference between an outright purchase or an irrevocable capital lease for four years. The Bestick Company uses the asset for its entire useful life and must pay for repairs, property taxes, and other operating costs under either plan.

Most lease rentals are paid at the *start* of each payment period, but to ease our computations we assume that each payment of $16,462 will occur at the end of the year. To make the comparison between leasing and purchasing, payments on the $50,000 loan in the purchase option must be calculated:

$$\text{Let } X = \text{loan payment}$$
$$\$50,000 = \text{PV of annuity of } X \text{ per year for 4 years at 12\%}$$
$$\$50,000 = 3.0373X$$
$$X = \$50,000 \div 3.0373$$
$$X = \$16,462 \text{ per year}$$

Note that this loan payment is exactly equal to the lease payment. Of course, we constructed the example this way deliberately because we want to stress the fundamental economic similarity between ownership and certain kinds of leases. Thus, from Bestick's perspective as lessee, both buying outright and leasing create an obligation for four $16,462 payments that have a present value of $50,000.

Suppose the lease contract were treated as an operating lease. Each year the journal entry would be:

```
Rent expense . . . . . . . . . . . . . . . . . . . . . .   16,462
    Cash . . . . . . . . . . . . . . . . . . . . . . . .           16,462
To record lease payment.
```

Table 1

Future Value of $1

$$FV = 1(1 + i)^n$$

Periods	3%	4%	5%	6%	7%	8%	10%	12%	14%	16%	18%	20%	22%	24%	25%
1	1.0300	1.0400	1.0500	1.0600	1.0700	1.0800	1.1000	1.1200	1.1400	1.1600	1.1800	1.2000	1.2200	1.2400	1.2500
2	1.0609	1.0816	1.1025	1.1236	1.1449	1.1664	1.2100	1.2544	1.2996	1.3456	1.3924	1.4400	1.4884	1.5376	1.5625
3	1.0927	1.1249	1.1576	1.1910	1.2250	1.2597	1.3310	1.4049	1.4815	1.5609	1.6430	1.7280	1.8158	1.9066	1.9531
4	1.1255	1.1699	1.2155	1.2625	1.3108	1.3605	1.4641	1.5735	1.6890	1.8106	1.9388	2.0736	2.2153	2.3642	2.4414
5	1.1593	1.2167	1.2763	1.3382	1.4026	1.4693	1.6105	1.7623	1.9254	2.1003	2.2878	2.4883	2.7027	2.9316	3.0518
6	1.1941	1.2653	1.3401	1.4185	1.5007	1.5869	1.7716	1.9738	2.1950	2.4364	2.6996	2.9860	3.2973	3.6352	3.8147
7	1.2299	1.3159	1.4071	1.5036	1.6058	1.7138	1.9487	2.2107	2.5023	2.8262	3.1855	3.5832	4.0227	4.5077	4.7684
8	1.2668	1.3686	1.4775	1.5938	1.7182	1.8509	2.1436	2.4760	2.8526	3.2784	3.7589	4.2998	4.9077	5.5895	5.9605
9	1.3048	1.4233	1.5513	1.6895	1.8385	1.9990	2.3579	2.7731	3.2519	3.8030	4.4355	5.1598	5.9874	6.9310	7.4506
10	1.3439	1.4802	1.6289	1.7908	1.9672	2.1589	2.5937	3.1058	3.7072	4.4114	5.2338	6.1917	7.3046	8.5944	9.3132
11	1.3842	1.5395	1.7103	1.8983	2.1049	2.3316	2.8531	3.4785	4.2262	5.1173	6.1759	7.4301	8.9117	10.6571	11.6415
12	1.4258	1.6010	1.7959	2.0122	2.2522	2.5182	3.1384	3.8960	4.8179	5.9360	7.2876	8.9161	10.8722	13.2148	14.5519
13	1.4685	1.6651	1.8856	2.1329	2.4098	2.7196	3.4523	4.3635	5.4924	6.8858	8.5994	10.6993	13.2641	16.3863	18.1899
14	1.5126	1.7317	1.9799	2.2609	2.5785	2.9372	3.7975	4.8871	6.2613	7.9875	10.1472	12.8392	16.1822	20.3191	22.7374
15	1.5580	1.8009	2.0789	2.3966	2.7590	3.1772	4.1772	5.4736	7.1379	9.2655	11.9737	15.4070	19.7423	25.1956	28.4217
16	1.6047	1.8730	2.1829	2.5404	2.9522	3.4259	4.5950	6.1304	8.1372	10.7480	14.1290	18.4884	24.0856	31.2426	35.5271
17	1.6528	1.9479	2.2920	2.6928	3.1588	3.7000	5.0545	6.8660	9.2765	12.4677	16.6722	22.1861	29.3844	38.7408	44.4089
18	1.7024	2.0258	2.4066	2.8543	3.3799	3.9960	5.5599	7.6900	10.5752	14.4625	19.6733	26.6233	35.8490	48.0386	55.5112
19	1.7535	2.1068	2.5270	3.0256	3.6165	4.3157	6.1159	8.6128	12.0557	16.7765	23.2144	31.9480	43.7358	59.5679	69.3889
20	1.8061	2.1911	2.6533	3.2071	3.8697	4.6610	6.7275	9.6463	13.7435	19.4608	27.3930	38.3376	53.3576	73.8641	86.7362
21	1.8603	2.2788	2.7860	3.3996	4.1406	5.0338	7.4002	10.8038	15.6676	22.5745	32.3238	46.0051	65.0963	91.5915	108.4202
22	1.9161	2.3699	2.9253	3.6035	4.4304	5.4365	8.1403	12.1003	17.8610	26.1864	38.1421	55.2061	79.4175	113.5735	135.5253
23	1.9736	2.4647	3.0715	3.8197	4.7405	5.8715	8.9543	13.5523	20.3616	30.3762	45.0076	66.2474	96.8894	140.8312	169.4066
24	2.0328	2.5633	3.2251	4.0489	5.0724	6.3412	9.8497	15.1786	23.2122	35.2364	53.1090	79.4968	118.2050	174.6306	211.7582
25	2.0938	2.6658	3.3864	4.2919	5.4274	6.8485	10.8347	17.0001	26.4619	40.8742	62.6686	95.3962	144.2101	216.5420	264.6978
26	2.1566	2.7725	3.5557	4.5494	5.8074	7.3964	11.9182	19.0401	30.1666	47.4141	73.9490	114.4755	175.9364	268.5121	330.8722
27	2.2213	2.8834	3.7335	4.8223	6.2139	7.9881	13.1100	21.3249	34.3899	55.0004	87.2598	137.3706	214.6424	332.9550	413.5903
28	2.2879	2.9987	3.9201	5.1117	6.6488	8.6271	14.4210	23.8839	39.2045	63.8004	102.9666	164.8447	261.8637	412.8642	516.9879
29	2.3566	3.1187	4.1161	5.4184	7.1143	9.3173	15.8631	26.7499	44.6931	74.0085	121.5005	197.8136	319.4737	511.9516	646.2349
30	2.4273	3.2434	4.3219	5.7435	7.6123	10.0627	17.4494	29.9599	50.9502	85.8499	143.3706	237.3763	389.7579	634.8199	807.7936

Table 2

Present Value of $1

$$PV = \frac{1}{(1+i)^n}$$

Periods	3%	4%	5%	6%	7%	8%	10%	12%	14%	16%	18%	20%	22%	24%	25%
1	.9709	.9615	.9524	.9434	.9346	.9259	.9091	.8929	.8772	.8621	.8475	.8333	.8197	.8065	.8000
2	.9426	.9246	.9070	.8900	.8734	.8573	.8264	.7972	.7695	.7432	.7182	.6944	.6719	.6504	.6400
3	.9151	.8890	.8638	.8396	.8163	.7938	.7513	.7118	.6750	.6407	.6086	.5787	.5507	.5245	.5120
4	.8885	.8548	.8227	.7921	.7629	.7350	.6830	.6355	.5921	.5523	.5158	.4823	.4514	.4230	.4096
5	.8626	.8219	.7835	.7473	.7130	.6806	.6209	.5674	.5194	.4761	.4371	.4019	.3700	.3411	.3277
6	.8375	.7903	.7462	.7050	.6663	.6302	.5645	.5066	.4556	.4104	.3704	.3349	.3033	.2751	.2621
7	.8131	.7599	.7107	.6651	.6227	.5835	.5132	.4523	.3996	.3538	.3139	.2791	.2486	.2218	.2097
8	.7894	.7307	.6768	.6274	.5820	.5403	.4665	.4039	.3506	.3050	.2660	.2326	.2038	.1789	.1678
9	.7664	.7026	.6446	.5919	.5439	.5002	.4241	.3606	.3075	.2630	.2255	.1938	.1670	.1443	.1342
10	.7441	.6756	.6139	.5584	.5083	.4632	.3855	.3220	.2697	.2267	.1911	.1615	.1369	.1164	.1074
11	.7224	.6496	.5847	.5268	.4751	.4289	.3505	.2875	.2366	.1954	.1619	.1346	.1122	.0938	.0859
12	.7014	.6246	.5568	.4970	.4440	.3971	.3186	.2567	.2076	.1685	.1372	.1122	.0920	.0757	.0687
13	.6810	.6006	.5303	.4688	.4150	.3677	.2897	.2292	.1821	.1452	.1163	.0935	.0754	.0610	.0550
14	.6611	.5775	.5051	.4423	.3878	.3405	.2633	.2046	.1597	.1252	.0985	.0779	.0618	.0492	.0440
15	.6419	.5553	.4810	.4173	.3624	.3152	.2394	.1827	.1401	.1079	.0835	.0649	.0507	.0397	.0352
16	.6232	.5339	.4581	.3936	.3387	.2919	.2176	.1631	.1229	.0930	.0708	.0541	.0415	.0320	.0281
17	.6050	.5134	.4363	.3714	.3166	.2703	.1978	.1456	.1078	.0802	.0600	.0451	.0340	.0258	.0225
18	.5874	.4936	.4155	.3503	.2959	.2502	.1799	.1300	.0946	.0691	.0508	.0376	.0279	.0208	.0180
19	.5703	.4746	.3957	.3305	.2765	.2317	.1635	.1161	.0829	.0596	.0431	.0313	.0229	.0168	.0144
20	.5537	.4564	.3769	.3118	.2584	.2145	.1486	.1037	.0728	.0514	.0365	.0261	.0187	.0135	.0115
21	.5375	.4388	.3589	.2942	.2415	.1987	.1351	.0926	.0638	.0443	.0309	.0217	.0154	.0109	.0092
22	.5219	.4220	.3418	.2775	.2257	.1839	.1228	.0826	.0560	.0382	.0262	.0181	.0126	.0088	.0074
23	.5067	.4057	.3256	.2618	.2109	.1703	.1117	.0738	.0491	.0329	.0222	.0151	.0103	.0071	.0059
24	.4919	.3901	.3101	.2470	.1971	.1577	.1015	.0659	.0431	.0284	.0188	.0126	.0085	.0057	.0047
25	.4776	.3751	.2953	.2330	.1842	.1460	.0923	.0588	.0378	.0245	.0160	.0105	.0069	.0046	.0038
26	.4637	.3607	.2812	.2198	.1722	.1352	.0839	.0525	.0331	.0211	.0135	.0087	.0057	.0037	.0030
27	.4502	.3468	.2678	.2074	.1609	.1252	.0763	.0469	.0291	.0182	.0115	.0073	.0047	.0030	.0024
28	.4371	.3335	.2551	.1956	.1504	.1159	.0693	.0419	.0255	.0157	.0097	.0061	.0038	.0024	.0019
29	.4243	.3207	.2429	.1846	.1406	.1073	.0630	.0374	.0224	.0135	.0082	.0051	.0031	.0020	.0015
30	.4120	.3083	.2314	.1741	.1314	.0994	.0573	.0334	.0195	.0116	.0070	.0042	.0026	.0016	.0012
40	.3066	.2083	.1420	.0972	.0668	.0460	.0221	.0107	.0053	.0026	.0013	.0007	.0004	.0002	.0001

Table 3

Present Value of Ordinary Annuity of $1

$$PV_A = \frac{1}{i}\left[1 - \frac{1}{(1+i)^n}\right]$$

Periods	3%	4%	5%	6%	7%	8%	10%	12%	14%	16%	18%	20%	22%	24%	25%
1	.9709	.9615	.9524	.9434	.9346	.9259	.9091	.8929	.8772	.8621	.8475	.8333	.8197	.8065	.8000
2	1.9135	1.8861	1.8594	1.8334	1.8080	1.7833	1.7355	1.6901	1.6467	1.6052	1.5656	1.5278	1.4915	1.4568	1.4400
3	2.8286	2.7751	2.7232	2.6730	2.6243	2.5771	2.4869	2.4018	2.3216	2.2459	2.1743	2.1065	2.0422	1.9813	1.9520
4	3.7171	3.6299	3.5460	3.4651	3.3872	3.3121	3.1699	3.0373	2.9137	2.7982	2.6901	2.5887	2.4936	2.4043	2.3616
5	4.5797	4.4518	4.3295	4.2124	4.1002	3.9927	3.7908	3.6048	3.4331	3.2743	3.1272	2.9906	2.8636	2.7454	2.6893
6	5.4172	5.2421	5.0757	4.9173	4.7665	4.6229	4.3553	4.1114	3.8887	3.6847	3.4976	3.3255	3.1669	3.0205	2.9514
7	6.2303	6.0021	5.7864	5.5824	5.3893	5.2064	4.8684	4.5638	4.2883	4.0386	3.8115	3.6046	3.4155	3.2423	3.1611
8	7.0197	6.7327	6.4632	6.2098	5.9713	5.7466	5.3349	4.9676	4.6389	4.3436	4.0776	3.8372	3.6193	3.4212	3.3289
9	7.7861	7.4353	7.1078	6.8017	6.5152	6.2469	5.7590	5.3282	4.9464	4.6065	4.3030	4.0310	3.7863	3.5655	3.4631
10	8.5302	8.1109	7.7217	7.3601	7.0236	6.7101	6.1446	5.6502	5.2161	4.8332	4.4941	4.1925	3.9232	3.6819	3.5705
11	9.2526	8.7605	8.3064	7.8869	7.4987	7.1390	6.4951	5.9377	5.4527	5.0286	4.6560	4.3271	4.0354	3.7757	3.6564
12	9.9540	9.3851	8.8633	8.3838	7.9427	7.5361	6.8137	6.1944	5.6603	5.1971	4.7932	4.4392	4.1274	3.8514	3.7251
13	10.6350	9.9856	9.3936	8.8527	8.3577	7.9038	7.1034	6.4235	5.8424	5.3423	4.9095	4.5327	4.2028	3.9124	3.7801
14	11.2961	10.5631	9.8986	9.2950	8.7455	8.2442	7.3667	6.6282	6.0021	5.4675	5.0081	4.6106	4.2646	3.9616	3.8241
15	11.9379	11.1184	10.3797	9.7122	9.1079	8.5595	7.6061	6.8109	6.1422	5.5755	5.0916	4.6755	4.3152	4.0013	3.8593
16	12.5611	11.6523	10.8378	10.1059	9.4466	8.8514	7.8237	6.9740	6.2651	5.6685	5.1624	4.7296	4.3567	4.0333	3.8874
17	13.1661	12.1657	11.2741	10.4773	9.7632	9.1216	8.0216	7.1196	6.3729	5.7487	5.2223	4.7746	4.3908	4.0591	3.9099
18	13.7535	12.6593	11.6896	10.8276	10.0591	9.3719	8.2014	7.2497	6.4674	5.8178	5.2732	4.8122	4.4187	4.0799	3.9279
19	14.3238	13.1339	12.0853	11.1581	10.3356	9.6036	8.3649	7.3658	6.5504	5.8775	5.3162	4.8435	4.4415	4.0967	3.9424
20	14.8775	13.5903	12.4622	11.4699	10.5940	9.8181	8.5136	7.4694	6.6231	5.9288	5.3527	4.8696	4.4603	4.1103	3.9539
21	15.4150	14.0292	12.8212	11.7641	10.8355	10.0168	8.6487	7.5620	6.6870	5.9731	5.3837	4.8913	4.4756	4.1212	3.9631
22	15.9369	14.4511	13.1630	12.0416	11.0612	10.2007	8.7715	7.6446	6.7429	6.0113	5.4099	4.9094	4.4882	4.1300	3.9705
23	16.4436	14.8568	13.4886	12.3034	11.2722	10.3711	8.8832	7.7184	6.7921	6.0442	5.4321	4.9245	4.4985	4.1371	3.9764
24	16.9355	15.2470	13.7986	12.5504	11.4693	10.5288	8.9847	7.7843	6.8351	6.0726	5.4509	4.9371	4.5070	4.1428	3.9811
25	17.4131	15.6221	14.0939	12.7834	11.6536	10.6748	9.0770	7.8431	6.8729	6.0971	5.4669	4.9476	4.5139	4.1474	3.9849
26	17.8768	15.9828	14.3752	13.0032	11.8258	10.8100	9.1609	7.8957	6.9061	6.1182	5.4804	4.9563	4.5196	4.1511	3.9879
27	18.3270	16.3296	14.6430	13.2105	11.9867	10.9352	9.2372	7.9426	6.9352	6.1364	5.4919	4.9636	4.5243	4.1542	3.9903
28	18.7641	16.6631	14.8981	13.4062	12.1371	11.0511	9.3066	7.9844	6.9607	6.1520	5.5016	4.9697	4.5281	4.1566	3.9923
29	19.1885	16.9837	15.1411	13.5907	12.2777	11.1584	9.3696	8.0218	6.9830	6.1656	5.5098	4.9747	4.5312	4.1585	3.9938
30	19.6004	17.2920	15.3725	13.7648	12.4090	11.2578	9.4269	8.0552	7.0027	6.1772	5.5168	4.9789	4.5338	4.1601	3.9950
40	23.1148	19.7928	17.1591	15.0463	13.3317	11.9246	9.7791	8.2438	7.1050	6.2335	5.5482	4.9966	4.5439	4.1659	3.9995

The total expense over the four years of the lease would be $65,848, the sum of four years of cash payments of $16,462 per year.

No leased asset or lease liability would appear on the balance sheet. However, under today's accounting rules, such a lease must be accounted for as a *capital lease*. This means that both a leased asset and a lease liability must be placed on the balance sheet at the present value of future lease payments, $50,000 in this illustration. The signing of the capital lease requires the following journal entry:

```
Truck leasehold . . . . . . . . . . . . . . . . . . . .   50,000
        Capital lease liability . . . . . . . . . . . .            50,000
To record lease payment.
```

At the end of each of the four years, the asset must be amortized. *Straight-line depreciation*, which is used almost without exception, is $50,000 ÷ 4 = $12,500 annually.

The yearly journal entries for the leased asset expense are:

```
Leased Amortization expense . . . . . . . . . .   12,500
        Truck leasehold . . . . . . . . . . . . . . .            12,500
```

In addition, the annual lease payment must be recorded. Each lease payment consists of interest expense plus an amount that reduces the outstanding liability. The *effective-interest method* is used, as Exhibit 10-15 demonstrates. Study the exhibit before proceeding.

The yearly journal entries for lease payments are:

	YEAR 1		YEAR 2		YEAR 3		YEAR 4	
Interest expense	6,000		4,745		3,339		1,764	
Lease liability	10,462		11,717		13,123		14,698	
Cash		16,462		16,462		16,462		16,462

Exhibit 10-15

Analytical Schedule of Capital Lease Payments

	(1) Capital Lease Liability at Beginning of Year	(2) Interest Expense at 12% Per Year	(3) Cash for Capital Lease Payment	(4) (3) – (2) Reduction in Lease Liability	(5) (1) – (4) Capital Lease Liability at End of Year
End of Year					
1	$50,000	$6,000	$16,462	10,462	$39,538
2	39,538	4,745	16,462	11,717	27,821
3	27,821	3,339	16,462	13,123	14,698
4	14,698	1,764	16,462	14,698	0

The Thomson Corporation specializes in information and publishing, newspaper publishing, and leisure travel. In its 1996 annual report the following two footnotes provided information on its capital (finance) leases.

Thomson Corporation
www.thomson.com/

6. Aircraft and spares	1996	1995
Aircraft and spares	251	278
Aircraft held under finance leases	724	658
	975	936
Accumulated depreciation	(225)	(174)
	750	762

9. Finance Leases

The fair values of finance lease obligations approximate their carrying amounts. The obligations, which are principally in respect of aircraft, are as follows:

	1996	1995
Total future minimum lease payments	351	432
Imputed interest	(81)	(128)
	272	304
Portion included in current liabilities	(21)	(19)
	251	285
Aircraft	266	254
Newspaper presses and other equipment	6	50
	272	304

Differences in Income Statements

Exhibit 10-16 shows the major differences between the accounting for operating leases and the accounting for capital leases. The cumulative expenses are the same, $65,848, but the timing differs. In comparison with the operating-lease approach, the capital-lease approach tends to bunch heavier charges in the early years. The longer the lease, the more pronounced the differences will be in the early years. Therefore, immediate reported income is hurt more under the capital-lease approach.

Exhibit 10-16   Comparison of Annual Expenses: Operating versus Capital Leases

	Operating-Lease Method	Capital-Lease Method			Differences	
Year	(a) Lease Payment*	(b) Amortization of Asset†	(c) Interest Expense‡	(d) (b) + (c) Total Expense	(e) (a) – (d) Difference in Pretax Income	(f) Cumulative Difference in Pretax Income
1	$16,462	$12,500	$ 6,000	$18,500	$(2,038)	$(2,038)
2	16,462	12,500	4,745	17,245	(783)	(2,821)
3	16,462	12,500	3,339	15,839	623	(2,198)
4	16,462	12,500	1,764	14,264	2,198	0
Cumulative expenses	$65,848	$50,000	$15,848	$65,848	$ 0	

* Rent expense for the year under the operating-lease method.
† $50,000 ÷ 4 = $12,500.
‡ From Exhibit 10-15.

An operating lease affects the income statement as rent expense, which is the amount of the lease payment. A capital lease affects the income statement as amortization (of the asset) plus interest expense (on the liability).

Accounting for capital leases is similar to Canadian GAAP in most developed countries around the world, such as the United States, Australia, Germany, and the United Kingdom. In France and Brazil most leases continue to be recorded as operating leases. However, in France extensive lease disclosures are required, and, at this writing, Brazil is contemplating adoption of a capitalization requirement.

Tests for Capital Leases

The capital lease approach was adopted after many years of controversy within the accounting profession regarding which leases deserve capitalization as balance sheet items. Until then, almost no leases were capitalized. Many companies were criticized for "invisible debt" or "off-balance sheet financing" in the sense that noncancelable leases existed but were not included as liabilities on the balance sheet.

A *capital lease* exists if *one* or more of the following conditions are met:

1. Title is transferred to the lessee by the end of the lease term.
2. An inexpensive purchase option is available to the lessee at the end of the lease.
3. The lease term equals or exceeds 75% of the estimated economic life of the property.
4. At the start of the lease term, the present value of minimum lease payments is at least 90% of the property's fair value.

The lease structure determines whether a lease is operating or capital. Managers cannot choose how to treat an existing lease. However, some managers seek to structure leases so that they do not meet any of the criteria of a capital lease and therefore are not shown on the balance sheet.

As you can readily visualize, accounting for leases can become enormously complicated. For further discussion, see a textbook on intermediate or advanced accounting.

Appendix 10C: Deferred Income Taxes

timing difference A situation that arises whenever revenue or expense items are recognized in one period for tax purposes and in another period for shareholder reporting.

Chapter 9 explained that companies use Capital Cost Allowance (CCA) to amortize assets for income tax reporting which is frequently different in amount from the amortization expense used for shareholder reporting. This appendix explores the meaning of the deferred income taxes that result from **timing differences** between the tax return and financial reports.

A Matter of Timing

Objective 11

Understand the concept of deferred income taxes

Consider the $100 million asset that is amortized using CCA for tax purposes and straight-line for shareholder reporting (in millions):

	Shareholder Reporting			Tax Reporting		
	Beginning Book Value	Amortization Expense	Ending Book Value	Beginning Book Value	Capital Cost Allowance	Ending Book Value
Year 1	$100	$20	$80	$100	$30	$70
Year 2	80	20	60	70	21	49
Year 3	60	20	40	49	15	34
Year 4	40	20	20	34	10	24
Year 5	20	20	0	24	7	17

Examine the situation at the end of Year 2. Under shareholder reporting, the book value is $60 million, meaning that $40 million of amortization expense has been charged and $60 million remains to be charged. For tax reporting, the book value is $49 million; $51 million of CCA has been charged and $49 million remains. The difference in book values is a result of the different timing of amortization expense. It is a *temporary* difference because higher amortization in the early years for tax purposes will be offset by higher amortization in later years for shareholder reporting.

Reporting Temporary Differences

How should these temporary differences affect *financial* or shareholder reporting? Suppose Cava Company is the owner of a $100 million asset. The company began on January 1, 19X1 with initial paid-in capital of $200 million cash. On January 2, 19X1, the company purchased the asset for $100 million cash. For shareholder reporting, the estimated useful life is ten years, the estimated residual value is zero, and the straight-line method is used. Prospective annual income before amortization and income taxes is $45 million. The income tax rate is 40% and is not expected to change over the life of the asset. Assume that the asset qualifies for a CCA rate of 20% on a declining-balance basis, after the first year in which a rate of 10% is allowed. Also assume that all taxes are paid early in the next year after the income is earned.

Compare the CCA used for tax purposes with the straight-line depreciation used for shareholder reporting (in millions):

	19X1	*19X2*	*19X3*	*19X4*	*19X5*	*19X6*	*Total*
Capital cost allowance*	$10	$18	$14	$12	$ 9	$ 7	$ 70
Straight-line depreciation	10	10	10	10	10	10	60
Difference	$ 0	$ 8	$ 4	$ 2	$ (1)	$(3)	$ 10

* Year 1: 100 × .10 = 10; Year 2: (100 − 10) .20 = 18; Year 3: (90 − 18) .2 = 14; Year 4: (72 − 14) .2 = 12; Year 5: (58 − 12) .2 = 9; Year 6: (46 − 9) .2 = 7; and so on.

Note that the *timing* of the charges differs. Consider 19X2. The income tax return would show:

Income before amortization	$45,000,000
Capital cost allowance	18,000,000
Taxable income	$27,000,000
Income tax to be paid:	
.40 × $27,000,000, or	$10,800.000

Consider 19X2. The income statement for shareholder reporting would show:

Income before amortization	$45,000,000
Straight-line depreciation	10,000,000
Income before income taxes	$35,000,000
Income tax expenses:	
−current	10,800,000
−deferred	3,200,000
	14,000,000*
Net income	$21,000,000

* $35 million × .40 = $14 million

Now examine the following, which shows the Cava Company's transactions as they would be prepared for shareholder reporting. Stop for a moment after transaction *d*. If straight-line depreciation is used for shareholder reporting purposes, should *income tax expense* be based on CCA or straight-line depreciation?

Analysis of Transactions for Reporting to Cava Company Shareholders (in millions of dollars)

	A		=	L		+	SE	
	Cash	Equipment		Income Tax Payable	Deferred Tax Liability		Paid-in Capital	Retained Earnings
a. Formation	+200		=				+200	
b. Acquisition of equipment	−100	+100	=					
c. Income before amortization and taxes	+ 45		=					+45
d. Straight-line depreciation		− 10	=					−10
e. Income tax expense—deferral			=	+10.8	+3.2			−14
Bal. Dec. 31, 19X1	+145	+ 90	=	+10.8	+3.2		+200	+21

GAAP requires that income tax expense be based on the amortization expense reported to shareholders, not on the typically higher CCA deducted on the tax return. Thus, tax expense (in millions) is calculated as $0.4 \times (45 - 10)$ = 14. Actual tax is calculated as $0.4 \times (45 - 18) - 10.8$. Entry *e* shows the effect on the accounting equation. The 10 of amortization expense reduces shareholders' equity, the 10.8 is shown as a liability to the government, and the difference of 3.2 appears as a *deferred tax liability*. Note that the 3.2 is exactly equal to the tax rate times the difference between CCA and straight-line depreciation $(0.40 \times [18 - 10] = 3.2)$. This represents additional taxes that will be paid in the future as the straight-line depreciation exceeds CCA in the later years.

tax deferral (interperiod tax allocation, tax allocation) A method that measures reported income as if it were subject to full current tax rate even though a more accelerated method was used for tax purposes.

This accounting is called **tax deferral**, or **interperiod tax allocation**, or simply **tax allocation.** Tax allocation produces a deferred tax liability account that fluctuates as the cumulative difference between tax amortization and financial reporting amortization fluctuates.

This topic has many complexities which are beyond the scope of this text. Students should refer to more advanced texts to study this topic further.

Assignment Material

QUESTIONS

10-1. Distinguish between *current liabilities* and *long-term liabilities*.

10-2. Name and briefly describe five items that are often classified as current liabilities.

10-3. "Withholding taxes really add to employer payroll costs." Do you agree? Explain.

10-4. Distinguish between *employee* payroll taxes and *employer* payroll taxes.

10-5. "Product warranties expense should not be recognized until the actual services are performed. Until then you don't know which products might require warranty repairs." Do you agree? Explain.

10-6. Distinguish between a *mortgage bond* and a *debenture*. Which is safer?

10-7. Distinguish between *subordinated* and *unsubordinated* debentures.

10-8. "The face amount of a bond is what you can sell it for." Do you agree? Explain.

10-9. "Protective covenants protect the shareholders' interests in cases of liquidation of assets." Do you agree? Explain.

10-10. Bond covenants usually restrict the borrower's rights in various ways. An example might be a restriction that no additional long-term debt could be issued unless the debt-to-total assets ratio was below 0.5. Who benefits from such a covenant? How?

10-11. Many callable bonds have a call premium for "early" calls. Who does the call premium benefit, the issuer or the purchaser of the bond? How?

10-12. "The quoted bond interest rates imply a rate per annum, but the bond markets do not mean that rate literally." Explain.

10-13. Contrast *nominal* and *effective* interest rates for bonds.

10-14. "Discount *accumulation* is a better descriptive term than discount *amortization*." What would be the justification for making this assertion?

10-15. Distinguish between *straight-line* depreciation and *effective-interest* amortization.

10-16. A company issued bonds with a nominal rate of 10%. At what market rates will the bonds be issued at a discount? At what market rates will they be issued at a premium?

10-17. What are the three main differences between accounting for a bond discount and accounting for a bond premium?

10-18. "A company that issues zero coupon bonds recognizes no interest expense until the bond matures." Do you agree? Explain.

10-19. "A contingent liability is a liability having an estimated amount." Do you agree? Explain.

10-20. "At the balance sheet date, a private high school has lost a court case for an uninsured football injury. The amount of damages has not been set. A reasonable estimate is between $800,000 and $2 million." How should this information be presented in the financial statements?

10-21. Suppose IBM won a lawsuit for $1 million against Innovative Software, a young company with assets of $20 million. Innovative has appealed the suit. How would each company disclose this event in financial statements prepared while the appeal was under way?

10-22. We observe higher debt levels in the automobile industry than in the pharmaceutical industry. Why?

10-23. Appendix 10A. "Future value and present value are two sides of the same coin." Explain.

10-24. Appendix 10B. Why might a company prefer to lease rather than to buy?

10-25. Certain leases are essentially equivalent to purchases. A company must account for such leases as if the asset had been purchased. Explain.

10-26. We observe greater use of capital leases by airlines as a method for financing planes. Why might this be true? Does it make the airline seem to have lower debt ratios?

10-27. Discuss which characteristics of a lease are evaluated in deciding whether it is a capital lease.

10-28. Suppose Consumers Gas signed a contract to deliver a specific quantity of natural gas each year for the next 20 years. How would this be disclosed in its financial statements?

10-29. "Because a company never knows how much it will have to pay for pensions, no pension liability is recognized. Pension obligations are simply explained in a footnote to the financial statements." Do you agree? Explain.

10-30. Variation in international practice in the accounting for pensions can be explained in part by different financial practices in different countries. Discuss.

EXERCISES FOR APPENDIX A IN CHAPTER 10

10–31 through 10–41 are arranged to correspond with Appendix 10A to provide practice for students newly familiar with present value concepts.

10-31 Exercises in Compound Interest

1. You deposit $5,000. How much will you have in four years at 8%, compounded annually? At 12%?

2. A savings and loan association offers depositors a lump-sum payment of $5,000 four years hence. If you desire an interest rate of 8% compounded annually, how much would you be willing to deposit? at an interest rate of 12%?

3. Repeat requirement 2, but assume that the interest rates are compounded semiannually.

10-32 Exercises in Compound Interest

A reliable friend has asked you for a loan. You are pondering various proposals for repayment.

1. Repayment of a lump sum of $40,000 four years hence. How much will you lend if your desired rate of return is (a) 10% compounded annually, (b) 20% compounded annually?

2. Repeat requirement 1, but assume that the interest rates are compounded semiannually.

3. Suppose the loan is to be paid in full by equal payments of $10,000 at the end of each of the next four years. How much will you lend if your desired rate of return is (a) 10% compounded annually, (b) 20% compounded annually?

10-33 Compound Interest and Journal Entries

Bruckner Company acquired equipment for a $250,000 promissory note, payable five years hence, non-interest-bearing, but having an implicit interest rate of 14% compounded annually. Prepare the journal entry for (1) the acquisition of the equipment and (2) interest expense for the first year.

10-34 Compound Interest and Journal Entries

A German company has bought some equipment on a contract entailing a DM 100,000 cash down payment and a DM 400,000 lump sum to be paid at the end of four years. The same equipment can be bought for DM 336,840 cash. DM refers to the German mark, a unit of currency.

Required

1. Prepare the journal entry for the acquisition of the equipment.

2. Prepare journal entries at the end of each of the first two years. Ignore entries for amortization.

10-35. Compound Interest and Journal Entries

A dry-cleaning company bought new presses for an $80,000 down payment and $100,000 to be paid at the end of each of four years. The applicable imputed interest rate is 10% on the unpaid balance. Prepare journal entries (1) for the acquisition and (2) at the end of the first year.

10-36 Exercises in Compound Interest

a. It is your sixtieth birthday. You plan to work five more years before retiring. Then you want to spend $10,000 for a Mediterranean cruise. What lump sum do you have to invest now in order to accumulate the $10,000? Assume that your minimum desired rate of return is

(1) 6%, compounded annually.

(2) 10%, compounded annually.

(3) 20%, compounded annually.

Required 1. Using the balance sheet equation format, prepare an analysis of transactions for CBA. Key your transactions as follows: (a) issuance, (b) first semiannual interest using effective-interest amortization of bond discount, and (c) payment of maturity value. Round all amounts to the nearest thousand.
   2. Prepare corresponding journal entries keyed (a), (b), and (c) as in requirement 1.
   3. Show how the bond-related accounts would appear on CBA's balance sheets as of December 31, 1995 and June 30, 1996. Assume that the semiannual interest payments and amortization have been recorded.

10-63 Early Extinguishment of Debt

On December 31, 1994, Lansing Landscaping issued $20 million of ten-year, 12% debentures. The market interest rate at issuance was 14%. On December 31, 1995 (after all interest payments and amortization had been recorded for 1995), the company purchased all the debentures for $18.5 million. Throughout their life, the debentures had been held by a large insurance company.

Required Show all amounts in thousands of dollars. Round to the nearest thousand.
   1. Compute the gain or loss on early extinguishment.
   2. Using the balance sheet equation, present an analysis of the transaction on the issuer's books.
   3. Show the appropriate journal entry.
   4. At what price on December 31, 1995 could Lansing Landscaping redeem the bonds and realize a $500,000 gain?

10-64 Early Extinguishment of Debt

(Alternate is 10-63.) On December 31, 1995, a local ski slope issued $10 million of ten-year, 12% debentures. The market interest rate at issuance was 12%. Suppose that on December 31, 1996 (after all interest payments and amortization had been recorded for 1996), the company purchased all the debentures for $9.8 million. The debentures had been held by a large insurance company throughout their life.

Required Show all amounts in thousands of dollars.
   1. Compute the gain or loss on early extinguishment.
   2. Using the balance sheet equation, present an analysis of the transaction on the issuer's books.
   3. Show the appropriate journal entry.

10-65 Retirement of Bonds

(J. Patell, adapted) This is a more difficult problem than others in this group.

On January 2, 1986, the Liverpool Financial Corporation sold a large issue of Series A $1,000 denomination bonds. The bonds had a stated coupon rate of 6% (annual), had a term to maturity of twenty years, and made semiannual coupon payments. Market conditions at the time were such that the bonds sold at their face value.

During the ensuing ten years, market interest rates fluctuated widely, and by January 2, 1996, the Liverpool bonds were trading at a price that provided an annual yield of 10%. Liverpool's management was considering purchasing the Series A bonds in the open market and retiring them; the necessary capital was to be raised by a new bond issue—the Series B bonds. Series B bonds were to be $1,000 denomination coupon (semiannual) bonds with a stated annual rate of 8% and a twenty-year term. Management felt that these bonds could be sold at a price yielding no more than 10%, especially if the Series A bonds were retired.

Required 1. On January 2, 1996, at what price could Liverpool Financial purchase the Series A bonds? *Hint*: The applicable factors are 5% and 20 periods.
   2. Show the journal entries necessary to record the following transactions:
   a. Issue of one Series B bond on January 2, 1996.
   b. Purchase and retirement of one Series A bond on January 2, 1996.

c. The first coupon payment on a Series B bond on July 2, 1996. Liverpool uses the effective-interest method of accounting for bond premium and discount.

d. The second coupon payment on a Series B bond on January 2, 1997.

10-66 Non-Interest Bearing Notes
(Alternate is 10-67.) A local theatre borrowed from a bank on a one-year note due on July 31, 19X0. The face value of the note was $200,000. However, the bank deducted its interest "in advance" at 18% of the face value.

Required
Show the effects on the borrower's records at inception and at the end of the month:
1. Using the balance sheet equation, prepare an analysis of transactions.
2. Prepare journal entries.
3. What was the real rate of interest?

10-67 Non-Interest Bearing Notes
(Alternate is 10-66.) On July 31, 1995, a local vineyard borrowed money from a bank on a two-year note due on July 31, 1997. The face value of the note was $25,000. However, the bank deducted interest of $5,070 "in advance."

Required
Show the effects on the borrower's records. Show the effects at July 31, 1995 and 1996.
1. Using the balance sheet equation, prepare an analysis of transactions.
2. Prepare journal entries.
3. Calculate the effective annual rate of interest.

10-68 Zero Coupon Bonds
Northern Company issued a ten-year zero coupon bond having a face amount of $20,000,000 to yield 10%. For simplicity, assume that the 10% yield is compounded annually.

Required
1. Prepare the journal entry for the issuer.
2. Prepare the journal entry for interest expense for the first full year and the second full year using (a) straight-line and (b) effective-interest amortization.
3. Assume an income tax rate of 40%. How much more income tax for the first year would the issuer have to pay because of applying effective-interest instead of straight-line depreciation?

10-69 Zero Coupon Bonds
Medical Holdings, Inc. operates acute care facilities. The company included the following information on its balance sheet:

	August 31	
	1994	1993
Zero Coupon Guaranteed Bonds due 1997, and 2002, $179.3 million face value, net of $83.6 million unamortized discount at August 31, 1994	$95,714,000	$84,577,000

Assume that none of the bonds was issued or retired in fiscal 1994.

Required
1. Assume that the bonds were issued on August 31, 1993. Prepare the journal entry at issuance. Do not use a discount account.
2. Prepare the journal entry for recording interest expense on the bonds for fiscal 1994. Assume annual compounding of interest.
3. The bonds maturing in August of 1997 have a face value of $103 million and an effective annual interest rate of 14% compounded semiannually. Calculate their value at August 31, 1994.

1. Calculate the amortization on the warehouse and office building for the fiscal year ending January 31, 1994.
2. On what date was the building placed into service? (*Hint*: How long would it take to build up the accumulated amortization shown?)
3. The interest on the lease obligation was $464,000 in fiscal 1994. The total lease payment was $550,000. Reconstruct the 1994 journal entry.
4. Suppose this building had met the requirements for an operating lease rather than a capital lease. Calculate the operating income for Deb Shops in fiscal 1994.

10-85　Hudson's Bay Company Annual Report

Refer to the Hudson's Bay Company financial statements in Appendix A.

1. Footnote 13 provides short-term debt information. Calculate and compare the interest expense on short-term debt during 1996 and 1997. Did short-term borrowing increase or decrease from 1996 to 1997?
2. Assume that all payments of principal on long-term debt occur as planned during 1997. Prepare the journal entry to record 1997 principal payments. Also prepare the journal entry to reclassify the current portion of long-term debt as of January 31, 1997.
3. Compute the following three ratios at January 31, 1996 and 1997.
    (a) Debt-to-equity ratio
    (b) Debt-to-total-assets ratio
    (c) Interest-coverage ratio

10-86　Annual Report Disclosure

Identify a company's annual report of your choice.

Calculate and compare the following ratios.
1. Debt-to-equity ratio
2. Debt-to-total-assets ratio
3. Interest-coverage ratio

11 Shareholders' Equity

Learning Objectives

After studying this chapter, you should be able to

1 Describe the rights of shareholders.

2 Differentiate among authorized, issued, and outstanding shares.

3 Explain the characteristics of preferred stock.

4 Discuss similarities and differences between bonds and preferred stock.

5 Identify the economic characteristics of stock splits and dividends.

6 Explain the accounting for stock splits.

7 Differentiate between the accounting for large-percentage and small-percentage stock dividends.

8 Account for treasury stock transactions.

9 Explain and record conversions of preferred stock into common stock.

10 Describe the motivation for and importance of restrictions on retained earnings.

11 Define and use the rate of return on common equity and book value per share.

Business entities obtain economic resources from two sources: debt and equity. The shareholders' equity section of the balance sheet and its related footnotes provide substantial information about the investments made by the owners of the firm. In this chapter we consider two types of equity securities—preferred and common stock—and discuss how to classify and report transactions involving them. Such transactions include issuance, redemption, and reissuance of securities and various types of distributions to the owners of the shares. These distributions may involve cash or other assets, and sometimes, as with stock splits, these distributions may alter the characteristics of the securities. Many of these transactions lead to changes in the retained earnings account.

Sole proprietorships and partnerships are more common business entities than are corporations, but the majority of business activity in terms of volume is conducted by corporations. Therefore, we concentrate on the accounting for ownership in the corporate form. A number of the accounting practices for shareholders' equity are based on legal characteristics of corporations, so the chapter includes frequent reference to the rights and privileges of shareholders and the consequences of various financing decisions on the firm and its owners.

Internationally there is substantial variation in the structure of corporate activity and in accounting procedures used to disclose results. At the most basic level we are observing the conversion of many planned economies from state-owned-and-operated business entities into private ones. In regions of the former USSR, decisions are now being made about the geographic boundaries, the form of government, and the structure of private businesses *and* how to own and account for those businesses. Even in the West we increasingly observe that government is selling "public companies" to the private sector. Examples range from Canada's privatization of Air Canada, to the United Kingdom's privatization of British Petroleum in the mid-1980s to New York City's 1994 sale of its public television station. From an accounting perspective, the key point is that many diverse legal structures worldwide lead to plentiful variation in accounting for shareholders' equity internationally.

■ SHAREHOLDERS' EQUITY IN PERSPECTIVE

CSX Corporation
www.csx.com/

The owners of a business have a *residual interest* in the assets of the firm after both current and long-term liabilities have been deducted. In prior chapters this residual interest has been separated into *paid-in* (or *contributed*) *capital* and *retained earnings*, which is the result of profitable operations in prior years. The following balance sheet presentation is condensed from the 1994 annual report of CSX Corporation, a family of international transportation companies offering a variety of rail-freight, container-shipping, and other transportation, warehousing, and distribution services.

	December 31	
	1994	1993
Common stock, $1 par value	$ 105	$ 104
Other capital	1,368	1,307
Retained earnings	2,258	1,769
Total shareholders' equity	$3,731	$3,180

In the footnotes to the financial statements, CSX provides additional disclosures, including the fact that almost 1 million new shares were issued during the year for approximately $57 million. The summary journal entry to record these new shares would be (in millions):

```
Cash . . . . . . . . . . . . . . . . . . . . . . . . . . . . .   57
        Common stock . . . . . . . . . . . . . . . .          1
        Other capital  . . . . . . . . . . . . . . . .        56
```

As the journal entry shows, the issue price is far in excess of the par value. CSX labels that excess simply "Contributed surplus," but the amounts in excess of par value appear under many different names in various corporate balance sheets. Examples are:

- Paid-in capital (Kelly Services, Inc.)
- Additional paid-in capital (Sara Lee Corporation)
- Capital in excess of par value of stock (Ford Motor Company)
- Capital surplus (Coca-Cola Company)

Recall that some jurisdictions require by law a minimum level of investment by the owners of a company, and this is the amount called par value. Some jurisdictions use a conceptually equivalent term called the *stated value*, and other jurisdictions permit issuance of common stock without either a par or a stated value. Thus, for antiquated legal reasons the corporation may have two accounts for its common stock, one for par or stated value and one for additional paid-in capital. However, the economic substance of the stock issuance by CSX could be portrayed with one account, as indicated by the following journal entry (in thousands):

```
Cash . . . . . . . . . . . . . . . . . . . . . . . . . . . . .   57
        Paid-in capital, common stock   . . . .          57
```

Indeed, as you pursue your study of this chapter, keep in mind that distinguishing between the par or stated value, the additional paid-in capital, and retained income has little practical importance for ongoing corporations. To keep perspective, whenever feasible think of shareholders' equity as a single amount. In Canada, most companies use only one account to report common stock, and there is no separation between amounts received as par or stated value and additional paid-in capital.

The highlights of the corporate form of ownership were covered in Chapter 1. In addition, Chapter 1 compared the sole proprietorship, partnership, and corporation on pages 16–18. Please review this material before proceeding.

Corporations are creatures of the government. They are artificial persons created by law. They exist separately from their owners. As persons, corporations may enter into contracts, may sue, and may even marry (by affiliating with another corporation) and produce offspring (corporation subsidiaries). Corporations are also subject to taxation as separate entities.

Shareholders' Rights

Objective 1

Describe the rights of shareholders.

Shareholders (or stockholders) are entitled to (1) vote, (2) share in corporate profits, (3) share residually in corporate assets upon liquidation, and (4) acquire more shares of subsequent issues of stock. The extent of the shareholders' powers is determined by the number and type of shares held.

(a) Common Share Transactions

Issued	Dec. 30/95 Shares	($000) Amount	Dec. 31/94 Shares	($000) Amount
Balance, beginning of period	29,336,571	94,428	29,336,571	94,428
Reduction on one-for-four consolidation (i)	(22,002,561)	(1)	—	—
Offset of deficit against Share Capital (II)	—	90,000	—	—
	7,334,010	4,427	29,336,571	94,428
Shares issued	250	1		
Increase in shares owned by Subsidiary Company	(43,750)	(654)	—	—
Balance, end of period	7,290,510	3,774	29,336,571	94,428

(I) On May 10, 1995, the Company's shareholders approved a consolidation of the Company's common shares on a one-for-four basis. This change was effective May 10, 1995.

(ii) On May 10, 1995, the Company's shareholders approved the reduction of the stated capital of the common shares of the Company by $90,000,000 with a corresponding reduction to deficit effective April 1, 1995.

(b) Preference Shares

The Class C and Class D Convertible Preference Shares are inter-convertible at the option of the shareholder on a one-for-one basis and rank equally with respect to dividends and in all other respects.

The Second Preference Shares are redeemable at their par value plus accrued and unpaid dividends. Cumulative dividends are payable quarterly at one-half the bank prime lending rate plus 3 percent. Dividends are in arrears at December 30, 1995 in the cumulative amount of $5,924,823 (1994: $4,495,060).

The Class C and Class D Preference Shares and the Second Preference Shares will be redeemable in full in the event of any redemption or purchase for cancellation of any shares of the Company.

(c) Share Option and Share Purchase Plans

The Company has a common share option plan for designated directors, officers and certain managers of the Company and of subsidiary companies, with outstanding options not to exceed 10 percent of the issued Common Shares. Options totaling 260,675 (1994: 265,475) Common Shares have been granted and are still outstanding at year end, at prices of $6.40 (1994: $6.40) to $20.50 (1994: $22.00), to be exercised at various times through the year 2002. During the year 250 Shares (1994: nil) were issued. The 1994 comparatives have been restated to reflect the one-for-four share consolidation in 1995.

The Company has an employee and crew member share purchase plan whereby the Compay will sell treasury Common Shares to the participants at market price or the plan will purchase shares on the stock markets, for the benefit of participants. The Company contributes $2.00 for each $10.00 contributed by the plan participants.

The Company has a share purchase plan which provides that the Company loan funds, interest free, to designated officers to purchase Common Shares in the Company. The shares are held by a trustee for the officers until the loan is repaid. There were no Common Shares issued under the plan during 1995 or 1994.

■ CASH DIVIDENDS

Dividends are proportional distributions of assets to shareholders to satisfy their claims arising from the generation of net income. It is infrequent for assets other than cash to be distributed. In Canada the tendency is for dividends to be paid in equal amounts each quarter, although the board may declare, change, or eliminate a dividend at any time. Some firms do tend to pay a special, larger dividend once a year.

declaration date
The date the board of directors declares a dividend.

The date on which the board formally announces that it will pay a dividend is called the **declaration date**. The board specifies a **date of record,** a future date that determines which shareholders will receive the dividend. A person who holds the stock on the declaration date but sells before the date of record will not receive the dividend. The person who owns it on the date of record will receive it. The actual **payment date** is the day the cheques are mailed and follows the date of record by a few days or weeks. ALLTEL has 61,141 shareholders who must be identified and to whom dividends must be paid. AT&T pays dividends to 2.3 million shareholders.

date of record The date when ownership is fixed for determining the right to receive a dividend.

The declaration will specify the amount of the dividend, and it becomes a liability on that date. No journal entry is required on the date of record, although the company's stock transfer agent must identify all parties to whom dividends will be paid as of that date. If a balance sheet is prepared between declaration and payment, a liability for the dividend payable will appear. The journal entries to record a $20,000 dividend declaration and its subsequent payment appear below:

payment date The date dividends are paid.

Date of Declaration	Sept. 26	Retained earnings	20,000	
		Dividends payable		20,000
		To record the declaration of dividends to be paid on November 15 to shareholders of record as of October 25.		
Date of Payment	Nov. 15	Dividends payable	20,000	
		Cash		20,000
		To pay dividends declared on September 26 to shareholders of record as of October 25.		

The amount of cash dividends declared by a board of directors depends on many factors. The least important factor is the amount of retained earnings, except in cases in which the company is on the brink of bankruptcy in which the company has just been incorporated. In these two cases, the wisdom of declaring dividends is highly questionable.

The more important factors that affect dividends include the stock market's expectations that have crystallized over a series of years, the current and predicted earnings, and the corporation's current cash position and financial plans regarding spending on plant assets and repayments of debts. Remember that payment of cash dividends requires *cash*. Large amounts of net income or retained earnings do not mean that the necessary cash is available.

Some corporations try to increase the attractiveness of their shares by maintaining a stable quarterly dividend payment on common shares (say, $1 per share each quarter). Others pay a predictable fraction of current earnings per share (say, 60% of whatever is earned in the current year). Some corporations also try to show steady growth in dividends by increasing the dividend per share each year. Sometimes an "extra" payment occurs at the end of an especially profitable year. General Motors has followed the latter practice.

If a company has maintained a series of uninterrupted dividends over a span of years, it will make an effort to continue such payments even in the face of net losses. Indeed, companies occasionally borrow money for the sole purpose of maintaining dividend payments.

■ DISTRIBUTIONS OF ADDITIONAL STOCK

Objective 5

Identify the economic characteristics of stock splits and dividends.

Companies occasionally issue additional shares to current shareholders. A common approach is to issue one additional share for every share currently owned. Suppose the Allstar Equipment Company has 100,000 shares outstanding with a market value of $150 per share. The total market value of the stock is thus $15,000,000. If Allstar Equipment gives each shareholder an additional share for each share owned, the total number of shares would increase to 200,000.

If nothing else changes, the shareholder is no better or worse off. Allstar Equipment is unchanged because the shareholders did not provide any new resources. Since Allstar has the same assets, liabilities, and equity, the total value of the firm should still be $15,000,000. With 200,000 shares outstanding, the market value per share should drop to $75.

In practice distributions of new shares take a variety of forms that may involve changing the par value of the shares and may involve smaller increases in the shares. Such minor differences in the distribution lead to the use of a different term for the transaction and to somewhat different accounting.

Stock Splits and Stock Dividends

stock split Issuance of additional shares to existing shareholders for no payments by the shareholders.

A **stock split** refers to the issuance of additional shares to existing shareholders without any additional cash payment to the firm. Issuance of one additional share for each share currently owned is called a "two-for-one" split. Typically, there is a corresponding adjustment to the par value. The following expands the Allstar Equipment example to show the whole shareholders' equity section. Suppose that 100,000 $10 par value shares of common are returned to Allstar in exchange for 200,000 $5 par value shares of common. Nothing changes in the shareholders' equity section of Allstar's balance sheet except the description of shares authorized, issued, and outstanding. As shown below, the aggregate par value is unchanged, no cash has changed hands, each owner has the same proportionate interest as before, and each has the same relative voting power:

	Before 2-for-1 Split	Changes	After 2-for-1 Split
Common stock, 100,000 shares @ $10 par	$ 1,000,000	[−100,000 shares @ $10 par + 200,000 shares @ $5 par]	$ 1,000,000
Additional paid-in capital	4,000,000		4,000,000
Total paid-in capital	$ 5,000,000		$ 5,000,000
Retained earnings	6,000,000		6,000,000
Shareholders' equity	$11,000,000		$11,000,000
Overall market value of stock @ assumed $150 per share	$15,000,000	@ assumed $75 per share	$15,000,000

stock dividends
Distribution to shareholders of additional shares of any class of the distributing company's stock, without any payment to the company by the shareholders.

Stock dividends are also issuances of additional shares to existing shareholders without additional cash payment, but the number of new shares issued is usually smaller than in a split, and the original par value is typically retained. For example, a 10% stock dividend involves issuance of one new share for every ten currently owned.

Why Use Stock Splits and Dividends?

Experts debate the importance of splits and stock dividends even as companies continue to use them. One observation is that most common stock sells at under $100 per share. In 1994, Wal-Mart stock sold for approximately $25 per share. During the prior thirteen years the stock split two-for-one on six occasions. An investor who purchased one share in 1981 would have sixty-four shares in 1994. Without any splits, one original Wal-Mart share would have been worth $1,600 in 1994. After these splits, a "round-lot" of 100 shares cost 100 × $25 = $2,500, a reasonable investment size. Without the splits, a round-lot would have cost $1,600 × 100 = $160,000. Thus, splits allow the company to maintain the stock price in a trading range accessible to small investors and company employees. If one share cost $1,600, Wal-Mart might not have as many shareholders.

Wal-Mart
www.wal-mart.com

Professor Willard Graham explained a stock split as being akin to taking a gallon of whiskey and pouring it into five individual bottles. The resulting packaging *might* attract a price for each fifth that would produce a higher total value than if the gallon had not been split. There is little evidence to suggest that Graham's speculation is true. But as he noted, there is some spillage when pouring the gallon into five bottles—that's the legal, printing, and clerical cost of physically issuing the new stock.

Often a stock split or stock dividend accompanies other announcements, such as new corporate investment strategies or changes in cash dividend levels. Suppose a company issues a 10% stock dividend, issuing one new share for each ten shares held. The company may not change the normal cash dividend per share, which means total cash dividends to each shareholder will increase by 10%. Why? Because dividends are received on eleven shares instead of ten. Or perhaps the firm has traditionally paid a special cash dividend at year-end but plans to expand production substantially, which will absorb available cash. The firm might combine the announcement of the planned expansion with an announcement of a small stock dividend. The small-percentage stock dividend will not draw on cash immediately but will provide shareholders with an increase in future cash dividends in proportion to the percentage of new shares issued.

Accounting for Stock Splits

Objective 6

Explain the accounting for stock splits.

In the Allstar Equipment Company's stock split, no entry occurs because the number of shares doubles and the par value is cut in half. Thus, the total par value in the common stock account is unchanged.

However, Allstar Equipment might have chosen a different procedure to implement their plan to increase the number of shares outstanding. If Allstar did not want to bother physically exchanging the old $10 par value stock certificates for new $5 par value certificates, it could simply have issued more of the $10 par value shares. Previously, no accounting entry was required because total par value was unchanged. Issuing more $10 par value shares requires that the common stock account be increased by a credit to common stock. Since the investors did not contribute more capital to the company, this accounting procedure is just a rearrangement of owners' equity. Normally, the increase to the common stock account is transferred from the Additional Paid-in Capital. If a company has a zero or an insufficient balance in "Additional Paid-in Capital," then the shortfall is transferred from Retained Earnings to increase the common stock account. In this case different language is used to describe the two-for-one stock split. We say it is "accounted for as a stock dividend." The three alternative implementations are summarized below:

Option 1.	Exchange 200,000 new $5.00 par value shares for the old ones	No Entry		
Option 2.	Issue 100,000 new $10.00 par value shares	Additional Paid-in Capital Common Stock	100,000	100,000
Option 3.	Issue 100,000 new $10.00 par value shares and "account for it as a stock dividend"	Retained Earnings Common Stock	100,000	100,000

Large-Percentage Stock Dividends

Objective 7

Differentiate between the accounting for large-percentage and small-percentage stock dividends.

Some companies may differentiate between the sizes of stock dividends, in that large-percentage stock dividends (typically those 20% or higher) are accounted for at par or stated value. As in the case of stock splits, the market value of the outstanding shares tends to adjust completely when additional shares are issued. When firms issue large-percentage stock dividends or splits, they usually lower the per-share dividend proportionately. Consider the Allstar Equipment Company and the effect of possible stock dividends on share price. Recall that the market value of the firm will be unchanged by simply changing the number of shares.

If the Allstar Equipment Company chose to double the outstanding number of shares by issuing a 100% stock dividend, the total amount of shareholders' equity would still be unaffected. However, its composition would change.

Possible Allstar Stock Dividends; Total Market Value $15,000,000	Stock Dividend	Shares			Price per Share
		Original	New	Total	
	None	100,000		100,000	$150.00
	20%	100,000	20,000	120,000	125.00
	40%	100,000	40,000	140,000	107.14
	60%	100,000	60,000	160,000	93.75
	80%	100,000	80,000	180,000	83.33
	100%	100,000	100,000	200,000	75.00

	Before 100% Stock Dividend	Changes	After 100% Stock Dividend
Common stock, 100,000 shares @ $10 par	$ 1,000,000	+ (100,000 shares @ $10 par = $1,000,000)	$ 2,000,000
Additional paid-in capital	4,000,000		4,000,000
Total paid-in capital	$ 5,000,000		$ 6,000,000
Retained earnings	6,000,000	–$1,000,000 par value of "dividend"	5,000,000
Shareholders' equity	$11,000,000		$11,000,000

In substance, there is absolutely no difference between the 100% stock dividend and the two-for-one stock split. *In form*, the shareholder receiving a dividend has $10 par shares rather than $5 par shares. The stock dividend is accounted for as in Option 3 above for stock splits. Note retained earnings is transferred to the par value account. Infrequently, a company will transfer amounts from additional paid-in capital, as in Option 2.

Small-Percentage Stock Dividends

When a stock dividend of less than 20% is issued, accountants require that the dividend be accounted for at market value, *not* at par value. This rule is not easy to defend. It is partly the result of tradition and partly because small-percentage stock dividends often accompany increases in the total dividend payments or other changes in the company's financial policies. It is argued that the decision to increase total dividends communicates management's conviction that future cash flows will rise to support these increased distributions, and this is a positive statement about the firm's prospects.

Reconsider our example of Allstar Equipment Company (before the split). Suppose the market value of common shares is $150 at the time of issuance of a 2% stock dividend. The effect on the shareholders' equity section is shown in the table on page 496.

As before, the individual shareholder receives no assets from the corporation. Moreover, the shareholders' fractional interest is unchanged; if the shareholders sell the dividend shares, their proportionate ownership interest in the company will decrease. The major possible economic effect of a stock dividend is to signal increased cash dividends. Suppose the company in our example consistently paid cash dividends of $1 per share. Often this cash dividend level per share is maintained after a stock dividend. The recipient of the stock dividend can now expect a future annual cash dividend of $1 × 1,020 = $1,020 rather than $1 × 1,000 = $1,000. In this case, when the dividend rate per share is maintained, announcing a stock dividend of 2% has the same effect as announcing an increase of 2% in the cash dividend.

	Before 2% Stock Dividend	Changes	After 2% Stock Dividend
Common stock, 100,000 shares @ $10 par	$ 1,000,000	+ (2,000 shares @ $10 par) = + 20,000	$ 1,020,000
Additional paid-in capital	4,000,000	+ [2,000 shares @ ($150 − $10)] = + 280,000	4,280,000
Retained earnings	6,000,000	− (2,000 @ $150)	5,700,000
Shareholders' equity	$11,000,000	= − 300,000	$11,000,000
Overall market value of stock @ assumed $150 per share	$15,000,000	@ assumed $147.06 per share*	$15,000,000
Total shares outstanding	100,000		102,000
Individual shareholder:			
Assumed ownership of shares	1,000		1,020
Percentage ownership interest	1%		Still 1%

* Many simultaneous events affect the level of stock prices, including expectations regarding the general economy, the industry, and the specific company. Thus, the market price of the stock may move in either direction when the stock dividend is declared. Theory and complicated case studies indicate that a small-percentage stock dividend should have zero effect on the total market value of the firm. Accordingly, the new market price per share should be $15,000,000 ÷ 102,000 shares = $147.06.

For small-percentage (under 20%) stock dividends the company records the transaction by transferring the *market value* of the additional shares from retained earnings to common stock and additional paid-in capital. The entry is often referred to as being a "capitalization of retained earnings." It is basically a signal to the shareholders that $300,000 of retained earnings is being invested for the long term in productive assets. In our example, the required journal entry would be:

```
Retained earnings . . . . . . . . . . . . . . . . . . . . .    300,000
        Common stock . . . . . . . . . . . . . . . . . . . .              20,000
        Additional paid-in capital . . . . . . . . . . .              280,000
To record a 2% common stock dividend,
resulting in the issuance of 2,000 shares.
Retained earnings is reduced at the rate of
the market value of $150 per share at date
of issuance.
```

The practice regarding the use of market values in accounting for small-percentage stock dividends is applied in Canada and the United States arbitrarily and is not consistently adopted worldwide. For example, in Japan these journal entries are recorded at par value. The Japanese practice is one most accountants would support.

Relation of Dividends and Splits

Companies typically use large-percentage stock dividends to accomplish exactly the same purpose as a stock split. That is, the companies want a material reduction in the market price of their shares or they want to signal an increase in total dividend payments to shareholders. Stock splits frequently occur in the form of a stock "dividend" to save clerical costs. After all, swapping old $10-par certificates for new $5 par certificates is more expensive than merely printing and mailing additional $10-par certificates.

Review the typical accounting for stock splits and stock dividends:

- Stock splits—
  1. Change par value—no accounting entry.
  2. Retain par value—rearranging owners' equity by transferring paid-in capital or retained earnings to common stock.
- Stock dividends—shift from retained earnings to paid-in capital:
  1. Small-percentage dividends—reduce retained earnings by *market value* of the additional shares issued.
  2. Large-percentage dividends—reduce retained earnings or additional paid-in capital by only the *par value* of the additional shares issued.

If the company has shares without a par or stated value, the accounting is simplified as follows:
- Small-percentage stock dividend—
  1. Rearrange owners' equity by transferring from retained earnings to common stock at market value.
- Stock split or large percentage stock dividend
  1. Adjust the number of issued shares.

Fractional Shares

Corporations ordinarily issue shares in whole units. However, some shareholders are entitled to stock dividends in amounts equal to fractional units. Consequently, corporations issue additional shares for whole units plus cash equal to the market value of the fractional amount.

For example, suppose a corporation issues a 3% stock dividend. A shareholder has 160 shares. The market value per share on the date of issuance is $40. Par value is $2. The shareholder would be entitled to 0.03 × 160 = 4.8 shares. The company would issue 4 shares plus 0.8($40) = $32 cash. The journal entry is:

Retained earnings (4.8 × $40)	192	
Common stock, at par (4 × $2)		8
Additional paid-in capital (4 × $38) .		152
Cash (0.8 × $40)		32
To issue a stock dividend of 3% to a holder of 160 shares.		

The Investor's Accounting for Dividends and Splits

So far we have focused on the corporation. What about the shareholder? Consider the *investor's* entries for the transactions described so far. Suppose Investor J is passive and takes no active voice in management. She bought 1,000 shares of the original issue of Allstar Equipment Company stock for $50 per share:

Investment in Allstar common stock	50,000	
Cash		50,000

To record investment in 1,000 shares of an original issue of Allstar Equipment Company common stock at $50 per share. The par value is $10 per share.

Investor J holds the shares indefinitely. However, if Investor J sold the shares to Investor K at a subsequent price other than $50, a gain or loss would be recorded by J, and K would carry the shares at the amount paid to J. Meanwhile, the shareholders' equity of Allstar Equipment Company would be completely unaffected by this sale by one investor to another. The company's underlying shareholder records would simply be changed to delete J and add K as a shareholder.

The following examples show how Investor J would record the stock split, cash dividends, and stock dividends, with each treated as an independent event, not as sequential events. Note that several events that produced journal entries for Allstar do not provide entries for Investor J:

a. Stock split at 2 for 1:

No journal entry, but a memorandum would be made in the investment account to show that 2,000 shares are now held at a cost of $25 each instead of 1,000 shares at a cost of $50 each.

b. Cash dividends of $2 per share:

Cash	2,000	
Dividend income		2,000

To record cash dividends on Allstar Equipment Company stock.

or:

Alternatively, the following two entries might be used:

Date of declaration:

Dividends receivable	2,000	
Dividend income		2,000

To record dividends declared by Allstar Equipment Company.

Date of receipt:

Cash	2,000	
Dividends receivable		2,000

To record the receipt of cash dividends.

c. Stock dividends of 2%:

No journal entry, but a memorandum would be made in the investment account to show that (assuming the stock split in a had not occurred) 1,020 shares are now owned at an average cost of $50,000 ÷ 1,020, or $49.02 per share.

d. Stock split in form of a 100% dividend:

No journal entry, but a memorandum would be made in the investment account to show that (assuming the stock splits and stock dividends in a and c had not occurred) 2,000 shares are now owned at an average cost of $25 instead of 1,000 shares @ $50. Note that this memorandum has the same effect as the memorandum in a above.

■ REPURCHASE OF SHARES

Companies repurchase their own shares for two main purposes: (1) to permanently reduce shareholder claims, called *retiring stock*, and (2) to temporarily hold shares for later use, most often to be granted as part of employee bonus or stock purchase plans. Temporarily held shares are called *treasury stock* or *treasury shares*. By repurchasing shares, for whatever reason, a company liquidates some shareholders' claims, and the following journal entry results:

```
Shareholders' equity . . . . . . . . . . . . . . . .   xxx
        Cash . . . . . . . . . . . . . . . . . . . . . . .         xxx
Repurchase of outstanding shares.
```

The purpose of the repurchase determines *which shareholders' equity accounts* are affected. Consider an illustration of the Brecht Company, whose stock has a market value of $15 per share:

Common stock, 1,000,000 shares at $1 par	$ 1,000,000
Additional paid-in capital	4,000,000
Total paid-in capital	$ 5,000,000
Retained earnings	6,000,000
Shareholders' equity	$11,000,000
Overall market value of stock @ assumed $15 per share	$15,000,000
Book value per share = $11,000,000 ÷ 1,000,000 = $11.	

Book value per share refers to the historical investment by the shareholders in the company. The total shareholders' equity of $11,000,000 combines the original purchase price of shares in the past (par value plus paid-in capital) with the periodic earnings of the firm that have remained in the business (retained earnings). Dividing the total shareholders' equity by the number of shares gives the average per share, in this case $11,000,000 ÷ 1,000,000 = $11.

Retirement of Shares

Suppose the board of directors has decided that the $15 market value of its shares is "too low." Even though the market value exceeds the book value by $4 per share ($15 – $11), the board may think the market is too pessimistic regarding the company's shares. Because of inflation and other factors, it is not unusual to have the market value vastly exceed the book value.

The board might believe that the best use of corporate cash would be to purchase and retire a portion of the outstanding shares. In this way, the remaining shareholders would have the sole benefit of the predicted eventual increase in market value per share. Other motives include the desire to change the proportion of debt and equity in use to finance the firm. The company may wish to return cash to shareholders without creating expectations of permanent increases in dividends.

Suppose the Board of Brecht Company purchases and retires 5% of its outstanding shares @ $15 for a total of 50,000 × $15, or $750,000 cash. The total shareholders' equity is reduced or contracted. The stock certificates are cancelled, and the shares are no longer issued and outstanding:

	Before Repurchase of 5% of Outstanding Shares	Changes Because of Retirement	After Repurchase of 5% of Outstanding Shares
Common stock, 1,000,000 shares @ $1 par	$ 1,000,000	−(50,000 shares @ $1 par) = −$50,000	$ 950,000
Additional paid-in capital	4,000,000	−(50,000 shares @ $4) = −$200,000	3,800,000
Total paid-in capital	$ 5,000,000		$ 4,750,000
Retained earnings	6,000,000	−(50,000 @ $10*) = −$500,000	5,500,000
Shareholders' equity	$11,000,000		$10,250,000
Book value per common share:			
$11,000,000 ÷ 1,000,000	$ 11.00		
$10,250,000 ÷ 950,000			$ 10.79

* $15 – the $5 (or $1 + $4) originally paid in.

The journal entry reverses the original average paid-in capital per share and charges the additional amount to retained earnings:

```
Common stock ...............................    50,000
Additional paid-in capital  ....................   200,000
Retained earnings  ...........................   500,000
      Cash  ....................................              750,000
To record retirement of 50,000 shares of stock for
$15 cash per share. The original paid-in capital
was $5 per share, so the additional $10 per share
is debited to Retained Earnings.
```

The additional $10 is sometimes described as being tantamount to a special cash dividend paid to the owners of the 50,000 retired shares. Note how the book value per share of the outstanding shares has declined from $11.00 to $10.79. The phenomenon is called *dilution* of the common shareholders' equity. **Dilution** is usually defined as a reduction in shareholders' equity per share or earnings per share that arises from some changes among shareholders' proportionate interests. As a rule, boards of directors avoid dilution. However, boards sometimes favour deliberate dilution if expected future profits will more than compensate for a temporary undesirable reduction in book value per share.

dilution Reduction in shareholders' equity per share or earnings per share that arises from some changes among shareholders' proportional interests.

Treasury Stock

Objective 8

Account for treasury stock transactions.

Suppose the Brecht Company's Board of Directors decides that the 50,000 repurchased shares will be held only temporarily and then resold. Perhaps the shares are needed for an employee stock purchase plan or for executive stock options. Such temporarily held shares are called *treasury stock*. The Canada Business Corporations Act (CBCA) does not allow companies incorporated under the CBCA to hold treasury stock. For these companies, shares repurchased are annulled. As in the retirement of shares, the repurchase is a *decrease* in shareholders' equity. Treasury stock is NOT an asset. It indicates a liquidation of the ownership claim of one or more shareholders. Cash dividends are not paid on shares held in the treasury; cash dividends are distributed only to the shares outstanding (in the hands of shareholders), and treasury stock is not outstanding:

Shares issued	1,000,000
Less: Treasury stock	50,000
Total shares outstanding	950,000

Brecht's shareholders' equity section would be affected as follows:

	Before Repurchase of 5% of Outstanding Shares	Changes Because of Treasury Stock	After Repurchase of 5% of Outstanding Shares
Common stock, 1,000,000 shares @ $1 par	$ 1,000,000		$ 1,000,000
Additional paid-in capital	4,000,000		4,000,000
Total paid-in capital	$ 5,000,000		$ 5,000,000
Retained earnings	6,000,000		6,000,000
Total	$11,000,000		$11,000,000
Deduct:			
Cost of treasury stock	—	–$750,000	750,000
Shareholders' equity	$11,000,000		$10,250,000

The journal entry is:

```
Treasury stock .............................  750,000
      Cash ....................................            750,000
To record acquisition of 50,000 shares of common
stock @ $15 (to be held as treasury stock).
```

The Treasury Stock account is a contra account to Owners' Equity just as Accumulated Depreciation is a contra account to related asset accounts. Like the retirement of shares, the purchase of treasury stock decreases shareholders' equity by $750,000. Unlike retirements, common stock at par value, additional paid-in capital, and retained earnings remain untouched by treasury stock purchases. A separate treasury stock account is a deduction from total shareholders' equity on the balance sheet.

Remember that treasury stock is not an asset. A company's holding of shares in *another company* is an asset; its holding of its *own shares* is a negative element of shareholders' equity.

Why Buy Back Your Own Shares?

During the three-year period 1988 through 1990, total net income for The Coca-Cola Company was $4.2 billion, an average of $1.4 billion per year. What did Coca-Cola do with this $4.2 billion in assets generated? It isn't surprising that some of it was distributed to shareholders in the form of cash dividends. Total cash dividends for the three-year period were $1.5 billion, resulting in a dividend payout ratio (cash dividends/net income) of 35.7%. What may be a bit surprising is that during this same period, Coca-Cola used $2.2 billion to buy back some of its own shares of stock. We often think that cash dividends are the primary method corporations employ to distribute cash to shareholders, but frequently, as in the case of Coca-Cola, cash used in stock purchases exceeds the amount paid in cash dividends.

One reason firms give is that idle resources within the company could be more efficiently used by individual shareholders. In announcing a $10 billion stock buyback plan in 1989 following an impressive series of acquisitions during the 1980s, General Electric stated that it saw no further acquisitions that looked attractive and, thus, would return excess funds to the shareholders. Such a strategy decreases the likelihood that a firm will be an object of a takeover bid since takeover artists frequently target firms holding large amounts of inefficiently used assets.

Firms also use stock purchases to demonstrate confidence in their own prospects. The thinking is that investors are more likely to believe company claims of rosy prospects if the investors see the company putting its money where its mouth is by buying its own shares. This tactic was employed extensively in the wake of the market crash of October 1987. At the time, in a bid to prop up falling share prices, over 600 firms announced plans to repurchase their own shares.

Both Coca-Cola and General Electric remain committed to share repurchase programs. In August of 1994, Coca-Cola began a repurchase program of up to 10 million shares. In December of 1994, GE's board of directors authorized the repurchase of up to $5 billion in common shares.

To put these numbers in perspective, GE has issued 1.8 billion shares historically and raised $594 million in equity investments in the process. As a result of continual repurchase activity, 8% of those shares are now in the treasury at a cost of $5.3 billion. Almost ten times as much has been used to reacquire shares as was originally raised. ■

Sources: 1990 and 1994 Annual Reports *of The Coca Cola Company; Amal Kumar Naj, "General Electric Buy-Back Plan Signals New Tack, Reflects Earnings Optimism,"* Wall Street Journal *(November 20, 1989), p. A3; 1994* Annual Report *of General Electric.*

General Electric
www.ge.com

Disposition of Treasury Stock

Treasury shares are often resold at a later date, perhaps in conjunction with an employee stock purchase plan. The sales price usually differs from the acquisition cost. Suppose the sales price is $18. The journal entry is:

Cash	900,000	
Treasury stock		750,000
Additional paid-in capital		150,000
To record sale of treasury stock, 50,000 shares @ $18. Cost was $15 per share.		

Suppose the price is $13:

Cash	650,000	
Additional paid-in capital	100,000	
Treasury stock		750,000
To record sale of treasury stock, 50,000 shares @ $13. Cost was $15 per share.		

If the treasury shares are resold below their cost, accountants tend to debit (decrease) Additional Paid-in Capital for the difference, $2 per share in this case. Additional Paid-in Capital is sometimes divided into several separate accounts that identify different sources of capital. For example:

- Additional paid-in capital—preferred stock
- Additional paid-in capital—common stock
- Additional paid-in capital—treasury stock transactions

If such accounts are used, a consistent accounting treatment would call for debiting only Additional Paid-in Capital—Treasury Stock Transactions (and no other paid-in capital account) for the excess of the cost over the resale price of treasury shares. If there is no balance in such a paid-in capital account, the debit should be made to Retained Earnings.

Suppose 25,000 of the treasury shares bought by Brecht are later sold for $17 and still later the other 25,000 shares are sold for $12. The company had no previous sales of treasury stock. The journal entries are:

Cash	425,000	
Treasury stock		375,000
Additional paid-in capital—treasury		
stock transactions		50,000
To record sale of treasury stock, 25,000 shares @ $17.		
Cost was $15 per share.		
Cash	300,000	
Additional paid-in capital—treasury		
stock transactions	50,000	
Additional paid-in capital*	25,000	
Treasury stock		375,000
To record sale of treasury stock, 25,000 shares @ $12.		
Cost was $15 per share.		

*If an insufficient balance exists in Additional paid-in capital, then Retained Earnings would be reduced.

Although the specific accounting for transactions in the company's own stock may vary from company to company, one rule is paramount. Any differences between the acquisition costs and the resale proceeds of treasury stock must never be reported as losses, expenses, revenues, or gains in the income statement. Why? A corporation's own capital stock is part of its capital structure. It is *not* an asset of the corporation. Nor is stock intended to be treated like merchandise for sale to customers at a profit. Therefore, changes in a corporation's capitalization should produce no gain or loss but should merely require direct adjustments to the owners' equity.

There is essentially no difference between unissued shares and treasury shares. In our example, Brecht Company could accomplish the same objective by (1) acquiring 50,000 shares, retiring them, and issuing 50,000 new shares, or (2) acquiring 50,000 shares and reselling them.

■ OTHER ISSUANCES OF COMMON STOCK

Not all common stock is issued in exchange for cash. In some cases other assets are given to the company in exchange for its stock. In other cases another corporate security—a bond or preferred stock—is *converted* into common

Noncash Exchanges

Often a company issues its stock to acquire land, a building, or even the common stock of another company. Such exchanges raise the question of the proper dollar value of the transaction to be recorded in both the buyer's and the seller's books. The proper amount is the "fair value" of either the securities or the exchanged assets, whichever is more objectively determinable. That amount should be used by both companies.

For example, suppose Company A acquires some equipment from Company B in exchange for 10,000 newly issued shares of A's common stock. The equipment was carried on B's books at the $200,000 original cost less accumulated amortization of $50,000. Company A's stock is listed on the Toronto Stock Exchange; its current market price is $18 per share. Its par value is $1 per share. In this case, the market price of A's common stock would be regarded as a more objectively determinable fair value than the book value or the undepreciated cost of B's equipment. The accounts are affected as follows:

	Assets	=	Liabilities	+	Shareholders' Equity	
	Equipment				*Common Stock*	*Additional Paid-in Capital*
Issuance of stock by A	+ 180,000	=			+10,000	+170,000

	Investment in A Common Stock	*Equipment*	*Accumulated Depreciation*		*Retained Earnings*	
Disposal of equipment by B	+ 180,000	−200,000	+50,000	=	+30,000	[gain on disposal of equipment]

The journal entries (without explanations) are:

On issuer's books (A):

Equipment	180,000	
Common stock		10,000
Additional paid-in capital		170,000

On investor's books (B):

Investment in A common stock	180,000	
Accumulated amortization, equipment	50,000	
Equipment		200,000
Gain on disposal of equipment		30,000

Conversion of Securities

Objective 9

Explain and record conversions of preferred stock into common stock.

When companies issue *convertible* bonds or preferred stock, the conversion feature makes the securities more attractive to investors and increases the price the issuer receives (or, equivalently, reduces the interest or dividend it must pay). Ultimately, the buyer or some subsequent owner may exercise the conversion privilege. Since the conversion is a transaction of form rather than substance, the accounts are simply adjusted as if the common stock had been issued initially.

For example, suppose Company B had paid $160,000 for an investment in 5,000 shares of the $1 par value convertible preferred stock of Company A in 19X1. The preferred stock was converted into 10,000 shares of Company A common stock ($1 par value) in 19X8. The accounts of Company A (the issuer) would be affected as shown in Exhibit 11-2.

Exhibit 11-2	Analysis of Convertible Preferred Stock					
	Assets =	**Liabilities** +		**Shareholders' Equity**		
	Cash		Preferred Stock	Additional Paid-in Capital, Preferred	Common Stock	Additional Paid-in Capital, Common
Issuance of preferred (19X1)	+ 160,000 =		+5,000	+155,000		
Conversion of preferred (19X8)	=		−5,000	−155,000	+10,000	+150,000

The journal entries would be as follows:

On issuer's books (A):

```
19X1  Cash ................................   160,000
          Preferred stock, convertible ...........          5,000
          Additional paid-in capital, preferred ....      155,000
      To record issuance of 5,000 shares of $1 par
      preferred stock convertible into two common
      shares for one preferred share.

19X8  Preferred stock, convertible ...............    5,000
      Additional paid-in capital, preferred .........  155,000
          Common stock .......................             10,000
          Additional paid-in capital, common  ....       150,000
      To record the conversion of 5,000 preferred
      shares to 10,000 common shares.
```

Company B (the investor) has experienced a change in form of the investment, with no change in historical cost. The carrying value, or book value, of the investment remains $160,000. To show that the form of the investment is now common stock rather than preferred stock, Company B might use a journal entry to transfer the $160,000 from one investment account to another. Alternatively, it might change subsidiary records that document the composition of a single general ledger account called Investments.

While preferred stock is common in some countries, it does not exist in others. Japan, for example, does not have this form of security. Other countries that have classes of preferred stock may not follow Canadian practice with respect to priority in liquidation or special features such as cumulative dividends, convertibility, or callability.

Objective 10

Describe the motivation for and importance of restrictions on retained earnings.

■ RETAINED EARNINGS RESTRICTIONS

Directors can make decisions that benefit shareholders but hurt creditors. For example, directors might pay such large dividends that payments of creditors' claims would be threatened. To protect creditors, dividend-declaring power is restricted by either laws or contractual obligations or both. Moreover, boards of directors can voluntarily restrict their declarations of dividends.

Laws typically do not permit dividends if shareholders' equity is less than total paid-in capital. Therefore, retained earnings must exceed the cost of treasury stock. If there is no treasury stock, retained earnings must be positive. This restriction limits dividend payments and protects the position of the creditors. For example, consider the following (in millions):

	Before Dividends	After Dividend Payments of $10	$4
Paid-in capital	$25	$25	$25
Retained earnings	10	—	6
Total	$35	$25	$31
Deduct:			
Cost of treasury stock	6	6	6
Shareholders' equity	$29	$19	$25

Without restricting dividends to the amount of retained earnings in excess of the cost of the treasury stock, the corporation could pay a dividend of $10 million. This would reduce the shareholders' equity below the paid-in capital of $25 million. With the restriction, unrestricted retained earnings (and maximum legal payment of dividends) would be $10 million – $6 million, or $4 million. The **restricted retained earnings** cannot be reduced by dividend declarations.

Most of the time, restrictions of retained earnings are disclosed by footnotes. Restrictions of retained earnings are also sometimes called **appropriated retained earnings** or *reserves*. The term *reserve* can be misleading. Accountants *never* use the word reserve to indicate cash set aside for a particular purpose; instead they call such assets a *fund*. The word **reserve** can have one of two meanings in Canada. It can designate a portion of retained earnings which cannot be distributed as dividends as stipulated by a contract or statute. It can also designate a portion of retained earnings which management appropriates to indicate its plan to reduce the dividends for a future purpose such as a major expansion.

The Canadian practice toward retained earnings reserves is very discrectionary, as it is in other countries, among them France, Germany, the Netherlands, and Japan. The U.S. practice on the other hand is very restrictive.

restricted retained earnings (appropriated retained income) Any part of retained earnings that may not be reduced by dividend declarations.

■ STOCK OPTIONS

stock options Special rights usually granted to executives to purchase a corporation's capital stock.

Stock options are rights often granted to executives to purchase a corporation's capital stock. Various conditions are specified for the options including the time period during which the stock may be purchased, the number of shares, and the price per share. Although options have assorted conditions, a typical option grants the holder the right to purchase shares (exercise the option) during some specified time in the *future* at *today's* market price (the exercise price, which is set at the date of grant).

Options are frequently given to corporate officers as a form of incentive compensation. For example, suppose Company A granted its top executives options to purchase 60,000 shares of $1 par value common stock at $15 per share, the market price today (date of grant). The options can be exercised over a five-year span, beginning three years hence. Such options clearly are valuable rights. The executives can gain the benefits of price increases without bearing the risks of price declines. However, measurement of the value of options at the time of grant is difficult because executive options may not be sold to others. Therefore, currently accepted accounting attributes zero value to most of them as long as the exercise price is the same as the market price at the date of the grant. Thus, the accounting approach is to make no entry at the time of grant. Subsequent financial statements must reveal (usually by a footnote) the number and type of options outstanding.

Suppose all options are exercised three years hence. The journal entry is:

Cash	900,000	
Common stock		60,000
Additional paid-in capital		840,000
To record issue of 60,000 shares upon exercise of options to acquire them @ $15 per share.		

Executives sometimes let their options lapse. For example, here the options will become worthless if the price of the common stock is no higher than $15 per share during the time they may be exercised. In such a case, no journal entry is made.

A company's share capital can change over the year for numerous reasons. Southam Inc. reported the following summary of its share transactions in 1993:

Southam Inc.
www.southam.com/

Summary of share transactions

Common shares:

	Shares	Amount
Issued at January 1	63,503,414	$282,813
Stock dividends	3,049	50
Employee stock investment plans	61,904	1,014
Treasury issues	12,857,343	180,004
Issued at December 31	76,425,710	$463,881
Average number of common shares outstanding (net of reciprocal holdings)	73,434,324	

Preference shares:

	Shares	Amount
Treasury issues during the year	386,013	$ 7,720
Issued at December 31	386,013	$ 7,720

■ FINANCIAL RATIOS RELATED TO SHAREHOLDERS' EQUITY

Many ratios aid in evaluating the performance of a company. One important question is how effectively the company uses resources provided by the shareholders. To assess this, analysts relate the net income generated by the firm to

Solution to Problem One

Dividends payable is a *liability*. It must therefore be excluded from a statement of share-holders' equity:

Sample Corporation
Statement of
Shareholders' Equity
December 31, 19X1

9% preferred stock, $50 par value, callable at $55, authorized 20,000 shares, issued and outstanding 12,000 shares		$ 600,000
Common stock, no par, stated value $2 per share, authorized 500,000 shares, issued 400,000 shares of which 25,000 shares are held in the treasury		800,000
Additional paid-in capital:		
Preferred	$ 50,000	
Common	1,000,000	1,050,000*
Retained earnings		2,000,000
Subtotal		$4,450,000
Less: Cost of 25,000 shares of common stock reacquired and held in treasury		250,000
Total shareholders' equity		$4,200,000

* Many presentations would not show the detailed breakdown of additional paid-in capital into preferred and common portions.

Problem Two

B Company splits its $10 par common stock 5 for 1. How will its balance sheet be affected? Its earnings per share? Assume 2,000 shares are originally outstanding.

Solution to Problem Two

The total amount of shareholders' equity would be unaffected, but there would be 10,000 outstanding shares (instead of 2,000) at $2 par rather than $10 par. Earnings per share would be one-fifth of that previously reported, assuming no change in total net income applicable to the common stock.

    Suppose the question were framed: the company recently issued a 5-for-1 stock split "accounted for" as a stock dividend. Then the par value per share would be retained, and a journal entry would increase the par value account for common stock by $80,000 (8,000 additional shares times $10 par value per share):

Retained earnings	80,000	
Common stock at par		80,000

Problem Three

C Company distributes a 2% stock dividend on its 1 million outstanding $5 par common shares. Its shareholders' equity section before the dividend was:

Common stock, 1,000,000 shares @ $5 par	$ 5,000,000
Paid-in capital in excess of par	20,000,000
Retained earnings	75,000,000
Total shareholders' equity	$100,000,000

The common was selling on the open market for $150 per share when the dividend was distributed.

    How will the shareholders' equity section be affected? If net income were $10.2 million next year, what would be the earnings per share before considering the effects of the stock dividend? After considering the effects of the stock dividend?

Solution to Problem Three

Shareholders' equity:

	Before 2% Stock Dividend	Changes	After 2% Stock Dividend
Common stock, 1,000,000 shares @ $5 par	$ 5,000,000	+ (20,000 @ $5)	$ 5,100,000
Paid-in capital	20,000,000	+ [20,000 @ ($150 – $5)]	22,900,000
Retained earnings	75,000,000	– (20,000 @ $150)	72,000,000
Total	$100,000,000		$100,000,000

Earnings per share before considering the effects of the stock dividend would be $10,200,000 ÷ 1,000,000, or $10.20. After the dividend: $10,200,000 ÷ 1,020,000, or $10.

Note that the dividend has no effect on net income, the numerator of the earnings-per-share computation. But it does affect the denominator and causes a mild dilution which, in theory, should be reflected by a slight decline in the market price of the stock.

Problem Four

Metro-Goldwyn-Mayer Film Co. declared and distributed a 3% stock dividend. The applicable market value per share was $7.75. The par value of the 966,000 additional shares issued was $1.00 each. The total cash paid to shareholders in lieu of issuing fractional shares was $70,000. Prepare the appropriate journal entry.

Solution to Problem Four

Retained earnings	7,556,500	
Common stock, $1.00 par value		966,000
Capital in excess of par value		6,520,500
Cash		70,000

To record 3% stock dividend. Total shares issued were 966,000 at $7.75, a total market value of $7,486,500. In addition, cash of $70,000 was paid in lieu of issuing fractional shares. Total charge to retained earnings was $70,000 + (966,000 × $7.75) = $7,556,500. The account Capital in Excess of Par Value was the description actually used by MGM.

Highlights to Remember

On the balance sheet, shareholders' equity is reported as the book values of the residual interests of a corporation's owners. By incorporating, the company provides limited liability for its owners and provides them with various rights, including the right to vote. Among equity holders, preferred shareholders have more senior claims to dividends and may have other special rights, including cumulative dividends, participating dividends, conversion privileges, and preference in liquidation. While bonds pay legally enforceable interest and principle payments at maturity, preferred stock has an infinite life, and dividend payments to shareholders become legal obligations only if the board declares the dividend.

Stock splits and stock dividends alter the number of shares held by the owners. Accounting for them involves rearranging the owners' equity account balances. Par value accounts, paid-in capital accounts, and retained earnings may be rearranged without changing the total owners' equity. The exact procedure depends on whether the par value of the new shares changes and on the number of additional shares. Similarly, a rearrangement of owners' equity arises when convertible preferred shares are exchanged for common shares.

Companies sometimes acquire treasury stock, which are shares of their own stock purchased in the open market. These shares may later be retired, resold, or used to meet obligations under option agreements. Transactions in the company's own stock never give rise to gains and losses and do not affect the income statement. Such transactions with the shareholders give rise only to changes in the equity accounts.

Cash dividends to preferred and common shareholders will be declared only when cash is available for payment. But in most provinces, dividends may be paid legally only to the extent that retained earnings exceed the cost of treasury stock. Additional restrictions on the right to pay cash dividends are often built into debt contracts.

Security analysts use the return on common shareholders' equity as a primary ratio to assess the effectiveness of management and the profitability of the firm. Analysts often compare the market value per share with the book value per share. A higher market value should be associated with growth prospects and possibly unrecorded assets, such as internally developed patents.

Assignment Material

QUESTIONS

11-1. In what ways are corporations "artificial persons"?

11-2. What is the purpose of preemptive rights?

11-3. Can a share of common stock be outstanding but not authorized or issued? Why?

11-4. In what way is preferred stock similar to debt? To common stock?

11-5. "Treasury stock is unissued stock." Do you agree? Explain.

11-6. "Cumulative dividends are liabilities that must be paid to preferred shareholders before any dividends are paid to common shareholders." Do you agree? Explain.

11-7. "The liquidating value of preferred stock is the amount of cash for which it can currently be exchanged." Do you agree? Explain.

11-8. "Common shareholders have limited liability." Explain.

11-9. List the characteristics that distinguish debt and equity.

11-10. What is the proper measure for an asset newly acquired through an exchange (e.g., an exchange of land for securities)? Explain.

11-11. What are convertible securities?

11-12. "The only real dividends are cash dividends." Do you agree? Explain.

11-13. "The term *stock dividends* is a misnomer." Why?

11-14. "A stock split can be achieved by means of a stock dividend." Do you agree? Explain.

11-15. "A 2% stock dividend increases every shareholder's fractional portion of the company by 2%." Do you agree? Explain.

11-16. "When a company retires shares, it must pay the shareholders an amount equal to the original par value and additional capital contributed for those shares plus the shareholders' fractional portion of retained earnings." Do you agree? Explain.

11-17. "Treasury stock is not an asset." Explain.

11-18. "Gains and losses are not possible from a corporation's acquiring or selling its own stock." Do you agree? Explain.

11-19. Restrictions on dividend-declaring power may be voluntary or involuntary. Give an example of each.

11-20. Why might a board of directors voluntarily restrict its dividend-declaring power?

11-21. How may the distinction between contributed and accumulated capital be blurred by traditional accounting?

11-22. Which are riskier, bonds or preferred stock? Why? Whose perspective are you taking, the issuer's or the investor's?

11-23. "A common stock selling on the market far below its book value is an attractive buy." Do you agree? Explain.

11-24. If you were about to lend a company a substantial amount of money, what kinds of restrictions might you want to place on the company's use of that money? What other conditions might you include in the loan to increase the probability that you would be repaid?

11-25. Why do you suppose companies offer their employees stock options rather than simply paying higher salaries?

EXERCISES

11-26   Distinctions Between Terms

Clean-up Services, Inc., a waste-management company, had 4 million shares of common stock authorized on August 31, 19X8. Shares issued were 2,073,178. There were 20,000 shares held in the treasury. How many shares were issued and outstanding? How many shares were unissued? Label your computations.

11-27   Preferences as to Assets

The following are account balances of Shopper's Mart, Inc. (in thousands): common stock and retained earnings, $300; accounts payable, $300; preferred stock (5,000 shares; $20 par and $24 liquidating value per share), $100; subordinated debentures, $300; and unsubordinated debentures, $100. Prepare a table showing the distribution of the cash proceeds upon liquidation and dissolution of the corporation. Assume cash proceeds of (in thousands): $1,400; $1,000; $790; $500; $400; and $200, respectively.

11-28   Cumulative Dividends

The Blackfoot Corporation was founded on January 1, 19X1:

Preferred stock, no par, cumulative, $6 annual dividend per share:	
Issued and outstanding, 1,000,000 shares	$ 40,000,000
Capital stock, no par, 6,000,000 shares	90,000,000
Total shareholders' equity	$130,000,000

The corporation's subsequent net incomes (losses) were:

19X1	$(5,000,000)
19X2	(4,000,000)
19X3	14,000,000
19X4	30,000,000
19X5	12,000,000

Required   Assume that the board of directors declared dividends to the maximum extent permissible by law. The laws prohibit dividend declarations that cause negative retained earnings.

1. Tabulate the annual dividend declarations on preferred and common shares. There is no treasury stock.
2. How would the total distribution to common shareholders change if the preferred were not cumulative?

of common stock in connection with the conversion of convertible debt. Conversions of convertible debt issued subsequent to October 1, 1982 into common stock and exercise of warrants were accounted for in accordance with the provisions of the Japanese Commercial Code by crediting one-half of the aggregate conversion price equally to the common stock account and the capital surplus account.

(10) Dividends and Legal Reserve

The Japanese Commercial Code provides that earnings in an amount equal to at least 10% of all appropriations of retained earnings that are paid in cash, such as cash dividends and bonuses to directors, shall be appropriated as a legal reserve until such reserve equals 25% of stated capital. This reserve is not available for dividends but may be used to reduce a deficit or may be transferred to stated capital. Certain foreign subsidiaries are also required to appropriate their earnings to legal reserves under laws of the respective countries of domicile.

Cash dividends and appropriations to the legal reserve charged to retained earnings during the years ended March 31, 1992, 1993, and 1994 represent dividends paid out during those years and the related appropriations to the legal reserve. The accompanying consolidated financial statements do not include any provision for the dividend of ¥7 ($0.07) per share aggregating ¥6,816 million ($66,079 thousand) to be proposed in June 1994 or for the related appropriation to legal reserve.

Required

1. Give journal entries to record the items shown for 1994 except the foreign currency translation.
2. Give the journal entry that Honda will make for the proposed dividend and transfer to the reserve in June 1994. Assume the transfer is 10% of the dividends.
3. If stated capital is defined as the common stock account, how much more must Honda pay in dividends and add to the legal reserve before the 25% limit is met?

11-61   Hudson's Bay Company Annual Report
Use the Hudson Bay Company's financial statements and notes contained in Appendix A to answer the following questions.

Required

1. Give the journal entry to record dividends declared in fiscal 1997.
2. What was the average price of shares issued for executive stock options during fiscal 1997?

11-62   Annual Report Disclosure
Select a company's annual report of your choice.

Required

1. Identify each transaction that affected Shareholders' Equity during the most recent year. Indicate which accounts were affected and by how much. List any transactions that appear unusual. For example, many companies have a change in shareholders' equity that arises from tax benefits related to stock options. This and a few other common transactions are beyond our scope in this introductory course.

PART 3

SPECIALIZED TOPICS

12 *Internal Control and Ethics*

Learning Objectives

After studying this chapter, you should be able to

1 Describe the elements of internal control.

2 Explain the role of the audit committee.

3 Judge an internal control system using the checklist of internal control.

4 Describe how computers have changed the internal control environment.

5 Explain the basics of controlling cash and inventories.

6 Incorporate ethical judgments into decision making.

This chapter focuses on the internal accounting controls that detect and prevent errors and generally safeguard the firm's assets. The chapter describes the elements of internal control and the roles of management and the audit committee. An internal control checklist is provided, and its applicability to computer systems is considered along with the special types of controls required for large computer systems. The chapter contains a special section on ethical standards that are essential to good internal control, and two appendices extending our discussion of cash and inventories.

CFO magazine reports that American businesses lose some $50 billion a year to internal thievery. At its simplest, this refers to employees walking out the door with their employers' assets, although the process is often more complicated. For example, an accounts payable clerk at a pharmaceuticals company embezzled $25,000 by writing cheques to companies that he created. Following a standard practice, his employer had an executive authorize payments by initialling invoices. The resulting cheques, for small amounts, were created by the clerk, mechanically signed and mailed. The extra payments to the clerk's companies were detected one day when the clerk called in sick and his coworker noted cheques written to an unfamiliar vendor. In another case, a bookkeeper wrote fraudulent payroll cheques to seasonal employees and cashed them himself. The theft was revealed when a seasonal employee objected that the T-4 form, sent to the government at year end to report his annual earnings for income tax purposes, reported too much income. Good systems of internal control would reduce such losses.

■ OVERVIEW OF INTERNAL CONTROL

The essence of internal control is the creation of a system of checks and balances that assures that all actions occurring within the company are in accord with organizational objectives and have the general approval of top management. At one level, this means that a highly placed manager should not expose the company to unauthorized, speculative losses from, for example, trading exotic derivatives securities. Here internal control seeks to tie daily decisions to corporate strategy. At another level it means that a salesperson at the clothing-store giant, The GAP, should not be able to walk out of the store with holiday gifts for the family without paying for them. Here internal control refers to protection of firm assets from theft and loss. Therefore, an electronic tag on a leather coat is an internal control device and so is the requirement that cheques over $200 have the approval of two people.

internal control
Refers to both internal administrative control and internal accounting control.

In its broadest sense, **internal control** refers to both *administrative* control and *accounting* control:

1. *Administrative controls* include the plan of organization (for example, the formal organizational chart concerning who reports to whom) and all methods and procedures that facilitate management planning and control of operations. Examples are departmental budgeting procedures, reports on performance, and procedures for granting credit to customers.

2. *Accounting controls* include the methods and procedures for authorizing transactions, safeguarding assets, and ensuring the accuracy of the financial records. Good accounting controls help *maximize* efficiency; and they help *minimize* waste, unintentional errors, and fraud.

Our focus is on internal accounting controls, which should provide reasonable assurance concerning

1. *Authorization.* Transactions are executed in accordance with management's general or specific intentions.

2. *Recording*. All authorized transactions are recorded in the correct amounts, periods, and accounts. No fictitious transactions are recorded.

3. *Safeguarding*. Precautions and procedures appropriately restrict access to assets.

4. *Reconciliation*. Records are compared with other independently kept records and physical counts. Such comparisons help ensure that other control objectives are attained.

5. *Valuation*. Recorded amounts are periodically reviewed for impairment of values and necessary write-downs.

Objective 1

Describe the elements of internal control.

accounting system A set of records, procedures, and equipment that routinely deals with the events affecting the financial performance and position of the entity.

The first three general objectives—authorization, recording, and safeguarding—relate to establishing the system of accountability and are aimed at *prevention* of errors and irregularities. The final two objectives—reconciliation and valuation—are aimed at *detection* of errors and irregularities.

A sixth objective of an internal control system should be added: *promoting operating efficiency*. Management should recognize that an internal control system's purpose is as much a positive one (promoting efficiency) as a negative one (preventing errors and fraud).

The Accounting System

An entity's **accounting system** is a set of records, procedures, and equipment that *routinely* deals with the events affecting the entity's financial performance and position. The system maintains accountability for the firm's assets and liabilities.

The $346,770 Overdraft

Karen Smith was amazed when her credit union notified her that her account was overdrawn by $346,770. How could that kind of money turn up missing? Did she mistakenly add three extra zeros to a cheque? No, but she did leave her bank card in her wallet, locked inside her van during a high school football game on a Friday night. Two thieves broke into the van, stole the bank card, and visited local cash machines.

Think about how bank internal control procedures should stop thieves. Automated teller machines (ATM) require the use of a customer's specific personal identification number (the "pin" number). As a secondary precaution, ATM machines normally restrict withdrawals to a maximum amount, perhaps $200 per day, per account. Thieves cannot randomly guess pin numbers. The computer tracks "unauthorized" accesses. After several incorrect pin numbers the ATM keeps the card and notifies the user to reclaim it at the bank.

Nonetheless, these thieves hit the jackpot. Karen stored her pin number on her social security card, in the stolen wallet. Luckier yet, the Oregon TelCo Credit Union was updating some computer programs and their $200 limit per account per day was inoperative. To access all the funds in Karen's account, the thieves put the card in and withdrew $200, time after time. Eventually the ATM ran out of bills, but the thieves visited many more on a circuitous, five county, 500 mile route.

A third internal control should have limited the thieves to the balance in Karen's account. Something else went wrong. Most financial institutions only permit immediate withdrawal of certified cheques or cheques drawn on accounts at the institution. Deposits may be unavailable for days while the institution verifies that the cheque is written on a good bank against a bonafide account with sufficient funds. Checks on in-state institutions may take two days to "clear" while out-of-state cheques take three or four days. Deposits into an ATM machine are generally unavailable until the next banking day so the bank can verify the deposit, subject to the rules just described.

Unfortunately, the TelCo system was giving immediate credit for deposits made into automated tellers. The thieves "deposited" $820,500, by inserting empty deposit envelopes and recording large deposits on the ATM keypad. They exhausted the cash in the ATM machines in their five county area by 2:30 a.m. on Monday and headed to Reno to buy a new truck and enjoy their wealth.

One piece of TelCo's internal control worked. Hidden cameras photographed the thieves. The perpetrators, David Gallagher and his wife Terry were easily identified. David has been in prison five times and has 21 felony convictions. Federal sentencing guidelines could bring up to 63 years in prison. ■

Source: The New York Times (*February 12, 1995*), p. 36.

Then the cash receipts are deposited, and the tape is forwarded to the accounting department as a basis for accounting entries. If cash from the till is sometimes used to pay suppliers, there is a serious internal control weakness.

3. All major disbursements should be made by serially numbered cheques. Gaps should be investigated. The *Wall Street Journal* cited an example of good controls used poorly: "A bookkeeping assistant [was] under strict orders to note every missing number.... But no one checked to see how many were missing or why."

4. Bank accounts should be reconciled monthly. (This recommendation also applies to personal banking accounts.) A **bank reconciliation** is an analysis that explains any difference between the cash balance shown by the depositor and that shown by the bank. It is surprising how many businesses (some of substantial size) do not reconcile their bank accounts regularly.

bank reconciliation
An analysis that explains any difference between the cash balance shown by the depositor and that shown by the bank.

Control of cash requires procedures for handling both cheques and currency. To control cheques, many organizations use cheque protectors that perforate or otherwise establish an unalterable amount on the face of each cheque. Dual signatures are frequently required on large cheques.

Currency is probably the most alluring form of cash. Businesses that handle much currency, such as gambling establishments, restaurants, and bars, are particularly subject to theft and false reporting. For example, many owners of small retail outlets do not record all of their cash receipts, a procedure known as *skimming*. Why? To save income taxes.

A recent news story reported: "Federal undercover agents in New York City opened an attack on the underground economy, which spawns billions of dollars yearly in untaxed income through off-the-books transactions." According to the affidavits, the establishments searched by the agents grossed more than $5 million while reporting on their tax returns only $3.6 million.

Recall from Chapter 8 that tax authorities often use known gross profit margins for an industry to assess the reasonableness of the profits based on reported revenues and costs of goods sold for a particular company. Measures such as industry average sales per square foot of store space allow assessment of the adequacy of reported revenue.

Comparing reported results with averages is not foolproof. An exclusive clothing store in San Francisco paid a percentage of sales for rent. Reported sales for a recent year were $11.2 million; an independent audit later disclosed actual sales of $20.5 million. The lessor always compared sales per square foot of floor space with those of similar stores. No clue to any impropriety arose. In fact, the lessor termed the reported sales per square foot "extraordinary" and the actual results as "unheard of."

Internal Control of Inventories

In many organizations, inventories are more easily accessible than cash. Therefore, they become a favourite target for thieves.

Retail merchants must contend with inventory shrinkage, a polite term for shoplifting by customers and embezzling by employees. *Inventory shrinkage* is the difference between (1) the value of inventory that would occur if there were no pilferage, misclassifications, breakage, or clerical errors and (2) the value of inventory when it is physically counted. Consider the following footnote from a recent annual report of Associated Dry Goods, one of the largest operators of department and discount stores in the country: "Physical inventories are taken twice each year.

Department store inventory shrinkage at retail, as a percent of retail sales, was 2.4% this year compared with 2.1% last year. Discount store inventory shrinkage as a percent of retail sales was 0.4% and 0.3%, respectively." Some department stores have suffered shrinkage losses of 4% to 5% of their sales volume. Compare this with the typical net profit margin of 5% to 6%.

A management consulting firm has demonstrated how widespread shoplifting has become. The firm concentrated on a midtown New York City department store. Five hundred shoppers, picked at random, were followed from the moment they entered the store to the time they departed. Forty-two shoppers, or one out of every twelve, took something. They stole $300 worth of merchandise, an average of $7.15 each. Similar experiments were conducted in Boston (1 of 20 shoplifted), Philadelphia (1 of 10), and again in New York (1 of 12).

Experts on controlling inventory shrinkage generally agree that the best deterrent is an alert employee at the point of sale. Retail stores use sensitized tags on merchandise; if not detached or neutralized by a salesclerk, these miniature transmitters trip an alarm as the culprit begins to leave the store. Many libraries use a similar system to safeguard their books. Macy's in New York has continuous surveillance with over fifty television cameras.

Retailers must also scrutinize their own personnel, because they account for at least 30% to 40% of inventory shortages. Some stores have actors pose as shoplifters, who are then subjected to fake arrests. If potential thieves see the arrests, they may be deterred. Such ploys have helped reduce thefts by employees at major retail chains.

The problem of stealing is not confined to profit-seeking entities. According to the student newspaper at Northwestern University, $14,000 worth of silverware, glasses, and china was stolen from the university dining halls annually. That amounts to $4.71 for every regular customer. Signs posted at the end of each school term requesting the return of "borrowed" goods have had little success. The food service director commented: "Two years ago, we put up really nice signs and set out boxes for returns. Kids saw the boxes and stole them for packing."

The imposing magnitude of retail inventory shrinkage demonstrates how management objectives may differ among industries. For example, consider the grocery business, where net income is about 1% of sales. You can readily see why a prime responsibility of the store manager is to control inventory shrinkage rather than boost gross sales volume. The trade-off is clear: If the operating profit is 2% of sales, to offset a $1,000 increase in shrinkage requires a $50,000 boost in gross sales.

Shrinkage in Perpetual and Periodic Inventory Systems

Measuring inventory shrinkage is straightforward for companies that use a perpetual inventory system. Shrinkage is simply the difference between the cost of inventory identified by a physical count and the clerical inventory balance. Consider the following example:

Sales	$100,000
Cost of goods sold (perpetual inventory system)	$ 80,000
Beginning inventory	$ 15,000
Purchases	$ 85,000
Ending inventory, per clerical records	$ 20,000
Ending inventory, per physical count	$ 18,000

Shrinkage is $20,000 − $18,000 = $2,000. The journal entries under a perpetual inventory system would be:

Inventory shrinkage	2,000	
Inventory		2,000
To adjust ending inventory to its balance per physical count.		
Cost of goods sold	2,000	
Inventory shrinkage		2,000
To close inventory shrinkage to cost of goods sold.		

The total cost of goods sold would be $80,000 + $2,000 = $82,000.

By definition, a periodic inventory system has no clerical balance of the inventory account. Inventory shrinkage is automatically included in cost of goods sold. Why? Because beginning inventory plus purchases less ending inventory measures all inventory that has flowed out, whether it went to customers, shoplifters, or embezzlers, or was simply lost or broken. Our example would show:

Beginning inventory	$ 15,000
Plus: Purchases	85,000
Goods available for sale	$100,000
Less: Ending inventory, per physical count	18,000
Cost of goods sold	$ 82,000

To assess shrinkage, we need some way to *estimate* what the ending inventory *should be*. The difference between this *estimate* and the physical count is inventory shrinkage. Appendix 12B describes how these estimates are made. No journal entries are necessary.

■ ETHICS AND INTERNAL CONTROL

Employees' ethical standards play a large part in internal control. Ethical failures that went undetected by internal control systems have led to widely publicized cases—from security traders benefitting from the use of inside information, to savings and loan executives diverting company funds for their own personal use, to managers lying about their company's financial prospects as they approach bankruptcy. Although such ethical failures are rare, there is a public perception that they are widespread. Most businesses realize that, as Roger Smith, former Chairman and CEO of General Motors said, "Ethical practice is, quite simply, good business."

Corporate Codes of Ethics

To help employees make ethical decisions, a majority of large companies have a "corporate code of ethics." For example, General Motors has a booklet, "Guidelines for Employee Conduct," which includes the following:

> It would be comforting to have a booklet which sets forth clear-cut rules that would apply in all our business dealings. This would help us balance the seemingly contradictory obligations we owe to our fellow stockholders, customers, dealers, sup-

General Motors
www.gm.com

pliers, communities—and to ourselves and families. But the world is not neat and orderly, and arriving at an ethical decision can be difficult. It has been wisely observed that: "It is easy to do what is right; it is hard to know what is right."... In the final analysis, each of us must exercise individual judgment and answer to our own conscience. As General Motors employees, we should never do anything we would be ashamed to explain to our family or afraid to see on the front page of the local newspaper.[3]

Some companies have a more detailed code, and some have less detail. Supporters of general guidelines maintain that a detailed list of "do's" and "don'ts" leads to a legalistic view of ethics—any action not prohibited by the code is seen as acceptable. Supporters of more detail say that general guidelines are unenforceable platitudes that are easily ignored. There is no easy answer.

Regardless of the exact form of the code, top management support is essential for its success in influencing employee behaviour. The code should be approved at the Board of Directors or CEO level, and the need to adhere to the code must be continually communicated throughout the organization. A common practice is to have employees sign a statement of compliance each year.

Professional Codes of Ethics

Accountants have an additional motivation to behave ethically. As professionals, they are expected to maintain higher standards of ethical conduct than other members of society. Professionals have an expertise that is hard for nonprofessionals to judge. Just as a patient lacks the knowledge to judge a physician, users of accounting information generally lack the expertise to evaluate the accountant who prepares or audits the information. Therefore, it is important that the public have confidence in accountants, that they be able to rely on accountants' honesty, integrity, and competence. To ensure this confidence, professional accounting organizations have developed codes of ethics for their members. They also have procedures for reviewing alleged behaviour that is not consistent with the standards and enforcing penalties for violators of the standards.

Professional accountants establish codes of conduct that include both broad basic philosophical principles and explicit rules of conduct. The *principles* set a target, an ideal standard to aim for. The *rules* set a minimum standard; conduct below the minimum standard is unsatisfactory and results in penalties. Topics for which rules of conduct exist include independence, integrity and objectivity, competence, confidential client information, contingent fees, and advertising. The Society of Management Accountants of Canada, which focuses on accountants in industry and government, has developed the *Code of Professional Ethics*.

Ethical Dilemmas

Despite corporate and professional codes of ethical conduct, making ethical choices is not always easy. Managers and accountants should have no difficulty choosing between clearly ethical and unethical alternatives. Unfortunately,

---

[3] R. B. Smith, "Ethics in Business: An Essential Element of Success," *Management Accounting* (June 1990), p. 50.

Bank Reconciliation
January 31, 19X2

Balance per books (also called *balance per cheque register, register balance*)	$ 8,000
Deduct: Bank service charges for January not recorded on the books (also include any other charges by the bank not yet deducted)*	20
Adjusted (corrected) balance per books	$ 7,980
Balance per bank (also called *bank statement balance, statement balance*)	$10,980
Add: Deposits not recorded by bank (also called *unrecorded deposits, deposits in transit*), deposit of 1/31	7,000
Total	$17,980
Deduct: Outstanding cheques, check of 1/29	10,000
Adjusted (corrected) balance per bank	$ 7,980

* Note that new entries on the depositor's books are required for all previously unrecorded additions and deductions made to achieve the adjusted balance per books.

As the bank reconciliation indicates, an adjustment is necessary on the books of the depositor:

Jan. 31 Bank service charge expense   20
        Cash   20
       To record bank charges for printing cheques.

This popular format has two major sections. The first section begins with the balance per books (that is, the balance in the Cash T-account). Adjustments are made for items not entered on the books but already entered by the *bank*, such as deduction of the $20 service charge. No additions are shown in the illustrated section, but an illustrative addition would be the bank's collection of a customer receivable on behalf of the company. The second section begins with the balance per bank. Adjustments are made for items not entered by the *bank* but already entered in the books. After adjustments, each section should end with identical adjusted cash balances. This is the amount that should appear as cash in bank on the depositor's balance sheet.

Paperless Bank Transactions

Each passing year brings us closer to so-called paperless banking. For example, many employees never see their payroll cheques. Instead the employer deposits the "cheques" in the employees' bank accounts. This is an example of an "automatic" deposit. If the employee were to forget to add the amount to his or her cheque register, the bank's books would show a higher balance than the depositor's books. Similarly, some 75% of transactions in "branch banking" offices occur at automatic teller machines (ATM). Many depositors may forget to record these, but will find them when they reconcile their bank statement with their books (cheque register).

Petty Cash

imprest basis A method of accounting for petty cash.

Every organization desires to minimize red tape—for example, avoiding unjustifiably complicated procedures for minor disbursements. Consequently, petty cash funds are usually created and accounted for on an **imprest basis**. An imprest petty cash fund is initiated with a fixed amount of currency and coins. As the currency is used, petty cash receipts or vouchers are prepared to show the purposes of the disbursements. When the balance of currency gets low, the fund is restored to its original level by drawing and cashing a single cheque for the exact amount of the needed cash replenishment. The following are typical journal entries:

Petty cash	100	
Cash in bank		100
To set up a fund for miscellaneous minor office disbursements. (A cheque is drawn, cashed, and proceeds placed with some responsible person.)		
Postage	10	
Freight in	40	
Miscellaneous office expenses	35	
Cash in bank		85
To replenish the petty cash fund and record expenses paid therefrom.		

Examples of petty cash outlays include special post office charges for certifying or insuring mail, collections by delivery personnel, and dinner money given to an employee when working overtime.

Note that after inception, the Petty Cash account itself is never directly charged or credited unless the $100 initial amount of the fund is increased or decreased. Further, the cash on hand plus the receipts (or vouchers) should always equal the $100 amount of the petty cash fund.

Appendix 12B: Inventory Control via Retail Method, Cost Ratios, and Cutoffs

Retail Method of Inventory Control

retail inventory method (retail method) A popular inventory costing method based on sales prices, often used as a control device and for obtaining an inventory valuation for financial statement purposes.

A popular inventory costing method, known as the **retail inventory method**, or simply **retail method**, is often used as a control device. Its role in obtaining an inventory valuation (at cost) for financial statement purposes will be discussed in the next section; for now, concentrate on its internal control characteristics. Consider how a food store might use the retail method to control grocery inventories. Merchandise is accounted for at *retail prices* as follows:

		Retail Prices
	Inventory, January 5 (by surprise count by branch auditors)	$ 15,000
	Purchases (shipments to store from branch warehouse)	101,000
	Additional retail price changes:	
	Markups (from initial retail prices)	2,000
	Markdowns (from initial retail prices)	(5,000)
(1)	Total merchandise to account for	$113,000
	Sales (per cash-register records)	$100,000
	Allowable shrinkage (shoplifting, breakage, etc., usually a predetermined percentage of sales)	1,000

continued

		Retail Prices
(2)	Total deductions	$101,000
(1) – (2)	Inventory, February 11 (should be)	$ 12,000
	Inventory, February 11 (by physical count)	11,100
	Excess shrinkage	$ 900

The total retail value of merchandise to account for is $113,000. What happens to it? Most is sold, some disappears as shrinkage, and some remains in ending inventory. Cash-register tabulations indicate sales of $100,000. If there were absolutely no shrinkage, the ending inventory at retail should be $113,000 – $100,000 = $13,000. But suppose "normal" shrinkage is 1% of sales, or $1,000. Therefore, the expected inventory is $13,000 – $1,000 = $12,000. The actual physical count provides a retail valuation of $11,100. Thus, the total shrinkage is $1,900, including $900 of excess shrinkage ($12,000 – $11,100 = $900). If the inventory shrinkage is not within predetermined limits, the manager usually bears prime responsibility.

Computerized checkout systems help to control inventory shrinkage. Such systems record each individual item that is sold, allowing a store to keep an item-by-item perpetual inventory. Pinpointing the items that are disappearing allows additional control measures to be applied to these items.

Role of Cost Ratios and Gross Profit Percentages

While retail inventory values provide a satisfactory basis for internal control, inventories in financial statements are reported at cost. Therefore, the retail values of inventories must be converted to costs. This is accomplished using the ratio of cost to retail value. Consider the data in our prior illustration with a "cost" column added.

		Retail Prices	Cost
	Inventory, January 5 (by surprise count by branch auditors)	$ 15,000	$12,300
	Purchases (shipments to store from branch warehouse)	101,000	78,100
	Additional retail price changes:		
	Markups (from initial retail prices)	2,000	
	Markdowns (from initial retail prices)	(5,000)	
(1)	Total merchandise to account for	$113,000	$90,400
	Ratio of cost to retail value		80%
	Sales (per cash-register records)	$100,000	$80,000
	Allowable shrinkage (shoplifting, breakage, etc., usually a predetermined percentage of sales)	1,000	800
(2)	Total deductions	$101,000	$80,800
(1) – (2)	Inventory, February 11 (should be)	$ 12,000	$ 9,600
	Inventory, February 11 (by physical count)	11,100	8,880
	Excess shrinkage	$ 900	$ 720

The line denoted as (1) provides the basis for a ratio of cost to retail value:

$90,400 ÷ $113,000 = .80

This critical ratio[5] is then used to develop the key subsequent amounts at cost:

	Retail Prices		Average Ratio of Cost to Retail Value		Cost
Allowable shrinkage	$ 1,000	×	.80	=	$ 800
Inventory per physical count	11,100	×	.80	=	8,880
Excess shrinkage	900	×	.80	=	720

These amounts can be used in an income statement for a company with a periodic inventory system:

Sales		$100,000
Cost of sales:		
Beginning inventory per physical count	$12,300	
Purchases	78,100	
Available for sale	$90,400	
Ending inventory per physical count	8,880	
Cost of sales (including $800 allowable shrinkage and $720 excess shrinkage)		81,520
Gross margin (after inventory shrinkage)		$ 18,480

This approach is used over and over again as periods unfold. The ending inventory of $8,880 becomes the beginning inventory of the next reporting period. Purchases are then added at cost, a new ratio of cost to retail value is developed, and shrinkage and ending inventory values are approximated:

1. Compute the goods available for sale at retail value and cost.
2. Compute the ratio of cost to retail value.
3. Count the ending inventory and value it at retail value.
4. Convert the retail value of the ending inventory to cost by using the ratio of cost to retail value.

The *cost* of shrinkage, which can be divided into normal and excess components, is approximated by using the ratio of cost to retail value.

Note that the ratio of cost to retail value is the complement of the gross profit ratio. In this illustration, the gross profit percentage is 100% − 80% = 20%. Thus, the gross profit percentage or its related ratio of cost to retail value is a key element of internal control.

---

[5] Both markdowns and markups are included in this illustrative computation. Many retailers prefer to exclude markdowns because a lower cost ratio is developed:

$90,400 ÷ ($113,000 + $5,000 Markdowns) = .7661

This ratio would provide a "more conservative" ending inventory. Advocates of this approach say that it yields a better approximation of the lower-of-cost-and-market method.

financial statement analysis Using financial statements to assess a company's performance.

This chapter focuses on **financial statement analysis,** which means using financial statement data to assess a company's performance. Sources of information about companies, the objectives of financial statement analysis, and methods for evaluating financial statements are covered. The majority of the chapter deals with ratios and how to understand the financial statements as prepared under GAAP. A few additional steps in producing the financial statements are presented, including calculating earnings per share and preparing segmental disclosures of the parts of the business.

Disclosure practices in Canada have evolved with the specific purpose of providing information to investors, creditors, managers, suppliers, customers—anyone who wants to know about a company's financial position or prospects. The preceding chapters concentrated on how information is collected, aggregated, and disclosed. We have frequently provided examples of ratios and other tools of analysis and have demonstrated how the information might aid in making decisions. In this chapter we integrate prior material and discuss additional tools for analyzing and evaluating the company's financial position.

Internationally, financial statement analysis is significantly complicated by a variety of factors. Throughout the text we have considered differences in accounting methods used. In addition, we should stress the obvious but easily forgotten differences in the language of reporting and the currency of measurement. For example, most Canadian analysts cannot read financial statements in Japanese and do not readily "have a feel for" the value of yen versus dollars. Last, but not least, is the fact that different structures for security markets, different tax laws, and different preferences among citizens of different countries all affect the relative value of financial assets.

■ SOURCES OF INFORMATION ABOUT COMPANIES

Objective 1

Describe many sources of financial and operating information about company performance.

Financial statement analysis focuses on techniques used by analysts external to the organization being analyzed, although managers use many of the same methods. These analysts rely on publicly available information.

Publicly available information refers primarily to published information and analysis that is broadly available to analysts and investors. Companies provide periodic press releases, which provide the financial community with news about company developments, including the following:

1. Changes in personnel.
2. Changes in dividends.
3. Issuance or retirement of debt.
4. Acquisition or sale of assets or business units.
5. New products.
6. New orders.
7. Changes in production plans.
8. Financial results.

Members of the financial press decide which information in press releases will be interesting and important. When a small company announces that thirty people will be laid off, *The Globe and Mail* or the the *Financial Post* may ignore the event, while it will be front page news in the company's home town where many citizens are affected. Similarly, in certain regions, an industry focus deter-

Calgary Herald
www.southam.com/
calgaryherald/

mines what news is carried. The *Calgary Herald* is a newspaper in Alberta that publishes more details about oil exploration and production, for example, oil rigs in use, newly discovered oil or gas deposits, and changes in management of petroleum companies.

A major source of information about an individual firm is the company's annual report. In addition to the financial statements (income statement, balance sheet, statement of changes in financial position, and statement of shareholders' equity), annual reports usually contain:

1. Footnotes to the financial statements.
2. A summary of the accounting principles used.
3. Management's discussion and analysis of the financial results.
4. The auditor's report.
5. Comparative financial data for a series of years.
6. Narrative information about the company.

To be useful, the financial statements and their accompanying footnotes and other disclosures must provide all significant or *material* information. Although analysts can learn much from the various parts of an annual report, we will focus most of our attention on the financial statements themselves.

Companies may also be required to file reports with a provincial securities commission. In some provinces, these reports are called annual information forms (AIF). Both annual reports and AIF reports are issued well after the events being reported have occurred. More timely information is often available from company press releases and articles in the business press. In addition, stockbrokers prepare company analyses for their clients, and private investment services and newsletters supply information to their subscribers.

Heavy financial commitments, whether by investors purchasing many shares of the common stock of a company or by banks making large loans to a new customer, are preceded by thorough investigations. These investigations use information from many sources. When the amounts being invested are significant, investors and creditors often ask for a set of projected financial statements. Such a **pro forma statement** is a carefully formulated expression of predicted results. Major creditors expect the projections to include a schedule of the amounts and timings of cash repayments.

pro forma statement
A carefully formulated expression of predicted results.

Most investors and creditors are not able to request specific information from companies. For example, the typical trade creditor cannot afford the time or resources for an exhaustive investigation of every customer. Instead, such creditors rely on published information and reports from credit agencies such as Dun & Bradstreet.

Dun & Bradstreet
www.dnb.com/

Because of the wide range of information available, this chapter on financial statement analysis covers only the most common methods used by financial analysts. Nevertheless, the techniques presented in this chapter constitute an important step in gaining a thorough understanding of a company's position and prospects.

Objective 2

Explain the different objectives of debt and equity investors in analyzing information.

■ OBJECTIVES OF FINANCIAL STATEMENT ANALYSIS

Investors purchase capital stock expecting to receive dividends and an increase in the value of the stock. Creditors make loans with the expectation of receiving interest and eventual repayment. However, both investors and creditors bear the risk that they will not receive their expected returns. They use financial statement analysis to (1) predict the amount of expected returns and (2) assess the risks associated with those returns.

Because creditors generally have specific fixed amounts to be received and have the first claim on assets, they are most concerned with assessing short-term liquidity and long-term solvency. **Short-term liquidity** is an organization's ability to meet current payments as they become due. **Long-term solvency** is the ability to generate enough cash to repay long-term debts as they mature.

In contrast, equity investors are more concerned with profitability, dividends, and future security prices. Why? Because dividend payments depend on profitable operations, and stock price appreciation depends on the market's assessment of the company's prospects. However, creditors also assess profitability. Why? Because profitable operations are the prime source of cash to repay loans.

How can financial statement analysis help creditors and investors? After all, financial statements report on past results and current position, but creditors and investors want to predict future returns and their risks. Financial statement analysis is useful because past performance is often a good indicator of future performance, and current position is the base on which future performance must be built. For example, trends in past sales, operating expenses, and net income may continue. Furthermore, evaluation of management's past performance gives clues to its ability to generate future returns. Finally, the assets a company owns, the liabilities it must pay, its levels of receivables and inventories, its cash balance, and other indicators of current position all provide clues to its future prospects.

short-term liquidity
An organization's ability to meet current payments as they become due.

long-term solvency
An organization's ability to generate enough cash to repay long-term debts as they mature.

■ EVALUATING TRENDS AND COMPONENTS OF THE BUSINESS

Objective 3

Describe trend analysis and approaches to analyzing the components of a business.

This section discusses methods used to analyze financial statement data. These methods focus on trend analysis and assessing the components of the business. Trend analysis examines changes over time. Component analysis can mean several things. One application concentrates on the components of the financial statements themselves, the relative size of current assets, the level of investment in fixed assets, the gross margin percentage, and so on. At another level, component analysis means sorting out the parts of the company's business. The company can be separated into different business units or kinds of businesses, different geographic areas of production or marketing, or different customer groups such as private versus government.

Trend Analysis

Financial statements contain both the current year's and the previous year's amounts. In addition, annual reports must include the amounts of key financial items for at least the last five years. Many companies include ten years of data. Using these data, financial analysts can examine in detail the changes in the past year and can examine longer-term trends in several important items.

Consider the balance sheets and income statements of Oxley Company in Exhibits 13-1 and 13-2. The amounts are identical to the financial statements introduced in Chapter 5 in the Oxley Company illustration. (Recall that Oxley is a retailer of lawn and garden products.) However, two columns have been added to aid the comparison of 19X2 results with those of 19X1. The first new column shows the amount of the change in each item from 19X1 to 19X2. The second shows the percentage change, computed as follows:

$$\text{Percentage change 19X1 to 19X2} = \frac{\text{Amount of change}}{\text{19X1 amount}} \times 100$$

The percentage change shows the percentage by which the current-year amount exceeds or falls short of the base-year amount, 19X1 in this case. For example, Oxley's accounts receivables increased from $70,000 at the end of 19X1 to $95,000 at the end of 19X2, an increase of 35.7%:

$$\text{Percentage change} = \frac{\$95,000 - \$70,000}{\$70,000} \times 100 = 35.7\%$$

Exhibit 13-1   **Oxley Company** Statement of Income (in thousands except earnings per share)

	For the Year Ended December 31, 19X2	For the Year Ended December 31, 19X1	Increase (Decrease) Amount	Increase (Decrease) Percentage
Sales	$999	$800	$199	24.9%
Cost of goods sold	399	336	63	18.8
Gross profit (or gross margin)	$600	$464	$136	29.3
Operating expenses:				
Wages	$214	$150	$ 64	42.7
Rent	120	120	0	0.0
Miscellaneous	100	50	50	100.0
Amortization	40	40	0	0.0
Total operating expenses	$474	$360	$114	31.7
Operating income (or operating profit)	$126	$104	$ 22	21.2
Other revenue and expense:				
Interest revenue	36	36	0	0.0
Deduct: Interest expense	(12)	(12)	0	0.0
Income before income taxes	$150	$128	$ 22	17.2
Income tax expense	60	48	12	25.0
Net income	$ 90	$ 80	$ 10	12.5
Earnings per common share*	$ .45	$ .40	$ .05	12.5%

* Dividends per share, $.40 and $.20, respectively. For publicly held companies, there is a requirement to show earnings per share on the face of the income statement or by way of a footnote, but it is not necessary to show dividends per share. Calculation of earnings per share: $90,000 ÷ 200,000 = $.45, and $80,000 ÷ 200,000 = $.40.

(Place a clip on this page for easy reference.)

Exhibit 13-2   **Oxley Company** Balance Sheet (in thousands)

	December 31		Increase (Decrease)	
	19X2	*19X1*	*Amount*	*Percentage*
ASSETS				
Current assets:				
Cash	$150	$ 57	$ 93	163.2%
Accounts receivable	95	70	25	35.7
Accrued interest receivable	15	15	0	0.0
Inventory of merchandise	20	60	(40)	(66.7)
Prepaid rent	10	—	10	*
Total current assets	$290	$202	$ 88	43.6
Long-term assets:				
Long-term note receivable	288	288	0	0.0
Equipment, less accumulated amortization				
of $120 and $80	80	120	(40)	(33.3)
Total assets	$658	$610	$ 48	7.9%
LIABILITIES AND SHAREHOLDERS' EQUITY				
Current liabilities:				
Accounts payable	$ 90	$ 65	$ 25	38.5%
Accrued wages payable	24	10	14	140.0
Accrued income taxes payable	16	12	4	33.3
Accrued interest payable	9	9	0	0.0
Unearned sales revenue	—	5	(5)	(100.0)
Note payable—current portion	80	—	80	*
Total current liabilities	$219	$101	$118	116.8
Long-term note payable	40	120	(80)	(66.7)
Total liabilities	$259	$221	$ 38	17.2
Shareholders' equity:				
Paid-in capital[†]	$102	$102	$ 0	0.0
Retained earnings	297	287	10	3.5
Total shareholders' equity	$399	$389	$ 10	2.6
Total liabilities and shareholders' equity	$658	$610	$ 48	7.9%

* When the base-year amount is zero, no percentage change can be computed.
† Details are often shown in a supplementary statement or in footnotes. In this case, there are 200,000 common shares outstanding, $.25 par per share, or 200,000 × $.25 = $50,000. Additional paid-in capital is $52,000.

Notice that each percentage change is independent of the others. Unlike the amounts of change, the percentage changes cannot be added or subtracted to obtain subtotals.

Changes must be interpreted carefully. Both the amount and the percentage changes should be examined. For example, the amount of the sales increase, $199,000, seems much larger than the increase in operating income, $22,000. But the base for sales is much larger, so the percentage increase is only slightly larger, 24.9% to 21.2%. Examination of percentage changes alone can also be misleading. For instance, the 140% increase in accrued wages payable seems to dominate the percentage increases. But the increase is only $14,000, a relatively small amount in the overall picture.

What would an analyst conclude from Oxley Company's changes from 19X1 to 19X2? Consider Exhibit 13-1, the income statement. The sales increase, 24.9%, is larger than the increase in cost of goods sold, 18.8%, causing a 29.3% increase in gross profit. That is the good news. The bad news is that operating expenses increased by 31.7%. This would be of special concern because huge increases in only two items, wages and miscellaneous expenses, caused the entire increase. In addition, income tax expense increased by a larger percentage than pretax income (25.0% to 17.2%), meaning that the effective tax rate must have increased. In total, the nearly 25% increase in sales led to only a 12.5% increase in net income.

Changes in dollar amount and percentage terms are used to identify patterns. This procedure focuses the analysts' attention and encourages questions that probe for underlying causes. Examination of the balance sheet changes in Exhibit 13-2 might lead the analysts to question why the composition of the assets changed so considerably, with current assets increasing by 43.6% while equipment decreased by 33.3%. Within the current assets, cash and accounts receivable had substantial increases, and inventories plummeted. Total liabilities increased by 17.2%, but most significant is the 116.8% increase in current liabilities and 66.7% decrease in long-term liabilities. This change is attributable primarily to $80,000 of the note payable becoming due within the next year, thereby qualifying as a current liability.

The large percentage fluctuations can now be understood. Cash is being accumulated to pay an imminent debt obligation and the equipment is depreciating quickly. A plan for replacement of the equipment should be considered.

Financial analysts often examine changes over a series of years, not just the current year's changes. Exhibit 13-3 shows a five-year summary of key items for Oxley Company. Percentage changes could be computed for each year, using the earlier year as the base year. For example, percentage changes in sales are:

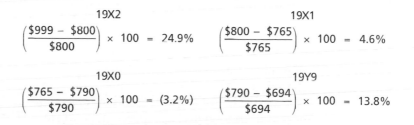

$$19X2 \qquad\qquad 19X1$$
$$\left(\frac{\$999 - \$800}{\$800}\right) \times 100 = 24.9\% \qquad \left(\frac{\$800 - \$765}{\$765}\right) \times 100 = 4.6\%$$

$$19X0 \qquad\qquad 19Y9$$
$$\left(\frac{\$765 - \$790}{\$790}\right) \times 100 = (3.2\%) \qquad \left(\frac{\$790 - \$694}{\$694}\right) \times 100 = 13.8\%$$

Sales growth rates are highly variable. In this business, weather might be one factor. Rates of new home construction might also play a role. Awareness of this variability may aid the analyst in determining the core economic factors that drive the business. We might learn that Oxley's sales decline in 19X0 was associated with a recession, or that the significant increase in 19X2 involved a new product.

EXHIBIT 13-3

Oxley Company

Five-Year Financial
Summary (in thou-
sands, except per
share amounts)

	For the Year Ended December 31				
	19X2	19X1	19X0	19Y9	19Y8
Income Statement Data:					
Sales	$999	$800	$765	$790	$694
Gross profit	600	464	448	460	410
Operating income	126	104	85	91	78
Net income	90	80	62	66	56
Earnings per share	.45	.40	.31	.33	.28
Dividends per share	.40	.20	.20	.20	.15
Balance Sheet Data (as of December 31):					
Total assets	$658	$610	$590	$585	$566
Total liabilities	259	221	241	258	265
Shareholders' equity	399	389	349	327	301

Common-Size Statements

To aid comparisons with a company's previous years and especially to aid the comparison of several companies that differ in size, income statements and balance sheets are often analyzed by percentage relationships, called **component percentages.** The resulting statements, in which the components are assigned a relative percentage, are called **common-size statements.** Consider Oxley Company's common-size statements in Exhibit 13-4. It is difficult to compare Oxley's $290,000 of current assets with a larger company's $480,000. But suppose the other company has total assets of $1 million. Oxley's 44% current asset *percentage* (shown in Exhibit 13-4) can be directly compared with the other company's $480,000 ÷ $1,000,000 = 48%.

The income statement percentages are usually based on sales = 100%. Oxley seems very profitable, but such percentages have more meaning when comparing the budgeted performance with another competitor's values, or with the industry average. Our concern that high margins attract price competition might be reduced if we learned that high margins were characteristic of the industry.

The behaviour of each expense in relation to changes in total revenue is often revealing. That is, which expenses go up or down as sales fluctuate? For example, during these two years, rent, amortization, and interest have been fixed in total but have decreased in relation to sales. In contrast, the wages have increased in total and as a percentage of sales. The latter is not a welcome sign. Exhibit 13-4 indicates that wages in 19X1 were $150 ÷ $800 = 19% of sales, whereas wages in 19X2 were $214 ÷ $999 = 21% of sales.

**component
percentages** Analysis
and presentation of
financial statements
in percentage form to
aid comparability.

**common-size
statement** Financial
statement expressed
in component
percentages.

The balance sheet percentages are usually based on total assets = 100%. See Exhibit 13-4. The most notable feature of the balance sheet percentages is that both current assets and current liabilities are more prominent at the end of 19X2. This arises from the $80,000 debt coming due, which was also highlighted in our review of percentage changes.

Exhibit 13-4

Oxley Company
Common-Size
Statements
(in thousands except
percentages)

	For the Year Ended December 31			
	19X2		**19X1**	
Statement of Income				
Sales	$999*	100%	$800	100%
Cost of goods sold	399	40	336	42
Gross profit (or gross margin)	$600*	60%	$464	58%
Wages	$214	21%	$150	19%
Rent	120	12	120	15
Miscellaneous	100	10	50	6
Amortization	40	4	40	5
Operating expenses	$474	47%	$360	45%
Operating income	$126	13%	$104	13%
Other revenue and expense	24	2	24	3
Pretax income	$150	15%	$128	16%
Income tax expense	60	6	48	6
Net income	$ 90	9%	$ 80	10%

	December 31			
	19X2		**19X1**	
Balance Sheet				
Current assets	$290	44%	$202	33%
Long-term note receivable	288	44	288	47
Equipment, net	80	12	120	20
Total assets	$658	100%	$610	100%
Current liabilities	$219	33%	$101	16%
Long-term note	40	6	120	20
Total liabilities	$259	39%	$221	36%
Shareholders' equity	399	61	389	64
Total liab. and sh. eq.	$658	100%	$610	100%
Working capital	$ 71		$101	

* Note the use of dollar signs in columns of numbers. Frequently, they are used at the top and bottom only and not for every subtotal. Their use by companies depends on the preference of management.

The Truth, the Whole Truth...

The Securities Exchange Commission is serious about full disclosure. You might characterize the SEC approach as a *no surprises* concept. Management should share *material* information with investors as it becomes known. "Management's Discussion and Analysis" is one place where information is shared. A recent enforcement action against Caterpillar, Inc., manufacturer of heavy equipment, illustrates both the concept of timely disclosure and the concept of material facts. A few months after the 1989 annual report and the first quarter 1990 report were issued, Caterpillar announced that 1990 earnings were expected to be *well below* earlier projections. The majority of the decrease was associated with an earnings decline in its Brazilian subsidiary. The stock price fell sharply on this news. The SEC believed that Caterpillar's disclosure about the negative Brazilian events constituted a case of too little information too late.

Ultimately, the problem was that Caterpillar's segment reporting did not identify the fact that 23% of its 1989 profit of $497 million was generated in Brazil. In December 1989 Brazil elected a new president, whose administration adopted severe programs to curb Brazil's hyperinflation. The subsequent decline in economic activity in Brazil substantially affected 1990 earnings of many multinationals, including Ford and GM. Yet, Caterpillar's *1989 Annual Report* observed only a potential decline in sales due to "post election politics" in Brazil. Worse yet, the first quarter 1990 report indicated increased demand worldwide while barely mentioning uncertain economic conditions in Brazil, in spite of disclosures by management to Caterpillar's board of directors in February 1990 that the economic conditions in Brazil would have major negative effects on 1990 results.

The action against Caterpillar stresses the SEC's commitment to increase disclosure. As James Lyons noted in a 1992 *Forbes* article, "... if management is worried about something, it should say so."

Segment reporting is the area of greatest concern to analysts. In order to assess the entity's performance to date and to predict future earnings, analysts want to know how the parts of the company are doing. In the Caterpillar case, the issue was geographic: How is the Brazilian business doing? In the chapter, the Pepsico information includes reference to future uncertainty regarding the consequences of the devaluation of the Mexican peso during 1994 to 1995. It is also important to know how different lines of business are performing. An analyst following Ford might want to separate the automobile business from the truck business and the financing business in order to refine his or her forecasts. An analyst following Pepsico might want to separate restaurants like Kentucky Fried Chicken (KFC) and Taco Bell from the soft drink business. As this text is being written, FASB is developing new rules to guide the nature and extent of segment data to be required. ■

Source: Forbes *(May 25, 1992).* Pepsico 1994 Annual Report

Securities Exchange Commission
www.sec.gov/

Caterpillar, Inc.
www.cat.com/

Segment Reporting

The purpose of consolidated financial statements is to provide an overall view of an economic entity. However, consolidated data can hide some of the details that might be useful in predicting profitability, risk, and growth. The purpose of segment disclosures is to facilitate such prediction.

Exhibit 13-5 lists the four types of disclosures required by GAAP. An *industry segment* is a product or service or a group of related products or services. Management has much discretion in defining industry segments. The nature of the product, the nature of the production process, and the markets or marketing methods should be considered in identifying a company's segments. Examples of industry segments include the following:

- The Oshawa Group Limited: wholesale and retail food; food service; drug stores
- Bombardier Inc.: Transportation equipment; motorized consumer products; aerospace; defence

If an industry segment meets any one of the three criteria for disclosure in Exhibit 13-5, the segment's revenue, profit, assets, amortization, and capital expenditures must be reported.

Companies with significant operations in foreign countries must separately disclose the results of operations by geographic area. For example, Magna reports revenue, profits, and assets for Canada, Europe, the USA and others. Even companies without foreign operations must disclose foreign *sales* by geographic area if such export sales are 10% or more of total revenues.

Finally, companies must report aggregate sales to any customer accounting for more than 10% of revenues. For example, Ball Corporation, maker of packaging materials, including metal beverage containers for brewers and soft drink companies, reports that 23% of its sales were to Anheuser-Busch and 20% were to various agencies of the United States government. Exhibit 13-6 shows the industry and geographic segment information from the Dominion Textile Inc. annual report.

Exhibit 13-5   Segment Reporting

Type of Disclosure	Criteria Disclosure	Items to Be Disclosed
1. Industry segment	a. Revenue at least 10% of company revenue, or b. Profit at least 10% of company profit, or c. Assets at least 10% of company assets.	a. Segment revenue b. Segment profit c. Segment assets d. Other (e.g., segment amortization and capital expenditures)
2. Geographic segment	a. Foreign operations contribute at least 10% of company's revenue, or b. Foreign operations use more than 10% of the company's assets	a. Segment revenue b. Segment profit c. Segment assets
3. Export disclosures	At least 10% of revenues from export sales	Export sales by geographic area
4. Major customers	Any customer providing more than 10% of company's revenue	Customer identity and amount of revenue

---

Exhibit 13-6   Dominion Textile Inc. 1996 Segmented Information

Segmented Information
The corporation operates in the following business segments:

Apparel Fabrics
The Apparel Fabrics Group produces denim, polycotton fabrics for careerwear and woven fabrics for protective apparel and industrial applications and markets these products on a worldwide basis.

Nonwovens
The Nonwovens Group produces and markets nonwoven fabrics used in hygiene, medical and industrial markets.

continued

Corporate and Other
Corporate and other include general corporate earnings and expenses. Identifiable assets include remaining assets of operations which were discontinued as well as corporate assets consisting principally of cash, investments and other.

Business groups

(in millions of dollars)	Apparel Fabrics	Nonwovens	Corporate and other	Total
1996				
Sales to customers	$ 963.3	$ 180.0	$ 2.8	$ 1,146.1
Earnings (loss) from operations	46.2	16.5	(19.8)	42.9
Identifiable assets	801.7	229.5	206.1	1,237.3
Capital expenditures	74.8	26.1	0.5	101.4
Depreciation and amortization	43.5	15.7	0.9	60.1

Geographic areas

(in millions of dollars)	Canada	United States	International	Eliminations	Total
1996					
Sales to customers (a)	$ 198.7	$ 635.8	$ 311.6	$ —	$ 1,146.1
Transfers between geographic areas (b)	10.9	24.3	—	(35.2)	—
	209.6	660.1	311.6	(35.2)	1,146.1
Earnings (loss) from operations	12.5	43.2	(12.8)	—	42.9
Identifiable assets					
– continuing operations	142.1	656.0	290.0	—	1,088.1
– discontinued operations	68.6	80.6	—	—	149.2

(a) Canadian sales include export sales of $94.7 million made primarily to the United States.
(b) Transfers between geographic areas are accounted for at prices comparable to open market prices for similar products and services.

Management's Discussion and Analysis

management's discussion and analysis (MD&A)
A required section of annual reports that concentrates on explaining the major changes in the income statement and the major changes in liquidity and capital resources.

Both trends and component percentages are generally discussed in a required section of annual reports called **management's discussion and analysis** (often called **MD&A**). The MD&A section explains the major changes in the income statement and the major changes in liquidity and capital resources. The space most companies devote to this section in annual reports has increased dramatically in recent years. For example, a recent Power Corporation of Canada annual report has an eighteen-page MD&A section.

Exhibit 13-7 contains excerpts from the letter to shareholders and management's discussion and analysis in the annual report of Consumers Packaging Inc. which provides an overview of the company's operating results and financial perspective from senior management's perspective. Consumers Packaging is a leading designer and producer of glass containers with headquarters in Canada.

Exhibit 13-7

Consumers
Packaging Inc.
1995 Letter to share-
holders and
Management
Discussion and
Analysis

Letter to Shareholders

The word that best describes Consumers Packaging's performance in 1995 is "progress." To be specific, in the past year the Company made solid progress towards the goal of becoming a leading global competitor in the packaging industry. Consumers recorded a second consecutive year of profitability following the Company's turnaround in 1994. We also significantly strengthened our capital resources through a successful equity offering, continued to invest in manufacturing capability, and furthered our expansion in international markets. We are proud to state that the result of this progress is a solid foundation on which to build a thriving enterprise.

Our record of progress in the past year is especially gratifying in light of the tough competitive environment for glass-packaging companies. In recent years, glass-packaging producers have been adversely impacted by the trend toward alternatives such as the plastic "PET" bottle. Additionally, excess plant capacity and financial stresses on competing manufacturers have often suppressed pricing. While industry consolidation and capacity reductions are improving conditions somewhat, 1995 was dominated by pricing pressures in the important U.S. market.

Consumers has responded to these conditions on several fronts. We have focused on improving quality and service, while continuing to upgrade our manufacturing infrastructure. The Company has targeted growth niches including customers requiring small runs and those in up-and-coming segments such as microbreweries and new-age beverages. To satisfy the needs of these customers, we have emphasized flexibility, technological innovation and service. And, we have gradually expanded our markets—moving first from Canada to the U.S. and Latin America, and now exploring other opportunities overseas.

Financial Overview

Consumers had profitable operations in 1995 despite very difficult industry conditions in the North American glass-container industry. Gross sales were $458.1 million in 1995, increasing 5% over the prior year due to substantially higher export sales. Net earnings from continuing operations were $26.2 million or 90¢ per share, fully diluted, compared with restated earnings of $24.8 million or 93¢ per share, fully diluted, in 1994. Net earnings in 1994 were $26.1 million after including a gain of $1.3 million or 4¢ per share, from discontinued operations. Cash flow before changes in non-cash operating working capital items remained strong at $56.1 million in 1995 compared with $59.1 million in 1994.

A key financial accomplishment was the Company's issuance of 4.6 million shares of common stock in September 1995, generating net proceeds of $57.2 million. This transaction enabled Consumers to reduce long-term indebtedness from $135.6 million to $79.0 million, and contributed to an increase in shareholders' equity from $89.9 million in 1994 to $173.2 at the end of 1995. With a ratio of long-term debt to equity of .46 to 1, we believe the Company is in a strong financial position for profitable growth.

Investing in Growth

Capital expenditures totalled $52.8 million in 1993, following on the previous year's strong level of $51.3 million. Among the investments made during the past year to support our continued growth were advanced production machinery with higher capacity, and the rebuild of a furnace in our Bramalea plant.

Such investments have enabled Consumers to serve the needs of a growing customer base representing some of the world's leading consumer products companies. During 1995, we significantly expanded our business with many of our customers and also added new relationships. Again, we would like to emphasize the growing export component of our business, which rose 51% last year.

continued

Exhibit 13-7

Consumers
Packaging Inc.
1995 Letter to share-
holders and
Management
Discussion and
Analysis
(*Continued*)

Looking Ahead
We believe there are many attractive opportunities for Consumers as we pursue
our strategy to position the Company as a sharply-focused, cost-efficient and ser-
vice-oriented packaging producer. As the industry continues to consolidate, we
can anticipate further reductions in capacity and more economically-prudent pricing behaviour by competitors. At the same time, we will pursue potential expansion in the U.S., with a focus on fast growing niche markets—and in emerging
nations—through joint ventures, technology exchanges or other affiliations. We
also would selectively consider business combinations that allow us to diversify
into complementary sectors of the packaging industry, although such moves must
be highly disciplined both strategically and financially. Consumers' future growth
will be supported by our healthy financial condition, reputation for quality and
service, and commitment to constructive relationships with our labour force.

We are encouraged by our progress to-date, despite a challenging industry
environment. And we look forward to producing increasing value for shareholders, quality products for customers, and a rewarding work experience for employees as we move forward.

John J. Ghaznavi
Chairman and Chief Executive Officer
February 6, 1996

Management's Discussion and Analysis
The following discussion has been prepared by management and is a review of
the operating results, financial condition, risks and outlook for the Company. This
discussion supplements the financial statements and the accompanying notes.

Operating Results
Sales in dollars increased by 5% in 1995 compared with 1994 with growth in
export sales offsetting a decline in the Canadian market. The Company's share of
the Canadian market remained at approximately 80% in 1995. Sales in units in
1995 were similar to 1994 with the extra revenue due to a change in mix to higher
value products.

Gross margins decreased from 32.8% of sales in 1994 to 30.9% in 1995 due to
pricing pressures, increased raw material costs, particularly linerboard, and a
decrease in productivity as the plants dealt with the impact of new products, customers and equipment.

Distribution costs increased largely as a result of carrying excessive levels of finished goods inventory for a large part of the year. This inventory was reduced significantly by year end.

Administration and selling expenses declined in 1995 compared with 1994 due
mainly to a reduction in an accrual for a proposed relocation of the Company's
administrative offices and reduced lease costs.

The Company changed certain of its accounting policies in 1995 to more closely
reflect industry practice. The changes included capitalizing and depreciating
moulds rather than the previous practice of expensing moulds cost as incurred. The
impact of the most significant of these changes, mould accounting, resulted in
prior years' results being restated with the effect on 1994 being to decrease earnings by $2.7 million. The effect on 1995 of the change in mould accounting was to
increase earnings by $1.8 million. In recognition of changes in industry conditions,

continued

Exhibit 13-7

Consumers
Packaging Inc.
1995 Letter to share-
holders and
Management
Discussion and
Analysis
(*Continued*)

the unit of production method of depreciation was applied to production equipment effective January 1, 1995. As a result of this change depreciation and amortization in total was $35.4 million in 1995 compared with a restated $38.6 million in the previous year. In addition, the Company instituted the practice of including fixed manufacturing costs, such as depreciation and amortization of production facilities, in the determination of the cost of finished goods inventory.

The high interest rate Senior Notes were retired in 1995 from the proceeds of an equity issue which resulted in a reduction of interest expense in 1995 compared with 1994.

Financial Condition

The Company significantly improved its financial condition in 1995 through an equity issue, the proceeds of which were used primarily to retire high interest rate Senior Notes with the balance used to repay a portion of long-term bank debt.

In 1995, the Company generated cash, before changes in non-cash working capital, of $56.1 million. The cash generated, together with provincial government assistance loans in the year of $6.9 million for the use in financing capital projects, was more than sufficient to meet the capital expenditure program of $52.8 million.

The increase in the level of non-cash working capital in 1995 of $36.0 million compared with 1994 was caused by higher than planned inventories and accounts receivable along with a reduction in accrued liabilities. Approximately a third of this was financed from internal funds with the balance financed by bank debt. For the year 1996, a small decrease in non-cash working capital is expected.

The Company's pension plan has a solvency deficit estimated to be $30.2 million at the end of 1995. This deficiency which has been reduced from $46 million at the end of 1992, will be amortized by payments of approximately $5 million per year.

At the end of 1995, the Company had unused credit lines of $15 million and a debt to equity ratio low enough to enable the Company to increase its long-term borrowing should it be desirable.

The Company expects to maintain its high level of capital expenditures, which have averaged $52.1 million a year for the last two years, including $8.6 million for moulds under the revised method of accounting for moulds, for another year or two. After 1997 capital expenditures are expected to be reduced to levels not significantly higher than the annual depreciation and amortization expense.

Risks

In the U.S., glass-container shipments declined in 1995 by approximately 5%, compared with 1994, due mainly to the conversion of soft drink containers from glass to plastic. This conversion had a relatively smaller direct impact in Canada but has created excess production capacity in the U.S. The excess capacity in the U.S. has a negative impact on the Company as U.S. manufacturers look to the Canadian market for additional business usually at suppressed pricing. As a result, the Company may lose some existing Canadian business or keep the business at lower prices. In addition, the Company's penetration of the U.S. market becomes more difficult in this highly competitive market place. U.S. manufacturers have responded to the excess capacity by closing plants with three plants closing in 1995 and the announcement of the closing of an additional two plants early in 1996. Margins in the glass-container industry have also been negatively affected by increases in the cost of raw materials such as soda ash and linerboard.

As a result of export and other sales denominated in U.S. dollars, which are only partially offset by U.S. dollar purchases, the Company has a net annual U.S. dollar cash inflow exceeding $100 million. At the end of 1995, the Company had sold forward approximately two-thirds of its 1996 net U.S. dollar cash flow at

continued

Exhibit 13-7

Consumers
Packaging Inc.
1995 Letter to share-
holders and
Management
Discussion and
Analysis
(*Continued*)

exchange rates more favourable than current rates. To manage its future exposure to fluctuations in the exchange rate of the U.S. and Canadian dollar the
Company plans to utilize options and/or forward sale agreements in amounts not
exceeding its anticipated net U.S. dollar cash flow.

The Company's interest rate exposure at December 31, 1995 has been reduced
by fixing the interest rate on $40 million of its bank debt at current rates. The bal-
ance of its other bank debt, which is at floating rates, may be fixed depending on
the movement of rates during the year.

The Company believes its labour and material costs at current rates of
exchange are comparable to those of U.S. glass-container manufacturers. The
Company expects that labour and material costs in Canada will not increase more
than comparable U.S. costs. Increased productivity attained through the
Company's capital expenditure program will enable the Company to remain competitive with U.S. manufacturers.

The Company's collective agreements with labour unions expire at four of its
seven manufacturing plants in 1996.

Outlook

The Company's business strategy, in view of its already dominant share of the
Canadian market, is to expand its business in the U.S. while maintaining its base
business in the Canadian market. The Company's current U.S. sales strategy is to
focus on the niche product segment of the market. Niche products include a variety of food products, specialty and microbrewery beers, wine and lower volume
liquor products. These niche markets generally enjoy a higher growth rate than
that of the overall glass-container market and tend to have higher margins than
the high volume commodity business. In addition this type of business is well
suited to the Company's design and flexible manufacturing capabilities.

The Company's share of the Canadian market has improved from 75% in 1993
to approximately 80% in 1995. Export sales increased by 87% in 1994 compared
with 1993 and by 51% in 1995 compared with 1994.

Objective 4

Review the basic
financial ratios.

■ FINANCIAL RATIOS

The cornerstone of financial statement analysis is the computation and interpretation of ratios. Exhibit 13-8 groups some of the most popular ratios into
four categories. Most of these ratios have been introduced in earlier chapters,
as indicated in the second column. (A dash in the column means that the ratio
is being introduced in this chapter for the first time.)

Evaluating Financial Ratios

**time-series
comparisons**
Comparisons of a
company's financial
ratios with its own his-
torical ratios.

bench marks General
rules of thumb specify-
ing appropriate levels
for financial ratios.

Evaluation of a financial ratio requires a comparison. There are three main
types of comparisons: (1) with a company's own historical ratios (called **time-
series comparisons**), (2) with general *rules of thumb* or **bench marks,** and (3)
with ratios of other companies or with industry averages (called **cross-
sectional comparisons**).

Much can be learned by examining the *time-series trend* of a company's
ratios. That is why annual reports typically contain a table of comparative
statistics for five or ten years. For example, some of the items listed in the 1996
annual report of Mark's Work Warehouse are:

cross-sectional comparisons
Comparisons of a company's financial ratios with the ratios of other companies or with industry averages.

	Jan 1996	Jan 1995	Jan 1994	Jan 1993
Earnings per share	0.13	0.27	0.06	(0.17)
Cash flow from operations per share	0.28	0.36	0.29	0.02
Price/Earnings ratio	9.62	6.30	23.33	(4.41)
Book value per share (year end)	1.31	1.19	0.90	0.86
Return on average shareholders' equity	10.2%	25.4%	70%	(20.8%)
Current ratio	1.74	1.80	1.62	1.64
Total debt-to-equity ratio	1.21	1.23	1.72	2.04
Inventory turnover	2.1	2.4	2.4	2.3

Ratios

Ratios are useful for financial analysis by investors because ratios capture critical dimensions of the economic performance of the entity. Where else might economic performance need to be measured? Where else might ratios pay off for managers? It turns out that ratios are increasingly a tool that managers use to guide, measure, and reward workers. If you compensate workers for actions that make the company more profitable, for actions that increase the value of the company's common stock, you are motivating the employees effectively.

Hewitt Associates, a compensation consulting firm, reports that 60% of the 1,941 large companies they surveyed in 1994 had profit-sharing programs. Such programs are based on the solid view that when profits rise, the company is doing the right thing. And when workers do the right thing, they should share in the benefits. The higher the profit, the more the workers should earn as their share.

Duke Power Co. in Charlotte, N.C., has decided that profit may not be the right measure. Suppose profit increases because you raise more capital and expand the company? Should the workers necessarily earn more? Duke Power decided to reward workers based on two factors: success in meeting goals and the return on equity (ROE). For one worker the goal might be defined as reduced injuries and for another as improved customer service. But everyone earns more for meeting ROE targets. ROE is a good measure of efficiency because it can be improved by increasing profitability (the return on sales) and also by increasing the efficiency with which assets are employed (asset turnover).

In 1991, many workers had never heard of ROE, but by 1995 workers were watching the monthly financial results as carefully as their chidren look both ways before crossing the street. Now workers participate, and bonuses can exceed the base pay. As a result a $9.00 per hour worker can earn $20.00 per hour by achieving targets. And management is delighted to pay these bonuses because they are only paid when worker productivity is exceptional. The surprise is that workers can and do turn in exceptional performances when they know it will be recognized—not just by kind words, but by a management that puts its money where its mouth is.

Tawn Nhan, in a *Washington Post* article, gave the example of Neely Ashe, an engineer responsible for the coal division who has begun to cooperate more actively with the nuclear division. As Ashe said about the nuclear group, "I want to see them do well; it has an effect on my pay." Other companies are following this pattern. Glenayre Technologies and Nucor are also centred in Charlotte, N.C., and have similar bonus plans. ■

Source: The Washington Post, *Sunday March 26, 1995, p. H5*

Broad *rules of thumb* often serve as bench marks for comparison. Historically, the most quoted bench mark is a current ratio of 2 to 1. Recently, changes in management practices have reduced cash and inventory levels, and average current ratios are moving toward 1 to 1. Other bench marks are described in *Industry Norms and Key Business Ratios* by Dun & Bradstreet, the financial services firm.

Bench marks are general guides. More specific comparisons come from cross-sectional comparisons; that is, by examining ratios of similar companies or from industry averages. Dun & Bradstreet informs its subscribers of the credit-worthiness of thousands of individual companies. In addition, the firm regularly compiles many ratios of the companies it monitors. Compare the ratios for Oxley Company in Exhibit 13-8 to some of the Dun & Bradstreet ratios for 1,712 retail nurseries and garden stores:

Dun & Bradstreet Ratios			Average Collection Period	Total Debt to Shareholders' Equity	Net Income on Sales	Net Income on Shareholders' Equity
	Current Ratio	Quick Ratio	(Days)	(Percent)	(Percent)	(Percent)
1,712 companies:						
Upper quartile	4.2	1.5	5.5	32.3	6.1	30.2
Median	2.0	0.5	11.3	92.8	2.5	12.6
Lower quartile	1.3	0.2	23.0	230.7	0.5	2.6
Oxley*	1.3	1.1	30.0	64.9	9.0	22.8

* Ratios are from Exhibit 13-8. Please consult that exhibit for an explanation of the components of each ratio.

The individual ratios are ranked from best to worst. The ratio ranked in the middle is the *median*. The upper quartile is the ratio ranked halfway between the median and the best value. The lower quartile is the ratio ranked halfway between the median and the worst value. The concept of best and worst must be considered carefully. Different constituencies may adopt different points of view. For example, a short-term creditor would think that a very high current ratio was good, because it means the assets are there to repay the debt. From management's perspective, however, it is possible that current assets are excessive.

Short-Term Liquidity Ratios

Questions concerning liquidity focus on whether there are sufficient current assets to satisfy current liabilities as they become due. The most commonly used liquidity ratio is the current ratio. The higher the current ratio, the more assurance the short-term creditor usually has about being paid in full and on time. As Exhibit 13-8 shows, Oxley's current ratio of 1.3 has declined from 2.0 and is unimpressive in relation to the industry median of 2.0, which is shown in the previous section.

The quick ratio measures shorter-term liquidity. The numerator includes only those current assets that can quickly be turned into cash: cash, marketable securities, and accounts receivable. Oxley's quick ratio has also declined in 19X2, from 1.3 to 1.1, but is still greater than the industry median of 0.5.

Liquidity is also affected by how soon accounts receivable will be collected and how soon inventory will be sold. The average collection period and

Exhibit 13-8   Some Typical Financial Ratios

Typical Name of Ratio	Introduced in Chapter	Numerator	Denominator	Using Appropriate Oxley Numbers Applied to December 31 of Year	
				19X2	19X1
Short-term liquidity ratios:					
Current ratio	4	Current assets	Current liabilities	$290 \div 219 = 1.3$	$202 \div 101 = 2.0$
Quick ratio	4	Cash + marketable securities + receivables	Current liabilities	$(150 + 0 + 95) \div 219 = 1.1$	$(57 + 0 + 70) \div 101 = 1.3$
Average collection period in days	7	Average accounts receivable × 365	Sales	$[1/2(95 + 70) \times 365] \div 999 = 30^{\dagger}$	Unknown*
Inventory turnover	8	Cost of goods sold	Average inventory at cost	$399 \div 1/2(20 + 60) = 10$	Unknown*
Long-term solvency ratios:					
Total debt to total assets	10	Total liabilities	Total assets	$259 \div 658 = 39.4\%$	$221 \div 610 = 36.2\%$
Total debt to equity	10	Total liabilities	Shareholders' equity	$259 \div 399 = 64.9\%$	$221 \div 389 = 56.8\%$
Interest coverage	10	Income before interest and taxes	Interest expense	$(150 + 12) \div 12 = 13.5$	$(128 + 12) \div 12 = 11.7$
Profitability ratios:					
Return or shareholders' equity	4,11	Net income	Average shareholders' equity	$90 \div 1/2(399 + 389) = 22.8\%$	Unknown*
Gross profit rate or percentage	4	Gross profit or gross margin	Sales	$600 \div 999 = 60\%$	$464 \div 800 = 58\%$
Return on sales	4	Net income	Sales	$90 \div 999 = 9\%$	$80 \div 800 = 10\%$
Asset turnover	—	Sales	Average total assets available	$999 \div 1/2(658 + 610) = 1.6$	Unknown*
Pretax return on operating assets	—	Operating income	Average total assets available	$126 \div 1/2(658 + 610) = 19.9\%$	Unknown*
Earnings per share	2	Net income less dividends on preferred stock, if any	Average common shares outstanding	$90 \div 200 = \$.45$	$80 \div 200 = \$.40$
Market price and dividend ratios:					
Price-earnings	2	Market price of common share (assume $4 and $3)	Earnings per share	$4 \div .45 = 8.9$	$3 \div .40 = 7.5$
Dividend-yield	2	Dividends per common share	Market price of common share (assume $4 and $3)	$.40 \div 4 = 10.0\%$	$.20 \div 3 = 6.7\%$
Dividend-payout	2	Dividends per common share	Earnings per share	$.40 \div .45 = 89\%$	$.20 \div .40 = 50\%$

* Insufficient data available because the *beginning* balance sheet balances for 19X1 are not provided. Without them, the *average* investment in receivables, inventory, total assets, or shareholders' equity during 19X1 cannot be computed.

† This may be easier to see as follows: Average receivables = $1/2(95 + 70) = 82.5$. Average receivables as a percentage of annual sales = $82.5 \div 999 = 8.25\%$. Average collection period = $8.25\% \times 365$ days = 30 days.

inventory turnover are closely watched signals. Deteriorations through time in these ratios can help alert investors and creditors to problem areas. For example, a decrease in inventory turnover may suggest slower-moving (or even unsalable) merchandise or a worsening coordination of the buying and selling functions. An increase in the average collection period of receivables may indicate increasing acceptance of poor credit risks or less-energetic collection efforts. Whether the inventory turnover of 10 and the average collection period of 30 days are "fast" or "slow" depends on past performance and the performance of similar companies. Inventory turnover is not available from Dun & Bradstreet on an industry-comparable basis. The average collection period for Oxley is nearly three times as long as the industry median of 11.3 days.

Many analysts use sales *on account* in the denominator of the average collection period. This ratio focuses attention on how long it takes to collect credit accounts, in contrast to how long it takes to receive payment on sales in general. A company with many cash sales may have a short average collection period for total sales, even though there may be long delays in receiving payments for items sold on credit. Suppose half of Oxley's sales were for cash (including bank cards) and only half on open credit. The average collection period for *credit sales* would be

$$\frac{(1/2)(95 + 70) \times 365}{(1/2)(999)} = 60 \text{ days}$$

To be compared with industry averages, the averages must also be adjusted for credit sales. Suppose only one-fourth of the sales in retail nurseries are on credit. The industry median collection period for credit accounts would be $10.2 \div (1/4) = 40.8$ days.

Long-Term Solvency Ratios

Ratios of debt to assets and debt to equity are used for solvency evaluation. Although the focus is on the ability to repay long-term creditors, both creditors and shareholders watch these ratios to judge the degree of risk of insolvency and the stability of profits. Typically, companies with heavy debt in relation to ownership capital are in greater danger of suffering net losses or even insolvency when business conditions sour. Why? Because revenues and many expenses decline, but interest expenses and maturity dates do not change. Oxley's debt-to-equity ratio of 64.9% is below the industry median of 92.8%, reflecting less-than-average uncertainty concerning the company's ability to pay its debts on time.

Another solvency measure is the interest coverage ratio. It shows how much danger there is that operations will not generate operating income (before interest expense) at least as large as the company's interest expense. A common rule of thumb is that the interest coverage ratio should be at least five. Oxley's ratio of 13.5 comfortably exceeds this bench mark. The interest coverage ratio was discussed in more detail in Chapter 10.

Profitability Ratios

Earnings per share (EPS) is the best known of all financial ratios. It measures the "bottom line," earnings available to the holder of a share of common stock. It was introduced in Chapter 2, and extended discussion appears later in this chapter, where we examine some issues that arise for more complex companies than Oxley.

A primary profitability measure is return on shareholders' equity. Abbreviated ROE, this ratio relates an accounting measure of income to the level of ownership capital used to generate the income. As defined in Chapter 4 and discussed more extensively in Chapter 11, the ratio is:

ROE = Net income / Average shareholders' equity

Oxley's return of 22.8% is above the 1994 industry median of 12.6% shown on page 588. What explains Oxley's superior performance? Two additional profitability ratios help explain it. The return on sales was introduced in Chapter 4. Exhibit 13-8 shows that the return on sales has fallen from 10% to 9%. But the 9% level, which indicates that 9 cents of every dollar of sales is profit, places Oxley well above the 75th percentile of nurseries and garden stores according to Dun & Bradstreet. The second key to assessing Oxley's superior ROE is the efficiency with which Oxley uses its asset structure to generate sales. To accomplish this, we now examine some distinctions between operating performance and financial performance.

■ OPERATING PERFORMANCE AND FINANCIAL PERFORMANCE

ROE, discussed above, is affected by financing choices. *Financial management* is concerned with where to get cash and how to use that cash to benefit the entity. Borrowed funds create interest costs and affect net income, the numerator of the ratio. *Operating management* is concerned with the day-to-day activities that generate revenues and expenses. Ratios to assess operating efficiency should not be affected by financial considerations.

Market Price and Dividend Ratios

Investors are particularly concerned with the market price of common shares. Both earnings and dividends are related to share price. The price-earnings (P/E) ratio shows how market participants value $1 of a company's earnings. Generally, high P/E means that investors expect earnings to grow faster than average, and a low P/E indicates small expected earnings growth. In 1997, P/E ratios averaged in the range of 18 to 22. However, some companies such as Bank of Montreal had a P/E ratio of 11 while IMAX had a P/E ratio of 35. Oxley's P/E of 8.9 is above the previous year's 7.5, but it is below the economy-wide average. Apparently, investors think Oxley has below-average growth potential.

Oxley doubled its dividend per share in 19X2, increasing the dividend yield to 10.0%. Therefore an investor who buys $1,000 of Oxley common stock will receive annual cash dividends of 10% × $1,000 = $100 if dividend rates do not change. Oxley is paying out 89% of earnings, as shown by the dividend-payout ratio. The high payout ratio may be one reason for the low projected growth; Oxley is not reinvesting much of its earnings.

Operating Performance

Objective 5

Explain the relationship between ROA and ROE in evaluating corporate performance.

In general, we evaluate the overall success of an investment by comparing what the investment returns to us with the investment we initially made. In general, the rate of return on investment can be defined as:

$$\text{Rate of return on investment} = \frac{\text{Income}}{\text{Invested capital}} \tag{1}$$

EBIT Earnings before interest and taxes.

In various settings, we find it useful to define *income* differently, sometimes as net earnings and sometimes as either pretax income from operations or earnings before interest and taxes (**EBIT**). We also define *invested capital* differently, sometimes as the shareholders' equity and other times as the total capital provided by both debt and equity sources. These choices are determined by the purpose of the analysis.

The measurement of *operating* performance (that is, how profitably assets are employed) should not be influenced by the management's *financial* decisions (that is, how assets are financed). Operating performance is best measured by **pretax operating rate of return on total assets:**

pretax operating rate of return on total assets
Operating income divided by average total assets available.

$$\begin{array}{c}\text{Pretax operating rate} \\ \text{of return on total assets}\end{array} = \frac{\text{Operating income}}{\text{Average total assets available}} \tag{2}$$

The right side of Equation 2 consists, in turn, of two important ratios:

$$\frac{\text{Operating income}}{\text{Average total assets available}} = \frac{\text{Operating income}}{\text{Sales}} \times \frac{\text{Sales}}{\text{Average total assets available}} \tag{3}$$

Using Exhibits 13-1 and 13-2, pages 575-576, we can compute the following 19X2 results for Oxley Company:

$$\frac{\$126}{\frac{1}{2}(\$658 + \$610)} = \frac{\$126}{\$999} \times \frac{\$999}{\$634} = 19.9\%$$

operating income percentage on sales
Operating income divided by sales.

These relationships are displayed in a boxed format in Exhibit 13-9.

The right-side terms in Equation 3 are often called the **operating income percentage on sales** and the **total asset turnover (asset turnover),** respectively. Equation 3 may be reexpressed:

total asset turnover (asset turnover)
Sales divided by average total assets available.

$$\begin{array}{c}\text{Pretax operating rate} \\ \text{of return on total assets}\end{array} = \text{Operating income percentage on sales} \times \text{Total asset turnover}$$
$$19.9\% = 12.6\% \times 1.576 \text{ times} \tag{4}$$

Exhibit 13-9

Major Ingredients of
Return on Total
Assets

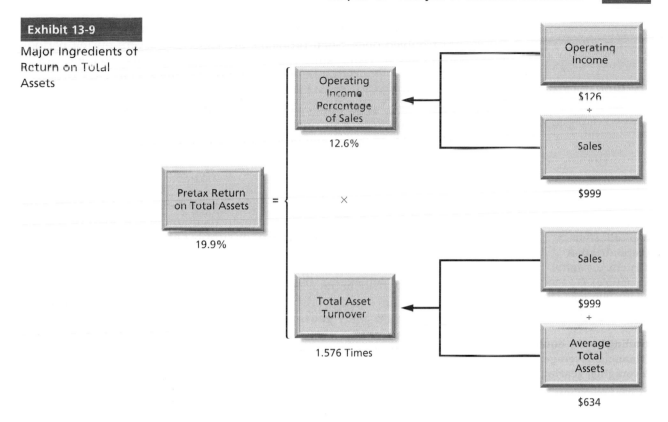

If ratios are used to evaluate operating performance, they should exclude extraordinary items that are regarded as nonrecurring items that do not reflect normal performance.

Equation 4 highlights two basic factors in profit making: operating margin percentage and turnover. An improvement in either will, by itself, increase the rate of return on total assets.

The ratios could be computed on the basis of figures after taxes, and often are. However, the peculiarities of the income tax laws may sometimes distort results—for example, the tax rate may change, or losses carried back or forward might eliminate the tax in certain years.

Financial Performance

A major aspect of financial performance is achieving an appropriate balance of debt and equity financing. Debt surrounds us. Governments issue debt securities of all kinds for many purposes. Businesses do likewise. Individuals have small loans (on refrigerators) and big loans (on homes).

In addition to a decision about how much debt is appropriate, a firm must choose how much to borrow short-term (e.g., accounts payable and some bank debt) and how much to borrow by issuing bonds or other longer-term debt. Short-term financing should ordinarily be for investments in current assets. Some entities have edged into deep financial water by using short-term debt for long-term investments (for example, plant and equipment).

The problem with short-term debt is that it must be quickly repaid or replaced with new financing. When the borrower encounters trouble and cannot

Objective 8

Explain the
importance of
efficient markets
to accounting
disclosures.

Research in finance and accounting during the past twenty years has reinforced the idea that financial ratios and other data such as reported earnings
provide inputs to predictions of such economic phenomena as financial failure
or earnings growth. Furthermore, many ratios are used simultaneously rather
than one at a time for such predictions. Above all, the research has shown that
accounting reports are only one source of information and that in the aggregate
the market is not fooled by companies that choose the least-conservative
accounting policies. In sum, the market as a whole sees through attempts by
companies to gain favour through the choice of accounting policies that tend to
boost immediate income. Thus, there is evidence that the stock markets may
indeed be relatively "efficient," at least in their reflection of most accounting
data. However, the stock market crash of October 1987 and other reported
"anomalies" prevent unqualified endorsement of stock market efficiency.

Suppose you are the chief executive officer of Company A. Reported earnings are $4 per share and the stock price is $40. You are contemplating changing your method of amortization for investor-reporting purposes from
accelerated to straight-line. Your competitors use straight-line. You think the
Company A stock price unjustifiably suffers in comparison with other companies in the same industry.

Southam Inc.
Consolidated
Statements of
Income (thousands
of dollars)

	Year Ended December 31
	1992
Revenue from Operations	
Newspapers	$ 809,517
Business communications	177,100
Book retailing	196,852
	1,183,469
Cost of Operations	
Operating expenses	1,109,869
Depreciation	36,398
Amortization of goodwill and circulation	7,878
Interest	31,549
	1,185,694
Operating Income (Loss) Before Unusual Items and Income Taxes	(2,225)
Unusual items	(160,351)
Operating Income (Loss) Before Income Taxes	(162,576)
Income taxes (recovered)	35,981
Operating income (loss)	(126,595)
Equity in earnings of associated business	3,744
Income (Loss) from Continuing Operations	(122,851)
Loss from discontinued operations	(140,000)
Net Income (Loss)	(262,851)
Income (Loss) Per Common Share	—
From continuing operations	—
Discontinued operations	—
Net income (loss)	—
Average number of common shares outstanding	61,630,096

If straight-line depreciation is adopted by Company A, reported earnings will be $5 instead of $4 per share. Would the stock price rise accordingly from $40 to $50? No, the empirical research on these issues indicates that the stock price would remain at $40 (all other things being equal).

Remember that the market is efficient only with respect to *publicly available* information. Therefore, accounting issues that deal with the disclosure of new information are important, but concerns about the format for reporting already available data are less important. William Beaver has commented on the implications of market efficiency for accounting regulators:

> Many reporting issues are trivial and do not warrant an expenditure of FASB resources. The properties of such issues are twofold: (1) There is essentially no difference in cost to the firm of reporting either method. (2) There is essentially no cost to statement users in adjusting from one method to the other. In such cases, there is a simple solution. Report one method, with sufficient footnote disclosure to permit adjustment to the other, and let the market interpret implications of the data for security prices.
>
> The FASB should shift its resources to those controversies where there is nontrivial additional cost to the firms or to investors in order to obtain certain types of information (for example, replacement cost accounting for depreciable assets). Whether such information should be a required part of reporting standards is a substantive issue.[1]

Be aware also that accounting statements are not the only source of financial information about companies, as newspapers, analyst reports, etc. all provide information to investors. However, financial statement information may be more directly related to the item of interest, and it may be more reliable, lower-cost, or more timely than information from alternative sources.

The research described above concentrates on the effects of accounting on investors in the aggregate. Individual investors must either incur the costs of conducting careful analyses or delegate that chore to professional analysts. In any event, intelligent analysis cannot be accomplished without an understanding of the assumptions and limitations of financial statements, including the presence of various alternative accounting methods.

Objective 9

Explain some effects on financial statements of translating foreign currencies.

foreign-currency exchange rates The number of units of one currency that can be exchanged for one unit of another currency.

■ FOREIGN-CURRENCY ISSUES

Today, companies conduct business in various countries and so must learn to do business using different currencies. Two problems arise. One problem is accounting for day-to-day transactions that occur in foreign currencies. Another problem is consolidating a subsidiary that exists in another country and does its own accounting in the currency of that country.

These issues are important because of fluctuating **foreign-currency exchange rates.** The foreign-currency exchange rate specifies how many units of one currency are required to obtain one unit of another currency. Recently, the conversion rate of Japanese yen into Canadian dollars has been approximately $.0112. This means that one yen buys 1.12 cents. The relation could be expressed as the conversion rate of Canadian dollars into Japanese yen, which would be ¥89.1. If conversion rates were constant, no accounting problems would arise, but the rates often change significantly. Forty years ago, the conversion rate of dollars into yen was ¥360. During this time the value of the yen increased relative to the value of the dollar.

---

[1] William H. Beaver, "What Should Be the FASB's Objectives?" *Journal of Accountancy,* Vol. 136, p. 32.

Markets Respond to Rumors

Still reeling from fending off a massive lawsuit and a hostile takeover bid, **Loewen Group Inc.** ■■■■ is under attack again from a barrage of rumors—denied by the company—of a looming earnings disappointment and an accounting dispute.

Shares in North America's second-biggest operator of funeral homes and cemeteries have fallen more than 5% this week to their lowest level since September.

The stock (LWN/TSE, LWN/NYSE) fell 55¢ in Toronto yesterday to close at $44.10, off its 52-week high of $58.75. And in New York, it fell US$1⅝ to US$31.

"There has been some modest trimming of earnings expectations and some negative sentiment surrounding the company," TD Securities Inc. analyst Darren Martin said.

The collapse of Loewen's stock price last year spurred Houston-based rival **Service Corp. International** to launch a US$2.9-billion hostile takeover bid. Loewen defeated the bid in January and has since campaigned to rebuild investors' trust. But the current turmoil is making shareholders edgy.

This week's pummelling of Loewen stock was triggered partly by a lowering of earnings expectations and talk the company might not meet investors' profit targets. Loewen is due to report fourth-quarter results next Wednesday.

The stock slide then gathered force largely because of murky rumors of a potential accounting problem. Various versions of the rumor have been circulating but all are untrue, said Loewen chief financial officer Paul Wagler.

The rumors range from talk that Loewen and its auditors are in a dispute over the financial statements, that one of the company's top internal accounting officers has quit over a rift with management and that Loewen plans to change its accounting methods because it fell short of fourth-quarter earnings expectations.

"We have no disagreements or difficulty in that area. Our expectation is that [earnings targets] will be achieved when results are announced," Wagler said. "There was never a contemplation of changing our accounting policy. The same people have been spreading the same rumors, and they are going to be terribly disappointed when we announce the results and our accountants sign off because they are in absolute and total agreement."

Speculation took the heaviest toll on Loewen shares Wednesday, the day after SCI met with analysts. Several analysts, who asked to remain anonymous, said Service highlighted what it considered to be Loewen's weaknesses and the rumors circulated at the meeting.

Nervousness over Loewen's underlying earnings performance is worrying investors and some analysts have lowered their forecasts. The current consensus is that Loewen will report fourth-quarter earnings from operations of US37¢ to US38¢ a share or US$21.5 million to US$22 million. Costs associated with fighting off the SCI bid are seen reducing net earnings by US$11 million (US18¢).

Wagler denied the company had changed its outlook. He said the lower estimates merely formalized earlier projections made by analysts. ■

Source: "Loewen hit by rumored accounting, profit troubles," *Financial Post* (February 28, 1997).

Accounting for Transactions in Foreign Currencies

If a Canadian firm exports an automobile to Japan for $10,000, the sale will often be on credit and *denominated* in yen. The customer owes ¥891,000 (because the conversion rate at the time of the sale was ¥89.1). The Canadian firm will record the sale in dollars, and the receivable would be $10,000 on its books. After one month, the buyer remits ¥891,000 to the seller. Suppose the yen has fallen (or weakened) against the dollar, and the new exchange rate is ¥92. When the yen is converted to dollars the seller ends up with only $9,684.78 (¥891,000 / ¥92). The transaction has given rise to a loss of $315.22, which would be recorded as follows:

Cash	$9,684.78	
Loss on currency fluctuation	315.22	
Accounts receivable		$10,000.00

Not surprisingly, the currency exchange rate could move in the other direction and give rise to a gain. Many companies use sophisticated financial transactions to eliminate the effect of currency fluctuations, but these hedging transactions and their accounting are covered in more advanced courses.

Consolidating International Subsidiaries

The previous section dealt with a company in one country doing business with a company in another country. A more complex problem arises in an international parent-subsidiary relationship. Suppose a Canadian company (parent) owns a Japanese company (subsidiary, or sub) doing business in Japan in yen. At the end of the year the parent must consolidate the sub's financial data with its own and create a single set of statements. What exchange rate should be used?

GAAP recognizes two perspectives when accounting for a foreign operation. In one case the foreign operation is viewed as operating independently from the parent, and is called a self-sustaining operation. The alternative perspective is that of an integrated foreign operation. For a self-sustaining operation, the assets and liabilities of the sub are translated at the year-end exchange rate. The common stock account is translated at the historic rate existing when the sub was created. The average exchange rate during the year is used to account for the transactions in the income statement. These translated net income figures annually increase the retained earnings of the parent. Over time, the parent's retained earnings reflect yen translations at different exchange rates. The problem is apparent. If the assets of the sub equal its liabilities plus its owners' equity in yen, and different rates are used to translate assets, liabilities, and equity, then the consolidated balance sheet is forced out of balance. To bring it back in balance a **translation adjustment** is created, which is reported as part of shareholders' equity. Details of computing this translation adjustment are beyond the scope of this text.

translation adjustment A contra account in shareholders' equity that arises when a foreign subsidiary is consolidated.

For an integrated operation, the foreign operation is accounted for as if the parent had directly performed the transaction and thus the existing exchange rates would be used to translate the foreign currency amounts. In this case any foreign exchange gains and losses are reported on the income statement. An exception exists if the foreign exchange gain or loss applies to a long-term asset or liability, then the gain or loss is spread out over the life of the asset or liability. The shareholders' equity sections of most multinational firms include foreign-currency translation adjustments. The title and amount of the translation adjustment and total shareholders' equity for some international companies follow:

Company	Account Name	Amount	Total SE
Bombardier	Deferred translation adjustments	33.7	$1,687.9 million
Placer Dome	Cumulative translation adjustment	(167)	$1,541
Power Corporation	Foreign currency translation adjustment	201	2,630

Summary Problem for Your Review

Problem

Exhibit 13-12 contains a condensed income statement and balance sheet for Gannett Company, Inc., a leading publisher of newspapers.

Required

1. Compute the following ratios: (a) current ratio, (b) quick ratio, (c) average collection period, (d) total debt to shareholders' equity, (e) return on sales, and (f) return on shareholders' equity.
2. Using the 1994 Gannett values provided below and the following Dun & Bradstreet 1994–95 ratios for 503 newspaper companies, assess Gannett's liquidity, solvency, and profitability.

	Current Ratio	Quick Ratio	Average Collection Period	Total Debt to Shareholders' Equity	Net Income on Sales	Net Income on Shareholders' Equity
Upper quartile	5.5	4.0	28.1	18.0	9.0	27.4
Median	2.2	1.7	37.6	47.0	4.2	11.8
Lower quartile	1.3	0.9	46.5	151.4	1.0	3.4

Using only the ratios in requirement 1, assess Gannett Company's liquidity, solvency, and profitability.

Solution

Gannett's 1994 ratios are also provided for comparison, although data for their calculation are not provided in the problem.

				1991	1994
1. a.	Current ratio $=$	$\dfrac{636,101}{443,835}$	$=$	1.4	1.2
b.	Quick ratio $=$	$\dfrac{70,673 + 444,568}{443,835}$	$=$	1.2	1.1
c.	Average collection period $=$	$\dfrac{(1/2)(444,568 + 469,701) \times 365}{3,382,035}$	$=$	49.3	44.7
d.	Total debt to shareholders' equity $=$	$\dfrac{2,144,593}{1,539,487}$	$=$	139.3%	103.0%

		1991	1994

e. Return on sales $= \dfrac{301,649}{3,382,035} =$ 8.9% 12.2%

f. Return on shareholders' equity $= \dfrac{301,649}{(1/2)(1,539,487 + 2,063,077)}$

$= 16.8\%$ 25.0%

Exhibit 13-12

Gannett
Company, Inc.
(in thousands)

Income Statement	For the Year Ended December 29, 1991
Revenues	$ 3,382,035
Operating expenses	(2,823,088)
Operating income	558,947
Interest expense	(71,057)
Interest and other income	14,859
Income before income taxes	502,749
Provision for income taxes	(201,100)
Net income	$ 301,649

Balance Sheets	For the Year Ended December 29, 1991	December 30, 1990
Assets		
Current assets:		
Cash and marketable securities	$ 70,673	$ 56,238
Receivables	444,568	469,071
Inventories	51,380	66,525
Prepaid expenses	69,480	76,856
Total current assets	636,101	668,690
Property, plant, and equipment, net	1,484,910	1,472,123
Intangible and other assets	1,563,069	1,685,332
Total assets	$ 3,684,080	$3,826,145
Liabilities and Shareholders' Equity		
Total current liabilities	$ 443,835	$ 500,203
Long-term liabilities	1,700,758	1,262,865
Total liabilities	2,144,593	1,763,068
Total shareholders' equity	1,539,487	2,063,077
Total liabilities and shareholders' equity	$ 3,684,080	$3,826,145

---

2. The measures of profitability improved significantly from 1991 to 1994. In 1994, Gannett continued to manage current assets aggressively while reducing the level of debt in the capital structure. In 1994, Gannett was below the median on liquidity measures and more leveraged than the median. However, profitability was very high.

Highlights to Remember

Financial and operating information is available from many sources, including annual reports and daily newspapers.

Financial information is provided to aid investors in assessing the risk and return of a potential investment. Investors in debt are particularly concerned about the solvency and liquidity of the issuer, while equity investors are more interested in profitability.

Trend analysis is a form of financial statement analysis that concentrates on changes in the financial statements through time. It involves comparing relationships for a period of years or quarters. Common-size financial statements are constructed by expressing the elements of the balance sheet as a percentage of total assets and the elements of the income statement as a percentage of total revenue. They enhance the ability to compare one company with another or to conduct a trend analysis over time.

The basic financial ratios allow us to put numbers in perspective. By relating one part of the financial statements to another they facilitate questions such as "Given the change in revenues, was the change in accounts receivable reasonable?" and "Is the company's inventory level, given its size, comparable to industry norms?" The chapter reviews the ratios presented throughout the text.

Liquidity ratios deal with the immediate ability to make payments. Solvency ratios deal with the longer-term ability to meet obligations. Both are often incorporated into debt covenants to ensure lenders' rights. Profitability ratios are used to assess operating efficiency and performance.

Return on equity (ROE) is the most fundamental profitability ratio because it relates income to the shareholder's investment. Return on assets is one of several related elements that focuses on the profitable use of all assets. It can be further divided into the return on sales and the total asset turnover.

Earnings per share (EPS) is a fundamental measure of performance. In this chapter three complexities in calculating this measure were identified and incorporated into the calculation. Since preferred shares receive preference to dividends, their dividends are deducted from earnings in the numerator. Since shares outstanding may change during the year, the denominator is calculated as a weighted average over the year. The presence of options and convertible securities creates a potential to issue new shares as a result of the actions of others. Therefore, EPS is calculated on both a basic and a fully diluted basis.

Special (unusual) items, extraordinary items, and discontinued operations are three categories of unusual and possibly nonrecurring items. Separately disclosing these allows analysts to refine forecasts of future performance based on current operations. Special (unusual) items are included with other expenses but identified separately. Extraordinary items and discontinued items are shown separately below earnings from operations and net of their individual tax effects.

Efficient markets refer to the probability that the actions of analysts to carefully evaluate disclosures lead to their incorporating all available information into the market price for securities. Evidence suggests this is substantially, but not totally, true. This fact means that complete disclosure is more important than the form of the disclosure. For example, investors are unlikely to be confused in their efforts to price securities by differences in the methods of amortization or inventory accounting in use.

Multinational companies do business in more than one country. Sometimes they export products produced in the home country to other markets. In this case, transactions with foreign customers are often in the customer's currency, although they are accounted for in the home currency. Exchange-rate fluctuations between the sale date and the collection date give rise to gains or losses, which appear in the seller's earnings statement and affect net earnings. In other cases, foreign subsidiaries manufacture and sell outside the home country. Foreign subsidiaries hold assets, conduct business, and account for it in their own currency. Translation problems arise when the subsidiary's financial statements are translated into the parent's currency for consolidation. In Canada such translations for consolidation give rise to translation adjustments recorded in shareholders' equity with no effect on consolidated net earnings.

Assignment Material

QUESTIONS

13-1. Why do decision makers use financial statement analysis?

13-2. In addition to the basic financial statements, what information is usually presented in a company's annual report?

13-3. Give three sources of information for investors besides accounting information.

13-4. "Financial statements report on *history*. Therefore they are not useful to creditors and investors who want to predict *future* returns and risk." Do you agree? Explain.

13-5. How do common-size statements aid comparisons with other companies?

13-6. What information is presented in the "management's discussion and analysis" (MD&A) section of annual reports?

13-7. Name three types of comparisons that are useful in evaluating financial ratios.

13-8. "Ratios are mechanical and incomplete." Explain.

13-9. Ratios are often grouped into four categories. What are the categories?

13-10. What two measures of operating performance are combined to give the pretax operating return on total assets?

13-11. "Trading on the equity means exchanging bonds for shares." Do you agree? Explain.

13-12. "Borrowing is a two-edged sword." Do you agree? Explain.

13-13. Why are companies with heavy debt in relation to ownership capital in greater danger when business conditions sour?

13-14. "The tax law discriminates against preferred stock and in favour of debt." Explain.

13-15. "An efficient capital market is one in which securities are traded through stockbrokers." Do you agree? Explain.

13-16. Suppose the president of your company wanted to switch amortization methods to increase reported net income: "Our stock is 10% below what I think it should be; changing the amortization method will increase income by 10%, thus getting our share price up to its proper level." How would you respond?

13-17. Evaluate the following quotation from *Forbes*: "If IBM had been forced to expense [the software development cost of] $785 million, its earnings would have been cut by 72 cents a share. With IBM selling at 14 times earnings, expensing the costs might have knocked over $10 off IBM's share price."

13-18. Suppose you wanted to compare the financial statements of Stelco and Dofasco. What concerns might you have in comparing their various ratios?

13-19. Suppose you wanted to evaluate the financial performance of Bombardier Inc. over the last ten years. What factors might affect the comparability of a firm's financial ratios over such a long period of time?

13-20. Suppose you worked for a small manufacturing company and the president said that you must improve your current ratio. Would you interpret this to mean that you should increase it or decrease it? How might you do so?

13-21. Suppose you work for a small local department store that manages its own accounts receivable with a private charge card. Your

This chapter provides an overview of the conceptual framework of accounting. It gives some insight into the development of accounting policy making as well as the political, social, and business forces that influence the accounting policy decisions. The chapter gathers some of the concepts introduced in earlier chapters and adds others to provide a more complete picture of the concepts that underlie accounting. It also provides a synopsis and integration of the international diversity that characterizes accounting practice. We have stressed throughout the text that Canadian practices represent only one of a number of possible choices. Here we revisit and extend examples from throughout the text.

■ CONCEPTUAL FRAMEWORK OF ACCOUNTING

For years, accountants have sought a consistent set of concepts underlying accounting practice. But they still have a patchwork of generally accepted accounting principles (GAAP) that has slowly evolved over many years of accounting practice and regulatory effort. As a result, various accounting rules seem inconsistent within any single framework. For example, the lower-of-cost-and-market basis is applied differently to inventories, to temporary investments, and to long-term investments.

Objective 1

Describe the conceptual framework of accounting.

Between 1978 and 1984 in the United States, the Financial Accounting Standards Board (FASB) issued four *Statements of Financial Accounting Concepts* (SFACs) relating to business enterprises.[1] Exhibit 14-1 summarizes the highlights of these SFACs. The statements provide the conceptual framework used by the FASB.

In Canada, the Canadian Institute of Chartered Accountants (CICA) substantially adopted FASB's concepts when in 1988 it issued its version of the conceptual framework in the first section of the *CICA Handbook*. The principal task of the FASB is **accounting policy making**, which is choosing the accounting measurement and disclosure methods required for financial reporting. Each of the CICA and the FASB is a policy-making body that exercises judgment to choose among alternatives. There are no objective criteria to guide the CICA and the FASB in making their decisions. The conceptual framework summarized in Exhibit 14-1 aids the exercise of judgment; it does not provide solutions to all the reporting issues faced by the accounting standard-setting bodies.

accounting policy making Choosing the accounting measurement and disclosure methods required for financial reporting.

Financial Accounting Standards Board
raw.rutgers.edu/raw/fasb/

Accounting policy making is complex. Progress will continue to come in fits and starts. It will always be considered as too fast by some critics and too slow by others. Most people favour "improvements" in accounting—the quicker the better. But one person's improvement is often another person's impairment. Resolving these trade-offs is the essence of policy making.

---

[1] The FASB has also issued two statements on a conceptual framework for nonbusiness organizations. These statements apply to "most human service organizations, churches, foundations, and some other organizations, such as those private nonprofit hospitals and nonprofit schools that receive a significant portion of their financial resources from sources other than the sale of goods and services." See Concepts Statement No. 4, "Objectives of Financial Reporting by Nonbusiness Organizations" (Stamford, CT: FASB, 1980); and Concepts Statement No. 6, "Elements of Financial Statements" (Stamford, CT: FASB, 1985).

	Statement*	Highlights
Exhibit 14-1 Statements of Financial Accounting Concepts for Business Enterprises	SFAC No. 1, Objectives of Financial Reporting by Business Enterprises	• Accounting should provide information useful for making economic decisions • Statements should focus on external users, e.g., creditors and investors • Information should aid the prediction of cash flows • Earnings based on accrual accounting provide a better measure of performance than do cash receipts and disbursements
	SFAC No. 2, Qualitative Characteristics of Accounting Information	• Usefulness is evaluated in relation to the purposes to be served • Different information is useful for different decisions • Decision usefulness is the primary characteristic in the hierarchy of desirable characteristics • Both relevance and reliability are necessary for information to be useful • Relevance requires timeliness and either predictive or feedback value • Reliable information must faithfully represent the item being measured and be verifiable and neutral • Comparability and consistency aid usefulness • To be useful, information must be material, that is, reported amounts must be large enough to make a difference in decisions • Benefits from using information should exceed its cost
	SFAC No. 3, Elements of Financial Statements of Business Enterprises	• Defines the ten building blocks that comprise financial statements: (1) assets, (2) liabilities, (3) equity, (4) investments by owners, (5) distributions to owners, (6) comprehensive income, (7) revenues, (8) expenses, (9) gains, and (10) losses.
	SFAC No. 5, Recognition and Measurement in Financial Statements of Business Enterprises	• Specifies what information should be included in financial statements and when • All components of financial statements are important, not just a single "bottom-line" number • A statement of financial position provides information about assets, liabilities, and equity; it does not show the market value of the entity • Earnings measure periodic performance; comprehensive income recognizes all effects on equity except investments by or distributions to owners • Financial statements are based on the concept of financial capital maintenance • Measurement is and will continue to be based on nominal units of money • Revenue is recognized when it is earned and realized (or realizable) • Information based on current prices, if reliable and more relevant than alternative information, should be reported if costs involved are not too high

* SFAC Nos. 4 and 6 relate to nonbusiness entities and are not summarized here.

Above all, students, accountants, managers, and others should recognize that the process of setting accounting standards is not confined to the development of a conceptual framework and its application to specific issues via exercises in impeccable logic and fact gathering. The process also includes the gaining of general acceptance and support. A major role of the conceptual framework is ultimately to enhance the likelihood that proposed statements will be generally accepted. The more plausible the logic and the more compelling the facts, the greater the chance of winning the support of diverse interests.

Lessons from History

All accounting regulatory bodies have been criticized for using piecemeal approaches, solving one accounting issue at a time. Again and again, critics have cited a need for a conceptual framework. As we saw earlier, the FASB has worked hard on constructing a conceptual framework. Meanwhile, the board also has had to contend with an unending stream of specific accounting controversies that demanded immediate attention. Is there a lesson here? Why has the piecemeal approach persisted? The answer lies in a careful look at the policy-making process.

The term *generally accepted* is a key part of the familiar term *generally accepted accounting principles*. The policy-making process is much more complicated than having intelligent, experienced regulators apply logic and evidence to an issue and then promulgate rules that are subsequently followed by the affected parties. The use of logic and evidence is absolutely necessary, but it is insufficient. When the CICA considers a financial accounting standard, assorted interested parties present arguments to support their favoured choices. The standards issued are often compromises among the contending interests; therefore, the standards are not necessarily products of airtight logic.

The CICA's task is not only technical, but also political and educational. When the term *political* is used in this context, it means the ways of convincing interested persons about the wisdom of the board's decisions. In short, they must tackle the task of obtaining general acceptance.

■ CHOOSING AMONG REPORTING ALTERNATIVES

The CICA must make difficult decisions about reporting requirements. For example, should reporting of income tax expense include deferred taxes? How should the expense for pensions and the associated pension liability be measured? Should liabilities be shown at historical cost or current market value? The list could go on and on. How does the CICA decide that one level of disclosure or one measurement method is acceptable and another is not?

The overriding criterion for choosing reporting alternatives is *cost/benefit*. Accounting should improve decision making. This is a benefit. But accounting information is an economic good that is costly to produce. A policy-making body such as the CICA must do its best to issue pronouncements whose perceived benefits exceed their perceived costs for the whole of society. The costs and benefits are hard to measure. They are widely diffused and fall unevenly throughout the economy. Nevertheless, the board should never lose sight of the fundamental cost-benefit test.

The costs of providing information include costs to both providers and users. Providers incur costs of data collecting and processing, of auditing, and of educating preparers. In addition, disclosure of sensitive information can lead to lost competitive advantages or increased labour union pressures. The costs to users of information include those passed on by the providers plus the costs of education, analysis, and interpretation.

The benefits of accounting information surely exist, but they are harder to pinpoint than the costs. A highly developed economy depends on accounting to inform investors and creditors whose collective decisions provide resources to sound and promising enterprises while withdrawing support from faltering entities.

An important concept in judging costs and benefits is materiality. Information is *material* when its inclusion or correct presentation would probably change the judgment of a reasonable person. Determining whether an item is material is a pervasive problem that is usually resolved by professional judgment on a case-by-case basis. The CICA should not get bogged down in issues whose effect is likely to be immaterial.

As part of its conceptual framework, the FASB has identified a hierarchy of characteristics of information that lead to increased benefits. These are shown in Exhibit 14-2. Foremost is decision usefulness. Without usefulness there would be no benefits. The rest of the items specify what characteristics make information useful.

Exhibit 14-2

Qualities that Increase the Value of Information

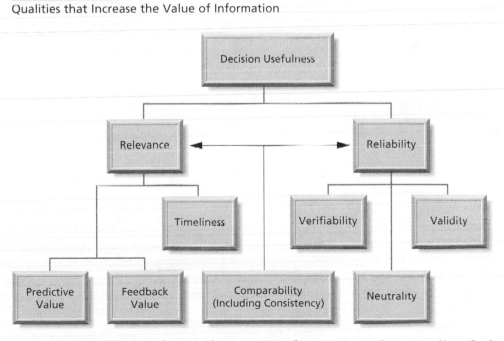

Source: Adapted from *Qualitative Characteristics of Accounting Information* (Stamford, CT: FASB, 1980), p. 15.

Relevance and Reliability

relevance The capability of information to make a difference to the decision maker.

Relevance and *reliability* are qualities that make accounting useful for decision making. **Relevance** is defined as the capability of information to make a difference to the decision maker. *Reliability* is defined in Chapter 1 as the quality of information that assures decision makers that the information captures the conditions or events that it purports to represent. The accounting literature is filled with arguments about the trade-offs between relevance and reliability. Consider the balance sheet value of Weyerhaeuser Company's timberlands, which are recorded at original cost. Most of the land was purchased more than fifty years ago. The historical cost is reliable, but not very relevant. In contrast, the current value of the land is more relevant, but estimates of this current value are subjective. The prevailing view in Canada is that many current market value estimates are not sufficiently reliable to be included in the accounting records, even though they are more relevant. However, in some countries current market values are routinely used. For example, British Petroleum subtracted the "replacement cost of sales" in obtaining "replacement cost operating profit" of £2,501 million in 1993.

Objective 2

Identify the qualities that make information valuable.

For information to be relevant, it must help decision makers either predict the outcomes of future events (*predictive value*) or confirm or update past predictions (*feedback value*). Relevant information must also be available on a timely basis, that is, before a decision maker has to act. Information that does not help predict or confirm predictions, or is not available when it is needed, is not relevant.

Reliability is enhanced by *verifiability* (or *objectivity*), *neutrality*, and *validity*. **Verifiability** means that there would be a high degree of consensus among independent measurers of an item. For example, the amount paid for assets is highly verifiable, but the predicted cost to replace the assets usually is not.

verifiability A quality of information such that there would be a high degree of consensus among independent measurers of an item.

Validity (also called **representational faithfulness**) means a correspondence between the accounting numbers and the resources or events those numbers purport to represent. Consider goodwill, which represents excess earning power when a group of assets is acquired (i.e., excess of cost over the fair market value of the net assets acquired). Suppose such earning power disappears before the goodwill is completely amortized. The amount of goodwill on the balance sheet would no longer be a valid measure of excess earning power.

validity (representational faithfulness) A correspondence between the accounting numbers and the resources or events those numbers purport to represent.

Neutrality, or *freedom from bias*, means choosing accounting policies without attempting to achieve purposes other than measuring economic impact. In other words, financial reporting rules should not be used to achieve social policy objectives, nor should they be used to give an advantage to certain types of companies. For example, amortization methods for reporting to shareholders should not be chosen to encourage or discourage investment.

neutrality Choosing accounting policies without attempting to achieve purposes other than measuring economic impact; freedom from bias.

Tampering with accounting policies (standards or principles) to promote national goals is a dangerous path. First, research has demonstrated that accounting measurements per se are unlikely to affect investors' decisions if the timing and amounts of the underlying cash flows are unaffected. Therefore, such tampering is not likely to achieve its objectives. Second, tampering with policies would quickly erode the credibility of financial reporting to the detriment of the public interest.

The quality of neutrality underscores a fundamental approach taken by the CICA. Arguments about accounting issues should concentrate on how measurements and disclosure can improve the communication of economic phenomena. These issues should be resolved, however imperfectly, by determining how economic information is best disseminated in light of the costs and benefits for society as a whole.

The final items affecting usefulness are *comparability* and *consistency*. Information is more useful if it can be compared with similar information about other companies or with similar information for other reporting periods. For example, financial results for two companies are hard to compare if one uses FIFO and the other uses LIFO. Because identifying trends for a single company is difficult if accounting methods are continually changed, consistency in applying accounting methods over time is desirable. Moreover, firms must disclose their accounting methods so that users can determine the extent to which the financial statements of two firms are comparable.

Overview of Key Concepts

Exhibit 14-3 presents an overview of key concepts covered in this chapter and elsewhere in the text. A concrete example of each is provided, as is a listing of the chapters in the text that contain the main discussions or examples of the individual concepts. This entire tabulation should be a convenient guide for recalling and comparing some major ingredients of accounting's conceptual framework.

■ ACCOUNTING STANDARDS THROUGHOUT THE WORLD

This text has focused on the principles of accounting that are generally accepted in Canada. Nevertheless, practices of other countries have been mentioned throughout. This section elaborates on some of the basic differences among accounting reports in various countries.[2]

Although differences exist among countries, the most basic aspects of accounting are consistent throughout the world. Double-entry systems, accrual accounting, and the income statement and balance sheet are used worldwide. Therefore, similarities in financial reporting exceed the differences.

Differences in Tax and Inflation Accounting

Objective 3

Present examples of accounting standards in other countries that differ from those in Canada

One major area of differences in financial reporting is the influence of the income tax law on reporting to shareholders. In Appendix 10C, we emphasized that methods in Canada for reporting to tax authorities differ from those used for reporting to shareholders. In contrast, tax reporting and shareholder reporting are identical in many countries. For example, France has a "Plan Compatible" that specifies a National Uniform Chart of Accounts that is used for both tax returns and reporting to shareholders. German financial reporting

---

[2] For elaboration of the material in this section see F. Choi and G. Mueller, *International Accounting* (Upper Saddle River, NJ: Prentice Hall, 1992), especially Chap. 3, pp. 77–136.

is also determined primarily by tax laws. If accounting records are not kept according to strict tax laws, the German tax authorities can reject the records as a basis for taxation.

In some countries, tax laws have a major influence on shareholder reporting even if tax and shareholder reports are not required to be identical. In Japan, for example, certain principles are allowed for tax purposes only if they are also used for shareholder reporting. When such principles provide tax advantages, there is a tendency for companies to use them for reporting to shareholders.

In addition to the influence of the tax law, financial reporting of income taxes differs among countries. For example, in Argentina income tax expenses are recognized in financial statements only when payments are made to the government; in contrast, most countries accrue taxes when the related income is recognized. Sweden and Switzerland are two other countries that do not recognize deferred taxes. However, Britain, the Netherlands, and the United States recognize deferred taxes in a manner similar to Canada.

Another significant difference among countries is the extent to which financial statements account for inflation. In the 1980s, the CICA experimented with requiring supplementary disclosure of inflation-adjusted numbers. After years of accounting research on the value of these disclosures, the CICA concluded that the costs exceeded the benefits. Now no requirements for such supplementary disclosure exist in Canada. In contrast, many countries require full or partial adjustments for inflation for reporting to both shareholders and tax authorities. For example, Brazil has experienced persistent double- and triple-digit inflation rates and requires all statements to be adjusted for changes in the general price level in the manner described later in this chapter. Such inflation-adjusted statements are used for both tax and shareholder reporting. Argentina requires dual reporting. Companies must include two columns in financial statements, one for traditional historical-cost numbers and one for general price-level-adjusted numbers.

The Netherlands has been a leader in the application of current replacement-cost measurements to financial accounts, although it has no formal requirement mandating either historical cost or replacement cost. French financial statements include a partial inflation adjustment, using replacement cost for fixed assets. Similarly, Sweden allows (but does not require) the revaluation of certain property, plant, and equipment. Mexico requires inflation adjustments, but allows either price-level adjustments or current-cost statements.

Not surprisingly, countries that have experienced the lowest inflation rates have been the slowest to recognize inflation in their accounting statements. Japan has no recognition of inflation, and Germany has recommended supplementary disclosures, but few companies have responded.

Accounting Principles in Selected Countries

Accounting practices differ among countries for a variety of reasons, such as differences in government, economic systems, culture, and traditions. Throughout the text, we have mentioned some of the differences between Canada and the United States. Now we will briefly discuss how accounting in the United Kingdom, France, Germany, and Japan differs from that in Canada and the United States.

The Companies' Laws in the *United Kingdom* provide general guidance for accounting standards, and details are specified by the Accounting Standards Board, a private-sector body sponsored by the accountancy profession. U.K. companies can use either historical-cost or current-cost accounting, or a mixture of the two. For example, British Petroleum reports both "Historical cost operating profit" and "Replacement cost operating profit" on its income statement. LIFO is not allowed for either tax or shareholder reporting; research expenditures are charged to expense, but development expenses can be capitalized; purchased goodwill is usually written off immediately.

France leads the way in national uniform accounting. Companies must use a National Uniform Chart of Accounts, and financial reporting requirements are extensive. Accounting records are considered legal control devices more than sources of information for decision makers. Accounting methods such as pooling-of-interests, LIFO, and capitalization of leases are not allowed. Research and development costs can be capitalized but must be amortized over no more than five years, and goodwill is amortized over five to twenty-five years. Future pension obligations are not recognized as liabilities. Two reporting requirements are unique to France: (1) companies must publish an annual social balance sheet relating to environmental matters and employee conditions and benefits, and (2) companies must publish comprehensive financial forecasts.

Tax law dominates financial reporting in *Germany*; whatever is reported to shareholders must also be reported to tax authorities. Therefore, accounting standards are based on statutes and court decisions, and they are not necessarily directed at producing statements useful for decision making. Both FIFO and LIFO are allowed, but they must correspond to the physical flow of inventory. Goodwill must be written off over fifteen years. Amortization is based on specific tax-amortization schedules. Statements of changes in financial position are not required, but many companies provide them anyway. Consolidated statements are required, but exceptions are granted for many companies. Although German accounting standards have grown closer to Canadian standards since World War II, they remain significantly different.

Accounting and finance play a smaller role in *Japanese* companies and in the Japanese economy than in other industrialized countries. Accounting is dominated by the central government, especially the Ministry of Finance. There is extensive cross-ownership among Japanese firms, and banks are often heavily involved with companies to whom they lend money. Debt capital is used much more than equity capital. Because large creditors can obtain extensive information easily, there is less need for public financial disclosure to capital market participants such as individual investors. Japan almost reveres historical cost accounting; current cost data cannot even be given as supplementary information. Consolidated statements are required, though many significant subsidiaries are still excluded from the consolidated statements. Goodwill is based on the difference between purchase price and book value (not fair market value) of net assets acquired. Goodwill, research and development expenditures, and many other intangible assets must be written off over five years or less. Few leases are capitalized, and pension obligations are not recognized as liabilities. In general, Japanese accounting standards are very conservative. One study showed that the average net income for a Japanese firm is 58% below the amount that would be reported using U.S. accounting standards. This is one of the reasons that price-earnings ratios of Japanese firms average more than double those of Canadian and U.S. firms.

TABLE OF CONTENTS

A BRIEF HISTORY

On May 2nd 1670, King Charles II granted a Charter to 18 investors incorporating them as the Governor and Company of Adventurers of England trading into Hudson's Bay ("HBC"). This followed the successful voyage of the ketch "Nonsuch", to trade for furs.

During its first century, HBC established forts on Hudson Bay and traded with the Native Peoples. In its second century, the Company ventured inland to meet growing competition from the North West Company. Over this two hundred year period the Company contributed in many ways to the discovery and development of the territory that was to become Canada. The two rival companies amalgamated in 1821 under the Hudson's Bay Company name.

Company Charter under inspection at Canadian Conservation Institute in Ottawa.

In 1870, two hundred years after the Company's formation, HBC's chartered territory, Ruperts Land, was transferred to the Government of Canada in return for farm lands in the prairie provinces. These lands were sold to settlers over the next 85 years.

Early in the 20th century, HBC turned its attention to retailing which became its most important activity. HBC built downtown department stores in each of the major cities of western Canada (1913 - 1968). It moved into eastern Canada through acquisitions (Morgans in 1960 and Freimans in 1971) and expanded to the suburbs of major Canadian cities beginning in the 1960's.

HBC acquired Zellers in 1978 and Simpsons the following year. Simpsons was merged into the Bay over the period 1986 -1991. Towers was acquired and merged into Zellers in 1990/1991. In 1993, stores in British Columbia and Alberta were acquired from the former Woodward's. Also in 1993, HBC acquired Linmark, a major buying organization in the Far East.

HBC acquired control of Markborough Properties in 1973 and real estate became an important segment of HBC's activities until Markborough was spun-off to HBC shareholders in 1990.

HBC had major investments in oil and gas (Hudson's Bay Oil & Gas, Siebens and Roxy Petroleum) between 1950 and 1987.

In the mid-1980's, HBC disposed of a number of "non-strategic" assets including its Northern Stores, Wholesale and Fur divisions.

In 1979, Kenneth R. Thomson and his family interests acquired a controlling interest in HBC. This was reduced to 25% by a secondary offering in 1992 and has subsequently declined to 22%.

At its three hundredth anniversary, in 1970, HBC was continued as a Canadian corporation.

Hudson's Bay Company

FINANCIAL HIGHLIGHTS

Hudson's Bay Company

	1996 $millions	1995 $millions
Sales and Revenue	6,007.2	5,984.5
Operating Profit	251.2	214.5
Net Earnings	36.1	34.6
Net Earnings before Restructuring Costs	72.5	34.6
Cash Flow From Earnings	188.5	162.0
Capital Expenditures	121.0	238.5
Debt:Equity Ratio	0.62:1	0.86:1

Per Share	$	$
Net Earnings	0.61	0.59
Net Earnings before Restructuring Costs	1.22	0.59
Cash Flow From Earnings	3.18	2.79
Dividends	0.72	0.92
Equity	29.92	30.24

the Bay

	1996 $millions	1995 $millions
Sales and Revenue	2,332.7	2,348.6
Operating Profit	131.1	121.1
Assets Employed	1,213.0	1,477.8

Zellers

	1996 $millions	1995 $millions
Sales and Revenue	3,578.5	3,536.6
Operating Profit	116.4	106.7
Assets Employed	1,567.8	1,694.1

Hudson's Bay Company

COMPANY PROFILE

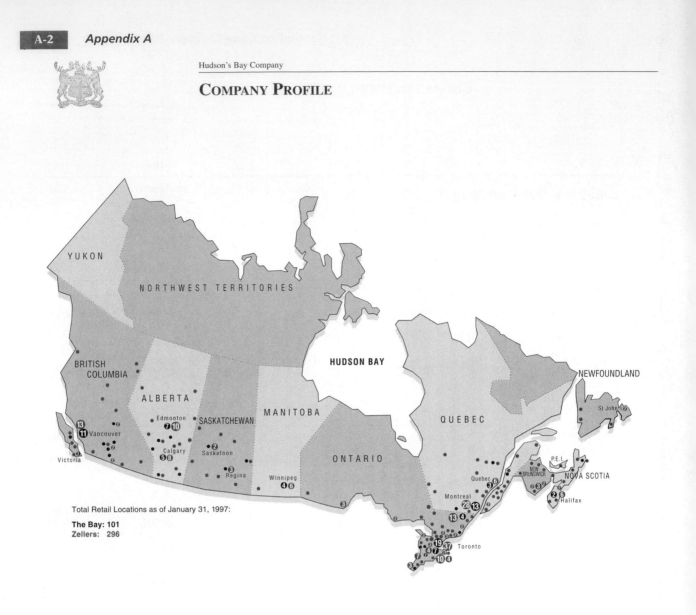

Total Retail Locations as of January 31, 1997:

The Bay: 101
Zellers: 296

Corporate

Hudson's Bay Company, established in 1670, is Canada's oldest corporation and its largest department store retailer.

Through its major operating divisions, the Bay and Zellers, Hudson's Bay Company covers the Canadian retail market across all price zones and from coast to coast. It accounts for approximately 39% of Canadian department store sales and almost 8% of all retail sales, other than food and automobiles.

The Company aims to develop its human and material resources and capitalize on its experience in merchandising to anticipate and satisfy the needs of customers for the goods and services they seek at fair prices, and thereby earn a satisfactory return for its shareholders.

The Bay

The Bay is Canada's fashion department store with 101 locations coast to coast. Stores are positioned in the mid-range urban and suburban markets, with a strong franchise in the downtown core of major cities. The Bay is predominately a soft goods retailer concentrating on fashion merchandise and soft home categories. Customers are offered quality merchandise at popular price points combined with traditional department store guarantees and services. The Bay promotes its own credit card and accepts major bank cards. Merchandise selection, procurement and sales promotion are centralized. A number of service functions are integrated on a corporate basis to reduce cost and improve operating efficiency.

Bay stores are marketed by price level and fashion appeal to fit the communities in which they are located. The stores vary in size from 21,000 square feet in Banff, Alberta to 890,000 square feet in downtown Toronto, with most suburban stores in the 140,000 to 180,000 square foot range.

Zellers

Zellers is the leading national chain of discount department stores. It targets the budget-minded customer with the assurance of the lowest price. Excellent values are offered in both national and private brand merchandise and these are communicated aggressively with frequent advertising in both print and electronic media. Zellers is further distinguished by Club Z, its customer loyalty rewards program. Zellers is successful in its competitive retail segment by operating with a low expense rate.

Zellers stores are characterized by self service and central checkout. Zellers markets its own credit card and accepts those of the major banks. Merchandising and sales promotion are centrally directed. Zellers operates 296 stores across Canada, mainly in shopping malls. The average store is 77,500 square feet with new stores in the 90,000 to 125,000 square foot range.

Store Statistics
(January 31, 1997)

	Stores	Square Feet (000's)
British Columbia	19	3,160
Alberta	17	2,517
Saskatchewan	3	457
Manitoba	4	1,044
Ontario	36	6,212
Quebec	19	3,008
Nova Scotia	3	384
	101	16,782

Store Statistics
(January 31, 1997)

	Stores	Square Feet (000's)
British Columbia	33	2,562
Alberta	29	2,248
Saskatchewan	13	812
Manitoba	7	525
Ontario	118	9,443
Quebec	61	5,018
New Brunswick	12	739
Nova Scotia	15	1,081
Prince Edward Island	3	209
Newfoundland	5	305
	296	22,942

"GROWTH IS AN ESSENTIAL PART OF OUR CORPORATE CULTURE"

During 1996, we implemented numerous major initiatives designed to return the Company to previous levels of profitability.

Vision and determination were key to the success of these initiatives, ensuring that what "must happen" in this radically changed competitive and economic environment would "actually happen".

We needed to move quickly and decisively...

However, before the necessary changes could be implemented, we engaged in a process of self-discovery and self-assessment – through identifying the deficiencies of the past – and the shortcomings of the present. This process has also allowed us to ensure the strengths of the past will be reinforced while we relentlessly pursue the opportunities for the future.

George J. Kosich
President and
Chief Executive Officer

With the evaluation stage behind us, the economic rejuvenation and human renewal of our corporation truly got under way. We needed to move quickly and decisively, and we needed the support and insight of our executives. We needed dynamic change that would capture the attention and commitment of our employees.

The solution, we discovered, has as much to do with "people" as it has with "strategy". To garner the maximum cost leverage and management expertise available, we needed a lightning-fast, proactive organizational change program that would enhance performance through both vertical and horizontal focus.

We refined our existing strategies in all facets of our businesses to neutralize our competition and to enhance our current and future strengths.

We also needed a quantified gross profit growth and protection strategy and a productivity improvement plan to ensure a reduced expense rate.

An initial stage of our new strategy was the relocation of Zellers' Administrative and Marketing Offices from Montreal to Toronto – a major step completed during the summer of 1996. All operating areas have now been effectively integrated with the operations of the Bay and Hudson's Bay Corporate. In addition, the organizational structures in all areas of operation have been redefined and provided with the tools and technology required to succeed.

Although our program of corporate re-engineering and restructuring is now largely complete, we also understand that the process of change is continuous.

Our concentration will be on growth.

One of our main objectives is "business growth". Sales growth in our existing store base, plus incremental growth from expanded and new stores, will be our top priority.

We make this commitment at a time when many retail companies have been shelving plans for expansion, focusing instead on rationalization, restructuring, downsizing and divestitures. We believe companies that pursue this strategy and abandon their faith in growth are mistaken.

It should never be forgotten that growth is an imperative at all times for all businesses in all sectors regardless of the economic climate or the competitive environment. Growth attracts investors, reinforces competitive positioning, energizes the total organization and attracts and retains the best employees. Growth is self-perpetuating fed by the belief in growth itself.

Some companies mistakenly assume that opportunities for growth are determined primarily by external factors such as competitors, technology and logistics.

However, the best companies, both in Canada and around the world, have managed to sustain consistent growth during poor economic cycles and in fiercely competitive industries. Growth is always possible when senior management believes in it and when that belief is instilled throughout the organization.

Persuading an organization to believe in endless possibilities for growth is every leader's responsibility. It is not automatic. We must create an environment in which people feel comfortable in challenging established beliefs. Leaders of growth companies must encourage risk-taking and discourage an "it-can't-be-done" attitude.

Growth creates a vital, enthusiastic corporation where people see genuine personal opportunity and personal satisfaction. They take calculated risks. They work harder, smarter and with greater job satisfaction. For that reason, growth must be an essential part of our corporate culture.

Our performance in 1996 shows a substantial improvement in operating results. With our new organizational structure, renewed determination and vision and our emphasis on growth, we are certain our results will show steady and continuous improvement in the years to come.

George J. Kosich
President and Chief Executive Officer

Growth creates a vital, enthusiastic corporation...

Hudson's Bay Company

DIRECTORS' REPORT TO SHAREHOLDERS

Summary

The year 1996 will almost certainly be remembered as an important and pivotal year for Hudson's Bay Company and its two operating companies: the Bay and Zellers.

Most immediately notable is the significant improvement in the Company's operating performance and earnings from disappointing results reported last year. Earnings before unusual items increased from $35 million to $73 million, or from $0.59 per share to $1.22.

For a full analysis of the 1996 financial results and a comparison with the prior two years, readers are referred to Management's Discussion & Analysis (MD&A) presented on pages 21-26 of this Report. The MD&A describes in some detail the factors that contributed to the operating profit improvement of $37 million – 17.2% on a 0.4% increase in revenues.

After a sustained period of economic sluggishness, the improvement in the Canadian economic climate contributed to the Company's improved performance.

More than that, however, the results of 1996 represent deeper structural changes within the Company itself. Over the past several years, the Company has engaged in a major process of internal re-evaluation. Guaging the impact of a permanently altered economic landscape... learning to react and respond to the most aggressive single competitor the Company has ever faced... and having the fortitude to undertake major internal realignments... these developments have given the Company a renewed sense of direction and dedication. As we prepare to go forward at the approach of the coming millennium, these are lessons – and survival skills – that will ably serve the Company, together with its family of employees, suppliers, customers and investors, to the year 2000 and well beyond.

David E. Mitchell
Governor

Significant Events

Foremost among the Company's behind-the-scenes activities of the past year was the consolidation of the administrative and marketing offices of Zellers with those of the Bay and Hudson's Bay Company. This entailed the move, completed in mid-summer 1996, of nearly 300 Zellers associates from Montreal to the corporate headquarters in Toronto. Although many of the activities which are not visible to our customers have been combined, each of the Bay and Zellers will continue to maintain its own unique identity and public image.

Henceforth, Canada's two largest retailers in their respective market categories will enjoy the added efficiencies of integrated buying and of support systems in accounting, control, distribution and management information systems.

In announcing the consolidation in March 1996, the Company indicated a total cost of $64 million, with a payback period of three and a half years. Savings achieved through combined purchasing power and increased efficiencies resulting from added leverage and the elimination of duplicate functions contributed to fourth quarter profits.

In addition to a new corporate home, 1996 also provided the Zellers organization with a new corporate leader. Millard E. Barron, a respected name in North American retailing circles, took over as President and Chief Operating Officer of Zellers in September. Mr. Barron also became an Executive Vice-President of Hudson's Bay Company.

Mr. Barron has rapidly gained the confidence of colleagues and associates as well as of the Board.

Near the close of the fiscal year, the Company announced that it had established a securitization program involving the sale of undivided ownership interests in pools of selected Bay and Zellers credit card receivables. Proceeds of the sale – an aggregate of $300 million – are being used to finance expansion and reduce outstanding debt.

Bay store in Richmond, B.C. underwent major expansion in 1996

The Marketplace

Ending a prolonged spell of lean economic conditions – with consumer spending taking a severe battering from weak economic fundamentals – 1996 finally offered the beginnings of the turnaround that retailers throughout the North American marketplace had long been awaiting. After more than 20 successive quarters of weakness, economic conditions finally began to brighten in the second quarter of 1996 and went on to end the year with a visible upward momentum.

Chief among the favourable features of 1996 was a continuous downward ratcheting of interest rates. A total of 10 rate reductions over as many months brought the prime tumbling to 4.75% by November – a historic 40-year low and the level at which it remained for the balance of the year. Equally, fiscal and monetary measures at the national level led to a reduction in the rate of increase in the Consumer Price Index (CPI), resulting in close to historic lows in the country's rate of inflation.

The combination of low interest rates and low inflation had an important stimulative impact on economic recovery, leading to a modest rise in consumer confidence in the second half of 1996. Fourth quarter economic growth of 2.3% , combined with a return to more active consumer spending over the all-important Christmas period, made an important contribution to retailers' bottom lines for the year as a whole.

In spite of the welcome surge occurring in the fourth quarter, overall economic growth during the year was 1.5%, a decline from the growth rate of 2.2% of the previous year. Social adjustment traumas, including layoffs, down-sizings and government cutbacks, continued to be felt intermittently in pockets throughout the country. Nevertheless, the economic mood brightened as the year progressed, with aggregate new job creation marginally exceeding job losses. Sales of Department Store Type Merchandise (DSTM) increased by 4.5% in the fourth quarter, bringing the increase for the whole year up to 2.6%.

Outlook for 1997

Entering 1997, improving economic factors show convincing signs of sustained momentum. Some degree of unevenness is expected on a regional basis, with economic performance expected to be highest in Ontario and Alberta while the rest of the country lags slightly behind. Growth projection for the Canadian economy as a whole for 1997 is 3.0%.

For the retail sector the outlook for 1997 is more buoyant than in recent years. In particular, the growth in housing starts – already showing signs of a healthy rebound – is a harbinger of increased consumer spending on household furnishings.

During 1997, the Hudson's Bay organization expects to realize the rewards of several years of sustained investment in new and expanded stores and in improved systems and operational refinements. Efficiencies achieved through the corporate restructuring, described above, are expected to impact the bottom line in 1997 and beyond.

Heritage

In April 1996, His Royal Highness The Prince of Wales presided at a ceremony at the Manitoba Museum of Man and Nature marking the official dedication of a new wing, to be completed in 1997, to house the Hudson's Bay Company Museum Collection.

On display at this ceremony was the original parchment document created nearly 327 years ago as the originating Charter of the Governor and Company of Adventurers of England trading into Hudson's Bay – the original and still official name of Hudson's Bay Company. This historic Charter document, granted and sealed by order of King Charles II on May 2nd 1670, was flown under escort to Winnipeg specifically for the royal visit.

On its return to Toronto, the Company arranged to have the condition of the Charter scientifically evaluated to determine the most appropriate means of ensuring its safety and preservation in perpetuity. We are deeply grateful to experts from both the Canadian Conservation Institute and the National Research Council of Canada who inspected and analyzed the document using the latest technology and equipment, some of which has only recently become available. Initial reports indicate that the Charter is in excellent condition – surprisingly so for a document of its age. We are committed to ensuring that it is maintained in similar condition for future generations.

Appreciation

Entering a new chapter in the Company's history – and especially mindful of the successful consolidation of all operations at corporate headquarters in Toronto – the directors wish to express their particular appreciation to all employees, staff and associates for the dedication and hard work that went into making 1996 a true "turnaround" year. The Board wishes to note with gratitude the employees of Zellers who coped with the difficulty of relocating their families during a time of exceptional work pressure.

Sincere thanks are in order to the Company's dedicated network of vendors, suppliers and private brand manufacturers – throughout Canada, North America and overseas. Through their tremendous talents and efforts, Hudson's Bay Company continues to be able to offer its customers a broad, competitively priced and most attractive selection of merchandise.

Ultimately, the Company has the consumers of Canada to thank for their demanding tastes. It is because of their high standards that Hudson's Bay Company finds itself constantly striving to reach new heights of excellence in all aspects of our mission and our work.

On behalf of the Board,

David E. Mitchell
Governor

George J. Kosich
President and Chief Executive Officer

March 6, 1997

Hudson's Bay Company

WINNING AT RETAILING

New Bay store in Cambridge Centre, Ontario

Setting the Stage

Much has changed since the days more than three centuries ago when the vast territories of newly discovered Canada seemed to many early explorers and settlers like an endless feeding-ground for blackflies and mosquitoes, and Canada's strategic potential on the world's stage was dismissed by European diplomats as "quelques arpents de neige" ("just a few acres of snow").

One thing that has not changed is the core mission of the Governor and Company of Adventurers of England trading into Hudson's Bay – meeting the needs of the customer of the day.

in so doing, changed the course of history. Today, nearly 327 years later, the same proud company is still at work, with its central mission, and many of the skills needed to support this mission, remaining fundamentally the same.

now, is providing consumers with the products they want – a complex, multi-disciplinary commercial activity at which HBC has been successfully engaged for longer than all but a very few other organizations anywhere in the world. ...continued on page 10

New Zellers store in Cambridge Centre, Ontario

The original driving goal of this, the first of all Canadian companies, was to locate, acquire, transport, package and deliver the specialty product – beaver pelts – that drove the buying habits of the consumer class of 17th century Europe. It was the fashion craze for beaver hats that mobilized capital and human energy – and,

Images of voyageur canoes, trappers' lines, wooden stockades and striped woolen blankets may seem little more than quaint foot notes to history. In fact, they are potent reminders that today's Hudson's Bay Company (HBC) remains part of an unbroken tradition of continuous business activity. That business, then as

Message from Bob Peter, President of the Bay

Front:
Bob Peter,
President of the Bay
Back Row:
Barry Agnew,
Vice-President, Sales
Promotion
Sheilagh Blight,
Vice-President,
Ready-To-Wear
Fashion Merchandise
Steve Wolfenden,
Vice-President,
Home Decorating,
Home Operating,
and Cosmetics

The Bay's mission and commitment to be Canada's fashion department store remains unchanged and, despite a soft market for most of the year, much was accomplished.

The addition of exciting new lines of women's and men's clothing as well as a wider selection of styles across most ready to wear and accessory departments combined to offer more choice for customers. Brand new names like Tommy Hilfiger and Nautica for ladies, Muskoka Lakes and Fila for men were added in 1996. Those, together with increasing the number of outlets for other lines like Carolee and Alfred Dunner enabled us to bring to consumers the best assortments of fashion merchandise across all price lines.

In addition to the new 130,000 square foot store in Cambridge, Ontario and the 50,000 square foot expansion (to 150,000 square feet) of the Richmond, B.C. store, minor renovations were completed in 12 stores, the majority on the fashion and cosmetic floors.

A very important factor in both of these strategies was, and is the partnership and joint planning with our key vendors. In 12 stores last year, Levis "North American Shops" were installed, showcasing a broad range of products in men's, ladies' and children's wear, accessories and jewelry. In cosmetics, vendor partnerships with Lauder, Clinique, Lancôme, MAC, Dior, Clarins, Nectar and Yves Rocher, produced new personalized installations across the country.

The Bay's exclusive brands, the final plank in creating the very best in fashionability, providing both value and quality, were also expanded during the year. Selected vendors produce clothing, footwear and many other products to the Bay's exacting standards.

For the future we see no major changes to these strategies save continual improvement and dedication to provide to all our customers the newest and latest styles at the best prices.

None of the above improvements would have come without the hard work and dedication of all the Bay's staff and associates and I express my thanks and appreciation to them. I would also like to acknowledge the help and cooperation of all of our vendors.

While there is no doubt that we operate in one of, if not the most competitive retail markets in the world, I am confident, that with the continued support of our vendor partners and the dedication of our associates, we will provide our customers with Canada's destination fashion department store.

Bob Peter, President, the Bay

Bay and Zellers Overview

By the early decades of the twentieth century, most of the dynamic factors shaping Canada's modern economic development were already set in place. Canada had grown westward through immigration, encouraged by settlement on lands formerly owned by HBC and the impact of the trans-continental railway. The Company's retailing activities had developed from trading posts supplying merchandise to meet the needs of trappers to small retail stores and continued to grow. As a leading buyer of goods for sale to consumers – both domestic and foreign – HBC began building large retail outlets (by then known as "department stores") in downtown locations in the major cities across western Canada.

Moving into the second half of the 20th century, HBC expanded its operations into eastern Canada through the acquisition of smaller, rival companies – Morgans of Montreal and Freimans of Ottawa. At the same time, HBC began its expansion from downtown locations into the newly emerging suburbs of major Canadian cities.

With the Canadian retail market already beginning to segment itself along the key differentials of price and consumer

Scratch & Save Day at the Bay...

...continued on page 11

Canadian Sourcing

As the leading – indeed, as the original – Canadian corporate citizen, Hudson's Bay Company is a committed supporter of the manufacturing industry in Canada – from garments to gadgets... from plastic to pantyhose... from telephones to towels.

Cambridge Towels in Cambridge, Ontario, manufactures quality towels for both the Bay and Zellers.

Whether at the Bay or at Zellers, the Company's policy on Canadian products is unequivocal and unwavering: "Whenever fashion, quality and value are the same or better, we will buy Canadian first".

Together the Bay and Zellers support in excess of 5,000 Canadian suppliers from whom they purchase a wide variety of merchandise to be found in just about every department in our stores.

Products from many of our domestic suppliers are automatically re-ordered on a weekly basis. Quick turnaround of these orders is achieved through the electronic sharing of sales data and the issuance of purchase orders directly from our computer to those of the vendors.

As well, many other merchandise lines, including greeting cards, music and video, hosiery and ties, are managed by our vendors on a store by store basis. This allows the Company to benefit from their product knowledge and expertise in meeting the specific needs of different stores and markets.

Doris Hosiery in Montreal, Quebec, makes fine panty-hose for Hudson's Bay Company.

Jeno Neuman & Fils in Boisbriand, Quebec, designs and manufactures private brand ladies' sportswear for the Bay.

Rubbermaid in Mississauga, Ontario manufactures a wide variety of plastic household products.

targets, HBC took the strategic step in 1978 of expanding its market reach by acquiring control of Montreal-based Zeller's Limited, by then an important force in a growing new category – "discount retailing" – with more than 150 stores across Canada. HBC's rapid grasp of retail segmentation was further reinforced less than three months later with the acquisition of Simpsons, Limited of Toronto – with 20 department stores in eastern Canada – known for its high-end customers and leadership in fashion retailing. As the pace of acquisitions quickened, HBC continued to consolidate its leadership position in Canadian retailing – both in traditional and, increasingly, in discount stores – with the purchase, in this decade, of the Woodwards traditional and Towers discount department store chains, in western and eastern Canada, respectively.

As the largest non-food retailer in Canada, HBC enjoys the leading position in two distinct franchises that drive the industry in Canada today: the traditional department store market and the discount segment. With past mergers now absorbed, the category of traditional stores is embodied in the Bay's 101 stores, and the discount segment is represented by Zellers 296 retail outlets, making it the leading force in discount marketing in Canada.

Clearly defining these market segments, differentiating their values, protecting their franchises and supporting them with a full arsenal of modern retailing techniques, lies at the heart of HBC's corporate mission in today's competitive retail marketplace.

...continued on page 12

and suburban markets, together with a strong franchise in many downtown city cores, as predominantly a soft goods retailer concentrating in fashion merchandise and soft home categories. As additional positioning elements, customers at the Bay are offered quality merchandise at popular price points combined with traditional department store guarantees and services.

Conversely, the elements determining the in-store shopping experience offered by Zellers are driven by different criteria. Zellers positions itself as the leading national chain in the discount department store category, targeting budget-minded customers with assurances of the lowest price. Zellers' choice of assortments is based on offering national and private brand merchandise priced to provide value to customers. Zellers has a policy of generating store traffic through frequent advertising in print and electronic media. Further, Zellers engages its

Designer fashion for ladies at the Bay

...continued on page 16

Distribution Network

While most Canadians are familiar with both Bay and Zellers stores, what they never see is the extensive behind-the-scenes network of support systems.

Once our buyers and merchants have identified specific items required in each and every store, a vast support structure takes over to ensure that the right products get to the right stores at the right time.

We determine with vendors the most effective shipment preparation and packing. We also decide whether to ship using vendors' equipment, common carriers or HBC's own fleet of trailers. For import shipments we decide which ocean carriers, consolidators and forwarders to use. While most shipments flow directly through the Company's eight major distribution centres, each centre can perform additional services including re-sorting, storage, hanging fashion merchandise and verifying incoming shipments.

Hudson's Bay Company was the first to use 53 foot containers

From distribution centres, the Company services stores as far apart as Newfoundland and Vancouver Island. Nearby stores are typically supplied by Company trucks, while railways are extensively used to regional depots en route to distant stores. Upon arrival at the store most merchandise is moved directly to the sales floor.

Every store sale is entered into one of more than 10,000 electronic cash registers where each item's unique code is scanned and recorded as is the method of payment. Credit and debit card transactions are authorized electronically. Radio frequency remote scanning devices are used to record transactions such as transfers.

An extensive communications network connects every company unit to the central computer where each transaction is recorded, accumulated and analyzed into formats required for decision making and control. Managers and associates company-wide, access this information through more than 6,000 computer terminals, personal computers and radio frequency devices. Appropriate access is available to third party credit authorizers and to vendors.

We are constantly improving the Company's supply chain management and are already capitalizing on the benefits offered through having a single organization supporting both the Bay and Zellers.

Private Brands

The HBC organization is the leader in the development of private brands. The mission of HBC's private brands department is to develop products which are similar to well known "national brands" but which offer "the same or better quality and fashionability at a better price".

Every season, HBC's private brands department – a staff of more than 50 experts in design, fashion, packaging, manufacturing technology and importing – undertakes the complex task of evaluating consumer trends and making calculated predictions about consumer buying habits.

To further enhance its expertise in product development, HBC has created a close relationship as a shareholder of the Atkins Group, a New York-based firm specializing in the development of private brands for retail clients around the world.

Both the Bay and Zellers offer a broad range of private brand products. As Canada's leading fashion store, private brands at the Bay are especially strong in clothing and linen goods. These successful in-house brands include Principles, Northern Spirit and Charter Collection. At Zellers, private brands include Caroll Reed, Home Styles, Northern Climate and Venture. In total, nearly 33% of the Company's sales can be attributed to private brands which were developed – and sourced either in Canada or overseas– by HBC's own in-house experts.

Our private brands are a major point of differentiation between ourselves and our competitors. We will continue to fine-tune their development and improve their fashionability.

Take the case of a "Principles" brand winter parka. The product development and buyers' team decided to combine the outer nylon shell from a supplier in Italy... the inner viscose lining from a Taiwanese mill... the hollofill insulation from a source in the United States... the zipper and fittings from a Japanese manufacturer... with the final product assembled in Korea. In addition to these complicated production elements, the other key features of the product – design, style, colour and fashionability – were selected five to six months in advance of the selling season.

Bay Fashion Leadership

Central to the strategic position of the Bay as Canada's largest department store is its continuing leadership in fashion. In all its dominant product lines, the Bay's choice of assortments is determined by a judicious balance between national brands ("brand names") and private brands (the Bay's own labels).

The Bay's customers are presented with leading products – often heavily advertised in national and international media and sought out on the basis of the "name". Once in the store, customers are exposed to an additional assortment of benchmark private brand products, created specifically by the Bay, against which perceptions of price, value and fashionability can be directly measured and tested.

During the past several years, the Bay has mapped out a deliberate "blueprint" of commodity areas targeted for fashion dominance and top-of-mind awareness. As a result of this strategy, the Bay today enjoys market leadership in a number of department store categories across Canada. These include: women's and men's clothing, cosmetics, intimate apparel, jewelry, linens, home "white goods" and housewares. As market leadership is achieved, new target categories are added. Once the Bay has identified product segments for leadership, the strategic initiatives needed to establish market domination are quickly rolled into place. Most important is the accurate targeting – and sourcing – of the appropriate mix of assortments.

In the clothing segment, for example, the Bay continues to pursue an aggressive approach towards building strong partnerships with manufacturers of leading national brands. Powerful relationships have been formed with many of the best known "brand names" in the fashion business today, including names such as Ralph Lauren, Tommy Hilfiger, Liz Claiborne, Jones New York, Nautica, Levis and Calvin Klein.

Spring fashion at St. Regis Room, downtown, Toronto, exclusively designed for the Bay by Yves St.Laurent under the "encore" label.

Two of the new wave fashion styles available at the Bay – Nautica and Tommy Hilfiger

customers directly through an active program of incentives and rewards – most notably through "Club Z", the largest and most successful customer loyalty program in North America.

Buying Decisions

Guided by a clear vision of their positioning in the marketplace, together with the demographics of target customers, both the Bay and Zellers are able to identify the precise mix of products – or "assortments" – to meet the needs and expectations of their respective customer base, refined to the level of each individual store.

Store Location Management

The Bay and Zellers pay the utmost attention to two critical details about each of the nearly 400 stores they operate: location and size.

The Bay and Zellers maintain vigilant tracking systems to measure the performance of every store on a regular basis. Indicators can quickly show whether a store is performing well – or whether it is out-of-step with the surrounding consumer demographic base.

The output from this steady, ongoing analysis provides a constant review, both for the Bay and Zellers, of their competitive positions in every marketplace they serve. It is from this raw data that key Company decisions are made. Stores opened... stores renovated... stores expanded... stores closed. The decision to open or close a store is strategically driven, supported by analytical data and underscored by a commitment from the Company to serve its customers by providing the best solution in the best location.

The Bay and Zellers operate with a keen awareness of the need to provide the ideal "customer shopping experience". As retailing trends continue to evolve, optimum store size is increasing. For the Bay, new stores are typically in the range of 140,000 to 180,000 square feet; new Zellers stores are smaller, at about 90,000 to 125,000 square feet.

Activity across Canada in 1996 demonstrated a number of strategic changes in store location and size. At the Bay, one new store was opened, one was renovated and expanded and one store was closed – for a net increase of 116,000 square feet of retail space. At Zellers, eight new locations were opened, 10 were renovated or expanded and 12 were closed – for a net gain of 360,000 square feet.

The Bay downtown, Vancouver, B.C.

Typical new Bay regional store

Typical new Zellers store

For its part, the Bay's buying decisions flow directly from its strategic mission to be the destination of choice as Canada's fashion store. In identifying the mix of product assortments it needs to maintain leadership in its market category, the Bay has targeted core departments that meet its marketing objectives and, equally, has identified a number of others to be de-emphasized. Broadly, the Bay is reducing its emphasis on commodity goods and general merchandise while moving to consolidate its position in fashion items and soft goods.

With equal clarity, Zellers has identified its own priority businesses and is concentrating on offering a leading combination of assortments – always within the price ranges appropriate for the Zellers customer.

Infrastructure: the powerhouse behind-the-scenes

A high percentage of Canadians are familiar with Bay and Zellers stores in their communities. In the case of Zellers alone, for example, the sheer number of active participants in the

...continued on page 18

Profile:
Walter P. Zeller

Like many a success story, it began as a modest venture, yet, even then, many naysayers considered it a daring risk.

The year was 1931. Canada was barely climbing out of the Great Depression when Walter P. Zeller, third generation son of a Swiss farming family from Kitchener-Waterloo, put together enough collateral to buy up the assets of a struggling chain of 14 drygoods stores scattered across central and southwestern Ontario. At age 41, Walter Zeller could only dream that his little business venture would grow steadily to become Canada's largest discount store organization.

The first stores bearing the "Zeller's" name and its newly-minted slogan – "Retailers to Thrifty Canadians" – set the stage for what was to become a pace-setting institution for value-conscious shoppers from coast to coast. Undeterred by near-bankruptcy in the company's second year, Walter P. worked slowly and steadily through the depression and the war years, successfully doubling the number of stores in the first decade and doubling them again in the second. Sales grew five-fold – then ten-fold. By the end of the first decade, the company broke through the magic threshold of $10 million in sales.

With the head office relocated to Montreal, centre of Canada's garment industry, Zeller's continuously set new industry standards as it grew – from ambitious in-store features including drugstores and luncheonettes to far-sighted company human resource policies. The innovative "Better Relations Committees" set the pace for labour-management relations in the retail sector when set up in 1942 and have remained in place ever since.

Ever loyal to the rules of the company he founded, Walter P. retired as President at age 65 in 1956, just one year short of the company's 25th anniversary and two years before his death. In his final letter to company shareholders, Walter P. thanked his fellow 2,800 employees for their "loyalty, progressiveness and energy" – qualities that continued to serve the company on its steady path toward becoming the largest discount retail store in Canada.

company's Club Z loyalty program – over nine million members – means that Zellers has regular customers almost equivalent in number to the official census of households in Canada.

In spite of this unparalleled level of corporate visibility, what most Canadians never see is the equally extensive behind-the-scenes network of technological and support systems which also form a vital part of the HBC organization.

As the largest single bulk purchaser of non-food consumer end-goods in Canada – both from Canadian-made sources and from overseas markets – the Hudson's Bay organization also entails a vast network of distribution, transportation and communications facilities and systems needed to bring these goods to market. Many elements of HBC's systems are regarded as state-of-the-art within the retailing industry worldwide.

Since the year-end, HBC has taken the further step of launching the Company on the World Wide Web, with a new HBC homepage inter-linking company information as well as on-line shopping services.

Going forward, HBC remains committed to maintaining its dominant position across all price zones within the Canadian retail sector through continuous investment and improvement in all aspects of its core businesses.

As HBC continues to play a leadership role within the Canadian retail sector, the Company

...continued on page 20

Community Involvement

Through a web of family, friends and neighbours, hundreds of communities and neighborhoods across Canada have direct, personal links with the familiar and reassuring presence of the Bay or Zellers operating in their midst. For many Canadians, the Bay and Zellers are also known as community-based businesses that stand behind a large number of civic and charitable activities.

Every year, a wide variety of community-based social and charitable events are made possible because men and

Moonwalkers... staff and family members from the Zellers store in Red Deer, Alberta

women from the Bay and Zellers give of their time, energies and talents as volunteers, planners and community activators. The Company supports these efforts with resources and supplies to help to bring these community events to life.

The Company and its employees are very significant contributors to United Way and Centraide campaigns across Canada

and a major commitment every year is the Bay's Christmas season "Charity Bear" program.

The Zellers "Moonwalk" attracts thousands of community volunteers. Based on the "walk-a-thon" concept – in this case, to march the equivalent distance from the Earth to the Moon, a total of 240,000 miles – the purpose is to raise money, through pledges, for one of Canada's most debilitating childhood diseases: cystic fibrosis. The 1996 Moonwalk successfully raised pledges of more than $1.5 million. Overall, during Zellers 12 years of annual sponsorship, the drive has raised more than $10.5 million for the Canadian Cystic Fibrosis Foundation.

Employees

Technology, systems, buildings and even the right merchandise at the right price can not make a successful department store company without a team of dedicated employees to bring it all together and ensure that customers are satisfied.

HBC is proud of its associates, almost 60,000 strong. We celebrate their involvement in all aspects of Company life – as they interact with our customers, our suppliers, our communities, and with one another.

John Cunningham
Vice-President, Operations, Hudson's Bay Company

John Cunningham retires April 1, 1997 after more than 43 years with the Company. From Management Trainee to Corporate Vice-President, John's long career encompassed everything from store management to overseeing operations, license departments and loss prevention for the entire Bay and Zellers organizations. John is a fine example of the many long serving, loyal employees who are ready to assume responsibility at all levels.

Claire Drolet,
Sales Associate in Men's Shirts, the Bay, Montreal Downtown store

Claire Drolet is an 18-year veteran on the sales side who has been consistently recognized for her outstanding customer service record. She expertly satisfies shoppers' needs while providing the kind of enjoyable in-store experience that keeps our customers coming back year after year.

Sophie Roux
Linguistic Services Supervisor
Hudson's Bay Company
Montreal

Sophie Roux has been with HBC Linguistic Services for 17 years. She has been in charge of the translation of the Annual Report for many years and is a highly experienced professional translator in many fields.

Jack Hoar
Store Manager at the Bay in Red Deer, Alberta

Jack Hoar, a 28 year veteran of the Bay, was particularly proud of an unusual marketing accomplishment in his store in 1996... the sale of $92,000 of merchandise and $461,000 worth of Bay gift certificates. This was the payoff from clever "outbound marketing" in which Jack and his team took advantage of the Alberta Medis Pharmaceutical trade show.

Angela Mirenzi
Buyer - the Bay

Angela Mirenzi is responsible for men's designer sportswear. Her area has shown outstanding sales and profit growth over the last few years. Angela's success has stemmed from her partnership efforts with Bay vendors, our stores and our Store Planning & Construction Department in the roll-out of new shops and fixturing programs. Her initiatives have established us as a leader in men's designer sportswear and provided the Bay with exciting, fashionable merchandise within cornerstone brands as anchors for our total men's wear business.

Historic Trust

No other corporation in Canada – indeed, few anywhere in the world – enjoys the rich and fabled history of the 327 years of the Hudson's Bay Company.

With this history, however, comes a major responsibility. As keeper of many of the oldest known records describing human settlement in the territory which now comprises a major part of Canada, the HBC organization considers it has a sacred trust in the name of all Canadians to ensure the preservation of these documents, artifacts and memorabilia providing irreplaceable links to the nation's past.

Three years ago, the Company donated its archival treasures and extensive museum collections, together valued in excess of $60 million, to the people of Canada. These now reside in the Manitoba Provincial Archives and the Manitoba Museum of Man and Nature. The ongoing maintenance of these collections is largely financed by contributions from a foundation established with further donations from the Company.

Most of the material in the archives can also be examined on microfilm at the National Archives in Ottawa and at the Public Records Office in London, England. A program is underway to have much of the museum collection recorded on CD-ROM.

During a royal visit to Winnipeg in April 1996 by HRH Prince Charles, a new wing of the Manitoba Museum of Man and Nature – due for completion

HRH Prince Charles with the Governor on board the Nonsuch at Museum of Man and Nature in Winnipeg

in the fall of 1997 – was dedicated to house the Hudson's Bay Company collection. The continuing commitment by HBC to the preservation of its unique historical heritage is evidenced by the donation of $2 million from the Hudson's Bay History Foundation towards the cost of constructing this new wing. A similar commitment has been made to the Manitoba Archives to upgrade the facility housing the Hudson's Bay Archives.

also intends to maintain an active corporate presence within the Canadian business community as a whole. This includes participating actively in policy discussions whenever joint industry issues have a direct effect on consumers and retailers throughout Canada as well as taking a responsible position in overseas markets whenever Canadian labour standards or other ethical issues appear to be at stake.

Ultimately, as a company that has survived and flourished doing business in Canada for more than three centuries, Hudson's Bay Company continues to take the long view – both of the country and of the entrepreneurial spirit of Canadians that continues to drive the nation forward. ❏

Hudson's Bay Company

MANAGEMENT'S DISCUSSION AND ANALYSIS

RESULTS OF OPERATIONS

Earnings per share, before deducting restructuring costs which are described below, improved to $1.22 in 1996, an increase of $0.63 or 107% over 1995. Earnings per share after deducting restructuring costs were $0.61.

Net earnings before deducting restructuring costs increased to $73 million from $34 million in 1995. After deducting restructuring costs, net earnings were $37 million. An analysis of earnings for the last three years is shown in the following table:

	1996	1995	1994
		(in millions of dollars)	
Sales and Revenue	6,007	5,984	5,829
Operating Profits:			
Major Retail Divisions	247	228	377
Other Operating Items, Net	4	(14)	(8)
	251	214	369
Interest Expense	(108)	(129)	(100)
Earnings before Income Taxes and Unusual Items	143	85	269
Income Taxes	(70)	(51)	(118)
Earnings before Unusual Items	73	34	151
Restructuring Costs	(64)	–	–
Income Tax Credits	28	–	33
Net Earnings	37	34	184
Weighted Average Number of Shares Outstanding (in millions)	59.3	58.1	57.0
Earnings per Share before Unusual Items	$1.22	$0.59	$2.66
Earnings per Share	$0.61	$0.59	$3.23

SALES AND REVENUE

Sales and revenue of each of HBC's major retail divisions for the past three years were as follows:

	1996	1995	1994
		(in millions of dollars)	
Sales and Revenue:			
The Bay	2,333	2,348	2,353
Zellers	3,578	3,537	3,375
	5,911	5,885	5,728

Combined sales and revenue for the Bay and Zellers in 1996 of $5,911 million were 0.4% higher than 1995's $5,885 million, which represented a 2.7% increase over 1994.

Sales and revenue at the Bay in 1996 were 0.7% lower than last year, with comparable store sales decreasing by 0.6%. Sales in men's wear, cosmetics/fragrances and housewares outperformed the other sales categories. The Bay's DSS market share decreased by 0.6% in 1996. Sales of $159 per square foot of retail selling space for 1996 represented a $2 per square foot decrease from 1995.

Zellers' 1996 sales and revenue were 1.2% higher than last year. This sales increase was primarily driven by new stores and expansions, with comparable store sales down 2.2% from 1995. Sales in cosmetics, home decor, housewares and seasonal outperformed the other categories. DSS market share for Zellers was down by 0.4% in 1996. Sales of $191 per square foot of retail selling space for 1996 represented a $3 per square foot decrease from 1995.

The following table shows the percentage of sales of HBC derived from each of the four geographical regions of Canada for the last three years:

	1996	1995	1994
	%	%	%
Sales:			
Western Canada	33.9	33.7	33.5
Ontario	40.4	39.8	40.2
Quebec	19.6	20.2	19.8
Maritimes	6.1	6.3	6.5
	100.0	100.0	100.0

The Bay's 1996 sales were unchanged in Western Canada, increased in Ontario and were down in Quebec and the Maritimes. Zellers' 1996 sales increased in Western Canada and Ontario and were virtually unchanged in Quebec and the Maritimes.

On a consistent basis from year to year, fourth quarter sales and revenue of HBC's major retail divisions are considerably higher than in other quarters of the year, which has a significantly leveraged impact on profits. This is illustrated by the following table:

	1996	1995	1994
		(in millions of dollars)	
Sales and Revenue of Major Retail Divisions:			
First Quarter	1,175	1,205	1,174
Second Quarter	1,353	1,373	1,286
Third Quarter	1,441	1,433	1,416
Fourth Quarter	1,942	1,874	1,852
Year	5,911	5,885	5,728

Sales and revenue of the Bay were up in the fourth quarter of 1996 after five consecutive quarters of decreases starting with the third quarter of 1995. Zellers, on the other hand, experienced sales increases in the last two quarters of 1996 and decreases in the first two quarters, after achieving eight consecutive quarters of sales increases in 1995 and 1994.

Expressing the sales and revenue of HBC's major retail divisions by quarter as a percentage of total sales for the year continues to show a very consistent pattern. In the last three years, with a minor amount of rounding, the percentages were approximately 21%, 23%, 24% and 32% for the first, second, third and fourth quarters, respectively.

OPERATING PROFITS

Major Retail Divisions

Operating profits of HBC's major retail divisions for the past three years were as follows:

	1996	1995	1994
		(in millions of dollars)	
Operating Profits:			
The Bay	131	121	161
Zellers	116	107	216
	247	228	377

Total operating profits of the major retail divisions in 1996 were higher than the depressed levels achieved in 1995, as the positive effects of the restructuring (see **RESTRUCTURING COSTS** below) began to be realized in the latter part of the year and the price war in the discount department store segment eased. Total operating profits were $247 million, an 8.3% increase compared to a 39.5% reduction in 1995.

This improvement was shared equally by the Bay and Zellers, with the Bay's operating profit increasing by $10 million to $131 million, an 8.3% increase, and Zellers up by $9 million to $116 million, an 8.4% increase. Zellers' operating profit in 1996 was achieved after deducting store closure costs of $16 million compared with $5 million in 1995. The Bay's 1995 operating profit of $121 million was down 24.8% from 1994 and Zellers' 1995 operating profit was down 50.5% from 1994.

Operating Profits (in $millions)

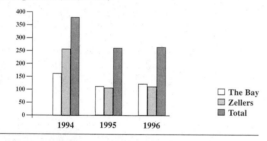

Since fourth quarter sales, which includes the Christmas shopping season, are considerably higher than in other quarters while expenses are spread somewhat more evenly throughout the year, a disproportionate share of the operating profits of the major retail divisions is earned in the fourth quarter as shown by the following table:

	1996	1995	1994
		(in millions of dollars)	
Operating Profits of Major Retail Divisions:			
First Quarter	**7**	17	36
Second Quarter	**35**	58	58
Third Quarter	**47**	42	77
Fourth Quarter	**158**	111	206
Year	**247**	228	377

In 1996 both the Bay and Zellers experienced accelerating operating profit increases in the last two quarters, following reductions in the first two quarters.

Operating Profits (in $millions)

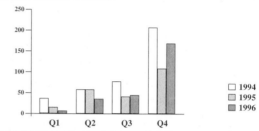

Other Operating Items, Net

Other operating items, net represents items that are not directly attributable to either of the major retail divisions. This category includes unallocated corporate expenses and miscellaneous profits and losses from various ongoing and non-recurring secondary activities. It also includes the operations of Linmark, a buying agency located in Asia, and Fields, a minor division which operates 102 small family clothing stores in smaller communities in Western Canada.

Net profits from these items were $4 million in 1996 compared to net losses of $14 million in 1995 and $8 million in 1994. Linmark's operating profit was $4.5 million in 1996, $5.3 million in 1995 and $4.7 million in 1994. For 1996, 1995 and 1994 operating losses of Fields were $1.8 million, $1.8 million and $1.7 million, respectively. The significant factors contributing to the improved profits in 1996 compared with 1995 were recoveries of amounts previously written off, profits from real estate activities and a $7.0 million reduction in the carrying value of a vacant department store building in 1995. There was no comparable write down in 1996.

INTEREST EXPENSE

Interest expense of $108.5 million in 1996 was well below 1995's $129.2 million as HBC reaped the benefits of lower interest rates throughout the year. In 1995 interest expense increased by $28.7 million as HBC's total debt and average interest rate increased during the year. HBC's average debt in 1996 was slightly higher than in 1995 but by year end was down by $418 million from 1995. $300 million of this decrease resulted from cash proceeds from the securitization of credit card receivables described below in *NET ASSETS, DEBT AND EQUITY*. HBC's average interest rate on fixed and swapped debt decreased to 9.0% from 10.5% in 1995 and 10.8% in 1994 and its average floating rate decreased to 5.3% from 7.3% in 1995 and 6.1% in 1994. HBC's total average interest rate decreased to 6.9% in 1996 from 8.4% in 1995 and 7.6% in 1994.

TAXES AND LEVIES

Income taxes represent a relatively small proportion of the total taxes and levies paid by HBC. The following table provides an analysis of the total amounts paid in each of the last three years:

	1996	1995	1994
	(in millions of dollars)		
Corporation income taxes	63	44	112
Large corporations tax	7	7	6
Income taxes	70	51	118
Other taxes and levies:			
Realty and business taxes	113	108	106
Customs duties	79	85	74
Canada Pension Plan and other payroll taxes	76	74	71
Sales taxes	13	14	13
Provincial capital taxes	7	11	9
Total other taxes and levies	288	292	273
Total	358	343	391

RESTRUCTURING COSTS

After a very disappointing Christmas season in 1995, HBC determined that it was essential that steps be taken to reduce overhead and other expenses in its major retail divisions in order to enhance its competitive position and improve overall profitability on an ongoing basis. As a result, in March 1996 HBC announced that it would amalgamate its Zellers administrative and marketing office, formerly located in Montreal, with that of the Bay and its Toronto corporate offices. Offers to move to Toronto were made to many employees and some were able to transfer to the Credit division with the relocation to Montreal of certain credit functions. The amalgamation was effectively completed by the end of the summer. HBC has estimated its costs to carry out this restructuring at approximately $64 million, before deducting income tax credits of approximately $28 million.

UNUSUAL INCOME TAX CREDITS

The 1996 unusual income tax credit of $28 million represents the reduction in income taxes relating to the restructuring costs of $64 million. The 1994 unusual income tax credits of $33 million consisted of $24 million derived from tax losses acquired on the amalgamation of Woodward's Limited with Zellers Inc. and $9 million from the donation of tax savings arising from the gift of HBC's historical archives collection to the Government of Manitoba.

EARNINGS PER SHARE

An analysis of earnings per share by quarter for the last three years is as follows:

	1996*	1995	1994**
Earnings per Share:			
First Quarter	($0.29)	($0.25)	$0.06
Second Quarter	$0.01	$0.10	$0.33
Third Quarter	$0.14	$0.04	$0.50
Fourth Quarter	$1.36	$0.70	$1.77
Year	$1.22	$0.59	$2.66

 * Excludes restructuring costs net of related income taxes of $0.61 per share, all recorded in the first quarter.
** Excludes unusual income tax credits of $0.57 per share (first quarter nil; second quarter $0.39; third quarter $0.14 and fourth quarter $0.04).

Earnings per Share before Unusual Items

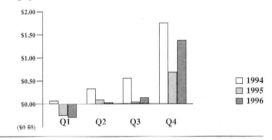

FINANCIAL CONDITION

NET ASSETS, DEBT AND EQUITY

The following summary shows details of HBC's net assets as financed by debt and equity for the last three years:

	1996	1995	1994
	(in millions of dollars)		
Net Assets:			
The Bay	1,213	1,478	1,440
Zellers	1,568	1,694	1,594
Other	256	281	241
	3,037	3,453	3,275
Financed By:			
Debt	1,113	1,531	1,364
Deferred Taxes	132	144	138
Equity	1,792	1,778	1,773
	3,037	3,453	3,275
Debt:Equity Ratio	0.62:1	0.86:1	0.77:1

Net assets at the 1996 year end were down from last year by $416 million, with virtually all of the decrease occurring in credit card receivables.

On January 27, 1997, HBC sold $300 million of its credit card receivables ($150 million each from the Bay and Zellers) to an independent trust. The sale reduced assets employed and the proceeds were used to reduce debt. This will improve the Company's liquidity and its financial ratios.

HBC's debt:equity ratio has improved to 0.62:1 from 0.86:1 at the 1995 year end.

CASH FLOW AND FUNDING

The following table shows an analysis of HBC's cash flow and funding for the past three years:

	1996	1995	1994
		(in millions of dollars)	
Cash Flow:			
From Earnings	**189**	162	346
Working Capital Changes	**52**	(70)	(252)
Cash Inflow From Operating			
Activities	**241**	92	94
Credit Card Receivables	**300**	–	–
Capital Expenditures	**(121)**	(238)	(202)
Dispositions of Fixed Assets			
and Investments	**32**	2	10
Dividends	**(43)**	(53)	(52)
Other	**(12)**	5	(40)
Net Cash Inflow (Outflow)	**397**	(192)	(190)
Funding:			
Debt	**(417)**	168	163
Equity	**20**	24	27
	(397)	192	190

Cash inflow from operating activities amounted to $241 million in 1996 compared with $92 million in 1995 and $94 million in 1994. Most of this improvement resulted from a $100 million reduction in credit card receivables, excluding the $300 million sale of receivables under a securitization program which is shown separately in the above table. Net cash inflow was $397 million compared with a net cash outflow of $192 million in 1995. As shown above, a decrease in capital expenditures of $117 million and a $30 million increase in cash flow from dispositions, together with the total reduction in credit card receivables, were the main factors in the improvement in net cash flow.

CAPITAL EXPENDITURES

Capital expenditures were $121 million in 1996, $238 million in 1995 and $202 million in 1994. Projected capital expenditures over the next three years will amount to approximately $500 million. Zellers expects to add up to 30 new stores and expand a similar number in the next three years. Zellers will take advantage of opportunities to add stores in locations that fit the long term strategy of the division and to enlarge existing stores. At this time the Bay has not committed to any new stores over this period, but will be expanding three stores in 1997 and 1998. Both divisions will renovate and upgrade existing stores where appropriate to maintain or enhance their desired marketing image. HBC remains committed to continu-

ing its expansion in communities where there are marketing opportunities, but will not hesitate to close unprofitable or underperforming stores where necessary and appropriate.

RETAIL RISK FACTORS

In management's view there are five key elements that combine to produce retail profits for HBC: Sales and Revenue, Gross Profit Rate, Expense Rate, Credit Earnings and Interest Expense. The following table shows the principal external and internal Retail Risk Factors that directly influence these elements.

These Retail Risk Factors interact and action taken to stimulate one factor often results in a negative effect on other factors. For example, store openings may increase sales but will also increase occupancy costs and payroll and interest expense; additional advertising may also increase sales but will almost certainly increase expenses; reducing levels of sales staff will lower payroll expense but may also reduce sales and increase stock shortages. Management's responsibility is to achieve an appropriate balance among these Retail Risk Factors in order to optimize profits.

Elements	Retail Risk Factors	
	External	**Internal**
Sales and Revenue	Competition Economy Inflation Weather	Customer Service Marketing Strategies Store Openings and Closings
Gross Profit Rate	Competition Consumer Price Resistance	Buying/Pricing Control of Inventories Sales Blend Stock Shortages
Expense Rate	Inflation Taxes	Advertising Occupancy Costs Payroll
Credit Earnings	Bad Debts Card Competition Government Legislation	Card Promotion Service Charge Rates
Interest Expense	Credit Rating Rates Government Policy	Debt Volume Foreign Exchange Exposure Fixed/Floating Blend Short/Long Term Blend

Sales and revenue and interest expense are reviewed above and each of the remaining key elements is analyzed in the following sections.

GROSS PROFIT RATE

The gross profit rate, which represents sales less the cost of goods sold, expressed as a percentage of retail sales, improved slightly at the Bay in 1996 but declined at Zellers.

The Bay's gross profit rate in 1996 improved slightly from 1995 primarily due to lower markdowns and an improved stock shortage position. At Zellers the gross profit rate was lower in 1996 as markdowns increased over 1995.

EXPENSE RATE

Expenses as a percentage of retail sales decreased in both major retail divisions. Favourable expense variances in the latter part of the year resulting from savings realized as a result of the restructuring overcame the impact of decreases in comparable store sales at both the Bay and Zellers and resulted in total expenses for the year decreasing in each division.

CREDIT EARNINGS

Credit earnings in 1996 increased slightly over 1995 earnings, in an environment of lower credit card receivable balances (at the 1996 year end $831 million after the securitization sale of $300 million referred to above under *NET ASSETS, DEBT AND EQUITY* compared to 1995's $1,231 million) and the resulting lower revenues. Earnings improvements were driven by decreases in bad debts from an all-time high in 1995. In 1996 the Bay and Zellers terminated the arrangement under which their credit cards had been accepted at automotive service locations.

FINANCING AND CREDIT RISK

The objectives of HBC with regard to financing its activities are:
- to maintain a debt:equity ratio which allows access to capital markets at all times;
- to maintain a level of leverage appropriate to the retail industry to generate superior returns for shareholders;
- to maintain a mix of debt which will provide adequate liquidity at the lowest cost of capital while providing reasonable protection from adverse movements in interest and foreign exchange rates; and
- to maintain a variety of financing sources.

Management believes that HBC continues to be successful in meeting these objectives.

Debt at the 1996 year end, after deducting $63 million in investments and short-term deposits, was $1,113 million, of which $1,110 million (including the $49 million due within one year) was long-term debt. The unusually low level of net short-term debt came as a result of the receipt of the $300 million on the securitization of credit card receivables in late January. Seasonal upswings in inventories and credit card receivables are normally financed by short-term borrowings. Management is confident that it will be able to raise any additional long-term funds that may be required.

The 1996 year end long-term debt comprised $451 million at fixed rates and $659 million at nominal floating rates. However, the rates on $475 million of nominal floating rate debt were fixed at an average rate of 7.25% through various interest rate swap agreements. Interest rates on a further $200 million were capped at rates ranging from 8.75% to 9.0%.

Assuming no change in the level of floating rate debt from year end, a 1% increase or decrease in floating interest rates that are below the maximum capped rate is projected to increase or decrease HBC's interest expense by $2.5 million. For a 1% increase in floating interest rates above 9.0%, interest expense would increase by only $0.5 million.

Foreign exchange and floating rate interest rate risks are managed by hedges, swaps and caps under guidelines established and reviewed periodically by the Board. Debt subject to foreign exchange rate risk amounts to approximately $10 million, representing the Canadian dollar equivalent of unhedged U.S. dollar and pound sterling obligations.

HBC negotiates unsecured lines of credit annually with a number of Canadian banks to provide for short-term financial needs and to back up HBC's commercial paper program. Management foresees no difficulty in negotiating lines of credit sufficient to meet its requirements in 1997.

Debt of HBC and its wholly-owned subsidiary, Hudson's Bay Company Acceptance Limited ("HBCAL"), is rated by the Canadian Bond Rating Service ("CBRS") and by the Dominion Bond Rating Service ("DBRS"). A summary of these ratings is provided in the following table:

	1996		1995	
	Rating	**Outlook**	Rating	Outlook
CBRS:				
HBC unsecured debentures	**B++(high)**	**Stable**	A1(low)	Negative
HBCAL secured debentures	**A**	**Stable**	A	Negative
HBC/HBCAL commercial paper	**A1(low)**	**Stable**	A1(low)	Negative
DBRS:				
HBC unsecured debentures	**BBB(high)**	**Stable**	A(low)	Negative
HBCAL secured debentures	**BBB(high)**	**Stable**	A(low)	Negative
HBC/HBCAL commercial paper	**R1(low)**	**Stable**	R1(low)	Stable

In April 1996, following publication of HBC's disappointing 1995 results, CBRS lowered its rating on HBC unsecured debentures and maintained the same ratings on HBCAL secured debentures and commercial paper. At the same time, DBRS lowered its ratings on the HBC and HBCAL debentures and maintained the same ratings on HBC and HBCAL commercial paper.

ASSET PROTECTION

The many programs which are in effect to protect the assets of HBC from loss and from liability claims from third parties are backed by contracts of insurance to cover major losses. The total cost of risk management, including insurance premiums and fees and self-insured losses, has been approximately $15 million for each of the last three years. The amount of self insured risk assumed by HBC is reviewed periodically by the Board of Directors.

RETAIL PROPERTIES

The number and aggregate gross areas in square feet of the retail stores of each of HBC's major retail divisions and of its distribution centres at the last three year ends were as follows:

	Number			Sq. Ft. (000's)		
	1996	1995	1994	**1996**	1995	1994
Retail Stores:						
The Bay	**101**	101	100	**16,782**	16,666	16,490
Zellers	**296**	300	292	**22,942**	22,609	21,089
	397	401	392	**39,724**	39,275	37,579
Distribution Centres	**9**	9	9	**2,927**	2,983	2,983

HBC owns the land and buildings of eight large downtown Bay stores, seven other Bay stores, 13 Zellers stores and three distribution centres. As well, HBC owns the Toronto Queen Street store building and approximately 60% of the related land, and the buildings (on leased land) of seven suburban Bay stores. The remaining stores are generally held under long-term leases. During 1996 Zellers opened 8 stores and closed 12. The Bay opened one store and closed one.

HBC's principal non-retail properties are The Simpson Tower, a 32 floor office building in Toronto, and a large downtown store in Montreal which has been closed and is being held for sale or development.

RETAIL ENVIRONMENT

The Canadian retail industry remained intensely competitive in 1996. Retailers engaged in aggressive marketing campaigns and continued to improve services and store presentations to attract customers to their stores. Some retailers were able to achieve sales increases and improved profit margins, while the rest continued to struggle. A few major retail chains expanded by opening new stores, while others upgraded existing stores. Consolidation and restructuring continued during the year. A few retailers were forced to liquidate their operations, while others continued to streamline their operations or closed their underperforming stores.

The Canadian economy grew by only 1.5% in 1996, the lowest rate reported since the early 90's. The slow economic growth was the result of continued government cutbacks and weak consumer and business confidence. In 1996, the labour market showed no improvement at all, with the unemployment rate remaining at 9.7%, slightly higher than the year before.

Although improving, consumer spending grew slowly during the year as Canadians were concerned about job security and high unemployment. However, the continued downward trend in interest rates throughout the year brought relief to debt-heavy consumers. Canadians were more optimistic about the future of the economy in the second half of the year, as reflected in the strong housing market activity and the surge in consumer spending.

Department Store Sales (DSS) were up 4.4% in 1996, the largest increase in seven years. The largest sales increases were achieved in the first and fourth quarters, both at 6.3%. Sales were up only 2.0% in the second and 2.6% in the third quarter. DSS outperformed DSTM sales in every quarter. The increases were largely attributable to strong sales in discount department stores (up 8.6% from 1995), which accounted for 56% of total DSS. The decline in traditional department stores sales continued (down 0.4%). Discount department stores continued to take market share from most other retailers, mostly due to their broader merchandise assortments and aggressive pricing strategies. HBC's DSS market share declined in the 1996 calendar year to 38.7% compared with 39.8% in 1995. The Bay's market share was 15.2% compared to 15.9% in 1995 and Zellers market share was 23.5% compared with 1995's 23.9%.

Among the DSS merchandise categories, the best performers were health and beauty aids, stationery/confectionery/consumables, seasonal and housewares, while the women's apparel group continued its sales decline for the third year in a row.

Spending on Department Store Type Merchandise (DSTM), which is total retail sales net of food and automotive sales, increased by 2.6% in 1996, as compared with the 1.2% increase in 1995. The retail stores that reported sales decreases included men's and women's clothing and furniture and appliances. The DSTM growth rate improved progressively in each quarter, from 1.4% in the first quarter to 4.5% in the fourth quarter, with the second and third quarters achieving sales increases of 1.5% and 2.1%, respectively. For the second year in a row, total DSTM sales gains were below those of DSS. Accordingly, DSS share as a percentage of DSTM sales increased to 19.9% from 19.6% in 1995. HBC's share of total DSTM was down 0.1% to 7.5%.

FUTURE PROSPECTS

The Canadian economy is expected to have stronger growth in 1997 and beyond. Low and stable inflation rates and low interest rates will have a continued positive impact on the economy. The housing market improved in the latter half of 1996 and this along with the strong growth in retail sales in the fourth quarter should continue into 1997.

The retail environment will continue to be very competitive in 1997. There will be more downsizing, consolidations and restructuring in the retail marketplace. Retailers must be able to adapt to the changing consumer environment. They must make shopping more efficient and entertaining for the consumer and be in a position to offer the newest merchandise and trends. HBC believes that the Bay and Zellers have these abilities and are fully capable of taking in the difficult challenges that lie ahead.

The company is encouraged by the improved results achieved in the second half of the year. The benefits of consolidating Zellers operational offices with the Bay's offices and HBC corporate started to show in the fourth quarter and will accelerate in 1997.

The increase in consumer spending in the fourth quarter of 1996 is expected to continue into 1997 and this, along with internal initiatives, should allow the company to continue to generate improved results.

Hudson's Bay Company

CONSOLIDATED STATEMENTS OF EARNINGS

	Notes	Years Ended January 31, 1997 $000's	1996 $000's
Sales and Revenue			
The Bay		**2,332,720**	2,348,571
Zellers		**3,578,488**	3,536,601
Other		**96,004**	99,346
		6,007,212	5,984,518
Operating Profit			
The Bay		**131,112**	121,108
Zellers		**116,388**	106,730
Other		**3,709**	(13,378)
Earnings before Interest, Unusual Item and Income Taxes		**251,209**	214,460
Interest Expense	3	**(108,505)**	(129,152)
Earnings before Unusual Item and Income Taxes		**142,704**	85,308
Restructuring Costs	4	**(64,000)**	–
Earnings before Income Taxes		**78,704**	85,308
Income Taxes on Earnings before Unusual Item and Income Taxes	5	**(70,163)**	(50,758)
Income Tax Credits on Restructuring Costs	4	**27,600**	–
Net Earnings		**36,141**	34,550
Earnings per Share	6	**$0.61**	$0.59

CONSOLIDATED STATEMENTS OF RETAINED EARNINGS

	Years Ended January 31, 1997 $000's	1996 $000's
Retained Earnings at Beginning of Year	**681,277**	700,210
Net Earnings	**36,141**	34,550
Dividends	**(42,700)**	(53,483)
Retained Earnings at End of Year	**674,718**	681,277

Hudson's Bay Company

CONSOLIDATED BALANCE SHEETS

	Notes	January 31, 1997 $000's	January 31, 1996 $000's
Current Assets			
Cash		**6,762**	7,563
Short-term deposits		**18,079**	16,283
Credit card receivables	7	**831,006**	1,231,190
Other accounts receivable		**123,793**	131,430
Merchandise inventories		**1,365,260**	1,308,676
Prepaid expenses		**47,287**	60,067
		2,392,187	2,755,209
Secured Receivables	8	**23,598**	12,033
Investments		**47,590**	52,561
Fixed Assets	9	**966,181**	989,458
Goodwill	10	**91,769**	96,859
Pensions	11	**200,429**	191,988
Other Assets	12	**94,515**	110,229
		3,816,269	4,208,337
Current Liabilities			
Short-term borrowings	13	**65,849**	115,395
Trade accounts payable		**300,576**	281,314
Other accounts payable and accrued expenses		**407,124**	386,051
Income taxes payable		**8,093**	20,788
Long-term debt due within one year	13	**49,122**	119,182
		830,764	922,730
Long-Term Debt	13	**1,061,453**	1,362,704
Deferred Income Taxes		**132,061**	144,558
Contingencies	19		
Shareholders' Equity			
Capital stock	14	**1,099,616**	1,079,411
Additional paid-in capital		**17,657**	17,657
Retained earnings		**674,718**	681,277
		1,791,991	1,778,345
		3,816,269	4,208,337

On behalf of the Board:

_____
Director

_____
Director

Hudson's Bay Company

CONSOLIDATED STATEMENTS OF CASH FLOW AND FUNDING

	Notes	Years Ended January 31,	
		1997	1996
		$000's	$000's
Operating Activities			
Earnings before income taxes		78,704	85,308
Current income tax expense		(55,013)	(44,776)
Items not affecting cash flow:			
Amortization	2	132,252	122,492
Pension credits		(4,800)	(1,000)
Restructuring Costs	4	37,381	–
Cash Inflow from Earnings (per share $3.18 and $2.79)		188,524	162,024
Net change in operating working capital	16	52,577	(69,903)
Net Cash Inflow from Operating Activities		241,101	92,121
Investing Activities			
Sale of credit card receivables	7	300,000	–
Capital expenditures		(121,015)	(238,481)
Fixed asset dispositions		32,171	1,897
Other		(12,279)	6,336
Net cash inflow from (outflow for) investing activities		198,877	(230,248)
Dividends (per share $0.72 and $0.92)		(42,700)	(53,483)
Net Cash Inflow from (Outflow for) Activities and Dividends		397,278	(191,610)
Funding			
Long-term debt:			
Issued		250,334	399,193
Redeemed		(621,796)	(138,725)
		(371,462)	260,468
Equity - common shares issued		20,205	24,388
Net Cash Inflow from (Outflow to Reduce) Funding		(351,257)	284,856
Decrease in Net Short-Term Borrowings		(46,021)	(93,246)
Net Short-Term Borrowings at Beginning of Year	13	48,705	141,951
Net Short-Term Borrowings at End of Year	13	2,684	48,705

Hudson's Bay Company

NOTES TO THE CONSOLIDATED FINANCIAL STATEMENTS
Years Ended January 31, 1997 and January 31, 1996

1. ACCOUNTING PRINCIPLES AND POLICIES

These consolidated financial statements have been prepared by management in accordance with accounting principles generally accepted in Canada. The significant accounting policies are as follows:

a) Consolidation

These consolidated financial statements include the accounts of Hudson's Bay Company and of all its subsidiary companies, with inter-company balances and transactions eliminated.

b) Segmentation

The Company's dominant industry segment is retailing, mainly through retail outlets which include full-line and discount department stores. Certain information within this segment has been shown separately in these consolidated financial statements for the principal operating divisions, the Bay and Zellers, both of which operate solely in Canada.

c) Foreign currency translation

Foreign currency assets and liabilities, which primarily are components of debt and accounts payable, are translated into Canadian dollars at exchange rates in effect at the balance sheet dates.

Foreign currency costs and earnings, predominantly interest, are translated into Canadian dollars at exchange rates in effect at the time they are incurred or earned.

The net exchange gain or loss arising from the translation of foreign currency denominated debt having a fixed term to maturity is included in other assets and amortized over the remaining life of the related issue.

d) Leases

Leases entered into by the Company as lessee that transfer substantially all the benefits and risks of ownership to the lessee are recorded as capital leases and included in fixed assets and long-term debt. All other leases are classified as operating leases under which leasing costs are recorded as expenses in the period in which they are incurred.

e) Earnings per share

Earnings per share are based on the weighted average number of shares outstanding during the year.

f) Capitalization of interest

Interest relating to properties that are under construction or vacant and held for sale or development is capitalized as part of the cost of these assets when their net carrying amount is lower than their estimated net recoverable amount.

g) Credit card receivables

Credit card receivables represent open-ended revolving credit card customer accounts and are shown net of an allowance for doubtful accounts. Reserves for estimated losses on receivables sold with limited recourse under securitization agreements are classified as other accounts payable.

In accordance with accepted retail industry practice, credit card receivables, of which a portion will not become due within one year, are classified as current assets.

h) Merchandise inventories

Merchandise inventories are carried at the lower of cost and net realizable value less normal profit margins. The cost of inventories is determined principally on an average basis by the use of the retail inventory method.

i) Investments

Investments consist principally of portfolio investments, comprising bonds held primarily to support funding obligations, carried at cost with discounts or premiums arising on purchase amortized to maturity.

j) Fixed assets

Fixed assets are carried at cost. The cost of buildings (excluding the office tower noted below), equipment, equipment held under capital leases and leasehold improvements is amortized on the straight-line method over their estimated useful lives. The cost of property for sale or development is not amortized, since it represents either land or vacant properties.

The amortization periods applicable to the various classes of fixed assets are as follows:

Asset	Amortization Periods
Buildings	20-40 years
Equipment	$3-12\frac{1}{2}$ years
Equipment held under capital leases	5-8 years
Leasehold improvements	10-40 years

Certain buildings acquired before February 1, 1995 are being amortized over the remainder of 50 year periods. Buildings include an office tower, the cost of which is being amortized on the sinking fund method at a rate of 3% over a 40 year period.

k) Goodwill

Goodwill comprises the unamortized balance of the excess of the cost to the Company over the fair value of its interest in the identifiable net assets of Zellers Inc., Towers Department Stores Inc. (subsequently amalgamated with Zellers Inc.) and the Linmark group of companies, at their respective dates of acquisition. These balances are amortized on the straight-line method over periods of 40 years, 20 years and 20 years, respectively.

Goodwill is regularly evaluated by reviewing the returns of the related business, taking into account the risk associated with the investment. Any permanent impairment would be written off against earnings.

l) Pensions

The Company maintains both defined contribution pension plans and defined benefit pension plans.

The costs of defined contribution pension plans, representing the Company's required contribution, and the costs of defined benefit pension plans, calculated under the accrued benefit method, are charged to earnings as incurred.

The excess of the value of defined benefit pension plan assets over the actuarial present value of accrued obligations as of February 1, 1986, together with adjustments arising from plan amendments, experience gains and losses and changes in actuarial assumptions since that date, is amortized to earnings over the expected average remaining service lives of the respective employee groups.

m) Other assets

Other assets include deferred and prepaid rent, post employment benefits other than pensions and merchandise systems development costs, which are amortized on the straight-line method over periods of up to 25 years, 10 years and five years, respectively.

Other assets also include debt discount and expense, costs of interest rate caps and unamortized exchange gains and losses on long-term debt denominated in foreign currency, which are amortized to interest expense on the straight-line method over the terms of the related issues or contracts.

n) Post employment benefits other than pensions

The Company's obligation to provide post employment benefits is limited to medical and dental care and life insurance commitments to certain former employees of acquired companies and to the continuation of staff discount privileges to eligible employees. Provision has been made for the limited obligation in respect of these former employees. The impact of staff discount to retired employees is absorbed as a reduction in sales when the discount is applied.

o) Off balance sheet financial instruments

To hedge its interest rate risks, the Company utilizes interest rate swaps, forward rate agreements and caps. Accrued interest receivable and payable under the interest rate swaps and forward rate agreements are included in other accounts receivable or other accounts payable. The up front fees paid under interest rate caps are amortized to interest expense on the straight-line method over the terms of the related contracts and the unamortized amounts are included in other assets.

The Company manages the risks associated with changes in foreign exchange rates affecting firm purchase commitments by use of forward contracts.

2. AMORTIZATION

Amortization of the cost of assets that is included in the Consolidated Statements of Earnings comprises the following:

	Years Ended January 31,	
	1997	1996
	$000's	$000's
Deducted in arriving at operating profit:		
Fixed assets	**111,200**	103,267
Goodwill	**5,090**	5,090
Merchandise systems development costs	**7,246**	6,683
Other	**7,582**	6,918
	131,118	121,958
Included in interest expense:		
Debt discount and expense	**1,047**	637
Foreign currency net losses (gains)	**87**	(103)
	1,134	534
	132,252	122,492

3. INTEREST EXPENSE

Interest expense arises from the following:

	Years Ended January 31,	
	1997	1996
	$000's	$000's
Long-term debt	**100,005**	109,068
Net short-term borrowings	**10,243**	23,454
	110,248	132,522
Less amounts capitalized	**(1,743)**	(3,370)
	108,505	129,152

4. RESTRUCTURING COSTS

The Company incurred restructuring costs in the year ended January 31, 1997 estimated to be $64,000,000 ($36,400,000 after deducting related income tax credits of $27,600,000). Of this total amount, $37,381,000 remained unpaid as of January 31, 1997. Included in these costs were lease termination costs, severance payments, moving expenses, asset write-downs and other related expenses incurred as a result of the consolidation of the operations of Zellers, formerly located in Montreal, with the Bay's office and the Company's corporate offices in Toronto.

5. INCOME TAXES

The average statutory Canadian income tax rates for the years ended January 31, 1997 and January 31, 1996 were 43.7% and 43.6%, respectively. A comparison of nominal tax provisions at these rates with the amounts provided in the Consolidated Statements of Earnings is as follows:

	Years Ended January 31,	
	1997	1996
	$000's	$000's
Earnings before unusual item and income taxes	**142,704**	85,308
Nominal tax provision at average statutory Canadian income tax rates	**62,362**	37,194
Increase (decrease) in income taxes resulting from:		
Large corporations tax	**6,913**	6,617
Tax rates in other jurisdictions	**1,107**	388
Net capital gains and losses	**(28)**	(128)
Other permanent differences	**(191)**	6,687
Archives donation:		
Decrease in income taxes	**–**	(4,396)
Payable to charitable foundations	**–**	4,396
Income taxes on earnings before unusual item and income taxes per Consolidated Statements of Earnings	**70,163**	50,758

In March 1995 the Canadian Cultural Property Review Board increased by $10,100,000 its determination of the fair value of the Company's archives collection that had been donated to the Provincial Archives of Manitoba during the year ended January 31, 1994. The resulting additional tax reduction of $4,396,000, after deducting expenses, was contributed to Hudson's Bay History Foundation and Hudson's Bay Charitable Foundation in October 1995. These amounts were offset in calculating income taxes on earnings for the year ended January 31, 1996.

6. EARNINGS PER SHARE

Fully diluted earnings per share for the years ended January 31, 1997 and January 31, 1996 are higher than the reported earnings per share, or anti-dilutive. The weighted average number of common shares outstanding are recalculated under the assumption that all outstanding stock options at January 31 of each year (both vested and unvested - see note 14) had been exercised as of the preceeding February 1, with the resulting proceeds used to reduce interest-bearing short-term borrowings.

7. CREDIT CARD RECEIVABLES

Under a securitization program, on January 27, 1997 the Company sold, with limited recourse, a $300 million undivided co-ownership interest in certain of its credit card receivables to an independent Trust. No gain or loss has been recorded by the Company as a result of this transaction. The Company is acting as the servicer of these accounts and pays to the Trust a portion of service charge revenues derived from the sold co-ownership interest equal to the Trust's stipulated share thereof.

8. SECURED RECEIVABLES

Secured receivables comprise the following:

	January 31,	
	1997	1996
	$000's	$000's
Mortgages	18,613	9,834
Employee share ownership plan loans	9,971	11,234
Total secured receivables	28,584	21,068
Less amounts due within one year classified as other accounts receivable	(4,986)	(9,035)
	23,598	12,033

Maturities of secured receivables are summarized as follows:

	$000's
Year ending January 31,	
1998	4,986
1999	3,688
2000	1,746
2001	1,898
2002	2,025
Subsequent periods	14,241
	28,584

The mortgages are secured by property and the employee share ownership plan loans are secured by shares of Hudson's Bay Company. The average interest rate on secured receivables is 3.5% at January 31, 1997 and 4.8% at January 31, 1996. Under certain conditions, the amounts due may be received prior to maturity.

9. FIXED ASSETS

Fixed assets comprise the following:

	January 31,	
	1997	1996
	$000's	$000's
Cost:		
Land	82,855	82,857
Buildings	322,414	317,636
Equipment	1,009,912	988,432
Equipment held under capital leases	7,093	7,093
Leasehold improvements	306,817	274,135
Property for sale or development	41,902	40,937
	1,770,993	1,711,090
Accumulated amortization:		
Buildings	(146,614)	(136,751)
Equipment	(573,094)	(518,722)
Equipment held under capital leases	(4,239)	(3,285)
Leasehold improvements	(80,865)	(62,874)
	(804,812)	(721,632)
	966,181	989,458

10. GOODWILL

Of the unamortized balance of goodwill that arose on the acquisitions of Zellers Inc., Towers Department Stores Inc. (since amalgamated with Zellers Inc.) and the Linmark group of companies, $47,802,000 will be amortized over the next 24 years, $27,577,000 over the next 14 years and $16,390,000 over the next 16 years, respectively.

11. PENSIONS

Pensions in the Consolidated Balance Sheets represents the recorded portion of the excess of the market value of defined benefit pension plan assets over the related accrued obligations.

In respect of defined benefit pension plans at January 31, 1997, the aggregate market value of assets is $791,000,000 and the aggregate actuarial present value of accrued obligations is $458,000,000. Corresponding aggregate asset and obligation amounts for defined benefit pension plans at January 31, 1996 were $701,000,000 and $442,000,000, respectively.

12. OTHER ASSETS

Other assets comprise the following:

	January 31,	
	1997	1996
	$000's	$000's
Deferred and prepaid rent	**61,146**	75,968
Merchandise systems development costs	**17,978**	22,186
Post employment benefits other than pensions	**2,101**	4,193
Debt discount and expense	**5,052**	3,244
Other	**8,238**	4,638
	94,515	110,229

13. DEBT

Total debt comprises the following:

	January 31,	
	1997	1996
	$000's	$000's
Short-term borrowings	**65,849**	115,395
Less short-term deposits	**(18,079)**	(16,283)
Less portfolio investments	**(45,086)**	(50,407)
Net short-term borrowings	**2,684**	48,705
Long-term debt due within one year	**49,122**	119,182
Long-term debt	**1,061,453**	1,362,704
	1,113,259	1,530,591

Short-term borrowings principally comprise commercial paper, which bears interest at an average rate of 3.1% at January 31, 1997 and 5.5% at January 31, 1996. The portfolio investments bear interest at an average rate of 7.6% at January 31, 1997 and 7.3% at January 31, 1996.

Long-term debt comprises the following:

	January 31,	
	1997	1996
	$000's	$000's
Secured on credit card receivables:		
Hudson's Bay Company Acceptance Limited		
11.56% debentures series N due 1996	**–**	25,000
11.23% debentures series N due 1996	**–**	25,000
13.75% debentures series G due 2001	**44,878**	44,544
Floating rate term loans due 1996	**–**	25,000
	44,878	119,544
Secured - other:		
Hudson's Bay Company		
Capital lease obligations at an average rate of 10.5% and maturing in 2000	**3,230**	4,210
Total secured	**48,108**	123,754
Unsecured:		
Hudson's Bay Company		
15.36% term loan due 1995-1997 (£1,541,000)	**3,342**	9,007
8.00% debentures series A due 2000	**150,000**	150,000
7.95% debentures series B due 2001	**125,000**	–
6.25% debentures series C due 2002	**125,000**	–
Floating rate debt:		
Term loans due 1998	**–**	470,000
Term loans due 1999	**200,000**	95,000
Term loans due 2000	**149,125**	634,125
Term loans due 2001	**310,000**	–
Total unsecured	**1,062,467**	1,358,132
	1,110,575	1,481,886
Less amounts due within one year	**(49,122)**	(119,182)
	1,061,453	1,362,704

Long-term floating rate debt shown above (including amounts due within one year) comprises term loans with several financial institutions.

The interest rate on $475,000,000 of this debt has been fixed at an average of 7.25% through a number of interest rate swap agreements, under which the Company agrees with a counterparty to exchange, at specified intervals and for a specified period, its floating interest rate for a fixed interest rate calculated on an agreed upon notional principal amount. These swaps effectively enable the Company to convert these floating rate interest obligations into fixed rate obligations.

The interest rate on a further $200,000,000 has been capped at rates ranging from 8.75% to 9.0% through several interest rate cap agreements under which, after payment of an up front fee to a counterparty, the Company is entitled to receive from the counterparty the amount, if any, by which the Company's interest payments exceed a predetermined level. These caps are used to limit the potential impact of major increases in interest rates on floating rate long-term debt while allowing the Company to participate fully in decreases in interest rates.

All of these agreements have been made with Canadian chartered banks.

On January 28, 1997 the Company announced its intention to redeem the 13.75% debentures series G at a premium of 0.75% above the face value, and the debentures were redeemed for $44,878,000 on February 28, 1997.

Most of the long-term debt issues are subject to cancellation or redemption at the option of the issuer at various times or under certain conditions.

Maturities of long-term debt are summarized as follows:

	$000's
Year ending January 31,	
1998	**49,122**
1999	**960**
2000	**201,059**
2001	**299,434**
2002	**435,000**
Subsequent periods	**125,000**
	1,110,575

14. CAPITAL STOCK

The authorized classes of shares of the Company consist of unlimited numbers of preferred shares and common shares, all without nominal or par value.

There are no outstanding preferred shares. The changes in common shares issued and outstanding during the two years ended January 31, 1997 are as follows:

	Number of Shares	$000's
Issued and outstanding at January 31, 1995	57,634,584	1,055,023
Issued:		
Under the dividend reinvestment plan	849,419	18,524
Under the executive stock option plan	245,019	3,604
Under the senior executive share purchase plan	87,220	2,260
Issued and outstanding at January 31, 1996	58,816,242	1,079,411
Issued:		
Under the dividend reinvestment plan	**677,973**	**13,623**
Under the executive stock option plan	**266,298**	**4,122**
Under the senior executive share purchase plan	**139,100**	**2,460**
Issued and outstanding at January 31, 1997	**59,899,613**	**1,099,616**

Weighted average numbers of common shares outstanding during each of the years ended January 31 are as follows:

1997	**59,284,836**
1996	58,109,024

At January 31, 1997, 5,000,296 common shares were reserved for issuance under the executive stock option plan and the directors' stock option plan. Under these plans, 4,174,862 options are outstanding to purchase common shares at exercise prices equivalent to their fair market value per share immediately preceding the respective dates on which the options were granted. These outstanding options have a weighted average issue price of $24.09 per share and expire at various dates up to November 2006. Of the outstanding options, 1,585,638, having a weighted average issue price of $27.50 per share, are vested at January 31, 1997; only 424,065 of these vested options, with a weighted average of $17.49, had an issue price lower than the closing price of $23.85 at January 31, 1997. A further 578,090 common shares are reserved for issuance under the senior executive share purchase plan.

At January 31, 1997 the holders of 31.2% of the common shares were participating in the dividend reinvestment plan. Under the terms of this plan, dividends are reinvested in common shares at 95% of their weighted average market price during the three business days immediately preceding the dividend payment date.

15. FINANCIAL INSTRUMENTS

a) Fair values of financial instruments

The Company has estimated the fair values of its financial instruments as of January 31, 1997 and January 31, 1996, using quoted market values where available and other information. These estimates are not necessarily indicative of the amounts the Company might pay or receive in actual market transactions and do not include other transaction costs and income taxes. A comparison of book values with related estimated fair values at January 31, 1997 and January 31, 1996 is as follows:

	January 31,			
	1997		1996	
	Book Value	Fair Value	Book Value	Fair Value
	$000's	$000's	$000's	$000's
Financial assets				
Secured receivables	23,598	17,500	12,033	8,000
Portfolio investments	45,086	46,500	50,407	51,000
Financial liabilities				
Fixed rate long-term debt	(451,450)	(468,000)	(257,761)	(266,000)
Off balance sheet financial instruments				
Interest rate swaps in a net payable position		(26,000)		(17,500)
Interest rate caps		100		500

The above table does not include cash, short-term deposits, credit card receivables, other accounts receivable, short-term borrowings, forward rate agreements, trade accounts payable, other accounts payable and income taxes payable, as due to the immediate or short-term maturity of these financial instruments their book values approximate fair values. The table also excludes floating rate long-term debt, as due to the floating nature of the interest rates their book value approximates fair value.

The fair values shown in the above table, which are estimated as at January 31, 1997 and January 31, 1996, change daily as they approach maturity and as interest rates increase or decrease. These fair values are estimated as follows:

- Secured receivables - by determining equivalent principal amounts bearing interest at bank prime interest rates;
- Portfolio investments - based upon quoted market prices;
- Fixed rate long-term debt - based on quoted values which represent debt with similar terms and maturities;
- Interest rate swaps and caps - based on the estimated net cost or proceeds of unwinding the agreements.

The Company has no intention of unwinding the interest rate swap and interest rate cap agreements and therefore does not anticipate any impact on earnings arising from the differences between book value and fair value.

b) Off balance sheet financial instruments

The Company enters into various interest rate swap and cap agreements with counterparties (see note 13) to manage its exposure to interest rate risks. The Company believes that its exposure to credit and market risks for these financial instruments is negligible.

Notional principal amounts on outstanding interest rate contracts are as follows:

	January 31,	
	1997	1996
	$000's	$000's
Interest rate swap	475,000	450,000
Interest rate cap	200,000	200,000

The credit exposure relating to interest rate swaps and caps are not shown in the above table since the amounts are insignificant. Credit exposure represents the fair value of contracts with a positive fair value. If a counterparty were to fail to meet the terms of a swap or cap agreement, the Company's exposure would be limited to the net amount that otherwise would have been received over the remaining life of the agreement. The notional principal amounts shown in the above table are those on which interest amounts to be exchanged under the contracts are based. The Company enters into these contracts to lower the net cost of financing, to diversify sources of funding and/or to reduce interest rate exposures.

The following table indicates the type of interest rate swaps in place and their average interest rates:

	January 31,	
	1997	1996
	%	%
Pay-fixed swaps		
Average pay rate %	7.25	7.28
Average receive rate %	4.59	6.93

The Company also enters into forward rate agreements, a form of swap that allows the Company to lock in interest rates on future short-term borrowings.

In addition to interest rate agreements, the Company enters into forward foreign exchange contracts to lock in prices in Canadian dollars for future contracted purchases of merchandise from foreign suppliers. At January 31, 1997, the amount of outstanding foreign exchange contracts bought forward was U.S.$15,000,000.

16. NET CHANGE IN OPERATING WORKING CAPITAL

The net change in operating working capital appearing in the operating activities section of the Consolidated Statements of Cash Flow and Funding comprises the following:

	Years Ended January 31,	
	1997	1996
	$000's	$000's
Decrease (increase) in:		
Cash	**801**	(859)
Credit card receivables	**100,184**	15,372
Other accounts receivable	**7,637**	(10,797)
Merchandise inventories	**(56,584)**	(79,317)
Prepaid expenses	**12,780**	(3,680)
Increase (decrease) in:		
Trade accounts payable	**19,262**	21,152
Other accounts payable and		
accrued expenses	**(18,808)**	(15,719)
Income taxes payable	**(12,695)**	3,945
	52,577	(69,903)

17. LEASES

a)   As lessee

The Company conducts a substantial part of its operations from leased stores in shopping centres. All shopping centre leases have been accounted for as operating leases.

Rental expenses related to operating leases charged to earnings in the years ended January 31, 1997 and January 31, 1996 were $176,000,000 and $167,000,000, respectively.

The future minimum rental payments required under leases having initial or remaining lease terms in excess of one year are summarized as follows:

	Operating Leases	Capital Leases
	$000's	**$000's**
Year ending January 31,		
1998	**162,300**	**1,200**
1999	**161,600**	**1,200**
2000	**156,100**	**1,100**
2001	**149,900**	**300**
2002	**141,000**	–
Subsequent periods	**1,192,000**	–
	1,962,900	**3,800**

In addition to these rental payments (and, in a few cases, relatively minor contingent rentals), the leases generally provide for the payment by the Company of real estate taxes and other related expenses.

b)   As lessor

Fixed assets in the Consolidated Balance Sheets at January 31, 1997 and January 31, 1996 include an office tower partially leased to others under operating leases, with a cost of $22,100,000 at January 31, 1997 and $22,000,000 at January 31, 1996 and accumulated amortization of $8,500,000 and $8,100,000, respectively. Sales and revenue for the years ended January 31, 1997 and January 31, 1996 include third party rentals from this property of $3,100,000 and $3,600,000, respectively.

18. RELATED PARTY TRANSACTIONS

Transactions with related parties, which are in the ordinary course of business, are not significant in relation to these consolidated financial statements.

19. CONTINGENCIES

As of January 31, 1997 there are a number of claims against the Company in varying amounts and for which provisions have been made in these consolidated financial statements as appropriate. It is not possible to determine the amounts that may ultimately be assessed against the Company with respect to these claims but management believes that any such amounts would not have a material impact on the business or financial position of the Company.

Hudson's Bay Company

MANAGEMENT'S STATEMENT ON FINANCIAL REPORTING

Front:
Gary J. Lukassen
Executive Vice-President and
Chief Financial Officer

Back row, from left.
Harold Chmara
Vice-President,
Planning and Tax

Bill Luciano
Vice-President, Control
HBC Retail Group

Brian Grose
Vice-President,
Secretary and Controller

The management of Hudson's Bay Company is responsible for the preparation, presentation and integrity of the consolidated financial statements contained on pages 27 to 36 of this annual report and for financial information, discussion and analysis consistent therewith, presented on other pages. The accounting principles which form the basis of the consolidated financial statements and the more significant accounting policies applied are described in note 1 on pages 30 and 31. Where appropriate and necessary, professional judgments and estimates have been made by management in preparing the consolidated financial statements.

In order to meet its responsibility, management has established a code of business conduct and maintains accounting systems and related internal controls designed to provide reasonable assurance that assets are safeguarded and that transactions and events are properly recorded and reported. An integral part of these controls is the maintenance of programs of internal audit coordinated with the programs of the external auditors.

Ultimate responsibility for financial reporting to shareholders rests with the Board of Directors. The Audit Committee of the Board, all members of which are outside directors, meets quarterly with management and with internal and external auditors to review audit results, internal accounting controls and accounting principles and procedures. Internal and external auditors have unlimited access to the Audit Committee. The Audit Committee recommends to the Board the accounting firm to be named in the resolution to appoint auditors at each annual meeting of shareholders. The Audit Committee reviews consolidated financial statements and the other contents of the Annual Report with management and the external auditors and reports to the directors prior to their approval for publication.

KPMG, independent auditors appointed by the shareholders, express an opinion on the fair presentation of the consolidated financial statements. They meet regularly with both the Audit Committee and management to discuss matters arising from their audit, which includes a review of accounting records and internal controls. The Auditors' Report to Shareholders is presented on page 38.

President and
Chief Executive Officer

Executive Vice-President and
Chief Financial Officer

Toronto, Canada
March 6, 1997

KPMG   AUDITORS' REPORT TO SHAREHOLDERS

We have audited the consolidated balance sheets of Hudson's Bay Company as at January 31, 1997 and January 31, 1996 and the consolidated statements of earnings, retained earnings and cash flow and funding for the years then ended. These financial statements are the responsibility of the Company's management. Our responsibility is to express an opinion on these financial statements based on our audits.

We conducted our audits in accordance with generally accepted auditing standards. Those standards require that we plan and perform an audit to obtain reasonable assurance whether the financial statements are free of material misstatement. An audit includes examining, on a test basis, evidence supporting the amounts and disclosures in the financial statements. An audit also includes assessing the accounting principles used and significant estimates made by management, as well as evaluating the overall financial statement presentation.

In our opinion, these consolidated financial statements present fairly, in all material respects, the financial position of the Company as at January 31, 1997 and January 31, 1996 and the results of its operations and the changes in its financial position for the years then ended in accordance with generally accepted accounting principles.

KPMG

Chartered Accountants

Toronto, Canada
March 6, 1997

Hudson's Bay Company

STATEMENT OF CORPORATE GOVERNANCE PRACTICES

The following statement, which describes the Company's Corporate Governance Practices, is provided in response to the requirements of both The Toronto Stock Exchange and the Montreal Exchange.

The statement has been approved by the Board of Directors on the recommendation of the Corporate Governance Committee.

Composition of the Board of Directors

The listing of the 13 directors, which appears on page 41 of this Annual Report, discloses the principal occupation and some brief additional information regarding each Board member. On a rigorous application of the definitions (see footnote), the Board believes that 10 of the current directors are both unrelated and outside directors, one unrelated director would be considered an inside director and the remaining two directors are both related and inside directors. In coming to this conclusion, the Board examined the factual circumstances of each director in the context of many factors.

Mr. David E. Mitchell O.C., appointed to the position of Governor in May 1994, serves as Chairman of the Board and is an unrelated director. As an officer of the Company, Mr. Mitchell would be considered an inside director even though he has never been a member of management.

The company has two related directors who are also inside directors, Mr. George J. Kosich and Mr. Gary J. Lukassen, the Chief Executive Officer and the Chief Financial Officer, respectively.

Several outside directors serve on the boards of banks and other corporations with which the Company does business from time to time. As a matter of course they declare their interests and abstain from voting on any resolutions which relate to dealings with the corporations on whose boards they serve. One director is a partner in a firm of lawyers which acts for the Corporation to a limited degree. In no case is the volume or nature of the business transacted sufficiently material to prejudice the independence of a director.

There is no significant shareholder, as defined, the largest beneficial shareholding being approximately 22%. Four (31%) of the 13 directors are associated with this shareholder. These directors were appointed between ten and 18 years

ago, at times when this largest shareholding exceeded 70%. The Board believes that their experience and knowledge of the Company and its business outweigh any perceived advantage that could result from requiring strictly proportionate representation and that their association does not affect the independence of their judgement.

When appropriate, to ensure Board independence from management, inside directors (other than the unrelated Governor) are requested to withdraw from meetings of the Board and similarly of any Board Committees which have inside members. At least one informal meeting is held annually to which only outside directors are invited.

No circumstances have yet arisen which would require the appointment of an outside adviser to an individual Board member. Any such appointment would be subject to prior approval by the Board.

The size of Board was reduced from 17 to 16 in 1994, to 14 in 1995 and to 13 in 1996. A Board of about the current size, including two executives, should suffice but the most appropriate number will be determined annually based on contemporary needs.

The directors' compensation package is reviewed annually and adjusted when deemed appropriate in reference to those of other corporations of similar size and complexity as well as to responsibilities and risks assumed.

New Board members are invited by the Governor to meet with himself, the C.E.O. and other senior officers for discussion and review prior to attending their first Board meeting. Tours of stores and other facilities are tailored to meet individual requirements. Each Board member receives a Directors' Handbook which provides much of the information directors need to have. Periodic educational sessions for experienced as well as new directors are held preceding Board meetings at which one or more of the unique aspects of the retail business are discussed in some detail.

Mandate of the Board of Directors

The mandate of the Board of Directors, as required by business corporation legislation, is to supervise the management of the business and affairs of the Company and act in the best interests of the Company.

In fulfilling this mandate the Board has assigned to Board Committees the responsibility for reviewing and making recommendations on many of the matters requiring its attention. Principal Board concerns, in addition to the matters listed by Committee below, include the approval of: strategies, long term objectives and major policies; succession plans for senior management and the Board itself; capital and operating budgets; and long range plans.

The Board meets regularly each quarter and, in addition, meets at the call of the chair when matters of Board significance require attention between regularly scheduled meetings. The frequency of meetings as well as the nature of agenda items vary depending on the state of the Company's affairs and the opportunities and challenges it faces. During the 1996 fiscal year the Board met on nine occasions.

It has been the practice for one Board meeting in each year of the last several years to be held in a city other than Toronto. This has enabled Board members to visit a varied selection of Bay and Zellers stores and to meet with local management with a view to better understanding regional differences in the business. Due to the pressure of other business this practice was not followed in 1996 but it is expected to be resumed in the current year.

Under corporate legislation there are a number of items which may not be delegated by a board of directors. In addition to these the Board has resolved that it will not delegate authority: to appoint officers of the Company; to approve projects in excess of a predetermined sum which have not been specifically included in the capital budget; or to approve sales of fixed assets or disposal of long-term leases with either proceeds or book values in excess of a predetermined sum.

The Board's first expectation of management is that the Board will be kept adequately informed on all material matters necessary for it to supervise the management of the business and affairs of the Company.

The Board holds management responsible for the overall performance of the Company within a sensible balance of both long and short-term objectives and for attention to the specific interests of shareholders. Management is required to submit a detailed strategic plan to the Board annually and a full day's meeting is devoted to a review of this plan prior to its adoption.

The Board expects that management will adhere to the established code of business conduct and will maintain the necessary systems, procedures and controls to manage the Company's business effectively and to enhance and safeguard its assets with due regard for environmental, health and safety concerns.

Communications of major significance are reviewed at Board or Committee level before release. Responsibility for other communications with shareholders, other stakeholders, suppliers, customers and the general public is delegated to the officer most appropriate to the topic to be communicated. Shareholder and other enquiries are responded to promptly by the Secretary or other appropriate officer of the Company.

Committees of the Board of Directors

There are six Standing Committees of the Board as follows:

Audit, Compensation, Corporate Governance, Executive, Pension and Social Responsibility.

In addition there is an Ad Hoc Succession Committee.

The list of directors, which appears on page 41 of this Annual Report, discloses the membership of each Board Committee. Apart from the Governor all members of Board Committees, other

than as noted for the Executive and Pension Committees and the Ad Hoc Succession Committee are outside unrelated directors.

The **Audit Committee,** comprising four unrelated outside directors, meets quarterly and advises the Board on matters relating to: external auditors; internal auditors; financial reporting; accounting policies, systems and procedures; and financial management. The Committee reviews principal risks and the integrity of internal control systems and of management information systems.

The **Compensation Committee,** comprising four unrelated directors, meets as required at the call of the chairman, who is an outside director. The Committee advises the Board regarding compensation policies and practices generally and the remuneration of senior executives in particular. During the 1996 fiscal year the Committee met on three occasions.

The **Corporate Governance Committee,** comprising four unrelated directors, is chaired by the Governor and meets as required at the call of the chair. It performs the functions of a nominating committee in addition to its responsibility for other aspects of corporate governance. The Committee has the responsibility to assess the effectiveness of the Board, its Committees and its members. During the 1996 fiscal year the Committee met on three occasions.

The **Executive Committee,** comprising five members, chaired by the Governor, includes both the Chief Executive Officer and the Chief Financial Officer as it is believed to be both necessary and appropriate for the effective operation of this Committee that these officers be full voting members. The Committee has eight scheduled meetings per year and, in addition, meets as required at the call of the chair. It reviews performance and deals with matters which do not require decisions of the full Board. Between Board meetings it may exercise the powers of the Board other than those which may not be delegated or which have been reserved by the Board. During the 1996 fiscal year the Committee met on 10 occasions.

The **Pension Committee,** comprising three members, meets quarterly. Membership includes the Chief Financial Officer as it is believed to be both necessary and appropriate for the effective operation of this Committee that this officer be a full voting member. The Committee oversees pension plans, including investment, safekeeping, procedural and administrative matters.

The **Social Responsibility Committee,** comprising four unrelated directors, meets quarterly to review compliance with legislation in a manner consistent with the legitimate best interests of the Company's customers, employees, shareholders and the communities in which it conducts its business. Principal areas of concern include health and safety, employment equity, environmental protection, legal and ethical compliance, government and community relations, and donations.

An **Ad Hoc Succession Committee,** comprising four members, was formed in 1995 to review, and advise the Board concerning, succession plans for the key senior executive positions. Membership includes both the Governor and the Chief Executive Officer. The Committee meets at the call of the chairman, who is an unrelated outside director.

Regardless of regularly scheduled meetings, the chairperson of a Board Committee would call a special purpose meeting at the request of any member of the Committee. In the case of the Audit Committee a meeting also would be called at the request of either the external or the internal auditor.

A copy of the minutes of each Committee meeting is distributed to every director. Committee chairpersons report as appropriate at each Board meeting and an opportunity is provided for dialogue between Committee members and the full Board.

Note: The guidelines set out in the report of The Toronto Stock Exchange Committee on Corporate Governance in Canada, dated December 1994, form the basis of this Statement of Practices. Terms such as "inside director", "unrelated director" and "significant shareholder" used in this statement are as defined in the TSE report.

Hudson's Bay Company

DIRECTORS

W. Michael Brown, Stamford, Ct.
President, The Thomson Corporation,
an information, publishing and leisure travel
company which is associated with the largest
shareholder of Hudson's Bay Company.

Elected 1985   (3)(7)

Dominic D'Alessandro, Toronto
President and Chief Executive Officer,
Manulife Financial,
a leading Canadian-based international life
insurance company.

Elected 1996   (2)

L. Yves Fortier, Montreal
Chairman and Senior Partner,
Ogilvy Renault, Barristers and Solicitors.
Mr. Fortier is a former Canadian Ambassador
to the United Nations.

Elected 1993   (1)(3)(5)

Barbara R. Hislop, Vancouver
Group Vice-President, Coastal Operations,
Canfor Corporation,
a forest industry company.

Elected 1993   (4)(5)

Gurth C. Hoyer Millar, London, England
Chairman, HW Park Place Limited,
a venture capital company.

Elected 1976   (4)(7)

George J. Kosich, Toronto
President and Chief Executive Officer,
Hudson's Bay Company.

Elected 1985   (1)(7)

Gary J. Lukassen, Toronto
Executive Vice-President and
Chief Financial Officer,
Hudson's Bay Company.

Elected 1987   (1)(6)

Dawn R. McKeag, Winnipeg
President, Walford Investments Ltd.
Mrs. McKeag is a director of a number
of major companies.

Elected 1975   (4)

Peter W. Mills, Toronto
Senior Vice-President and
General Counsel,
The Woodbridge Company Limited.
Mr. Mills is an officer and director of a
number of companies associated with the
largest shareholder of Hudson's Bay
Company.

Elected 1985   (2)(5)(6)

David E. Mitchell, Calgary
Governor of Hudson's Bay Company and
Chairman, Alberta Energy Company Ltd.,
an energy and resource development
company.

Elected 1984   (1)(2)(3)(4)(5)(7)

Guy St-Germain, Montreal
President, Placements Laugerma Inc.,
a private holding company.
Mr. St-Germain is a director of several
major Canadian corporations.

Elected 1994   (2)(6)

David K. R. Thomson, Toronto
Deputy Chairman,
The Woodbridge Company Limited.
Mr. Thomson is an associate of the largest
shareholder of Hudson's Bay Company.

Elected 1987

John A. Tory, Toronto
Deputy Chairman,
The Thomson Corporation.
Mr. Tory is an officer and director
of a number of companies associated with the
largest shareholder of
Hudson's Bay Company.

Elected 1979   (1)(3)

(1) Member of Executive Committee
(2) Member of Audit Committee
(3) Member of Compensation Committee
(4) Member of Social Responsibility Committee
(5) Member of Corporate Governance Committee
(6) Member of Pension Committee
(7) Member of Ad Hoc Succession Committee

OFFICERS

David E. Mitchell
Governor

13 years as a director
3 as an officer

George J. Kosich
President and
Chief Executive Officer

37 years service
12 as a director
13 as an officer

Gary J. Lukassen
Executive Vice-President and
Chief Financial Officer

22 years service
10 as a director
11 as an officer

N. R. (Bob) Peter
Executive Vice-President
also:
President, The Bay

28 years service
12 as an officer

Millard E. Barron
Executive Vice-President
also:
President, Zellers Inc.

1 year service
1 as an officer

Stuart W. Fraser
Executive Vice-President,
Logistics, Distribution and
Information Services

24 years service
3 as an officer

Robert N. D. Hogan
Executive Vice-President,
Credit and Financial
Marketing Services

24 years service
12 as an officer

Harold J. Chmara
Vice-President,
Planning and Tax

17 years service
4 as an officer

David J. Crisp
Vice-President,
Human Resources

12 years service
9 as an officer

Brian C. Grose
Vice-President,
Secretary and Controller

33 years service
18 as an officer

Donald C. Rogers
Vice-President,
Real Estate and
Development

24 years service
12 as an officer

Kenneth C. Wong
Assistant Treasurer

11 years service
11 as an officer

Hudson's Bay Company

Tᴇɴ Yᴇᴀʀ Fɪɴᴀɴᴄɪᴀʟ Sᴜᴍᴍᴀʀʏ

For the purpose of comparability, extraordinary items, unusual tax credits and restructuring costs and related taxes have been eliminated and certain other figures have been restated or reclassified.

	1996	1995
Number of weeks	52	52
Operations (in millions of dollars)		
Sales and revenue:		
The Bay	2,333	2,348
Zellers	3,578	3,537
Other	96	99
Total sales and revenue	6,007	5,984
Operating profit:		
The Bay	131	121
Zellers	116	107
Other	4	(14)
Earnings before interest and income taxes	251	214
Interest expense	(108)	(129)
Earnings before income taxes	143	85
Income taxes	(70)	(51)
Earnings	73	34
Cash flow:		
From earnings	189	162
From changes in operating working capital	52	(70)
From operations	241	92
Securitization of receivables	300	–
Capital expenditures	(121)	(238)
Investments	–	–
Common dividends	(43)	(53)
Other (including preferred dividends from 1987 to 1991 inclusive)	20	7
Net cash inflow from (outflow for) activities and dividends	397	(192)
Assets Employed (in millions of dollars)		
The Bay	1,213	1,478
Zellers	1,568	1,694
Other	256	281
Assets employed	3,037	3,453
Funding thereof:		
Debt	1,113	1,531
Deferred income taxes	132	144
Shareholders' equity	1,792	1,778
	3,037	3,453
Debt:Equity Ratio	0.6:1	0.9:1
Per Common Share (in dollars)		
Earnings	1.22	0.59
Cash flow from earnings	3.18	2.79
Dividends	0.72	0.92
Equity	29.92	30.24
Shareholders		
Number of registered common shareholders	6,700	6,800
Common shares outstanding (in millions):		
Year end	59.9	58.8
Weighted average	59.3	58.1
Range in common share price during year (in dollars):		
After Markborough spin-off	25-16	29-17
Before Markborough spin-off		
The Economy (% change)		
Gross domestic product (GDP)	1.5	2.3
Consumer price index (CPI)	1.6	2.1
Department store sales (DSS)	4.4	4.1
Department store type merchandise sales (DSTM)	2.6	1.7

1994	1993	1992	1991	1990	1989	1988	1987
52	52	53	52	52	52	52	52
2,353	2,183	2,017	2,118	2,322	2,296	2,334	2,356
3,375	3,159	3,021	2,789	2,330	2,150	2,011	1,845
101	99	114	125	318	158	146	144
5,829	5,441	5,152	5,032	4,970	4,604	4,491	4,345
161	122	91	59	122	129	89	81
216	256	229	218	200	180	142	93
(8)	(14)	7	7	(5)	6	(3)	7
369	364	327	284	317	315	228	181
(100)	(97)	(128)	(144)	(155)	(158)	(171)	(168)
269	267	199	140	162	157	57	13
(118)	(119)	(82)	(57)	(64)	(59)	(20)	–
151	148	117	83	98	98	37	13
346	325	230	170	203	190	104	119
(252)	(172)	6	(91)	16	44	44	(134)
94	153	236	79	219	234	148	(15)
–	–		–	–	–	–	–
(202)	(153)	(128)	(122)	(120)	(92)	(36)	(30)
–	(107)	–	(36)	(142)	–	–	–
(52)	(44)	(40)	(40)	(36)	(21)	(18)	(18)
(30)	2	20	9	(32)	10	(10)	43
(190)	(149)	88	(110)	(111)	131	84	(20)
1,440	1,373	1,220	1,237	1,294	1,270	1,301	1,288
1,594	1,344	1,229	1,170	934	757	703	700
241	180	188	181	173	171	227	400
3,275	2,897	2,637	2,588	2,401	2,198	2,231	2,388
1,364	1,200	1,239	1,335	1,243	1,147	1,441	1,549
138	83	82	27	(14)	6	(1)	(42)
1,773	1,614	1,316	1,226	1,172	1,045	791	881
3,275	2,897	2,637	2,588	2,401	2,198	2,231	2,388
0.8:1	0.7:1	0.9:1	1.1:1	1.1:1	1.1:1	1.8:1	1.8:1
2.66	2.72	2.32	1.61	2.01	2.26	0.32	(0.51)
6.07	5.98	4.57	3.36	4.35	5.02	2.53	3.05
0.92	0.80	0.80	0.80	0.80	0.60	0.60	0.60
30.76	28.56	25.92	24.43	23.53	21.09	14.41	16.33
6,900	7,100	6,800	7,000	7,400	7,800	8,900	9,300
57.6	56.5	50.8	49.8	45.6	44.6	31.0	30.2
57.0	54.2	50.3	49.0	45.0	33.5	30.6	29.8
33-23	41-29	32-26	37-24	24-16			
				34-28	38-25	26-19	29-18
4.1	2.2	0.8	(1.8)	(0.2)	2.4	5.0	4.2
0.2	1.8	1.5	5.6	4.8	5.0	4.0	4.4
3.9	(1.7)	0.8	(5.7)	2.0	4.8	2.8	1.4
4.9	4.4	3.2	(3.5)	1.7	5.1	7.0	8.6

automotive sales between 1992 and 1993 (12.9 million to 13.9 million) as well as the upward turn in home and industrial construction lead to an increased demand for steel. At the same time as increased demand and corresponding increases in prices reshaped the market, most producers also cut costs and upgraded operations. A drop of approximately 10% in the value of the Canadian dollar since 1990 also helped the steel industry make its products more attractive in foreign markets.

In 1994 and the first half of 1995 low interest rates and continued increasing demand for flat-rolled steel products furthered the recovery of the steel industry. In fact, in 1994 demand grew by 16% in Canada because of economic recovery and booming auto sales. This level of demand was actually 11% higher than the previous peak demand in 1988.

By the fourth quarter of 1995, the Canadian steel industry was again faced with weak demand, low prices, and high inventory levels, due to high import levels, a continued slump in the housing market, and a shaky Canadian economy. It is predicted that the steel industry will rebound in 1996 and 1997 due to further reductions in interest rates, an increase in demand, and higher prices. Contributing to the positive outlook for the steel industry is the rapidly rising prices for lumber, which makes steel more attractive as a substitute for wood. However, tempering the positive outlook for the industry are the high levels of imports which are expected to continue to pose a threat to the Canadian steel industry unless dumping by American producers is eliminated.

Technological Changes

The biggest technological change in the industry has been the growth and success of the mini-mill and the corresponding move away from fully integrated steel manufacturing mills. Declining demand for steel sheets, increasing markets for structural steel (which is used in the housing market), as well as lower costs are largely responsible for this shift.

Mini-mills are smaller, cheaper steel makers that use scrap steel and electric arc furnaces (as opposed to oxygen and blast furnaces) to produce structural steel. This process was developed over the past 20 years, and is considered to be more efficient than the old-fashioned method of producing steel from iron and coke in large, expensive blast furnaces. Mini-mill technology is also less complex than technology employed in fully integrated operations, allowing for lower costs due to less material handling, less processing time, lower energy consumption requirements, and lower direct labour requirements.

Mini-mills require approximately 0.6 labour hours to produce one ton of steel through the hot rolling process, while integrated manufacturers require 2.5 to 3 labour hours to produce the same amount. Nucor Corporation, a mini-mill located in Charlotte, North Carolina, has even pushed mini-mills into the last exclusive domain of integrated steel producers: the flat-rolled steel market. As a result, by the end of 1993, mini-mills had gained approximately 95% of the market for structural steel, and were beginning to gain market share in the flat-rolled steel product sector.

Mini-mills do face some disadvantages in comparison to integrated producers. At present they are unable to make certain coated steel and high quality, high technical specification steel required for car fenders and appliances. Mini-mills also face limited capacity which must be overcome if they are to compete over the long haul with fully integrated producers in the flat-rolled steel market.

Restructuring

Labour disputes, decreased demand, increased use of substitutes, the recession, and increased competition from the United States' steel producers has led to vast restructuring and downsizing in the Canadian steel industry. In fact, during the ten year period between 1983 and 1993 Canadians employed in the steel industry decreased from 42,000 to 32,000. This was partly due to the decreasing demand for steel sheets and the increasing market for structural steel, which is used in housing, and produced in mini-mills. The mini-mills require less direct labour, which contributed to the downsizing trend. As a result, the three major steel producers in Canada were forced to refocus their attentions on core activities by divesting themselves of non-core activities, reorganizing their business centres, and controlling expenditures.

The restructuring and reorganization efforts met with stiff resistance from the steel producers' unionized labour forces.[1] While the steel producers were chiefly concerned with survival during the recession of the early 1990s, the steel workers' unions were trying to negotiate new collective bargaining agreements which would minimize the job losses and pay reductions. As a result, in 1990 both Stelco and Algoma faced damaging lengthy strikes. The issues in these strikes included job security, contracting out, pension security, wage increases, and the general mistrust between the unions and management. Both companies eventually recovered from the lengthy strikes and were able to concentrate on paying down their debts and strengthening their balance sheets.

Trade Disputes

Despite the implementation of NAFTA, many trade disputes between American and Canadian steel producers continue to plague the industry. One of the main reasons that trade disputes continue between the countries is the failure of the respective governments to implement one of the key provisions of the Canada-U.S. Free Trade Agreement—a set of bilateral trading rules. The NAFTA deadline for negotiating common trade rules expired in December 1995.

The contrast between the domestic trading laws of each country is detrimental to Canadian steel producers. According to Canadian trading regulations domestic manufacturers have the onus to prove they have been injured by imports. Even when a finding of "dumping"[2] is made by the Canadian International Trade Tribunal (the CITT), no penalty need ever be paid provided the importer prices its products above average variable cost. Lastly, rulings made by the CITT are enforced for a period of five years. Conversely, under U.S. trade law, Canadian exporters must prove that they are not causing injury to the American industry. Further, U.S. law requires that the foreign producer post a duty deposit for more than a year, even when dumping is not proven. Finally, U.S. trade rulings are enforced indefinitely.

The amount of steel imported into Canada doubled between 1985 and 1991, and has continued to rise. Canadian producers claim that their American counterparts are dumping steel into Canada because lower American labour costs and taxes make it difficult for the Canadian producers to compete on price.

---

[1] Stelco and Algoma are unionized, while Dofasco is not.

[2] Dumping is defined as selling products in a foreign market for less than the price in the domestic market.

Since the trade pacts were signed between the three parties to NAFTA, the U.S. has launched five steel trade actions against Canadian producers, while Canada has filed four challenges against U.S. companies. Canadian steel producers continue to lobby the federal government to change the process by which the CITT administers Canadian trade regulations until common trade rules are negotiated between the two countries.

In 1995, the United States steel industry lost its appeal of the CITT's finding of injury against galvanized and cold-rolled steel shipments into Canada. Conversely, Dofasco is awaiting a final determination by the U.S. department of Commerce of the appropriate duty rate to be applied to galvanized steel products shipped into the U.S., while it continues to pay a rate of 11.71%.

CASE 2   Stelco Inc.

Background

Since the Steel Company of Canada was originally incorporated in 1910 by a financier named Max Aitken, Stelco Inc. (Stelco) has grown to become Canada's largest producer of steel. The company was organized into its present form in 1969 from the amalgamation of a variety of companies including: The Steel Company of Canada, Page-Hersey Tubes Ltd., Premium Steel Mills Ltd., and the Canadian Drawn Steel Company. In the late 1980s and 1990 Stelco had two separate operating divisions—Stelco Steel and Stelco Corporation. In 1991 both these companies were combined to form the Stelco Corporation, which is the holding company for all Stelco businesses, including wholly owned business units, subsidiaries, and joint ventures.

Stelco is an integrated maker of steel, which means that it produces steel from its basic components of iron ore, coal, and lime in a blast furnace. The steel is then rolled into a variety of products, including flat-rolled products (sheet, strip, and plate), long products (rods and bars), tubular products such as diameter pipe, and a variety of wire and wire products.

Stelco's two main facilities are its wholly owned Hilton Works and Lake Erie Works. Hilton Works is located in Hamilton and occupies 1,100 acres, and has harbour facilities on site. In the late 1980s and early 1990s the Hilton Works facility was Stelco's highest cost steel mill. However, as Stelco has rebounded from the difficulties of the recession, the Hilton Works facility has become more cost efficient and has continued to improve the quality of its products. By 1995 Hilton Works had attained the ISO 9002 certification in its six product areas (the hot strip mill, plate mill, cold mill, galvanized department, no. 1 bar mill, and no. 2 rod mill). This is an impressive achievement in light of the fact that Hilton Works is one of the most product-diversified steel plants in North America.

Stelco's other main steel producing facility, Lake Erie Works, was commissioned from 1980 to 1983. Its principal product is high quality rolled steel sheets, and the focus of the plant is production for one segment of the marketplace (the automotive sector). The hot strip mill functioned at peak levels and attained record levels of output in 1994 and 1995, achieving 173,205 net tons of output in October 1995. The hot strip mill was also awarded ISO 9002 certification in 1995. Finally, the steel plant scrapped a $100 million improvement plan, which would have increased capacity and employment, after it failed to reach a new collective agreement with its 1,000 member local of the United Steelworkers of

America, 14 months prior to the expiration of the previously existing collective agreement. Financing for the Lake Erie upgrade was conditional on an early collective agreement, which was required to ensure operational continuity. The project had been planned to coincide with the scheduled 33-day shutdown in the summer of 1996 to complete a $32 million relining of the blast furnace. The improvements would have provided the facility with improved production quality by upgrading the slab caster and hot strip mill, which in turn would have ensured the competitiveness of the site for the foreseeable future.

Strategic Priorities and Direction

Stelco, much like its competitors, was significantly affected by the recession of the early 1990s. As a result, Stelco embarked on a cost cutting and restructuring plan to revitalize its operations and position itself for a strong recovery. Stelco downsized its labour force by more than 4,000 employees, and began to divest itself of non-core assets, in order to concentrate on its core steel making operations. This resulted in the sale of Kautex of Canada, a manufacturer of plastic automobiles, in 1991, and in 1994 Stelco finalized its sale of Stelco Technology Services to Hatch Associates.

Stelco also embarked on a business reorganization of its operating units. Previously, Stelco's production units had been centrally controlled by the head office in Hamilton, Ontario. As part of Stelco's strategic plan, senior management decided to reorganize its business centres and its traditional method of approving projects. Since 1991, senior management has turned Stelco's 14 major wholly owned subsidiaries into separate viable business units, each of which is responsible for justifying its own projects. Under this cost centre approach, each plant must come up with its own projects as well as the necessary financing. As a result, Stelco will now only allow capital projects that are cash flow neutral or better, so as not to hurt the company's improving balance sheet. This approach to approving capital expenditures is part of Stelco's overall plan of reducing costs and not incurring any further debt.

Stelco has managed to repair much of the damage caused by the company's 1991 cash flow crisis, which was brought on by the recessionary steel markets and the long strikes of 1991. Stelco managed to survive the crisis by drastically cutting costs, issuing common shares and warrants for a total of $364 million in net proceeds, and temporarily suspending preferred dividends. As well, the strong turnaround in the steel market in 1994 and the consequent improvement in the company's cash flow position were crucial to Stelco's survival. As a result Stelco learned a difficult lesson and now considers reaching zero debt to be its top priority, in order to avoid a liquidity squeeze the next time the steel cycle bottoms out. Stelco believes that its approach to retiring debt before it matures, along with the project financing policy, should help the company reach its goal of generating positive cash flow at the bottom of the steel cycle. By maintaining close control of costs the company will ensure its competitiveness.

The next strategic goal of continually investing in research and development, while more generic than the other goals, is perhaps the company's most overarching goal. In fact, the company's emphasis on research and development will help Stelco meet all of its other goals including: maintaining its asset base by keeping its operating facilities productive and up to date, delivering continually improving levels of quality and service to its customers, achieving superior levels of output and productivity, creating and maintaining healthy and safe workplaces, and preserving the environment in company plant locations through responsible and environmentally oriented operating practices.

Management

In 1995 Stelco focussed on human resourcessed development through its training and educational program W-I-N (Winning in the Nineties). Phase I of the process was designed to give more than 800 participants an understanding of contemporary management principles and to encourage thinking in a holistic manner. W-I-N II sessions, which cover organizational structure and clarity, were also held in 1995. These sessions are aimed at individuals who are in a position to have a direct influence on the organizational structure of the various businesses. W-I-N III sessions which began in late 1995 and continued in 1996, are designed to provide managers with concrete tools to more effectively run their businesses for ongoing improvement. Senior management believes that the principles behind this training and educational process, and their implementation, have been a catalyst in the return to profitability at Stelco.

During 1995, there was a significant change to the board of directors. The retirement of John D. Allan from the board ended a distinguished 48-year association with Stelco. Mr. Allan had previously retired in 1990 as chair and CEO, but had remained as a director of the corporation. In 1996, Robert Milbourne, the 54-year-old executive who had served as both Stelco's president and chief operating officer announced that he was stepping down in order to concentrate on furthering the human resources agenda of the company and to relocate with his family to the West Coast. Milbourne will be replaced by James Alfano, the 45-year-old vice-president and general manager of Hilton Works. Alfano, who is considered to be not as tough as his predecessor, has also successfully run the Lake Erie Works integrated steel mill in the past. The new president and chief operating officer's task is not nearly as daunting as the one which faced Robert Milbourne when he took the reigns in 1991. Since that time Milbourne has steered the company through a large-scale downsizing, divestitures, and union negotiations, while restructuring the company into business units with identifiable costs.

Main Products

Stelco manufactures and competes in a wide variety of products, although the company has focussed on the high value-added end of the market which is less susceptible to competition from the mini-mills. This includes flat-rolled steel products (sheet, strip, and plate), long products (rods and bars), tubular products including large diameter pipe, and a large variety of wire and wire products. The company's largest facility, Hilton Works, produces an extensive range of products including plate, hot- and cold-rolled sheet, galvanized sheet, tin mill products, rods, bar, and other shapes. As mentioned above, the Lake Erie Works facility's single customer is the automotive sector, and its main product is high quality rolled sheet. In general, a potential growth sector for Stelco is the construction sector because of the increase in steel used in residential construction. Stelco presently produces steel for frames and foundations in houses.

Unique Processes/Capabilities

As mentioned above, two of the company's strategic goals are improved competitiveness and enhanced environmental performance. The Pulverized Coal

Injection facility at Hilton Works includes state-of-the-art technology which injects coal directly into the blast furnaces in order to achieve both of these goals. Similarly, a new Bloom Mill reheat furnace and enhancements to the Plate Mill at the Hilton Works facility are expected to advance operating technology and improve competitiveness in the rod, bar, and plate products markets through better quality and reductions in costs. As well, the use of natural gas injection to supplement heavy liquid injection at the Lake Erie Works blast furnace, resulted in reduced coke usage, more efficient production, and a significant enhancement in air quality. As a result, the Lake Erie Works received a National Gas Award from the Canadian Gas Association for superior environmental performance.

The Hamilton Works facility's continued preservation and enhancement of the environment includes the development of an innovative technology which recycles the spent alkali solution from the steel making process. The Ministry of Environment and Energy awarded the cold roll and coated division with a P4 status—the highest level of the ministry's Pollution Pledge Programme. This ultrafiltration technology, together with other Stelco-developed technology, is being marketed all over the world by Steltech Ltd., which is an operating unit of Hatch Associates Ltd.

Stelco also considers producing higher quality steel and reducing costs for its automotive customers to be a top priority. Towards this end the Hilton Works plant has maintained its position as the foremost North America producer of hot-dipped free zinc coated sheets for automotive exposed applications. Two new products were developed by the cold roll and coated division in order to address the automotive industry's need to control costs and reduce vehicle weight. The first new product is a high surface quality hot-dipped galvanized coated steel suitable for exposed body applications. The second product is a high strength, galvanized steel that is 50% more dent resistant and weighs considerably less than conventional steels when used for outer body panels.

The company's research and development division continues to provide the company with new capabilities and processes. Towards this end, the research and development division spearheaded a significant refurbishing of the Sinter Plant and also made significant improvements in steel-making procedures. This realized both environmental and cost benefits by increasing productivity by 20% and expanding the consumption of recycled materials. The research and development division has also created a technology, new to the steel industry, for filtering rolling solutions which will come into commercial operation in the first quarter of 1996. The same technology is now being utilized in recycling rolling mill detergent. At the Lake Erie Works facility, HSLA hot-rolled sheet grades were developed to meet the automotive requirements for excellent surface quality, weldability, formability, and uniformity of properties. As a result, Stelmax 80, a new high strength steel for use in many automotive stamping operations, was introduced to the market in 1994 and has experienced a steady increase in demand since.

Required

Through an analysis of the information provided, identify the financial strengths and weaknesses of Stelco Inc.

Stelco Inc. Consolidated Statements of Income and Retained Earnings (in millions)

Year Ending December 31	1996	1995	1994	1993	1992
Revenue	$ 2,941	$ 2,926	$ 2,916	$ 2,500	$ 2,200
Cost of Sales, exclusive of the following:	$ 2,480	$ 2,369	$ 2,388	$ 2,166	$ 2,033
Depreciation	132	130	138	122	128
Corporate Services	23	22	28	32	40
Gov't payment other than income taxes	135	130	137	125	121
	2,770	2,651	2,691	2,445	2,322
Income (Loss) from Operations	171	275	225	55	(122)
Non-Recurring Items	0	0	0	0	21
Financial Expense					
Interest on long-term debt	(46)	(63)	(75)	(78)	(82)
Other interest (net)	6	12	2	(7)	(8)
Income (loss) before income taxes	131	224	152	(30)	(191)
Income taxes — current	49	6	14	(7)	(4)
— deferred	3	62	23	1	68
Net Income	$ 79	$ 156	115	(36)	(127)
Retained Earnings					
Balance at beginning of year	274	165	67	107	234
Net income	71	156	115	(36)	(127)
Dividends	(13)	(47)	(17)	(4)	0
Balance at end of year	$ 340	$ 274	$ 165	$ 67	$ 107
Income per Common Share	$ 0.63	$ 1.35	$ 1.01	($ 0.62)	($ 1.76)
Dividends per common share	—	—	—	—	—

Stelco Inc. Consolidated Balance Sheets (in millions)

Year Ending December 31	1996	1995	1994	1993	1992
Common share price High	$ 8.75	$ 8.50	$ 9.88	$ 8.88	$ 6.63
Low	$ 5.50	$ 5.25	$ 7.13	$ 1.17	$ .90
Current Assets					
Cash and short-term investments	$ 165	$ 190	$ 267	$ 111	$ 68
Accounts receivable	426	406	476	396	343
Inventories	582	582	475	407	449
Prepaid expenses	13	12	11	13	7
	1,186	1,190	1,229	927	867
Fixed and Other Assets					
Fixed assets	$ 1,129	$1,223	$ 1,277	$ 1,194	$ 1,309
Long-term investments	0	0	0	193	193
Other	74	25	24	13	17
Deferred pension cost	99	96	57	37	37
	1,302	1,334	1,358	1,437	1,556
Total Assets	$ 2,488	$2,534	$ 2,587	$ 2,364	$ 2,423
Current Liabilities					
Bank Borrowings	$ 7	$ 67	$ 156	$ 176	$ 190
Accounts payable and accrued charges	457	466	465	368	352
Income and other taxes payable	41	415	42	32	20
Cash dividends payable	3	3	4	4	0
Current requirements on long-term debt	48	38	39	48	26
	566	615	706	628	588
Long-Term Liabilities					
Provision for blast furnace — beyond 1 yr.	80	78	91	87	74
Long-term debt	393	457	581	695	767
Deferred income taxes	123	120	49	25	27
	596	655	721	807	868
Total Liabilities	1,162	1,270	1,427	1,435	1,456
Shareholders' Equity					
Capital Stock	973	977	982	849	847
Contributed Surplus	13	13	13	13	13
Retained earnings	340	274	165	67	107
	1,326	1,264	1,160	929	967
Total Liabilities and Shareholders' Equity	$ 2,488	$2,534	$2,587	$ 2,364	$ 2,423

Stelco Inc. Consolidated Statements of Changes in Financial Position (in millions)

Year Ending December 31	1996	1995	1994	1993	1992
Cash Provided by (used for)					
Operating Activities					
Net income (loss)	$ 79	$156	$115	($ 36)	($127)
Charges (credits) to income not affecting cash					
Depreciation	132	130	138	122	128
Deferred income taxes	3	62	23	(1)	(68)
Provision for blast furnace relines	7	14	6	13	16
Gain on sales of assets	(5)	(3)	(14)	—	—
Equity income (loss) net of dividends	—	—	—	6	20
Non-recurring items	—	—	—	—	(21)
Other—net	2	—	3	11	16
	218	359	271	115	(36)
Net change in deferred pension cost	(3)	(39)	(20)	—	(22)
Changes in operating elements of working capital (see below)	(30)	(39)	10	11	29
Other — net	6	(15)	(8)	(1)	(24)
	191	266	253	125	(53)
Investment Activities					
Advance to joint venture—net of repayments	(62)	—	—	—	—
Proceeds from sale of assets	21	5	46	—	47
Expenditures for fixed assets	(53)	(79)	(23)	(8)	(12)
Long-term investments — net	—	—	—	(10)	(9)
	(94)	(74)	23	(18)	26

continued

Stelco Inc. Consolidated Statements of Changes in Financial Position (in millions)

Year Ending December 31	1996	1995	1994	1993	1992
Financing Activities					
Net proceeds from issue of long-term debt	11	80	—	—	—
Net proceeds from issue of common shares	1	1	134	2	1
Purchase of preferred shares	(6)	(6)	—	—	(5)
Reduction of long-term debt	(65)	(207)	(202)	(52)	(27)
	(59)	(132)	(68)	(50)	(31)
Cash Dividends Paid	(13)	(48)	(17)	—	—
Net Increase (Decrease) in Cash Position	25	12	191	57	(58)
Balance at beginning of year	123	111	(80)	(122)	(64)
Balance at end of year	$148	$ 123	$111	($ 65)	($122)
Changes in Operating Elements of Working Capital					
Accounts receivable	($ 20)	$ 70	($ 30)	($ 53)	($ 39)
Inventories	—	(107)	(26)	42	49
Prepaid expenses	(1)	(1)	3	(6)	2
Accounts payable and accrued	(3)	1	53	16	10
Income and other taxes	—	(2)	10	12	7
	($ 33)	($ 39)	$ 10	$ 11	$ 29

CASE 3   Dofasco Inc.

Background

Dofasco Inc. (Dofasco), one of Canada's largest fully integrated steel producers, was founded in 1912 and was previously known as Dominion Foundries and Steel in Hamilton, Ontario. Dofasco produces high quality flat-rolled steels from its operations located in both Canada and the U.S. in order to service its customers throughout North America. The company has undergone major changes, which began in the 1980s, and have included acquisitions, divestitures, downsizing, and investments in new steel-making technology.

One of many changes for Dofasco took place in 1987, when it began steel making using continuous casting technology, which uses slabs in the production process. In 1988 Dofasco acquired control of The Algoma Steel Corporation (Algoma), Canada's third largest integrated steel producer, for a total cost of $562.5 million. This acquisition enabled Dofasco to boast that it had surpassed Stelco, and now was Canada's largest fully integrated steel producer. In 1990 Dofasco ceased its mining operations at the Adams Mine and the Sherman Mine, and provided $72 million for the write-down of assets and for other expenses. By the end of the year, Dofasco wrote off its entire investment of $713 million due to the financial difficulties Algoma was experiencing, and in 1991 Dofasco decided to provide no further funding to Algoma. Also in 1991, Dofasco sold its American subsidiary's wholly owned operating division, Whittar Steel Strip located in Detroit.

Algoma was brought back from the brink of bankruptcy in 1992 with a corporate reorganization that issued 60% of new common shares to employees. Dofasco agreed to pay $30 million over three installments to Algoma in order to utilize Algoma's non-capital tax losses. It was in 1993 that the company began to carve out its new direction. Dofasco sold its remaining investment in Algoma for $39 million in cash, and closed its outdated ingot cast facility. The company agreed to form a joint venture with Co-Steel Inc. of Toronto, to create a mini-mill in Kentucky. The Gallatin Steel Company project (each partner owns 50%) cost over US $300 million, has an annual capacity of 1.2 million tons, and was created to mimic the mini-mill success of Nucor Inc. by combining cheap labour, cheap power, and expensive technology to melt cheap scrap metal. The Gallatin Steel Company intends to exceed the success of other mini-mills, because it will be one of the first mini-mills in the world that will turn recycled steel into a flat-rolled product that can be utilized by the automotive industry.

Dofasco continued its divestitures and consolidation in 1994, as the company sold wholly owned National Steel Car Limited of Hamilton, which manufactured railway cars, for $16.5 million cash and wholly owned Prudential Steel Limited of Calgary, which produced tubular products for the oil and gas industry, for $95 million. Finally in 1995, Dofasco continued to finance its Gallatin Steel joint venture, which experienced problems in its start-up, and unveiled plans for a $200 million expansion at the company's Hamilton site. The expansion will consist of an electric arc furnace that will melt scrap steel, as well as a continuous slab caster that flattens 8.5 inch thick slabs of hot steel, and it is expected to be completed by the end of 1996.

Strategic Direction and Priorities

After Dofasco's decision to purchase the outstanding shares in Algoma in order to become the country's number one producer of steel products, the industry suffered huge setbacks in terms of world demand and steel prices. As a result, the company was forced to change its priorities and develop a new strategic direction. Initially the company reorganized its Hamilton operations into five core divisions: commercial, manufacturing, technology, financial, and administration. The company also began to downsize, reduce debt, and divest itself of non-core activities. At the same time Dofasco took steps to become more flexible and to shift some of its production to mini-mills. As part of Dofasco's plan to become more flexible, in 1993 the company closed its ingot processes which were an obsolete manner of producing flat-rolled steel. As well, by purchasing cast steel slabs for use in the production process, Dofasco hoped to increase throughput and productivity.

Dofasco's strategic focus in 1996 and 1997 will include reducing debt further, and focussing on operational excellence by upgrading its Hamilton facility and doubling capacity at Gallatin Steel. Firstly, in order to strengthen its balance sheet, and increase the value of its common shares, Dofasco will pay down its liabilities, including $806 million in long-term debt.[1] Towards this end, Dofasco will utilize excess cash reserves which are not needed to finance the Hamilton expansion and the Gallatin Steel operation. This may be accomplished by redeeming $325 million worth of 8% class C preferred shares and/or the early repayment of the long-term debt.

Secondly, Dofasco will increase its operational capabilities, efficiencies, flexibility, and quality by upgrading existing facilities. Dofasco's manufacturing base in Hamilton contains a full range of fully integrated facilities, from coke, iron, and steel-making operations through to finishing and coating mills. In addition, Dofasco will add 1.35 million tons of annual steel-making capacity. This new capacity will make it possible to replace the 900,000 tons of cast steel that it presently buys on world markets, which is used to replace the production of steel slabs from its old ingot cast facility. This expansion will raise total capacity at the Hamilton plant to four million tons. The difference between producing steel slabs and purchasing them on the world markets, depending on prices, will save Dofasco anywhere from $50 million to $150 million annually. In addition, Gallatin Steel, which started in 1995, ran at approximately 50% of its 1.2 million annual capacity. The goal at Gallatin Steel is to meet its operational targets by the end of 1996, and then move forward with the planned expansion in 1997.

Dofasco's strategic direction includes focussing on growth with a global focus on the company's core competencies of steel manufacturing and processing. Also, Dofasco intends to differentiate itself from its competitors by developing close relationships with customers in order to provide products and services which meet customers' needs. Dofasco plans to build an organization with a flexible, competent workforce of enthusiastic people working towards shared, customer-driven goals.

---

[1] As seen in the Consolidated Balance Sheets at the end of 1995.

Management

The senior management team at Dofasco has embarked on a long-term plan which will evolve over the next several years, and will ensure that the company reaches its strategic goals. The board of directors will continue to have input in this process through a series of planning sessions with the senior management. Dofasco's two top officers are Charles H. Hantho, and John T. Mayberry. Mr. Hantho has been an active member of Dofasco's board since 1989, and sits on the audit, human resources and nominating and corporate governance committees. He was elected to the position of chair of the board in 1995. Mr. Mayberry was appointed president and CEO of Dofasco in 1993, and has served as a director since that time. Prior to being appointed to that position Mr. Mayberry was employed by Dofasco for a period of 26 years in a variety of positions.

Both Mr. Hantho and Mr. Mayberry publicly agree that Dofasco's priorities include expanding and updating the facility in Hamilton, ensuring that Gallatin Steel meets expectations, and paying down the company's debt. In 1995 Milan Kosanovich, the president of Gallatin Steel, was replaced with John Holditch. The replacement was due to disagreements about the future direction of Gallatin Steel. Mr. Holditch, a 26-year Dofasco veteran, is expected to act more in line with the goals of the senior executives at Dofasco and Co-Steel. His most recent position at Dofasco's Hamilton facility was in the capacity of general manager of primary manufacturing.

Main Products

Dofasco serves its customers throughout North America from its production facilities located in Hamilton and its joint venture, Gallatin Steel in Kentucky. The fully integrated steel-making facility in Hamilton produces hot-rolled, cold-rolled, galvanized, chromium-coated and pre-painted steels. Gallatin Steel produces low cost, hot-rolled steels from its mini-mill facility. Dofasco sells this full range of flat-rolled steel products to its customers in the automotive, construction, energy, manufacturing, pipe and tube appliance, container, and steel distribution industries.

In recent years Dofasco has begun to capitalize on the increasing number of home-builders using light-gauge galvanized steel instead of lumber for residential framing. In order to position itself as the number one supplier of steel in residential construction, Dofasco is working closely with builders and manufacturers. In addition, Dofasco is Canada's only producer of tinplate steel, which is used mainly by the food canning industry, including the fishing industry on both coasts.

Dofasco is also actively participating with over 30 of the world's leading steel companies in an automotive product development project, which intends to create an ultra-light steel auto body. The goal of this study is to demonstrate steel's capability to reduce the weight of the auto body shell, while increasing safety, comfort level, driving performance, and fuel economy. The results of the design and engineering phase show that the weight of the basic vehicle can be reduced by up to 35%.

Differentiating Capabilities/Processes

In order to differentiate itself from its competitors Dofasco continues to develop new technology and strong relationships with its customers. Firstly, the $200 million investment in upgrading the Hamilton facility will link mini-mill technology with existing blast furnaces. Once completed, the Hamilton mini-mill will be able to use up to 30% liquid iron mix from the company's coke ovens and blast furnaces. The expected advantages of this improvement include: reducing the mills' reliance on scrap metal in the event of a price increase, and an increase in the quality of the steel which the mill produces. Dofasco is Canada's only producer of tinplate steel, which is mostly used by the food canning industry, including Canada's fishing industry. In line with the company's strategic goal of providing its North American customers with quality steel products and the highest possible level of customer service, Dofasco opened a subsidiary in the U.S. in 1994. Dofasco USA Inc., which is located in Southfield Michigan, is responsible for the sales and distribution of Dofasco's 50% of the products from Gallatin Steel, as well as providing superior service to U.S. customers who buy their products from Dofasco's Hamilton facility. Lastly, Dofasco's Gallatin Steel project provides the company with a different manner of coping with the U.S.-Canada trade disputes. Dofasco will avoid duties on a growing percentage of its annual production by shifting approximately 600,000 tons of annual production to the American side of the border.

Required

Through an analysis of the information provided, identify the financial strengths and weaknesses of Dofasco Inc.

Dofasco Inc. Consolidated Statements of Income and Retained Earnings (in millions)

Year Ending December 31	1996	1995	1994	1993	1992
Revenue	$2,942	$2,636	$2,425	$2,103	$1,953
Cost of sales exclusive of the following	2,317	2,047	1,936	1,778	1,737
Depreciation and amortization	228	208	211	180	167
Employees' profit sharing plan	41	46	24	7	8
Interest on long-term debt	79	86	88	89	91
Interest on other income	(27)	(40)	(28)	(17)	(12)
Income (loss) from operations	304	289	194	66	(38)
Unusual items	0	0	67	75	(324)
Income (loss) before income taxes	304	289	261	141	(362)
Income tax expense (recovery)	97	93	40	(3)	(166)
Loss from equity investments	0	0	0	(5)	(11)
Net income (loss) for the year	$ 207	$ 196	$ 221	$ 139	$ (207)
Retained earnings					
Balance at beginning of year	$ 643	$ 545	$ 376	$ 265	$ 510
Net income (loss) for the year	207	196	221	139	(207)
	850	741	597	404	303
Dividends declared					
Preferred shares	26	27	27	28	27
Common shares	73	68	25	0	11
Premium on purchase of common shares	13	3	0	0	0
	112	98	52	28	38
Balance at end of year	$ 738	$ 643	$ 545	$ 376	$ 265
Earnings per common share — basic	$ 2.12	$ 1.98	$ 2.33	$ 1.41	($ 2.96)
— fully diluted	n/a	n/a	n/a	1.35	(2.96)
Dividends per common share	$ 0.85	$ 0.80	$ 0.30	—	$ 0.15
Common share price High	$26.55	$20.38	$26.38	$23.50	$19.00
Low	$17.13	$16.00	$17.13	$ 9.50	$ 7.25

continued

Dofasco Inc. Consolidated Balance Sheets (in millions)

Year Ending December 31	1996	1995	1994	1993	1992
Current Assets					
Cash and short-term investments	$ 444	$ 411	$ 552	$ 228	$ 215
Accounts receivable	364	395	375	262	226
Inventories	687	781	592	629	597
Deferred income taxes & other	17	13	14	39	73
	1,512	1,600	1,533	1,158	1,111
Fixed and Other Assets					
Fixed assets	2,198	2,134	2,110	1,917	2,004
Investment at equity	0	0	0	101	106
Investments at cost and other assets	65	66	69	32	33
Deferred pension cost	0	23	22	10	13
	2,263	2,223	2,201	2,060	2,156
Total Assets	$ 3,775	$ 3,823	$ 3,734	$ 3,218	$ 3,267
Current Liabilities					
Bank borrowings	$ 55	$ 35	$ 14	$ 0	$ 0
Accounts payable and accrued charges	328	360	287	278	349
Income and other taxes payable	0	105	25	0	0
Dividends payable	28	18	12	6	6
Current requirements on long-term debt	64	29	74	11	27
	475	547	412	295	382
Long-Term Liabilities					
Long-term debt	794	806	885	833	928
Accruals for:					
Relining blast furnaces and other	59	54	78	46	36
Pension and post-employment benefits	162	188	195	194	159
	1,015	1,048	1,158	1,073	1,123
Deferred Income Taxes	316	354	400	367	392
Shareholders' Equity					
Preferred shares	331	331	338	340	340
Common shares	900	895	878	767	764
Dividends distributable in common shares	0	5	3	0	1
Retained earnings	738	643	545	376	265
	1,969	1,874	1,764	1,483	1,370
Total Liabilities and Shareholders' Equity	$ 3,775	$ 3,823	$ 3,734	$ 3,218	$ 3,267

Dofasco Inc. Consolidated Statements of Changes in Financial Position (in millions)

Year Ending December 31	1996	1995	1994	1993	1992
Cash Derived from Operations					
Net income for year	$207.3	$195.8	$220.9	$138.6	$(207.1)
Items not involving cash					
Unusual items	—	—	(67.0)	(74.8)	323.9
Depreciation and amortization	228.2	207.8	181.0	179.8	166.8
Deferred income taxes	(33.9)	(44.9)	4.5	(11.9)	(163.8)
Loss (income) from equity investments	—	—	(8.5)	4.8	10.5
Pension and other post-employment benefits	(3.9)	(8.0)	2.9	6.5	(2.7)
Other	5.4	(14.5)	18.7	12.3	4.6
Changes in operating working capital	6.4	(76.1)	(52.0)	(74.7)	46.8
	$409.5	$260.1	$300.5	$180.6	$ 179.0
Cash Used for Investment Activities					
New facilities and investments	317.3	219.9	182.8	72.1	129.1
Sale of subsidiaries					
Proceeds	—	—	(110.5)	—	22.0
Bank indebtedness assumed by purchasers	—	—	(21.4)	—	—
Net proceeds from sale of Algoma preferred shares	—	—	—	(39.0)	—
Net proceeds from sale of BeachviLime Limited	—	—	50.9	33.1	(46.2)
	317.3	219.9	50.9	33.1	104.9
Dividends Paid	94.5	86.3	43.6	26.7	54.2
Cash Derived from (used for) Financing Activities					
Increase (decrease) in long-term debt	21.8	(121.4)	(12.4)	(109.7)	46
Redemption of preferred shares	(0.3)	(6.8)	(1.0)	(0.6)	(0.4)
Common shares issued	18.8	21.0	111.6	2.4	14.5
Common shares purchased	(26.0)	(7.6)	—	—	—
	14.3	(114.8)	98.2	(107.9)	92.4
Cash and Short-Term Investments					
Less Short-Term Bank Borrowings					
Increase (decrease) for year	12.0	(160.9)	304.2	12.9	112.3
Balance at beginning of year	376.5	537.4	227.8	214.9	102.6
Balance at end of year	$388.5	$376.5	$532.0	$227.8	$ 214.9

C

Accountants/Luca Pacioli

Synopsis

The double entry accounting system is the basis for today's accounting practices. In 1494 Luca Pacioli authored the first book on double entry bookkeeping. The video focuses on a conference organized by two professors who decided that the 500th anniversary of the publication of Pacioli's book should be celebrated.

When one reflects upon the changes over the past 500 years, one must be impressed by the ability of the simple formula of assets equals liabilities plus owners' equity to survive the test of time. In Pacioli's time, merchants were beginning to sail the world in search of trade. In today's world corporations continually look for ways to compete in the global economy. While the essence of the objectives of business people remains the same, the means and practices by which they achieve the objectives has changed considerably. The double entry system remains as relevant today as it has been for the past 500 years.

Video Resource: "Accountants/Luca Pacioli," *Venture* 507 (September 25, 1994).

QUESTIONS

1. What is double entry accounting?
2. Describe what may have existed as assets, liabilities and owner's equity on the balance sheet of a merchant in Pacioli's time.

CBC ❄ VIDEO CASE 2

Consumers Distributing
Synopsis

Consumers Distributing was a major Canadian retailer. Consumers Distributing introduced the concept of large scale discount purchasing to the Canadian market and thus established itself as a major player in the Canadian retail market. The video addresses some of the implications of their demise and the impact on their suppliers.

When suppliers ship goods to a company such as Consumers Distributing, the goods are typically shipped without any security or interest charged on the debt. In accounting terms, Consumers Distributing would record accounts payable and the suppliers would record accounts receivable. Given that these debts of consumers do not normally bear an interest charge, it is in a company's best interest to defer payment to their suppliers. Alternatively the suppliers would prefer payment as soon as possible. While there is a bias for Consumers Distributing to delay payment, it is also important for a company to maintain good supplier relations. Without the shipment of necessary products, Consumers Distributing would not have any inventory to sell. Thus the timing of payments to suppliers tends to be based upon the question of who needs who the most. As the video mentions, suppliers needed Consumers Distributing perhaps more than Consumers Distributing needed the suppliers. Consumers Distributing appears to have been in a position to find alternative sources of supply for many of their products. Thus they would be able to extend their accounts payable for a longer period than otherwise may have existed.

When Consumers Distributing went into bankruptcy because it could not pay its debts, the suppliers would need to revalue their accounts receivable given that they would likely receive almost no payment for their receivables. The eventual outcome was the financial demise of some of the suppliers such as Jolly Jumper. Financial statements can be used to provide suppliers with information to identify the likelihood of the financial demise of a company. The video raises the issue that perhaps all of the information from Consumers Distributing may not have been as accurate and complete as it should have been.

Video Resource: "Consumers Distributing," *Venture* 608 (September 15, 1996).

QUESTIONS

1. How can financial statements be used to assess the financial viability of a company?
2. Identify some of the implications that may result from the bankruptcy of a major company.
3. Identify some of the reasons why a company such as Consumers Distributing may not be able to meet its debt payments.

CBC ❖ VIDEO CASE 3

Multiple Unit Transporter (MUT)
Synopsis

Income statements record the revenues and expenses of a business. However, accounting practices focus on those revenues and expenses that are easily quantified in financial terms. There are numerous other factors that are relevant to the overall wealth of an organization that are not captured within our accounting practices. The video examines the situation of an entrepreneur from Newfoundland, Kevin McCarthy, and his efforts to develop and sell his product called MUT (Multiple Unit Transporter).

The case identifies many of the concerns that entrepreneurs face in the start-up of a new business. First it is important that an entrepreneur identifies and develops the product being marketed. The video examines Kevin McCarthy's efforts in marketing his new product at a trade show. Financing is always a concern for new business ventures, in particular as they attempt to expand their operations. For Kevin McCarthy, the local Business Development Corporation provided some funds to allow the business to expand. The video also examines some of the other important non-financial issues that are seen in many new venture start-ups. For example, Kevin McCarthy discusses openly the difficulties in maintaining close family relationships and friends as he attempts to develop his business. The entrepreneur's work week typically far exceeds the normal work week for employees. Kevin McCarthy works approximately 20 hours per day, 7 days a week. The physical implications of his work week are described by Kevin McCarthy as "burn out" in which he no longer is able to function in a manner in which he would prefer. Despite all of Kevin McCarthy's investments of money, time, energy and personal relationships, it is evident that the success of his new business is not guaranteed. Sometimes one needs to look beyond the normal financial statements in order to give a true understanding of the cost of operating a business.

Video Resource: "MUT (Newf.)," *Venture* 618 (November 24, 1996).

QUESTIONS

1. Net income is a measure of increase in worth of a business. Identify some revenues and expenses that may not be included in a typical income statement for an entrepreneur.
2. What advice would you provide to Kevin McCarthy as he attempts to develop his business?

CBC ✺ VIDEO CASE 4

$100 Bills
Synopsis

Similar to the role of the auditor of companies to ensure that the companies comply with the accounting standards, the Canadian government has a role to ensure that companies comply with the laws of the country. There has always been general agreement that a portion of our economy is "underground" in that the transactions are conducted and not reported for taxation purposes. By not reporting the business activities, businesses attempt to avoid paying income taxes, goods and services taxes, and provincial sales taxes. This tax evasion can lead to significant sums of money. There has been debate on the topic of the size of the Canadian underground economy. This video case draws a conclusion that the underground economy has grown through the evidence of the increased use of $100 bills.

In today's business environment there is an increased access to paperless transactions. Large sums of money can be transferred through the use of computers and not through the use of currency. However, the video highlights that the use of currency is increasing despite the fact that technology reduces the need for individuals to carry currency. Through this analysis, the video concludes that the underground unreported economy is large and increasing.

Video Resource: "$100 Bills," *Venture* 495 (July 3, 1994).

QUESTIONS

1. What are some of the implications of the existence of the Canadian underground economy?

CBC ✺ VIDEO CASE 5

Body Shop
Synopsis

Being socially responsible and ethical in today's business environment is an issue of increased importance to companies. The issues are far ranging and include such topics as the fair treatment of employees, preserving the environment, support for indigenous people, the support for non-animal testing, etc.

The Body Shop is a company that has staked its reputation on ethical business practices. In particular, it reports that its products have not used animals in their testing and in addition they support indigenous people by selling their products. The Body Shop has been able to establish itself as a major corporation without the use of advertising, but rather through the development of a socially responsible marketing plan. Thus, the Body Shop has been able to create a strategic niche for its products.

Video Resource: "Body Shop," *Venture* 510 (October 16, 1994).

QUESTIONS

1. Why is it important for a company to be socially responsible?
2. What are the benefits and risks of a company who uses a strategic niche in the marketplace?

CBC ⚙ VIDEO CASE 6

CN Sale
Synopsis

The potential privatization of CN Rail highlights an increasing trend that is found in many countries. Historically, countries would attempt to establish industries in the country for public policy reasons. Thus, the creation of crown corporations and monopolies in the Canadian economy has been common. Air Canada, Petro Canada, CN Rail, and Ontario Hydro are all examples of companies that have been created for the benefit of the economy. Recently Air Canada and Petro Canada have been privatized through the sale of shares on public stock markets. Considerable discussion still surrounds the potential privatization of companies like CN Rail and Ontario Hydro. The primary arguments for privatization focusses on the potential efficiencies that can be realized when companies must compete in the world economy for their customers and capital.

Video Resource: "CN Sale," *Venture* 544 (June 11, 1995).

QUESTIONS

1. What are the potential costs and benefits of privatizing CN Rail?

Glossary

accelerated depreciation (p. 385) Any depreciation method that writes off depreciable costs more quickly than the ordinary straight-line method based on expected useful life.

account (p. 11) A summary record of the changes in a particular asset, liability, or owners' equity.

account format (p. 149) A classified balance sheet with the assets at the left.

account payable (p. 12) A liability that results from a purchase of goods or services on open account.

Accounting Principles Board (APB) (p. 63) The predecessor to the Financial Accounting Standards Board.

accounting cycle (p. 174) The multistage process by which accountants produce an entity's financial statements.

accounting policy making (p. 624) Choosing the accounting measurement and disclosure methods required for financial reporting.

Accounting Standards Board (p. 63) The committee of the Canadian Institute of Chartered Accountants (CICA) responsible for setting Canadian accounting standards.

accounting system (p. 529) A set of records, procedures and equipment that routinely deals with the events affecting the financial performance and position of the entity.

accounts receivable (p. 290) Amounts owed to a company by customers as a result of delivering goods or services and extending credit in the ordinary course of business.

accounts receivable turnover (p. 298) Credit sales divided by average accounts receivable.

accrual basis (p. 42) Accounting method that recognizes the impact of transactions on the financial statements in the time periods when revenues and expenses occur.

accrue (p. 133) Accumulation of a receivable or payable during a given period even though no explicit transaction occurs.

accumulated amortization (p. 98) The cumulative sum of all amortization recognized since the date of acquisition of the particular assets described.

adjustments (p. 132) The key final process (before the computation of ending account balances) of assigning the financial effects of transactions to the appropriate time-periods.

adjusting entries See adjustments

affiliated company (p. 304) A company that has 20% to 50% of its voting shares owned by another company.

aging of accounts receivable (p. 297) An analysis of the elements of individual accounts receivable according to the time elapsed after the dates of billing.

AICPA (p. 64) American Institute of Certified Public Accountants, the leading organization of the auditors of corporate financial reports in the U.S.

allowance for bad debts See allowance for uncollectible accounts

allowance for amortization (depreciation) See accumulated amortization.

allowance for doubtful accounts See accumulated depreciation.

allowance for uncollectible accounts (p. 293) A contra asset account that offsets total receivables by an estimated amount that will probably not be collected.

allowance method (p. 293) Method of accounting for bad debt losses using estimates of the amount of sales that will ultimately be uncollectible and a contra asset account, allowance for doubtful accounts.

amortization (depreciation) (p. 46) The systematic allocation of the acquisition cost of long-lived or fixed assets to the expense accounts of particular periods that benefit from the use of the assets.

amortization (p. 381) The systematic reduction of a lump-sum amount. When referring to long-lived assets, it usually means the allocation of the costs of such assets to the periods that benefit from these assets.

amortization schedule (p. 384) The listing of amortization accounts for each year of an asset's useful life.

annual report (p. 5) A combination of financial statements, management discussion and analysis, and graphs and charts that is provided annually to investors.

annuity (p. 455) Equal cash flows to take place during successive periods of equal length.

appropriated retained income *See* restricted retained income.

assets (p. 7) Economic resources that are expected to benefit future cash inflows or help reduce future cash outflows.

asset turnover *See* total asset turnover.

audit (p. 21) An examination of transactions and financial statements made in accordance with generally accepted auditing standards.

audit committee (p. 531) A committee of the board of directors that oversees the internal accounting controls, financial statements, and financial affairs of the corporation.

auditor (p. 195) An accountant who provides an independent examination of the financial statements.

auditor's opinion (p. 21) A report describing the auditor's examination of transactions and financial statements. It is included with the financial statements in an annual report issued by the corporation.

authorized shares (p. 486) The total number of shares that may legally be issued under the articles of incorporation.

average collection period *See* days to collect accounts receivable.

bad debts *See* uncollectible accounts.

bad debt recoveries (p. 298) Accounts receivable that were written off as uncollectible but then were collected at a later date.

bad debts expense (p. 290) The cost of granting credit that arises from uncollectible accounts.

balance (p. 86) The difference between the total left-side and right-side amounts in an account at any particular time.

balance sheet ((p. 6) A financial statement that shows the financial status of a business entity at a particular instant in time.

balance sheet equation (p. 7) Assets = Liabilities + Owners' equity.

bank reconciliation (p. 540) An analysis that explains any difference between the cash balance shown by the depositor and that shown by the bank.

basic earnings per share (p. 598) EPS calculated by dividing net income less preferred share dividends by the weighted-average number of outstanding common shares.

basket purchase (p. 382) The acquisition of two or more types of assets for a lump-sum cost.

bearer instrument *See* unregistered instrument.

bench marks (p. 586) General rules of thumb specifying appropriate levels for financial ratios.

betterment *See* improvement

bonds (p. 430) Formal certificates of indebtedness that are typically accompanied by (1) a promise to pay interest in cash at a specified annual rate plus (2) a promise to pay the principal at a specific maturity date.

book of original entry (p. 89) A formal chronological record of how the entity's transactions affect the balances in pertinent accounts.

book value (p. 98) The balance of an account shown on the books, net of any contra accounts. For example, the book value of equipment is its acquisition cost minus accumulated amortization.

book value per share of common stock (p. 511) Shareholders' equity attributable to common stock divided by the number of shares outstanding.

call premium (p. 432) The amount by which the redemption price exceeds par.

callable (p. 490) A characteristic of bonds or preferred stock that gives the issuer the right to redeem the security at a fixed price.

callable bonds (p. 432) Bonds subject to redemption before maturity at the option of the issuer.

Canadian Institute of Chartered Accountants (CICA) (p. 21) A professional accounting organization of Chartered Accountants (CA).

capital (p. 17) A term used to identify owners' equities for proprietorships and partnerships.

capital cost allowance (CCA) (p. 387) The term used to describe the amortization method permitted by the Income Tax Act in Canada.

capital improvement See improvement.

capital lease (p. 457) A lease that transfers substantially all the risks and benefits of ownership to the lessee.

capital stock certificate (p. 17) Formal evidence of ownership shares in a corporation.

capital structure See capitalization.

capitalization (p. 594) Owners' equity plus long-term debt.

capitalization structure See capitalization.

capitalized (p. 382) A cost that is added to an asset account, as distinguished from being expensed immediately.

carrying amount See book value.

carrying value See book value.

cash basis (p. 42) Accounting method that recognizes the impact of transactions on the financial statements only when cash is received or disbursed.

cash discounts (p. 285) Reductions of invoice prices awarded for prompt payment.

cash dividends (p. 57) Distributions of cash to shareholders that reduce retained earnings.

cash equivalents (p. 288) Highly liquid temporary investments that can easily be converted into cash.

cash flow (p. 238) Usually refers to net cash provided by operating activities.

cash flows from financing activities (p. 245) The third major section of the statement of changes in financial position describing flows to and from providers of capital.

cash flows from investing activities (p. 245) The second major section of the statement of changes in financial position describing purchase or sale of plant, property, equipment, and other long-lived assets.

cash flows from operating activities (p. 236) The first major section of the statement of changes in financial position. It shows the cash effects of transactions that affect the income statement.

cash flow statement See statement of changes in financial position.

certificates of deposit (p. 303) Short-term obligations of banks.

certified general accountant (CGA) (p. 23) The professional accountant designation issued by the Certified General Accountants Association of Canada (CGAAC).

Certified General Accountants Association of Canada (CGAAC) (p. 21) A professional accounting organization of Certified General Accountants (CGA).

certified management accountant (CMA) (p. 23) The professional accountant designation issued by the Society of Management Accountants of Canada (SMAC).

charge (p. 87) A word often used instead of debit.

chart of accounts (p. 90) A numbered or coded list of all account titles.

chartered accountant (CA) (p. 23) The professional accountant designation issued by the Canadian Institute of Chartered Accountants (CICA).

classified balance sheet (p. 144) A balance sheet that groups the accounts into subcategories to help readers quickly gain a perspective on the company's financial position.

closing entries (p. 190) Entries that transfer the revenues, expenses, and dividends declared balances from their respective accounts to the retained earnings account.

closing the books (p. 190) The final step taken in the accounting cycle to update retained earnings and facilitate the recording of the next year's transactions.

commercial paper (p. 303) Short-term notes payable issued by large corporations with top credit ratings.

common stock (p. 19) Stock representing the class of owners having a "residual" ownership of a corporation.

common-size statement (p. 578) Financial statement expressed in component percentages.

comparative financial statements (p. 176) Statements that present data for two or more reporting periods.

compensating balances (p. 289) Required minimum cash balances on deposit when money is borrowed from banks.

component percentages (p. 578) Analysis and presentation of financial statements in percentage form to aid comparability.

compound entry (p. 12, 93) An entry for a transaction that affects more than two accounts.

compound interest (p. 452) For any period, interest rate multiplied by an increasing principal amount. The unpaid interest is added to the principal to become the principal for the new period.

compound interest method *See* effective-interest amortization.

conservatism (p. 345) Selecting the methods of measurement that yield lower net income, lower assets, and lower shareholders' equity.

consignment (p. 556) Goods shipped for future sales, title remaining with the shipper (consignor), for which the receiver (consignee), upon his or her acceptance, is accountable. The goods are part of the consignor's inventory until sold.

consistency (p. 341) Conformity from period to period with unchanging policies and procedures.

consolidated statements (p. 306) Combinations of the financial positions and earnings reports of the parent company with those of various subsidiaries into an overall report as a single entity.

contingent liability (p. 445) A potential liability that depends on a future event arising out of a past transaction.

continuity convention *See* going concern convention.

contra account (p. 98) A separate but related account that offsets or is a deduction from a companion account. An example is accumulated amortization.

contra asset (p. 98) A contra account that offsets an asset.

contractual rate *See* nominal interest rate.

coupon rate *See* nominal interest rate.

convertible (p. 490) A characteristic of bonds or preferred stock that gives the holder the right to exchange the security for common stock.

convertible bonds (p. 432) Bonds that may, at the holder's option, be exchanged for other securities.

copyrights (p. 399) Exclusive rights to reproduce and sell a book, musical composition, film, or similar products.

corporate proxy (p. 486) A written authority granted by individual shareholders to others to cast the shareholders' votes.

corporation (p. 16) An organization that is an "artificial being" created by law.

cost of goods available for sale (p. 332) Sum of beginning inventory plus current year purchases.

cost of goods sold (p. 62) The original acquisition cost of the inventory that was sold to customers during the reporting period.

cost method (p. 304) Accounting for an investment carried at cost and dividends received recorded as revenues.

cost recovery (p. 43) The concept by which some purchases of goods or services are recorded as assets because their costs are expected to be recovered in the form of cash inflows (or reduced cash outflows) in future periods.

cost of sales *See* cost of goods sold.

cost valuation (p. 330) Process of assigning specific historical costs to items counted in the physical inventory.

cost-benefit criterion (p. 109) As a system is changed, its expected additional benefits should exceed its expected additional costs.

coupon rate *See* nominal interest rate.

covenant *See* protective covenant.

credit (p. 91) An entry or balance on the right side of an account.

creditor (p. 87) One to whom money is owed.

cross-referencing *See* keying of entries.

cross-sectional comparisons (p. 587) Comparisons of a company's financial ratios with the ratios of other companies or with industry averages.

cumulative (p. 487) A characteristic of preferred stock that requires that undeclared dividends accumulate and must be paid in the future before common dividends.

current assets (p. 145) Cash plus assets that are expected to be converted to cash or sold or consumed during the next twelve months or within the normal operating cycle if longer than a year.

current liabilities (p. 145) Liabilities that fall due within the coming year or within the normal operating cycle if longer than a year.

current ratio (p. 147) Current assets divided by current liabilities.

current yield (p. 431) Annual interest payments divided by the current price of a bond.

cutoff error (p. 556) Failure to record transactions in the correct time period.

data processing (p. 106) The totality of the procedures used to record, analyze, store, and report on chosen activities.

date of record (p. 493) The date when ownership is fixed for determining the right to receive a dividend.

days to collect accounts receivable (p. 299) 365 divided by accounts receivable turnover.

debenture (p. 431) A debt security with a general claim against all assets rather than a specific claim against particular assets.

debit (p. 87) An entry or balance on the left side of an account.

debtor (p. 15) One who owes money.

declaration date (p. 493) The date the board of directors declares a dividend.

deferred charges (p. 401) Similar to prepaid expenses, but they have longer-term benefits.

deferred credit See unearned revenue.

deferred revenue See unearned revenue.

depletion (p. 381) The process of allocating the cost of natural resources to the period in which the resources are used.

depreciable value (p. 383) The amount of the acquisition cost to be allocated as amortization over the total useful life of an asset. It is the difference between the total acquisition cost and the predicted residual value.

dilution (p. 502) Reduction in shareholders' equity per share or earnings per share that arises from some changes among shareholders' proportional interests.

direct method (p. 236) In a statement of changes in financial position, the method that calculates net cash provided by operating activities as collections minus operating disbursements.

discontinued operations (p. 601) The termination of a business segment reported separately, net of tax, in the income statement.

discount amortization (p. 437) The spreading of bond discount over the life of the bonds as expense.

discount on bonds (p. 433) The excess of face amount over the proceeds upon issuance of a bond.

discount rates (p. 454) The interest rates used in determining present values.

disposal value See residual value.

dividend arrears (p. 488) Accumulated unpaid dividends on preferred stock.

double-declining-balance depreciation (DDB) (p. 385) The most popular form of accelerated depreciation. It is computed by doubling the straight-line rate and multiplying the resulting DDB rate by the beginning book value.

double-entry system (p. 84) The method usually followed for recording transactions, whereby at least two accounts are always affected by each transaction.

earnings See income.

EBIT (p. 592) Earnings before interest and taxes.

economic life See useful life.

effective-interest amortization (p. 437) An amortization method that uses a constant interest rate.

effective interest rate See yield to maturity.

efficient capital market (p. 601) One in which market prices "fully reflect" all information available to the public.

entity (p. 8) An organization or a section of an organization that stands apart from other organizations and individuals as a separate economic unit.

equity method (p. 304) Accounting for an investment at acquisition cost adjusted for the investor's share of dividends and earnings or losses of the investee subsequent to the date of investment.

expenditures (p. 393) The purchases of goods or services, whether for cash or on credit.

expenses (p. 40) Decreases in owners' equity that arise because goods or services are delivered to customers.

explicit transactions (p. 132) Events such as cash receipts and disbursements, credit purchases, and credit sales that trigger nearly all day-to-day routine entries.

extraordinary items (p. 601) Items that are unusual in nature and infrequent in occurrence that are shown separately, net of tax, in the income statement.

F.O.B. destination (p. 335) Seller pays freight costs from the shipping point of the seller to the receiving point of the buyer.

F.O.B. shipping point (p. 335) Buyer pays freight costs from the shipping point of the seller to the receiving point of the buyer.

face amount (p. 430) The principal as indicated on the certificates of bonds or other debt instruments.

FASB Statements (p. 64) The FASB's rulings on generally accepted accounting principles.

financial accounting (p. 6) The field of accounting that serves external decision makers, such as shareholders, suppliers, banks, and government agencies.

Financial Accounting Standards Board (FASB) (p. 63) A private-sector body that determines generally accepted accounting standards in the United States.

financial leverage *See* trading on the equity.

financial management (p. 234) Is mainly concerned with where to get cash and how to use cash for the benefit of the entity.

financial statement analysis (p. 572) Using financial statements to assess a company's performance.

financing activities (p. 235) In the statement of changes in financial position, obtaining resources as a borrower or issuer of securities and repaying creditors and owners.

financing lease *See* capital lease

finished goods inventory (p. 360) The accumulated costs of manufacture for goods that are complete and ready for sale.

first-in, first-out (FIFO) (p. 339) This method of accounting for inventory assumes that the units acquired earliest are used or sold first.

fiscal year (p. 39) The year established for accounting purposes.

fixed assets *See* tangible assets.

foreign-currency exchange rates (p. 603) The number of units of one currency that can be exchanged for one unit of another currency.

franchises (p. 399) Privileges granted by a government, manufacturer, or distributor to sell a product or service in accordance with specified conditions.

freight in (p. 335) An additional cost of the goods acquired during the period, which is often shown in the purchases section of an income statement.

freight out (p. 335) The transportation costs borne by the seller of merchandise and often shown as a "shipping expense."

fully diluted EPS (p. 598) An earnings-per-share figure on common stock that assumes that all potentially dilutive convertible securities and stock options are exchanged for common stock.

future value (p. 453) The amount accumulated, including principal and interest.

gearing *See* trading on the equity.

general controls (p. 539) Internal accounting controls that focus on the organization and operation of the data-processing activity.

general journal (p. 89) The most common example of a book of original entry; a complete chronological record of transactions.

general ledger (p. 85) The collection of accounts that accumulates the amounts reported in the major financial statements.

generally accepted accounting principles (GAAP) (p. 8) A term that applies to the broad concepts or guidelines and detailed practices in accounting, including all the conventions, rules, and procedures that together make up accepted accounting practice at a given time.

going concern convention (p. 108) The assumption that in all ordinary situations an entity persists indefinitely.

goodwill (p. 399) The excess of the cost of an acquired company over the sum of the fair market value of its identifiable individual assets less the liabilities.

gross margin *See* gross profit.

gross margin percentage *See* gross profit percentage.

gross profit (p. 150) The excess of sales revenue over the cost of the inventory that was sold.

gross profit percentage (p. 154) Gross profit divided by sales.

gross profit test (p. 354) The comparing of gross profit percentages to detect any phenomenon worth investigating.

gross sales (p. 284) Total sales revenue before deducting sales returns and allowances.

holding gain (p. 344) Increase in the replacement cost or other measure of current value of the inventory held during the current period.

implicit interest (p. 443) An interest expense that is not explicitly recognized in a loan agreement.

implicit transactions (p. 132) Events (such as the passage of time) that are temporarily ignored in day-to-day recording procedures and are recognized via end-of-period adjustments.

imprest basis (p. 552) A method of accounting for petty cash.

improvement (betterment, capital improvement) (p. 394) An expenditure that is intended to add to the future benefits from an existing fixed asset.

imputed interest See implicit interest.

imputed interest rate (p. 443) The market interest rate that equates the proceeds from a loan with the present value of the loan payments.

income (p. 40) The excess of revenues over expenses.

income statement (p. 48) A report of all revenues and expenses pertaining to a specific time period.

independent opinion See auditor's opinion.

indirect method (p. 236) In a statement of changes in financial position, the method that adjusts the accrual net income to reflect only cash receipts and outlays.

input controls (p. 539) Internal accounting controls that help guard against the entry of false or erroneous data.

intangible assets (p. 380) Rights or economic benefits, such as franchises, patents, trademarks, copyrights, and goodwill, that are not physical in nature.

interest coverage (p. 597) Income before interest expense and income taxes divided by interest expense.

interest period (p. 452) The time period over which the interest rate applies.

interest rate (p. 452) The percentage applied to a principal amount to calculate the interest charged.

interim periods (p. 40) The time spans established for accounting purposes that are less than a year.

internal control (p. 528) A system of both internal administrative control and internal accounting control.

interperiod tax allocation See tax deferral

International Accounting Standards Committee (IASC) (p. 64) An organization representing over one hundred accountancy boards from over seventy-five countries that is developing a common set of accounting standards to be used throughout the world.

inventory (p. 11) Goods held by a company for the purpose of sale to customers.

inventory profit See holding gain.

inventory shrinkage (p. 333) Difference between (a) the value of inventory that would occur if there were no theft, breakage, or losses of inventory and (b) the value of inventory when it is physically counted.

interperiod tax allocation See tax deferral.

inventory turnover (p. 351) The cost of goods sold divided by the average inventory held during the period.

investing activities (p. 234) Activities that involve (1) providing and collecting cash as a lender or as an owner of securities and (2) acquiring and disposing of plant, property, equipment, and other long-term productive assets.

inward transportation See freight in.

issued shares (p. 486) The aggregate number of shares potentially in the hands of shareholders.

journal entry (p. 89) An analysis of the effects of a transaction on the accounts, usually accompanied by an explanation.

journalizing (p. 89) The process of entering transactions into the journal.

keying of entries (p. 91) The process of numbering or otherwise specifically identifying each journal entry and each posting.

last-in, first-out (LIFO) (p. 339) This inventory method assumes that the units acquired most recently are used or sold first.

lease (p. 456) A contract whereby an owner (lessor) grants the use of property to a second party (lessee) for rental payments.

leasehold improvement (p. 401) Investments by a lessee in items that are not permitted to be removed from the premises when a lease expires, such as installation of new fixtures, panels, walls, and air-conditioning equipment.

leasehold (p. 401) The right to use a fixed asset for a specified period of time, typically beyond one year.

ledger (p. 85) A group of related accounts kept current in a systematic manner.

leveraging *See* trading on the equity.

liabilities (p. 7) Economic obligations of the organization to outsiders or claims against its assets by outsiders.

licences *See* franchises.

limited liability (p. 17) A feature of the corporate form of organization whereby corporate creditors ordinarily have claims against the corporate assets only. The owners' personal assets are not subject to the creditors' grasp.

line of credit (p. 424) An agreement with a bank to provide automatically short-term loans up to some preestablished maximum.

liquidating value (p. 489) A measure of the preference to receive assets in the event of corporate liquidation.

long-lived assets (p. 380) Resources that are held for an extended time, such as land, buildings, equipment, natural resources, and patents.

long-term liabilities (p. 423) Obligations that fall due beyond one year from the balance sheet date.

long-term solvency (p. 574) An organization's ability to generate enough cash to repay long-term debts as they mature.

lower-of-cost-and-market method (LCM) (p. 345) The superimposition of a market-price test on an inventory cost method.

management accounting (p. 6) The field of accounting that serves internal decision makers, such as top executives, department heads, university deans, hospital administrators, and people at other management levels within an organization.

management reports (p. 530) Explicit statements in annual reports of publicly held companies that state management is responsible for all audited and unaudited information in the annual report.

management's discussion and analysis (MD&A) (p. 582) A required section of annual reports that concentrates on explaining the major changes in the income statement and the major changes in liquidity and capital resources.

market rate *See* yield to maturity.

marketable securities (p. 302) Any notes, bonds, or stocks that can readily be sold via public markets. The term is often used as a synonym for short-term investments.

matching (p. 43) The recording of expenses in the same time period as the related revenues are recognized.

materiality convention (p. 108) The concept that states that a financial statement item is material if its omission or misstatement would tend to mislead the reader of the financial statements under consideration.

mortgage bond (p. 430) A form of long-term debt that is secured by the pledge of specific property.

multiple-step income statement (p. 150) An income statement that contains one or more subtotals that highlight significant relationships.

net book value *See* book value.

net income (p. 48) The remainder after all expenses have been deducted from revenues.

net sales (p. 284) Total sales revenue reduced by sales returns and allowances.

neutrality (p. 628) Choosing accounting policies without attempting to achieve purposes other than measuring economic impact; freedom from bias.

nominal interest rate (p. 430) A contractual rate of interest paid on bonds.

non-controlling interests (p. 311) The outside shareholders' interests, as opposed to the parent's interests, in a subsidiary corporation.

notes payable (p. 7) Promissory notes that are evidence of a debt and state the terms of payment.

open account (p. 12) Buying or selling on credit, usually by just an "authorized signature" of the buyer.

operating activities (p. 234) Transactions that affect the income statement.

operating cycle (p. 39) The time span during which cash is used to acquire goods and services, which in turn are sold to customers, who in turn pay for their purchases with cash.

operating income (p. 150) Gross profit less all operating expenses.

operating income percentage on sales (p. 592) Operating income divided by sales.

operating lease (p. 457) A lease that should be accounted for by the lessee as ordinary rent expenses.

operating management (p. 234) Is mainly concerned with the major day-to-day activities that generate revenues and expenses.

operating profit *See* operating income.

operating statement *See* statement of income.

other postretirement benefits (p. 444) Benefits provided to retired workers in addition to a pension, such as life and health insurance.

output controls (p. 539) Internal accounting controls that check output against input and ensure that only authorized persons receive reports.

outstanding shares (p. 486) Shares in the hands of shareholders equal to issued shares less treasury shares.

owners' equity (p. 7) The residual interest in, or remaining claim against, the organization's assets after deducting liabilities.

P&L statement *See* statement of income.

paid-in capital (p. 18) The total capital investment in a corporation by its owners at the inception of business and subsequently.

paid-in capital in excess of par value (p. 18) When issuing stock, the difference between the total amount received and the par value.

par value (p. 18) The nominal dollar amount printed on stock certificates. *See* face amount

parent company (p. 306) A company owning more than 50% of the voting shares of another company, called the subsidiary company.

participating (p. 489) A characteristic of preferred stock that provides increasing dividends when common dividends increase.

partnership (p. 16) A special form of organization that joins two or more individuals together as co-owners.

patents (p. 398) Grants by the federal government to an inventor, bestowing the exclusive right to produce and sell the invention.

payment date (p. 493) The date dividends are paid.

pensions (p. 444) Payments to former employees after they retire.

percentage of accounts receivable method (p. 296) An approach to estimating bad debts expense and uncollectible accounts at year end using the historical relations of uncollectibles to accounts receivable.

percentage of sales method (p. 295) An approach to estimating bad debts expense and uncollectible accounts based on the historical relations between credit sales and uncollectibles.

period costs (p. 43) Items identified directly as expenses of the time period in which they are incurred.

periodic inventory system (p. 332) The system in which the cost of goods sold is computed periodically by relying solely on physical counts without keeping day-to-day records of units sold or on hand.

permanent accounts (p. 195) Balance sheet accounts.

perpetual inventory system (p. 331) A system that keeps a running, continuous record that tracks inventories and the cost of goods sold on a day-to-day basis.

physical count (p. 333) The process of counting all the items in inventory at a moment in time.

plant assets *See* tangible assets.

posting (p. 91) The transferring of amounts from the journal to the appropriate accounts in the ledger.

preemptive rights (p. 486) The rights to acquire a pro-rata amount of any new issues of capital stock.

preferred stock (p. 487) Stock that has some priority over other shares regarding dividends or the distribution of assets upon liquidation.

premium on bonds (p. 433) The excess of the proceeds over the face amount of a bond.

present value (p. 454) The value today of a future cash inflow or outflow.

pretax income (p. 139) Income before income taxes.

pretax operating rate of return on total assets (p. 592) Operating income divided by average total assets available.

private accounting (p. 22) Accountants who work for businesses, government agencies, and other nonprofit organizations.

private placement (p. 430) A process whereby notes are issued by corporations when money is borrowed from a few sources, not from the general public.

privately owned (p. 16) A corporation owned by a family, a small group of shareholders, or a single individual, in which shares of ownership are not publicly sold.

pro forma statement (p. 573) A carefully formulated expression of predicted results.

processing controls (p. 539) Internal accounting controls relating to the design, programming, and operation of the system.

product costs (p. 43) Costs that are linked with revenues and are charged as expenses when the related revenue is recognized.

professional corporation (p. 486) A form of corporation providing professional people some corporate benefits without limited liability.

profit See income.

profitability evaluation (p. 153) The assessment of the likelihood that a company will provide investors with a particular rate of return on their investment.

promissory note (p. 424) A written promise to repay principal plus interest at specific future dates.

protective covenant (p. 431) A provision stated in a bond, usually to protect the bondholders' interests.

public accounting (p. 22) The field of accounting in which services are offered to the general public on a fee basis.

publicly owned (p. 16) A corporation in which shares in the ownership are sold to the public.

purchase allowance See sales allowance.

purchase returns See sales returns.

rate of return on common equity (ROE) (p. 510) Net income less preferred dividends divided by average common equity.

rate of return on shareholders' equity (ROE) (p. 594) Net income divided by average shareholders' equity.

raw material inventory (p. 360) Includes the cost of materials held for use in the manufacturing of a product.

receivables See accounts receivable.

recognition (p. 43) A test for determining whether revenues should be recorded in the financial statements of a given period. To be recognized, revenues must be earned and realized.

reconcile a bank statement (p. 289) To verify that the bank balance for cash is consistent with the accounting records.

redemption price (p. 490) The call price, which is typically 5% to 10% above the par value of the bond or stock.

registered instrument (p. 432) Bonds that require the interest and maturity payments to be made to specific owners.

reinvested earnings See retained earnings.

relevance (p. 628) The capability of information to make a difference to the decision maker.

reliability (p. 9) The quality of information that assures decision makers that the information captures the conditions or events it purports to represent.

replacement cost (p. 344) The cost at which an inventory item could be acquired today.

report format (p. 149) A classified balance sheet with the assets at the top.

representational faithfulness See validity.

reserve for doubtful accounts See allowance for uncollectible accounts.

residual value (p. 383) The amount received from disposal of a long-lived asset at the end of its useful life.

restricted retained earnings (p. 508) Any part of retained income that may not be reduced by dividend declarations.

results of operations See statement of income.

retail method See retail inventory method.

retail inventory method (p. 553) A popular inventory costing method based on sales prices, often used as a control device and for obtaining an inventory valuation for financial statement purposes.

retailer (p. 350) A company that sells items directly to the final users, individuals.

retained earnings (p. 61) A synonym for retained income.

retained income (p. 40) Additional owners' equity generated by income or profits.

return on sales ratio (p. 154) Net income divided by sales.

return on shareholders' equity ratio (p. 154) Net income divided by invested capital (measured by average shareholders' equity).

return on total assets (ROA) (p. 594) Income before interest expense divided by average total assets.

revenues (p. 40) Gross increases in owners' equity arising from increases in assets received in exchange for the delivery of goods or services to customers.

reversing entries (p. 205) Entries that switch back all debits and credits made in a related preceding adjusting entry.

sales (p. 61) A synonym for revenues.

sales allowance (p. 284) Reduction of the selling price (the original price previously agreed upon).

sales returns (p. 284) Products returned by the customer.

sales revenues See sales.

salvage value See residual value.

scrap value See residual value.

series (p. 490) Different groups of preferred shares issued at different times with different features.

shareholders' equity (stockholders' equity) (p. 18) Owners' equity of a corporation. The excess of assets over liabilities of a corporation.

short-term debt securities (p. 302) Largely notes and bonds with maturities of one year or less.

short-term equity securities (p. 303) Capital stock in other corporations held with the intention to liquidate within one year as needed.

short-term liquidity (p. 574) An organization's ability to meet current payments as they become due.

simple entry (p. 92) An entry for a transaction that affects only two accounts.

simple interest (p. 452) For any period, interest rate multiplied by an unchanging principal amount.

single-step income statement (p. 150) An income statement that groups all revenues together and then lists and deducts all expenses together without drawing any intermediate subtotals.

sinking fund (p. 432) Cash or securities segregated for meeting obligations on bonded debt.

sinking fund bonds (p. 432) Bonds with indentures that require the issuer to make annual payments to a sinking fund.

Society of Management Accountants of Canada (SMAC) (p. 21) A professional accounting organization of Certified Management Accountants (CMA).

sole proprietorship (p. 16) A separate organization with a single owner.

solvency (p. 147) An entity's ability to meet its financial obligations as they become due.

source documents (p. 87) The supporting original records of any transaction; they are memoranda of what happened.

special (unusual) items (p. 599) Expenses that are large enough and unusual enough to warrant separate disclosure.

special journals (p. 205) Journals used to record particular types of voluminous transactions; examples are the sales journal and the cash receipts journal.

specific identification method (p. 339) This inventory method concentrates on the physical tracing of the particular items sold.

specific write-off method (p. 292) This method of accounting for bad debt losses assumes all sales are fully collectible until proved otherwise.

stated rate *See* nominal interest rate.

stated value *See* par value.

statement of changes in financial position (p. 51) A required statement that reports the cash receipts and cash payments of an entity during a particular period.

statement of earnings *See* statement of income.

statement of financial condition *See* balance sheet.

statement of financial position *See* balance sheet.

statement of income (p. 61) A synonym for income statement.

statement of income and retained earnings (p. 59) A statement that includes a statement of retained earnings at the bottom of an income statement.

statement of operations *See* statement of income

statement of retained earnings (p. 58) A statement that lists the beginning balance in retained earnings, followed by a description of any changes that occurred during the period, and the ending balance.

statement of revenues and expenses *See* statement of income.

stock certificate *See* capital stock certificate.

stock dividends (p. 495) Distribution to shareholders of additional shares of any class of the distributing company's stock, without any payment to the company by the shareholders.

stock options (p. 508) Special rights usually granted to executives to purchase a corporation's capital stock.

stock split (p. 494) Issuance of additional shares to existing shareholders for no payments by the shareholders.

straight-line depreciation (p. 384) A method that spreads the depreciable value evenly over the useful life of an asset.

subordinated debentures (p. 431) Debt securities whose holders have claims against only the assets that remain after the claims of certain secured creditors are satisfied.

subsidiary (p. 306) A corporation owned or controlled by a parent company through the ownership of more than 50% of the voting stock.

T-account (p. 85) Simplified version of ledger accounts that takes the form of the capital letter T.

tangible assets (p. 380) Physical items that can be seen and touched, such as land, natural resources, buildings, and equipment.

tax deferral (p. 465) A method that measures reported income as if it were subject to the full current tax rate even though a more advantageous accounting method was used for tax purposes.

temporary accounts (p. 195) Accounts that are subjected to periodic closing, i.e., revenue, expense, and dividends declared accounts.

temporary (short-term) investment (p. 302) A temporary investment in marketable securities of otherwise idle cash.

terminal value *See* residual value.

time-series comparisons (p. 586) Comparisons of a company's financial ratios with its own historical ratios.

times interest earned *See* interest coverage.

timing difference (p. 463) A situation that arises whenever revenue or expense items are recognized in one period for tax purposes and in another period for shareholder reporting.

total asset turnover (p. 592) Sales divided by average total assets available.

trade discounts (p. 285) Reductions to the gross selling price for a particular class of customers to arrive at the actual selling price (invoice price).

trade receivables *See* accounts receivable.

trademarks (p. 399) Distinctive identifications of a manufactured product or of a service taking the form of a name, a sign, a slogan, a logo, or an emblem.

trading on the equity (p. 594) Using borrowed money at fixed interest rates with the objective of enhancing the rate of return on common equity.

transaction (p. 9) Any event that both affects the financial position of an entity and can be reliably recorded in money terms.

translation adjustment (p. 605) A contra-account in shareholders' equity that arises when a foreign subsidiary is consolidated.

Treasury bills (p. 303) Interest-bearing notes, bonds, and bills issued by the government.

treasury stock (p. 486) A corporation's issued stock that has subsequently been repurchased by the company and not retired.

trial balance (p. 100) A list of all accounts with their balances.

trust indenture (p. 431) A contract whereby the issuing corporation of a bond promises a trustee that it will abide by stated provisions.

turnover (p. 287) Often a synonym for sales or revenues outside North America.

uncollectible accounts (p. 290) Receivables determined to be uncollectible because debtors are unable or unwilling to pay their debts.

underwriters (p. 433) A group of investment bankers that buys an entire bond or stock issue from a corporation and then sells the bonds to the general investing public.

unearned revenue (p. 133) Revenue received and recorded before it is earned.

unit depreciation (p. 384) A method based on units of service when physical wear and tear is the dominating influence on the useful life of the asset.

unlimited liability (p. 486) Legal responsibility not limited by law or contract; personal assets can be seized to satisfy corporate debts.

unregistered instrument (p. 432) Bonds requiring interest to be paid to the individual who presents the interest coupons attached to the bond.

unsubordinated debenture (p. 437) A bond that is unsecured by specific pledged assets, giving its owner a general claim with a priority like an account payable.

useful life (p. 383) The time period over which an asset is amortized.

validity (p. 628) A correspondence between the accounting numbers and the resources or events those numbers purport to represent.

verifiability (p. 628) A quality of information such that there would be a high degree of consensus among independent measurers of an item.

weighted-average cost (p. 339) This inventory method computes a unit cost by dividing the total acquisition cost of all items available for sale by the number of units available for sale.

wholesaler (p. 350) An intermediary that sells inventory items to retailers.

work in process inventory (p. 360) Includes the cost incurred for partially completed items, including raw materials, labour, and other costs.

work sheet (p. 198) A columnar approach to moving from a trial balance to the finished financial statements.

working capital (p. 146) The excess of current assets over current liabilities.

working capital ratio *See* current ratio.

write-down (p. 346) A reduction in carrying value to below cost in response to a decline in value.

working paper *See* work sheet.

yield to maturity (p. 433) The interest rate that equates market price at a particular date to the present value of principal and interest.

Index of Companies

Subject Index